Microsoft® Office 2003

ILLUSTRATED SECOND COURSE

SECOND COURSE

(2 of 2)

Beskeen • Cram • Duffy • Friedrichsen •
Reding • Wermers

THOMSON
COURSE TECHNOLOGY™

Australia • Canada • Mexico • Singapore • Spain • United Kingdom • United States

THOMSON
™
COURSE TECHNOLOGY

Microsoft® Office 2003 - Illustrated Second Course
Beskeen/Cram/Duffy/Friedrichsen/Wermers

Executive Editor:
Nicole Jones Pinard

Production Editors:
Anne Valsangiacomo, Aimee Poirier, Philippa Lehar, Daphne Barbas, Melissa Panagos

QA Manuscript Reviewers:
Chris Carvalho, John Freitas, Chris Kunciw, Burt LaFontaine, Jeff Schwartz, Maxwell Prior, Susan Whelen, Alex White

Product Manager:
Jane Hosie-Bounar

Developmental Editors:
Rachel Biheller Bunin, Barbara Clemens, Pamela Conrad, Jeanne Herring, Jane Hosie-Bounar, Lisa Ruffolo, Barbara Waxer

Text Designer:
Joseph Lee, Black Fish Design

Associate Product Manager:
Emilie Perreault

Editorial Assistant:
Abbey Reider

Composition House:
GEX Publishing Services

Contributing Authors:
Jennifer T. Campbell
Elizabeth Eisner Reding

The Illustrated Series Vision

Teaching and writing about computer applications can be extremely rewarding and challenging. How do we engage students and keep their interest? How do we teach them skills that they can easily apply on the job? As we set out to write this book, our goals were to develop a textbook that:

- works for a beginning student
- provides varied, flexible and meaningful exercises and projects to reinforce the skills
- serves as a reference tool
- makes your job as an educator easier, by providing resources above and beyond the textbook to help you teach your course

Our popular, streamlined format is based on advice from instructional designers and customers. This flexible design presents each lesson on a two-page spread, with step-by-step instructions on the left, and screen illustrations on the right. This signature style, coupled with high-caliber content, provides a comprehensive yet manageable introduction to Microsoft Office 2003—it is a teaching package for the instructor and a learning experience for the student.

Author Acknowledgments

David Beskeen I would like to thank Rachel Biheller Bunin for her tireless efforts and editorial insights, which have made my work better. I would also like to thank Course Technology for all of their vision and support over the last 10 years; I look forward to many more!

Jennifer Campbell Thanks to my wonderful family, Mike, Emma, and Lucy, and to Barbara Waxer for her insight, expertise, and humor.

Carol Cram A big thank you to developmental editor Jeanne Herring for her patience, good humor, and insight! And, as always, everything I do is made possible by Gregg and Julia. They make everything worthwhile.

Jennifer Duffy Many talented people at Course Technology helped to shape this book— thank you all. I am especially indebted to Pam Conrad for her precision editing and endless good cheer throughout the many months of writing. On the home front, I am ever grateful to my family for their patience, and to Nancy Macalaster, who so lovingly cared for my babies during the long hours I needed to be at my desk.

Lisa Friedrichsen The Access portion is dedicated to my students, and all who are using this book to teach and learn about Access. Thank you. Also, thank you to all of the professionals who helped me create this book.

Lynn Wermers I would like to thank Barbara Clemens for her insightful contributions and guidance. I would also like to thank Christina Kling Garrett for patiently answering and researching my endless questions.

Preface

Welcome to *Microsoft® Office 2003–Illustrated Second Course*. Each lesson in this book contains elements pictured to the right.

How is the book organized?

The book is organized into sections, by application, illustrated by the brightly colored tabs on the sides of the pages: Reviewing Office 2003, Word, Excel, Access, PowerPoint, and Publisher. Three units of integration projects follow the Excel, Access, and PowerPoint sections.

What kinds of assignments are included in the book? At what level of difficulty?

The lessons use MediaLoft, a fictional chain of bookstores, as the case study. The assignments on the light purple pages at the end of each unit increase in difficulty. Data Files and case studies, with many international examples, provide a great variety of interesting and relevant business applications. Assignments include the following:

- **Concepts Reviews** include multiple choice, matching, and screen identification questions.

- **Skills Reviews** provide additional hands-on, step-by-step reinforcement.

- **Independent Challenges** are case projects requiring critical thinking and application of the unit skills. The Independent Challenges increase in difficulty, with the first one in each unit being the easiest (most step-by-step with detailed instructions). Independent Challenges 2 and 3 become increasingly open-ended, requiring more independent problem solving.

- **E-Quest Independent Challenges** are case projects with a Web focus. E-Quests require the use of the World Wide Web to conduct research to complete the project.

- **Advanced Challenge Exercises** set within the Independent Challenges provide *optional* steps for more advanced students.

- **Visual Workshops** are practical, self-graded capstone projects that require independent problem solving.

Each 2-page spread focuses on a single skill.

Concise text introduces the basic principles in the lesson and integrates a real-world case study.

UNIT F
Word 2003

Resizing Graphics

Once you insert a graphic into a document, you can change its shape or size by using the mouse to drag a sizing handle or by using the Picture command on the Format menu to specify an exact height and width for the graphic. Resizing a graphic with the mouse allows you to see how the image looks as you modify it. Using the Picture command to alter a graphic's shape or size allows you to set precise measurements. You enlarge the MediaLoft logo.

STEPS

QUICK TIP
Click Ruler on the View menu to display the rulers.

1. **Click the logo graphic to select it, place the pointer over the middle-right sizing handle, when the pointer changes to ↔, drag to the right until the graphic is about 1¾" wide**
As you drag, the dotted outline indicates the size and shape of the graphic. You can refer to the ruler to gauge the measurements as you drag. When you release the mouse button, the image is stretched to be wider. Dragging a side, top, or bottom sizing handle changes only the width or height of a graphic.

QUICK TIP
If you enlarge a bitmap graphic too much, the dots that make up the picture become visible and the graphic is distorted.

2. **Click the Undo button 🔲 on the Standard toolbar, place the pointer over the upper-right sizing handle, when the pointer changes to ⤢ drag up and to the right until the graphic is about 2" tall and 1¾" wide as shown in Figure F-4, then release the mouse button**
The image is enlarged. Dragging a corner sizing handle resizes the graphic proportionally so that its width and height are reduced or enlarged by the same percentage. Table F-1 describes other ways to resize objects using the mouse.

3. **Double-click the logo graphic**
The Format Picture dialog box opens. It includes options for changing the coloring, size, scale, text wrapping, and position of a graphic. You can double-click any graphic object or use the Picture command on the Format menu to open the Format Picture dialog box.

4. **Click the Size tab**
The Size tab, shown in Figure F-5, allows you to enter precise height and width measurements for a graphic or to scale a graphic by entering the percentage by which you want to reduce or enlarge it. When a graphic is sized to scale, its height to width ratio remains the same.

TROUBLE
Your height measurement might differ slightly.

5. **Select the measurement in the Width text box in the Size and rotate section, type 1.5, then click the Height text box in the Size and rotate section**
The height measurement automatically changes to 1.68". When the Lock aspect ratio check box is selected, you need to enter only a height or width measurement. Word calculates the other measurement so that the resized graphic is proportional.

6. **Click OK, then save your changes**
The logo is resized to be precisely 1.5" wide and approximately 1.68" tall.

TABLE F-1: Methods for resizing an object using the mouse

do this	to
Drag a corner sizing handle	Resize a clip art or bitmap graphic proportionally from a corner
Press [Shift] and drag a corner sizing handle	Resize a drawing object, such as an AutoShape or a WordArt object, proportionally from a corner
Press [Ctrl] and drag a side, top, or bottom sizing handle	Resize any graphic object vertically or horizontally while keeping the center position fixed
Press [Ctrl] and drag a corner sizing handle	Resize any graphic object diagonally while keeping the center position fixed
Press [Shift][Ctrl] and drag a corner sizing handle	Resize any graphic object proportionally while keeping the center position fixed

WORD F-4 ILLUSTRATING DOCUMENTS WITH GRAPHICS

Tips as well as troubleshooting advice, right where you need it—next to the step itself.

Tables provide quickly accessible summaries of key terms, toolbar buttons, or keyboard alternatives connected with the lesson material. Students can refer easily to this information when working on their own projects at a later time.

Every lesson features large, full-color representations of what the screen should look like as students complete the numbered steps.

Brightly colored tabs indicate which section of the book you are in.

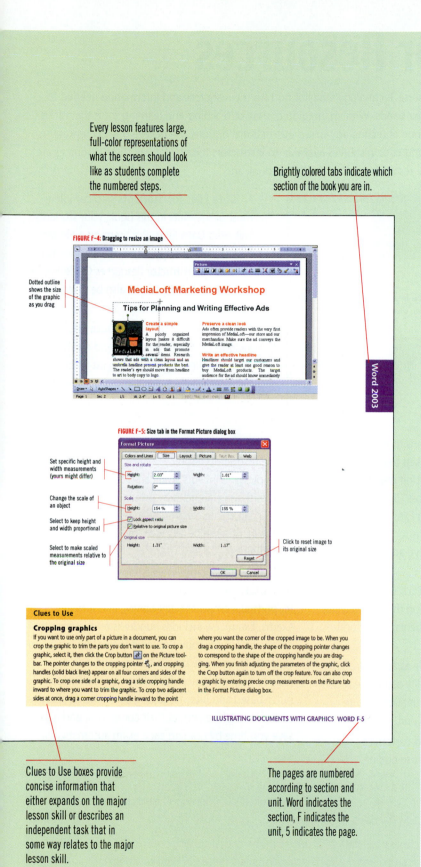

Dotted outline shows the size of the graphic as you drag

FIGURE F-4: Dragging to resize an image

Set specific height and width measurements (yours might differ)

Change the scale of an object

Select to keep height and width proportional

Select to make scaled measurements relative to the original size

Click to reset image to its original size

FIGURE F-5: Size tab in the Format Picture dialog box

Clues to Use

Cropping graphics

If you want to use only part of a picture in a document, you can crop the graphic to trim the parts you don't want to use. To crop a graphic, select it, then click the Crop button on the Picture toolbar. The pointer changes to the cropping pointer, and cropping handles (solid black lines) appear on all four corners and sides of the graphic. To crop one side of a graphic, drag a side cropping handle inward to where you want to trim the graphic. To crop two adjacent sides at once, drag a corner cropping handle inward to the point where you want the corner of the cropped image to be. When you drag a cropping handle, the shape of the cropping pointer changes to correspond to the shape of the cropping handle you are dragging. When you finish adjusting the parameters of the graphic, click the Crop button again to turn off the crop feature. You can also crop a graphic by entering precise crop measurements on the Picture tab in the Format Picture dialog box.

ILLUSTRATING DOCUMENTS WITH GRAPHICS WORD F-5

Clues to Use boxes provide concise information that either expands on the major lesson skill or describes an independent task that in some way relates to the major lesson skill.

The pages are numbered according to section and unit. Word indicates the section, F indicates the unit, 5 indicates the page.

Is this book Microsoft Office Specialist Certified?

When used in conjunction with *Microsoft Office 2003 – Illustrated Introductory*, this book covers the Specialist objectives for Word, Excel, Access, and PowerPoint. See the inside front cover for more information on other Illustrated titles meeting Microsoft Office Specialist certification.

The first page of each unit includes objectives set in red to indicate which skills covered in the unit are Microsoft Office Specialist skills. A grid in the Review Pack and on the Instructor Resources disk lists all the exam objectives and cross-references the skills with the lessons and exercises.

What online content solutions are available to accompany this book?

Visit www.course.com for more information on our online content for Illustrated titles. Options include:

MyCourse 2.0

Need a quick, simple tool to help you manage your course? Try MyCourse 2.0, the easiest to use, most flexible syllabus and content management tool available. MyCourse 2.0 offers you brand new content, including Topic Reviews, Extra Case Projects, and Quizzes, to accompany this book.

WebCT

Course Technology and WebCT have partnered to provide you with the highest quality online resources and Web-based tools for your class. Course Technology offers content for this book to help you create your WebCT class, such as a suggested Syllabus, Lecture Notes, Practice Test questions, and more.

Blackboard

Course Technology and Blackboard have also partnered to provide you with the highest quality online resources and Web-based tools for your class. Course Technology offers content for this book to help you create your Blackboard class, such as a suggested Syllabus, Lecture Notes, Practice Test questions, and more.

Instructor Resources

The Instructor Resources CD is Course Technology's way of putting the resources and information needed to teach and learn effectively into your hands. With an integrated array of teaching and learning tools that offers you and your students a broad range of technology-based instructional options, we believe this CD represents the highest quality and most cutting edge resources available to instructors today. Many of these resources are available at www.course.com. The resources available with this book are:

• **Data Files for Students**—To complete most of the units in this book, your students will need **Data Files**. Put them on a file server for students to copy. The Data Files are available on the Instructor Resources CD-ROM, in the Review Pack, and can also be downloaded from www.course.com.

Instruct students to use the **Data Files List** included in the Review Pack and on the Instructor Resources CD. This list gives instructions for copying and organizing files.

• **Solutions to Exercises**—Solutions to Exercises contains every file students are asked to create or modify in the lessons and End-of-Unit material. A Help file on the Instructor Resources CD includes information for using the Solution Files. There is also a document outlining the solutions for the End-of-Unit Concepts Review, Skills Review, and Independent Challenges.

• **PowerPoint Presentations**—Each unit has a corresponding PowerPoint presentation that you can use in a lecture, distribute to your students, or customize to suit your course.

• **Instructor's Manual**—Available as an electronic file, the Instructor's Manual is quality-assurance tested and includes unit overviews, and detailed lecture topics with teaching tips for each unit.

• **Sample Syllabus**—Prepare and customize your course easily using this sample course outline.

• **Figure Files**—The figures in the text are provided on the Instructor Resources CD to help you illustrate key topics or concepts. You can create traditional overhead transparencies by printing the figure files. Or you can create electronic slide shows by using the figures in a presentation program such as PowerPoint.

• **ExamView**—ExamView is a powerful testing software package that allows you to create and administer printed, computer (LAN-based), and Internet exams. ExamView includes hundreds of questions that correspond to the topics covered in this text, enabling students to generate detailed study guides that include page references for further review. The computer-based and Internet testing components allow students to take exams at their computers, and also save you time by grading each exam automatically.

SAM 2003 Assessment & Training

SAM 2003 helps you energize your class exams and training assignments by allowing students to learn and test important computer skills in an active, hands-on environment.

With SAM 2003 Assessment, you create powerful interactive exams on critical applications such as Word, Outlook, PowerPoint, Windows, the Internet, and much more. The exams simulate the application environment, allowing your students to demonstrate their knowledge and think through the skills by performing real-world tasks.

Designed to be used with the Illustrated series, SAM 2003 Assessment & Training includes built-in page references so students can create study guides that match the Illustrated textbooks you use in class. Powerful administrative options allow you to schedule exams and assignments, secure your tests, and run reports with almost limitless flexibility.

Brief Contents

Brief Contents

Contents

EXCEL 2003

Working with Formulas and Functions   E-1

EXCEL 2003

Managing Workbooks and Preparing Them for the Web   F-1

EXCEL 2003

Automating Worksheet Tasks   G-1

ACCESS 2003

INTEGRATION

POWERPOINT 2003

POWERPOINT 2003

POWERPOINT 2003

POWERPOINT 2003

Using Advanced Features   H-1

INTEGRATION

Integrating Word, Excel, Access, and PowerPoint   F-1

PUBLISHER 2003

Getting Started with Publisher 2003   A-1

PUBLISHER 2003

Working with Text and Graphics   B-1

Read This Before You Begin

Software Information and Required Installation

This book was written and tested using Microsoft Office 2003 - Professional Edition, with a typical installation on Microsoft Windows XP, including the most recent Windows XP Service Pack, and with Internet Explorer 6.0 or higher. Some of the exercises in this book assume that your computer is connected to the Internet. If you are not connected to the Internet, see your instructor.

Tips for Students

What are Data Files?

To complete many of the units in this book, you need to use Data Files. A Data File contains a partially completed file, so that you don't have to type in all the information in the file yourself. Your instructor will either provide you with copies of the Data Files or ask you to make your own copies. Your instructor can also give you instructions on how to organize your files, as well as a complete file listing, or you can find the list and the instructions for organizing your files in the Review Pack. Because Excel has no Data Files for Unit G, you will need to create a Unit G folder at the same level as the other unit folders so that you have a place to save the files you create in Unit G.

In addition, keep the following things in mind:

- If you are using floppy disks for your Data Files, you'll need to consider the important information about Access Data Files on page xvi as you organize your files for this book.

- Also, if you are using floppy disks to complete the exercises in this book, then you will need to use multiple disks to complete all of the work in PowerPoint Unit G, and some of the work in Office B and Publisher (depending on the size of the graphics files you use). Integration Units E and F will also require more than one disk per unit.

- Because of the size of the Data Files in PowerPoint Unit H and the nature of some of PowerPoint's features, it will be necessary for you to use some hard disk space to complete the exercises.

Why is my screen different from the book?

Your desktop components and some dialog box options might be different if you are using an operating system other than Windows XP.

Depending on your computer hardware and the XP Display settings, you may also notice the following differences even if you are using Windows XP:

- Your screen may look larger or smaller because of your screen resolution (the height and width of your screen).

- Your title bars and dialog boxes may not display file extensions. To display file extensions, click Start on the taskbar, click Control Panel, click Appearance and Themes, then click Folder Options. Click the View tab if necessary, click Hide extensions for known file types to deselect it, and then click OK.

- The colors of the title bar in your screen may be a solid blue, and the cells in Excel may appear different from the orange and gray because of your color settings.

- Depending on your Office settings, your toolbars may be displayed on a single row and your menus may display a shortened list of frequently used commands. Office menus and toolbars can modify themselves to your working style by displaying only the most frequently used buttons and menu commands, as shown here.

Toolbars in one row

Toolbars in two rows

To view buttons not currently displayed, click a Toolbar Options button ⬛ at the end of either the Standard or Formatting toolbar. To view the full list of menu commands, click the double arrow at the bottom of the menu.

In order to have your toolbars displayed in two rows, showing all buttons, and to have the full menus displayed, you must turn off the personalized menus and toolbars feature. Click Tools on the menu bar, click Customize, select the show Standard and Formatting toolbars on two rows and Always show full menus check boxes on the Options tab, and then click Close. This book assumes you are displaying toolbars in two rows and displaying full menus.

Important Information for Access Units if you are using floppy disks

Compact on Close?

If you are storing your Access databases on floppy disks, *you should **not** use the Compact on Close option* (available from the Tools menu). While the Compact on Close feature works well if your database is stored on your hard drive or on another large storage device, it can cause problems if your database is stored on a floppy when the size of your database is greater than the available free space on the floppy. Here's why: When you close a database with the Compact on Close feature turned on, the process creates a temporary file that is just as large as the original database file. In a successful compact process, this temporary file is deleted after the compact procedure is completed. But if there is not enough available space on your floppy to create this temporary file, the compact process never finishes, which means that your original database is never closed properly. If you do not close an Access database properly before attempting to use it again, you can corrupt it beyond repair. *Therefore, if you use floppies to complete these exercises, please follow the Review Pack guidelines on how to organize your databases or ask your instructor for directions so that you do not run out of room on a floppy disk or corrupt your database.*

Closing a Database Properly

It is extremely important to close your databases properly before copying, moving, e-mailing the database file, or before ejecting the Data Files floppy disk from the disk drive. Access database files are inherently multi-user, which means that multiple people can work on the same database file at the same time. To accomplish this capability, Access creates temporary files to keep track of which record you are working on while the database is open. These temporary files must be closed properly before you attempt to copy, move, or e-mail the database. They must also be closed before you eject a floppy that contains the database. If these temporary files do not get closed properly, the database can be corrupted beyond repair. Fortunately, Access closes these temporary files automatically when you close the Access application window. So to be sure that you have properly closed a database that is stored on a floppy, *close not only the database window, but also **close the Access application window*** *before copying, moving, or e-mailing a database file, as well as before ejecting a floppy that stores the database.*

2000 vs. 2002/2003 File Format

New databases created in Access 2003 default to an Access 2000 file format, which is why "Access 2000 file format" is shown in the database window title bar for the figures in this book. This also means that Access databases now support seamless backward compatibility with prior versions of Access including Access 2000 and Access 2002, like other products in the Microsoft Office suite, such as Word and Excel.

But while the Data Files for this book can be opened and used in Access 2000 or Access 2002, the figures in this book present the Access 2003 application, use the Access 2003 menus and toolbars, and highlight the new features of Access 2003 including new smart tags, new error indicators, the ability to easily locate object dependencies, the ability to update properties automatically, a new backup tool, new themes for forms, and improvements to PivotTables and PivotCharts.

Microsoft Jet database engine

You may not have the latest version of the Microsoft Jet database engine. To obtain the latest update, follow the prompts in the dialog box that appears when you open a database. (This dialog box will only appear if you do not have the latest version of the Microsoft Jet database engine.)

Reviewing Microsoft Office 2003

OBJECTIVES

Review Office 2003 programs

Review Word: Task Reference

Use Word: Visual Workshop

Review Excel: Task Reference

Use Excel: Visual Workshop

Review Access: Task Reference

Use Access: Visual Workshop

Review PowerPoint: Task Reference

Use PowerPoint: Visual Workshop

As you know from your experience with Microsoft Office 2003, the programs help you complete tasks quickly and work more efficiently. MediaLoft, a chain of café bookstores, uses Office 2003 programs every day in memos, worksheets, presentations, databases, publications, Web pages, and artwork.  Elizabeth Reed, a MediaLoft vice president, has asked you to use Office programs to help her plan and prepare for an executive retreat for MediaLoft managers.

Reviewing Office 2003 Programs

The programs included in Microsoft Office 2003 provide the tools you need to complete common business tasks. Each program provides tools to meet specific needs. As you have learned, Office 2003 programs include common tools such as task panes and the Office Clipboard to provide you with rapid access to the information you need. As you use Office, you identify which programs have the best tools for each job at hand, and how you can use them together to produce effective documents as efficiently as possible. Elizabeth Reed, a MediaLoft vice president, is planning a retreat for MediaLoft store managers. She has asked you to help her create the letter, workbook, database, and presentation she will need; the information listed on this page provides an overview of each document. The Visual Workshops that follow contain specific instructions. As you work, you can review the features you will need in the Task Reference for each program.

DETAILS

- ### Edit and format a multi-page Word document
  Elizabeth wants to send a multi-page letter to managers to prepare them for the retreat. Because the document will have more than one page, you will use the header and footer feature, as well as section and column breaks. To add visual interest, you will add formatting attributes, as well as a table and a graphic to help illustrate important points.

- ### Create a spreadsheet that contains sales calculations, projections, and a chart
  Elizabeth wants you to use Excel tools to create a budget for the retreat. You will use the powerful Excel calculation features and include an Excel chart to display her data in an informative and engaging way.

- ### Query an existing database for hotel information
  Elizabeth gives you an Access database containing specific information about hotels in the area. You'll use forms, queries, and reports to determine the best hotel for the retreat.

- ### Create a presentation for group meetings
  Elizabeth wants you to create an impressive PowerPoint presentation that she will use in her main address to the managers. It will incorporate text, graphics, timing, and transitions that will both communicate information clearly and provide visual interest.

- ### Integrate Office documents
  As you complete the Independent Challenges at the end of this unit, you will practice not only individual program skills, but also the powerful Office integration features. Integration ensures that you only have to create information once; you can then use it in documents created in other programs to save time.

Reviewing Word: Task Reference

This task reference lists the most common tasks covered in Units A through D of Microsoft Office Word Illustrated. It is designed as a refresher to help you find the button, dialog box, or tab you can use to perform each task.

task	method	task	method
Getting Started with Word 2003		Help, display list of recently asked questions	Click Type a question for help list arrow on menu bar
Action, undo	Click	Hyperlink, open	Press [Ctrl], click with pointer
Align text	, , , or	New Document task pane, display	Click File, New
AutoCorrect change, undo	Click , click Undo	Outline view, change to	Click on status bar
Back, go	Click	Preview, close	Click Close on Preview toolbar
Button, select	Click with pointer	Preview, document	Click on Standard toolbar
Button not visible, display	Click	Preview, magnify	Click document preview with pointer
Delete characters to the left	Click pointer after character, press [Backspace]	Preview, reduce	Click document preview with pointer
Delete characters to the right	Click pointer before character, press [Delete]	Program, exit	Click File, Exit
Document, close	Click File, Close	Program, start	Click start , point to Microsoft Office Word 2003 or point to All Programs, click Microsoft Office, click Microsoft Office Word 2003
Document, create	Click or click Create a new document hyperlink in Getting Started task pane		
Document, save	Click	Reading Layout view, change to	Click Read on Standard toolbar
Document, save under different name	Click File, Save As	Smart Tag, show	Position pointer over
Document, preview	Click	Toolbars, change display options	Click Tools, Customize, Options tab, select/deselect Show Standard and Formatting toolbars on two rows
Document, print	Click		
Folder, create	Click in Open or Save As dialog box	View, change to Full Screen	Click View, Full Screen
Folder, delete	Click in Open or Save As dialog box	View, change to Normal	Click on status bar
		View, change to Print Layout	Click on status bar
Help, search	Click , type word or question in the Type a question for help box, press [Enter]	View, change to Web Layout	Click on status bar
		Web, search	Click in Open or Save As dialog box
Help, hide the Office Assistant	Click Help, Hide the Office Assistant		
Help, show the Office Assistant	Click Help, Show the Office Assistant	Zoom, change	Click 100%
		Zoom tool, use in Print Preview	Move or pointer over document, click area

Word Task Reference (Continued)

task	method	task	method
Editing Documents		**Formatting Text and Paragraphs**	
Copied selection, embed	Click Edit, Paste Special, Paste	Action, repeat last	Press [F4]
Document, create from template	Click Templates in New Document task pane	Beginning of document, move to	Press [Ctrl][Home]
Document, open from task pane	Click Open or More hyperlink in Getting Started task pane	Bold attribute, apply	Select text, click **B**
Document, open	Click 📂	Border, add	Select text, click ▦ ▾
Document, save with a new name	Click File, Save As	Bullets, add or remove	Select text, click ☰
Document, select all text in	Press [Ctrl][A]	Bullet style, change	Select text, right-click list, click Bullets and Numbering
Entry, undo	Click ↺	Case, change	Select text, click Format, Change Case
Last action, repeat	Press [F4]		
Line, select	Click ⟋ pointer to the left of the line	Character spacing, change	Select text, click Format, Font, click Character Spacing tab
Nonconsecutive text blocks, select	Hold [Ctrl] while selecting each block	Drop Cap, add	Select paragraph, click Format, Drop Cap
Office Clipboard, open	Click Edit, Office Clipboard	First Line Indent, change	Drag ▽ on ruler
Paragraph, select	Triple-click paragraph	Font, change	Select text, click Times New Roman ▾, select font
Selection, copy	Click 📋	Font color, change	Select text, click **A** ▾
Selection, cut	Click ✂	Font size, change	Select text, click 12 ▾
Selection, paste	Click 📋	Format, paint	Click in source text, click 🖌, click in target text
Sentence, select	Press [Ctrl] while clicking sentence	Formats, clear	Click Edit, Clear, Formats
Special characters, Show/Hide	Click ¶	Formats, compare	Select text, click Format, Reveal Formatting, click Compare to another selection check box
Spelling, check	Click 🔤, click Change or Ignore to accept or reject suggestions		
Task pane, display	Click View, Task Pane	Hanging indent, change	Drag ⌂ on ruler
Text, delete	Select text, press [Delete]	Indent, decrease	Click in text, click ⇤
Text, find	Click Edit, Find	Indent, increase	Click in text, click ⇥
Text, replace	Click Edit, Replace	Italics, apply	Select text, click *I*
Text, select	Drag with I pointer	Left indent, change	Click in text, drag ▭ on ruler
Text, select all in document	[Ctrl][A]	Line spacing, change	Select text, click ⇳☰ ▾
Text block, select	Click selection beginning, hold [Shift], click end of selection	Numbering, add or remove	Click in or select text, click ☷
		Numbering style, change	Select list, right-click list, click Bullets and Numbering
Typing over characters, turn on/off	Double-click OVR on status bar	Outdent, create	Click in text, drag ▽ on ruler
Word, select	Double-click word		

Word Task Reference (Continued)

task	method	task	method
Outline list, create	Click Format, Bullets and Numbering, click Outline Numbered tab	AutoText, create	Select text, click Insert, AutoText, New
Reveal Formatting task pane, show	Click Format, Reveal Formatting	AutoText, insert	Click Insert, AutoText
Right indent, change	Click in text, drag △ on the right side of ruler	Clip art, add	Click Insert, Picture, Clip Art; enter search text, click desired clip
Scale characters, change	Click Scale list arrow in the Font dialog box	Clip art, wrap text around	Double-click image, click Layout tab
		Column break, create	Click Insert, Break
Shading, add	Click Format, Borders and Shading, click Shading tab	Columns, create	Click 🔳
Spacing above and below paragraphs, change	Click paragraph, click Format, Paragraph, click Indents and Spacing tab	Date, insert in header/footer	Click 🔳
		Font color, change	Select text, click 🅰 ▾, click color
Style, apply character or paragraph	Select text, select style in Styles and Formatting task pane list	Header and Footer, add	Click View, Header and Footer, click 🔳 to switch between header and footer
Styles and Formatting task pane, open	Click 🄰🄰	Header/Footer setup, modify	Click 🔳 on Header and Footer toolbar
Tab, insert center	Click in paragraph, click left side of ruler to display ⊥, click in ruler at tab location	Header/Footer, switch between	Click 🔳
		Margins, set	Click File, Page Setup, Margins tab
Tab, insert decimal	Click in paragraph, click left side of ruler to display ⊥, click in ruler at tab location	Mirrored margins, create	Click File, Page Setup, Margins tab, click Multiple pages list arrow
		Multiple pages, preview	Click 🔳 on Preview toolbar
Tab, insert left	Click in paragraph, click left side of ruler to display L, click in ruler at tab location	Number of pages, insert in header/footer	Click 🔳
Tab, insert right	Click in paragraph, click left side of ruler to display ⌐, click in ruler at tab location	Page break, insert	Press [Ctrl][Enter]
		Page number, insert in header/footer	Click 🔳
Tab leader, insert	Click in text, click Format, Tabs	Page numbers, add	Click Insert, Page Numbers
Tab stops, display a paragraph's	Click in paragraph, see horizontal ruler	Paper orientation, change	Click File, Page Setup, click Margins tab
Text, align	Click in or select text, click 🔳, 🔳, 🔳, or 🔳	Picture file, add	Click Insert, Picture, From File
		Section break, create	Click Insert, Break
		Symbol, insert	Click Insert, Symbol
Text, highlight	Click 🔳 ▾, select color, select text	Table, insert	Click 🔳
Underline, apply	Select text, click U	Template, create document based on	Click File, New, click On my computer hyperlink under Templates
Formatting Documents		Time, insert in header/footer	Click 🔳
Alignment, change vertical	Click in text, click File, Page Setup, click Layout tab	WordArt, insert	Click Insert, Picture, WordArt

Using Word: Visual Workshop

Open the file Office B-1.doc from the drive and folder where your Data Files are stored, then save it as **MediaLoft Update Memo**. Modify the document using Figure B-1 as a guide. Replace the text Elizabeth Reed with **your name**, save the document, then print it. As you modify the document, do the following:

- Create bulleted text
- Adjust line spacing and paragraph order
- Check the spelling
- Add formatting attributes (*Hint*: The Summary box uses Gray-20% shading.)
- Add a graphic image (*Hint*: Search on the keyword **globe**.) If you don't have access to the graphic shown, use another of your choice.
- Use sections and columns

- Use Find and Replace (*Hint*: Replace **locations** with **sites**.)
- Create a table (Select the table, then apply the Table Contemporary AutoFormat style, using the AutoFormat command on the Table menu. Resize the columns using the AutoFit and AutoFit to Contents commands on the Table menu. Then choose the Table Properties command on the Table menu, click the Table tab, and center the table.)
- Add a header and page number (*Hint*: Use a bottom border under the header, which is on the Section 1 header; there is no header or footer in the First Page Header.)

FIGURE B-1: Word document with artwork and formatting

MediaLoft

Memo

To:	MediaLoft Employees
From:	Elizabeth Reed, Vice President
CC:	Leilani Ho, President
Date:	6/20/2006
Re:	Progress Report for Author Retreat

Summary

The success MediaLoft is experiencing is due to your hard work. We would like to take this time to give you a progress report, and discuss some upcoming plans.

Expansion Plans

There are several new stores being planned (although this is still top secret) in the United States, and we plan on expanding in Europe, Canada, and Asia. Possible new sites include the following cities:

- Paris, France
- Toronto, Canada
- Beijing, China

Think about these potential sites. Are there other international sites we should consider? How should we implement such an expansion? These are topics we will be discussing at the retreat.

Reviewing Excel: Task Reference

This task reference lists the most common tasks covered in Units A through D of Microsoft Office Excel Illustrated. It is designed as a refresher to help you find the button, dialog box, or tab you can use to perform each task.

task	method	task	method
Getting Started with Excel 2003		Program, start	Click [start], click Microsoft Office Excel 2003 or point to All Programs, click Microsoft Office, click Microsoft Office Excel 2003
Button not visible, display	Click	Sheet tab, change color	Right-click sheet tab, click Tab Color
Cell, delete contents	Click Edit, Clear, Contents, or press [Delete]	Sheet tab, change location	Drag tab with pointer
Cell, select	Click the cell, or use [↑], [↓], [←], [→], or click Edit, Go To	Sheet tab, rename	Double-click current name, type new name, press [Enter]
Character, delete to the left	Press [Backspace]	Toolbars, change display	Click Tools, Customize, Options tab, deselect Show Standard and Formatting toolbars on two rows
Character, delete to the right	Press [Delete]	Value, enter	Click cell, type value, click or press [Enter]
Entry, accept	Click ✓	Workbook, close	Click File, Close
Entry, cancel	Click ✗	Workbook, create	Click or click New Workbook in the Getting Started or New Workbook task pane
First active cell, return to	Press [Ctrl][Home]	Workbook, open	Click or click workbook name or Open in the Getting Started task pane
Folder, create	Click	Workbook, open using template	Click Other Task Panes list arrow in the Getting Started task pane, click New Workbook, click Templates
Getting Started task pane, display	Click	Workbook, save	Click
Help, search	Click , type keyword/question, click → or click Type a question for help box on menu bar, type question, press [Enter]	Workbook, save with a new name	Click File, Save As
Help, hide the Office Assistant	Click Help, Hide the Office Assistant	Worksheet, copy	Press [Ctrl], drag sheet tab
Help, show the Office Assistant	Click Help, Show the Office Assistant	Worksheet, delete	Click sheet tab, click Edit, Delete Sheet, or right-click Sheet tab, click Delete
Help, display list of recently asked questions	Click Type a question for help list arrow on menu bar	Worksheet, display next screen of	Press [Page Up] or [Page Down]
Label, enter	Make cell active, type label, click ✓ or press [Enter]	Worksheet, insert	Display sheet you want to follow new sheet, click Insert, Worksheet
Label, enter number as	Type apostrophe (') before number	Worksheet, move	Drag sheet tab to new location, release mouse button when triangle pointer is correctly positioned
Menu, open	Click menu name on the menu bar		
Office Assistant, change	Right-click Office Assistant, click Options, click Gallery tab, click Back/Next on Gallery tab, click OK	Worksheet, preview	Click
Office Assistant, hide	Click Help, Hide the Office Assistant	Worksheet, print using existing settings	Click
Preview, magnify	Click preview with pointer		
Preview, reduce	Click preview with pointer	Worksheet, rename	Right-click sheet tab, click Rename, type a new name
Program, exit	Click File, Exit		

task	method	task	method
Building and Editing Worksheets		Border, add	Click [⊞ ▾]
Absolute cell reference, make	Highlight or click in reference on formula bar, press [F4]	Cell A1, go to	Press [Ctrl][Home]
Cells, delete	Select cells, click Edit, Delete	Clip art, insert	Click Insert, point to Picture, click Clip Art
Cells, insert	Click Insert, Cells	Color, fill a cell with	Click [🪣 ▾]
Cell entry, copy	Click [📋]	Column, delete	Click column heading, click Edit, Delete
Cell entry, cut	Click [✂]	Column, hide	Click Format, point to Column, click Hide
Cell entry, edit	Double-click cell, or press [F2]	Column, unhide	Click Format, point to Column, click Unhide
Cell entry, paste	Click [📋]		
Characters to the left, delete	Press [Backspace]	Column, insert	Right-click cell in column, click Insert, select Entire column option, click OK
Characters to the right, delete	Press [Delete]		
Clipboard, open	Click Edit, Office Clipboard	Column width, size to widest entry	Double-click ✛ pointer between columns
Clipboard entry, paste	Click item in Clipboard task pane	Comma format, apply	Click [,]
Drag-and-drop method, copy using	Select cell(s), press and hold [Ctrl], drag with pointer	Comment, add	Click Insert, Comment
Drag-and-drop method, move using	Select cell(s), drag pointer	Comment, edit	Click cell with comment, click Insert, Edit Comment
Entry, confirm	Click [✓]	Comments, view	Click View, Comments
Entry, copy to right	Select entry or formula and range to right, click Edit, Fill, Right	Conditional format, create	Click Format, Conditional Formatting
		Conditional format, delete	Click Format, Conditional Formatting, Delete
Entry, undo	Click [↶]		
Fill sequence, complete	Click Edit, point to Fill, click Series	Currency format, apply	Click [$]
Formula, enter	Press =, click value, press +, -, *, or /, click another value, click [✓]	Date format, apply	Click Format, Cells, click Number tab, click Date, select type, click OK
Function, enter	Click [fx]	Decimals, decrease	Click [.00→]
Moving border, turn off	Press [Esc]	Decimals, increase	Click [←.0.00]
Named range, go to	Click Name box list arrow, click range name	Font, change	Click [Arial ▾]
Range, name	Select range, click Name box, type name, press [Enter]	Font color, change	Click [A ▾]
		Font size, change	Click [10 ▾]
Series, fill	Select first two series cells, drag fill handle	Format, copy	Click [🖌]
		Format Painter, turn off	Press [Esc] or click [🖌]
Sum, calculate	Click [Σ]	Indent, decrease	Click [⸫]
Formatting a Worksheet		Indent, increase	Click [⸫]
AutoFormat, apply	Click Format, AutoFormat	Italics, apply	Click [I]
Bold attribute, apply	Click [B]	Merge and Center, apply	Click [⊞]

Excel Task Reference (Continued)

task	method	task	method
Picture, insert	Click Insert, point to Picture, click Clip Art, From File, or From Scanner or Camera	Arrow, add	Click ✎
Picture, insert in header or footer	Click 🖼	Chart, create	Click 📊
		Chart, delete	Click chart, press [Delete]
Range, select contiguous	Click top-left cell, press and hold [Shift], click bottom-right cell	Chart, deselect	Click outside chart
		Chart, move	Drag chart with ↔ pointer
Range, select noncontiguous	Select range, press and hold [Ctrl], select additional cells	Chart, resize	Select chart, drag corner with ↕, ↔, ⬊, or ⬈ pointer
Row, delete	Click row heading, click Edit, Delete	Chart, preview	Click 🔍
Row, insert	Right-click row heading, click Insert	Chart, print	Click 🖨
		Chart, select	Click chart
Row height, size to tallest entry	Double-click bottom of row heading with ✛ pointer	Chart, change location	Click Chart, click Location, click As new sheet or As object in option button, click OK
Row, hide	Click Format, point to Row, click Hide		
Row, unhide	Click Format, point to Row, click Unhide	Chart title, add	Select chart, click Chart, Chart Options, Titles tab
Row contents, delete	Select row, press [Delete]	Chart type, change	Click 📈 ▼ on Chart toolbar
Spelling, check	Click ✓	Data series color, edit	Double-click data series, select color on Patterns tab, click OK
Text, center	Click ▤		
Underline, apply	Click U	Drawing toolbar, display	Click ✎
Value to label, change	Type apostrophe (') before value	Gridlines, add	Select chart, click Chart, Chart Options, click Gridlines tab
Workbook, send electronically	Click 📧	Paper orientation, change	Click 🔍, Setup, Page tab, select orientation option
Working with Charts			
3-D chart, rotate	Click axes, drag handles	Pie slice, explode	Click pie chart, click slice, drag slice from pie

Using Excel: Visual Workshop

Open the workbook Office B-2.xls from the drive and folder where your Data Files are stored, then save it as **MediaLoft Retreat Budget**. Use your Excel skills to make the Data File look like the sample shown in Figure B-2. Enter your name in cell A30, preview the worksheet, then change the page orientation to landscape. Save and print your results. As you modify the worksheet, consider the need for the following:

- Adding, editing, and moving text and values; entering formulas

- Formatting the title and AutoFormatting the data

- Using Conditional Formatting (for prices over $200)

- Clip art (search on **meeting**). If you cannot find this clip, select another one.

- Naming and coloring the sheet tab

- Formatting chart data points (*Hint*: Change the label display to percentages by clicking Chart on the menu bar, clicking Chart Options, clicking the Data Labels tab, then clicking the Percentage check box.)

- Moving and resizing the chart legend (*Hint*: Change the legend font size to 8 point.)

FIGURE B-2: Excel data and chart

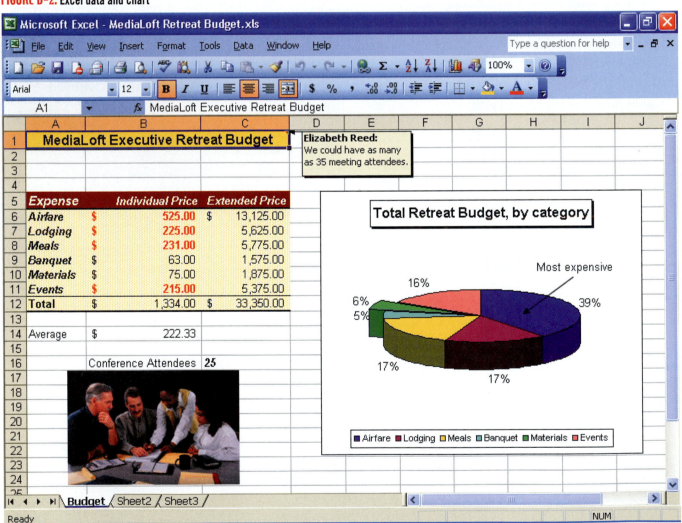

Reviewing Access: Task Reference

This task reference lists the most common tasks covered in Units A through D of Microsoft Office Access Illustrated. It is designed as a refresher to help you find the button, dialog box, or tab you can use to perform each task.

task	method	task	method
Getting Started with Access 2003		Field, move to last in last record	Press [Ctrl][End]
Action, undo	Click	Field, move to previous in current record	Press [Shift][Tab]
Changes to current field, undo	Press [Esc]	Field, move to next	Press [Tab] or [Enter]
Changes to current record, undo	Press [Esc][Esc]	Help, search	Click, type question, click Search, or click Ask a Question box on menu bar, type question, press [Enter]
Character, delete to the left	Press [Backspace]	Help, hide the Office Assistant	Click Help, Hide the Office Assistant
Character, delete to the right	Press [Delete]	Help, show the Office Assistant	Click Help, Show the Office Assistant
Columns, move	Click column to be moved, then drag to new location	Help questions, display list of recently asked	Click Type a question for help list arrow on menu bar
Column, resize	Drag or double-click column header line with ✛ pointer	Menu, open	Click menu name on the menu bar
Date, insert current	Press [Ctrl][;]	Modes, switch between	Press [F2]
Database, close	Click File, Close	Navigation mode, return to	Press [Tab] or [Enter]
Database, compact	Click Tools, Options, click the General Tab	Object, create	Click in Database window
Database, open	Click	Office Assistant, hide	Click Help, Hide the Office Assistant
Database, save	Click	Office Assistant, change	Right-click Office Assistant, click Choose Assistant
Database object, print	Click	Paper orientation, change	Click File, Page Setup, Page tab
Datasheet, preview	Click	Preview, magnify	Click Preview with 🔍 pointer
Datasheet, print on close	Click	Preview pages, view two or more	Click or
Field, display	Click Format, Unhide Columns	Print Preview, close	Click Close
Field, hide	Click Format, Hide Columns	Print Preview, view	Click
Field, move to current in first record	Press [Ctrl][↑]	Program, exit	Click File, Exit
Field, move to current in last record	Press [Ctrl][↓]	Program, start	Click start, point to Microsoft Office Access 2003 or point to All Programs, click Microsoft Office, click Microsoft Office Access 2003
Field, move to current in next record	Press [↓]	Record, create new	Click
Field, move to current in previous record	Press [↑]	Record, delete	Click
Field, move to first in current record	Press [Home]	Record, go to	Press [F5], type record number, press [Enter]
Field, move to first in first record	Press [Ctrl][Home]	Spelling, check	Press [F7] or click
Field, move to last in current record	Press [End]		

Access Task Reference (Continued)

task	method	task	method
Table, open	In Database window, click Tables, click table name, click ▣	Records, sort descending	Click ▣
Toolbars, customize	Click Tools, Customize, Options tab	Relationships, view database	Click ▣
Value from previous record's field, insert	Press [Ctrl][']	Single field, select	Click ▣
View, change objects	Click ▣ , ▣ , ▣ , or ▣ in Database window	Table, create	Double-click Create table by using wizard in Database window
Using Tables and Queries		Table, display the Create table by using wizard shortcut	Click Tools, Options, click View tab, click New object shortcuts
Database, create	Click ▣ on Database toolbar or Blank Database hyperlink in New section of task pane	Task pane, display	Click File, New
		Text, find	Click ▣
Datasheet, view	Click ▣	Wildcard, single character	Type question mark (?)
Design, view	Click ▣	Wildcard, single digit	Type pound (#)
Fields, select All	Click ▣	Wildcard, any character	Type asterisk (*)
Filter, apply/remove	Click ▣	**Using Forms**	
Filter by form	Click ▣	Action, redo	Click Edit, Redo (Last Command)
Filter by selection	Click ▣	AutoForm, create form using	Click ▣ on Database toolbar
First page, display in print preview	Click ▣	Control, move single	Drag ▣ pointer
Font, change	Click Format, Font, click font from list	Control, move all selected	Drag ▣ pointer
Formatting toolbar, display in datasheet	Click View, Toolbars, Formatting (Datasheet)	Control, resize	Drag pointer when over handle
Grid, clear	Click ▣ on the Query toolbar	Controls, selecting multiple	Click control, press [Shift], click additional controls, or drag selection box around controls
Gridlines, change color in datasheet	Click ▣	Fields, select all in Form Wizard	Click ▣
Gridlines, change display of	Click ▣	Field List, toggle on/off	Click ▣ on Design View toolbar
Last page, display in print preview	Click ▣	Font color, change	Click ▣
Line/Border color, change	Click ▣	Font size, change	Click ▣
Next page, display in print preview	Click ▣	Form, create	Click ▣ in Database window
Previous page, display in print preview	Click ▣	Image, insert	Click ▣ on Form Design toolbox
Query, create	Double-click Create query by using wizard in Database window	Label, align text in	Click label, click ▣ , ▣ , or ▣
		Label, modify	Click label, click ▣ on Form Design toolbar, click Format tab
Record, find	Click ▣	Properties, display	Select object, click ▣
Records, sort ascending	Click ▣	Record, enter new	Click ▣
		Record, move to next in Form View	Click ▣

Access Task Reference (Continued)

task	method	task	method
Record, move to previous in Form View	Click ◀	Field, select single for report	Click >
Record, move to first in Form View	Click I◀	Fields, select all for report	Click >>
Record, move to last in Form view	Click ▶I	Fill color, change	Click 🪣▾
Tab order, modify	Click ✎, click View, Tab Order	Fit to page, magnify	Click Fit ▾
Text box, create	Click ab	Italics, apply	Click *I*
Toolbox toolbar, toggle on/off	Click 🛠 on Form Design toolbar	Line/Border color, change	Click ✎▾
Using Reports		Line/Border width, change	Click ▾
AutoReport, create	Click ⚡▾, AutoReport	Margins, change	Click File, Page Setup
Bold , apply	Click **B**	Property sheet, open	Double-click control
Controls, align	Click Format, Align	Sorting or Grouping, create	Click ▤
Controls, move 1 pixel at a time	Press and hold [Ctrl] while pressing arrow keys	Special effect, apply	Click ▭▾
		Text, left-align	Click ≡
Controls, resize 1 pixel at a time	Press and hold [Shift] while pressing arrow keys	Text, right-align	Click ≡
		Text, center	Click ≡
Field, add to report	Click ▤	Toolbox, display	Click 🛠
		Underline, apply	Click U

Office 2003

Using Access: Visual Workshop

Open the Access database Office B-3.mdb from the drive and folder where your Data Files are stored. (*Hint*: Since there is no Save As feature in Access, you should make a copy of Office B-3.mdb on another disk prior to starting this project.)

- Modify the **Hotels table** using Figure B-3 and Figure B-4 as guides.
- Replace **Garden** in the Hilton Garden record with your own name.
- Create the **Hotel Short List Query** using the field order shown in Figure B-5. Display all the fields in the Hotel table for accommodations having in-room data ports and more than two conference rooms. Sort the query in ascending order by zip code, then descending order by hotel name. Use the Hotel Short List Query as the data source. The results of your query should look like Figure B-5.
- Use the Form Wizard and the Hotel Short List Query to create a columnar form that contains all the fields. Accept the default name, use the Expedition style, arrange the fields in a pleasing manner, then adjust the tab order.
- Use the Report Wizard and the Hotel Short List Query to create a columnar report that contains all the fields. Group the report by the number of conference rooms, sorting the hotels in ascending order by hotel name, using the Stepped layout and the Corporate style. Accept the default name, then modify the design so the full field names are displayed. Change the formatting of the Hotel Name label control to red. Change the alignment of the Zip Code field so it is centered under its label control. Add an unbound expression that calculates the average room rate for each group. Make sure the expression is italicized, formatted as currency, and aligned beneath the Room Rate data. Print this report.
- Create and print labels for participants' suitcases using the Hotel Short List Query, showing each hotel name, and the zip code. (*Hint*: Labels in Access are produced with the Report Wizard. Click Reports, click New, then click Label Wizard.) Use the label with the Avery product number C2242, use the default font and font size, place the Hotel Name field on the first line and the Zip Code field on the second line, use the default name, and sort by hotel name.

FIGURE B-3: Access table in Design view

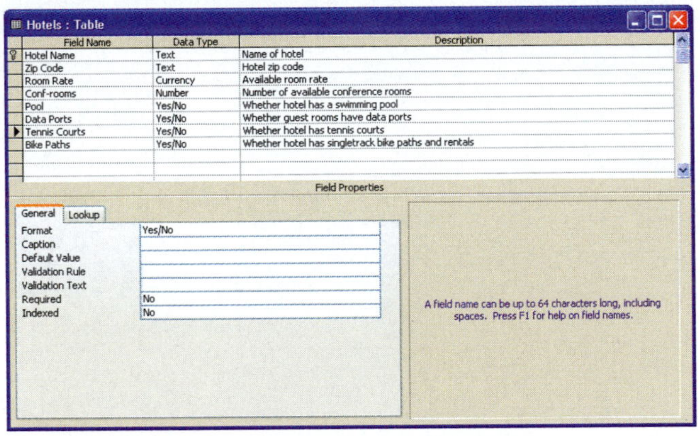

Field Name	Data Type	Description
Hotel Name	Text	Name of hotel
Zip Code	Text	Hotel zip code
Room Rate	Currency	Available room rate
Conf-rooms	Number	Number of available conference rooms
Pool	Yes/No	Whether hotel has a swimming pool
Data Ports	Yes/No	Whether guest rooms have data ports
Tennis Courts	Yes/No	Whether hotel has tennis courts
Bike Paths	Yes/No	Whether hotel has singletrack bike paths and rentals

FIGURE B-4: Access table in datasheet

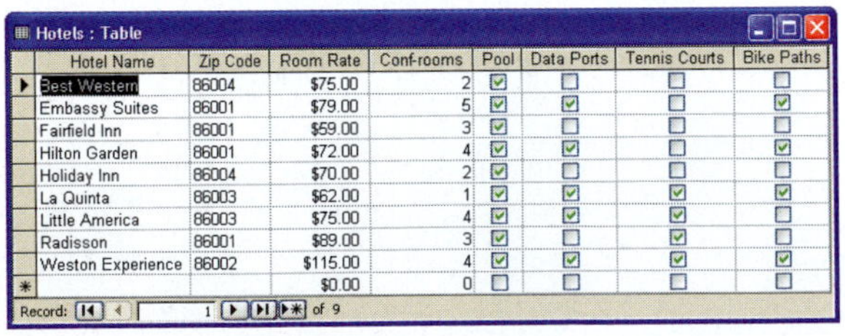

Hotel Name	Zip Code	Room Rate	Conf-rooms	Pool	Data Ports	Tennis Courts	Bike Paths
Best Western	86004	$75.00	2	☑	☐	☐	☐
Embassy Suites	86001	$79.00	5	☑	☑	☐	☑
Fairfield Inn	86001	$59.00	3	☑	☐	☐	☐
Hilton Garden	86001	$72.00	4	☑	☑	☐	☑
Holiday Inn	86004	$70.00	2	☑	☐	☐	☐
La Quinta	86003	$62.00	1	☑	☑	☑	☑
Little America	86003	$75.00	4	☑	☑	☑	☐
Radisson	86001	$89.00	3	☑	☐	☑	☐
Weston Experience	86002	$115.00	4	☑	☑	☑	☑
*		$0.00	0	☐	☐	☐	☐

FIGURE B-5: Access query datasheet

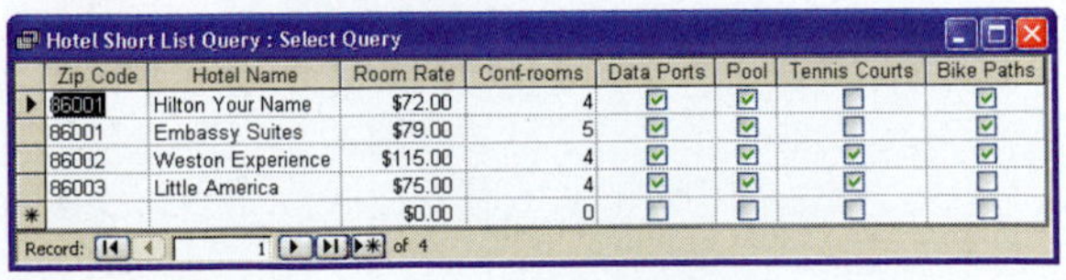

Zip Code	Hotel Name	Room Rate	Conf-rooms	Data Ports	Pool	Tennis Courts	Bike Paths
86001	Hilton Your Name	$72.00	4	☑	☑	☐	☑
86001	Embassy Suites	$79.00	5	☑	☑	☐	☑
86002	Weston Experience	$115.00	4	☑	☑	☑	☑
86003	Little America	$75.00	4	☑	☑	☑	☐
*		$0.00	0	☐	☐	☐	☐

Reviewing PowerPoint: Task Reference

This task reference lists the most common tasks covered in Units A through D of Microsoft Office PowerPoint Illustrated. It is designed as a refresher to help you find the button, dialog box, or tab you can use to perform each task.

task	method	task	method
Getting Started with PowerPoint 2003		Toolbars, change display of	Click Tools, Customize, Options tab, select or deselect Show Standard and Formatting toolbars on two rows
Button not visible, display	Click ⬚		
File, print	Click 🖨	View, change to Normal	Click 🔳
Fonts, save with presentation	Click File, Save As, Tools, Save Options, select Embed TrueType fonts	View, change to Notes page	Click View, Notes Page
		View, change to Slide Show	Click 🖥
Grayscale, view presentation in	Click 🔲	View, change to Slide Sorter	Click 🔳
Help, display list of recently asked questions	Click Type a question for help list arrow on menu bar	**Creating a Presentation**	
		Automatic spell checking, turn off	Click Tools, Options, Spelling and Style tab, clear Check spelling as you type option
Help, hide the Office Assistant	Click Help, Hide the Office Assistant		
Help, search	Click 🔵, type question, click Search or click Type a question for help box on menu bar, type question, press [Enter]	Bullet, convert to new slide	In Outline view, click in bullet, press [Shift][Tab]
		Bullet, move in Outline view	Point to left of bullet, drag up or down
		Bulleted list, insert	Click 📋 in placeholder
Help, show the Office Assistant	Click Help, Show the Office Assistant	Character, delete from placeholder	Click after character, press [Backspace]
Menu, open	Click menu name on the menu bar	Chart, insert	Click 📊 in placeholder
Office Assistant, turn off	Right-click Assistant, click Options, deselect Use the Office Assistant	Content, insert	Click 🖼 in placeholder
Overhead transparencies, print presentation for	Click File, Page Setup, click Slides sized for list arrow, click Overhead	Design Template, apply	Click Other Task Panes list arrow, click Slide Design, click template
Presentation, close	Click File, Close	Diagram or Organization Chart, insert	Click 🔷 in placeholder
Presentation, create from Wizard	Click From AutoContent Wizard hyperlink in New Presentation task pane	Entry, undo	Click ↩
Previous slide, move to	Click ⬆	Graphic, insert on Notes page	Click View, Notes Page, insert graphic using Insert Clip Art task pane
Presentation, preview	Click 🔍		
Presentation, print with current Print options	Click 🖨	Header and Footer, add	Click View, Header and Footer
		Insertion point, move to next placeholder	Press [Ctrl][Enter]
Presentation, save	Click 💾		
Program, exit	Click File, Exit	Media Clip, insert	Click 🎞 in placeholder
Program, start	Click 🟢start, point to Microsoft Office PowerPoint 2003 or click All Programs, click Microsoft Office, click Microsoft Office PowerPoint 2003	Notes, enter slide	Click in Notes pane, type text
		Outline, display presentation	Click Outline tab in tab pane on left side of screen
		Outlining toolbar, display	Click View, point to Toolbars, click Outlining

task	method	task	method
Slide show, end	Press [Esc]	Font size, change	Click 10 ▾
Slide text, enter	Click placeholder, type text	Guide, add to slide	Click existing guide, press [Ctrl], drag guide
Slide, create new	Click ▦	Guide, move	Drag to new position
Slide, create new, with specific layout	Point to layout in task pane, click Layout list arrow, click Insert New Slide	Guides, display	Right-click blank area, click Grid and Guides
Spelling, check	Click ✓	Italics, apply	Click *I*
Table, insert	Click ▦ in placeholder	Line color, add	Click ✎
Task pane, display a different	Click Other Task Panes list arrow	Nonwrapping text label, create	Click ▤, click, slide, type text
Template, apply to all slides	Click Template list arrow in Slide Design task pane, click Apply to All slides	Object color, add	Click ▨ ▾
Template, apply to selected slides	Select slides, point to Template list arrow in Slide Design task pane, click Apply to Selected slides	Object, add or modify 3-D effect	Click ▣
		Object, rotate	Click object, drag rotate handle
Template, create	Create desired presentation, click File, Save As, click Save as type list arrow, choose Design Template, name the template, click Save	Objects, align or distribute	Select objects, click Draw on Drawing toolbar, point to Align or Distribute
		Objects, group or ungroup	Select objects, click Draw on Drawing toolbar, click Group or Ungroup
Text, delete from slide	Select text, press [Backspace] or [Delete]	Paste Options, apply	Click ▦ next to pasted object
Text, demote in Outline view	Click ➡ on Outlining toolbar	Permission, set	Click ⊘
Modifying a Presentation		Presentation, open	Click 📂
Attributes, replace	Click Tools, Options, Spelling and Style tab	Presentation, save as	Click File, Save As
AutoShape, apply shaded background to	Right-click AutoShape, click Format AutoShape	Presentation, send electronically	Click File, Send to, Mail Recipient (as Attachment)
AutoShape, change color	Click AutoShape, click ▨ ▾	Preview, display in Open dialog box	Click ▦ ▾, select Preview
AutoShape, create	Click AutoShapes ▾ on Drawing toolbar	Slides, import	Click Insert, Slides from Files, click Browse, locate presentation
AutoShape text, wrap	Right-click AutoShape, click Format AutoShape, click Text Box tab	Text, center align	Click in text, click ▤
Background, change	Click Format, Background	Text, import	Click Insert, Slides from Outline
Color scheme, change hyperlink	Click Design, click Color Schemes	Text, left-align	Click in text, click ▤
		Text, replace	Click Edit, Replace
Font, change	Click Arial ▾	Text, right-align	Click in text, click ▤
Font color, change	Click **A** ▾	Text box, create	Click ▤

PowerPoint Task Reference (Continued)

task	method	task	method
Enhancing a Presentation		Order, change object's stacking	Click [Draw ▾], point to Order
Animation effects, apply	Click Other Task Panes list arrow, Slide Design - Animation Schemes	Picture, crop	Select picture, click [icon] on Picture toolbar, drag handle
Annotation, create	In slide show, click [icon] on the Slide Show toolbar	Picture, insert	Click [icon]
Annotation drawing, erase	In slide show, press [E]	Picture, recolor	Click [icon]
Automatic Layout Options, change	Click [icon]	Picture, resize and reposition	Click [icon] on Picture toolbar, click Size and Position tabs
Bold, apply	Click [B]	Previous slide, return to	Press [PageUp]
Border, add	Click [icon ▾]	Rehearse Timings, set	Click [icon]
Chart, insert	Click [icon], enter data on datasheet	Screen to black, change	Press [B] during slide show
Chart data, format	Double-click chart, close datasheet, select chart element, click formatting buttons	Screen to white, change	Press [W] during slide show
		Shadow, add	Select object, click [icon] on Drawing toolbar
Clip art, insert	Click [icon] on Drawing toolbar	Slide Show pointer, change to arrow	Press [Ctrl][A]
Clip art, resize	Drag sizing handle		
Currency format, apply	Click [$]	Slide show pointer, change to pencil	Press [Ctrl][P]
Decrease decimal, apply	Click [icon]	Slide show, pause	Press [S]
First slide in slide show, move to	Press [Home]	Slide show, stop	Press [Esc]
		Slide transition, add	Click [Transition] on Slide Sorter toolbar
Format, copy	Click in source, click [icon], click destination	Table, insert	Click [icon]
Graphic, save slide as a	Click File, Save As, click Save as type list arrow, select desired format, name file	Text box, center vertically	Click text block, click Format, Placeholder, click Text Box tab, click Text Anchor point list arrow
Hidden slide, display	Press [H]		
Last slide in Slide show, move to	Press [End]	Timing, change slide show	Click [icon], click [Transition], type number in Automatically after text box
Line style, modify	Click [icon]	Timing, rehearse slide show	Click [icon] on Slide Sorter toolbar, present show
Next slide, advance to in slide show	Press [Enter], [Spacebar], [PageDown], [N], [↓], [↑]		
		Transparent color, apply	Click [icon]
Object, resize	Select object, drag sizing handle	Underline, apply	Click [U]
Object, resize proportionally	Select object, press and hold [Shift], drag sizing handle	Value to label, change	Type an apostrophe (') before entering value

Using PowerPoint: Visual Workshop

Open the file Office B-4.ppt from the location where your Data Files are stored, then save it as **MediaLoft Retreat Presentation**. Use Figure B-6 as a guide as you work on the modifications below. Enter your name in the footer of the master slide, save your work, then print the slides. As you create the presentation, do the following:

- Apply the Network design template.

- Change the slide order, using Figure B-7 as a guide.

- Add the AutoShape shown, then add text to the shape. (*Hint*: Use a bold, 32-point Times New Roman font.)

- Create a chart on the MediaLoft Stores, By Size slide using the data in Table B-1, then relocate the legend above the chart.

- Copy and paste the MediaLoftLogo picture displayed in Slide 1 to the lower-left corner of the master slide.

- Add the clip art image shown in Figure B-7 (or one similar to it), create an oval shape, add Shadow Style 2 to the oval, arrange the objects as shown, then group the objects.

- Add your own timing, animations, and transitions to the slides, then spell check the presentation.

TABLE B-1: Chart data

location	square feet
Boston	60000
Chicago	150000
Houston	75000
Kansas City	130000
New York	90000
San Diego	50000
San Francisco	80000
Seattle	65000

FIGURE B-6: PowerPoint slide in Normal view

FIGURE B-7: PowerPoint slides in Slide Sorter view

Your timing will be different

 **▼ INDEPENDENT CHALLENGE 1**

As the human resources director and training coordinator for Hailey Dow Attorneys-at-Law, you want to create a letter that your department can easily adapt to send to job applicants. You use Word formatting features to create a letter that is both informative and visually appealing.

a. Open the Word document Office B-5.doc, then save it as **HD Multi-Page Letter** in the drive and folder where your Data Files are stored. Create the letter using Figure B-8 as a guide.

b. Insert the Scales clip art file (shown in Figure B-8) at the top of the document. (*Hint*: Search clip art using the keyword **law**. Substitute another piece of clip art if you do not have the image shown.) Use this artwork and the existing text to create a logo. (*Hint*: Use a blue, bold, 48-point Times New Roman font with an embossed effect for the company name, and a blue, 20-point Times New Roman font with a Shadow effect for the **Attorneys-at-Law** text.)

c. Replace Elizabeth Reed with **your name** in the signature area of each document.

d. Spell check the document, preview it for accuracy, save, then print the document.

FIGURE B-8: Multi-page document

▼ INDEPENDENT CHALLENGE 2

As an assistant professor at University College, London, you have decided to examine the population of Inner London (formerly London County), and the Outer Boroughs from 1951 to 1996. Your research assistant has gathered some raw data for you, and you are ready to create worksheets that will help you analyze the data further.

a. Open the Excel workbook Office B-6.xls from the drive and folder where your Data Files are stored, then save it as **London Demographics**.

b. The sheet for Inner London has already been created. Copy all the data on the Data sheet to a new sheet that will be used to summarize the Outer Boroughs, then delete the data for Inner London. Name the sheets accordingly, then apply a different color to each of the two sheet tabs.

c. Replace the column label in cell D3 with **Outer Boroughs**, then enter the population data shown in Figure B-9 for the Outer Boroughs.

d. In each of the two sheets, make sure that you include the following elements:

• Formatted labels and values, and appropriate column widths. (*Hint*: Population values should all use the comma format rounded to the nearest whole number.)

• A formula that calculates the square mile area in cell A17 and D17 on both sheets (rounded to the nearest whole number). Apply borders and a fill color to this information.

• Formulas that calculate the maximum, minimum, and average populations during the 1951–1996 time period in the appropriate cells for All London, Inner London, and the Outer Boroughs. (*Hint*: You can round the average to the nearest whole number.) Surround this information with borders and add a fill color.

• Formulas that contain an absolute reference. (*Hint*: Estimate the population in the Inner and Outer Boroughs in 2010 with a 20% increase. Use cell H3 in the cell reference, which includes a value of .20 for the 20% projected increase.) Place the results in the Speculation columns.

• At least one chart for the data on each sheet using appropriate formatting

• Formulas that contain conditional formatting

• Formulas that determine the percentage of London's total population represented by the Inner and Outer Boroughs; place the information in the percentage columns.

e. In each sheet, delete the rows for the years 1998–2004.

f. Copy data from Sheets 1 and 2 to Sheet 3 so that you have the following information for the years 1951–1996: population for all of London, population for Inner London, and population for Outer London. Name this sheet **Total Population**, and apply any color you choose to the tab.

g. Move the Total Population sheet so that it is the first sheet in the workbook.

h. Create a 3-D bar chart that displays the data for all three areas. Create your own title (using a shadow box), make necessary formatting improvements, and position the legend appropriately.

i. Format the title of each worksheet (in cell A1) so that it is larger and a different color from the rest of the sheet, then change the row height of cell A1 (in each worksheet) to 22.

j. Insert **your name** in each worksheet, spell check your work, save, then print the worksheets.

k. E-mail the workbook to your instructor. (Check with your instructor to make sure this is acceptable.)

FIGURE B-9: London demographic data

	Year	Population	Pop./Sq. Mi.	Inner London (Former London County) Population	Pop./Sq. Mi.	Outer Boroughs Population	Pop./Sq. Mi.
Inner London & Outer London							
Population & Density History							
2004		7,284,000	11,716				
2002		7,244,000	11,652				
2000		7,188,000	11,562				
1998		7,187,000	11,560				
1996		7,074,300	11,379	2,707,800	22,967	4,366,500	8,667
1991		6,679,699	10,744	2,504,451	21,242	4,175,248	8,288
1981		6,696,008	10,770	2,497,978	21,187	4,198,030	8,333
1971		8,119,246	13,060	3,045,436	25,831	5,073,810	10,071
1961		8,171,902	13,144	3,195,114	27,100	4,976,788	9,878
1951		8,348,023	13,428	3,347,982	28,397	5,000,041	9,925

▼ INDEPENDENT CHALLENGE 3

You have just taken over the management of the Competitive Edge Real Estate office. This five-year-old business specializes in residential properties. The market is booming, and since no one has ever created a database for the listings, you have decided to make this your mission.

a. Open the file Office B-7.mdb from the drive and folder where your Data Files are stored. (*Hint*: Since there is no Save As feature in Access, you should make a copy of Office B-7.mdb prior to starting this project.)

b. Resize the fields in the Listings table so all the data is displayed, then check the spelling of the records. (*Hint*: There are easily recognizable spelling errors in the table. All the street names are spelled correctly.)

c. Format the Asking Price field as Currency, displaying no decimal places.

d. Add a new record (Property ID=10020) to the Listings table for your own street address, but use the zip code 87111. Include Radiant Floor heat and Cooling System=Yes in this record, using your own data for the remaining fields. (*Hint*: Make sure your listing has a value over 3100 for the square footage.)

e. Use all the fields in the Listings table to create a columnar form (using any layout, design, and style you choose) that can be used for data entry, called **All Listings**. Add bold formatting to the Zip Code and Asking Price fields.

f. Add any enhancing formatting. Move the fields from their original order to another logical order, then change the tab order.

g. Use the Listings table to create a query that finds all records with radiant floor heat, called **Radiant Floor Heat**. The query should display the following fields: Property ID, Address, Zip Code, Square Feet, Central Heat, and Asking Price. Print the datasheet.

h. Modify the **Radiant Floor Heat** query so it includes only those listings that are over 3100 square feet.

i. Use the Radiant Floor Heat query to create a report called **Radiant Floor Heat Listings** that includes all the fields in the query. Group the records by zip code. Sort the records in descending order by the asking price, then print.

j. Create a calculated control that determines the average price in each grouping. Use the Currency format, displaying no decimal places, and use a color of your choice. Align the control beneath the Asking Price values.

k. Modify the report so that the labels and the contents of all the fields are displayed. Center-align the data in the Property ID field.

l. Use the Listings table to create a label using Avery product number C2160. This label should use the default text attributes and contain the following information: (Line 1) Property ID / Zip Code / Asking Price, (Line 2) Address, (Line 3) Square Feet / Bedrooms / Bathrooms. Sort the labels by zip code, then accept the default name.

▼ INDEPENDENT CHALLENGE 4

As director of software training for the Quest Public Relations firm, you want to create a presentation for the first day of training that generates enthusiasm for the Microsoft Office products. You decide to focus on the benefits of using Word, Access, Excel, and PowerPoint.

a. Open the file Office B-8.ppt from the location where your Data Files are stored, then save it as **Office 2003 Programs**.

b. Modify the slides for the four basic programs in the Office 2003 suite so that they contain text describing your favorite features of each program. Use Figure B-10 as a guide.

c. Apply the design template of your choice to all the slides. Customize the color scheme so that the title text has enough contrast with your chosen color scheme.

d. Italicize the subtitle text on the first slide.

e. Add a text box to the Word slide that contains the following text: **Word is fun to use!**

FIGURE B-10: Modified PowerPoint slides

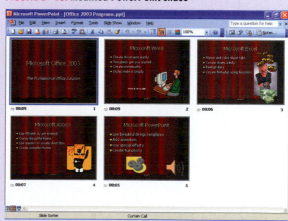

▼ INDEPENDENT CHALLENGE 4 (CONTINUED)

   f. Include clip art on each of the four program slides, resizing and moving objects as necessary. On the Access slide, copy and paste the graphic image you chose, scale it, then position it above the original image.

   g. Apply custom animation to the Microsoft Word slide. Change the animation order of this slide to the following: Slide title, bulleted text. The title text should fly in, and the bulleted text should fly out.

   h. Add three clip art images to the Excel slide, then scale, align, and group them. (*Hint*: Search on the keyword **money**.)

   i. Use drawing tools to create at least three shapes on the PowerPoint slide. Arrange the order of these shapes using your own judgment, then group the objects.

   j. Create brief notes for each slide.

   k. Insert your name in the footer of every slide except the title slide.

   l. Rehearse timings, then be prepared to present this slide show.

   m. Check the spelling, save, then print the slides as handouts.

▼ INDEPENDENT CHALLENGE 5

You are in charge of your local hospital's annual blood drive program. Since you are an experienced Office 2003 user, you want to use your skills to develop an exciting array of documents to promote the event.

   a. Open the file Office B-9.doc from the drive and folder where your Data Files are stored, then save it as **Blood Drive Events**.

   b. Replace Your Name at the end of the document with your name. Replace the date placeholder with the current date, then save and print the document. Save and close the document, then exit Word.

   c. Open the file Office B-10.mdb from the drive and folder where your Data Files are stored. (*Hint*: Since there is no Save As feature in Access, you may want to make a copy of Office B-10.mdb on a separate disk prior to starting this project.)

   d. Open the Blood Donors table, change the name and zip code in the last record of the **Blood Donors** table to your own, then modify the age and blood type to your own. Save your work and close the table.

   e. Open the Previous Donor Query, then merge this query with the Blood Drive Events document. In the Blood Drive Events document, replace the Address Block and Greeting Here placeholders using the Mail Merge hyperlinks and a format you feel is appropriate. Then examine the letter and insert the Blood Type field in the first paragraph of the letter.

   f. Merge the document. (*Hint*: You will create multiple documents later.)

   g. Open the file Office B-11.ppt from the drive and folder where your Data Files are stored, then save it as **Blood Drive Promotion**.

   h. Add a new slide after Slide 4, then add the title **Statistics From Previous Year**. Apply the Title Only slide layout.

   i. Open the file Office B-12.xls, then save it as **Blood Donation Statistics** in the drive and folder where your Data Files are stored.

   j. Copy the chart, then link it to Slide 5 in the Blood Drive Promotion presentation. Move and resize the chart so it is large enough for viewers to see clearly.

   k. Link the chart to the merged Blood Drive Events document, placing it in the second empty line following the paragraph starting with Blood donations are important**....**

l. Tile the PowerPoint and Excel windows. Modify the June data in cell B9 of the Blood Donation Statistics workbook so it is 1540 (from 525), then save the workbook. Your screen should look similar to Figure B-11.

m. Verify that the links in the Blood Drive Events document and Slide 5 of the Blood Drive Promotion presentation have been updated, then save the updated files.

n. Print the merged letter for the last record in the Blood Drive Events document, then close the document and exit Word.

o. Print Slide 4 in the Blood Drive Promotion presentation, then close the presentation and exit PowerPoint.

p. Export the Previous Donor Query in Office B-10.mdb to Excel. (*Hint*: The **Previous Donor Query.xls** workbook will be created.)

q. Enter your name in cell A35 in the Previous Donor Query, change the orientation to landscape, save and print the worksheet, then close the file and exit Excel.

r. Close the Office B-10 database, then exit Access.

Office 2003

FIGURE B-11: Tiled PowerPoint and Excel windows

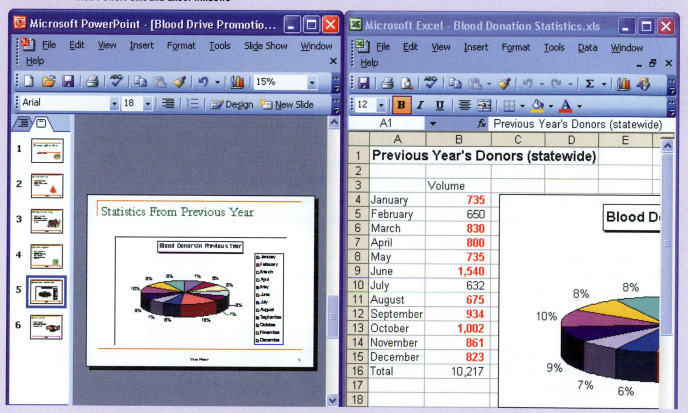

▼ INDEPENDENT CHALLENGE 6

As coordinator of a local historical society, one of your jobs is to create documents for special events. Your club periodically investigates events and shares information with other organizations. A few members of your club have researched the well-known Roswell, New Mexico, incident in which an alleged UFO landing was reported in 1947. Although the members are not convinced there was a UFO, the case remains intriguing—particularly to conspiracy buffs. The historical society members regard it as an interesting piece of history; they also want to strengthen the society's ties to the community and other historical societies. The organization will sponsor a large-scale event on the anniversary of the "landing." You decide to use your Microsoft Office 2003 skills to create professional documents for the event that generate excitement within your organization. You want to prepare the preliminary documents to show other club members before proceeding further.

a. Open the file Office B-13.mdb from the drive and folder where your Data Files are stored. (*Hint*: Since there is no Save As feature for database files, you may want to make a copy of Office B-13.mdb on a separate disk prior to starting this project.)

b. Modify the last record in the Preliminary Partnering Club Members table so that it contains your name, address, and telephone number.

c. Publish the Attending Club Members query in Word. (*Hint*: The Attending Club Members.rtf document will be created.)

d. Change the paper orientation of the Attending Club Members.rtf document to landscape, save your work, then print and close the file.

e. Open the Word document Office B-14.doc, then save it in the drive and folder where your Data Files are stored as **Roswell Mailing Letter**.

f. Insert your name in the signature area of this document, then save and close the document and exit Word.

g. Open the PowerPoint presentation Office B-15.ppt from the drive and folder where your Data Files are stored, then save it as **Roswell Presentation**.

h. Insert your name in the footer of each slide, except the title slide.

i. Insert additional slides after Slide 4 (What Was It?) using the Slides from Outline feature and the file Office B-16.doc located in the drive and folder where your Data Files are stored.

j. Open the file Office B-17.xls, then save it in the drive and folder where your Data Files are stored as **Roswell Special Event**.

k. Link the Partnering Historical Societies data (cells A3:F24) to the last slide (Estimated Attendance). (*Hint*: Resize the linked object so it is as large as possible. You may not be able to read the linked data until the next step is completed.)

l. Draw a rectangle, position the shape behind the linked object, then use a fill color that makes the text in the linked object stand out.

m. In the Excel workbook, change the data in cell B10 to 1575 (from 620), then save your work and exit Excel.

n. Update the link in PowerPoint if necessary, save your work, print the last slide, then exit PowerPoint.

o. Open the Attending Club Members query in the Office B-13.mdb, then merge this query with the Roswell Mailing Letter document.

p. Replace the Address Block and Greeting Here placeholders in the Roswell Mailing Letter document using the Mail Merge hyperlinks and a format you feel is appropriate.

q. Merge all records to a new document, save your work as **Merged Roswell Letters**, then print the letter for the last record.

r. Close the document, then exit Word.

s. Close Office B-13.mdb, then exit Access.

Creating and Formatting Tables

OBJECTIVES

Insert a table

Insert and delete rows and columns

Modify table rows and columns

Sort table data

Split and merge cells

Perform calculations in tables

Use Table AutoFormat

Create a custom format for a table

If you have a SAM user profile, you may have access to hands-on instruction, practice, and assessment of the skills covered in this unit. Log in to your SAM account and go to your assignments page to see what your instructor has assigned.

Tables are commonly used to display information for quick reference and analysis. In this unit, you learn how to create and modify a table in Word, how to sort table data and perform calculations, and how to format a table with borders and shading. You also learn how to use a table to structure the layout of a page. You are preparing a summary budget for an advertising campaign aimed at the Boston market. The goal of the ad campaign is to promote MediaLoft Online, the MediaLoft Web site. You decide to format the budget information as a table so that it is easy to read and analyze.

Inserting a Table

A **table** is a grid made up of rows and columns of cells that you can fill with text and graphics. A **cell** is the box formed by the intersection of a column and a row. The lines that divide the columns and rows and help you see the grid-like structure of a table are called **borders**. You can create a table in a document by using the Insert Table button on the Standard toolbar or the Insert command on the Table menu. Once you have created a table, you can add text and graphics to it. ▓▓▓ You begin by inserting a blank table into the document and then adding text to it.

STEPS

1. **Start Word, close the Getting Started task pane, click the Print Layout View button 🔲 on the horizontal scroll bar if it is not already selected, click the Zoom list arrow on the Standard toolbar, then click Page Width**

   A blank document appears in Print Layout view.

2. **Click the Insert Table button 🔲 on the Standard toolbar**

   A grid opens below the button. You move the pointer across this grid to select the number of columns and rows you want the table to contain. If you want to create a table with more than five columns or more than four rows, then expand the grid by dragging the lower-right corner.

3. **Point to the second box in the fourth row to select 4x2 Table, then click**

   A table with two columns and four rows is inserted in the document, as shown in Figure E-1. Black borders surround the table cells. The insertion point is in the first cell in the first row.

4. **Type Location, then press [Tab]**

   Pressing [Tab] moves the insertion point to the next cell in the row.

5. **Type Cost, press [Tab], then type Boston Sunday Globe**

   Pressing [Tab] at the end of a row moves the insertion point to the first cell in the next row.

6. **Press [Tab], type 27,600, press [Tab], then type the following text in the table, pressing [Tab] to move from cell to cell**

Boston.com	**25,000**
Taxi tops	**18,000**

7. **Press [Tab]**

   Pressing [Tab] at the end of the last cell of a table creates a new row at the bottom of the table, as shown in Figure E-2. The insertion point is located in the first cell in the new row.

TROUBLE
If you pressed [Tab] after the last row, click the Undo button ⟲ on the Standard toolbar to remove the new blank row.

8. **Type the following, pressing [Tab] to move from cell to cell and to create new rows**

Boston Herald	**18,760**
Townonline.com	**3,250**
Bus stops	**12,000**
Boston Magazine	**12,400**

9. **Click the Save button 🔲 on the Standard toolbar, then save the document with the file-name Boston Ad Budget to the drive and folder where your Data Files are located**

   The table is shown in Figure E-3.

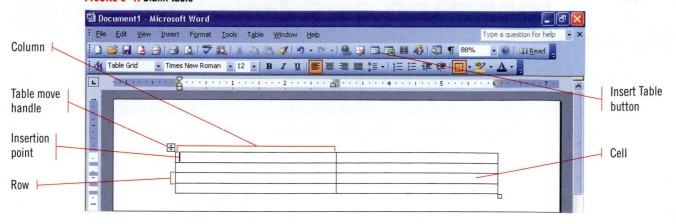

FIGURE E-1: Blank table

Column

Table move handle

Insertion point

Row

Insert Table button

Cell

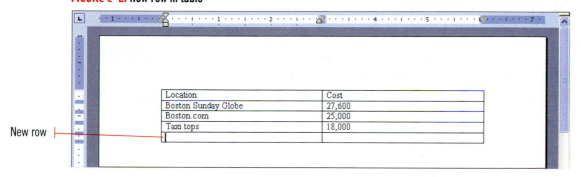

FIGURE E-2: New row in table

New row

Location	Cost
Boston Sunday Globe	27,600
Boston.com	25,000
Taxi tops	18,000

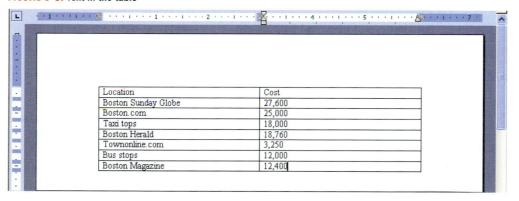

FIGURE E-3: Text in the table

Location	Cost
Boston Sunday Globe	27,600
Boston.com	25,000
Taxi tops	18,000
Boston Herald	18,760
Townonline.com	3,250
Bus stops	12,000
Boston Magazine	12,400

Clues to Use

Converting text to a table and a table to text

Another way to create a table is to convert text that is separated by a tab, a comma, or another separator character into a table. For example, if you want to create a two-column table of last and first names, you could type the names as a list with a comma separating the last and first name in each line, and then convert the text to a table. The separator character—a comma in this example—indicates where you want to divide the table into columns, and a paragraph mark indicates where you want to begin a new row. To convert tabbed or comma-delimited text to a table, select the text, point to

Convert on the Table menu, and then click Text to Table. In the Text to Table dialog box, select from the options for structuring and formatting the table, and then click OK to create the table. You can also select the text and then click the Insert Table button on the Standard toolbar to convert the text to a table.

Conversely, you can convert a table to text that is separated by tabs, commas, or some other character by selecting the table, pointing to Convert on the Table menu, and then clicking Table to Text.

Inserting and Deleting Rows and Columns

You can easily modify the structure of a table by adding and removing rows and columns. First, you must select an existing row or column in the table to indicate where you want to insert or delete information. You can select any element of a table using the Select command on the Table menu, but it is often easier to select rows and columns using the mouse: click in the margin to the left of a row to select the row; click the top border of a column to select the column. Alternatively, you can drag across a row or down a column to select it. To insert rows and columns, use the Insert command on the Table menu or the Insert Rows and Insert Columns buttons on the Standard toolbar. To delete rows and columns, use the Delete command on the Table menu. You add a new row to the table and delete an unnecessary row. You also add new columns to the table to provide more detailed information.

STEPS

1. **Click the Show/Hide ¶ button ¶ on the Standard toolbar to display formatting marks**
    An end of cell mark appears at the end of each cell and an end of row mark appears at the end of each row.

2. **Place the pointer in the margin to the left of the Townonline.com row until the pointer changes to ⬁, then click**
    The entire row is selected, including the end of row mark. If the end of row mark is not selected, you have selected only the text in a row, not the row itself. When a row is selected, the Insert Table button changes to the Insert Rows button.

3. **Click the Insert Rows button ⬛ on the Standard toolbar**
    A new row is inserted above the Townonline.com row, as shown in Figure E-4.

4. **Click the first cell of the new row, type Boston Phoenix, press [Tab], then type 15,300**
    Clicking in a cell moves the insertion point to that cell.

5. **Select the Boston Herald row, right-click the selected row, then click Delete Rows on the shortcut menu**
    The selected row is deleted. If you select a row and press [Delete], you delete only the contents of the row, not the row itself.

6. **Place the pointer over the top border of the Location column until the pointer changes to ⬇, then click**
    The entire column is selected. When a column is selected, the Insert Table button changes to the Insert Columns button.

7. **Click the Insert Columns button ⬛ on the Standard toolbar, then type Type**
    A new column is inserted to the left of the Location column, as shown in Figure E-5.

8. **Click in the Location column, click Table on the menu bar, point to Insert, click Columns to the Right, then type Details in the first cell of the new column**
    A new column is added to the right of the Location column. You can also use the Insert command to add columns to the left of the active column or to insert rows above or below the active row.

9. **Press [⬇] to move the insertion point to the next cell in the Details column, enter the text shown in Figure E-6 in each cell in the Details and Type columns, click ¶ to turn off the display of formatting marks, then save your changes**
    You can use the arrow keys to move the insertion point from cell to cell. Notice that text wraps to the next line in the cell as you type. Compare your table to Figure E-6.

FIGURE E-4: Inserted row

Insert Rows button

End of cell mark

End of row mark

New row is selected by default

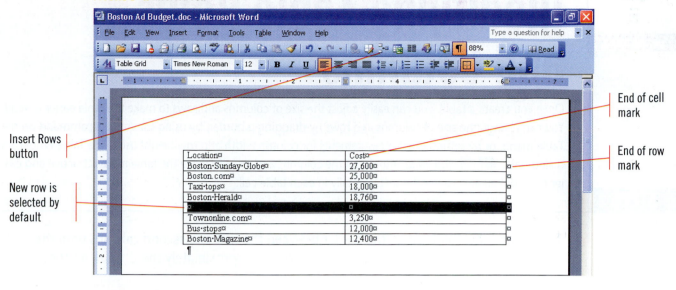

FIGURE E-5: Inserted column

New column

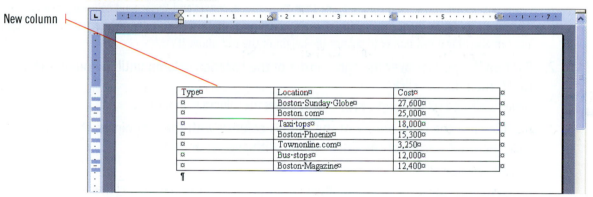

FIGURE E-6: Text in Type and Details columns

Text wraps to the next line

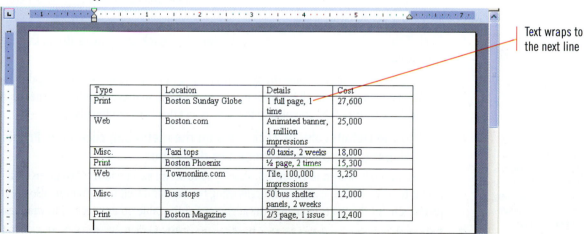

Type	Location	Details	Cost
Print	Boston Sunday Globe	1 full page, 1 time	27,600
Web	Boston.com	Animated banner, 1 million impressions	25,000
Misc.	Taxi tops	60 taxis, 2 weeks	18,000
Print	Boston Phoenix	½ page, 2 times	15,300
Web	Townonline.com	Tile, 100,000 impressions	3,250
Misc.	Bus stops	50 bus shelter panels, 2 weeks	12,000
Print	Boston Magazine	2/3 page, 1 issue	12,400

Clues to Use

Copying and moving rows and columns

You can copy and move rows and columns within a table in the same manner you copy and move text. Select the row or column you want to move, then use the Copy or Cut button to place the selection on the Clipboard. Place the insertion point in the location you want to insert the row or column, then click the Paste button to paste the selection. Rows are inserted above the row containing the insertion point; columns are inserted to the left of the column containing the insertion point. You can also copy or move columns and rows by selecting them and using the pointer to drag them to a new location in the table.

Modifying Table Rows and Columns

Once you create a table, you can easily adjust the size of columns and rows to make the table easier to read. You can change the size of columns and rows by dragging a border, by using the AutoFit command on the Table menu, or by setting exact measurements for column width and row height using the Table Properties dialog box. ████ You adjust the size of the columns and rows to make the table more attractive and easier to read. You also center the text vertically in each table cell.

STEPS

QUICK TIP

Press [Alt] as you drag a border to display the column width or row height measurements on the ruler.

1. **Position the pointer over the border between the first and second columns until the pointer changes to ╫, then drag the border to approximately the ½" mark on the horizontal ruler**

   The dotted line that appears as you drag represents the border. Dragging the column border changes the width of the first and second columns: the first column is narrower and the second column is wider. When dragging a border to change the width of an entire column, make sure no cells are selected in the column. You can also drag a row border to change the height of the row above it.

2. **Position the pointer over the right border of the Location column until the pointer changes to ╫, then double-click**

   Double-clicking a column border automatically resizes the column to fit the text.

3. **Double-click the right border of the Details column with the ╫ pointer, then double-click the right border of the Cost column with the ╫ pointer**

   The widths of the Details and Cost columns are adjusted.

4. **Move the pointer over the table, then click the table move handle ⊞ that appears outside the upper-left corner of the table**

   Clicking the table move handle selects the entire table. You can also use the Select command on the Table menu to select an entire table.

QUICK TIP

Quickly resize a table by dragging the table resize handle to a new location.

5. **Click Table on the menu bar, point to AutoFit, click Distribute Rows Evenly, then deselect the table**

   All the rows in the table become the same height, as shown in Figure E-7. You can also use the commands on the AutoFit menu to make all the columns the same width, to make the width of the columns fit the text, and to adjust the width of the columns so the table is justified between the margins.

QUICK TIP

To change the margins in all the cells in a table, click Options on the Table tab, then enter new margin settings in the Table Options dialog box.

6. **Click in the Details column, click Table on the menu bar, click Table Properties, then click the Column tab in the Table Properties dialog box**

   The Column tab, shown in Figure E-8, allows you to set an exact width for columns. You can specify an exact height for rows and an exact size for cells using the Row and Cell tabs. You can also use the Table tab to set a precise size for the table, to change the alignment of the table on a page, and to wrap text around a table.

7. **Select the measurement in the Preferred width text box, type 3, then click OK**

   The width of the Details column changes to 3".

QUICK TIP

Quickly center a table on a page by selecting the table and clicking the Center button ≡ on the Formatting toolbar.

8. **Click ⊞ to select the table, click Table on the menu bar, click Table Properties, click the Cell tab, click the Center box in the Vertical alignment section, click OK, deselect the table, then save your changes**

   The text is centered vertically in each table cell, as shown in Figure E-9.

FIGURE E-7: Resized columns and rows

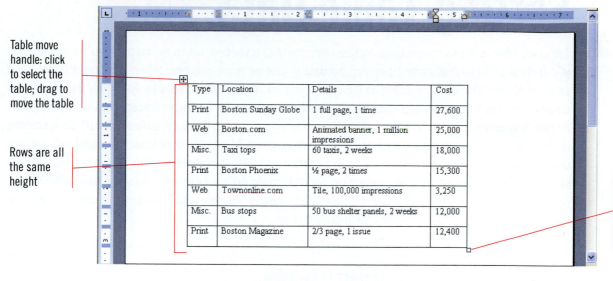

Table move handle: click to select the table; drag to move the table

Rows are all the same height

Table resize handle; drag to change the size of all the rows and columns

FIGURE E-8: Table Properties dialog box

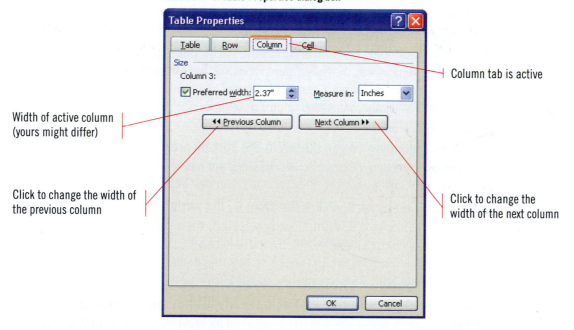

Column tab is active

Width of active column (yours might differ)

Click to change the width of the previous column

Click to change the width of the next column

FIGURE E-9: Text centered vertically in cells

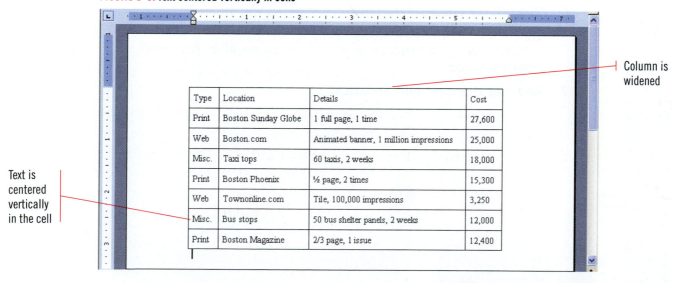

Column is widened

Text is centered vertically in the cell

Sorting Table Data

Tables are often easier to interpret and analyze when the data is **sorted**, which means the rows are organized in alphabetical or sequential order based on the data in one or more columns. When you sort a table, Word arranges all the table data according to the criteria you set. You set sort criteria by specifying the column (or columns) by which you want to sort, and indicating the sort order—ascending or descending—you want to use. **Ascending order** lists data alphabetically or sequentially (from A to Z, 0 to 9, or earliest to latest). **Descending order** lists data in reverse alphabetical or sequential order (from Z to A, 9 to 0, or latest to earliest). You can sort using the data in one column or multiple columns. When you sort by multiple columns you must select primary, secondary, and tertiary sort criteria. You use the Sort command on the Table menu to sort a table. ⬛ You sort the table so that all ads of the same type are listed together. You also add secondary sort criteria so that the ads within each type are listed in descending order by cost.

STEPS

1. **Place the insertion point anywhere in the table**

   To sort an entire table, you simply need to place the insertion point anywhere in the table. If you want to sort specific rows only, then you must select the rows you want to sort.

QUICK TIP

To quickly sort a table by a single column, click in the column, then click the Sort Ascending [A↓] or Sort Descending button [Z↓] on the Tables and Borders toolbar. When you use these buttons, Word does not include the header row in the sort.

2. **Click Table on the menu bar, then click Sort**

   The Sort dialog box opens, as shown in Figure E-10. You use this dialog box to specify the column or columns by which you want to sort, the type of information you are sorting (text, numbers, or dates), and the sort order (ascending or descending). Column 1 is selected by default in the Sort by list box. Since you want to sort your table first by the information in the first column—the type of ad (Print, Web, or Misc.)—you don't change the Sort by criteria.

3. **Click the Descending option button in the Sort by area**

   The ad type information will be sorted in descending—or reverse alphabetical—order, so that the "Web" ads will be listed first, followed by the "Print" ads, and then the "Misc." ads.

4. **In the first Then by section click the Then by list arrow, click Column 4, click the Type list arrow, click Number if it is not already selected, then click the Descending option button**

   Within the Web, Print, and Misc. groups, the rows will be sorted by the cost of the ad—the information contained in the fourth column, which is numbers, not dates or text. The rows will appear in descending order within each group, with the most expensive ad listed first.

5. **Click the Header row option button in the My list has section to select it**

   The table includes a header row that you do not want included in the sort. A **header row** is the first row of a table that contains the column headings.

6. **Click OK, then deselect the table**

   The rows in the table are sorted first by the information in the Type column and second by the information in the Cost column, as shown in Figure E-11. The first row of the table, which is the header row, is not included in the sort.

7. **Save your changes to the document**

FIGURE E-10: Sort dialog box

Select the primary sort column

Select the secondary sort criteria

Select the tertiary (third) sort criteria

Choose to include or exclude the header row in the sort

Choose the sort order

Select the type of data in the sort column

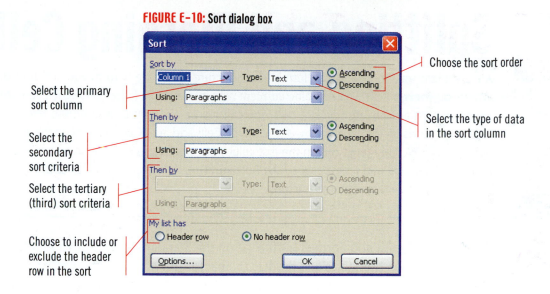

FIGURE E-11: Sorted table

Header row is not included in the sort

First, rows are sorted by type in descending order

Second, within each type, rows are sorted by cost in descending order

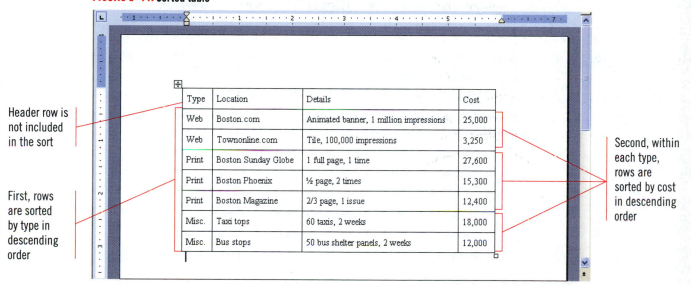

Type	Location	Details	Cost
Web	Boston.com	Animated banner, 1 million impressions	25,000
Web	Townonline.com	Tile, 100,000 impressions	3,250
Print	Boston Sunday Globe	1 full page, 1 time	27,600
Print	Boston Phoenix	½ page, 2 times	15,300
Print	Boston Magazine	2/3 page, 1 issue	12,400
Misc.	Taxi tops	60 taxis, 2 weeks	18,000
Misc.	Bus stops	50 bus shelter panels, 2 weeks	12,000

Clues to Use

Sorting lists and paragraphs

In addition to sorting table data, you can use the Sort command on the Table menu to sort lists and paragraphs. For example, you might want to sort a list of names alphabetically. To sort lists and paragraphs, select the items you want included in the sort, click Table on the menu bar, and then click Sort. In the Sort Text dialog box, use the Sort by list arrow to select the sort by criteria (paragraphs or fields), use the Type list arrow to select the type of data (text, numbers, or dates), and then click the Ascending or Descending option button to choose a sort order.

When sorting text information in a document, the term "fields" refers to text or numbers that are separated by a character, such as a tab or a comma. For example, if the names you want to sort are listed in "Last name, First name" order, then last name and first name are each considered a field. You can choose to sort the list in alphabetical order by last name or by first name. Use the Options button in the Sort Text dialog box to specify the character that separates the fields in your lists or paragraphs, along with other sort options.

Splitting and Merging Cells

A convenient way to change the format and structure of a table is to merge and split the table cells. When you **merge** cells, you combine adjacent cells into a single larger cell. When you **split** a cell, you divide an existing cell into multiple cells. You can merge and split cells using the Merge Cells and Split Cells commands on the Table menu, or the Merge Cells and Split Cells buttons on the Tables and Borders toolbar. 🎨 You merge cells in the first column to create a single cell for each ad type—Web, Print, and Misc. You also add a new row to the bottom of the table, and split the cells in the row to create three new rows with a different structure.

STEPS

TROUBLE
To move the Tables and Borders toolbar, click its title bar and drag it to a new location.

1. **Click the Tables and Borders button** 🔲 **on the Standard toolbar, then click the Draw Table button** 🔲 **on the Tables and Borders toolbar to turn off the Draw pointer** ✏ **if necessary**

   The Tables and Borders toolbar, which includes buttons for formatting and working with tables, opens. See Table E-1.

2. **Select the two Web cells in the first column of the table, click the Merge Cells button** 🔳 **on the Tables and Borders toolbar, then deselect the text**

   The two Web cells merge to become a single cell. When you merge cells, Word converts the text in each cell into a separate paragraph in the merged cell.

3. **Select the first Web in the cell, then press [Delete]**

4. **Select the three Print cells in the first column, click** 🔳 **, type Print, select the two Misc. cells, click** 🔳 **, then type Misc.**

   The three Print cells merge to become one cell and the two Misc. cells merge to become one cell.

5. **Click the Bus stops cell, click the Insert Table list arrow** 🔳▾ **on the Tables and Borders toolbar, then click Insert Rows Below**

   A row is added to the bottom of the table. The Insert Table button on the Tables and Borders toolbar also changes to the Insert Rows Below button. The active buttons on the Tables and Borders toolbar reflect the most recently used commands. You can see a menu of related commands by clicking the list arrow next to a button.

6. **Select the first three cells in the new last row of the table, click** 🔳 **, then deselect the cell**

   The three cells in the row merge to become a single cell.

QUICK TIP
To split a table in two, click the row you want to be the first row in the second table, click Table on the menu bar, then click Split Table.

7. **Click the first cell in the last row, then click the Split Cells button** 🔳 **on the Tables and Borders toolbar**

   The Split Cells dialog box opens, as shown in Figure E-12. You use this dialog box to split the selected cell or cells into a specific number of columns and rows.

8. **Type 1 in the Number of columns text box, press [Tab], type 3 in the Number of rows text box, click OK, then deselect the cells**

   The single cell is divided into three rows of equal height. When you split a cell into multiple rows and/or columns, the width of the original column does not change. If the cell you split contains text, all the text appears in the upper-left cell.

9. **Click the last cell in the Cost column, click** 🔳 **, repeat Step 8, then save your changes**

   The cell is split into three rows, as shown in Figure E-13. The last three rows of the table now have only two columns.

FIGURE E-12: Split Cells dialog box

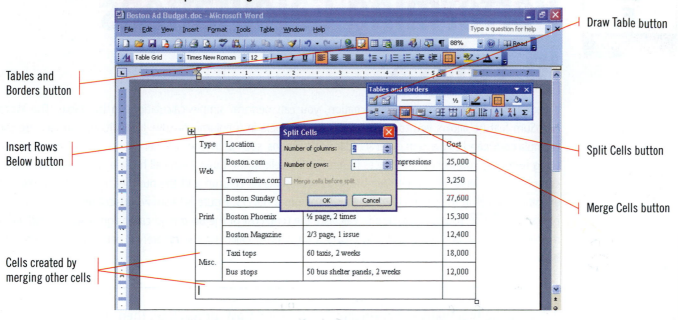

Tables and Borders button

Draw Table button

Insert Rows Below button

Split Cells button

Merge Cells button

Cells created by merging other cells

FIGURE E-13: Cells split into three rows

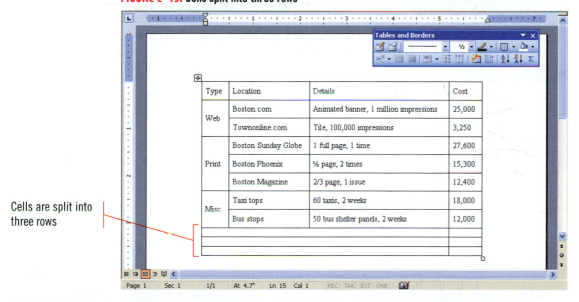

Cells are split into three rows

TABLE E-1: Buttons on the Tables and Borders toolbar

button	use to	button	use to
	Draw a table or cells		Divide a cell into multiple cells
	Remove a border between cells		Change the alignment of text in cells
	Change border line style		Make rows the same height
½	Change the thickness of borders		Make columns the same width
	Change the border color		Format the table with a Table AutoFormat table style
	Add or remove individual borders		Change the orientation of text
	Change the shading color of cells		Sort rows in ascending order
	Insert rows, columns, cells, or a table, and AutoFit columns		Sort rows in descending order
	Combine the selected cells into a single cell	Σ	Calculate the sum of values above or to the left of the active cell

Performing Calculations in Tables

If your table includes numerical information, you can perform simple calculations in the table. The Word AutoSum feature allows you to quickly total the numbers in a column or row. In addition, you can use the Formula command to perform other standard calculations, such as averages. When you calculate data in a table using formulas, you use cell references to refer to the cells in the table. Each cell has a unique **cell reference** composed of a letter and a number; the letter represents its column and the number represents its row. For example, the cell in the third row of the fourth column is cell D3. Figure E-14 shows the cell references in a simple table.  You use AutoSum to calculate the total cost of the Boston ad campaign. You also add information about the budgeted cost and create a formula to calculate the difference between the actual and budgeted costs.

STEPS

QUICK TIP

If a column or row contains blank cells, you must type a zero in any blank cell before using AutoSum.

1. **Click the first blank cell in column 1, type Total Cost, press [Tab], then click the AutoSum button Σ on the Tables and Borders toolbar**

   Word totals the numbers in the cells above the active cell and inserts the sum as a field. You can use the AutoSum button to quickly total the numbers in a column or a row. If the cell you select is at the bottom of a column of numbers, AutoSum totals the column. If the cell is at the right end of a row of numbers, AutoSum totals the row.

2. **Select 12,000 in the cell above the total, then type 13,500**

   If you change a number that is part of a calculation, you must recalculate the field result.

QUICK TIP

To change a field result to regular text, click the field, then press [Ctrl][Shift][F9].

3. **Press [↓], then press [F9]**

   When the insertion point is in a cell that contains a formula, pressing [F9] updates the field result.

4. **Press [Tab], type Budgeted, press [Tab], type 113,780, press [Tab], type Difference, then press [Tab]**

   The insertion point is in the last cell of the table.

5. **Click Table on the menu bar, then click Formula**

   The Formula dialog box opens, as shown in Figure E-15. The SUM formula appears in the Formula text box. Word proposes to sum the numbers above the active cell, but you want to insert a formula that calculates the difference between the actual and budgeted costs. You can type simple custom formulas using a plus sign (+) for addition, a minus sign (-) for subtraction, an asterisk (*) for multiplication, and a slash (/) for division.

TROUBLE

Cell references are determined by the number of columns in each row, not by the number of columns in the table. Therefore, rows 9 and 10 have only two columns.

6. **Select =SUM(ABOVE) in the Formula text box, then type =B9-B10**

   You must type an equal sign (=) to indicate that the text following it is a formula. You want to subtract the budgeted cost in the second column of row 10 from the actual cost in the second column of row 9; therefore, you type a formula to subtract the value in cell B10 from the value in cell B9.

7. **Click OK, then save your changes**

   The difference appears in the cell, as shown in Figure E-16.

FIGURE E-14: Cell references in a table

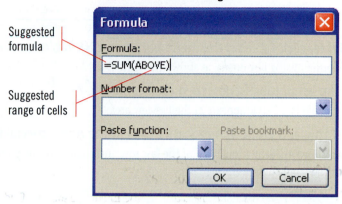

Column D (fourth column)

Cell reference indicates the cell's column and row

Row 3

	A	B	C	D
1	A1	B1	C1	D1
2	A2	B2	C2	D2
3	A3	B3	C3	D3

FIGURE E-15: Formula dialog box

Suggested formula

Suggested range of cells

Formula

Formula:
=SUM(ABOVE)

Number format:

Paste function:

Paste bookmark:

OK   Cancel

FIGURE E-16: Difference calculated in table

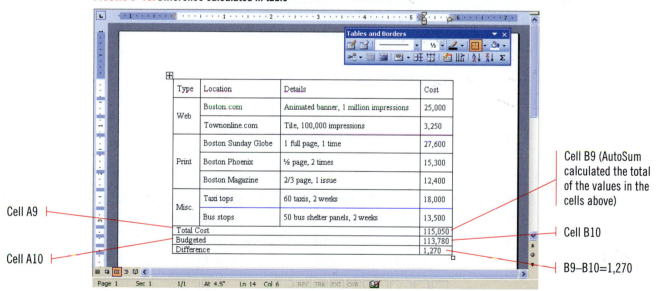

Cell A9

Cell A10

Cell B9 (AutoSum calculated the total of the values in the cells above)

Cell B10

B9–B10=1,270

Clues to Use

Working with formulas

In addition to the SUM function, Word includes formulas for averaging, counting, and rounding data, to name a few. To use a Word formula, click the Paste function list arrow in the Formula dialog box, select a function, and then insert the cell references of the cells you want included in the calculation in parentheses after the name of the function. When entering formulas, you must separate cell references by a comma. For example, if you want to average the values in cells A1, B3, and C4, enter the formula =AVERAGE(A1,B3,C4). You must also separate cell ranges by a colon. For example, to total the values in cells A1 through A9, enter the formula =SUM(A1:A9). To display the result of a calculation in a particular number format, such as a decimal percentage (0.00%), click the Number format list arrow in the Formula dialog box and select a number format. Word inserts the result of a calculation as a field in the selected cell.

Using Table AutoFormat

Adding shading and other design elements to a table can help give it a polished appearance and make the data easier to read. The Word Table AutoFormat feature allows you to quickly apply a table style to a table. Table styles include borders, shading, fonts, alignment, colors, and other formatting effects. You can apply a table style to a table using the Table AutoFormat command on the Table menu or the Table AutoFormat button on the Tables and Borders toolbar. You want to enhance the appearance of the table with shading, borders, and other formats. You use the Table AutoFormat feature to quickly apply a table style to the table.

STEPS

1. **Click in the table, click Table on the menu bar, then click Table AutoFormat**
   The Table AutoFormat dialog box opens, as shown in Figure E-17.

2. **Scroll down the list of table styles, then click Table List 7**
   A preview of the Table List 7 style appears in the Preview area.

3. **Clear the Last row and Last column check boxes in the Apply special formats to section**
   The Preview area shows that the formatting of the last row and column of the table now match the formatting of the other rows and columns in the table.

QUICK TIP
Use the Reveal Formatting task pane to view the format settings applied to tables and cells.

4. **Click Apply**
   The Table List 7 style is applied to the table, as shown in Figure E-18. Because of the structure of the table, this style neither enhances the table nor helps make the data more readable.

5. **With the insertion point in the table, click the Table AutoFormat button 🗔 on the Tables and Borders toolbar, scroll down the list of table styles in the Table AutoFormat dialog box, click Table Professional, then click Apply**
   The Table Professional style is applied to the table. This style works with the structure of the table.

TROUBLE
When you select the Type column, the first column in the last three rows is also selected.

6. **Select the Type column, click the Center button 🗉 on the Formatting toolbar, select the Cost column, then click the Align Right button 🗉 on the Formatting toolbar**
   The data in the Type column is centered, and the data in the Cost column is right-aligned.

7. **Select the last three rows of the table, click 🗉, then click the Bold button 🅱 on the Formatting toolbar**
   The text in the last three rows is right-aligned and bold is applied.

8. **Select the first row of the table, click 🗉, click the Font Size list arrow on the Formatting toolbar, click 16, deselect the row, then save your changes**
   The text in the header row is centered and enlarged, as shown in Figure E-19.

Clues to Use

Using tables to lay out a page

Tables are often used to display information for quick reference and analysis, but you can also use tables to structure the layout of a page. You can insert any kind of information in the cell of a table—including graphics, bulleted lists, charts, and other tables (called **nested tables**). For example, you might use a table to lay out a resume, a newsletter, or a Web page. When you use a table to lay out a page, you generally remove the table borders to hide the table structure from the reader. After you remove borders, it can be helpful to display the table gridlines onscreen while you work. **Gridlines** are light gray lines that show the boundaries of cells, but do not print. If your document will be viewed online—for example, if you are planning to e-mail your resume to potential employers—you should turn off the display of gridlines before you distribute the document so that it looks the same online as it looks when printed. To turn gridlines off or on, click the Hide Gridlines or Show Gridlines command on the Table menu.

FIGURE E-17: Table AutoFormat dialog box

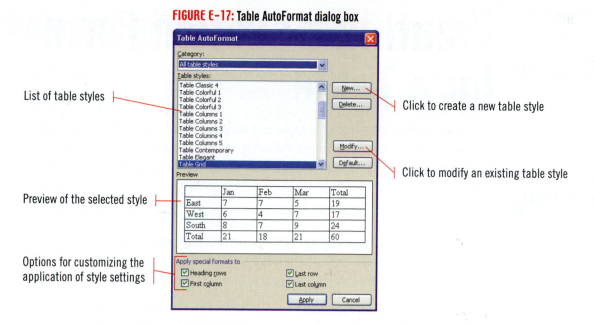

List of table styles

Click to create a new table style

Click to modify an existing table style

Preview of the selected style

Options for customizing the application of style settings

FIGURE E-18: Table List 7 style applied to table

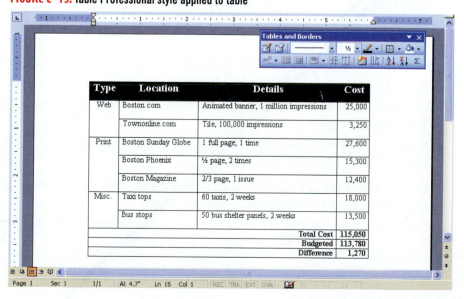

The shading applied to the merged cells is confusing

FIGURE E-19: Table Professional style applied to table

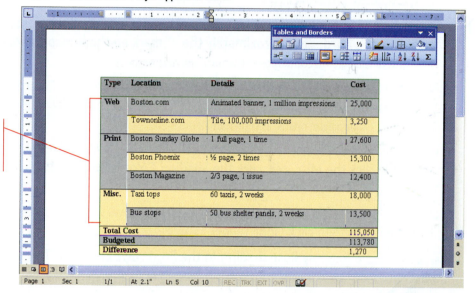

UNIT
E

Word 2003

Creating a Custom Format for a Table

You can also use the buttons on the Tables and Borders toolbar to create your own table designs. For example, you can add or remove borders and shading, vary the line style, thickness, and color of borders, change the orientation of text from horizontal to vertical, and change the alignment of text in cells. You adjust the text direction, shading, and borders in the table to make it easier to understand at a glance.

STEPS

1. **Select the Type and Location cells in the first row, click the Merge Cells button on the Tables and Borders toolbar, then type Ad Location**

   The two cells are combined into a single cell containing the text "Ad Location."

2. **Select the Web, Print, and Misc. cells in the first column, click the Change Text Direction button on the Tables and Borders toolbar twice, then deselect the cells**

   The text is rotated 270 degrees.

3. **Position the pointer over the right border of the Web cell until the pointer changes to +‖+, then drag the border to approximately the ¼" mark on the horizontal ruler**

   The width of the column containing the vertical text narrows.

QUICK TIP

In cells with vertical text, the I-beam pointer is rotated 90 degrees.

4. **Place the insertion point in the Web cell, then click the Shading Color list arrow on the Tables and Borders toolbar**

   The Shading Color palette opens, as shown in Figure E-20.

5. **Click Gold on the palette, click the Print cell, click the Shading Color list arrow, click Pink, click the Misc. cell, click the Shading Color list arrow, then click Aqua**

   Shading is applied to each cell.

6. **Drag to select the six white cells in the Web rows (rows 2 and 3), click the Shading Color list arrow, then click Light Yellow**

7. **Repeat Step 6 to apply Rose shading to the Print rows and Light Turquoise shading to the Misc. rows**

   Shading is applied to all the cells in rows 1–8.

TROUBLE

If gridlines appear, click Table on the menu bar, then click Hide Gridlines.

8. **Select the last three rows of the table, click the Outside Border list arrow on the Tables and Borders toolbar, click the No Border button on the menu that appears, then deselect the rows**

   The top, bottom, left, and right borders are removed from each cell in the selected rows.

QUICK TIP

On the Borders button menu, click the button that corresponds to the border you want to add or remove.

9. **Select the Total Cost row, click the No Border list arrow, click the Top Border button, click the 113,780 cell, click the Top Border list arrow, then click the Bottom Border button**

   A top border is added to each cell in the Total Cost row, and a bottom border is added below 113,780. The completed table is shown in Figure E-21.

10. **Press [Ctrl][Home], press [Enter], type your name, save your changes, print a copy of the document, close the document, then exit Word**

    Press [Enter] at the beginning of a table to move the table down one line in a document.

FIGURE E-20: Shading Color palette

Merged cell

Text is rotated in the cell

Pink
Gold
Aqua

Light Turquoise
Light Yellow
Rose

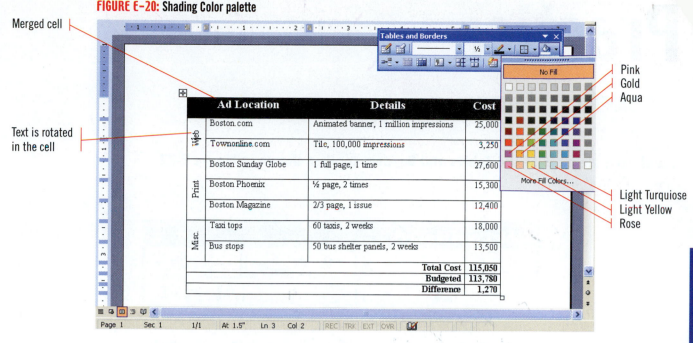

FIGURE E-21: Completed table

Top border added to Total Cost row

Bottom border added to cell

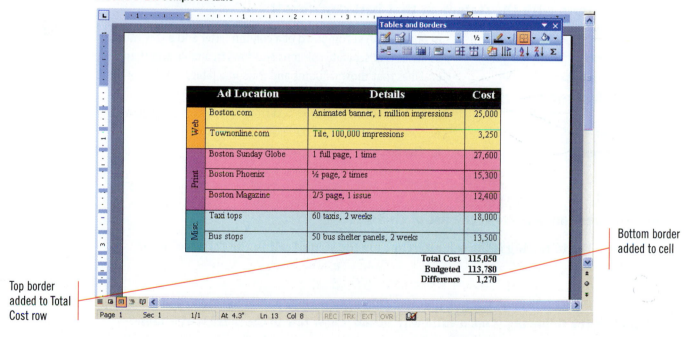

Clues to Use

Drawing a table

The Word Draw Table feature allows you to draw table cells exactly where you want them. To draw a table, click the Draw Table button on the Tables and Borders toolbar to turn on the Draw pointer, and then click and drag to draw a cell. Using the same method, you can draw borders within the cell to create columns and rows, or draw additional cells attached to the first cell. Click the Draw Table button to turn off the draw feature.

If you want to remove a border from a table, click the Eraser button on the Tables and Borders toolbar to activate the Eraser pointer, and then click the border you want to remove. Click the Eraser button to turn off the erase feature. You can use the Draw pointer and the Eraser pointer to change the structure of any table, not just the tables you draw from scratch.

ractice

▼ CONCEPTS REVIEW

Label each element of the Tables and Borders toolbar shown in Figure E-22.

FIGURE E-22

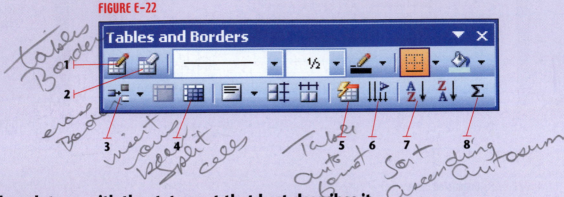

Handwritten labels:
1 — Tables Border
2 — erase Border
3 — insert rows
4 — split cell
5 — Table auto format
6 —
7 — Sort Ascending
8 — Autosum

Match each term with the statement that best describes it.

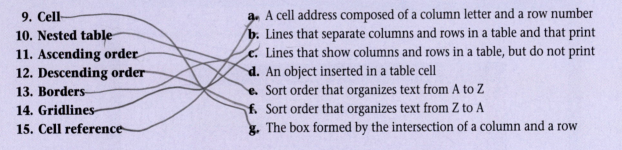

9. Cell
10. Nested table
11. Ascending order
12. Descending order
13. Borders
14. Gridlines
15. Cell reference

a. A cell address composed of a column letter and a row number
b. Lines that separate columns and rows in a table and that print
c. Lines that show columns and rows in a table, but do not print
d. An object inserted in a table cell
e. Sort order that organizes text from A to Z
f. Sort order that organizes text from Z to A
g. The box formed by the intersection of a column and a row

Select the best answer from the list of choices.

16. Which of the following is the cell reference for the second cell in the third column?
   a. C2
   b. 2C
   c. 3B
   d. B3

17. Which of the following is *not* a valid way to add a new row to the bottom of a table?
   a. Click in the bottom row, then click the Insert Rows Below button on the Tables and Borders toolbar
   b. Click in the bottom row, point to Insert on the Table menu, then click Rows Below
   c. Place the insertion point in the last cell of the last row, then press [Tab]
   d. Click in the bottom row, then click the Insert Rows button on the Standard toolbar

18. Which button do you use to change the orientation of text in a cell?
   a. [image button]
   b. [image button]
   c. [image button]
   d. [image button]

19. Which of the following is *not* a correct formula for adding the values in cells A1, A2, and A3?

    a. =SUM(A1:A3)

    b. =SUM(A1, A2, A3)

    c. =SUM(A1~A3)

    d. =A1+A2+A3

20. What happens when you double-click a column border?

    a. A new column is added to the left

    b. The column width is adjusted to fit the text

    c. The columns in the table are distributed evenly

    d. A new column is added to the right

▼ SKILLS REVIEW

1. Insert a table.

    a. Start Word, close the Getting Started task pane, then save the new blank document as **Mutual Funds** to the drive and folder where your Data Files are located.

    b. Type your name, press [Enter] twice, type **Mutual Fund Performance**, then press [Enter].

    c. Insert a table that contains four columns and four rows.

    d. Type the text shown in Figure E-23, pressing [Tab] to add rows as necessary.

    e. Save your changes.

FIGURE E-23

Fund Name	1 Year	5 Year	10 Year
Computers	16.47	25.56	27.09
Europe	-6.15	13.89	10.61
Natural Resources	19.47	12.30	15.38
Health Care	32.45	24.26	23.25
Financial Services	22.18	21.07	24.44
500 Index	9.13	15.34	13.69

2. Insert and delete rows and columns.

    a. Insert a row above the Health Care row, then type the following text in the new row:

    Canada 8.24   8.12   8.56

    b. Delete the Europe row.

    c. Insert a column to the right of the 10 Year column, type **Date Purchased** in the header row, then enter a date in each cell in the column using the format MM/DD/YY (for example, 11/27/98).

    d. Move the Date Purchased column to the right of the Fund Name column, then save your changes.

3. Modify table rows and columns.

    a. Double-click the border between the first and second columns to resize the columns.

    b. Drag the border between the second and third columns to the 2¼" mark on the horizontal ruler.

    c. Double-click the right border of the 1 Year, 5 Year, and 10 Year columns.

    d. Select the 1 Year, 5 Year, and 10 Year columns, then distribute the columns evenly.

    e. Select rows 2–7, use the Table Properties dialog box to set the row height to exactly .3", then save your changes.

4. Sort table data.

    a. Sort the table data in descending order by the information in the 1 Year column.

    b. Sort the table data in ascending order by date purchased.

    c. Sort the table data by fund name in alphabetical order, then save your changes.

...erge cells.

...v above the header row.

...rst cell in the new row with the Fund Name cell.

...ge the second cell in the new row with the Date Purchased cell.

d. Merge the three remaining blank cells in the first row into a single cell, then type **Average Annual Returns** in the merged cell.

e. Add a new row to the bottom of the table.

f. Merge the first two cells in the new row, then type **Average Return** in the merged cell.

g. Select the first seven cells in the first column (from Fund Name to Natural Resources), open the Split Cells dialog box, clear the Merge cells before split check box, then split the cells into two columns.

h. Type **Trading Symbol** as the heading for the new column, then enter the following text in the remaining cells in the column: **FINX**, **CAND**, **COMP**, **FINS**, **HCRX**, **NARS**.

i. Double-click the right border of the first column to resize the column, double-click the right border of the last column, then save your changes.

6. Perform calculations in tables.

a. Place the insertion point in the last cell in the 1 Year column, then open the Formula dialog box.

b. Delete the text in the Formula text box, type **=average(above)**, click the Number Format list arrow, click 0.00%, then click OK.

c. Repeat Step b to insert the average return in the last cell in the 5 Year and 10 Year columns.

d. Change the value of the 1-year average return for the Natural Resources fund to **10.35**.

e. Use [F9] to recalculate the average return for 1 year, then save your changes.

7. Using Table AutoFormat.

a. Open the Table AutoFormat dialog box, select an appropriate table style for the table, then apply the style to the table. Was the style you chose effective?

b. Using Table AutoFormat, apply the Table List 3 style to the table.

c. Change the font of all the text in the table to 10-point Arial. (*Hint*: Select the entire table.)

d. Apply bold to the 1 Year, 5 Year, and 10 Year column headings, and to the bottom row of the table.

e. Center the table between the margins, center the table title **Mutual Fund Performance**, format the title in 14-point Arial, apply bold, then save your changes.

8. Create a custom format for a table.

a. Select the entire table, then use the Align Center button on the Tables and Borders toolbar to center the text in every cell vertically and horizontally.

b. Right-align the dates in column 3 and the numbers in columns 4–6.

c. Left-align the fund names and trading symbols in columns 1 and 2.

d. Right-align the text in the bottom row. Make sure the text in the header row is still centered.

e. Select all the cells in the header row, including the 1 Year, 5 Year, and 10 Year column headings, change the shading color to indigo, then change the font color to white.

f. Apply rose shading to the cells containing the fund names and trading symbols.

g. Apply pale blue, light yellow, and lavender shading to the cells containing the 1 Year, 5 Year, and 10 Year data, respectively. Do not apply shading to the bottom row of the table.

h. Remove all the borders in the table.

i. Add a ½-point white bottom border to the Average Annual Returns cell. (*Hint*: Use the Tables and Borders toolbar.)

j. Add a 2¼-point black border around the outside of the table. Also add a top border to the last row of the table.

k. Examine the table, make any necessary adjustments, then save your changes.

l. Preview the table in Print Preview, print a copy, close the file, then exit Word.

▼ INDEPENDENT CHALLENGE 1

You are the director of sales for a publishing company with branch offices in six cities around the globe. In preparation for the upcoming sales meeting, you create a table showing your sales projections for the fiscal year 2006.

a. Start Word, then save the new blank document as **2006 Sales** to the drive and folder where your Data Files are located.

b. Type the table heading **Projected Sales in Millions, Fiscal Year 2006** at the top of the document, then press [Enter] twice.

c. Insert a table with five columns and four rows, then enter the data shown in Figure E-24 into the table, adding rows as necessary.

d. Resize the columns to fit the text.

e. Sort the table rows in alphabetical order by Office.

f. Add a new row to the bottom of the table, type **Total** in the first cell, then enter a formula in each remaining cell in the new row to calculate the sum of the cells above it.

g. Add a new column at the right end of the table, type **Total** in the first cell, then enter a formula in each remaining cell in the new column to calculate the sum of the cells to the left of it. (*Hint*: Make sure the formula you insert in each cell sums the cells to the left, not the cells above.)

h. Using Table AutoFormat, apply a table style to the table. Select a style that enhances the information contained in the table.

i. Center the text in the header row, left-align the remaining text in the first column, then right-align the numerical data in the table.

j. Enhance the table with fonts, font colors, shading, and borders to make the table attractive and easy to read at a glance.

k. Increase the font size of the table heading to 18 points, then center the table heading and the table on the page.

l. Press [Ctrl][End], press [Enter], type your name, save your changes, print the table, close the file, then exit Word.

FIGURE E-24

Office	Q1	Q2	Q3	Q4
Paris	9500	5800	3900	9800
Tokyo	6700	8900	4500	4900
Berlin	8800	8500	6800	7400
Shanghai	5800	7200	4700	8200
New York	8500	7800	9800	9400
Melbourne	7900	6800	3800	6200

▼ INDEPENDENT CHALLENGE 2

You have been invited to speak to your local board of realtors about the economic benefits of living in your city. To illustrate some of your points, you want to distribute a handout comparing the cost of living and other economic indicators in the U.S. cities that offer features similar to your city. You decide to format the data as a table.

a. Start Word, open the file WD E-1.doc, then save it as **US Cities** to the drive and folder where your Data Files are located.

b. Format the table heading in 18-point Arial, apply bold, then center the heading.

c. Turn on formatting marks, select the tabbed text in the document, then convert the text to a table.

d. Add a row above the first row in the table, then enter the following column headings in the new header row: **City**, **Cost of Living**, **Median Income**, **Average House Cost**, **Bachelor Degree Rate**.

e. Format the table text in 10-point Arial.

f. Apply an appropriate Table AutoFormat style to the table. Apply bold to the header row if necessary.

g. Adjust the column widths so that the table is attractive and readable. (*Hint*: Put the column headings on two lines.)

h. Make the height of each row at least .25".

i. Center Left align the text in each cell in the first column, including the column head.

j. Center Right align the text in each cell in the remaining columns, including the column heads.

k. Center the entire table on the page.

l. Sort the table by cost of living in descending order. (*Hint*: Use the Sort dialog box.)

▼ INDEPENDENT CHALLENGE 2 (CONTINUED)

Advanced Challenge Exercise

- Add a new row to the bottom of the table, then type **Average** in the first cell in the new row.
- In each subsequent cell in the Average row, insert a formula that calculates the averages of the cells above it. (*Hint:* For each cell, replace SUM with AVERAGE in the Formula text box, but do not make other changes.)
- Change the font color of the text in the Average row to a color of your choice.

m. On the blank line below the table, type **Note: The average cost of living in the United States is 100.**, italicize the text, then use a tab stop and indents to align the text with the left side of the table if it is not aligned.

n. Enhance the table with borders, shading, fonts, and other formats, if necessary to make it attractive and readable.

o. Type your name at the bottom of the document, save your changes, print a copy of the table, close the document, then exit Word.

▼ INDEPENDENT CHALLENGE 3

You work in the advertising department at a magazine. Your boss has asked you to create a fact sheet on the ad dimensions for the magazine. The fact sheet should include the dimensions for each type of ad. As a bonus, you could also add a visual representation of the different ad shapes and sizes, shown in Figure E-25. You'll use tables to lay out the fact sheet, present the dimension information, and, if you are performing the ACE steps, illustrate the ad shapes and sizes.

a. Start Word, open the file WD E-2.doc from the drive and folder where your Data Files are located, then save it as **Ad Dimensions**. Read the document to get a feel for its contents.

b. Drag the border between the first and second column to approximately the 2¾" mark on the horizontal ruler, resize the second and third columns to fit the text, then use the Table Properties dialog box to make each row in the table at least .5".

c. Change the alignment of the text in the first column to center left, then change the alignment of the text in the second and third columns to center right.

d. Remove all the borders from the table, then apply a 2¼-point, red, dotted line, inside horizontal border to the entire table. This creates a red dotted line between each row.

e. In the second blank paragraph under the table heading, insert a new table with three columns and four rows, then merge the cells in the third column of the new blank table.

f. Drag the border between the first and second columns of the new blank table to the 1¼" mark on the horizontal ruler. Drag the border between the second and third columns to the 1½" mark.

g. Select the table that contains text, cut it to the Clipboard, then paste it in the merged cell in the blank table. The table with text is now a nested table in the main table.

h. Split the nested table above the Unit Size (Bleed) row. (*Hint*: Place the insertion point in the Unit Size (Bleed) row, then use the Split Table command on the Table menu.)

i. Scroll up, merge the four cells in the first column of the main table, then merge the four cells in the second column.

j. Split the first column into one column and seven rows.

k. Using the Row tab in the Table Properties dialog box, change the row height of each cell in the first column so that the rows alternate between exactly 1.8" and .25" in height. Make the height of the first, third, fifth, and seventh rows 1.8".

l. Add red shading to the first, third, fifth, and seventh cells in the first column, then remove all the borders from the main table.

▼ INDEPENDENT CHALLENGE 3 (CONTINUED)

Advanced Challenge Exercise

- In the first red cell, type **Full Page**, change the font color to white, then center the text vertically in the cell.
- On the Tables and Borders toolbar, change the Line Style to a single line, change the Line Weight to 1, then change the Border Color to white.
- Activate the Draw Table pointer, then, referring to Figure E-25, draw a vertical border that divides the second red cell into ⅔ and ⅓. (*Hint*: You can also divide the cell using the Split Cells and Merge Cells buttons.)
- Label the cells and align the text as shown in the figure. (*Hint*: Change the text direction and alignment before typing text. Take care not to change the size of the cells when you type. If necessary, press [Enter] to start a new line of text in a cell, or reduce the font size of the text.)
- Referring to Figure E-25, divide the third and fourth red cells, then label the cells as shown in the figure.

m. Examine the document for errors, then make any necessary adjustments.

n. Press [Ctrl][End], type your name, save your changes to the document, preview it, print a copy, close the file, then exit Word.

FIGURE E-25

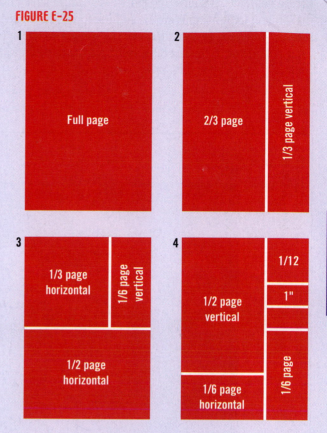

▼ INDEPENDENT CHALLENGE 4

A well-written and well-formatted resume gives you a leg up on getting a job interview. In a winning resume, the content and format support your career objective and effectively present your background and qualifications. One simple way to create a resume is to lay out the page using a table. In this exercise you research guidelines for writing and formatting resumes. You then create your own resume using a table for its layout.

a. Use your favorite search engine to search the Web for information on writing and formatting resumes. Use the keywords **resume templates**.

b. Print helpful advice on writing and formatting resumes from at least two Web sites.

c. Think about the information you want to include in your resume. The header should include your name, address, telephone number, and e-mail address. The body should include your career objective and information on your education, work experience, and skills. You may want to add additional information.

d. Sketch a layout for your resume using a table as the underlying grid. Include the table rows and columns in your sketch.

e. Start Word, open a new blank document, then save it as **My Resume** to the drive and folder where your Data Files are located.

f. Set appropriate margins, then insert a table to serve as the underlying grid for your resume. Split and merge cells and adjust the size of the table columns as necessary.

g. Type your resume in the table cells. Take care to use a professional tone and keep your language to the point.

h. Format your resume with fonts, bullets, and other formatting features. Adjust the spacing between sections by resizing the table columns and rows.

i. When you are satisfied with the content and format of your resume, remove the borders from the table, then hide the gridlines if they are visible.

j. Check your resume for spelling and grammar errors.

k. Save your changes, preview your resume, print a copy, close the file, then exit Word.

▼ VISUAL WORKSHOP

Create the calendar shown in Figure E-26 using a table to lay out the entire page. (*Hints*: The top and bottom margins are .7", the left and right margins are 1", and the font is Century Gothic. The clip art image is inserted in the table. The clip art image is found using the keyword **beach**. Use a different clip art image or font if the ones shown in the figure are not available.) Type your name in the last table cell, save the calendar with the filename **August 2006** to the drive and folder where your Data Files are located, then print a copy.

FIGURE E-26

August 2006

Sunday	Monday	Tuesday	Wednesday	Thursday	Friday	Saturday
		1	2	3	4	5
6	7	8	9	10	11	12
13	14	15	16	17	18	19
20	21	22	23	24	25	26
27	28	29	30	31		

Illustrating Documents with Graphics

OBJECTIVES

Add graphics

Resize graphics

Position graphics

Create text boxes

Create AutoShapes

Use the drawing canvas

Format WordArt

Create charts

SAM

If you have a SAM user profile, you may have access to hands-on instruction, practice, and assessment of the skills covered in this unit. Log in to your SAM account and go to your assignments page to see what your instructor has assigned.

Graphics can help illustrate the ideas in your documents, provide visual interest on a page, and give your documents punch and flair. In addition to clip art, you can add graphics created in other programs to a document, or you can use the drawing features of Word to create your own images. In this unit, you learn how to insert, modify, and position graphics, how to draw your own images, and how to illustrate a document with WordArt and charts. You are preparing materials for a workshop for new members of the MediaLoft marketing staff. You use the graphic features of Word to illustrate three handouts on marketing issues of interest to MediaLoft.

Adding Graphics

Graphic images you can insert in a document include the clip art images that come with Word, photos taken with a digital camera, scanned art, and graphics created in other graphics programs. When you first insert a graphic it is an **inline graphic**—part of the line of text in which it is inserted. You move an inline graphic just as you would move text. To be able to move a graphic independently of text, you must apply a text-wrapping style to it to make it a **floating graphic**, which can be moved anywhere on a page. To insert clip art or another graphic file into a document, you use the Picture command on the Insert menu. You have written a handout containing tips for writing and designing ads. You want to illustrate the handout with the MediaLoft logo, a graphic created in another graphics program. You use the Picture, From File command to insert the logo in the document, and then wrap the text around the logo.

STEPS

1. **Start Word, open the file WD F-1.doc from the drive and folder where your Data Files are located, save it as Ad Tips, then read the document to get a feel for its contents**

   The document opens in Print Layout view.

2. **Click the Show/Hide ¶ button ¶ on the Standard toolbar to display formatting marks, then click the Drawing button 🖉 on the Standard toolbar to display the Drawing toolbar if it is not already displayed**

   The Drawing toolbar, located below the document window, includes buttons for inserting, creating, and modifying graphics.

3. **Click before the heading Create a simple layout, click Insert on the menu bar, point to Picture, then click From File**

   The Insert Picture dialog box opens. You use this dialog box to locate and insert graphic files. Most graphic files are **bitmap graphics**, which are composed of a series of small dots, called **pixels**, that define color and intensity. Bitmap graphics are often saved with a .bmp, .png, .jpg, .wmf, .tif, or .gif file extension. To view all the graphic files in a particular location, use the Files of type list arrow to select All Pictures. To view a particular type of graphic, use the Files of type list arrow to select the graphic type.

4. **Click the Files of type list arrow, click All Pictures if it is not already selected, use the Look in list arrow to navigate to the drive and folder where your Data Files are located, click the file MLoft.jpg, then click Insert**

   The logo is inserted as an inline graphic at the location of the insertion point. Unless you want a graphic to be part of a line of text, usually the first thing you do after inserting it is to wrap text around it so it becomes a floating graphic. To be able to position a graphic anywhere on a page, you must apply a text-wrapping style to it even if there is no text on the page.

5. **Click the logo graphic to select it**

   Squares, called **sizing handles**, appear on the sides and corners of the graphic when it is selected, as shown in Figure F-1. The Picture toolbar also opens. The Picture toolbar includes buttons for modifying graphics.

6. **Click the Text Wrapping button 🖼 on the Picture toolbar**

   A menu of text-wrapping styles opens.

7. **Click Tight**

   The text wraps around the sides of the graphic, as shown in Figure F-2. Notice that the sizing handles change to circles, indicating the graphic is a floating graphic, and an anchor and a green rotate handle appear. The anchor indicates the floating graphic is **anchored** to the nearest paragraph, so that the graphic moves with the paragraph if the paragraph is moved. The anchor symbol appears only when formatting marks are displayed.

8. **Click ¶, deselect the graphic, then click the Save button 🖫 on the Standard toolbar to save your changes**

FIGURE F-1: Inline graphic

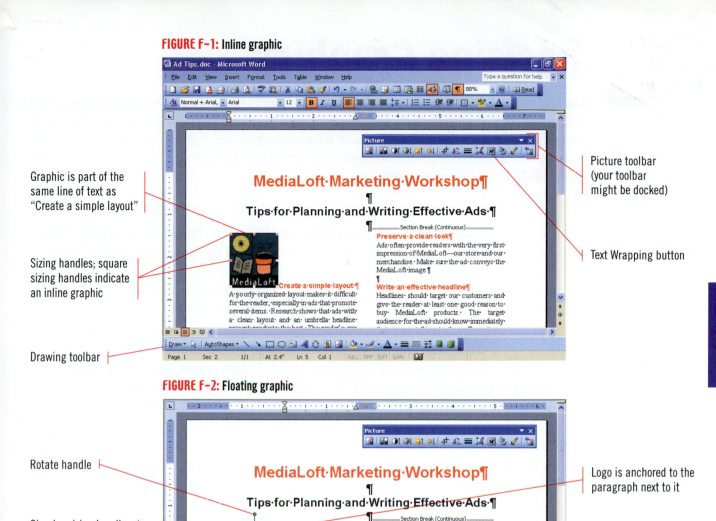

Graphic is part of the same line of text as "Create a simple layout"

Sizing handles; square sizing handles indicate an inline graphic

Drawing toolbar

Picture toolbar (your toolbar might be docked)

Text Wrapping button

FIGURE F-2: Floating graphic

Rotate handle

Circular sizing handles indicate a floating graphic

Text wraps around the shape of the graphic

Logo is anchored to the paragraph next to it

Clues to Use

Narrowing a search for clip art

Searching for clip art with an active Internet connection gives you access to the thousands of clips available on the Microsoft Office Online Web site. With so many clips to choose from, your search can be more productive if you set specific search criteria. To perform an initial search for a clip, type a word or words that describe the clip you want to find in the Search text box in the Clip Art task pane, shown in Figure F-3, and then click Go. If the clips returned in the Results box are too numerous or don't match the criteria you set, you can try using more keywords. For example, rather than "family," you might type "mother father baby" to return only clips associated with all three keywords. You can also narrow your search by reducing the number of collections to search, or by limiting your search to a specific media type, such as photographs. To search specific collections, click the Search in list arrow in the task pane, and then deselect the check box next to each collection you want to omit from the search. To search a specific media type, click the Results should be list arrow, and then deselect the check box next to each type of clip you want to omit from the search. In both lists, you can click a plus sign next to a collection name or media type to expand the list of options. To read more hints on searching for clips, click the Tips for finding clips hyperlink in the Clip Art task pane.

FIGURE F-3: Clip Art task pane

Resizing Graphics

Once you insert a graphic into a document, you can change its shape or size by using the mouse to drag a sizing handle or by using the Picture command on the Format menu to specify an exact height and width for the graphic. Resizing a graphic with the mouse allows you to see how the image looks as you modify it. Using the Picture command to alter a graphic's shape or size allows you to set precise measurements. You enlarge the MediaLoft logo.

STEPS

QUICK TIP

Click Ruler on the View menu to display the rulers.

1. **Click the logo graphic to select it, place the pointer over the middle-right sizing handle, when the pointer changes to ↔, drag to the right until the graphic is about 1¾" wide**

   As you drag, the dotted outline indicates the size and shape of the graphic. You can refer to the ruler to gauge the measurements as you drag. When you release the mouse button, the image is stretched to be wider. Dragging a side, top, or bottom sizing handle changes only the width or height of a graphic.

QUICK TIP

If you enlarge a bitmap graphic too much, the dots that make up the picture become visible and the graphic is distorted.

2. **Click the Undo button 🔄 on the Standard toolbar, place the pointer over the upper-right sizing handle, when the pointer changes to ↗ drag up and to the right until the graphic is about 2" tall and 1¾" wide as shown in Figure F-4, then release the mouse button**

   The image is enlarged. Dragging a corner sizing handle resizes the graphic proportionally so that its width and height are reduced or enlarged by the same percentage. Table F-1 describes other ways to resize objects using the mouse.

3. **Double-click the logo graphic**

   The Format Picture dialog box opens. It includes options for changing the coloring, size, scale, text wrapping, and position of a graphic. You can double-click any graphic object or use the Picture command on the Format menu to open the Format Picture dialog box.

4. **Click the Size tab**

   The Size tab, shown in Figure F-5, allows you to enter precise height and width measurements for a graphic or to scale a graphic by entering the percentage by which you want to reduce or enlarge it. When a graphic is sized to **scale**, its height to width ratio remains the same.

TROUBLE

Your height measurement might differ slightly.

5. **Select the measurement in the Width text box in the Size and rotate section, type 1.5, then click the Height text box in the Size and rotate section**

   The height measurement automatically changes to 1.68". When the Lock aspect ratio check box is selected, you need to enter only a height or width measurement. Word calculates the other measurement so that the resized graphic is proportional.

6. **Click OK, then save your changes**

   The logo is resized to be precisely 1.5" wide and approximately 1.68" tall.

TABLE F-1: Methods for resizing an object using the mouse

do this	to
Drag a corner sizing handle	Resize a clip art or bitmap graphic proportionally from a corner
Press [Shift] and drag a corner sizing handle	Resize a drawing object, such as an AutoShape or a WordArt object, proportionally from a corner
Press [Ctrl] and drag a side, top, or bottom sizing handle	Resize any graphic object vertically or horizontally while keeping the center position fixed
Press [Ctrl] and drag a corner sizing handle	Resize any graphic object diagonally while keeping the center position fixed
Press [Shift][Ctrl] and drag a corner sizing handle	Resize any graphic object proportionally while keeping the center position fixed

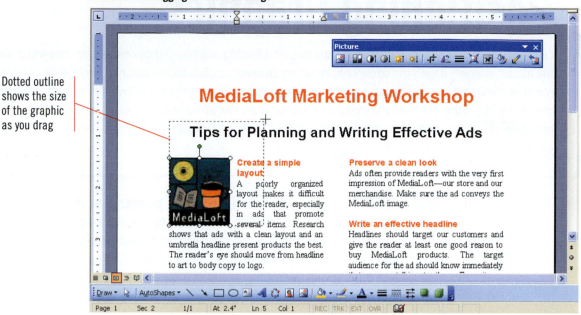

FIGURE F-4: Dragging to resize an image

Dotted outline shows the size of the graphic as you drag

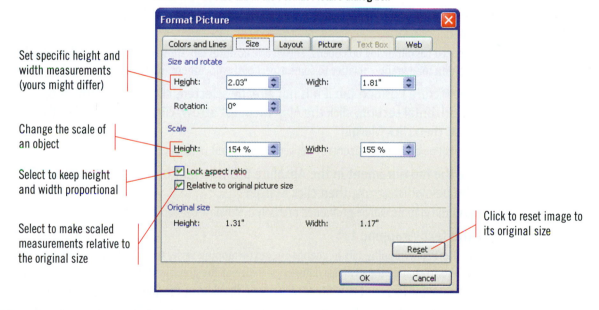

FIGURE F-5: Size tab in the Format Picture dialog box

Set specific height and width measurements (yours might differ)

Change the scale of an object

Select to keep height and width proportional

Select to make scaled measurements relative to the original size

Click to reset image to its original size

Clues to Use

Cropping graphics

If you want to use only part of a picture in a document, you can crop the graphic to trim the parts you don't want to use. To crop a graphic, select it, then click the Crop button ⊞ on the Picture toolbar. The pointer changes to the cropping pointer ⌐, and cropping handles (solid black lines) appear on all four corners and sides of the graphic. To crop one side of a graphic, drag a side cropping handle inward to where you want to trim the graphic. To crop two adjacent sides at once, drag a corner cropping handle inward to the point where you want the corner of the cropped image to be. When you drag a cropping handle, the shape of the cropping pointer changes to correspond to the shape of the cropping handle you are dragging. When you finish adjusting the parameters of the graphic, click the Crop button again to turn off the crop feature. You can also crop a graphic by entering precise crop measurements on the Picture tab in the Format Picture dialog box.

UNIT F

Word 2003

Positioning Graphics

Once you insert a graphic into a document and make it a floating graphic, you can move it by dragging it with the mouse, nudging it with the arrow keys, or setting an exact location for the graphic using the Picture command on the Format menu. Dragging an object with the mouse or using the arrow keys allows you to position a graphic visually. Using the Picture command to position a graphic allows you to place an object precisely on a page. You experiment with different positions for the MediaLoft logo to determine which position enhances the document the most.

STEPS

QUICK TIP

To move an object only horizontally or vertically, press [Shift] as you drag.

QUICK TIP

You can place a floating graphic anywhere on a page, including outside the margins.

TROUBLE

If the Picture toolbar remains open after you deselect the graphic, close the toolbar.

1. **Select the logo graphic if it is not already selected, move the pointer over the graphic, when the pointer changes to ✥, drag the graphic down and to the right as shown in Figure F-6 so its top aligns with the top of the Create a simple layout heading**

   As you drag, the dotted outline indicates the position of the graphic. When you release the mouse button, the graphic is moved and the text wraps around the graphic. Notice that the Create a simple layout heading is now above the graphic.

2. **With the graphic selected, press [←] four times, then press [↑] three times**

   Each time you press an arrow key the graphic is **nudged**—moved a small amount—in that direction. You can also press [Ctrl] and an arrow key to nudge an object in even smaller (one pixel) increments. Nudging the graphic did not position it exactly where you want it to be.

3. **Double-click the graphic, click the Layout tab in the Format Picture dialog box, then click Advanced**

   The Advanced Layout dialog box opens. The Picture Position tab, shown in Figure F-7, allows you to specify an exact position for a graphic relative to some aspect of the document, such as a margin, column, or paragraph.

4. **Click the Picture Position tab if it is not already selected, click the Alignment option button in the Horizontal section, click the Alignment list arrow, click Centered, click the relative to list arrow, then click Margin**

   The logo will be centered horizontally between the left and right page margins.

5. **Change the measurement in the Absolute position text box in the Vertical section to 1.5, click the below list arrow, then click Margin**

   The top of the graphic will be positioned precisely 1.5" below the top margin.

6. **Click the Text Wrapping tab**

   You use the Text Wrapping tab to change the text-wrapping style, to wrap text around only one side of a graphic, and to change the distance between the edge of the graphic and the edge of the wrapped text. You want to increase the amount of white space between the sides of the graphic and the wrapped text.

7. **Select Square, select 0.13 in the Left text box, type .3, press [Tab], then type .3 in the Right text box**

   The distance between the graphic and the edge of the wrapped text will be .3" on either side.

8. **Click OK to close the Advanced Layout dialog box, click OK to close the Format Picture dialog box, deselect the graphic, then save your changes**

   The logo is centered between the margins, the top of the graphic is positioned 1.5" below the top margin, and the amount of white space between the left and right sides of the graphic and the wrapped text is increased to .3", as shown in Figure F-8.

FIGURE F-6: Dragging a graphic to move it

Top of graphic aligns with the top of the text

Dotted outline shows the position as you drag

FIGURE F-7: Picture Position tab in the Advanced Layout dialog box

Select to horizontally align a graphic relative to an aspect of the document

Select to position a graphic a precise distance from an aspect of the document (your measurements might differ)

Select the aspect of the document you want to position the graphic relative to

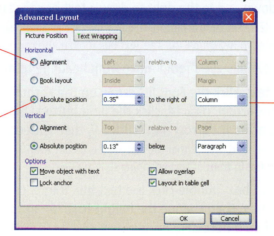

FIGURE F-8: Repositioned logo

Logo is centered and its top is 1.5" from the top margin

1.5" mark on the ruler

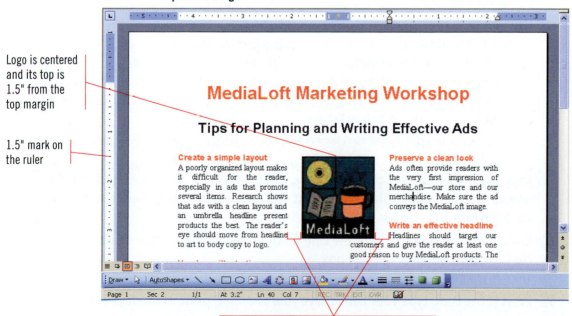

Space between the graphic and the text is increased

Creating Text Boxes

When you want to illustrate your documents with text, you can create a text box. A **text box** is a container that you can fill with text and graphics. Like other drawing objects, text boxes can be resized, formatted with colors, lines, and text-wrapping, and positioned anywhere on a page. You create a text box using the Text Box button on the Drawing toolbar or the Text Box command on the Insert menu. When you insert a text box or another drawing object, a drawing canvas opens in the document. A **drawing canvas** is a workspace for creating your own graphics. You can choose to draw the text box directly in the document, or to draw it in the drawing canvas.  You want to add a pull quote to call attention to the main point of the handout. You draw a text box, add the pull quote text to it, format the text, and then position the text box on the page.

STEPS

1. **Scroll down, click before the Use large illustrations heading, then click the Text Box button** 🄰 **on the Drawing toolbar**

   A drawing canvas opens in the document, as shown in Figure F-9, and the pointer changes to ╋. You'll draw a text box outside the drawing canvas.

2. **Move the** ╋ **pointer directly under the lower-left corner of the MediaLoft logo, then click and drag down and to the right to draw a text box that is about 1½" wide and 2¾" tall**

   When you release the mouse button, the drawing canvas disappears and the insertion point is located in the text box, as shown in Figure F-10. The Text Box toolbar also opens.

3. **Type The reader's eye should move from headline to art to body copy to logo**

4. **Select the text, click the Font list arrow on the Formatting toolbar, click Arial, click the Font Size list arrow, click 14, click the Bold button** B **, click the Center button** ▤ **, click the Line Spacing list arrow** ≣▾ **, click 2.0, then click outside the text box**

   The text is formatted. Notice that the body text does not wrap around the text box. By default, text boxes are inserted with the In front of text-wrapping style applied.

5. **Click the text box, double-click the text box frame, click the Size tab in the Format Text Box dialog box, then change the height to 2.75" and the width to 1.5" in the Size and rotate section, if necessary**

   When you click a text box with the I pointer, the insertion point moves inside the text box and sizing handles appear. Clicking the frame of a text box with the ⬚ pointer selects the text box object itself. Double-clicking the frame opens the Format Text Box dialog box.

6. **Click the Layout tab, click Advanced, click the Picture Position tab, click the Alignment option button in the Horizontal section, click the Alignment list arrow, click Centered, click the relative to list arrow, click Margin, make sure the Absolute position option button in the Vertical section is selected, change the measurement in the Absolute position text box to 3.4, click the below list arrow, then click Margin**

   The text box will be centered between the left and right margins, and its top will be precisely 3.4" below the top margin.

7. **Click the Text Wrapping tab, click Square, change the Top, Bottom, Left, and Right measurements to .3" in the Distance from text section, click OK twice, then deselect the text box**

   The text is wrapped in a square around the text box.

8. **Click inside the text box, click the Line Color list arrow** 🖌▾ **on the Drawing toolbar, click No Line, then deselect the text box**

   The thin black border around the text box is removed, as shown in Figure F-11.

9. **Press [Ctrl][End], type your name, save your changes, print, then close the file**

FIGURE F-9: Drawing canvas

Drawing canvas

Drawing Canvas toolbar

FIGURE F-10: Text box

Insertion point in text box

Text box frame

Text Box toolbar

Text Box button

Line Color list arrow

Word 2003

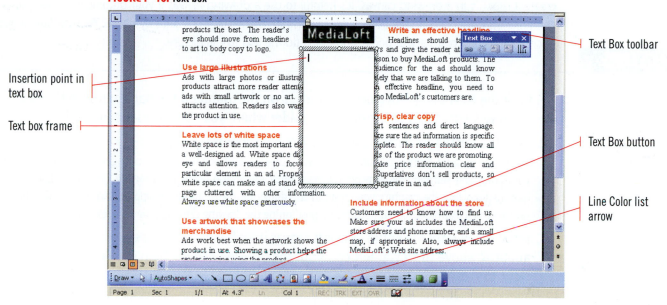

FIGURE F-11: Completed handout with text box

Formatted text in text box

Text wraps around the text box

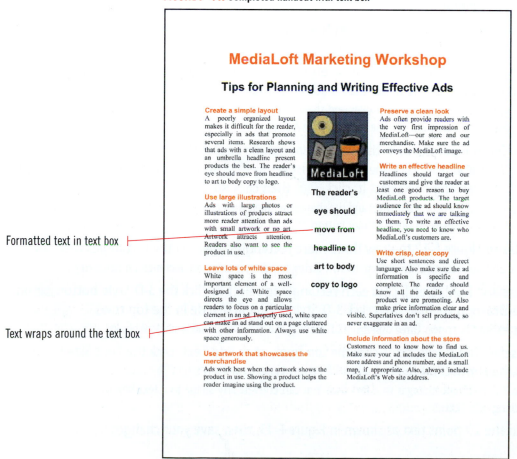

MediaLoft Marketing Workshop

Tips for Planning and Writing Effective Ads

Create a simple layout
A poorly organized layout makes it difficult for the reader, especially in ads that promote several items. Research shows that ads with a clean layout and an umbrella headline present products the best. The reader's eye should move from headline to art to body copy to logo.

Use large illustrations
Ads with large photos or illustrations of products attract more reader attention than ads with small artwork or no art. Artwork attracts attention. Readers also want to see the product in use.

Leave lots of white space
White space is the most important element of a well-designed ad. White space directs the eye and allows readers to focus on a particular element in an ad. Properly used, white space can make an ad stand out on a page cluttered with other information. Always use white space generously.

Use artwork that showcases the merchandise
Ads work best when the artwork shows the product in use. Showing a product helps the reader imagine using the product.

The reader's eye should move from headline to art to body copy to logo

Preserve a clean look
Ads often provide readers with the very first impression of MediaLoft—our store and our merchandise. Make sure the ad conveys the MediaLoft image.

Write an effective headline
Headlines should target our customers and give the reader at least one good reason to buy MediaLoft products. The target audience for the ad should know immediately that we are talking to them. To write an effective headline, you need to know who MediaLoft's customers are.

Write crisp, clear copy
Use short sentences and direct language. Also make sure the ad information is specific and complete. The reader should know all the details of the product we are promoting. Also make price information clear and visible. Superlatives don't sell products, so never exaggerate in an ad.

Include information about the store
Customers need to know how to find us. Make sure your ad includes the MediaLoft store address and phone number, and a small map, if appropriate. Also, always include MediaLoft's Web site address.

Creating AutoShapes

One way you can create your own graphics in Word is to use AutoShapes. **AutoShapes** are the rectangles, ovals, triangles, lines, block arrows, stars, banners, lightning bolts, hearts, suns, and other drawing objects you can create using the tools on the Drawing toolbar. The Drawing toolbar also includes tools for adding colors, shadows, fills, and three-dimensional effects to your graphics. Table F-2 describes the buttons on the Drawing toolbar. You can choose to draw a line or shape exactly where you want it in a document, or you can create a graphic in a drawing canvas. It's helpful to use a drawing canvas if your graphic includes multiple items.  Your second handout needs to illustrate MediaLoft book sales by genre. You use AutoShapes to create a picture of a stack of books, and then add the text to the picture.

STEPS

1. Click the **New Blank Document button** on the Standard toolbar, then save the document as **Genre Sales** to the drive and folder where your Data Files are located

2. Click the **Rectangle button** on the Drawing toolbar

   When you click an AutoShape button, a drawing canvas opens and the pointer changes to ╋. Depending on your computer settings, the Drawing Canvas toolbar might also open. The Drawing Canvas toolbar contains buttons for sizing the graphics you create in the drawing canvas, and for wrapping text around the drawing canvas. You'll learn more about resizing and positioning the drawing canvas in the next lesson.

3. Scroll down until the entire drawing canvas is visible on your screen, place the pointer about ¾" above the lower-left corner of the drawing canvas, then drag down and to the right to create a rectangle that is about **5" wide and ½" tall**

   You do not need to be exact in your measurements as you drag. When you release the mouse button, sizing handles appear around the rectangle to indicate it is selected. Cropping handles also appear around the edges of the drawing canvas.

4. Click **AutoShapes** on the Drawing toolbar, point to **Basic Shapes**, then click the **Sun**

   The AutoShapes menu contains categories of shapes and lines that you can draw.

5. Place the ╋ pointer in the upper-left corner of the drawing canvas, then drag down and to the right to create a sun that is about ½" wide

   The sun shape includes a yellow diamond-shaped adjustment handle. You can drag an **adjustment handle** to change the shape, but not the size, of many AutoShapes.

6. Position the pointer over the adjustment handle until it changes to ▷, drag the handle to the right about ¼", click the **Fill Color list arrow** on the Drawing toolbar, click **Gold**, click the **rectangle** to select it, click , then click **Rose**

   The sun shape becomes narrower and the shapes are filled with color. Notice that when you select a color, the active color changes on the Fill Color button.

7. Refer to Figure F-12 to draw three more rectangles, then fill the rectangles with color

   After all four rectangles are drawn, use the sizing handles to resize the rectangles if necessary.

8. Press and hold **[Shift]**, click each **rectangle** to select it, click the **3-D Style button** on the Drawing toolbar, then click **3-D Style 1** (the first style in the top row)

   The rectangles appear three-dimensional, making the group look like a stack of books.

9. Deselect the books, right-click the **top book**, click **Add Text**, click the **Font Size list arrow** on the Formatting toolbar, click **20**, then type **Children's - 17%**

   The 3-D rectangle changes to a text box. You can convert any shape to a text box by right-clicking it and clicking Add Text.

10. Add the 20-point text as shown in Figure F-13, then save your changes

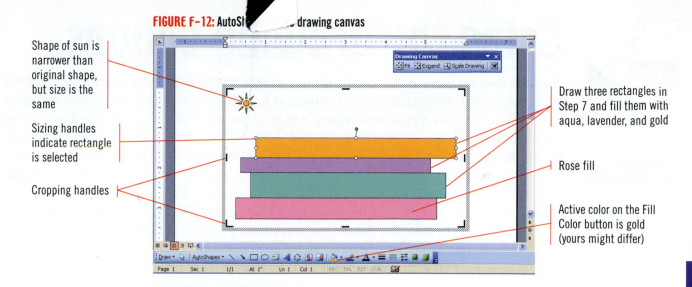

FIGURE F-12: AutoSh... drawing canvas

Shape of sun is narrower than original shape, but size is the same

Sizing handles indicate rectangle is selected

Cropping handles

Draw three rectangles in Step 7 and fill them with aqua, lavender, and gold

Rose fill

Active color on the Fill Color button is gold (yours might differ)

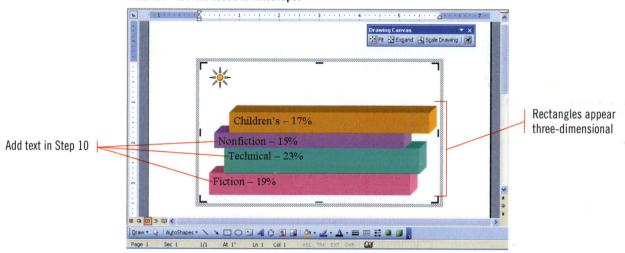

FIGURE F-13: Text added to AutoShapes

Add text in Step 10

Rectangles appear three-dimensional

TABLE F-2: Buttons on the Drawing toolbar

button	use to	button	use to
Draw ▾	Open a menu of commands for grouping, positioning, rotating, and wrapping text around graphics, and for changing an AutoShape to a different shape		Insert a clip art graphic
	Select graphic objects		Insert a picture from a file
AutoShapes ▾	Open a menu of drawing options for lines, shapes, and callouts		Fill a shape with a color, a texture, a gradient, or a pattern
\	Draw a straight line		Change the color of a line, an arrow, or a line around a shape
↘	Draw a straight line with an arrowhead	A ▾	Change the color of text
▭	Draw a rectangle or square	≡	Change the style and weight of a line, an arrow, or a line around a shape
○	Draw an oval or circle		Change the dash style of a line, an arrow, or a line around a shape
	Insert a text box	⇄	Change a line to an arrow; change the style of an arrow
	Insert a WordArt graphic		Add a shadow to a graphic object
	Insert a diagram or an organization chart		Make a graphic object three-dimensional

ILLUSTRATING DOCUMENTS WITH GRAPHICS WORD F-11

Word 2003

Using the Drawing Canvas

When multiple shapes are contained in a drawing canvas, you can resize and move them as a single graphic object. The Drawing Canvas toolbar includes buttons for sizing a drawing canvas and for wrapping text around it. Once you apply a text-wrapping style to a drawing canvas, you can position it anywhere in a document.  You want to add another three books to the stack. You enlarge the drawing canvas, add the shapes, size the drawing as a single object, and then move it to the bottom of the page.

STEPS

1. Click the Zoom list arrow on the Standard toolbar, click 75%, then click the stack of books graphic to make the drawing canvas visible if it is not visible

   Cropping handles appear around the edges of the drawing canvas.

2. Place the pointer over the top-middle cropping handle, when the pointer changes to ⊥, drag the handle to the top of the page, then release the mouse button

   The drawing canvas is enlarged from the top, but the size of the graphic does not change. Dragging a cropping handle resizes the drawing canvas, but not the graphic.

3. Select the sun, position the pointer over it until the pointer changes to 🕀, drag the sun on top of the right end of the Technical book, then release the mouse button

   The sun shape is moved to the spine of the book, but is hidden beneath the rectangle shape.

4. With the sun shape selected, click the Draw button on the Drawing toolbar, point to Order, then click Bring to Front

   The sun shape is moved on top of the rectangle shape.

5. Double-click the Rectangle button ▭ on the Drawing toolbar to activate the rectangle tool, draw three more rectangles on top of the stack of books, click ▭ to turn off the tool, then right-click each rectangle and add the 20-point text shown in Figure F-14

6. Select each rectangle, fill it with any color, then apply the 3-D Style 1

7. Click the Fit Drawing to Contents button ⊞Fit on the Drawing Canvas toolbar

   The drawing canvas is automatically resized to fit the graphic within it.

8. Click the Zoom list arrow, click Whole Page, then click the Scale Drawing button 🔲 Scale Drawing on the Drawing Canvas toolbar

   The cropping handles on the drawing canvas change to sizing handles. You can now use the drawing canvas frame to resize the contents of the drawing canvas as a single graphic.

9. Drag the bottom-middle sizing handle down until the graphic is about 6" tall

   Resizing the drawing canvas resizes all the shapes within it. Dragging a top, bottom, or side handle stretches the graphic. Dragging a corner handle resizes the graphic proportionally.

10. Click the Text Wrapping button ⊠ on the Drawing Canvas toolbar, click Square, place the pointer over the drawing canvas frame so it changes to 🕀, drag the drawing canvas down and position it so it is centered in the bottom part of the page, deselect the drawing canvas, then save your changes

    Compare your document to Figure F-15. You must wrap text around a drawing canvas to be able to position it anywhere on a page.

FIGURE F-14: New rectangles in drawing canvas

Draw rectangles and add text in Step 5

Scale Drawing button

Fit Drawing to Contents button

Sun shape moved to the spine of the book

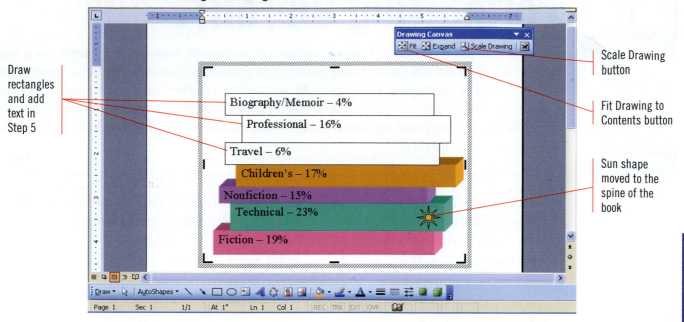

FIGURE F-15: Resized and repositioned graphic

Graphic is stretched to be taller and narrower

Graphic is centered at the bottom of the page

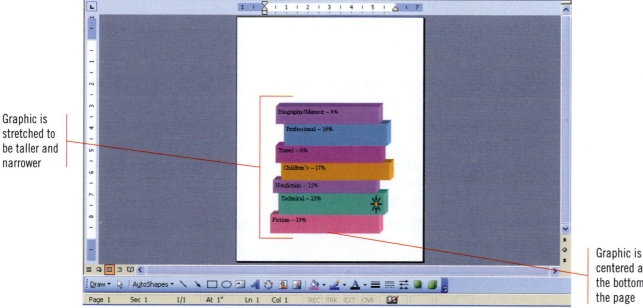

Clues to Use

Drawing lines

In addition to drawing straight lines and arrows, you can use the Lines tools on the AutoShapes menu to draw curved, freeform, and scribble lines. Click AutoShapes on the Drawing toolbar, point to Lines, then select the type of line you want to draw. Choose Curve ⌇ to draw an object with smooth curves, choose Freeform ⌒ to draw an object with both freehand and straight-line segments, or choose Scribble ✏ to draw a freehand object that looks like it was drawn with a pencil. The lines you draw include vertexes—a **vertex** is either a point where two straight lines meet or the highest point in a curve. To create a curve or freeform line, click the location you want the line to begin, move the mouse, click to insert a vertex, move the mouse, and so on. Double-click to end a curve or freeform line or click near the starting point to close a shape, if that's what you have drawn. Drawing scribble lines is similar to drawing with a pencil: drag the pointer to draw the line, and then release the mouse button when you are finished. The best way to learn about drawing curve, freeform, and scribble lines is to experiment. Once you draw a line, you can modify its shape by right-clicking it, clicking Edit Points, and then dragging a vertex to a different location.

Formatting WordArt

Another way to give your documents punch and flair is to use WordArt. **WordArt** is a drawing object that contains text formatted with special shapes, patterns, and orientations. You create WordArt using either the WordArt button on the Drawing toolbar or the Picture, WordArt command on the Insert menu. Once you have created a WordArt object, you can use the buttons on the WordArt toolbar to format it with different shapes, fonts, colors, and other effects to create the impact you desire. You use WordArt to create a fun heading for your handout.

STEPS

1. **Press [Ctrl][Home], press [Enter], click the Zoom list arrow on the Standard toolbar, click Page Width, then click the Insert WordArt button on the Drawing toolbar**
   The WordArt Gallery opens. It includes the styles you can choose for your WordArt.

2. **Click the first style in the third row, then click OK**
   The Edit WordArt Text dialog box opens. You type the text you want to format as WordArt in this dialog box and, if you wish, change the font and font size of the WordArt text.

3. **Type Genre Sales, then click OK**
   The WordArt object appears at the location of the insertion point. Like other graphic objects, the WordArt object is an inline graphic until you wrap text around it.

4. **Click the WordArt object to select it**
   The WordArt toolbar opens when a WordArt object is selected. It includes buttons for editing and modifying WordArt.

5. **Drag the lower-right corner sizing handle down and to the right to make the object about 2" tall and 6" wide**
   The WordArt is enlarged to span the page between the left and right margins, as shown in Figure F-16.

6. **Click the WordArt Character Spacing button on the WordArt toolbar, click Tight, click the WordArt Shape button on the WordArt toolbar, then click the Can Up shape (the third shape in the third row)**
   The spacing between the characters is decreased and the shape of the WordArt text changes.

7. **Click the Format WordArt button on the WordArt toolbar, then click the Colors and Lines tab**
   The Format WordArt dialog box opens. You use the Colors and Lines tab to change the fill color of WordArt, to change the transparency of the fill color, and to change the color or style of the line surrounding the WordArt characters.

8. **Click the Color list arrow in the Fill section, then click Fill Effects**
   The Fill Effects dialog box opens, as shown in Figure F-17. You use this dialog box to change the fill colors and effects of the WordArt object. Using the Gradient tab, you can select a preset gradient effect or choose colors and shading styles to create your own gradient effect. You can also apply a preset texture using the Texture tab, design a two-color pattern using the Pattern tab, or fill the object with a graphic using the Picture tab.

9. **Make sure the Two colors option button is selected in the Colors section on the Gradient tab, click the Color 1 list arrow, click Indigo, click the Color 2 list arrow, click Pink, click the Diagonal up option button in the Shading styles section, click the lower-right box in the Variants section, then click OK twice**
   The new fill effects are applied to the WordArt. The completed handout is shown in Figure F-18.

10. **Press [Ctrl][Home], type your name, save your changes, print the document, then close the file**

FIGURE F-16: Resized WordArt

WordArt object is enlarged

WordArt toolbar (yours might open in a different location)

WordArt Character Spacing button

WordArt Shape button

WordArt Gallery button

Biography/Memoir – 4%

FIGURE F-17: Fill Effects dialog box

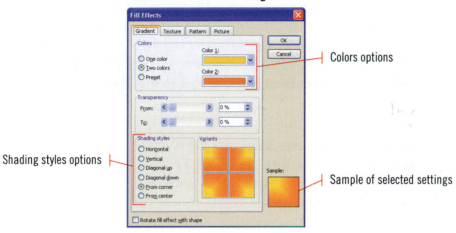

Colors options

Shading styles options

Sample of selected settings

FIGURE F-18: Completed handout with WordArt

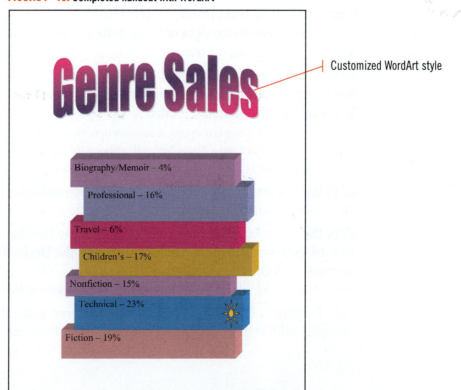

Customized WordArt style

Creating Charts

Adding a chart can be an attractive way to illustrate a document that includes numerical information. A **chart** is a visual representation of numerical data and usually is used to illustrate trends, patterns, or relationships. The Word chart feature allows you to create many types of charts, including bar, column, pie, area, and line charts. You can add a chart to a document using the Picture, Chart command on the Insert menu. You create a handout that includes a chart showing the distribution of MediaLoft customers by age and gender.

STEPS

1. **Open the file WD F-2.doc from the drive and folder where your Data Files are located, save it as Age and Gender, then press [Ctrl][End]**

   The insertion point is centered under the title.

QUICK TIP

To show the toolbars on two rows, click the Toolbar Options button at the end of the Formatting toolbar, then click Show Buttons on Two Rows.

2. **Click Insert on the menu bar, point to Picture, then click Chart**

   A table opens in a datasheet window and a column chart appears in the document. The datasheet and the chart contain placeholder data that you replace with your own data. The chart is based on the data in the datasheet. Any change you make to the data in the datasheet is made automatically to the chart. Notice that when a chart object is open, the Standard toolbar includes buttons for working with charts.

3. **Click the datasheet title bar and drag it so that the chart is visible, then move the pointer over the datasheet**

   The pointer changes to ⊹. You use this pointer to select the cells in the datasheet.

QUICK TIP

Click the Chart Type list arrow on the Standard toolbar to change the type of chart.

4. **Click the East cell, type Male, click the West cell, type Female, click the gray 3 cell to select the third row, then press [Delete]**

   When you click a cell and type, the data in the cell is replaced with the text you type. As you edit the datasheet, the changes you make are reflected in the chart.

5. **Replace the remaining placeholder text with the data shown in Figure F-19, then click outside the chart to deselect it**

6. **Click the chart to select the object, press [Ctrl], then drag the lower-right corner sizing handle down and to the right until the outline of the chart is approximately 7" wide**

   The chart is enlarged and still centered.

QUICK TIP

Point to any part of a chart to see a ScreenTip that identifies the part. You can also use the Chart Objects list arrow on the Standard toolbar to select a part of a chart.

7. **Double-click the chart to open it, click the View Datasheet button 📄 on the Standard toolbar to close the datasheet, click the legend to select it, then click the Format Legend button 🖼 on the Standard toolbar**

   The Format Legend dialog box opens. It includes options for modifying the legend. Select any part of a chart object and use 🖼 to open a dialog box with options for formatting that part of the chart. In this case, the name of the button is Format Legend because the legend is selected.

8. **Click the Placement tab, click the Bottom option button, then click OK**

   The legend moves below the chart.

9. **Click the Value Axis (the y-axis), click 🖼, click the Number tab in the Format Axis dialog box, click Percentage in the Category list, click the Decimal places down arrow twice so 0 appears, click OK, then deselect the chart**

   Percent signs are added to the y-axis. The completed handout is shown in Figure F-20.

10. **Type Prepared by followed by your name centered in the document footer, save your changes, print the handout, close the document, then exit Word**

FIGURE F-19: Datasheet and chart object

Format button

Datasheet window

Chart reflects data in datasheet after all data is entered

Value axis (y-axis)

Toolbar Options button

View Datasheet button

Chart object

Legend

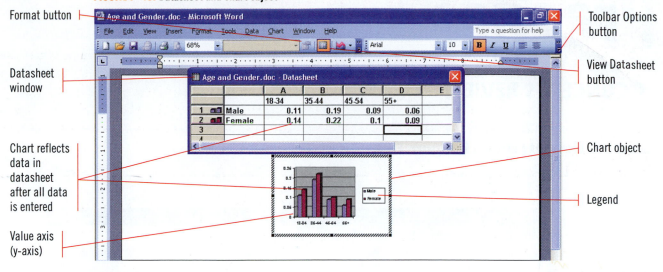

FIGURE F-20: Completed handout with chart

Percent signs added to the value axis

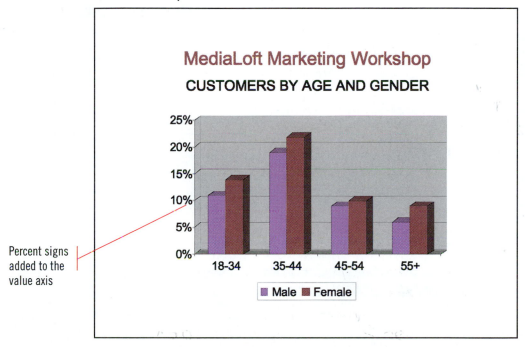

MediaLoft Marketing Workshop

CUSTOMERS BY AGE AND GENDER

■ Male ■ Female

Clues to Use

Creating diagrams and organization charts

Diagrams are another way to illustrate concepts in your documents. Word includes a diagram feature that allows you to quickly create and format several types of diagrams, including pyramid, Venn, target, cycle, and radial diagrams, as well as organization charts. To insert a diagram or an organization chart, click the Insert Diagram or Organization Chart button  on the Drawing toolbar or use the Diagram command on the Insert menu to open the Diagram Gallery, shown in Figure F-21. Select a diagram type in the Diagram Gallery, then click OK. The diagram appears in a drawing canvas with placeholder text, and the Diagram toolbar opens. The Diagram toolbar contains buttons for customizing and formatting the diagram, and for sizing and positioning the drawing canvas. Use the AutoFormat button on the Diagram toolbar to apply colors and shading to your diagram.

FIGURE F-21: Diagram Gallery

Practice

▼ CONCEPTS REVIEW

Label the elements shown in Figure F-22.

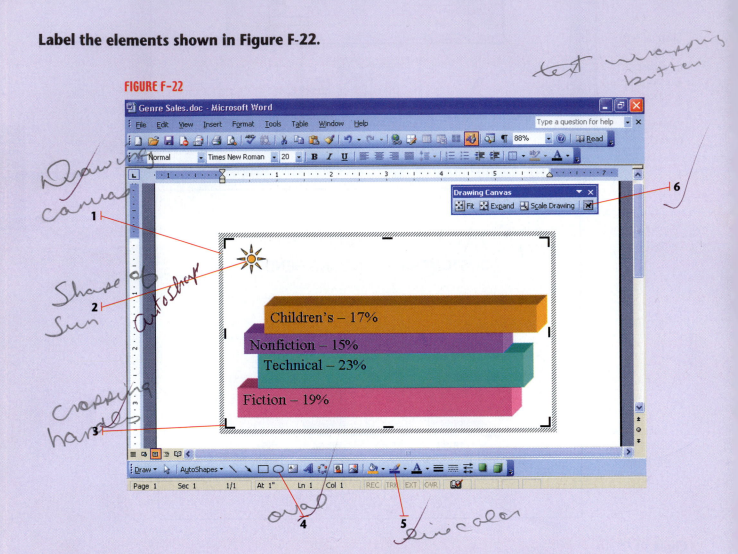

FIGURE F-22

Handwritten annotations:
- text wrapping button (pointing to 6)
- Drawing canvas (1)
- Shape of Sun / Autoshape (2)
- crossing handles (3)
- oval (4)
- line color (5)

Match each term with the statement that best describes it.

7. Text box _d_
8. Drawing canvas _b_
9. AutoShape _a_
10. Bitmap graphic _c_
11. Chart _f_
12. WordArt _g_
13. Pixels _e_
14. Vertex _h_

a. A graphic object drawn using the tools on the Drawing toolbar
b. A workspace for creating graphics
c. A graphic that is composed of a series of small dots
d. A graphic object that is a container for text and graphics
e. Dots that define color and intensity in a graphic
f. A visual representation of numerical data
g. A graphic object composed of specially formatted text
h. The intersection of two line sections or the highest point on a curve

Select the best answer from the list of choices.

15. Which button can be used to create a text box?

   a.   **c.**

   b.   **d.**

16. What must you do to a drawing canvas before moving it to a different location?

   a. Scale the drawing canvas.

   b. Enter a precise position for the drawing canvas in the Format Drawing Canvas dialog box.

   c. Fit the drawing canvas to the contents.

   d. Wrap text around the drawing canvas.

17. What do you drag to change an AutoShape's shape, but not its size or dimensions?

   a. Sizing handle

   b. Rotate handle

   c. Cropping handle

   d. Adjustment handle

18. Which method do you use to nudge a picture?

   a. Select the picture, then press an arrow key.

   b. Select the picture, then drag a top, bottom, or side sizing handle.

   c. Select the picture, then drag a corner sizing handle.

   d. Select the picture, then drag it to a new location.

19. If you want to create an oval that contains formatted text, what kind of graphic object would you create?

   a. A text box

   b. WordArt

   c. A pie chart

   d. An AutoShape

20. What style of text wrapping is applied to a text box by default?

   a. Square

   b. In line with text

   c. In front of text

   d. Tight

▼ SKILLS REVIEW

1. Add graphics.

   a. Start Word, open the file WD F-3.doc from the drive and folder where your Data Files are located, then save it as **Farm Flyer**.

   b. Press [Ctrl][End], then insert the file **Farm.jpg** from the drive and folder where your Data Files are located.

   c. Select the photo, apply the Square text-wrapping style to it, then save your changes.

Word Art Toolbar

2. Resize graphics.

   a. Scroll down so that the graphic is at the top of your screen.

   b. Drag the lower-right sizing handle to enlarge the graphic proportionally so that it is about 4" wide and 3" high.

   c. Click the Crop button on the Picture toolbar.

   d. Drag the bottom-middle cropping handle up approximately 1", then click the Crop button again.

   e. Double-click the photo, click the Size tab, then change the width of the photo to 6". (*Hint*: Make sure the Lock aspect ratio check box is selected.)

   f. Save your changes.

that its top is aligned with the top margin.

to, click the Layout tab, then click Advanced.

ion tab, change the horizontal alignment to centered relative to the margins.

on, change the absolute position to 2" below the margin.

pping tab, change the wrapping style to Top and bottom, change the Top measurement to 2", then

e Bottom measurement to .3".

ck OK to close the Advanced Layout and Format Picture dialog boxes, then save your changes.

4. Create text boxes.

a. Change the zoom level to Whole Page, then draw a 1.5" x 6" text box at the bottom of the page. (*Note*: Do not draw the text box in the drawing canvas if it opens.)

b. Change the zoom level to Page Width, type **Mountain Realty** in the text box, format the text in 18-point Arial, bold, then center it in the text box.

c. Press [Enter], type **603-555-3466**, press [Enter], type **www.mountainrealty.com**, then format the two lines of text in 11-point Arial, bold.

d. Resize the text box to be 1" high and 4" wide, then move it to the lower-left corner of the page, aligned with the left and bottom margin.

e. Fill the text box with Blue-Gray, change the font color of the text to White, then remove the line from around the text box.

f. With the text box selected, click Draw on the Drawing toolbar, point to Change AutoShape, point to Basic Shapes, then click the Oval. (*Note*: Adjust the text size or oval size if necessary.)

g. Deselect the text box, then save your changes.

5. Create AutoShapes.

a. Place the insertion point in the paragraph of text above the oval, click AutoShapes on the Drawing toolbar, point to Basic Shapes, then click the Isosceles Triangle shape.

b. Draw an isosceles triangle in the drawing canvas, then fill it with Violet. (*Note*: The drawing canvas appears on a new page 2. You resize and position the drawing canvas after you finish drawing in it.)

c. Draw three more isosceles triangles in the drawing canvas, then fill them with Lavender, Blue-Gray, and Indigo.

d. Drag the triangles to position them so they overlap each other to look like mountains.

e. Draw a sun shape in the drawing canvas, fill it with Gold, then position it so it overlaps the tops of the mountains. Resize the sun if necessary.

f. Select the sun, click Draw on the Drawing toolbar, point to Order, then click Send to Back.

g. Use the Order commands to change the order of the triangles and the sun so that the shapes look like a mountain range with the sun setting behind it. Resize and reposition the shapes as necessary to create a mountain effect, then save your changes.

6. Use the drawing canvas.

a. Fit the drawing canvas to the mountain range graphic. (*Hint*: You might need to scroll the document to locate the drawing canvas after you fit the drawing canvas to it.)

b. Apply the Square text-wrapping style to the drawing canvas.

c. Click the Scale Drawing button, then resize the drawing canvas so the graphic is approximately 1.5" wide and 1" tall. Adjust the shapes in the drawing canvas if the graphic looks awkward after resizing it.

d. Change the zoom level to Whole Page, move the drawing canvas to the lower-right corner of the page, aligned with the right and bottom margins, then deselect the drawing canvas.

e. Save your changes, then press [Ctrl][Home] to move the insertion point to the top of the document (the beginning of the text).

7. Format WordArt.

   a. Insert a WordArt object, select any horizontal WordArt style, type **Farmhouse**, then click OK.

   b. Apply Square text wrapping to the WordArt object, then move it above the photograph if necessary.

   c. Resize the WordArt object to be 6" wide and 1.25" tall, then position it so it is centered between the margins and 1" below the top of the page.

   d. Open the WordArt Gallery, then change the style to the fifth style in the second row.

   e. Open the Format WordArt dialog box, open the Fill Effects dialog box, select the Preset color Nightfall, select any Shading style and Variant, then apply the settings to the WordArt object.

   e. Type **Contact** followed by your name in the document footer, center the text, then format it in 12-point Arial.

   f. Save your changes to the flyer, print a copy, then close the file.

8. Create charts.

   a. Open a new, blank document, then save it as **Realty Sales** to the drive and folder where your Data Files are located.

   b. Click the Center button, type **Mountain Realty 2006 Sales**, then format the text in 26-point Arial, bold.

   c. Press [Enter] twice, then insert a chart.

   d. Click the Chart Type list arrow on the Standard toolbar, then click Pie Chart. (*Hint*: Use the Toolbar Options button as needed to locate the Chart Type button.)

   e. Select the second and third rows in the datasheet, then press [Delete].

   f. Replace the data in the datasheet with the data shown in Figure F-23, then close the datasheet. (*Hint*: If the label in your datasheet is East, replace it with **Pie 1**.)

   g. Select the legend, click the Format Legend button, then change the placement of the legend to Bottom.

   h. Use the Chart Objects list arrow to select the Plot Area, open the Format Plot Area dialog box, then change the Border and Area patterns to None.

FIGURE F-23

		A	B	C	D	E
		Houses	Land	Farms	Businesses	
1	Pie 1	15.7	11.8	6.7	12.2	
2						
3						

   i. Use the Chart Objects list arrow to select Series "Pie 1," open the Format Data Series dialog box, click the Data Labels tab, then make the data labels show the percentage.

   j. Resize the chart object proportionally so it is about 5" wide and 3" tall.

   k. Type **Prepared by** followed by your name centered in the document footer, save your changes, print the document, close the file, then exit Word.

▼ INDEPENDENT CHALLENGE 1

You are starting a business and need to design a letterhead. Your letterhead needs to include a logo, which you design using AutoShapes, as well as your name and contact information. Figure F-24 shows a sample letterhead.

   a. Start Word, open a new blank document, then save it as **Letterhead** to the drive and folder where your Data Files are located.

   b. Identify the nature of your business, then examine the shapes available on the AutoShapes menus and decide what kind of logo to create.

   c. Using pencil and paper, sketch a design for your letterhead. Determine the positions for your logo, name, address, and any other design elements you want to include. You will create and organize all the elements of your letterhead in a drawing canvas.

FIGURE F-24

Georgia J. McQueeney
Architect/Planner
54 Erie Street • Syracuse, NY 13219 • 315-555-3288 • gjmcq@earthlink.net

▼ INDEPENDENT CHALLENGE 1 (CONTINUED)

d. Using AutoShapes, create your logo in a drawing canvas. Use the buttons on the Drawing toolbar to enhance the logo with color, text, lines, shadows, and other effects.

e. Resize the logo and position it in the drawing canvas.

f. In the drawing canvas, create a text box that includes your name, address, and other important contact information. Format the text and the text box using the buttons on the Formatting and Drawing toolbars.

g. Resize the text box as necessary and position it in the drawing canvas.

h. Add to the drawing canvas any other design elements you want to include.

i. When you are satisfied with the layout of your letterhead in the drawing canvas, fit the drawing canvas to its contents, then resize the drawing canvas as necessary.

j. Wrap text around the drawing canvas, then position it on the page.

k. Save your changes, preview the letterhead, print a copy, close the file, then exit Word.

▼ INDEPENDENT CHALLENGE 2

FIGURE F-25

You design ads for GoTroppo.com, a company that specializes in discounted travel to tropical destinations. Your next assignment is to design a full-page ad for a travel magazine. Your ad needs to contain a photograph of a vacation scene, shown in Figure F-25, the text "Your vacation begins here and now," and the Web address "www.gotroppo.com." If you are performing the ACE steps, your ad will also include a company logo.

a. Start Word, open a new, blank document, then save it as **GoTroppo Ad** to the drive and folder where your Data Files are located.

b. Change all four page margins to .7".

c. Insert the file **Vacation.jpg** from the drive and folder where your Data Files are located, then examine the photo. Think about how you can use this photo effectively in your ad.

d. Using pencil and paper, sketch the layout for your ad. You can use AutoShapes, lines, text boxes, WordArt, and any other design elements in your ad to make it powerful and eye-catching.

e. Apply a text-wrapping style to the photograph to make it a floating graphic, then format the photograph as you planned. You can crop it, resize it, move it, and combine it with other design elements.

f. Using text boxes or WordArt, add the text **Your vacation begins here and now** and the Web address **www.gotroppo.com** to the ad.

g. Use the buttons on the Drawing and Formatting toolbars to format the graphic objects.

Advanced Challenge Exercise

■ Using AutoShapes and a text box in a drawing canvas, create a logo that includes a sun setting over the ocean and the company name **gotroppo.com**. Figure F-26 shows a sample logo.

FIGURE F-26

■ Using the Fill Effects dialog box, fill the AutoShapes with color, gradients, patterns, or textures.

■ Resize the drawing canvas to suit your needs, then move the logo to where you want it in the ad.

h. Adjust the layout and design of the ad: adjust the colors, add or remove design elements, and resize and reposition the objects as necessary.

i. When you are satisfied with your ad, type your name in the document header, save your changes, print a copy, close the document, then exit Word.

▼ INDEPENDENT CHALLENGE 3

You are a graphic designer. The public library has hired you to design a bookmark for Literacy Week. Their only request is that the bookmark includes the words Literacy Week. You'll create three different bookmarks for the library.

a. Start Word, open a new, blank document, then save it as **Bookmarks** to the drive and folder where your Data Files are located.

b. Change all four page margins to .7", change the page orientation to landscape, and change the zoom level to Whole Page.

c. Draw three rectangles in a drawing canvas. Resize the rectangles to be 2.5" x 6.5" and move them so they do not overlap. Each rectangle will become a bookmark. (*Hint*: If you use the Format AutoShape dialog box to resize the rectangles, make sure the Lock aspect ratio check box is not selected.)

d. In the first rectangle, design a bookmark using AutoShapes.

e. In the second rectangle, design a bookmark using WordArt.

f. In the third rectangle, design a bookmark using clip art.

Advanced Challenge Exercise

- Fill one bookmark with a gradient, one with a texture, and one with a pattern. You might need to revise some aspects of the bookmarks you created in the previous steps.
- To one bookmark, add a photograph.
- To one bookmark, add curved, scribble, or freeform lines.

g. Use the buttons on the Drawing toolbar to format the bookmarks with fills, colors, lines, and other effects. Be sure to add the words Literacy Week to each bookmark.

h. Type your name in the document header, save your changes, print, close the document, then exit Word.

▼ INDEPENDENT CHALLENGE 4

One way to find graphic images to use in your documents is to download them from the Web. Many Web sites feature images that are in the public domain, which means they have no copyright restrictions and permission is not required to use the images. You are free to download these images and use them in your documents, although you must acknowledge the artist or identify the source. Other Web sites include images that are copyrighted and require written permission, and often payment, to use. Before downloading and using graphics from the Web, it's important to research and establish their copyright status and permission requirements. In this exercise you download photographs from the Web and research their copyright restrictions.

a. Start Word, open the file WD F-4.doc from the drive and folder where your Data Files are located, then save it as **Copyright Info**. This document contains a table that you will fill with the photos you find on the Web and the copyright restrictions for those photos.

b. Use your favorite search engine to search the Web for photographs. Use the keywords **photo archives** to conduct your search.

c. Find at least three Web sites that contain photos you could use in a document. Save a photo from each Web site to your computer, and note the URL and copyright restrictions. To save an image from a Web page, right-click the image, then click the appropriate command on the shortcut menu.

d. Insert the photos you saved from the Web in the Photo column of the table. Resize the photos proportionally so that they are no more than 1.5" tall or 1.5" wide. Wrap text around the photos and center them in the table cells.

e. For each photo, enter the URL and the copyright restrictions for the photo in the table. In the Copyright Restrictions column, indicate if the photo is copyrighted or in the public domain, and note the requirements for using that photo in a document.

f. Type your name in the document header, save your changes, print a copy, close the file, then exit Word.

Using the files WD F-5.doc and Surfing.jpg (found in the drive and folder where your Data Files are located), create the flyer shown in Figure F-27. Type your name in the header, save the flyer as **Surf Safe**, then print a copy.

FIGURE F-27

Surf Safe

NEVER SURF ALONE

Follow the rules
All beginning surfers need to follow basic safety rules before heading into the waves. The key to safe surfing is caution and awareness.

Wear sunscreen
Sunscreen helps prevent skin cancer and aging of the skin. 30+ SPF broad spectrum sunscreen screens out both UVA and UVB rays and provides more than 30 times your natural sunburn protection. Apply sunscreen at least 15 minutes before exposing yourself to the sun, and reapply it every two hours or after swimming, drying with a towel, or excessive perspiration. Zinc cream also helps prevent sunburn and guards against harmful UV rays.

Dress appropriately
Wear a wet suit or a rash vest. Choose a wet suit that is appropriate for the water temperature. Rash vests help protect against UV rays.

Use a safe surfboard
A safe surfboard is a surfboard that suits your ability. Beginners need a big, thick surfboard for stability.

Learn how to escape rips
A rip current is a volume of water moving out to sea: the bigger the surf, the stronger the rips associated with it. Indicators of rips include:

- Brown water caused by stirred up sand
- Foam on the surface of the water that trails past the break
- Waves breaking on both sides of a rip current
- A rippled appearance between calm water
- Debris floating out to sea

If you are dragged out by a rip, don't panic! Stay calm and examine the rip conditions before trying to escape the current. Poor swimmers should ride the rip out from the beach and then swim parallel to the shore for 30 or 40 meters. Once you have escaped the rip, swim toward the shore where the waves are breaking. You can also probe with your feet to see if a sand bar has formed near the edge of the rip. Strong swimmers should swim at a 45 degree angle across the rip.

Study the surf
Always study the surf before going in. Select a safe beach with waves under 1 meter, and pick waves that are suitable for your ability.

Creating a Web Page

OBJECTIVES

| Plan a Web page |
| Create a Web page |
| Format a Web page with themes |
| Illustrate a Web page with graphics |
| Save a document as a Web page |
| Add hyperlinks |
| Modify hyperlinks |
| Preview a Web page in a browser |

If you have a SAM user profile, you may have access to hands-on instruction, practice, and assessment of the skills covered in this unit. Log in to your SAM account and go to your assignments page to see what your instructor has assigned.

Creating a Web page and posting it on the World Wide Web or an intranet is a powerful way to share information with other people. The Web page formatting features of Word allow you to easily create professional looking Web pages from scratch or to save an existing document in HTML format so it can be viewed using a browser. In this unit, you learn how to create a new Web page and how to save an existing document as a Web page. You also learn how to edit and format Web pages, create and modify hyperlinks, and preview a Web page in a browser. MediaLoft is sponsoring the Seattle Writers Festival, a major public event featuring prominent writers from around the world. You need to create a Web site for the Seattle Writers Festival to promote the event and provide information to the public. You plan to post the Web site on the World Wide Web.

Planning a Web Page

A **Web page** is a document that can be stored on a computer called a Web server and viewed on the World Wide Web or on an intranet using a **browser**, a software program used to access and display Web pages. A **Web site** is a group of associated Web pages that are linked together with hyperlinks. Before creating a Web page or a Web site, it's important to plan its content and organization. The **home page** is the main page of a Web site, and the first Web page viewers see when they visit a site. Usually, it is the first page you plan and create. The Seattle Writers Festival Web site will include a home page that serves both as an introduction to the festival and as a table of contents for the other Web pages in the site. Before creating the home page, you identify the content you want to include, plan the organization of the Web site, and sketch the design for each Web page.

- ## Identify the goal of the Web site

  A successful Web site has a clear purpose. For example, it might promote a product, communicate information, or facilitate a transaction. Your Web site will communicate information about the Seattle Writers Festival to the public.

- ## Sketch the Web site

  Identify the information you want to include on each Web page, sketch the layout and design of each Web page, and map the links between the pages in the Web site. A well-designed Web site is visually interesting and easy for viewers to use. Figure G-1 shows a sketch of the Seattle Writers Festival Web site.

- ## Create each Web page and save it in HTML format

  You can create a Web page from scratch in Word or convert an existing document to a Web page. When you create a Web page in Word, you save it in HTML format. **HTML** (Hypertext Markup Language) is the programming language used to describe how each element of a Web page should appear when viewed with a browser. You will use a blank Web page template to create the home page. You will create the Program of Events Web page by saving an existing document in HTML format. Files saved in HTML format can be recognized by their .htm, .html, .mht, or .mhtml file extension.

- ## Determine the file-naming convention to use

  Different operating systems place various restrictions on Web site filenames. Many Web page designers follow the standard eight-dot-three file-naming convention, which specifies that a filename have a maximum of eight characters followed by a period and a three-letter file extension—mypage.htm or chap_1.htm, for example. You will use the eight-dot-three naming convention for your Web pages.

- ## Format each Web page

  You can use the standard Word formatting features to enhance Web pages with fonts, backgrounds, graphics, lines, tables, and other format effects. Word also includes visual themes that you can apply to Web pages to format them quickly. The look of a Web page has as much of an impact on the viewer as its content, so it's important to select fonts, colors, and graphics that complement the goal of your Web site. You plan to apply a theme that expresses the spirit of the writers festival to each Web page. A consistent look between Web pages is an important factor in Web site design.

- ## Create the hyperlinks between Web pages

  Hyperlinks are text or graphics that viewers can click to open a file, another Web page, or an e-mail message, or that viewers can click to jump to a specific location in the same file. Hyperlinks are commonly used to link the pages of a Web site to each other. You will add hyperlinks that link the home page to other Web pages in your Web site. You will also add links from the home page to other Web sites on the Internet and to an e-mail message to MediaLoft.

- ## View the Web site using a browser

  Before publishing your Web site to the Web or an intranet, it's important to view your Web pages in a browser to make sure they look and work as you intended. You will use the Web Page Preview feature to check the formatting of each Web page in your browser and to test the hyperlinks.

FIGURE G-1: Sketch of the Seattle Writers Festival Web site

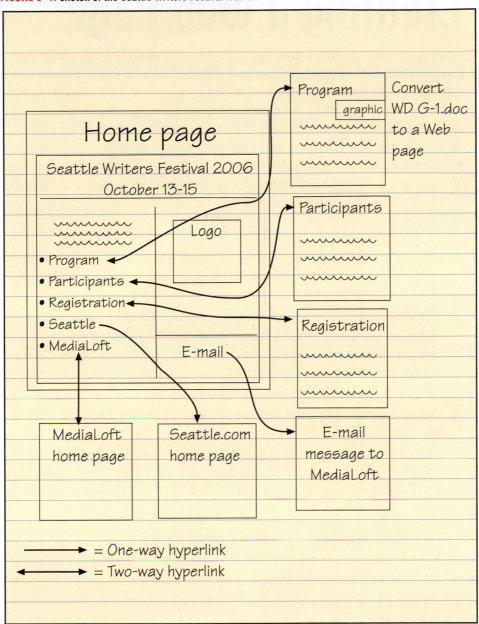

Clues to Use

Choosing a Web page file format

When you save a document as a Web page in Word, you save it in one of several HTML formats, which ensures the HTML codes are embedded in the file. You have the option of saving the document in Single File Web Page (.mht or .mhtml) format or in Web Page (.htm or .html) format. In a single file Web page, all the elements of the Web page, including the text and graphics, are saved together in a single MIME encapsulated aggregate HTML (MHTML) file, making it simple to publish your Web page or send it via e-mail. By contrast, if you choose to save a Web page as an .htm file, Word automatically creates a supporting folder in the same location as the .htm file. This folder has the same name as the .htm file plus the suffix _files, and it houses the supporting files associated with the Web page. For example, when you create a new Web page or save an existing document as an .htm file, each graphic—including the bullets, background textures, horizontal lines, and other graphics included on the Web page—is automatically converted to a GIF or JPEG format file and saved in the supporting folder. Be aware that if you copy or move a Web page saved in .htm format to a different location, it's important that you copy or move the supporting folder (and all the files in it) along with the .htm file, otherwise the links between the .htm file and the supporting files may be broken. If a browser cannot locate the graphic files associated with a Web page, the browser displays a placeholder (often a red X) instead of a graphic. By default, Word saves a Web page as a single file Web page using the .mht file extension.

Creating a Web Page

Creating a Web page involves creating a document that uses HTML formatting. HTML places codes, called **tags**, around the elements of a Web page to describe how each element should appear when viewed with a browser. When you create a Web page in Word, you use the usual Word buttons and commands to edit and format the text, graphics, and other elements, and Word automatically inserts the HTML tags for you. A quick way to create a new Web page is to start with the blank Web page template and add text and graphics to it. Because text and graphics align and position differently on Web pages than in Word documents, it's helpful to use a table to structure the layout of a Web page. You begin by creating the home page. You start with a new blank Web page, insert a table to structure the layout of the home page, add text, and then save the Web page in single file Web Page format.

STEPS

1. **Start Word, click Create a new document in the Getting Started task pane, then click Web page in the New Document task pane**

   A blank Web page opens in the document window in Web Layout view.

2. **Click the Zoom list arrow on the Standard toolbar, click 100% if necessary, click the Insert Table button on the Standard toolbar, point to the second box in the third row of the grid to create a 3 x 2 Table, then click**

   A table with three rows and two columns is inserted. After you finish using the table to help lay out the design of the Web page, you will remove the table borders.

3. **Select the two cells in the first row, click Table on the menu bar, click Merge Cells, then deselect the row**

   Two cells in the first row merge to become a single cell.

4. **Click in the first row, type Seattle Writers Festival 2006, press [Enter] twice, type October 13-15, then press [Enter]**

5. **Select the two cells in the second and third rows of the first column, click Table on the menu bar, click Merge Cells, then deselect the cell**

   The two cells in the first column merge to become a single cell.

6. **Type the text shown in Figure G-2 in the table cells**

7. **Click the Save button on the Standard toolbar**

   The Save As dialog box opens. Word assigns a default page title and filename for the Web page and indicates Single File Web Page (*.mht; *.mhtml) as the Save as type. If you prefer to save the Web page as an .htm file with a supporting folder for the associated files, click the Save as type list arrow, and then click Web Page (*.htm, *.html).

8. **Click Change Title, type Seattle Writers Festival - Home (Your Name) in the Set Page Title dialog box, then click OK**

   The page title appears in the title bar when the Web page is viewed with a browser. It's important to assign a page title that describes the Web page for visitors.

9. **Drag to select Seattle Writers Festival 2006.mht in the File name text box, type swfhome, use the Save in list arrow to navigate to the drive and folder where your Data Files are located, then compare your Save As dialog box with Figure G-3**

   The filename appears in the title bar when the Web page is viewed in Word.

10. **Click Save**

   The filename swfhome.mht appears in the title bar. Depending on your Windows settings, the file extension may or may not appear after the filename.

FIGURE G-2: Web page in Web Layout view

New Web Page button

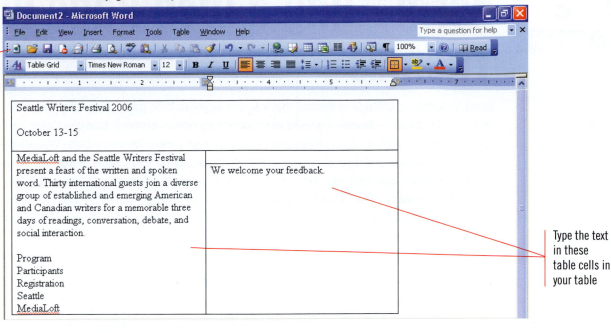

Type the text in these table cells in your table

FIGURE G-3: Save As dialog box

Page title of Web page (yours will include your name)

Filename of Web page

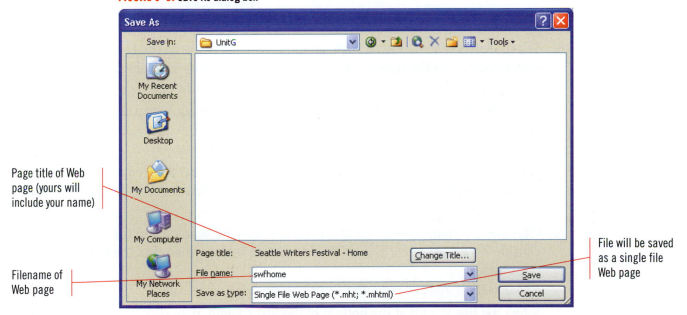

File will be saved as a single file Web page

Clues to Use

Adding frames to a Web page

Many Web pages you visit on the Internet include frames for displaying fixed information. A **frame** is a section of a Web page window in which a separate Web page can be displayed. Frames commonly contain hyperlinks and other navigation elements that help visitors browse a Web site. A header that remains at the top of the screen while visitors browse a Web site is one example of a frame; a left column that contains hyperlinks to each page in the Web site and stays on the screen while readers visit different pages is another example. You can add a frame to a Web page by pointing to Frames on the Format menu, and then clicking the type of frame you want to add.

Click New Frames Page to open the Frames toolbar, which you can use to select a location (left, right, above, or below) for a new, empty frame. Alternately, if you have applied heading styles to text in the current Web page, you can click Table of Contents in Frame to create a frame that includes hyperlinks to each heading in the Web page. Once you have created a frames page, you can resize the frames by dragging a frame border. To hide or show the frame borders or specify which page first appears in a frame, point to Frames on the Format menu, click Frame Properties, and then change the settings in the Frame Properties dialog box.

Formatting a Web Page with Themes

Word includes a multitude of themes that you can apply to Web pages to quickly give them an attractive and consistent look. A **theme** is a set of complementary design elements that you can apply to Web pages, e-mail messages, and other documents that are viewed on screen. Themes include Web page backgrounds, styles for headings and hyperlinks, picture bullets, horizontal lines, table borders, and other specially designed formats that work well together. To apply a theme to a Web page, you use the Theme command on the Format menu. You apply a theme to the Web page, format the text using the theme styles, and add a horizontal line and bullets. You then experiment with alternate themes to find a design that more closely matches the character of the Writers Festival.

STEPS

1. **Click Format on the menu bar, click Theme, then click Blends in the Choose a Theme list box**

   A preview of the Blends theme appears in the Theme dialog box, as shown in Figure G-4. The theme includes a background and styles for text, hyperlinks, bullet characters, and horizontal lines.

QUICK TIP

To create a custom background, point to Background on the Format menu. For a solid color background, select a standard color or click More Colors. For a background with a gradient, texture, pattern, or picture, click Fill Effects.

2. **Click OK**

   The theme background is added to the Web page and the Normal style that comes with the theme is applied to the text.

3. **Select Seattle Writers Festival 2006, click the Style list arrow on the Formatting toolbar, click Heading 1 in the Style list, then click the heading to deselect the text**

   The Heading 1 style—16-point Trebuchet MS bold—is applied to the heading text.

4. **Select October 13-15, click the Style list arrow, click Heading 2, then click the date to deselect the text**

   The Heading 2 style—14-point Trebuchet MS—is applied to the date text.

5. **Select the heading and the date, click the Center button on the Formatting toolbar, move the pointer over the table, click the table move handle to select the table, then click**

   The heading, date, and table are centered on the Web page.

QUICK TIP

To change the size or alignment of a line, double-click the line to open the Format Horizontal Line dialog box, then adjust the settings on the Horizontal Line tab.

6. **Place the insertion point in the blank line between the heading and the date, click the Outside Border list arrow on the Formatting toolbar, then click the Horizontal Line button**

   A horizontal line formatted in the theme design is added below the heading.

7. **Select the five-line list at the bottom of the first column, then click the Bullets button on the Formatting toolbar**

   The list is formatted using bullets from the Blends theme design.

QUICK TIP

Backgrounds are visible only in Web Layout view and do not print.

8. **Click Format on the menu bar, click Theme, scroll down the Choose a Theme list box, click Pixel, then click OK**

   The background and the text, line, and bullet styles applied to the Web page change to the designs used in the Pixel theme. You do not need to reapply the styles to a Web page when you change its theme.

9. **Select Seattle Writers Festival 2006, click the Font Size list arrow on the Formatting toolbar, click 26, click the Font Color list arrow on the Formatting toolbar, click Indigo, deselect the text, then save your changes**

   The font size of the heading is increased and the color changes to Indigo. Once you have applied styles to text you can customize the format to suit your purpose. Compare your Web page with Figure G-5.

FIGURE G-4: Blends theme in the Theme dialog box

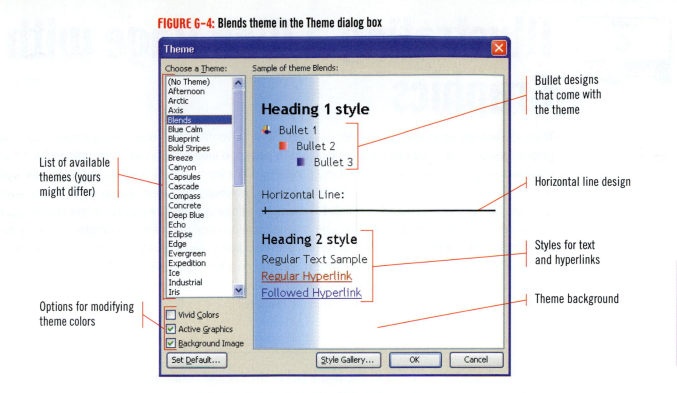

List of available themes (yours might differ)

Options for modifying theme colors

Bullet designs that come with the theme

Horizontal line design

Styles for text and hyperlinks

Theme background

FIGURE G-5: Pixel theme applied to the Web page

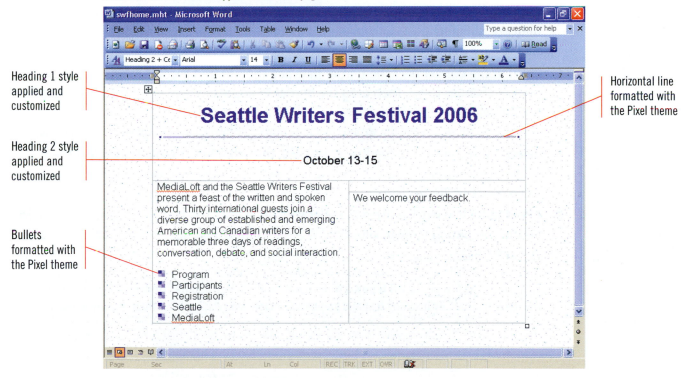

Heading 1 style applied and customized

Heading 2 style applied and customized

Bullets formatted with the Pixel theme

Horizontal line formatted with the Pixel theme

Illustrating a Web Page with Graphics

You can illustrate your Web pages with pictures, clip art, WordArt, text boxes, AutoShapes, and other graphic objects. When you insert a graphic on a Web page, it is inserted as an inline graphic and you must apply text wrapping to be able to move it independently of the line of text. Floating graphics align and position differently on Web pages than in Word documents, however, because browsers do not support the same graphic-formatting options as Word. For example, a floating graphic with square text wrapping can only be left- or right-aligned on a Web page, whereas you can position a floating graphic anywhere in a Word document. For this reason, it's important to use Web Layout view to position graphics on a Web page. If you want to position floating graphics or text precisely on a Web page, you can create a table and then insert the text or graphics in the table cells. You want the MediaLoft logo to appear to the right of center on the Web page. You insert the logo in the blank cell in the table, and then adjust the table formatting to make the Web page attractive.

STEPS

1. **Place the insertion point in the blank cell in the second column of the table, click Insert on the menu bar, point to Picture, then click From File**
   The Insert Picture dialog box opens.

2. **Use the Look in list arrow to navigate to the drive and folder where your Data Files are located, click the file mloft.jpg, then click Insert**
   The logo is inserted in the cell as an inline graphic.

3. **Click the logo to select it, click the Center button ≣ on the Formatting toolbar, press [→], then press [Enter]**
   The graphic is centered in the table cell and a blank line is inserted under the logo.

4. **Position the pointer over the border between the first and second columns until the pointer changes to +‖+, then drag the border to approximately the 4 ¼" mark on the horizontal ruler**
   The first column widens and the second column narrows. The logo remains centered in the table cell.

5. **Select We welcome your feedback., click ≣, then click in the table to deselect the text**
   The text is centered in the table cell, as shown in Figure G-6. In Web Layout view, text and graphics are positioned as they are in a Web browser.

6. **Click the table move handle ⊞ to select the table, click the Horizontal Line list arrow ≣▾ on the Formatting toolbar, click the No Border button ▦, deselect the table, then save your changes**
   Removing the table borders masks that the underlying structure of the Web page is a table, as shown in Figure G-7. The text on the left is now a wide column and the logo and text under the logo are positioned to the right of center. By inserting text and graphics in a table, you can position them exactly where you want.

FIGURE G-6: Logo and text centered in the second column

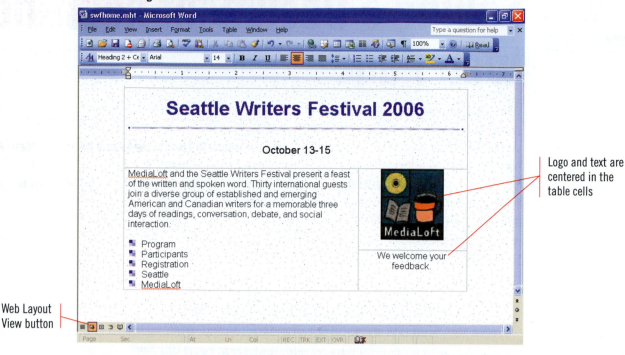

Logo and text are centered in the table cells

Web Layout View button

FIGURE G-7: Web page with table borders removed

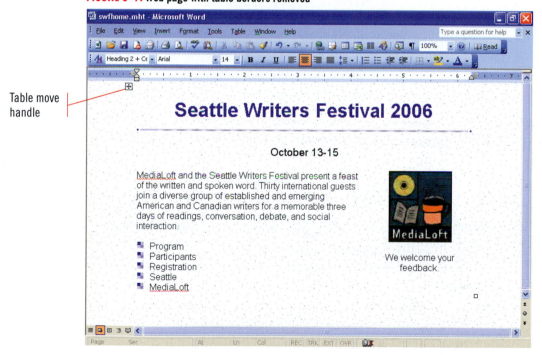

Table move handle

Adding alternate text for graphics

Graphics can take a long time to appear on a Web page. Some people turn off the display of graphics in their browsers so that they can download and view Web pages more quickly. If you don't want visitors to your Web page to see empty space in place of a graphic, you can add alternate text to appear on the Web page instead of the graphic. Alternate text appears in some browsers while the graphic is loading, and is used by search engines to find Web pages. To add alternate text to a Web page, select the graphic, and then click the Picture command on the Format menu. On the Web tab in the Format Picture dialog box, type the text you want to appear in lieu of the graphic, and then click OK.

Saving a Document as a Web Page

When you save an existing document as a Web page, Word converts the content and formatting of the Word file to HTML and displays the Web page as it will appear in a browser. Any formatting that is not supported by Web browsers is either converted to similar supported formatting or removed from the Web page. For example, if you save a document that contains a floating graphic in HTML format, the graphic will be left- or right-aligned on the Web page. Table G-1 describes several common formatting elements that are not supported by Web browsers. To save a document as a Web page, you use the Save as Web Page command on the File menu.  You want to add a Web page that includes the festival program of events to your Web site. Rather than create the Web page from scratch, you convert an existing document to HTML format. You then adjust the formatting of the new Web page and apply the Pixel theme.

STEPS

QUICK TIP

To create a Web page that is compatible with a specific browser, click Tools on the menu bar, click Options, click the General tab, click Web Options, then select from the options on the Browsers tab in the Web Options dialog box.

1. **Open the file WD G-1.doc from the drive and folder where your Data Files are located, click the Zoom list arrow on the Standard toolbar, then click Two Pages**

   The document opens in Print Layout view, as shown in Figure G-8. Notice that the document is two pages long, the text is formatted in three columns, and the graphic on the first page is centered.

2. **Click File on the menu bar, click Save as Web Page, click Change Title, type Seattle Writers Festival – Program of Events (Your Name) in the Set Page Title dialog box, click OK, select WD G-1.mht in the Filename text box, type swfevent, then click Save**

   A dialog box opens and informs you that browsers do not support some of the formatting features of the document, including that the floating graphic will be left- or right-aligned in the Web page.

TROUBLE

If the Web page appears in a different view, click the Web Layout View button on the horizontal scroll bar.

3. **Click Continue**

   A copy of the document is saved in HTML format with the filename "swfevent" and the page title "Seattle Writers Festival – Program of Events (Your Name)." The Web page appears in Web Layout view. Notice that the graphic is now left-aligned on the Web page.

4. **Click the Zoom list arrow on the Standard toolbar, click 100% if necessary, then scroll to the bottom of the Web page**

   The text is now formatted in a single column, there are no margins on the Web page, and the document is one long page.

5. **Press [Ctrl][Home], double-click the graphic to open the Format Picture dialog box, click the Size tab, select 3.76 in the Height text box, type 2, then click OK**

   The size of the graphic is reduced.

QUICK TIP

To be able to position a graphic precisely on a Web page, you must insert the graphic in a table or make it an inline graphic.

6 **Drag the graphic to the upper-right corner of the Web page, then deselect the graphic**

   The graphic jumps into place in the upper-right corner when you release the mouse button.

7. **Click Format on the menu bar, click Theme, click Pixel in the Choose a Theme list box, click OK, then save your changes**

   The Pixel theme is applied to the Web page, giving it a look that is consistent with the home page. Notice that the bullet characters change to the bullet design included with the theme. The font of the body text also changes to the Normal style font used in the theme (12-point Arial). Compare your Web page with Figure G-9.

FIGURE G-8: Word document in Print Layout view

Text is formatted in columns

Floating graphic is centered

Document is two pages long

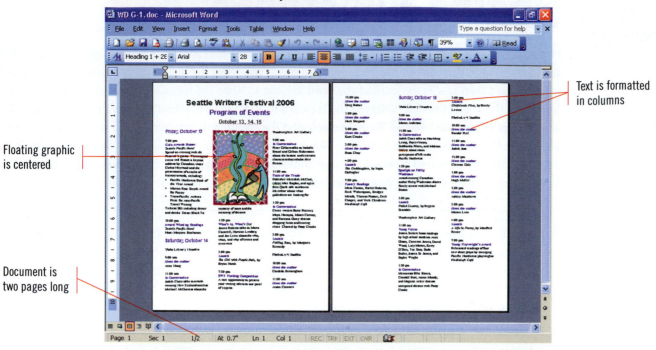

FIGURE G-9: Web page in Web Layout view

Graphic is moved to the upper-right corner

Body text changes to Pixel theme Normal style

Bullets change to Pixel theme bullets

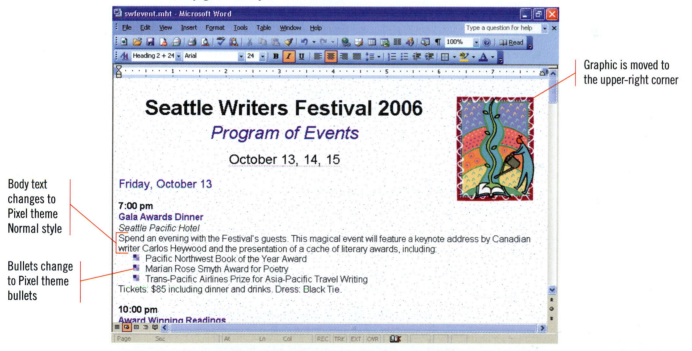

TABLE G-1: Word features that are not supported by Web browsers

feature	result when viewed with a browser
Character formatting	Shadow text becomes bold; small caps become all caps; embossed, engraved, and outline text becomes solid; character scale changes to 100%; and drop caps are removed
Paragraph formatting	Indents are removed, tabs might not align correctly, and border and shading styles might change
Page layout	Margins, columns, page numbers, page borders, and headers and footers are removed; all footnotes are moved to the end of the document
Graphics	Floating graphics, including pictures, AutoShapes, text boxes, and WordArt, are left- or right-aligned
Tables	Decorative cell borders become box borders, diagonal borders are removed, vertical text is changed to horizontal

Adding Hyperlinks

Hyperlinks allow readers to link (or "jump") to a Web page, an e-mail address, a file, or a specific location in a document. When you create a hyperlink in a document, you select the text or graphic you want to use as a hyperlink and then specify the location you want to jump to when the hyperlink is clicked. You create hyperlinks using the Insert Hyperlink button on the Standard toolbar. Text that is formatted as a hyperlink appears as colored, underlined text.  To make navigating the Events Web page easier, you create hyperlinks that jump from the dates in the third line of the Web page to the schedule for those dates farther down the Web page. You then insert several hyperlinks on your home page: one to link to the Events Web page, one to link to the Seattle.com Web site on the Internet, and one to link to an e-mail message to MediaLoft.

STEPS

1. **Select 15 in the third line of the Events Web page, then click the Insert Hyperlink button 🌐 on the Standard toolbar**

   The Insert Hyperlink dialog box opens. You use this dialog box to specify the location of the Web page, file, e-mail address, or position in the current document you want to jump to when the hyperlink—in this case, the text "15"—is clicked.

2. **Click Place in This Document in the Link to section**

   All the headings in the Web page are displayed in the dialog box, as shown in Figure G-10. In this context, a "heading" is any text to which a heading style has been applied.

   > **QUICK TIP**
   > Press [Ctrl] and click any hyperlink in Word to follow the hyperlink.

3. **Click Sunday, October 15 in the Select a place in this document section, then click OK**

   The selected text, "15", is formatted in blue and underlined, the hyperlink style when the Pixel theme is applied. When the Web page is viewed in a browser, clicking the 15 hyperlink jumps the viewer to the heading "Sunday, October 15" farther down the Web page.

4. **Select 14, click 🌐, click Saturday, October 14 in the Insert Hyperlink dialog box, click OK, select 13, click 🌐, click Friday, October 13, click OK, save your changes, then close the file**

   The numbers 14 and 13 are formatted as hyperlinks to the headings for those dates in the Web page. After you save and close the file, the home page appears in the document window.

5. **Select Program in the bulleted list, click 🌐, click Existing File or Web Page in the Link to section, use the Look in list arrow to navigate to the drive and folder where your Data Files are located, then click swfevent.mht**

   The filename swfevent.mht appears in the Address text box, as shown in Figure G-11.

   > **QUICK TIP**
   > To create a ScreenTip that appears in a browser, click ScreenTip in the Insert Hyperlink dialog box, then in the Set Hyperlink ScreenTip dialog box, type the text you want to appear.

6. **Click OK**

   "Program" is formatted as a hyperlink to the Program of Events Web page. If you point to a hyperlink in Word, the address of the file or Web page it links to appears in a ScreenTip.

7. **Select Seattle in the list, click 🌐, type www.seattle.com in the Address text box in the Insert Hyperlink dialog box, then click OK**

   As you type the Web address, Word automatically adds "http://" in front of "www." A Web address is also called a **URL**, which stands for Uniform Resource Locator. The word "Seattle" is formatted as a hyperlink to the Seattle.com Web site on the Internet.

   > **QUICK TIP**
   > By default, Word automatically creates a hyperlink to an e-mail address or URL when you type the address or URL in a document or Web page.

8. **Select feedback under the logo, click 🌐, then click E-mail Address in the Link to section of the Insert Hyperlink dialog box**

   The Insert Hyperlink dialog box changes so you can create a link to an e-mail message.

9. **Type swf@media-loft.com in the E-mail address text box, type Seattle Writers Festival in the Subject text box, click OK, then save your changes**

   The word "feedback" is formatted as a hyperlink, as shown in Figure G-12.

Create a hyperlink to a Web page or file

Create a hyperlink to a location in the current file

Create a hyperlink to a new blank document

Create a hyperlink to an e-mail address

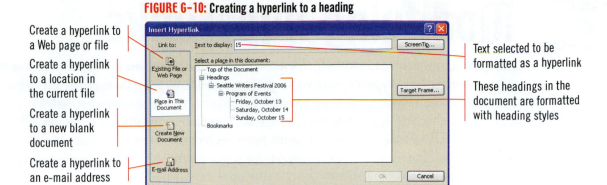

Text selected to be formatted as a hyperlink

These headings in the document are formatted with heading styles

FIGURE G-11: Creating a hyperlink to a file

Click to change the default ScreenTip for the hyperlink

Click to browse the Internet for a specific URL to link to

File to jump to when the hyperlink is clicked

Files in the active drive or folder (yours might differ)

FIGURE G-12: Hyperlinks in the Web page

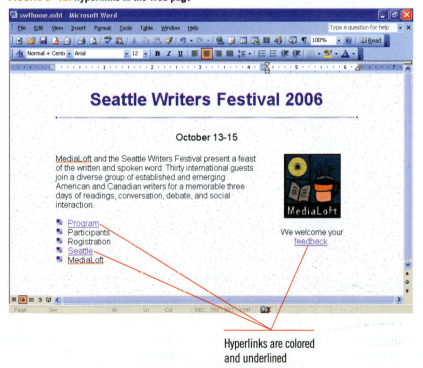

Hyperlinks are colored and underlined

Clues to Use

Pasting text as a hyperlink

You can quickly create a hyperlink to a specific location in any document by copying text from the destination location and pasting it as a hyperlink. To copy and paste text as a hyperlink, select the text you want to jump to, copy it to the Clipboard, place the insertion point in the location you want to insert the hyperlink, click Edit on the menu bar, then click Paste as Hyperlink. The text you copied is pasted and formatted as a hyperlink.

Word 2003

Modifying Hyperlinks

Over time, you might need to edit the hyperlinks on your Web pages with new information or remove them altogether. When you edit a hyperlink, you can change the hyperlink destination, the hyperlink text, or the ScreenTip that appears when a viewer points to the hyperlink. You can easily update or remove a hyperlink by right-clicking it and selecting the Edit Hyperlink or Remove Hyperlink command on the shortcut menu. You change the hyperlink text for the Program and Seattle hyperlinks to make them more descriptive. You also add a ScreenTip to the Seattle hyperlink so that visitors to the Seattle Writers Festival 2006 home page will better understand what the link offers.

STEPS

1. **Right-click Program, then click Edit Hyperlink on the shortcut menu**
   The Edit Hyperlink dialog box opens.

2. **Click after Program in the Text to display text box, press [Spacebar], type of Festival Events, then click OK**
   The hyperlink text changes to "Program of Festival Events" on the Web page.

3. **Right-click Seattle, click Edit Hyperlink, then click ScreenTip in the Edit Hyperlink dialog box**
   The Set Hyperlink ScreenTip dialog box opens, as shown in Figure G-13. Any text you type in this dialog box appears as a ScreenTip when a viewer points to the hyperlink.

4. **Type Hotels, dining, and entertainment in Seattle in the ScreenTip text box, then click OK**

5. **Click in front of Seattle in the Text to display text box in the Edit Hyperlink dialog box, type Visiting, press [Spacebar], click OK, then save your changes**
   The hyperlink text changes to "Visiting Seattle."

6. **Point to Visiting Seattle**
   The ScreenTip you added appears, as shown in Figure G-14.

Clues to Use

E-mailing a document from Word

Another way to share information online is to e-mail a Word document to others. Using the Send To command on the File menu, you can send a document directly from Word, either as an e-mail message or as an attachment to an e-mail message. To e-mail a document as a message, open the document, point to Send To on the File menu, and then click Mail Recipient. A message header opens above the document window. You can also click the E-mail button on the Standard toolbar to open a message header. Type the e-mail address(es) of the recipient(s) in the To and Cc text boxes in the message header, separating multiple addresses with a comma or a semicolon. When you are ready to send the file, click Send a Copy on the e-mail header toolbar.

To send a file as an attachment to an e-mail message, open the file, point to Send To on the File menu, and then click Mail Recipient (for Review) or Mail Recipient (as Attachment). When you select Mail Recipient (for Review), a message window opens that includes the request "Please review the attached document" in the body of the message. When you click Mail Recipient (as Attachment), a blank message window opens. Type the e-mail addresses in the To and Cc text boxes, any message you want in the message window, and then click the Send button on the message window toolbar to send the message. When you send a document from Word, your default e-mail program sends a copy of the document to each recipient.

FIGURE G-13: Set Hyperlink ScreenTip dialog box

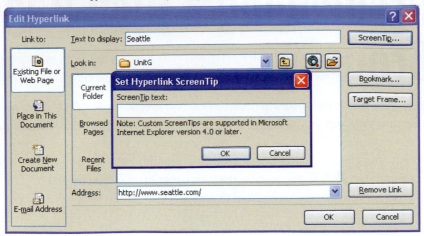

FIGURE G-14: ScreenTip and edited hyperlinks

Hyperlink text
is revised

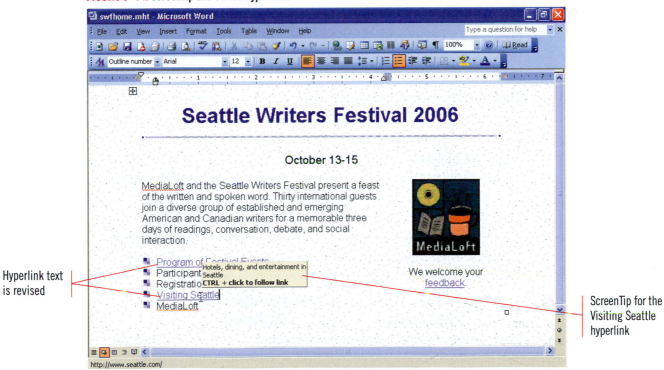

ScreenTip for the
Visiting Seattle
hyperlink

Previewing a Web Page in a Browser

Before you publish Web pages to the Web or an intranet, it's important to preview the pages in a browser to make sure they look as you intended. You can use the Web Page Preview command on the File menu to open a copy of a Web page in your default browser. When previewing a Web page, you should check for formatting errors and test each hyperlink. To complete this lesson, you must have a Web browser installed on your computer. ◆ You preview the Web pages in your browser and test the hyperlinks. After viewing the Program Web page, you use Word to adjust its formatting.

STEPS

1. **Click File on the menu bar, click Web Page Preview, then click the Maximize button on the browser title bar if necessary**

   The browser opens and the home page is displayed in the browser window, as shown in Figure G-15. Notice that the page title—Seattle Writers Festival - Home—appears in the browser title bar. Your page title will also include your name.

   > **TROUBLE**
   > If the hyperlink does not work, click File on the browser menu bar, click Open, click Browse, navigate to the swfevent.mht file, click Open, then continue with Step 3.

2. **Click the Program of Festival Events hyperlink**

   The Seattle Writers Festival – Program of Events Web page opens in the browser window.

3. **Click the 15 hyperlink**

   The browser jumps down the page and displays the program for Sunday, October 15 in the browser window.

4. **Click the Back button ⊙ Back on the browser toolbar**

   The top of the Program of Events Web page is displayed in the browser window. The browser toolbar includes buttons for navigating between Web pages, searching the Internet, and printing and editing the current Web page.

   > **TROUBLE**
   > If the Edit with Microsoft Office Word button is not available in your browser, click the Word Program button on the taskbar to switch to Word, and then open swfevent.mht.

5. **Click the Edit with Microsoft Office Word button 🗎 on the browser toolbar**

   The Program of Events Web page appears in a Word document window.

6. **Click the Zoom list arrow on the Standard toolbar, click 100% if necessary, select Tickets under the bulleted list, press and hold [Ctrl], select Dress in the same line, release [Ctrl], click the Bold button 🅱 on the Formatting toolbar, save your changes, then close the file**

   The home page appears in the Word document window. You want to check that your changes to the Program of Events Web page will preview correctly in the browser.

   > **TROUBLE**
   > If the hyperlink does not work, open the swfevent.mht file in the browser, then click the Refresh button.

7. **Click File on the menu bar, click Web Page Preview, click the Program of Festival Events hyperlink, then click the Refresh button 🗎 on the browser toolbar**

   The revised Program of Events Web page appears in the browser, as shown in Figure G-16.

8. **Click the Print button 🖨 on the browser toolbar to print a copy of the swfevent Web page, click ⊙ Back, then point to the Visiting Seattle hyperlink**

   The ScreenTip you created for the hyperlink appears. The URL of the Seattle.com Web site also appears in the status bar. If you are connected to the Internet you can click the Visiting Seattle hyperlink to open the Seattle.com Web site in your browser window. Click the Back button on the browser toolbar to return to the Seattle Writers Festival home page when you are finished.

   > **TROUBLE**
   > If an e-mail message does not open, continue with Step 10.

9. **Click the feedback hyperlink**

   An e-mail message that is automatically addressed to swf@media-loft.com with the subject "Seattle Writers Festival" opens in your default e-mail program.

10. **Close the e-mail message, click 🖨 to print the swfhome Web page, exit your browser, then exit Word**

FIGURE G-15: Home page in Internet Explorer

Page title (yours will include your name)

If your default browser is not Internet Explorer 6, your screens might differ

Edit with Microsoft Office Word button

FIGURE G-16: Revised Program of Events page in Internet Explorer

Print button

Text is bold

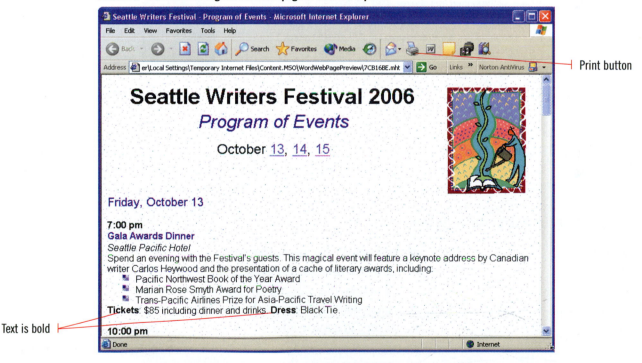

Clues to Use

Posting a Web site to the World Wide Web or an intranet

To make your Web site available to others, you must post (or publish) it to the Web or to a local intranet. Publishing a Web site involves copying the HTML files and any supporting folders and files to a Web server—either your Internet service provider's (ISPs) server, if you want to publish it to the Internet, or the server for your local intranet. Check with your ISP or your network administrator for instructions on how to post your Web pages to the correct server.

Practice

▼ CONCEPTS REVIEW

Label each element shown in Figure G-17.

FIGURE G-17

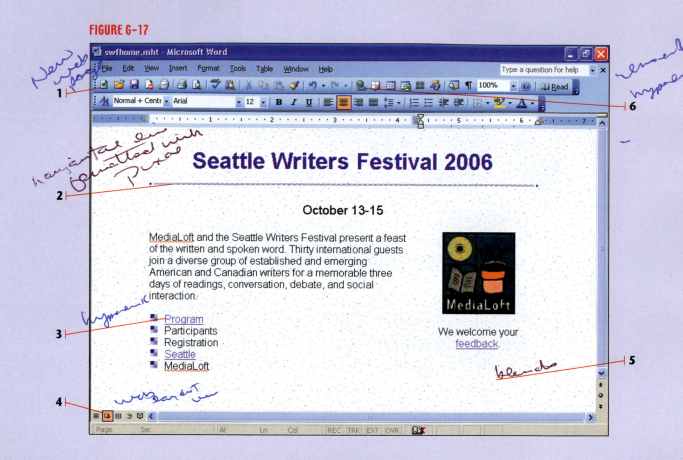

Match each term with the statement that best describes it.

7. Hyperlink
8. Web page
9. Home page
10. HTML
11. Theme
12. Web site
13. Browser
14. URL

a. A document that can be viewed using a browser
b. A group of associated Web pages
c. The address of a Web page on the World Wide Web
d. A programming language used to create Web pages
e. Text or a graphic that jumps the viewer to a different location when clicked
f. A set of common design elements that can be applied to a Web page
g. The main page of a Web site
h. A software program used to access and display Web pages

Select the best answer from the list of choices.

15. **Which of the following is *not* a design element included in a theme?**
   a. Bullet design
   b. Frame design
   c. Horizontal line style
   d. Web page background

16. **Which of the following *cannot* be opened using a hyperlink?**
   a. Files
   b. E-mail messages
   c. Web pages
   d. Support folders

17. **Which of the following formats is supported by Web browsers?**
   a. Inline graphics
   b. Columns of text
   c. Page numbers
   d. Headers and footers

18. **What does using the Save as Web Page command accomplish?**
   a. Converts the current file to HTML format
   b. Opens the current file in a browser
   c. Converts floating graphics to inline graphics
   d. Applies a Web theme to the current file

19. **Where does the page title of a Web page appear?**
   a. In the Word title bar
   b. On the home page
   c. In the browser title bar
   d. In the name of the supporting folder

20. **Which of the following statements is false?**
   a. A Web page saved as an .mht file does not need a supporting folder.
   b. When you save a document as a Web page, Word adds HTML tags to the file.
   c. You can use the Center button to center a floating graphic in Web Layout view.
   d. Hyperlink text is underlined.

▼ SKILLS REVIEW

1. **Create a Web page.**
   a. Study the sketch for the Web site devoted to literacy issues shown in Figure G-18.
   b. Start Word and create a blank Web page.
   c. Create a table with two columns and three rows, select the table, then AutoFit the table to fit the window. (*Hint:* Click Table on the menu bar, point to AutoFit, then click AutoFit to Window.)
   d. Type **Literacy Facts** in column 2, cell 1.
   e. Merge cells 2 and 3 in column 2, click Insert on the menu bar, click File, navigate to the drive and folder where your Data Files are located, select WD G-2.doc, then click Insert.
   f. In column 1, cell 3, type the following three-item list: **What you can do**, **ProLiteracy Worldwide**, **Contact us**.
   g. Save the file as a single file Web page to the drive and folder where your Data Files are located with the page title **Literacy Facts – Home** and the filename **literacy**.

2. **Format a Web page with themes.**
   a. Apply the Network theme to the Web page. (*Note:* Select a different theme if Network is not available to you.)
   b. Format Literacy Facts in the Heading 1 style, center the text, then press [Enter].

FIGURE G-18

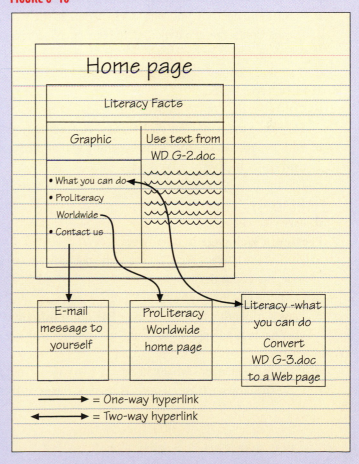

    c. Insert a horizontal line below the heading.

    d. Apply bullets to the list in column 1, cell 3, then save your changes.

3. Illustrate a Web page with graphics.

    a. In the blank cell in the first column, second row, insert the graphic file reader.gif from the drive and folder where your Data Files are located.

    b. Center the graphic in the cell, press [Enter], type **Literacy is not just reading and writing; the ability to perform basic math and solve problems is also important.**, press [Enter], then change the font size of the text to 10.

    c. Click Format on the menu bar, point to Background, click Fill Effects, click the Gradient tab, select the Two colors option button in the Colors section, click the Color 1 list arrow, click Gold, click the Color 2 list arrow, click Light Yellow, select any shading style and variant, then click OK.

    d. Select the table, remove the table borders, hide the gridlines, then save your changes.

4. Save a document as a Web page.

    a. Open the file WD G-3.doc from the drive and folder where your Data Files are located.

    b. Examine the document, then save it as a single file Web page with the page title **Literacy – what you can do** and the filename **whattodo**.

    c. Read the message about formatting changes, then click Continue.

    d. Apply the Network theme (or the theme you used with the Literacy page) to the Web page, then apply the Heading 1 style to the heading.

    e. Double-click the graphic, click the Layout tab, change its text-wrapping style to In line with text, then move it before Literacy in the heading.

    f. Change the background to a gold and light yellow gradient. (*Hint:* See Step 3c).

    g. Save your changes, then close the file.

5. Add hyperlinks.

    a. In the Literacy Facts file, select What you can do, then format it as a hyperlink to the whattodo.mht file.

    b. Format ProLiteracy Worldwide as a hyperlink to the Web address **www.proliteracy.org**.

    c. Format Contact us as a hyperlink to your e-mail address with the message subject **Literacy information**. (*Note:* If you do not have an e-mail address, skip this step.)

    d. Save your changes.

6. Modify hyperlinks.

    a. Right-click the Contact us hyperlink, click Edit Hyperlink, change the Text to display to your name, click OK, then type **For more information on literacy, contact** in front of your name on the Web page.

    b. Edit the ProLiteracy Worldwide hyperlink so that the ScreenTip says **Information on ProLiteracy Worldwide and links to literacy Web sites**.

    c. Edit the What you can do hyperlink so that the ScreenTip says **Simple actions you can take to help eliminate illiteracy**.

    d. Save your changes.

7. Preview a Web page in a browser.

    a. Preview the Literacy Facts Web page in your browser, test all the hyperlinks, print a copy of the Literacy Facts Web page, then close the browser.

    b. Open the whattodo.mht file in Word.

    c. Press [Ctrl][End], press [Enter], type **For more information, contact** followed by your name and a period, format your name as a hyperlink to your e-mail address with the subject line **Literacy Information**, then save your changes.

    d. Preview the Literacy - what you can do Web page in your browser, test the hyperlink, then print the page.

    e. Close the browser, close all open Word files, then exit Word.

▼ INDEPENDENT CHALLENGE 1

You have written a story about a recent hiking expedition you took and want to share it and some photos with your family and friends. You decide to create a Web page. Figure G-19 shows how you will arrange the photos.

FIGURE G-19

a. Start Word, open a blank Web page, save the Web page as a single file Web page with the page title **Conquering Rising Wolf** and the filename **risewolf** to the drive and folder where your Data Files are located, then change the zoom level to 100% if necessary.

b. Insert a table with two columns and four rows, merge the two cells in the first row, merge the three cells in the second column, select the table, then AutoFit the table to fit the window. (*Hint:* Use the AutoFit command on the Table menu.)

c. Type **Conquering Rising Wolf** in the first row of the table, then press [Enter].

d. Click in the second column, then insert the file WD G-4.doc from the drive and folder where your Data Files are located. (*Hint:* Use the File command on the Insert menu.)

e. Click in the first blank cell in the first column, then insert the graphic file rwolf.jpg from the drive and folder where your Data Files are located.

f. Press [Enter], then type **Rising Wolf Mountain (elev. 9513 feet)**.

g. In the last blank cell in the first column, insert the graphic file Derek.jpg from the drive and folder where your Data Files are located, then resize the photo proportionally to be the same width as the Rising Wolf Mountain photo.

h. Press [Enter], then type **Derek enjoying the view**.

i. Drag the border between the first and second columns left to approximately the 3¼" mark.

j. Apply a theme, then format the Web page using theme elements and other formatting features.

k. Select Glacier National Park in the first paragraph in the second column, format it as a hyperlink to the URL **www.nps.gov/glac/home.htm** with the ScreenTip **Glacier National Park Website Visitor Center**.

l. Press [Ctrl][End], press [Enter], type **E-mail** followed by your name, center the text, then format your name as a hyperlink to your e-mail address, if you have one. Type **Conquering Rising Wolf** as the message subject.

m. Resize the table rows and columns as necessary to make the Web page attractive, remove the borders from the table, save your changes, preview the Web page in your browser, then test the hyperlinks.

n. Switch to Word, make any necessary adjustments, save your changes, preview the Web page in your browser, print a copy, close the browser, close the file in Word, then exit Word.

Rising Wolf Mountain (elev. 9513 feet)

Derek enjoying the view

INDEPENDENT CHALLENGE 2

You and your business partner have just started a mail-order business called Monet's Garden. You create a home page for your business. As your business grows, you plan to add additional pages to the Web site.

a. Start Word, then create a new frames page. (*Hint:* Point to Frames on the Format menu, then click New Frames Page.)

b. Click the New Frame Left button on the Frames toolbar, close the toolbar, then drag the frame border to the left so that the left frame is about one quarter the width of the Web page.

c. Save the frames page as a single file Web Page with the page title **Welcome to Monet's Garden** and the filename **monet**.

d. In the left frame, type **Welcome to Monet's Garden**, press [Enter] four times, then type **1-800-555-2837**.

e. Insert an appropriate clip art graphic between the two lines of text in the left frame. Resize the graphic to fit the frame. (*Hint:* You might need to enlarge the frame temporarily to resize the graphic.)

f. In the right frame, insert the text file WD G-5.doc from the drive and folder where your Data Files are located. (*Hint:* Click File on the Insert menu.)

g. Insert an appropriate clip art graphic in the empty cell in the right frame.

h. Add a solid color background to the right frame, then format the frame with lines, fonts, colors, shading, and any other formatting features.

INDEPENDENT CHALLENGE 2 (CONTINUED)

i. Resize the graphic and table as needed, then remove the table borders. (*Note:* You do not need to remove the borders from the nested table.)

j. At the bottom of the right frame, replace Your Name with your name, then format it as a hyperlink to the e-mail address **info@monetsgarden.com** with the subject **Product Information**.

k. Add a different solid color background to the left frame, then format the frame with lines, fonts, colors, and any other formatting features.

l. Adjust the formatting of the Web page to make it attractive and readable, then save your changes.

Advanced Challenge Exercise

- Place the insertion point in the left frame, then open the Frame Properties dialog box. (*Hint*: Point to Frames on the Format menu.)
- On the Borders tab, click the No borders option button, click the Show scroll bars in browser list arrow, click Never, then click OK.
- Place the insertion point in the right frame, open the Frame Properties dialog box, set the scroll bar to show if needed, then save your changes.

m. Preview the Web page in your browser, test the hyperlink, adjust the formatting of the Web page as needed, then save your changes. (*Note:* Depending on your browser settings, the frames page might not preview correctly in your browser.)

n. Print a copy of the Web page, exit your browser, close the file, then exit Word.

▼ INDEPENDENT CHALLENGE 3

You are in charge of publicity for the Sydney Triathlon 2006 World Cup. One of your responsibilities is to create a Web site to provide details of the event. You have created the content for the Web pages as Word documents, and now need to save and format them as Web pages. Your Web site will include a home page and three other Web pages. One of the Web pages is shown in Figure G-20.

a. Start Word, open the file WD G-6.doc from the drive and folder where your Data Files are located, then save it as a single file Web page with the page title **Sydney Triathlon 2006 World Cup - Home** and the filename **tri_home**.

b. Apply the Slate or Breeze theme. (*Note:* Use a different theme if neither of these themes is available to you.)

FIGURE G-20

c. Press [Ctrl][A], then change the font size to 10.

d. Apply the Heading 1 style to the heading Sydney Triathlon 2006 World Cup in the first row of the table, right-align the text, apply italic, select Triathlon 2006, then change the font color to a different color.

e. Apply the Heading 3 style to Welcome to the Sydney Triathlon 2006 World Cup! in the upper-left cell of the table, apply bold, then center the text.

f. Read the remaining text on the Web page, then format it with heading styles, fonts, font colors, and other formatting effects to make it look attractive. Preview the Web page in your browser.

g. Remove the table borders, press [Ctrl][End], type your name, save your changes, then close the file.

▼ INDEPENDENT CHALLENGE 3

h. Open each file listed in Table G-2 from the drive and folder where your Data Files are located, save it as a single file Web Page with the page title and filename listed in the table, follow Steps b–g to format it using the same theme and other formatting features you used to format the home page, then close the file.

TABLE G-2

data file	page title	filename
WD G-7.doc	Sydney Triathlon 2006 World Cup – Best Views	tri_view
WD G-8.doc	Sydney Triathlon 2006 World Cup – Getting There	tri_get
WD G-9.doc	Sydney Triathlon 2006 World Cup – The Athletes	tri_athl

i. In Word, open the tri_home.mht file, then change the zoom level to 100% if necessary.

j. Select Best Views, then format it as a hyperlink to the tri_view.mht file. Format Getting There and The Athletes as hyperlinks to the tri_get.mht and tri_athl.mht files, then save your changes.

k. Open each of the remaining three files—tri_view.mht, tri_get.mht, and tri_athl.mht—and format the text in the left column of each Web page as a hyperlink to the appropriate file. Save your changes, then close each Web page.

l. Be sure tri_home.mht is the active document. Preview the home page in your browser. Test each hyperlink on the home page and on the other Web pages. (If the hyperlinks do not work in your browser, test them in Word.)

m. Examine each Web page in your browser, make any necessary formatting adjustments in Word, print a copy of each Web page from your browser, then close your browser, close all open files, and exit Word.

▼ INDEPENDENT CHALLENGE 4

In this Independent Challenge you will create a Web page that provides information about you and your interests. Your Web page will include text, a graphic, and links to Web sites that you think will be useful to people who visit your Web page.

a. Start Word, open the file WD G-10.doc from the drive and folder where your Data Files are stored, save it as a single file Web page, include your name in the page title, and save it with the filename **my_page**.

b. At the top of the Web page, replace Your Name with your name.

c. Under the heading Contents, format each item in the list as a hyperlink to that heading in the Web page.

d. Under the heading Biographical Information, type at least one paragraph about your background and interests.

e. Under the heading Personal Interests, type a list of your hobbies and interests. Format this list as a bulleted list.

f. Use your favorite search engine to search for Web sites related to your interests. Write down the page titles and URLs of at least three Web sites that you think are worth visiting.

g. Under the heading Favorite Links, type the names of the three Web sites you liked. Format each name as a hyperlink to the Web site, and create a ScreenTip that explains why you think it's a good Web site.

h. Under the heading Contact Information, enter your e-mail address, Web site address, and telephone numbers, if any. Delete any headings that do not apply. Format your e-mail and Web addresses as hyperlinks to those addresses.

i. In each section, format the text Back to top as a hyperlink to your name at the top of the Web page.

j. Illustrate the Web page with a photo of yourself or another graphic. Use a clip art graphic if another graphic is not available to you. Create a table to position the graphic if necessary.

k. Apply a theme, then format the Web page with different formatting features such as bullets and colors.

l. Save your changes, preview the Web page, test each hyperlink, make adjustments, then save again.

Advanced Challenge Exercise

- In Word, send a copy of the Web page to someone in an e-mail message.
- In Word, send a copy of the Web page to someone for review as an attachment to an e-mail message.
- Using the Web Options dialog box, save the Web page for a target browser, then post the Web page to the Web or an intranet if instructed to do so by your instructor.

m. Print a copy of the Web page, close the browser, close the file, then exit Word.

▼ VISUAL WORKSHOP

Create the Web pages shown in Figure G-21 using the graphic files rest.jpg, bridge.jpg, and studlamp.jpg, found on the drive and folder where your Data Files are located. Save the home page with the page title **Gallery Azul Home (Your Name)** and the filename **azulhome.mht**. Save the exhibit page with the page title **Gallery Azul Exhibit (Your Name)** and the filename **azulexhb.mht**. On the home page, create a hyperlink to the exhibit page and a hyperlink to the e-mail address **GalleryAzul@ptown.net**. On the Exhibit page, create a hyperlink to the home page. View the Web pages in your browser, then print a copy of each Web page.

FIGURE G-21

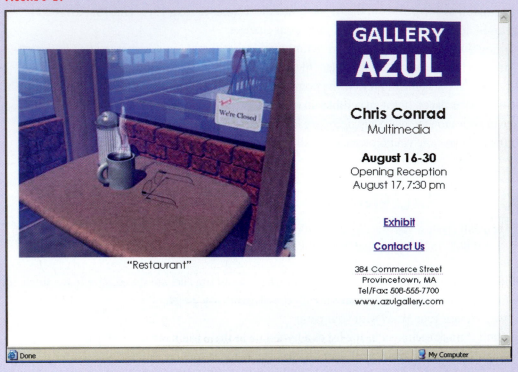

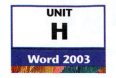

Merging Word Documents

OBJECTIVES

Understand mail merge

Create a main document

Design a data source

Enter and edit records

Add merge fields

Merge data

Create labels

Sort and filter records

If you have a SAM user profile, you may have access to hands-on instruction, practice, and assessment of the skills covered in this unit. Log in to your SAM account and go to your assignments page to see what your instructor has assigned.

A mail merge operation combines a standard document, such as a form letter, with customized data, such as a set of names and addresses, to create a set of personalized documents. You can perform a mail merge to create documents used in mass mailings, such as letters and labels. You also can use mail merge to create documents that include customized information, such as business cards. In this unit you learn how to use the Mail Merge task pane to set up and perform a mail merge. You need to send a welcome letter to the new members of the MediaLoft Coffee Club, a program designed to attract customers to the MediaLoft Café. You also need to send a brochure to all the members of the club. You use mail merge to create a personalized form letter and mailing labels for the brochure.

Understanding Mail Merge

When you perform a mail merge, you merge a standard Word document with a file that contains customized information for many individuals or items. The standard document is called the **main document**. The file with the unique data for individual people or items is called the **data source**. Merging the main document with a data source results in a merged document that contains customized versions of the main document, as shown in Figure H-1. The Mail Merge task pane steps you through the process of setting up and performing a mail merge.  You use the Mail Merge task pane to create your form letters and mailing labels. Before beginning, you explore the steps involved in performing a mail merge.

DETAILS

- ### Create the main document
  The main document contains the text—often called **boilerplate text**—that appears in every version of the merged document. The main document also includes the merge fields, which indicate where the customized information is inserted when you perform the merge. You insert the merge fields in the main document after you have created or selected the data source. You use the Mail Merge task pane to create a main document using either the current document, a template, or an existing document.

- ### Create a data source or select an existing data source
  The data source is a file that contains the unique information for each individual or item. It provides the information that varies in every version of the merged document. A data source is composed of data fields and data records. A **data field** is a category of information, such as last name, first name, street address, city, or postal code. A **data record** is a complete set of related information for an individual or an item, such as one person's name and address. It is easiest to think of a data source file as a table: the header row contains the names of the data fields (the **field names**), and each row in the table is an individual data record. You can use the Mail Merge task pane to create a new data source, or you can merge a main document with an existing data source, such as a data source created in Word, an Outlook contact list, or an Access database.

- ### Identify the fields to include in the data source and enter the records
  When you create a new data source, you must first identify the fields to include. It's important to think of and include all the fields before you begin to enter data. For example, if you are creating a data source that includes addresses, you might need to include fields for a person's middle name, title, department name, or country, even though every address in the data source does not include that information. Once you have identified the fields and set up your data source, you are ready to enter the data for each record.

- ### Add merge fields to the main document
  A merge field is a placeholder that you insert in the main document to indicate where the data from each record should be inserted when you perform the merge. For example, in the location you want to insert a zip code, you insert a zip code merge field. The merge fields in a main document must correspond with the field names in the associated data source. Merge fields must be inserted, not typed, in the main document. The Mail Merge task pane provides access to the dialog boxes you use to insert merge fields.

- ### Merge the data from the data source into the main document
  Once you have established your data source and inserted the merge fields in the main document, you are ready to perform the merge. You can merge to a new file, which contains a customized version of the main document for each record in the data source, or you can merge directly to a printer, fax, or e-mail message.

FIGURE H-1: Mail merge process

Data source document

Field name

Store	Title	First Name	Last Name	Address Line 1	City	State	Zip Code	Country
Seattle	Ms.	Linda	Barker	62 Cloud St.	Bellevue	WA	83459	US
Boston	Mr.	Bob	Cruz	23 Plum St.	Boston	MA	02483	US
Chicago	Ms.	Joan	Yatco	456 Elm St.	Chicago	IL	60603	US
Seattle	Ms.	Anne	Butler	48 East Ave.	Vancouver	BC	V6F 1AH	CANADA
Boston	Mr.	Fred	Silver	56 Pearl St.	Cambridge	MA	02139	US

Data record

Main document

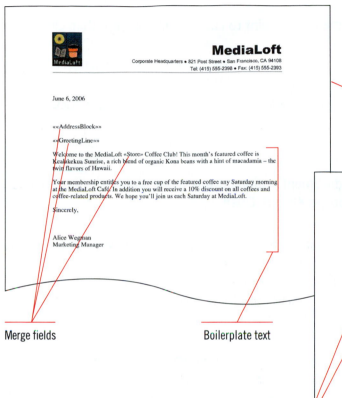

Merged document

Merge fields

Boilerplate text

Customized information

Creating a Main Document

The first step in performing a mail merge is to create the main document—the file that contains the boiler-plate text. You can create a main document from scratch, save an existing document as a main document, or use a mail merge template to create a main document. The Mail Merge task pane walks you through the process of selecting the type of main document to create. You use an existing form letter for your main document. You begin by opening the Mail Merge task pane.

STEPS

1. **Start Word, click Tools on the menu bar, point to Letters and Mailings, then click Mail Merge**

   The Mail Merge task pane opens, as shown in Figure H-2, and displays information for the first step in the mail merge process: selecting the type of merge document to create.

2. **Make sure the Letters option button is selected, then click Next: Starting document to continue with the next step**

   The task pane displays the options for the second step: selecting the main document. You can use the current document, start with a mail merge template, or use an existing file.

3. **Select the Start from existing document option button, make sure More files is selected in the Start from existing list box, then click Open**

   The Open dialog box opens.

4. **Use the Look in list arrow to navigate to the drive and folder where your Data Files are located, select the file WD H-1.doc, then click Open**

   The letter that opens contains the boilerplate text for the main document. Notice the filename in the title bar is Document1. When you create a main document that is based on an existing document, Word gives the main document a default temporary filename.

5. **Click the Save button 🖫 on the Standard toolbar, then save the main document with the filename Coffee Letter Main to the drive and folder where your Data Files are located**

   It's a good idea to include "main" in the filename so that you can easily recognize the file as a main document.

6. **Click the Zoom list arrow on the Standard toolbar, click Text Width, select April 9, 2006 in the letter, type today's date, scroll down, select Alice Wegman, type your name, press [Ctrl][Home], then save your changes**

   The edited main document is shown in Figure H-3.

7. **Click Next: Select recipients to continue with the next step**

   You continue with Step 3 of 6 in the next lesson.

Clues to Use

Using a mail merge template

If you are creating a letter, fax, or directory, you can use a mail merge template to start your main document. Each template includes boiler-plate text, which you can customize, and merge fields, which you can match to the field names in your data source. To create a main document that is based on a mail merge template, click the Start from a template option button in the Step 2 of 6 Mail Merge task pane, then click Select template. In the Select Template dialog box, select a template on the Mail Merge tab, then click OK to create the document. Once you have created the main document, you can customize it with your own information: edit the boilerplate text, change the document format, or add, remove, or modify the merge fields. Before performing the merge, make sure to match the names of the address merge fields used in the template with the field names used in your data source. To match the field names, click the Match Fields button 🖳 on the Mail Merge toolbar, and then use the list arrows in the Match Fields dialog box to select the field name in your data source that corresponds to each address field component in the main document.

FIGURE H-2: Step 1 of 6 Mail Merge task pane

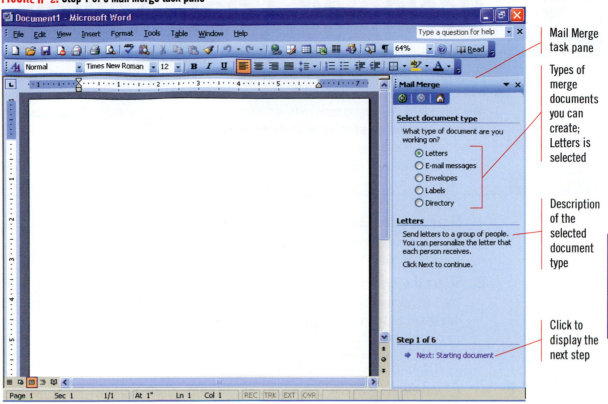

Mail Merge task pane

Types of merge documents you can create; Letters is selected

Description of the selected document type

Click to display the next step

FIGURE H-3: Main document with the Step 2 of 6 Mail Merge task pane

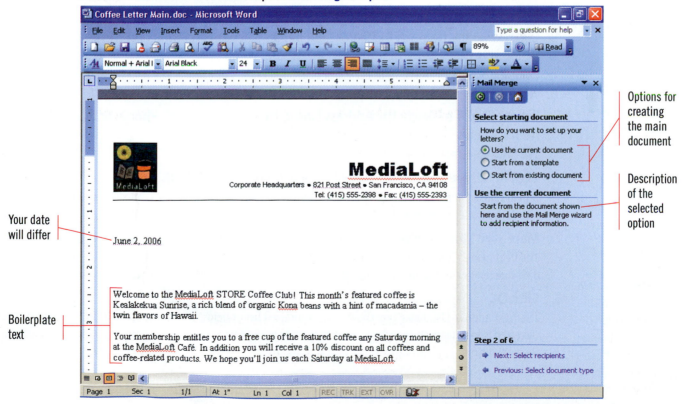

Options for creating the main document

Description of the selected option

Your date will differ

Boilerplate text

Designing a Data Source

Once you have identified the main document, the next step in the mail merge process is to identify the data source, the file that contains the information that differs in each version of the merge document. You can use an existing data source that already contains the records you want to include in your merge, or you can create a new data source. When you create a new data source you must determine the fields to include—the categories of information, such as a first name, last name, city, or zip code—and then add the records.  You create a new data source that includes fields for the name, address, and MediaLoft store location of each new member of the Coffee Club.

STEPS

1. **Make sure Step 3 of 6 is displayed at the bottom of the Mail Merge task pane**

   Step 3 of 6 involves selecting a data source to use for the merge. You can use an existing data source, a list of contacts created in Microsoft Outlook, or a new data source.

2. **Select the Type a new list option button, then click Create**

   The New Address List dialog box opens, as shown in Figure H-4. You use this dialog box both to design your data source and to enter records. The Enter Address information section of the dialog box includes fields that are commonly used in form letters, but you can customize your data source by adding and removing fields from this list. A data source can be merged with more than one main document, so it's important to design a data source to be flexible. The more fields you include in a data source, the more flexible it is. For example, if you include separate fields for a person's title, first name, middle name, and last name, you can use the same data source to create an envelope addressed to "Mr. John Montgomery Smith" and a form letter addressed to "Dear John."

3. **Click Customize**

   The Customize Address List dialog box opens, as shown in Figure H-5. You use this dialog box to add, delete, rename, and reorder the fields in the data source.

4. **Click Company Name in the list of field names, click Delete, then click Yes in the warning dialog box that opens**

   Company Name is removed from the list of field names. The Company Name field is no longer a part of the data source.

5. **Repeat Step 4 to delete the Address Line 2, Home Phone, Work Phone, and E-mail Address fields**

   The fields are removed from the data source.

6. **Click Add, type Store in the Add Field dialog box, then click OK**

   A field called "Store," which you will use to indicate the location of the MediaLoft store where the customer joined the Coffee Club, is added to the data source.

7. **Make sure Store is selected in the list of field names, then click Move Up eight times**

   The field name "Store" is moved to the top of the list. Although the order of field names does not matter in a data source, it's convenient to arrange the field names logically to make it easier to enter and edit records.

8. **Click OK**

   The New Address List dialog box shows the customized list of fields, with the Store field first in the list. The next step is to enter each record you want to include in the data source. You add records to the data source in the next lesson.

FIGURE H-4: New Address List dialog box

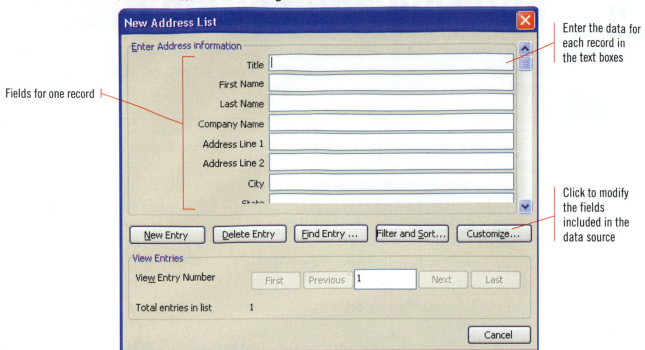

Fields for one record

Enter the data for each record in the text boxes

Click to modify the fields included in the data source

Word 2003

FIGURE H-5: Customize Address List dialog box

Fields in the data source

Clues to Use

Merging with an Outlook data source

If you maintain lists of contacts in Microsoft Outlook, you can use one of your Outlook contact lists as a data source for a merge. To merge with an Outlook data source, click the Select from Outlook contacts option button in the Step 3 of 6 Mail Merge task pane, then click Choose Contacts Folder to open the Select Contact List Folder dialog box. In this dialog box, select the contact list you want to use as the data source, and then click OK. All the contacts included in the selected folder appear in the Mail Merge Recipients dialog box. Here you can refine the list of recipients to include in the merge by sorting and filtering the records. When you are satisfied, click OK in the Mail Merge Recipients dialog box.

Entering and Editing Records

Once you have established the structure of a data source, the next step is to enter the records. Each record includes the complete set of information for each individual or item you include in the data source.  You create a record for each new member of the Coffee Club.

QUICK TIP

Be careful not to add spaces or extra punctuation after an entry in a field, or these will appear when the data is merged.

1. **Place the insertion point in the Store text box in the New Address List dialog box, type Seattle, then press [Tab]**

   "Seattle" appears in the Store field and the insertion point moves to the next field in the list, the Title field.

2. **Type Ms., press [Tab], type Linda, press [Tab], type Barker, press [Tab], type 62 Cloud St., press [Tab], type Bellevue, press [Tab], type WA, press [Tab], type 83459, press [Tab], then type US**

   Compare your New Address List dialog box with Figure H-6.

QUICK TIP

It's OK to leave a field blank if you do not need it for a record.

3. **Click New Entry**

   The record for Linda Barker is added to the data source and the dialog box displays empty fields for the next record, record 2.

4. **Enter the following four records, pressing [Tab] to move from field to field, and clicking New Entry at the end of each record except the last:**

Store	Title	First Name	Last Name	Address Line 1	City	State	ZIP Code	Country
Boston	Mr.	Bob	Cruz	23 Plum St.	Boston	MA	02483	US
Chicago	Ms.	Joan	Yatco	456 Elm St.	Chicago	IL	60603	US
Seattle	Ms.	Anne	Butler	48 East Ave.	Vancouver	BC	V6F 1AH	CANADA
Boston	Mr.	Fred	Silver	56 Pearl St.	Cambridge	MA	02139	US

5. **Click Close**

   The Save Address List dialog box opens. Data sources are saved by default in the My Data Sources folder so that you can easily locate them to use in other merge operations. Data sources you create in Word are saved in Microsoft Office Address Lists (*.mdb) format.

TROUBLE

If a check mark appears in the blank record under Fred Silver, click the check mark to eliminate the record from the merge.

6. **Type New Coffee Club Data in the File name text box, use the Save in list arrow to navigate to the drive and folder where your Data Files are located, then click Save**

   The data source is saved, and the Mail Merge Recipients dialog box opens, as shown in Figure H-7. The dialog box shows the records in the data source in table format. You can use the dialog box to edit, sort, and filter records, and to select the recipients to include in the mail merge. You will learn more about sorting and filtering in a later lesson. The check marks in the first column indicate the records that will be included in the merge.

7. **Click the Joan Yatco record, click Edit, select Ms. in the Title text box in the New Coffee Club Data.mdb dialog box, type Dr., then click Close**

   The data in the Title field for Joan Yatco changes from "Ms." to "Dr." and the New Coffee Club Data.mdb dialog box closes.

QUICK TIP

If you want to add new records or modify existing records, click Edit recipient list in the task pane.

8. **Click OK in the Mail Merge Recipients dialog box**

   The dialog box closes. The file type and filename of the data source attached to the main document now appear under Use an existing list in the Mail Merge task pane, as shown in Figure H-8. The Mail Merge toolbar also appears in the program window when you close the data source. You learn more about the Mail Merge toolbar in later lessons.

FIGURE H-6: Record in New Address List dialog box

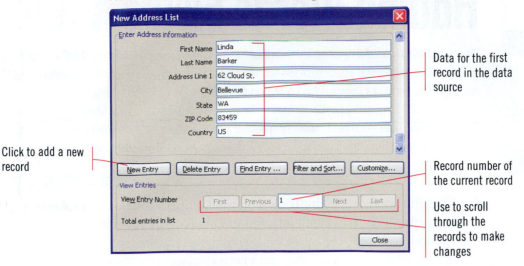

Data for the first record in the data source

Click to add a new record

Record number of the current record

Use to scroll through the records to make changes

FIGURE H-7: Mail Merge Recipients dialog box

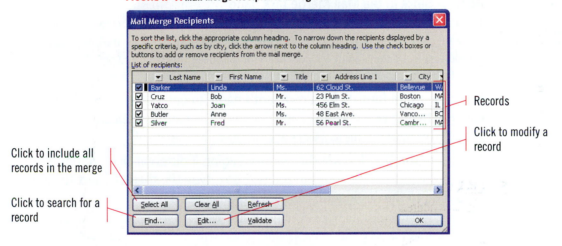

Records

Click to modify a record

Click to include all records in the merge

Click to search for a record

FIGURE H-8: Data source attached to the main document

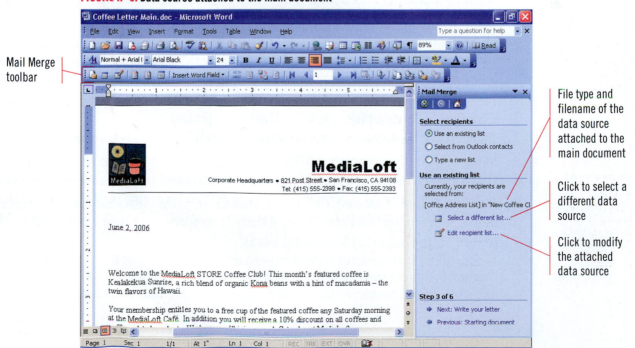

Mail Merge toolbar

File type and filename of the data source attached to the main document

Click to select a different data source

Click to modify the attached data source

Adding Merge Fields

After you have created and identified the data source, the next step is to insert the merge fields in the main document. Merge fields serve as placeholders for text that is inserted when the main document and the data source are merged. The names of merge fields correspond to the field names in the data source. You can insert merge fields using the Mail Merge task pane or the Insert Merge Field button on the Mail Merge toolbar. You cannot type merge fields into the main document.  You use the Mail Merge task pane to insert merge fields for the inside address and greeting of the letter. You also insert a merge field for the store location in the body of the letter.

STEPS

1. **Click the Show/Hide ¶ button ¶ on the Standard toolbar to display formatting marks, then click Next: Write your letter in the Mail Merge task pane**

   The Mail Merge task pane shows the options for Step 4 of 6, writing the letter and inserting the merge fields in the main document. Since your form letter is already written, you are ready to add the merge fields to it.

> **QUICK TIP**
>
> You can also click the Insert Address Block button 📄 on the Mail Merge toolbar to insert an address block.

2. **Place the insertion point in the blank line above the first body paragraph, then click Address block in the Mail Merge task pane**

   The Insert Address Block dialog box opens, as shown in Figure H-9. You use this dialog box to specify the fields you want to include in an address block. In this merge, the address block is the inside address of the form letter. An address block automatically includes fields for the street, city, state, and postal code, but you can select the format for the recipient's name and indicate whether to include a company name or country in the address.

3. **Scroll the list of formats for a recipient's name to get a feel for the kinds of formats you can use, then click Mr. Joshua Randall Jr. if it is not already selected**

   The selected format uses the recipient's title, first name, and last name.

4. **Make sure the Only include the country/region if different than: option button is selected, select United States in the text box, type US, then deselect the Format address according to the destination country/region check box**

   You only need to include the country in the address block if the country is different from the United States, so you indicate that all entries in the Country field except "US" should be included in the printed address.

> **QUICK TIP**
>
> You cannot simply type chevrons around a field name. You must insert merge fields using the Mail Merge task pane or the buttons on the Mail Merge toolbar.

5. **Click OK, then press [Enter] twice**

   The merge field AddressBlock is added to the main document. Chevrons (<< and >>) surround a merge field to distinguish it from the boilerplate text.

6. **Click Greeting line in the Mail Merge task pane**

   The Greeting Line dialog box opens. You want to use the format "Dear Mr. Randall:" (the recipient's title and last name, followed by a colon) for a greeting. The default format uses a comma, so you have to change the comma to a colon.

7. **Click the , list arrow, click :, click OK, then press [Enter]**

   The merge field GreetingLine is added to the main document.

> **QUICK TIP**
>
> You can also click the Insert Merge Fields button 📄 on the Mail Merge toolbar to insert a merge field.

8. **In the body of the letter select STORE, then click More items in the Mail Merge task pane**

   The Insert Merge Field dialog box opens and displays the list of field names included in the data source.

9. **Make sure Store is selected, click Insert, click Close, press [Spacebar] to add a space between the merge field and Coffee if there is no space, save your changes, then click ¶ to turn off the display of formatting marks**

   The merge field Store is inserted in the main document, as shown in Figure H-10. You must type spaces and punctuation between merge fields if you want spaces and punctuation to appear between the data in the merged documents. You preview the merged data and perform the merge in the next lesson.

FIGURE H-9: Insert Address Block dialog box

Formats for the
recipient's name

Click to match the
default address field
names to the field
names used in your
data source

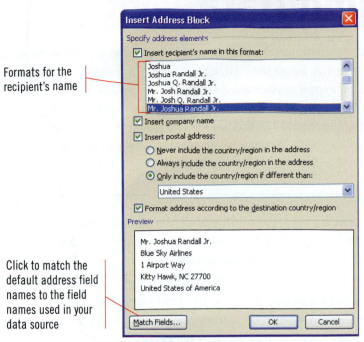

FIGURE H-10: Merge fields in the main document

Merge fields

Clues to Use

Matching fields

The merge fields you insert in a main document must correspond with the field names in the associated data source. If you are using the Address Block merge field, you must make sure that the default address field names correspond with the field names used in your data source. If the default address field names do not match the field names in your data source, click Match Fields in the Insert Address Block dialog box, then use the list arrows in the Match Fields dialog box to select the field name in the data source that corresponds to each default address field name.

Merging Data

Once you have added records to your data source and inserted merge fields in the main document, you are ready to perform the merge. Before merging, it's a good idea to preview the merged data to make sure the printed documents will appear as you want them to. You can preview the merge using the task pane or the View Merged Data button on the Mail Merge toolbar. When you merge the main document with the data source, you must choose between merging to a new file or directly to a printer.  Before merging the form letter with the data source, you preview the merge to make sure the data appears in the letter as you intended. You then merge the two files to a new document.

STEPS

QUICK TIP

To adjust the main document, click the View Merged Data button ABC on the Mail Merge toolbar, then make any necessary changes. Click ABC again to preview the merged data.

1. **Click Next: Preview your letters in the Mail Merge task pane**

   The data from the first record in the data source appears in place of the merge fields in the main document, as shown in Figure H-11. Always check the preview document to make sure the merge fields, punctuation, page breaks, and spacing all appear as you intend before you perform the merge.

2. **Click the Next Recipient button >> in the Mail Merge task pane**

   The data from the second record in the data source appears in place of the merge fields.

3. **Click the Go to Record text box on the Mail Merge toolbar, press [Backspace], type 4, then press [Enter]**

   The data for the fourth record appears in the document window. The non-US country name, in this case Canada, is included in the address block, just as you specified. You can also use the First Record ◀I, Previous Record ◀, Next Record ▶, and Last Record I▶ buttons on the Mail Merge toolbar to preview the merged data. Table H-1 describes other buttons on the Mail Merge toolbar.

QUICK TIP

If your data source contains many records, you can merge directly to a printer to avoid creating a large file.

4. **Click Next: Complete the merge in the Mail Merge task pane**

   The options for Step 6 of 6 appear in the Mail Merge task pane. Merging to a new file creates a document with one letter for each record in the data source. This allows you to edit the individual letters.

5. **Click Edit individual letters to merge the data to a new document**

   The Merge to New Document dialog box opens. You can use this dialog box to specify the records to include in the merge.

QUICK TIP

To restore a main document to a regular Word document, click the Main document setup button on the Mail Merge toolbar, then click Normal Word document. Restoring a main document removes the associated data source from it.

6. **Make sure the All option button is selected, then click OK**

   The main document and the data source are merged to a new document called Letters1, which contains a customized form letter for each record in the data source. You can now further personalize the letters without affecting the main document or the data source.

7. **Click the Zoom list arrow on the Standard toolbar, click Page Width, scroll to the fourth letter (addressed to Ms. Anne Butler), place the insertion point before V6F in the address block, then press [Enter]**

   The postal code is now consistent with the proper format for a Canadian address.

8. **Click the Save button on the Standard toolbar to open the Save As dialog box, then save the merge document as Coffee Letter Merge to the drive and folder where your Data Files are located**

   You may decide not to save a merged file if your data source is large. Once you have created the main document and the data source, you can create the letters by performing the merge again.

9. **Click File on the menu bar, click Print, click the Current Page option button in the Page range section of the Print dialog box, click OK, then close all open Word files, saving changes if prompted**

   The letter to Anne Butler prints.

FIGURE H-11: Preview of merged data

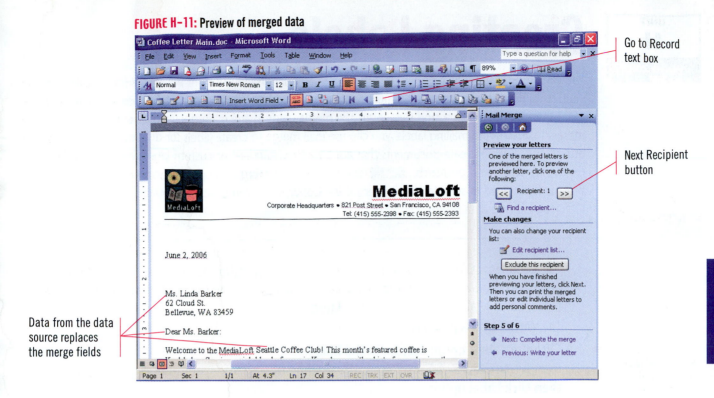

Go to Record text box

Next Recipient button

Data from the data source replaces the merge fields

TABLE H-1: Buttons on the Mail Merge toolbar

button	use to	button	use to
	Change the main document to a different type, or convert it to a normal Word document		Highlight the merge fields in the main document
	Select an existing data source		Match address fields with the field names used in the data source
	Edit, sort, or filter the associated data source		Search for a record in the merged documents
	Insert an Address Block merge field		Check for errors in the merged documents
	Insert a Greeting Line merge field		Merge the data to a new document and display it on screen
	Insert a merge field from the data source		Print the merged documents without first reviewing them on screen
	Switch between viewing the main document with merge fields and with merged data		

Creating Labels

You can also use the Mail Merge task pane to create mailing labels or print envelopes for a mailing. When you create labels or envelopes, you must select a standard label or envelope size to use as the main document, select a data source, and then insert the merge fields in the main document before performing the merge. In addition to mailing labels, you can use mail merge to create labels for diskettes, CDs, videos, and other items, and to create documents that are based on standard or custom label sizes, such as business cards, nametags, and postcards.  You use the Mail Merge task pane to create mailing labels for a brochure you need to send to all members of the Coffee Club. You create a new label main document and attach an existing data source.

STEPS

1. **Click the New Blank Document button**  **on the Standard toolbar, click the Zoom list arrow on the Standard toolbar, click Page Width, click Tools on the menu bar, point to Letters and Mailings, then click Mail Merge**

   The Mail Merge task pane opens.

TROUBLE

If your dialog box does not show Avery standard, click the Label products list arrow, then click Avery standard.

2. **Click the Labels option button in the Mail Merge task pane, click Next: Starting document to move to Step 2 of 6, make sure the Change document layout option button is selected, then click Label options**

   The Label Options dialog box opens, as shown in Figure H-12. You use this dialog box to select a label size for your labels and to specify the type of printer you plan to use. The default brand name Avery standard appears in the Label products list box. You can use the Label products list arrow to select other label products or a custom label. The many standard types of Avery labels for mailings, file folders, diskettes, post cards, and other types of labels are listed in the Product number list box. The type, height, width, and paper size for the selected product are displayed in the Label information section.

TROUBLE

If your gridlines are not visible, click Table on the menu bar, then click Show Gridlines.

3. **Scroll down the Product number list, click 5161 – Address, then click OK**

   A table with gridlines appears in the main document, as shown in Figure H-13. Each table cell is the size of a label for the label product you selected.

4. **Save the label main document with the filename Coffee Labels Main to the drive and folder where your Data Files are located**

   Next you need to select a data source for the labels.

5. **Click Next: Select recipients to move to Step 3 of 6, make sure the Use an existing list option button is selected, then click Browse**

   The Select Data Source dialog box opens.

6. **Use the Look in list arrow to navigate to the drive and folder where your Data Files are located, then open the file WD H-2.mdb**

   The Mail Merge Recipients dialog box opens and displays all the records in the data source. In the next lesson you sort and filter the records before performing the mail merge.

FIGURE H-12: Label Options dialog box

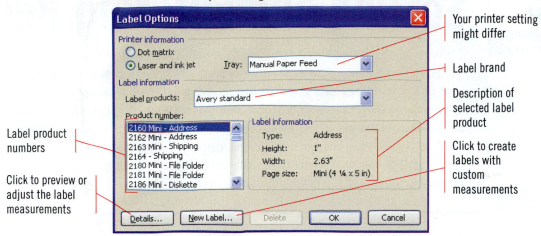

Label product numbers

Click to preview or adjust the label measurements

Your printer setting might differ

Label brand

Description of selected label product

Click to create labels with custom measurements

FIGURE H-13: Label main document

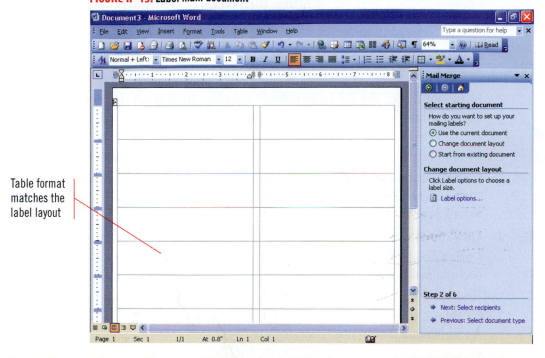

Table format matches the label layout

Clues to Use

Printing individual envelopes and labels

The Mail Merge task pane enables you to easily print envelopes and labels for mass mailings, but you can also quickly format and print individual envelopes and labels using the Envelopes and Labels dialog box. To open the Envelopes and Labels dialog box, point to Letters and Mailings on the Tools menu, then click Envelopes and Labels. On the Envelopes tab, shown in Figure H-14, type the recipient's address in the Delivery address box and the return address in the Return address box. Click Options to open the Envelope Options dialog box, which you can use to select the envelope size, add a postal bar code, change the font and font size of the delivery and return addresses, and change the printing options. When you are ready to print the envelope, click Print in the Envelopes and Labels dialog box. The procedure for printing an individual label is similar to printing an individual envelope: enter the recipient's address on

the Labels tab, click Options to select a label product number, click OK, then click Print.

FIGURE H-14: Envelopes and Labels dialog box

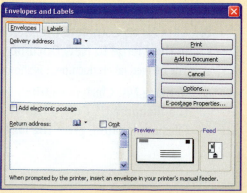

Sorting and Filtering Records

If you are using a large data source, you might want to sort and/or filter the records before performing a merge. Sorting the records determines the order in which the records are merged. For example, you might want to sort an address data source so that records are merged alphabetically by last name or in zip code order. Filtering the records pulls out the records that meet specific criteria and includes only those records in the merge. For instance, you might want to filter a data source to send a mailing only to people who live in the state of New York. You can use the Mail Merge Recipients dialog box both to sort and to filter a data source. 🎨 You apply a filter to the data source so that only United States addresses are included in the merge. You then sort those records so that they merge in zip code order.

STEPS

1. **In the Mail Merge Recipients dialog box, scroll right to display the Country field, click the Country column heading list arrow, then click US on the menu that opens**

   A filter is applied to the data source so that only the records with "US" in the Country field will be merged. The blue arrow in the Country column heading indicates that a filter has been applied to the column. You can filter a data source by as many criteria as you like. To remove a filter, click a column heading list arrow, then click "All."

2. **Scroll right, click the ZIP Code column heading, then scroll right again to see the ZIP Code column**

   The Mail Merge Recipients dialog box now displays only the records with a US address sorted in zip code order, as shown in Figure H-15. If you want to reverse the sort order, you can click a column heading again.

3. **Click OK, then click Next: Arrange your labels in the Mail Merge task pane**

   The sort and filter criteria you set are saved for the current merge, and the options for Step 4 of 6 appear in the task pane.

4. **Click Postal bar code in the task pane, then click OK in the Insert Postal Bar Code dialog box**

   A merge field for a U.S. postal bar code is inserted in the first label in the main document. When the main document is merged with the data source, a customized postal bar code determined by the recipient's zip code and street address will appear on every label.

5. **Press [→], press [Enter], click Address block in the task pane, then click OK in the Insert Address Block dialog box**

   The Address Block merge field is added to the first label.

6. **Point to the down arrow at the bottom of the task pane to scroll down, then click Update all labels in the task pane**

   The merge fields are copied from the first label to every label in the main document.

7. **Click Next: Preview your labels in the task pane**

   A preview of the merged label data appears in the main document. Only U.S. addresses are included, and the labels are organized in zip code order.

8. **Click Next: Complete the merge in the task pane, click Edit individual labels, then click OK in the Merge to New Document dialog box**

   The merged labels document is shown in Figure H-16.

9. **Replace Ms. Clarissa Landfair with your name in the first label, save the document with the filename US Coffee Labels Zip Code Merge to the drive and folder where your Data Files are located, print the labels, save and close all open files, then exit Word**

FIGURE H-15: US records sorted in zip code order

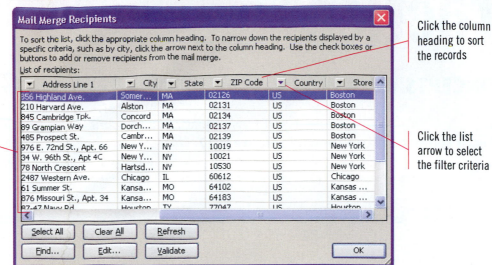

Click the column heading to sort the records

Click the list arrow to select the filter criteria

All records with a US address are sorted by zip code in ascending order

FIGURE H-16: Merged labels

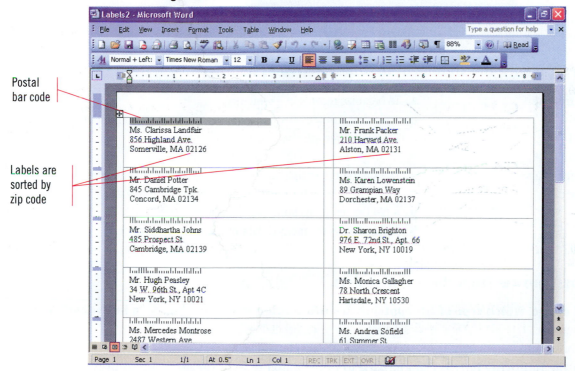

Postal bar code

Labels are sorted by zip code

Clues to Use

Inserting individual merge fields

You must include proper punctuation, spacing, and blank lines between the merge fields in a main document if you want punctuation, spaces, and blank lines to appear between the data in the merge documents. For example, to create an address line with a city, state, and zip code, you insert the City merge field, type a comma and a space, insert the State merge field, type a space, and then insert the Zip Code merge field: <<City>>, <<State>> <<Zip Code>>.

You can insert an individual merge field by selecting the field name in the Insert Merge Fields dialog box, clicking Insert, and then clicking Close. You can also insert several merge fields at once by clicking a field name in the Insert Merge Field dialog box, clicking Insert, clicking another field name, clicking Insert, and so on. When you have finished inserting the merge fields, click Close. You can then add spaces, punctuation, and lines between the merge fields you inserted in the main document.

Practice

▼ CONCEPTS REVIEW

Label each toolbar button shown in Figure H-17.

Figure H-17

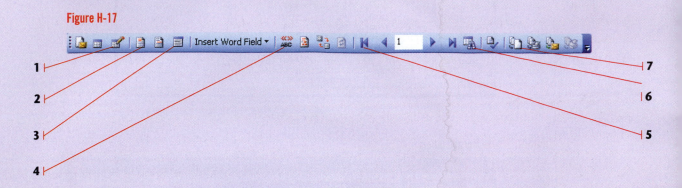

1

2

3

4

7

6

5

Match each term with the statement that best describes it.

8. Main document

9. Merge field

10. Data field

11. Boilerplate text

12. Data source

13. Data record

14. Filter

15. Sort

a. To organize records in a sequence

b. A file that contains customized information for each item or individual

c. To pull out records that meet certain criteria

d. A category of information in a data source

e. The standard text that appears in every version of a merged document

f. A complete set of information for one item or individual

g. A file that contains boilerplate text and merge fields

h. A placeholder for merged data in the main document

Select the best answer from the list of choices.

16. In a mail merge, which type of file contains the information that varies for each individual or item?

   a. Data source

   b. Main document

   c. Label document

   d. Merge document

17. Which of the following buttons can be used to insert a merge field for an inside address?

   a.

   b.

   c.

   d.

18. Which of the following buttons can be used to preview the merged data in the main document?

   a.

   b.

   c.

   d.

19. To change the font of merged data, which element should you format?

   a. Data record

   b. Merge field

   c. Field name

   d. Boilerplate text

20. Which of the following is included in a data source?

   a. Records

   b. Boilerplate text

   c. Labels

   d. Merge fields

▼ SKILLS REVIEW

1. Create a main document.

   a. Start Word, then open the Mail Merge task pane.

   b. Use the Mail Merge task pane to create a letter main document, click Next, then select the current (blank) document.

   c. At the top of the blank document, press [Enter] four times, type today's date, press [Enter] five times, then type **We are delighted to receive your generous contribution of AMOUNT to the New England Humanities Council (NEHC)**.

   d. Press [Enter] twice, then type **Whether we are helping adult new readers learn to read or bringing humanities programs into our public schools, senior centers, and prisons, NEHC depends upon private contributions to ensure that free public humanities programs continue to flourish in CITY and throughout the REGION region. I hope we will see you at a humanities event soon.**

   e. Press [Enter] twice, type **Sincerely**, and press [Enter] four times, type your name, press [Enter], then type **Executive Director**.

   f. Save the main document as **Donor Thank You Main** to the drive and folder where your Data Files are located.

2. Design a data source.

   a. Click Next, select the Type a new list option button in the Step 3 of 6 Mail Merge task pane, then click Create.

   b. Click Customize in the New Address List dialog box, then remove these fields from the data source: Company Name, Address Line 2, Country, Home Phone, Work Phone, and E-mail Address.

   c. Add an **Amount** field and a **Region** field to the data source. Be sure these fields follow the ZIP Code field.

   d. Rename the Address Line 1 field **Street**, then click OK to close the Customize Address List dialog box.

3. Enter and edit records.

   a. Add the following records to the data source:

Title	First Name	Last Name	Street	City	State	Zip Code	Amount	Region
Mr.	John	Conlin	34 Mill St.	Exeter	NH	03833	$250	Seacoast
Mr.	Bill	Webster	289 Sugar Hill Rd.	Franconia	NH	03632	$1000	Seacoast
Ms.	Susan	Janak	742 Main St.	Derby	VT	04634	$25	North Country
Mr.	Derek	Gray	987 Ocean Rd.	Portsmouth	NH	03828	$50	Seacoast
Ms.	Rita	Murphy	73 Bay Rd.	Durham	NH	03814	$500	Seacoast
Ms.	Amy	Hunt	67 Apple St.	Northfield	MA	01360	$75	Pioneer Valley
Ms.	Eliza	Perkins	287 Mountain Rd.	Dublin	NH	03436	$100	Pioneer Valley

   b. Save the data source as **Donor Data** to the drive and folder where your Data Files are located.

   c. Change the region for record 2 (Bill Webster) from Seacoast to **White Mountain**.

   d. Click OK to close the Mail Merge Recipients dialog box.

4. Add merge fields.

   a. Click Next, then in the blank line above the first body paragraph, insert an Address Block merge field.

   b. In the Insert Address Block dialog box, click Match Fields.

   c. Click the list arrow next to Address 1 in the Match Fields dialog box, click Street, then click OK.

   d. In the Insert Address Block dialog box, select the Never include the country/region in the address option button, then click OK.

   e. Press [Enter] twice, insert a Greeting Line merge field using the default greeting line format, then press [Enter].

   f. In the first body paragraph, replace AMOUNT with the Amount merge field.

   g. In the second body paragraph, replace CITY with the City merge field and REGION with the Region merge field. (*Note*: Make sure to insert a space before or after each merge field as needed.)

   h. Save your changes to the main document.

5. **Merge data**.
   a. Click Next to preview the merged data, then scroll through each letter.
   b. Click the View Merged Data button on the Mail Merge toolbar, place the insertion point before "I hope" in the second sentence of the second body paragraph, then press [Enter] twice to create a new paragraph.
   c. Combine the first and second body paragraphs into a single paragraph.
   d. Make any other necessary adjustments to the letter, save your changes, then click the View Merged Data button to return to the preview of the document.
   e. Click Next, click Edit individual letters, then merge all the records to a new file.
   f. Save the merged document as **Donor Thank You Merge** to the drive and folder where your Data Files are located, print a copy of the first letter, then save and close all open files.

6. **Create labels**.
   a. Open a new blank document, then open the Mail Merge task pane.
   b. Create a label main document, click Next, then select the Change document layout option button if necessary in the Step 2 of 6 Mail Merge task pane.
   c. Open the Label Options dialog box, select Avery standard 5162 – Address labels, then click OK.
   d. Save the label main document as **Donor Labels Main** to the drive and folder where your Data Files are located, then click Next.
   e. Select the Use an existing list option button, click Browse, then open the Donor Data.mdb file you created.

7. **Sort and filter records**.
   a. Filter the records so that only the records with NH in the State field are included in the merge.
   b. Sort the records in zip code order, then click OK.
   c. If the Mail Merge toolbar is not open, point to Toolbars on the View menu, then click Mail Merge.
   d. Click Next, insert a Postal bar code merge field using the default settings, press [➤], then press [Enter].
   e. Insert an Address Block merge field using the default settings, click the View Merged Data button on the Mail Merge toolbar, then notice that the street address is missing and the address block includes the region.
   f. Click the View Merged Data button again, click the Address Block merge field in the upper-left table cell to select it if necessary, then click Address block in the Mail Merge task pane.
   g. Click Match Fields in the Insert Address Block dialog box to open the Match Fields dialog box.
   h. Click the list arrow next to Address 1, click Street, scroll down, click the list arrow next to Country or Region, click (not matched), click OK, then click OK again.
   i. Click the View Merged Data button to preview the merged data, and notice that the address block now includes the street address and the region name is missing.
   j. Click Update all labels in the Mail Merge task pane, then click Next to move to Step 5.
   k. Examine the merged data for errors, then click Next to move to Step 6.
   l. Click Edit individual labels, merge all the records, then save the merged file as **NH Donor Labels Merge** to the drive and folder where your Data Files are located.
   m. In the first label, change Ms. Eliza Perkins to your name, save the document, then print it.
   n. Save and close all open Word files, then exit Word.

▼ INDEPENDENT CHALLENGE 1

You are the director of the Emerson Arts Center (EAC). The EAC is hosting an exhibit of ceramic art in th[e]
Massachusetts, and you want to send a letter advertising the exhibit to all EAC members with a Cambridge
Mail Merge to create the letter. If you are performing the ACE steps and are able to print envelopes on your p[rinter, you can]
also use Word to print an envelope for one letter.

a. Start Word, then use the Mail Merge task pane to create a letter main document using the file WD H-3.doc,
the drive and folder where your Data Files are located.

b. Replace Your Name with your name in the signature block, then save the main document as **Member Letter M[ain]**
the drive and folder where your Data Files are located.

c. Use the file WD H-4.mdb, found on the drive and folder where your Data Files are located, as the data source.

d. Sort the data source by last name, then filter the data so that only records with Cambridge as the city are included in
the merge.

e. Insert an Address Block and a Greeting Line merge field in the main document, preview the merged letters, then make
any necessary adjustments.

f. Merge all the records to a new document, then save it as **Member Letter Merge** to the drive and folder where your
Data Files are located.

g. Print the first letter.

Advanced Challenge Exercise

- ■ If you can print envelopes, select the inside address in the first merge letter, click Tools on the menu bar, point to
Letters and Mailings, then click Envelopes and Labels.
- ■ On the Envelopes tab, verify that no check mark appears in the check box next to Omit, type your name in the Return
address text box, type **60 Crandall Street, Concord, MA 01742**, click Options, make sure the Envelope size is set to
Size 10, then change the font of the Delivery address and the Return address to 12-point Times New Roman.
- ■ On the Printing Options tab, select the appropriate Feed method for your printer, then click OK.
- ■ Click Print, then click No to save the return address as the default.

h. Close all open Word files, saving changes, and then exit Word.

▼ INDEPENDENT CHALLENGE 2

One of your responsibilities at JDE Enterprises, a growing information technology company, is to create business cards for the
staff. You use mail merge to create the cards so that you can easily produce standard business cards for future employees.

a. Start Word, then use the Mail Merge task pane to create labels using the current blank document as the main document.

b. Select Avery standard 3612 – Business Card labels.

c. Create a new data source that includes the following fields: Title, First Name, Last Name, Phone, Fax, E-mail, and Hire
Date. Add the following records to the data source:

Title	First Name	Last Name	Phone	Fax	E-mail	Hire Date
President	Sandra	Bryson	(312) 555-3982	(312) 555-6654	sbryson@jde.com	1/12/01
Vice President	Philip	Holm	(312) 555-2323	(312) 555-4956	pholm@jde.com	1/12/01

d. Add six more records to the data source, including one with your name as the Administrative Assistant.

e. Save the data source with the filename **Employee Data** to the drive and folder where your Data Files are located, then
sort the data by Title.

INDEPENDENT CHALLENGE 2

f. In the first table cell, create the JDE Enterprises business card. Figure H-18 shows a sample JDE business card, but you should create your own design. Include the company name, a street address, and the Web site address www.jde.com. Also include a First Name, Last Name, Title, Phone, Fax, and E-mail merge fields. (*Hint*: If your design includes a graphic, insert the graphic before inserting the merge fields. Use the Insert Merge Field dialog box to insert each merge field, adjusting the spacing between merge fields as necessary.)

g. Format the business card with fonts, colors, and other formatting features. (*Note*: Use the Other Task Panes list arrow to reopen the Mail Merge task pane if necessary.)

FIGURE H-18

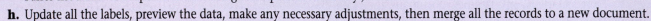

JDE Enterprises

Sandra Bryson
President

234 Walden Street, Dublin, PA 32183
Tel: (312) 555-3982; Fax: (312) 555-6654
E-mail: sbryson@jde.com
www.jde.com

h. Update all the labels, preview the data, make any necessary adjustments, then merge all the records to a new document.

i. Save the merge document with the filename **Business Cards Merge** to the drive and folder where your Data Files are located, print a copy, then close the file.

j. Save the main document with the filename **Business Cards Main** to the drive and folder where your Data Files are located, close the file, then exit Word.

▼ INDEPENDENT CHALLENGE 3

You need to create a team roster for the children's softball team you coach. You decide to use mail merge to create the team roster. If you are completing the ACE steps, you will also use mail merge to create mailing labels.

a. Start Word, then use the Mail Merge task pane to create a directory using the current blank document.

b. Create a new data source that includes the following fields: First Name, Last Name, Age, Position, Parent First Name, Parent Last Name, Address, City, State, Zip Code, and Home Phone.

c. Enter the following records in the data source:

First Name	Last Name	Age	Position	Parent First Name	Parent Last Name	Address	City	State	Zip Code	Home Phone
Sophie	Wright	8	Shortstop	Kerry	Wright	58 Main St.	Camillus	NY	13031	555-2345
Will	Jacob	7	Catcher	Bob	Jacob	32 North Way	Camillus	NY	13031	555-9827
Brett	Eliot	8	First base	Olivia	Eliot	289 Sylvan Way	Marcellus	NY	13032	555-9724
Abby	Herman	7	Pitcher	Sarah	Thomas	438 Lariat St.	Marcellus	NY	13032	555-8347

d. Add five additional records to the data source using the following last names and positions:

O'Keefe, Second base

George, Third base

Goleman, Left field

Siebert, Center field

Choy, Right field

Make up the remaining information for these five records.

e. Save the data source as **Softball Team Data** to the drive and folder where your Data Files are located.

f. Sort the records by last name, then click Next in the Mail Merge task pane.

g. Insert a table that includes five columns and one row in the main document.

h. In the first table cell, insert the First Name and Last Name merge fields, separated by a space.

i. In the second cell, insert the Position merge field.

j. In the third cell, insert the Address and City merge fields, separated by a comma and a space.

k. In the fourth cell, insert the Home Phone merge field.

l. In the fifth cell, insert the Parent First Name and Parent Last Name merge fields, separated by a space.

m. Preview the merged data and make any necessary adjustments. (*Hint*: Only one record is displayed at a time when you preview the data.)

n. Merge all the records to a new document, then save the document with the filename **Softball Roster Merge** to the drive and folder where your Data Files are located.

o. Press [Ctrl][Home], press [Enter], type **Wildcats Team Roster** at the top of the document, press [Enter], type **Coach:**, followed by your name, then press [Enter] twice.

p. Insert a new row at the top of the table, then type the following column headings in the new row: **Name, Position, Address, Phone, Parent Name**.

q. Format the roster to make it attractive and readable, save your changes, print a copy, then close the file.

r. Close the main document without saving changes.

Advanced Challenge Exercise

■ Open a new blank document, then use the Mail Merge task pane to create mailing labels using Avery standard 5162 – Address labels.

■ Use the Softball Team Data data source you created, and sort the records in zip code order.

■ In the first table cell, create your own address block using the Parent First Name, Parent Last Name, Address, City, State, and Zip Code merge fields. Be sure to include proper spacing and punctuation.

■ Update all the labels, preview the merged data, merge all the records to a new document, then type your name centered in the document header.

■ Save the document with the filename **Softball Labels Merge ACE** to the drive and folder where your Data Files are located, print a copy, close the file, then close the main document without saving changes.

s. Exit Word.

▼ INDEPENDENT CHALLENGE 4

Your boss has given you the task of purchasing mailing labels for a mass mailing of your company's annual report. The annual report will be sent to 55,000 people. Your company plans to use Avery standard 5160 white labels for a laser printer, or their equivalent, for the mailing. In this independent challenge, you will search for Web sites that sell Avery labels, compare the costs, and then write a memo to your boss detailing your purchasing recommendations.

a. Use your favorite search engine to search for Web sites that sell Avery labels or the equivalent. Use the keywords **Avery labels** to conduct your search.

b. Find at least three Web sites that sell Avery 5160 white labels for a laser printer, or their equivalent. Note the URL of the Web sites and the price and quantity of the labels. You need to purchase enough labels for a mailing of 55,000, plus enough extras in case you make mistakes.

c. Start Word, then use the Professional Memo template to create a memo to your boss. Save the memo as **5160 Labels Memo** to the drive and folder where your Data Files are located.

d. In the memo, make up information to replace the placeholder text in the memo header, be sure to include your name in the memo header, then type the body of your memo.

e. In the body, include a table that shows the URL of each Web site, the product name, the unit cost, the number of labels in each unit, the number of units you need to purchase, and the total cost of purchasing the labels. Also make a brief recommendation to your boss.

f. Format the memo so it is attractive and readable, save your changes, print a copy, close the file, then exit Word.

Using the Mail Merge task pane, create the post cards shown in Figure H-19. Use Avery standard 3611 – Post Card labels for the main document and create a data source that contains at least four records. Save the data source as **Party Data**, save the main document as **Party Card Main**, and save the merge document as **Party Card Merge**, all to the drive and folder where your Data Files are located. (*Hint:* Use a table to lay out the postcard; the clip art graphic uses the keywords "party cake balloon"; and the font is Comic Sans MS.) Print a copy of the postcards.

FIGURE H-19

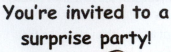

You're invited to a
surprise party!

||.|..|..|..|..|..||..|||..||.|.|.|
Grace Pappas
186 Buena Vista Terrace
Apt. 5C
San Francisco, CA 94117

For: Claudette Summer
When: August 3rd, 7:00 p.m.
Where: The Wharf Grill
Given by: Your Name

You're invited to a
surprise party!

||.|..|..|..|..|..|.||..|||.|.|.|
Mika Takeda
456 Parker Ave.
San Francisco, CA 94118

For: Claudette Summer
When: August 3rd, 7:00 p.m.
Where: The Wharf Grill
Given by: Your Name

Collaborating on Documents

OBJECTIVES

Track changes

Insert, view, and edit comments

Compare and merge documents

If you have a SAM user profile, you may have access to hands-on instruction, practice, and assessment of the skills covered in this unit. Log in to your SAM account and go to your assignments page to see what your instructor has assigned.

Several Word features make it easier to create and edit documents in cooperation with other people. The Track Changes, Comment, and Compare and Merge features in Word facilitate collaboration when two or more people are working on the same document. In this appendix, you learn how to track and review changes to a document, how to insert and work with comments, and how to compare and merge two documents. You have circulated a copy of the Chicago Marketing Report to two of your colleagues for feedback. You use the Track Changes, Comment, and Compare and Merge features to review their suggestions for changes and to combine their feedback into a final document.

Tracking Changes

A **tracked change** is a mark that shows where an insertion, deletion, or formatting change has been made in a document. When the Track Changes feature is turned on, each change that you or another reviewer makes to a document is tracked. In Print Layout view, text that is inserted in a document is displayed as colored, underlined text. Formatting changes and text that is deleted are shown in balloons in the right margin of the document. As you review the tracked changes in a document, you can choose to accept or reject each change. When you accept a change it becomes part of the document. When you reject a change, the text or formatting is restored to its original state. To turn tracked changes on and off, you use the Track Changes button on the Reviewing toolbar or the Track Changes command on the Tools menu. 🎨 Your boss, Alice Wegman, has used Track Changes to suggest revisions to your draft report. You review Alice's tracked changes, accepting or rejecting them as you go, and then edit the document with your additional changes.

STEPS

1. **Start Word, open the file WD AP-1.doc from the drive and folder where your Data Files are located, then save it as Chicago Draft 1**

   The document, which contains tracked changes, opens in Print Layout view, as shown in Figure AP-1. Notice that the Track Changes button on the Reviewing toolbar is enabled, indicating that tracked changes are turned on in the document. Any change you make to the document will be marked as a tracked change.

2. **Click the Next button 📄 on the Reviewing toolbar**

   The insertion point moves to the first tracked change in the document, in this case, a sentence inserted in the introductory paragraph.

3. **Click the Accept Change button 📄 on the Reviewing toolbar, then click 📄**

   The sentence becomes part of the document and the insertion point moves to a balloon containing a comment. You will work with comments in the next lesson, so you skip over the comment for now.

4. **Click 📄**

   The insertion point moves to the balloon containing the deleted text "Half."

5. **Click the Reject Change/Delete Comment button 📄 on the Reviewing toolbar, click 📄, then click 📄**

   The deleted word "Half" is restored to the document, the insertion point moves to the inserted word "Full," and then "Full" is removed from the document, returning the text to its original state, as shown in Figure AP-2.

6. **Click 📄 to select the next tracked change, right-click the selected text, then click Accept Insertion on the shortcut menu**

   The sentence becomes part of the document text. You can accept or reject any tracked change by right-clicking it and then selecting the appropriate command on the shortcut menu.

7. **Scroll down until the heading Travel Writers & Photographers Conference on page 2 is at the top of your screen, select sixth in the first sentence under the heading, type seventh, place the insertion point in front of discussion in the next line of text, then type spirited followed by a space**

   Your tracked changes are added to the document using a different color, as shown in Figure AP-3.

8. **Click the Track Changes button 📄 on the Reviewing toolbar to turn off the Track Changes feature, press [Ctrl][Home], replace Your Name with your name at the top of the document, then click the Save button 📄 on the Standard toolbar to save your changes**

FIGURE AP-1: Reviewing toolbar and tracked changes

Reviewing toolbar

Track Changes button

Inserted text (your color might differ)

Vertical bars indicate the adjacent line includes a tracked change

Comment in a balloon

Deleted text in a balloon

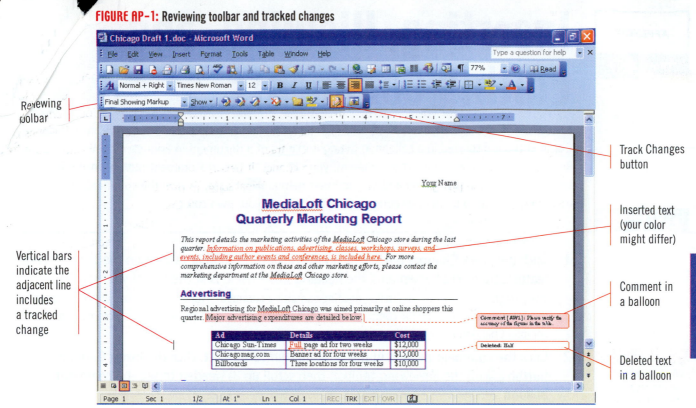

FIGURE AP-2: Text restored to its original state

Tracked change text becomes part of the document

Text is restored to the original state

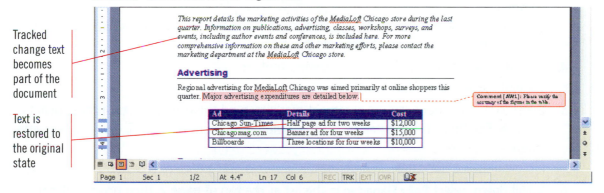

FIGURE AP-3: Tracked changes in the document

Deleted text

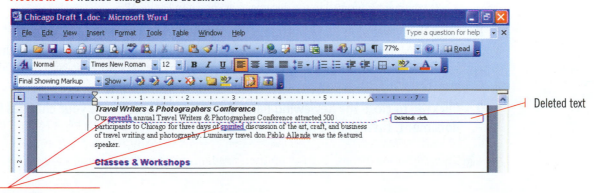

Your tracked changes appear in a color that is different than Alice's tracked changes (your color might differ)

Inserting, Viewing, and Editing Comments

A **comment** is an embedded note or annotation that an author or reviewer adds to a document. Comments are displayed in a balloon in the right margin of a document in Print Layout, Web Layout, and Reading Layout views. To insert a comment, you can use the Insert Comment button on the Reviewing toolbar or the Comment command on the Insert menu. You review the comments in the document, responding to them or deleting them, and then add your own comments.

STEPS

1. **Click the Track Changes button on the Reviewing toolbar to turn on the Track Changes feature, then scroll down until the heading Advertising is at the top of your screen**
   The paragraph under the Advertising heading contains a comment. Notice that a comment mark appears in the document at the point the comment was inserted, and a dashed line leads from the comment mark to the comment balloon in the margin.

2. **Click the comment balloon in the right margin to select it, click the Insert Comment button on the Reviewing toolbar, then scroll up as needed to see the comment balloon**
   A blank comment balloon is inserted in the document using a different color (the same color as your tracked changes). You respond to a comment by selecting the comment and then inserting your own comment.

3. **Type The numbers are correct., then click outside the comment balloon to deselect the comment**
   The text is added to the comment balloon, as shown in Figure AP-4. You can edit comment text by placing the insertion point in a comment balloon and then typing.

4. **Click the Next button on the Reviewing toolbar**
   The next comment in the document is selected.

5. **Point to the text between the comment markers, read the comment text that appears in a ScreenTip, then click the Reject Change/Delete Comment button on the Reviewing toolbar**
   The comment is removed from the manuscript.

6. **Scroll down, select Polly Flanagan in the list at the top of page 2, then press [Delete]**
   Polly Flanagan is removed from the list and the list is renumbered.

7. **Click , then type Polly Flanagan is the least likely to accept an invitation to speak.**
   A new comment is inserted in the document, as shown in Figure AP-5.

8. **Click the Reviewing Pane button on the Reviewing toolbar**
   The comments and tracked changes in the document are listed in the Reviewing Pane at the bottom of the screen. It's useful to view comments and tracked changes in the Reviewing Pane when the full text of a comment or tracked change does not fit in the balloon.

9. **Click to close the Reviewing Pane, press [Ctrl][Home], save your changes to the document, then print a copy**

FIGURE AP-4: Response comment in the document

Comment marks surround the text at the location the comment was inserted

Alice Wegman's comment

Your response comment in a color that is different than Alice's (your color might differ)

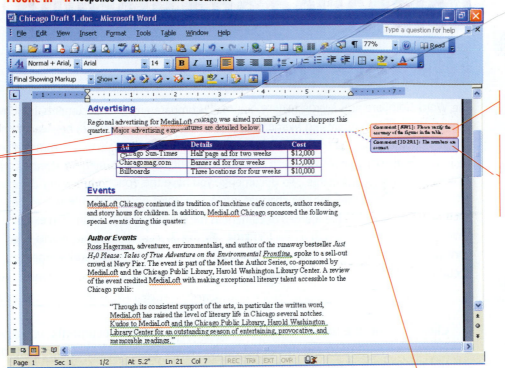

Dashed line connects the comment mark and the comment balloon

FIGURE AP-5: New comment in the document

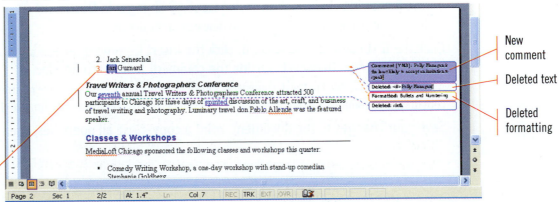

New comment

Deleted text

Deleted formatting

List is renumbered automatically

Comparing and Merging Documents

The Word Compare and Merge feature is used to compare any two documents to show the differences between the two. Compare and Merge is often used to show the differences between an original document and an edited copy of the original. It is also used to merge the changes and comments of multiple reviewers into a single document when each reviewer edits the document using a separate copy of the original. When you compare and merge two documents, you have the option of merging the changes into one of the documents or of merging the changes into a new third document. The differences between the two documents are shown in the merged document as tracked changes. You can then examine the merged document, edit it, and save it with a new filename. ★ A second colleague, Nazila Sharif, returns her revisions to you in a separate copy of the document. You use the Compare and Merge feature to merge your document with Nazila's to create a new document that shows the differences between the two copies.

STEPS

1. **Click Tools on the menu bar, click Compare and Merge Documents, use the Look in list arrow to navigate to the drive and folder where your Data Files are located, then select the file WD AP-2.doc in the Compare and Merge Documents dialog box**

   The Compare and Merge Documents dialog box is shown in Figure AP-6. You use this dialog box to select the document that you want to merge with the current document. The file WD AP-2.doc is the file that contains Nazila's comments and tracked changes.

2. **Click the Merge button list arrow in the dialog box, then click Merge into new document**

   Your document is merged with Nazila's copy into a new document, as shown in Figure AP-7. Notice that each reviewer's comments and tracked changes are displayed in a different color in the merged document.

3. **Save the document as Chicago Draft 2 to the drive and folder where your Data Files are stored**

   The document is saved with a new filename.

4. **Read the document to review the tracked changes, click the Accept Change list arrow 🖉▾ on the Reviewing toolbar, then click Accept All Changes in Document**

   All the tracked changes are accepted and become part of the document.

5. **Click the first comment to select it, click the Insert Comment button 📷 on the Reviewing toolbar, type No., then click outside the comment balloon to deselect it**

   A new comment is added to the document, as shown in Figure AP-8. After you have returned a copy of the file containing the comments to your colleagues, you will delete the comments and finalize the document.

6. **Save your changes to the document, print a copy, close all open files, then exit Word**

FIGURE AP-6: Compare and Merge Documents dialog box

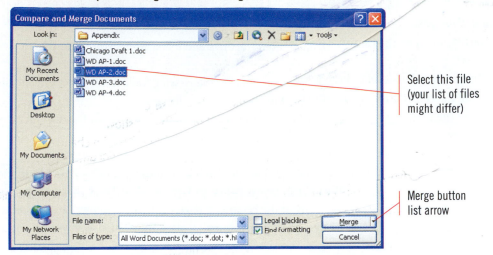

Select this file
(your list of files
might differ)

Merge button
list arrow

FIGURE AP-7: Merged document showing changes from each reviewer

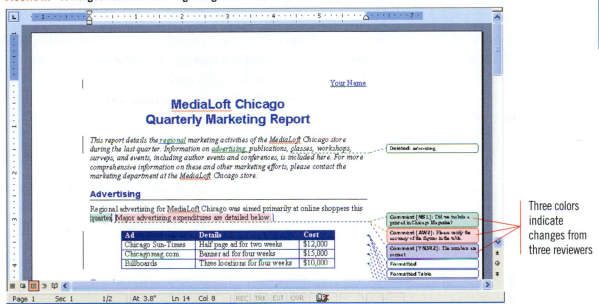

Three colors
indicate
changes from
three reviewers

FIGURE AP-8: New comment

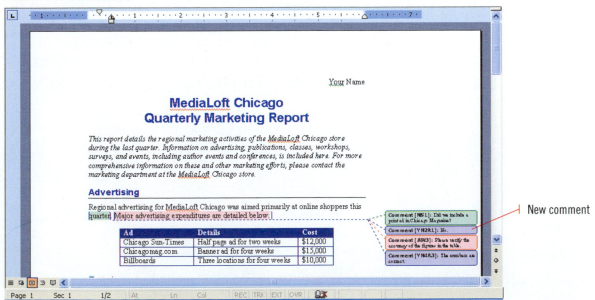

New comment

▼ SKILLS REVIEW

1. Track changes.

   a. Start Word, open the file WD AP-3.doc from the drive and folder where your Data Files are located, then save it as **EDA Draft 1**.

   b. Change the zoom level to Page Width, then open the Reviewing toolbar if it is not already displayed.

   c. Using the Next button, review the tracked changes in the document.

   d. Reject the first tracked change, then accept all remaining tracked changes in the document. Skip over the comments for now.

   e. Make sure the Track Changes feature is turned on.

   f. In the first sentence under the Guiding Principals heading, change Five to **Six**. Then, add the following sentence as point number six in the numbered list: **Open space in the rural district must be preserved.**

   g. Under the Proposed Actions heading at the bottom of page 2, delete the sentence Sponsor an e-commerce workshop.

   h. Turn off the Track Changes feature, press [Ctrl][Home], replace Your Name with your name at the top of the document, then save your changes.

2. Insert, view, and edit comments.

   a. Scroll down, select the first comment, then delete the comment.

   b. Scroll down, select 84% under the Issues heading, insert a new comment, then type **Should this be 86%?**

   c. Scroll down, select the next comment, insert a new comment, then type **We can only estimate.**

   d. Press [Ctrl][Home], save your changes to the document, then print a copy.

3. Compare and merge documents.

   a. Open the Compare and Merge Documents dialog box.

   b. Navigate to the drive and folder where your Data Files are located, select the file WD AP-4.doc, click the Merge button list arrow, then click Merge into new document.

   c. Choose to keep the formatting changes from your document, then continue with the merge.

   d. Save the merged document as **EDA Draft 2** to the drive and folder where your Data Files are located.

   e. Review the tracked changes in the document, then accept all the tracked changes.

   f. Delete all the comments.

   g. Save your changes to the document, print a copy, close all open files, then exit Word.

Working with Formulas and Functions

OBJECTIVES

Create a formula with several operators

Use names in a formula

Generate multiple totals with AutoSum

Use dates in calculations

Build a conditional formula with the IF function

Use statistical functions

Calculate payments with the PMT function

Display and print formula contents

If you have a SAM user profile, you may have access to hands-on instruction, practice, and assessment of the skills covered in this unit. Log in to your SAM account and go to your assignments page to see what your instructor has assigned.

Without formulas, Excel would simply be an electronic grid with text and numbers. Used with formulas, Excel becomes a powerful data analysis tool. As you learn how to analyze data using different types of formulas, including those containing functions, you will discover more ways to use Excel. In this unit, you will gain a further understanding of Excel formulas and learn how to use several Excel functions. 🎨 Top management at MediaLoft has asked marketing director Jim Fernandez to analyze various company data. To do this, Jim creates several worksheets that require formulas and functions. Because management is considering raising salaries for store managers, Jim has asked you to create a report that compares the payroll deductions and net pay for store managers before and after a proposed raise.

Creating a Formula with Several Operators

You can create formulas that contain a combination of cell references (for example, Z100 or B2), operators (for example, * for multiplication or – for subtraction), and values (for example, 99 or 1.56). Formulas can also contain functions. You have used AutoSum to insert the SUM function into a cell. You can also create a single formula that performs several calculations. If you enter a formula with more than one operator, Excel performs the calculations in a particular sequence based on algebraic rules, called the **order of precedence** (also called the order of operations); that is, Excel performs the operation(s) within parentheses first, then calculates exponents, then any multiplication and division from left to right. Finally, it calculates addition and subtraction, from left to right. See Table E-1 for examples. 🎨 Jim has received the gross pay and deductions for the monthly payroll and needs to complete his analysis. He has also preformatted, with the Comma style, any cells that are to contain values. He asks you to enter a formula for net pay that subtracts the payroll deductions from gross pay.

STEPS

1. **Start Excel if necessary, open the Data File EX E-1.xls from the drive and folder where your Data Files are stored, then save it as Company Data**

   The green triangles in the cells indicate that the formulas differ from the surrounding formulas. In this case, the formulas are correct, so you can ignore the triangles. The first part of the net pay formula should go in cell B11.

2. **Click Edit on the menu bar, click Go To, type B11 in the Reference box, then click OK**

   Cell B11 is now the active cell. The Go To command is especially useful when you want to select a cell in a large worksheet.

3. **Type =, click cell B6, type –, then click the Insert Function button 𝑓𝑥 on the formula bar to open the Insert Function dialog box**

   You type the equal sign (=) to indicate that a formula follows. B6 references the cell containing the gross pay, and the minus sign (–) indicates that the next entry, a sum, is subtracted from cell B6. The Insert Function dialog box allows you to choose from a list of available functions or search for a specific function. See Figure E-1.

4. **Type sum in the Search for a function text box, click Go, click SUM in the Select a function list, then click OK**

   B6:B10 appears in the Number1 text box. You want to sum the range B7:B10.

5. **With the Number1 argument selected in the Function Arguments dialog box, click the Number1 Collapse Dialog Box button 📊, select the range B7:B10 in the worksheet, click the Redisplay Dialog Box button 📊, then click OK**

   Collapsing the dialog box allows you to enter the range by selecting it. The net pay for Payroll Period 1 appears in cell B11.

6. **Copy the formula in cell B11 into cells C11:F11, then press [Ctrl][Home] to return to cell A1**

   The net pay for each column appears in row 11. See Figure E-2.

7. **Save the workbook**

FIGURE E-1: Insert Function dialog box

Type a function description

Click to start a function search

Your function listing may be different

Click to select the highlighted function

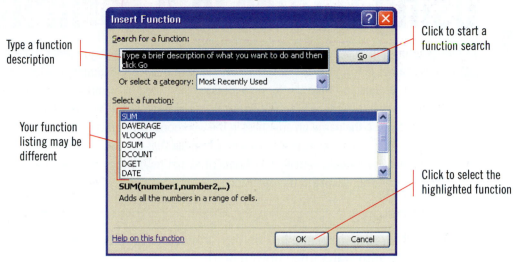

FIGURE E-2: Worksheet with copied formulas

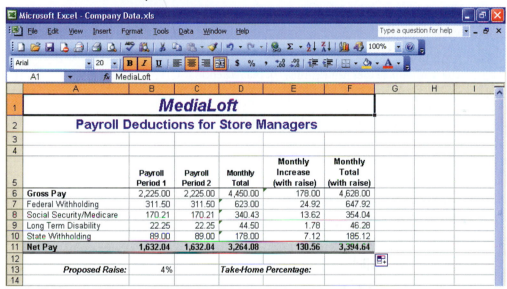

TABLE E-1: Sample formulas using parentheses and several operators

formula	order of precedence	calculated result
=10–20/10–5	Divide 20 by 10; subtract the result from 10, then subtract 5	3
=(10–20)/10–5	Subtract 20 from 10; divide that by 10; then subtract 5	–6
=(10*2)*(10+2)	Multiply 10 by 2; add 10 to 2; then multiply the results	240

Clues to Use

Using Paste Special

You can use the Paste Special command to enter formulas and values quickly or even to perform quick calculations. Click the cell(s) containing the formula or value you want to copy, click the Copy button on the Standard toolbar, then right-click the cell where you want the result to appear. In the shortcut menu, click Paste Special, choose the feature you want to paste, then click OK.

Using Names in a Formula

To reduce errors and make your worksheet easier to follow, you can assign names to cells and ranges. You can also use names in formulas to make formulas easier to build. For example, the formula Revenue-Cost is much easier to understand than the formula A2-D3. When used in formulas, names become absolute cell references by default. Names can use uppercase or lowercase letters as well as digits. After you name a cell or range, you can use the name on any sheet in the workbook. If you move a named cell or range, its name moves with it. 🎨 Jim wants you to include a formula that calculates the percentage of monthly gross pay that the managers would actually take home (their net pay) if they received a 4% raise. You decide to name the cells that you will use in the calculation.

STEPS

QUICK TIP

You can also assign names to ranges of cells. Select the range, click the name box, then type in the range name. You can also name a range by pointing to Name on the Insert menu, then clicking Define and typing the name.

1. **Click cell F6, click the name box on the formula bar to select the active cell reference, type Gross_with_Raise, then press [Enter]**

   The name assigned to cell F6, Gross_with_Raise, appears in the name box. Note that you must type underscores instead of spaces between words. Cell F6 is now named Gross_with_Raise to refer to the monthly gross pay amount that includes the 4% raise. The name box displays as much of the name as fits (Gross_with_...). The total net pay cell needs a name.

2. **Click cell F11, click the name box, type Net_with_Raise, then press [Enter]**

   The new formula uses names instead of cell references.

QUICK TIP

You can use the Label Ranges dialog box (Insert menu, Name submenu, Label command) to designate existing column or row headings as labels. Then instead of using cell references for the column or row in formulas, you can use the labels.

3. **Click cell F13, type =, click Insert on the menu bar, point to Name, click Paste, click Net_with_Raise, then click OK**

   The name is inserted and the color of the name matches the outline around the cell reference.

4. **Type /, click Insert on the menu bar, point to Name, click Paste, click Gross_with_Raise, click OK, then click the Enter button ✓ on the formula bar**

   The formula appears in the formula bar and the result, 0.7335, appears in the cell. Cell F13 needs to be formatted in Percent style.

QUICK TIP

To replace cell references in existing formulas with the corresponding names you have added, click Insert on the menu bar, point to Name, click Apply, click the name or names, then click OK.

5. **Select cell F13 if necessary, click Format on the menu bar, click Style, click the Style name list arrow, click Percent, then click OK**

   The result shown in cell F13, 73%, is rounded to the nearest whole percent, as shown in Figure E-3. A **style** is a combination of formatting characteristics, such as bold, italic, and zero decimal places. You can use the Style dialog box instead of the Formatting toolbar to apply styles.

6. **Enter your name in cell A20, save the workbook, then preview and print the worksheet**

Clues to Use

Defining and removing styles

To define your own style (such as bold, italic, 14 point numbers with commas and zero decimal places), select a cell, format it using the Formatting toolbar, open the Style dialog box and type a name for your style, then click Add. Later, you can apply all of your formatting characteristics by applying your new style from the Style dialog box. You can also use the Style dialog box to remove styles by selecting the cell that has a style and then selecting Normal in the Style name list.

FIGURE E-3: Worksheet formula that includes cell names

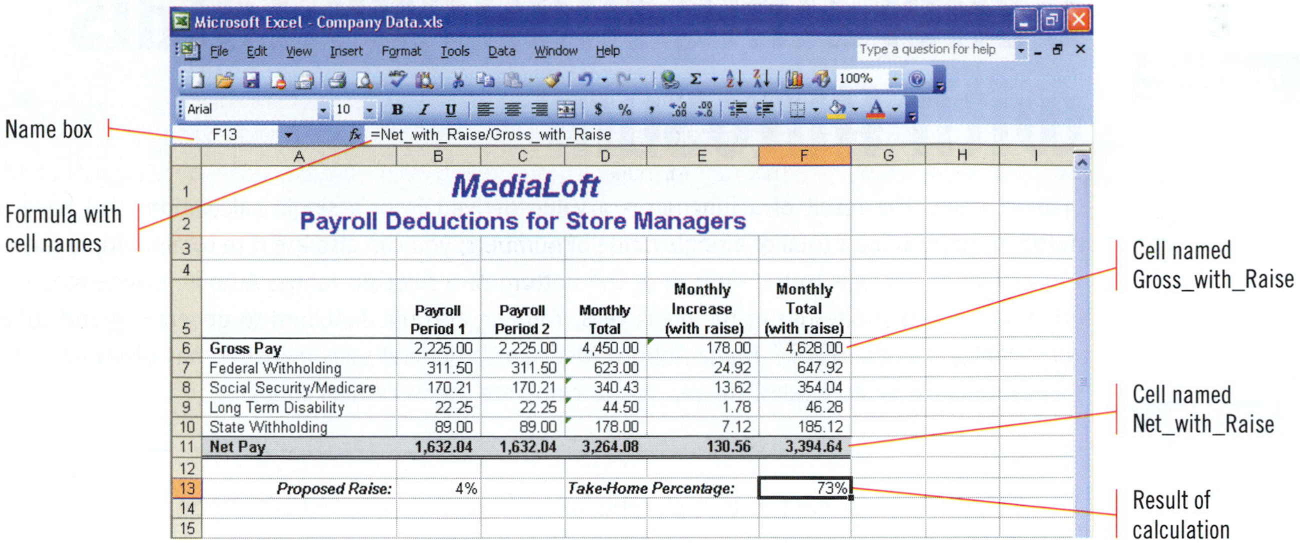

Name box

Formula with cell names

Cell named Gross_with_Raise

Cell named Net_with_Raise

Result of calculation

Clues to Use

Producing a list of names

You might want to verify the names you have assigned in a workbook and the cells they reference. To paste a list of names in a workbook, select a blank cell that has several blank cells beside and beneath it. Click Insert on the menu bar, point to Name, then click Paste. In the Paste Name dialog box, click Paste List. Excel produces a list of names that includes the sheet name followed by an exclamation point and the cell or range the name identifies. See Figure E-4.

FIGURE E-4: Worksheet with pasted list of names

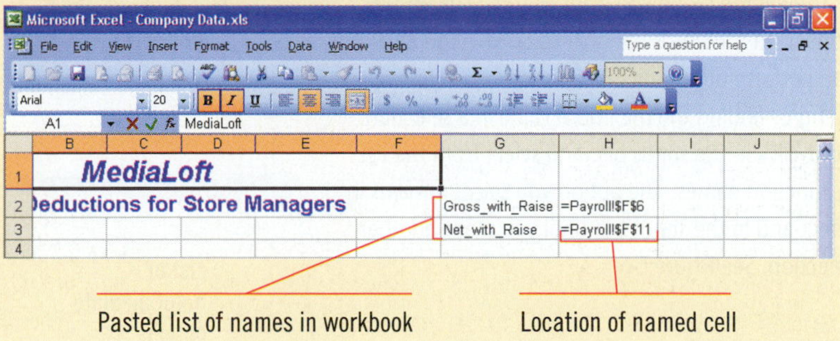

Pasted list of names in workbook

Location of named cell

UNIT
E
Excel 2003

Generating Multiple Totals with AutoSum

In most cases, the result of a function is a value derived from a single calculation. You have used AutoSum to produce a total of a single range of numbers; you can also use it to total multiple ranges. If you include blank cells to the right or at the bottom of a selected range, AutoSum generates several totals and enters the results in the blank cells. You can also use AutoSum to generate grand totals of worksheet subtotals. Maria Abbott, MediaLoft's general sales manager, has given Jim a worksheet summarizing store sales. He asks you to complete the worksheet totals.

STEPS

TROUBLE

If you select the wrong combination of cells, click a single cell and begin again.

1. **Click the Sales sheet tab to make the Sales sheet active, select the range B5:E9, press and hold [Ctrl], then select the range B11:E15**

   To select nonadjacent cells, you must press and hold [Ctrl] while selecting the additional cells. Compare your selections with Figure E-6. Jim would like totals to appear in the last line of each selection.

2. **Click the AutoSum button Σ on the Standard toolbar**

   When the selected range you want to sum (B5:E9 and B11:E15, in this example) includes a blank cell with data values above it, AutoSum enters the total in the blank cell.

3. **Select the range B5:F17, then click Σ**

   Although Excel generates totals when you click the AutoSum button, it is a good idea to check the results.

QUICK TIP

Excel uses commas to separate multiple arguments in all functions, not just in SUM.

4. **Click cell B17**

   The formula bar reads =SUM(B15,B9). In this case, Excel ignores the data values and it totals only the sums. See Figure E-7. When generating grand totals, Excel separates the cell references with a comma.

5. **Enter your name in cell A20, save the workbook, then preview and print the worksheet**

Clues to Use

Quick calculations with AutoCalculate

To view a total quickly without entering a formula, just select the range you want to sum. The answer appears in the status bar next to SUM=. You also can perform other quick calculations, such as averaging or finding the minimum value in a selection: right-click in the status bar, and select from the list of function names. The option you select remains in effect and in the status bar until you make another selection. See Figure E-5.

FIGURE E-5: Using AutoCalculate

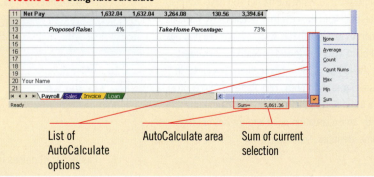

List of AutoCalculate options   AutoCalculate area   Sum of current selection

FIGURE E-6: Selecting nonadjacent ranges using [Ctrl]

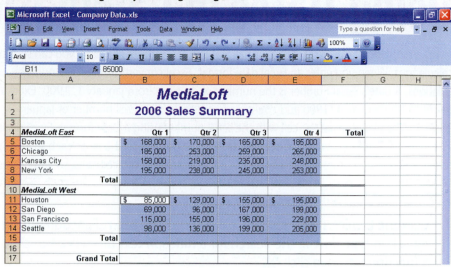

FIGURE E-7: Completed worksheet

Comma separates multiple arguments

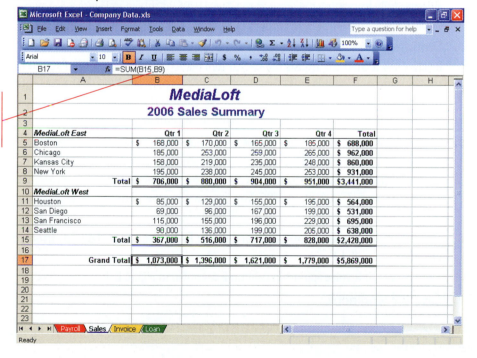

Using Dates in Calculations

If you enter dates in a worksheet in a format that Excel recognizes as a date, you can sort them and perform date calculations. When you enter an Excel date format, Excel converts it to a serial number so it can be used in calculations. A date's serial number is the number of days it is from January 1, 1900. Excel assigns the serial number of "1" to January 1, 1900 and counts up from there; the serial number of January 1, 2006, for example, is 38,718. When you format the cell with the serial number using a Date format, Excel displays the serial number as a date.  Jim wants you to calculate the due date and age of each invoice on his worksheet. He reminds you to enter the worksheet dates in a format that Excel recognizes, so you can use date calculations.

STEPS

1. **Click the Invoice sheet tab, click cell C4, click the Insert Function button f_x on the formula bar, type date in the Search for a function text box, click Go, click DATE in the Select a function list, then click OK**

   Your calculations need to be based on a current date of 4/1/06.

TROUBLE

If the year appears with four digits instead of two, your system administrator may have set a four-digit year display. You can continue with the lesson.

2. **Enter 2006 in the Year text box, enter 4 in the Month text box, enter 1 in the Day text box, then click OK**

   The Date function uses the format DATE(year, month, day). The date appears in cell C4 as 4/1/06. Your formula in cell E7 should calculate the invoice due date, which is 30 days from the invoice date. The formula adds 30 days to the invoice date.

3. **Click cell E7, type =, click cell B7, type +30, then click the Enter button ✓ on the formula bar**

   Excel calculates the result by converting the 3/2/06 invoice date to a serial date number, adding 30 to it, then automatically formatting the result as the date 4/1/06, as shown in Figure E-8. You can use the same formula to calculate the due dates of the other invoices.

QUICK TIP

You can also perform time calculations in Excel. For example, you can enter an employee's starting and ending time, then calculate how long he or she worked. You must enter time in an Excel time format.

4. **Drag the fill handle to copy the formula in cell E7 into cells E8:E13**

   Relative cell referencing adjusts the copied formula to contain the appropriate cell references. Now you are ready to enter the formula that calculates the age of each invoice. You do this by subtracting the invoice date from the current date. Because each invoice age formula must refer to the current date, you must make cell C4, the current date cell, an absolute reference in the formula.

5. **Click cell F7, type =, click cell C4, press [F4] to add the absolute reference symbols ($), type –, click cell B7, then click ✓**

   The formula bar displays the formula $C$4–B7. The numerical result, 30, appears in cell F7 because there are 30 days between 3/2/06 and 4/1/06. You can use the same formula to calculate the age of the remaining invoices.

QUICK TIP

You can also insert the current date into a cell by using the TODAY() function. The NOW() function inserts the current date and time into a cell. If you leave the argument area within its parentheses blank, it automatically displays today's date.

6. **Drag the fill handle to copy the formula in F7 to the range F8:F13, then press [Ctrl][Home] to return to cell A1**

   The age of each invoice appears in column F, as shown in Figure E-9.

7. **Save the workbook**

FIGURE E-8: Worksheet with calculated invoice due date

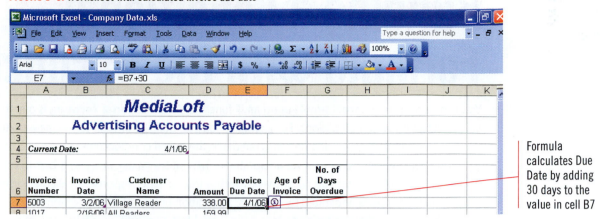

Formula calculates Due Date by adding 30 days to the value in cell B7

FIGURE E-9: Worksheet with copied formulas

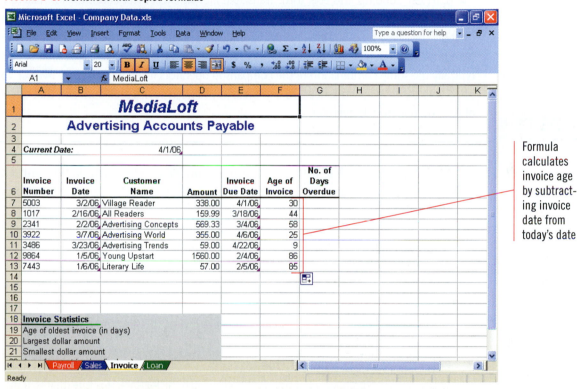

Formula calculates invoice age by subtracting invoice date from today's date

---

Clues to Use

Applying and creating custom number and date formats

When you use numbers and dates in worksheets or calculations, you can apply built-in Excel formats or create your own. To apply number formats, click Format on the menu bar, click Cells, then if necessary click the Number tab. In the Category list, click a category, then click the exact format in the list or scroll box to the right. To create a custom format, click Custom in the category list, then click a format that resembles the one you want. For example the value $3,789 uses the number format $#,### where # represents positive numbers. In the Type box, edit the symbols until they represent the format you want, then click OK. See Figure E-10.

FIGURE E-10: Custom formats on the Number tab in the Format Cells dialog box

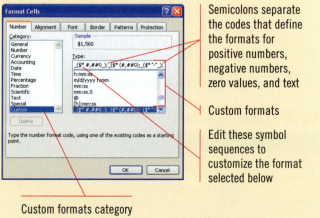

Semicolons separate the codes that define the formats for positive numbers, negative numbers, zero values, and text

Custom formats

Edit these symbol sequences to customize the format selected below

Custom formats category

Building a Conditional Formula with the IF Function

You can build a conditional formula using an IF function. A **conditional formula** is one that makes calculations based on stated conditions. For example, you can build a formula to calculate bonuses based on a person's performance rating. If a person is rated a 5 (the stated condition) on a scale of 1 to 5, with 5 being the highest rating, he or she receives an additional 10% of his or her salary as a bonus; otherwise, there is no bonus. A condition that can be answered with a true or false response is called a **logical test**. The IF function has three parts, separated by commas: a condition or logical test, an action to take if the logical test or condition is true, then an action to take if the logical test or condition is false. Another way of expressing this is: IF(test_cond,do_this,else_this). Translated into an Excel IF function, the formula to calculate bonuses would look something like this: IF(Rating=5,Salary*0.10,0). The translation would be: If the rating equals 5, multiply the salary by 0.10 (the decimal equivalent of 10%), then place the result in the selected cell; if the rating does not equal 5, place a 0 in the cell. When entering the logical test portion of an IF statement, you typically use some combination of the comparison operators listed in Table E-2. You are almost finished with the invoice worksheet. To complete it, you need to use an IF function that calculates the number of days each invoice is overdue.

STEPS

1. **Click cell G7, click the Insert Function button 𝑓𝑥 on the formula bar, enter conditional in the Search for a function text box, click Go, click IF in the Select a function list box, then click OK**

   You want the function to calculate the number of days overdue as follows: if the age of the invoice is greater than 30, calculate the days overdue (Age of Invoice – 30), and place the result in cell G7; otherwise, place a 0 (zero) in the cell.

2. **Enter F7>30 in the Logical_test text box**

   The symbol (>) represents "greater than." So far, the formula reads: if Age of Invoice is greater than 30 (in other words, if the invoice is overdue). The next part of the function tells Excel the action to take if the invoice is over 30 days old.

3. **Enter F7–30 in the Value_if_true text box**

   This part of the formula is what you want Excel to do if the logical test is true (that is, if the age of the invoice is over 30). Continuing the translation of the formula, this part means: take the Age of Invoice value and subtract 30. The last part of the formula tells Excel the action to take if the logical test is false (that is, if the age of the invoice is 30 days or less).

4. **Enter 0 in the Value_if_false text box, then click OK**

   The function is complete, and the result, 0 (the number of days overdue), appears in cell G7. See Figure E-11.

5. **Copy the formula in cell G7 into cells G8:G13, then press [Ctrl][Home] to return to cell A1**

   Compare your results with Figure E-12.

6. **Save the workbook**

TABLE E-2: Comparison operators

operator	meaning	operator	meaning
<	Less than	<=	Less than or equal to
>	Greater than	>=	Greater than or equal to
=	Equal to	<>	Not equal to

FIGURE E-11: Worksheet with IF function

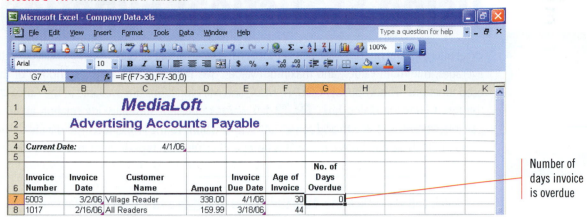

Number of days invoice is overdue

FIGURE E-12: Completed worksheet

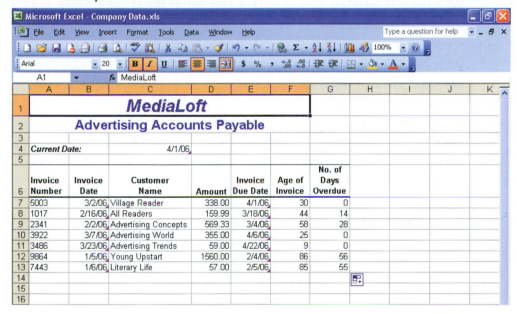

Clues to Use

Correcting circular references

A cell with a circular reference contains a formula that refers to its own cell location. If you accidentally enter a formula with a circular reference, a warning box opens alerting you to the problem. Click OK to display the Circular Reference toolbar or HELP to open a Help window explaining how to find the circular reference. In simple formulas, a circular reference is easy to spot. To correct it, edit the formula to remove any reference to the cell where the formula is located.

Using Statistical Functions

Excel offers several hundred worksheet functions. A small group of these functions calculate statistics such as averages, minimum values, and maximum values. See Table E-3 for a brief description of these commonly used functions. The AVERAGE, COUNT, MAX, and MIN functions are available in the AutoSum list as well as the Insert Function dialog box. ▰▰▰▰▰ Jim wants to present summary information about open accounts payable, and he asks you to add some statistical functions to the worksheet. You decide to use the AutoSum list to insert these functions because it is faster and easier than typing them into the worksheet.

STEPS

1. **Click cell D19, click the AutoSum list arrow Σ ▾ and then click Max**

   The invoice age information is in cells F7:F13.

2. **Select the range F7:F13, then press [Enter]**

   The age of the oldest invoice (or maximum value in range F7:F13) is 86 days, as shown in Figure E-13. Jim needs to know the largest dollar amount among the outstanding invoices.

3. **With cell D20 selected, click Σ ▾, click Max, select the range D7:D13, then press [Enter]**

   The largest outstanding invoice, for 1560.00, is shown in cell D20. The MIN function finds the smallest dollar amount and the age of the newest invoice.

   <table><tr><td>

   QUICK TIP

   You can cut, copy, and paste functions from one worksheet area to another or from one workbook to another.
   </td></tr></table>

4. **With cell D21 selected, click Σ ▾, click Min, select the range D7:D13, then press [Enter]**

   The smallest dollar amount owed is 57.00, as shown in cell D21. Jim wants to know the age of the newest invoice.

5. **With cell D22 selected, click Σ ▾, click Min, select the range F7:F13, then press [Enter]**

   The newest invoice is 9 days old. The COUNT function calculates the number of invoices by counting the number of entries in column A.

6. **With cell D23 selected, click Σ ▾, click COUNT, select the range A7:A13, then press [Enter]**

   Cell D23 confirms that there are seven invoices. Compare your worksheet with Figure E-14.

7. **Enter your name in cell A26, save the workbook, then print the worksheet**

TABLE E-3: Commonly used statistical functions

function	worksheet action	function	worksheet action
AVERAGE	Calculates an average value	MAX	Finds the largest value
COUNT	Counts cells that contain numbers	MIN	Finds the smallest value
COUNTA	Counts cells that contain nonblank entries	MEDIAN	Finds the middle value

FIGURE E-13: Worksheet with age of oldest invoice

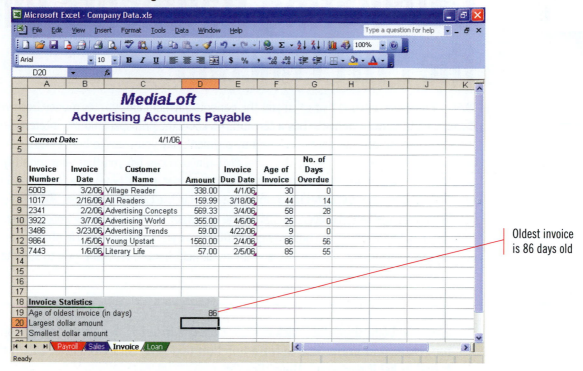

Oldest invoice is 86 days old

FIGURE E-14: Worksheet with invoice statistics

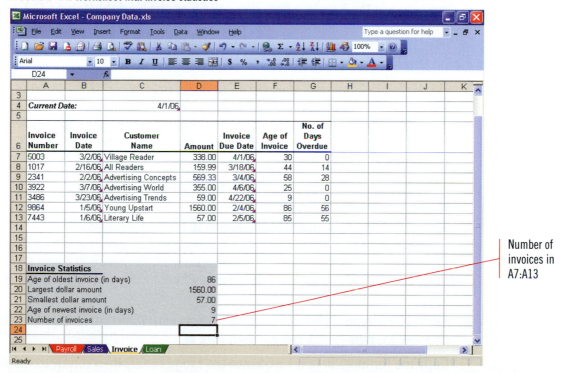

Number of invoices in A7:A13

Clues to Use

Using the COUNTA function

The COUNT function counts the number of cells that contain numeric data. If the cell entries that you are trying to count contain nonnumerical data (such as invoice numbers with text entries), the COUNT function does not work and displays a count of zero. There is another function, COUNTA, that counts the number of cells that are not empty and therefore can be used to count the number of entries that contain text.

Calculating Payments with the PMT Function

PMT is a financial function that calculates the periodic payment amount for money borrowed. For example, if you want to borrow money to buy a car, and you know the principal amount, interest rate, and loan term, the PMT function can calculate your monthly payment. Say you want to borrow $15,000 at 8.5% interest and pay the loan off in five years. The Excel PMT function can tell you that your monthly payment will be $307.75 The parts of the PMT function are: PMT(rate, nper, pv, fv, type). See Figure E-15 for an illustration of a PMT function that calculates the monthly payment in the car loan example. For several months, MediaLoft management has been discussing the expansion of the San Diego store. Jim has obtained quotes from three different lenders on borrowing $29,000 to begin the expansion. He obtained loan quotes from a commercial bank, a venture capitalist, and an investment banker. He wants you to summarize the information, using the Excel PMT function.

STEPS

1. Click the **Loan sheet tab**, click cell **E5**, click the **Insert Function button** on the formula bar, enter **pmt** in the Search for a function text box, click **Go**, click **PMT** in the Select a function list if necessary, then click **OK**

2. Move the Function Arguments dialog box so you can see row 5 of the worksheet; with the cursor in the Rate text box, click cell **C5** on the worksheet, type **/12**, then press **[Tab]**

   You must divide the annual interest by 12 because you are calculating monthly, not annual, payments.

> **QUICK TIP**
> You must be consistent about the units you use for rate and nper. If you express nper as the number of monthly payments, then you must express the interest rate as a monthly rate.

3. With the cursor in the Nper text box, click cell **D5**; click the **Pv text box**, click cell **B5**, then click **OK**

   The FV and Type are optional arguments. Note that the payment of ($581.10) in cell E5 appears in red, indicating that it is a negative amount. Excel displays the result of a PMT function as a negative value to reflect the negative cash flow the loan represents to the borrower. To show the monthly payment as a positive number, you place a minus sign in front of the Pv cell reference in the function.

4. Edit cell **E5** so it reads **=PMT(C5/12,D5,–B5)**, then click the **Enter button**

   A positive value of $581.10 now appears in cell E5. See Figure E-16. You can use the same formula to generate the monthly payments for the other loans.

5. With cell **E5** selected, drag the fill handle to fill the range **E6:E7**

   A monthly payment of $895.44 for the venture capitalist loan appears in cell E6. A monthly payment of $1,296.43 for the investment banker loan appears in cell E7. The loans with shorter terms have much higher payments. You will not know the entire financial picture until you calculate the total payments and total interest for each lender.

6. Click cell **F5**, type **=**, click cell **E5**, type *****, click cell **D5**, then press **[Tab]**; in cell **G5**, type **=**, click cell **F5**, type **–**, click cell **B5**, then click

> **QUICK TIP**
> You can evaluate and check for errors in worksheet formulas using the Formula Auditing toolbar. Right-click any toolbar and click Formula Auditing to display the toolbar.

7. Copy the formulas in cells **F5:G5** into the range **F6:G7**, then return to cell **A1**

   Compare your results with those in Figure E-17. You can experiment with different interest rates, loan amounts, or terms for any one of the lenders; the PMT function generates a new set of values automatically.

8. Enter your name in cell **A13**, save the workbook, then preview and print the worksheet

FIGURE E-15: Example of PMT function for car loan

$$PMT(0.085/12, 60, 15000) = \$307.75$$

Interest rate per period (rate)   Number of payments (nper)   Present value of loan amount (pv)   Monthly payment calculated

FIGURE E-16: PMT function calculating monthly loan payment

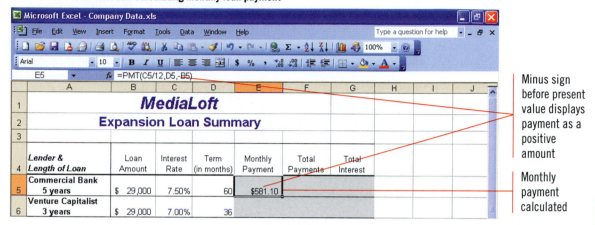

Minus sign before present value displays payment as a positive amount

Monthly payment calculated

FIGURE E-17: Completed worksheet

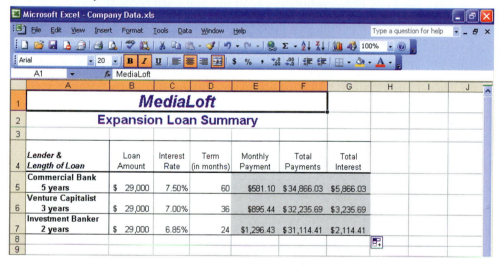

Clues to Use

Calculating future value with the FV function

You can use the FV (Future Value) function to determine the amount of money a given monthly investment will amount to, at a given interest rate after a given number of payment periods. The syntax is similar to that of the PMT function: FV(rate,nper,pmt,pv,type). For example, suppose you want to invest $1000 every month for the next 12 months into an account that pays 12% a year, and you want to know how much you will have at the end of 12 months (that is, its future value). You enter the function FV(.01,12,–1000), and Excel returns the value $12,682.50 as the future value of your investment. As with the PMT function, the units for the rate and nper must be consistent. If you made monthly payments on a three-year loan at 6% annual interest, you use the rate .06/12 and 36 periods (12*3). The arguments pv and type are optional; pv is the present value, or the total amount the series of payments is worth now. If you omit it, Excel assumes the pv is 0. The "type" argument indicates when the payments are made; 0 is the end of the period, and 1 is the beginning of the period.

Displaying and Printing Formula Contents

Excel usually displays the result of formula calculations in the worksheet area and displays formula contents for the active cell in the formula bar. However, you can instruct Excel to display the formulas directly in the worksheet cells in which they were entered. You can document worksheet formulas by first displaying the formulas, then printing them. These formula printouts are valuable paper-based worksheet documentation. Because formulas are often longer than their corresponding values, landscape orientation is the best choice for printing formulas. Jim wants you to produce a formula printout to submit with the Loan worksheet.

STEPS

1. **Click Tools on the menu bar, click Options, then click the View tab if necessary**

   The View tab of the Options dialog box appears, as shown in Figure E-18.

> **QUICK TIP**
>
> The worksheet formulas can also be displayed by selecting Formula Auditing Mode from the Formula Auditing option on the Tools menu.

2. **Under Window options, click the Formulas check box to select it, then click OK**

   The columns widen and retain their original formats. If the Formula Auditing toolbar is displayed, you can close it.

3. **Scroll horizontally to bring columns E through G into view**

   Instead of displaying formula results in the cells, Excel shows the actual formulas and automatically adjusts the column widths to accommodate them.

4. **Click the Print Preview button 🔍 on the Standard toolbar**

   The status bar reads Preview: Page 1 of 2, indicating that the worksheet will print on two pages. You want to print it on one page and include the row number and column letter headings.

> **QUICK TIP**
>
> All Page Setup options—such as Landscape orientation and Fit to scaling—apply to the active worksheet and are saved with the workbook.

5. **Click Setup in the Print Preview window, then click the Page tab if necessary**

6. **Under Orientation, click the Landscape option button; then under Scaling, click the Fit to option button and note that the wide and tall check boxes contain the number "1"**

   Selecting Landscape instructs Excel to print the worksheet sideways on the page. The Fit to option ensures that the document is printed on a single page.

> **QUICK TIP**
>
> To print row and column labels on every page of a multiple-page worksheet, click the Sheet tab, and fill in the Rows to repeat at top and the Columns to repeat at left in the Print titles section.

7. **Click the Sheet tab, in the Print section, click the Row and column headings check box to select it, click OK, then position the Zoom pointer 🔍 over column A and click**

   The worksheet formulas now appear on a single page, in landscape orientation, with row (number) and column (letter) headings. See Figure E-19.

8. **Click Print in the Print Preview window, then click OK**

   After you retrieve the printout, you want to return the worksheet to displaying formula results. You can do this easily by using a key combination.

9. **Press [Ctrl][`] to redisplay formula results**

   [Ctrl][`] (grave accent mark) toggles between displaying formula results and displaying formula contents.

10. **Save the workbook, then close it and exit Excel**

    The completed payroll worksheet is displayed in Figure E-3; the completed sales worksheet is displayed in Figure E-7; the completed invoice worksheet is shown in Figure E-14, and the completed loan worksheets are displayed in Figures E-17 and E-19.

FIGURE E-18: View tab of the Options dialog box

Select this option to view formulas

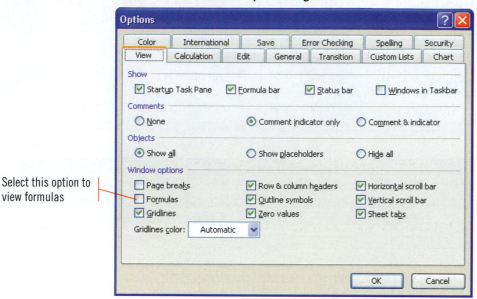

FIGURE E-19: Print Preview window

Column headings

Row headings

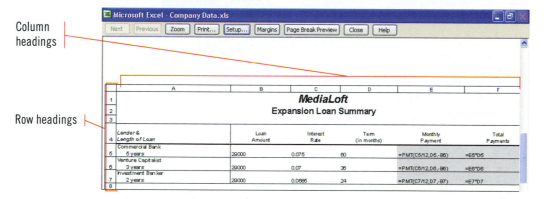

Clues to Use

Setting margins and alignment when printing part of a worksheet

You can set custom margins to print smaller sections of a worksheet. Select the range you want to print, click File on the menu bar, click Print, in the Print what section click Selection, then click Preview. In the Print Preview window, click Setup, then click the Margins tab. See Figure E-20. Double-click the margin numbers and type new ones. Use the Center on page check boxes to center the range horizontally or vertically. If you plan to print the range again, save the view after you print: click View on the menu bar, click Custom Views, click Add, then type a view name and click OK.

FIGURE E-20: Margins tab in the Page Setup dialog box

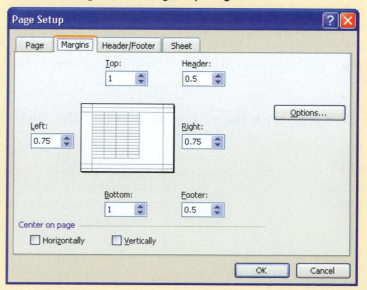

Practice

▼ CONCEPTS REVIEW

FIGURE E-21

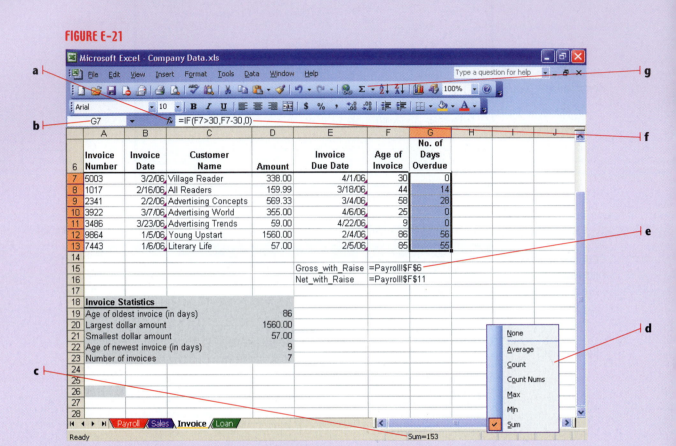

1. Which element points to the area where a name is assigned to a cell?
2. Which element points to a conditional formula?
3. Which element points to the AutoCalculate options?
4. Which element points to a list of the names assigned in the worksheet?
5. Which element do you click to insert a function into a worksheet?
6. Which element points to the result of an AutoCalculate option?
7. Which element do you click to enter a total of adjacent values into a blank cell?

Match each term with the statement that best describes it.

8. Style
9. COUNTA
10. test_cond
11. COUNT
12. pv

a. Function used to count the number of nonblank entries
b. A combination of formatting characteristics
c. Part of the PMT function that represents the loan amount
d. Part of the IF function in which the conditions are stated
e. Function used to count the number of numerical entries

Select the best answer from the list of choices.

13. To generate a positive payment value when using the PMT function, you must:
    a. Enter the function arguments as positive values.
    b. Enter the function arguments as negative values.
    c. Enter the interest rate divisor as a negative value.
    d. Enter the amount being borrowed as a negative value.

14. When you enter the rate and nper arguments in a PMT function, you must:
    a. Be consistent in the units used.
    b. Multiply both units by 12.
    c. Divide both values by 12.
    d. Use monthly units instead of annual units.

15. To express conditions such as less than or equal to, you can use a(n):
    a. Statistical function.
    b. PMT function.
    c. AutoCalculate formula.
    d. Comparison operator.

16. Which of the following statements is false?
    a. You can use only existing number and date formats in Excel.
    b. You can create custom number and date formats in Excel.
    c. Dates are stored in Excel as serial numbers.
    d. m/d/yy is an Excel date format.

▼ SKILLS REVIEW

1. **Create a formula with several operators.**
   a. Start Excel, open the Data File EX E-2.xls from the drive and folder where your Data Files are stored, then save the workbook as **Manager Bonuses**.
   b. On the Bonuses worksheet, select cell C13 using the Go To command.
   c. Enter the formula **.2*AVERAGE(C4:C10)**.
   d. Enter the formula **.1*C13** in cell **C14**.
   e. Use the Paste Special command to paste the values and formats in B4:B10 to G4:G10, then save your work.

2. **Use names in a formula.**
   a. Name cell C13 **Dept_Bonus**.
   b. Name cell C14 **Project_Bonus**.
   c. Select the range C4:C10 and name it **Base_Pay**.
   d. In cell E4, enter the formula **Dept_Bonus*D4+Project_Bonus**.
   e. Copy the formula in cell E4 into the range E5:E10.
   f. Format range E4:E10 with the Comma style, using the Style dialog box.
   g. Select the range E4:E10, if necessary, and name it **Bonus_Total**.
   h. In cell F4, enter a formula that sums Base_Pay and Bonus_Total.
   i. Copy the formula in cell F4 into the range F5:F10.
   j. Format range F4:F10 with the Comma style, using the Style dialog box.
   k. Save your work.

3. **Generate multiple totals with AutoSum.**
   a. Select range E4:F11.
   b. Enter the totals using AutoSum.
   c. Check the formulas in cells E11:F11 to make sure they are correct.
   d. Format range E11:F11 with the Currency style, using the Style dialog box.
   e. Enter your name in cell A18, save your work, then preview and print this worksheet.

▼ SKILLS REVIEW (CONTINUED)

4. Use dates in calculations.

   a. Make the Merit Pay sheet active.

   b. In cell D6, enter the formula **B6+183**.

   c. Copy the formula in cell D6 into the range D7:D14.

   d. Use the NOW function to insert the date and time in cell A3.

   e. In cell E18, enter the text **Last Pay Date for Year**, and in cell G18, use the Date function to enter the date **12/31/2006**.

   f. Save your work.

5. Build a conditional formula with the IF function.

   a. In cell F6, use the Function dialog box to enter the formula **IF(C6=5,E6*0.05,0)**.

   b. Copy the formula in cell F6 into the range F7:F14.

   c. Make sure the total in cell F15 is correct.

   d. Apply the Comma style with no decimal places to F6:F14.

   e. Save your work.

6. Use statistical functions.

   a. In cell C19, enter a function to calculate the average salary in the range E6:E14.

   b. In cell C20, enter a function to calculate the largest bonus in the range F6:F14.

   c. In cell C21, enter a function to calculate the lowest performance rating in the range C6:C14.

   d. In cell C22, enter a function to calculate the number of entries in range A6:A14.

   e. Apply the Comma style with no decimal places to C19:C22. Compare your results with Figure E-22.

   f. Enter your name into cell A28, then save, preview, and print the worksheet.

FIGURE E-22

18	**Department Statistics**	
19	Average Salary	30,560
20	Highest Bonus	1,825
21	Lowest Performance Rating	3
22	Number of Employees	9
23		
24		
25		
26		
27		
28		
29		
30		

◄◄ ◄ ► ►◄ \ Bonuses \ **Merit Pay** \ Loan \

Ready

7. Calculate payments with the PMT function.

   a. Make the Loan sheet active.

   b. In cell B9, use the Insert Function dialog box to enter the formula **PMT(B5/12,B6,–B4)**.

   c. In cell B10, enter the formula **B9*B6**.

   d. AutoFit column B, if necessary.

   e. In cell B11, enter the formula **B10–B4**.

   f. Enter your name in cell A15, then save, preview, and print the worksheet.

8. Display and print formula contents.

   a. Use the View tab in the Options dialog box to display formulas in the worksheet. If the Formula Auditing toolbar opens, you can close it.

   b. Adjust the column widths as necessary.

   c. Save, preview, and print this worksheet on one page in landscape orientation with the row and column headings.

   d. Redisplay the formula results in the worksheet, then resize columns as necessary.

   e. Close the workbook, then exit Excel.

▼ INDEPENDENT CHALLENGE 1

As manager of Mike's Ice Cream Parlor, you have been asked to create a worksheet that totals the monthly sales of all store products. Your monthly report should include the following:

- Sales totals for the current month for each product
- Sales totals for the last month for each product
- The percent change in sales from last month to this month

To document the report further, you decide to include a printout of the worksheet formulas.

a. Start Excel, open the Data File EX E-3.xls from the drive and folder where your Data Files are stored, then save it as **Mike's Sales**.

b. Use the TODAY function to enter today's date in cell A3.

c. Create and apply a custom format for the date entry.

d. Use AutoSum to enter totals for each week, and current month totals for each product.

e. Calculate the percent change in sales from the previous month for regular ice cream. (*Hint*: The formula in words would be (Current Month-Last Month)/Last Month.)

f. Copy the percent change formula down the column for the other products using AutoFill, then format the column with the Percent style using the Formatting toolbar.

g. Apply a Comma style with no decimal places to all weekly figures and totals, using the Formatting toolbar.

h. Enter your name into cell A15, then save, preview, and print the worksheet on a single page.

i. Display and preview the worksheet formulas, then print the formulas in landscape orientation on one page with row and column headings.

j. Close the workbook without saving the changes for displaying formulas, then exit Excel.

▼ INDEPENDENT CHALLENGE 2

You are an auditor with a certified public accounting firm. Fly Away, a manufacturer of skating products, has contacted you to audit its financial records. The management at Fly Away is considering opening a branch in Great Britain and needs its records audited to prepare the business plan. The managers at Fly Away have asked you to assist them in preparing their year-end sales summary as part of this audit. Specifically, they want to add expenses and show the percent of annual expenses that each expense category represents. They also want to show what percent of annual sales each expense category represents. You will include a formula calculating the difference between sales and expenses and another formula calculating expenses divided by sales. The expense categories and their respective dollar amounts are as follows: Building Lease $50,000; Equipment $208,000; Office $25,000; Salary $355,000; Taxes $310,000. Use these expense amounts to prepare the year-end sales and expenses summary for Fly Away.

a. Start Excel, open the Data File EX E-4.xls from the drive and folder where your Data Files are stored, then save the workbook as **Fly Away Sales**.

b. Name the cell containing the formula for total annual expenses **Annual_Expenses**. Use the name Annual_Expenses in cell C12 to create a formula calculating percent of annual expenses. Copy this formula as necessary and apply the Percent style. Add a formula that sums all the values for percent of annual expenses, which should equal 100%.

c. In cell D12, enter a formula calculating the percent of annual sales each expense category represents. Use the name **Annual_Sales** in the formula (cell B9 has been named Annual_Sales). Copy this formula as necessary and apply the Percent style. Include a formula that sums all the values for percent of annual sales.

d. Enter the formula calculating Net Profit in cell B19, using the names Annual_Sales and Annual_Expenses.

e. Enter the formula for Expenses as a percent of sales in cell B20, using the names Annual_Sales and Annual_Expenses.

f. Format cell B19 as Currency with two decimal places. Format cell B20 using the Percentage style with two decimal places. Widen the columns as necessary to display cell contents.

g. Enter your name into cell A22.

▼ INDEPENDENT CHALLENGE 2 (CONTINUED)

Advanced Challenge Exercise

■ Display the Formula Auditing toolbar and check the worksheet for errors.
■ Use the Formula Auditing toolbar to evaluate the formula in cell B20.
■ Close the Formula Auditing toolbar.

h. Save, preview, and print the worksheet.
i. Close the workbook, then exit Excel.

▼ INDEPENDENT CHALLENGE 3

As the owner of Custom Fit, a general contracting firm specializing in home-storage projects, you are facing a business challenge at your firm. Because jobs are taking longer than expected, you decide to take out a $10,000 loan to purchase some new power tools. You check three loan sources: the Small Business Administration (SBA), your local bank, and a consortium of investors. The SBA will lend you the money at 7% interest, but you have to pay it off in three years. The local bank offers you the loan at 7.75% interest over four years. The consortium offers you a 6.75% loan, but they require you to pay it back in two years. To analyze all three loan options, you decide to build a loan summary worksheet. Using the loan terms provided, build a worksheet summarizing your options.

a. Start Excel, open a new workbook, then save it as **Custom Fit Loan Options** in the drive and folder where your Data Files are stored.
b. Enter today's date in cell A3, using the TODAY function.
c. Using Figure E-23 as a guide, enter labels and worksheet data for the three loan sources.
d. Enter the monthly payment formula for your first loan source (making sure to show the payment as a positive amount), copy the formula as appropriate, then name the range containing the monthly payment formulas **Monthly_Payment**.

FIGURE E-23

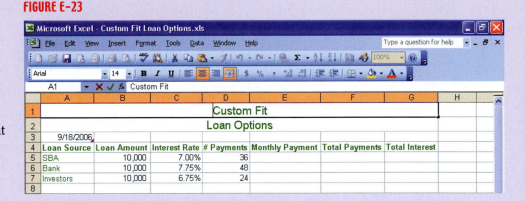

e. Name the cell range containing the number of payments, **Number_Payments**.
f. Enter the formula for total payments for your first loan source using the named ranges **Monthly_Payment** and **Number_Payments**, then copy the formula as necessary.
g. Name the cell range containing the formulas for Total payments, **Total_Payments**. Name the cell range containing the loan amounts, **Loan_Amount**.
h. Enter the formula for total interest for your first loan source using the named ranges **Total_Payments** and **Loan_Amount**, then copy the formula as necessary.
i. Format the worksheet using formatting appropriate to the worksheet purpose, then enter your name in cell A14.

Advanced Challenge Exercise

■ Paste the range names for the worksheet starting in cell E9.
■ Name the cell range C5:C7 as Interest_Rate. Name the range G5:G7 as Total_Interest.
■ Delete the pasted list of names and paste the new list.

j. Save, preview, and print the worksheet on a single page. Print the worksheet formulas showing row and column headings using landscape orientation. Do not save the worksheet with the formula settings.
k. Close the workbook then exit Excel.

▼ INDEPENDENT CHALLENGE 4

You have been asked to research IRA rates for your company's human resources department. The company plans to deposit $4000 in the employees' accounts at the beginning of each year. You have been asked to research current rates at financial institutions. You will use the Web to find this information. You will use the rate information to determine the value of the deposited money after five years.

a. Open your browser, then go to the search engine of your choice and search for **IRA rates** in the search text box. Find IRA rates offered by three institutions for a $4000 deposit, then write down the institution name, the rate, and the minimum deposit in the table below.

b. Start Excel, open a new workbook, then save it as **IRA Rates** in the drive and folder where your Data Files are stored.

c. Enter the column headings, row headings, and, research results from the table below into your IRA Rates workbook.

IRA Worksheet

Institution	Rate	Minimum Deposit	Number of Years	Amount Deposited (Yearly)	Future Value
			5	4000	
			5	4000	
			5	4000	
Highest Rate					
Average Rate					
Highest Future Value					

d. Use the FV function to calculate the future value of a $4000 yearly deposit over 35 years for each institution, making sure it appears as a positive number. Assume that the payments are made at the beginning of the period, so the Type argument equals 1.

e. Use Excel functions to enter the highest rate, the average rate, and the highest future value into the workbook.

f. Enter your name in cell A15, then save, preview, and print the worksheet on a single page with one inch left and right margins.

g. Display and print the formulas for the worksheet on a single page using landscape orientation. Do not save the worksheet with the formulas displayed.

h. Close the workbook then exit Excel.

Excel 2003

▼ VISUAL WORKSHOP

Create the worksheet shown in Figure E-24. (*Hints:* Use IF formulas to enter the bonus amounts. An employee with a performance rating of seven or higher receives a bonus of $1000. If the rating is less than seven, no bonus is awarded. The summary information in cells A15:C18 uses the SUM function and statistical functions.) Enter your name in cell A20, and save the workbook as **Bonus Pay**. Preview and then print the worksheet.

FIGURE E-24

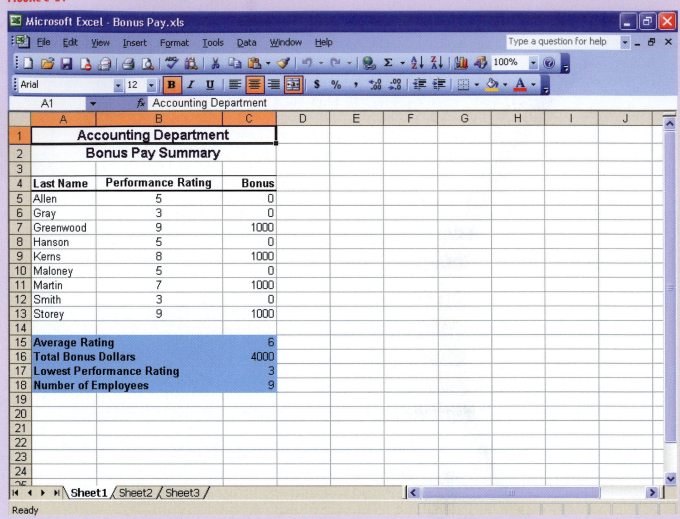

Managing Workbooks and Preparing Them for the Web

OBJECTIVES

Freeze columns and rows

Insert and delete worksheets

Consolidate data with 3-D references

Hide and protect worksheet areas

Save custom views of a worksheet

Control page breaks and page numbering

Create a hyperlink between Excel files

Save an Excel file as a Web page

If you have a SAM user profile, you may have access to hands-on instruction, practice, and assessment of the skills covered in this unit. Log in to your SAM account and go to your assignments page to see what your instructor has assigned.

In this unit you will learn several Excel features to help you manage and print workbook data. You will also learn how to prepare workbooks for publication on the World Wide Web. The MediaLoft Accounting Department asks its marketing director Jim Fernandez to design a timecard summary worksheet to track salary costs for hourly workers. When the worksheet is complete, the Accounting Department will add the rest of the employees and place it on the MediaLoft intranet site for review by store managers. Jim asks you to design a worksheet using some employees from the MediaLoft Houston store. He wants you to save the worksheet as a Web page for viewing on the company's intranet site.

Freezing Columns and Rows

As rows and columns fill up with data, you might need to scroll through the worksheet to add, delete, modify, and view information, and the column or row headings may scroll out of view. Looking at information without row or column labels can be confusing. In Excel, you can temporarily freeze columns and rows, so you can keep the headings in view as you scroll. **Panes** are the columns and rows that **freeze**, or remain in place, while you scroll through your worksheet. ✎ Jim asks you to check the total hours worked, hourly pay rate, and total pay for salespeople Paul Cristifano and Virginia Young. Because the worksheet is becoming more difficult to read as its size increases, you want to freeze the column and row labels.

STEPS

1. **Start Excel if necessary, open the Data File EX F-1.xls from the drive and folder where your Data Files are stored, then save it as Timecard Summary**

2. **Scroll through the Monday worksheet to view the data, then click cell D6**

    You select cell D6 because Excel freezes the columns to the left and the rows above the selected cell. You want to freeze columns A, B, and C as well as rows 1 through 5. By doing so, you can see each employee's last name, first name, and timecard number on the screen when you scroll to the right, and you can also read the labels in rows 1 through 5 when you scroll down.

3. **Click Window on the menu bar, then click Freeze Panes**

    A thin line appears along the column border to the left of the active cell, and another line appears along the row above the active cell, indicating that columns A through C and rows 1 through 5 are frozen.

4. **Scroll to the right until columns A through C and L through O are visible**

    Because columns A, B, and C are frozen, they remain on the screen; columns D through K are temporarily hidden from view. Notice that the information you are looking for in row 13 (last name, total hours, hourly pay rate, and total pay for Paul Cristifano) is readily available. Paul's data appears to be correct, but you still need to check Virginia Young's information.

5. **Scroll down until row 26 is visible**

    In addition to columns A through C, rows 1 through 5 remain on the screen. See Figure F-1. You are now able to verify Virginia Young's information. Even though a pane is frozen, you can click in the frozen area of the worksheet and edit the contents of the cells there, if necessary.

6. **Press [Ctrl][Home]**

    Because the panes are frozen, the cell pointer moves to cell D6, not A1.

7. **Click Window on the menu bar, then click Unfreeze Panes**

    The freeze lines no longer appear and the columns and rows are no longer frozen.

8. **Press [Ctrl][Home] to return to cell A1, then save the workbook**

Clues to Use

Viewing and arranging worksheets

In a multiple-sheet workbook, you can use the scrolling buttons to the left of the horizontal scroll bar. To scroll several tabs at once, press [Shift] while clicking one of the middle tab scrolling buttons. You can view multiple worksheets by clicking the sheet you want to view and then clicking New Window on the Window menu. Repeat this for each sheet you want to view. Each sheet becomes a button on the taskbar. To arrange the windows, click Arrange on the Window menu and choose a layout.

FIGURE F-1: Scrolled worksheet with frozen rows and columns

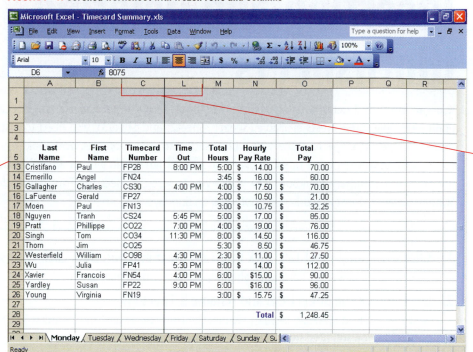

Break in row numbers due to frozen rows 1 through 5

Break in column letters due to frozen columns A through C

Clues to Use

Splitting the worksheet into multiple panes

Excel lets you split the worksheet area into vertical and/or horizontal panes, so that you can click inside any one pane and scroll to locate information in that pane while the other panes remain in place. See Figure F-2. To split a worksheet area into multiple panes, drag the split box (the small box at the top of the vertical scroll bar or at the right end of the horizontal scroll bar) in the direction you want the split to appear. To remove the split, move the pointer over the split until the pointer changes to a double-headed arrow ⇕, then double-click.

FIGURE F-2: Worksheet split into two horizontal and two vertical panes

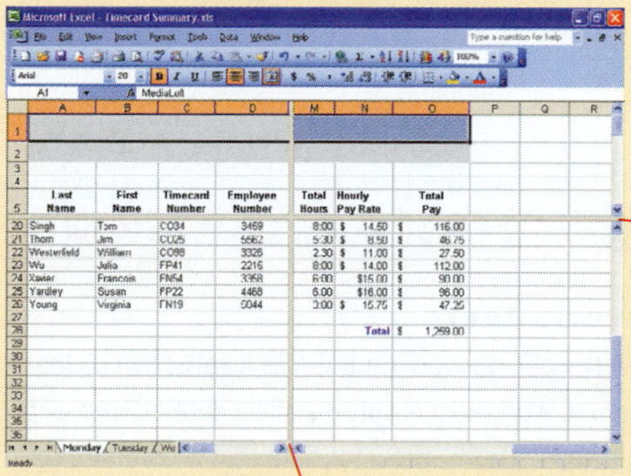

Horizontal split box

Vertical split box

Inserting and Deleting Worksheets

You can insert and delete worksheets in a workbook at any time. For example, because new workbooks open with only three sheets available (Sheet1, Sheet2, and Sheet3), you need to insert at least one more sheet if you want to have four quarterly worksheets in an annual budget workbook. You can do this by using commands on the menu bar or shortcut menu. ▦▦▦▦▦ Jim was in a hurry when he added the sheet tabs to the Timecard Summary workbook. He wants you to insert a sheet for Thursday and delete the sheet for Sunday because Houston workers do not work on Sundays.

STEPS

QUICK TIP

You can copy a selected worksheet by clicking Edit on the menu bar, then clicking Move or Copy Sheet. Choose the sheet you want the copy to precede, click the Create a copy check box, then click OK.

1. **Click the Friday sheet tab, click Insert on the menu bar, then click Worksheet**

   Excel inserts a new sheet tab labeled Sheet1 to the left of the Friday sheet.

2. **Double-click the Sheet1 tab and rename it Thursday**

   Now the tabs read Monday, Tuesday, Wednesday, Thursday, Friday, and Saturday. The tab for the Summary is not visible. You still need to delete the Sunday worksheet.

3. **Right-click the Sunday sheet tab, then click Delete on the shortcut menu shown in Figure F-3**

   The shortcut menu allows you to insert, delete, rename, move, or copy sheets; it also allows you to select all the sheets and change the tab color of a worksheet.

4. **Move the mouse pointer over any tab scrolling button, then right-click**

   Excel opens a shortcut menu of the worksheets in the active workbook. Compare your list with Figure F-4.

5. **Click Monday on the shortcut menu, then save the workbook**

Clues to Use

Grouping worksheets

You can group worksheets to work on them as a collection so that data entered into one worksheet is automatically entered into all of the selected worksheets. This is useful for data that is common to every sheet of a workbook such as headers and footers. Grouping worksheets can also be used to print multiple worksheets at one time. To group worksheets, press and hold [Ctrl] and click the tabs for the sheets you want to group. If the sheets that you want to group are adjacent, then click the first sheet and hold [Shift] while clicking the last sheet in the group.

FIGURE F-3: Worksheet shortcut menu

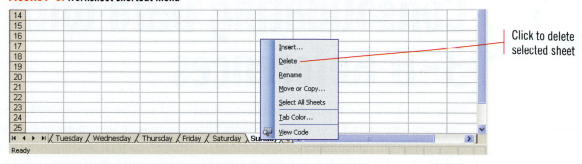

Click to delete selected sheet

FIGURE F-4: Workbook with worksheets menu

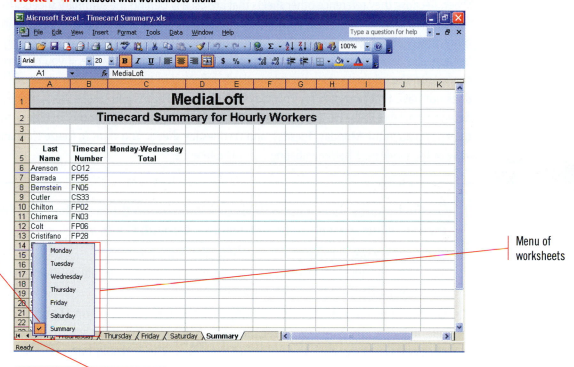

Active worksheet

Menu of worksheets

Right-click any tab scrolling button to display the menu of worksheets

Clues to Use

Specifying headers and footers

As you prepare a workbook for others to view, it is helpful to provide as much data as possible about the worksheets, such as the number of pages, who created it, and when. You can do this easily in a **header** or **footer**, which is information that prints at the top or bottom of each printed page. Headers and footers are visible on the screen only in Print Preview. To add a header, for example, click View on the menu bar, click Header and Footer, then click Custom Header. You see a dialog box similar to that in Figure F-5. Both the header and the footer are divided into three sections, and you can enter information in any or all of them. You can type information, such as your name, and click the icons to enter the page number 🔲, total pages 🔲, date 🔲, time 🔲, file path 🔲, filename 🔲, or sheet name 🔲. You can insert a picture by clicking the Insert Picture icon 🔲, and you can format the picture by clicking the Format picture icon 🔲 and selecting formatting options. When you click an

icon, Excel inserts a symbol in the footer section containing an ampersand (&) and the element name in brackets. When you are finished, click OK, click the Print Preview button on the Header/Footer tab to see your header and footer, then click Close.

FIGURE F-5: Header dialog box

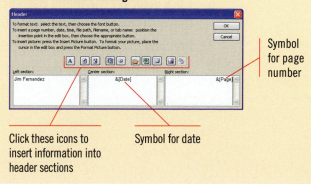

Symbol for page number

Click these icons to insert information into header sections

Symbol for date

Consolidating Data with 3-D References

When you want to summarize similar data that exists in different sheets or workbooks, you can combine and display it in one sheet. For example, you might have departmental sales figures on four different store sheets that you want to **consolidate** on one summary sheet showing total departmental sales for all stores. The best way to consolidate data is to use cell references to the various sheets on a consolidation, or summary, sheet. Because they reference other sheets that are usually behind the summary sheet, such references effectively create another dimension in the workbook and are called **3-D references**. You can reference data in other sheets and in other workbooks. Referencing cells is a better method than retyping calculated results because the data values on which calculated totals depend might change. If you reference the values, any changes to the original values are automatically reflected in the consolidation sheet. Although Jim does not have timecard data for Thursday and Friday, he wants you to use the Summary sheet to consolidate the available data. He asks you to do this by creating a formula on the Summary sheet that adds the total pay data in the Monday, Tuesday, and Wednesday sheets. You want to freeze the panes to improve the view of the worksheet before initiating the 3-D reference.

STEPS

1. **On the Monday sheet, click cell D6, click Window on the menu bar, click Freeze Panes, then scroll horizontally to bring columns L through O into view**

2. **Right-click a tab scrolling button, then click Summary**
   Because the Summary sheet (which is the consolidation sheet) will contain the reference, the cell pointer must reside there when you initiate the reference.

3. **On the Summary sheet, click cell C6, click the AutoSum button Σ on the Standard toolbar, activate the Monday sheet, press and hold [Shift] and click the Wednesday sheet tab, click cell O6, then click the Enter button ✔ on the formula bar**
   The Summary sheet becomes active, and the formula bar reads =SUM(Monday:Wednesday!O6). See Figure F-6. Monday:Wednesday references the Monday, Tuesday and Wednesday sheets. The ! (exclamation point) is an **external reference indicator**, meaning that the cells referenced are outside the active sheet; O6 is the actual cell reference in the external sheets. The result, $168.80, appears in cell C6 of the Summary sheet, showing the sum of the total pay referenced in cell O6 of the Monday, Tuesday, and Wednesday sheets.

4. **In the Summary sheet, copy cell C6 into cells C7:C26**
   Excel copies the 3-D formula in cell C6. You can test a consolidation reference by changing one cell value on which the formula is based and seeing if the formula result changes.

5. **Activate the Monday sheet, edit cell L6 to read 6:30 PM, then activate the Summary sheet**
   The sum of Beryl Arenson's pay was automatically updated in the Summary sheet. See Figure F-7.

6. **Click View on the menu bar, click Header and Footer, click Custom Footer, enter your name in the Left section text box, click OK, then click OK**

7. **Preview the worksheet, then print it**

8. **Activate the Monday sheet, unfreeze the panes, then save the workbook**

FIGURE F-6: Worksheet showing total pay

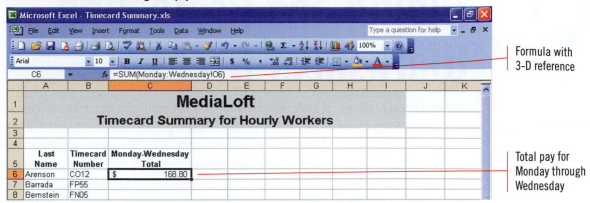

Formula with 3-D reference

Total pay for Monday through Wednesday

FIGURE F-7: Summary worksheet with updated total

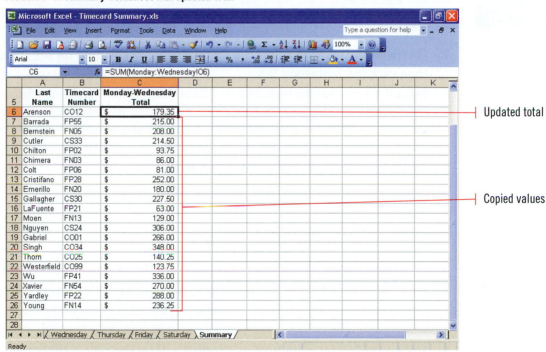

Updated total

Copied values

Clues to Use

Linking data between workbooks

Just as you can reference data between cells in a worksheet and between sheets, you can dynamically reference data between workbooks so that changes made in referenced cells in one workbook are reflected in the consolidation sheet in the other workbook. This dynamic referencing is called **linking**. To link a single cell between workbooks, open both workbooks, select the cell to receive the linked data, type = (the equal sign), select the cell in the other workbook containing the data to be linked, then press [Enter]. Excel automatically inserts the name of the referenced workbook in the cell reference. For example, if the linked data is contained in cell C7 of worksheet New in the Products workbook, the cell entry reads =′[Product.xls]New′!$C$7. To perform calculations, enter formulas on the consolidation sheet using cells in the supporting sheets. If you are linking more than one cell, you can copy the linked data to the Clipboard, select the upper-left cell in the workbook to receive the link, click Edit on the menu bar, click Paste Special, then click Paste Link.

UNIT
F
Excel 2003

Hiding and Protecting Worksheet Areas

Worksheets may contain sensitive information that you don't want others to view or alter. To protect such information, Excel gives you two options. You can **hide** the formulas in selected cells (or rows, columns, or entire sheets), and you can **lock** selected cells, in which case other people are able to view the data (values, numbers, labels, formulas, etc.) in those cells, but not change it. See Table F-1 for a list of options you can use to protect a worksheet. You set the lock and hide options in the Format Cells dialog box. Excel locks all cells by default, but this protection does not take effect until you activate the Excel protection feature on the Tools menu. A common worksheet protection strategy is to unlock cells in which data will be changed, sometimes referred to as the **data entry area**, and to lock cells in which the data should not be changed. Then, when you protect the worksheet, the unlocked areas can still be changed. 🎨 Because Jim will assign an employee to enter the sensitive timecard information into the worksheet, he wants you to hide and lock selected areas of the worksheet.

STEPS

1. **On the Monday sheet, select the range I6:L26, click Format on the menu bar, click Cells, then click the Protection tab**

   Notice that the Locked box in the Protection tab is already checked, as shown in Figure F-8. The Locked check box is selected by default, meaning that all the cells in a new workbook start out locked. (Note, however, that cell locking is not applied unless the protection feature is also activated. The protection feature is inactive by default.) You do not want the Time In and Time Out cells to be locked when the protection feature is activated.

2. **Click the Locked check box to deselect it, then click OK**

   Excel stores time as a fraction of a 24-hour day. In the formula for total pay, hours must be multiplied by 24. This concept might be confusing to the data entry person, so you hide the formulas.

3. **Select range O6:O26, click Format on the menu bar, click Cells, click the Protection tab, click the Hidden check box to select it, then click OK**

   The data remains the same (unhidden and unlocked) until you set the protection in the next step.

QUICK TIP

To turn off worksheet protection, click Tools on the menu bar, point to Protection, then click Unprotect Sheet. If prompted for a password, type the password, then click OK. Remember that passwords are case sensitive. If you assign the password "phone" and try to open the workbook using "Phone" or "PHONE," you will not be able to open the workbook.

4. **Click Tools on the menu bar, point to Protection, then click Protect Sheet**

   The Protect Sheet dialog box opens. The default options allow you to protect the worksheet while allowing users to select locked or unlocked cells only. You choose not to use a password.

5. **Make sure Protect worksheet and contents of locked cells is checked in the Protect Sheet dialog box, then click OK**

   You are ready to test the new worksheet protection.

6. **Click cell O6**

   The formula bar is empty because of the hidden formula setting.

7. **In cell O6, type T to confirm that locked cells cannot be changed, then click OK**

   When you attempt to change a locked cell, a message box reminds you of the protected cell's read-only status. See Figure F-9.

8. **Click cell I6, type 9, and notice that Excel allows you to begin the entry, press [Esc] to cancel the entry, then save the workbook**

   Because you unlocked the cells in columns I through L before you protected the worksheet, you can make changes to these cells. The Time In and Time Out data can be changed as necessary.

FIGURE F-8: Protection tab in Format Cells dialog box

Click to remove check mark

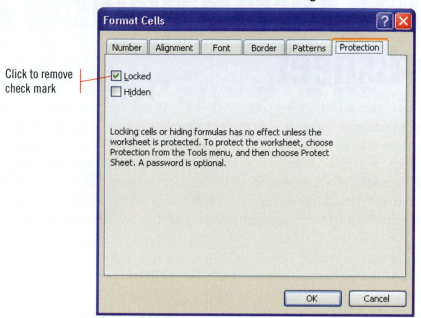

FIGURE F-9: Reminder of protected cell's read-only status

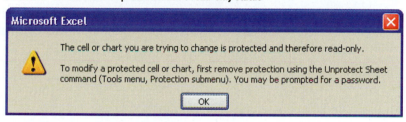

TABLE F-1: Options for hiding and protecting workbook elements

task	menu commands
Hide/Unhide a column	Format, Column, Hide or Unhide
Hide/Unhide a formula	Format, Cells, Protection tab, select/deselect Hidden check box
Hide/Unhide a row	Format, Row, Hide or Unhide
Hide/Unhide a sheet	Format, Sheet, Hide or Unhide
Hide/Unhide a workbook	Window, Hide or Unhide
Protect workbook	Tools, Protection, Protect Workbook, assign optional password
Protect worksheet	Tools, Protection, Protect Sheet, assign optional password
Unlock/Relock cells	Format, Cells, Protection tab, deselect/select Locked check box

(*Note*: Some of the hide and protect options do not take effect until protection is enabled. To enable protection, click Tools on the menu bar, point to Protection, then click Protect Sheet.)

Clues to Use

Changing workbook properties

You can also use a password to protect an entire workbook from being opened or modified by changing its file properties. Click File on the menu bar, click Save As, click Tools, then click General Options. Specify the password(s) for opening or modifying the workbook. To remove a workbook password, you can double-click the asterisks in the Password to open or Password to modify text boxes and press [Delete]. You can also use this dialog box to offer users an option to open the workbook in read-only format so that they can open, but not change it. Another way to make an entire workbook read-only is to right-click Start on the taskbar, then click Explore. Locate and right-click the filename, click Properties, click the General tab, then, in the Attributes section, select the Read-only check box.

UNIT
F

Excel 2003

Saving Custom Views of a Worksheet

A **view** is a set of display and/or print settings that you can name and save, then access at a later time. By using the Excel Custom Views feature, you can create several different views of a worksheet without having to create separate sheets. For example, if you often switch between portrait and landscape orientations when printing different parts of a worksheet, you can create two views with the appropriate print settings for each view. You set the display and/or print settings first, then name the view. Because Jim wants to generate several reports from his data, he asks you to save the current print and display settings as a custom view. To better view the data, he wants you to use the Zoom box to display the entire worksheet on one screen.

STEPS

> **QUICK TIP**
>
> After selecting the Zoom box, you can also pick a magnification percentage from the list or type the desired percentage.

1. **With the Monday sheet active, select range A1:O28, click the Zoom list arrow on the Standard toolbar, click Selection, then press [Ctrl][Home] to return to cell A1**

   Excel adjusts the display magnification so that the selected data fits on one screen. See Figure F-10.

2. **Click View on the menu bar, then click Custom Views**

   The Custom Views dialog box opens. Any previously defined views for the active worksheet appear in the Views box. In this case, Jim has created a custom view named Generic containing default print and display settings. See Figure F-11.

> **QUICK TIP**
>
> To delete views from the active worksheet, select the view in the Views list box, then click Delete.

3. **Click Add**

   The Add View dialog box opens, as shown in Figure F-12. Here, you enter a name for the view and decide whether to include print settings and hidden rows, columns, and filter settings. You want to include the selected options.

4. **In the Name box, type Complete Daily Worksheet, then click OK**

   After creating a custom view, you return to the worksheet. You are ready to test the two custom views. In case the views require a change to the worksheet, it's a good idea to turn off worksheet protection.

5. **Click Tools on the menu bar, point to Protection, then click Unprotect Sheet**

6. **Click View on the menu bar, then click Custom Views**

   The Custom Views dialog box opens, listing both the Complete Daily Worksheet and Generic views.

> **TROUBLE**
>
> If you receive the message "Some view settings could not be applied," repeat Step 5 to ensure that worksheet protection is turned off.

7. **Click Generic in the Views list, click Show, preview the worksheet, then close the Preview window**

   The Generic custom view returns the worksheet to the Excel default print and display settings. Now you are ready to test the new custom view.

8. **Click View on the menu bar, click Custom Views, click Complete Daily Worksheet in the Views list box if necessary, then click Show**

   The entire worksheet fits on the screen.

9. **Return to the Generic view, then save your work**

FIGURE F-10: Selected data fitted to one screen

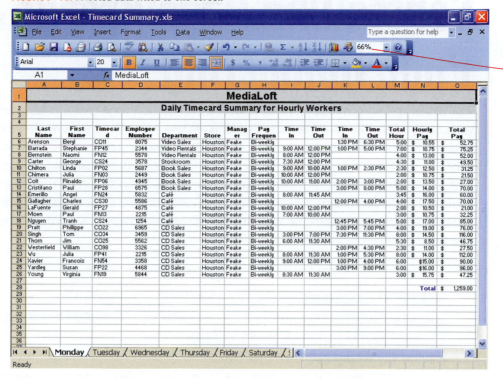

Zoom box showing current magnification

FIGURE F-11: Custom Views dialog box

Existing custom views appear here

Click to create new view

FIGURE F-12: Add View dialog box

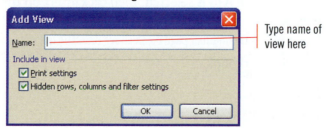

Type name of view here

Clues to Use

Creating a workspace

If you work with several workbooks at a time, you can group them so you can open them in one step by creating a **workspace**, a file with an .xlw extension. Then, instead of opening each workbook individually, you can open the workspace. To create a workspace, open the workbooks you wish to group and position and size them as you would like them to appear. Click File on the menu bar, click Save Workspace, type a name for the workspace file, then click Save. Remember, however, that the workspace file does not contain the workbooks themselves, so you still have to save any changes you make to the original workbook files. To have the workbooks automatically open in the workspace when you start Excel, place the workspace file in your XLStart folder (C:\Program Files\Microsoft Office\Office11\XLStart).

Controlling Page Breaks and Page Numbering

The vertical and horizontal dashed lines in worksheets represent page breaks. Excel automatically inserts a page break when your worksheet data doesn't fit on one page. These page breaks are **dynamic**, which means they adjust automatically when you insert or delete rows and columns and when you change column widths or row heights. Everything to the left of the first vertical dashed line and above the first horizontal dashed line is printed on the first page. You can override the automatic breaks by choosing the Page Break command on the Insert menu. Table F-2 describes the different types of page breaks you can use. Jim wants another report displaying no more than half the hourly workers on each page. To accomplish this, he asks you to insert a manual page break.

STEPS

1. **Click cell A16, click Insert on the menu bar, then click Page Break**

   A dashed line appears between rows 15 and 16, indicating a horizontal page break. See Figure F-13. After you set page breaks, it's a good idea to preview each page.

2. **Preview the worksheet, then click Zoom**

   Notice that the status bar reads "Page 1 of 4" and that the data for the employees up through Charles Gallagher appears on the first page. You decide to place the date in the footer.

3. **While in the Print Preview window, click Setup, click the Header/Footer tab, click Custom Footer, click the Right section box, then click the Date button**

4. **Click the Left section box, type your name, then click OK**

   Your name, the page number, and the date appear in the Footer preview area.

5. **In the Page Setup dialog box, click OK, and while still in Print Preview, check to make sure that all the pages show your name, the page numbers, and the date, click Close, save the workbook, then print the worksheet**

6. **Click View on the menu bar, click Custom Views, click Add, type Half and Half, then click OK**

   Your new custom view has the page breaks and all current print settings.

7. **Make sure cell A16 is selected, then click Insert on the menu bar and click Remove Page Break**

   Excel removes the manual page break above or to the left of the active cell.

8. **Save the workbook**

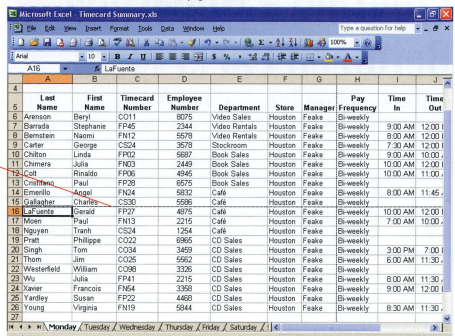
FIGURE F-13: Worksheet with horizontal page break

Dashed line indicates horizontal break after row 15

TABLE F-2: Page break options

type of page break	where to position cell pointer
Both horizontal and vertical page breaks	Select the cell below and to the right of the gridline where you want the breaks to occur
Only a horizontal page break	Select the cell in column A that is directly below the gridline where you want the page to break
Only a vertical page break	Select a cell in row 1 that is to the right of the gridline where you want the page to break

Clues to Use

Using Page Break Preview

You can view and change page breaks manually by clicking View on the menu bar, then clicking Page Break Preview, or clicking Page Break Preview in the Print Preview window. (If you see a Welcome to Page Break Preview dialog box, click OK to close it.) You can drag the page break lines to the desired location. See Figure F-14. If you drag a page break to the right to include more data on a page, Excel shrinks the type to fit the data on that page. To exit Page Break Preview, click View on the menu bar, then click Normal.

FIGURE F-14: Page Break Preview window

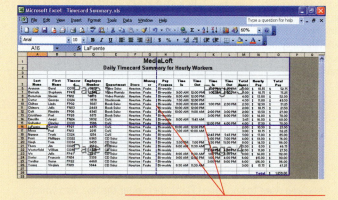

Drag page break lines to change page breaks

Creating a Hyperlink Between Excel Files

As you manage the content and appearance of your workbooks, you may want the workbook user to view information in another location. It might be nonessential information or data that is too detailed to place in the workbook itself. In these cases, you can create a **hyperlink**, an object (a filename, a word, a phrase, or a graphic) in a worksheet that, when you click it, displays, or "jumps to," another worksheet, called the **target**. The target can also be a document or a site on the World Wide Web. Hyperlinks are navigational tools between worksheets and are not used to exchange information. For example, in a worksheet that lists customer invoices, at each customer's name, you might create a hyperlink to an Excel file containing payment terms for each customer. Jim wants managers who view the Timecard Summary workbook to be able to view the pay categories for MediaLoft store employees. He asks you to create a hyperlink at the Hourly Pay Rate column heading. Users can click the hyperlink to view the Pay Rate worksheet.

STEPS

1. **Click cell N5 (the cell containing the text Hourly Pay Rate) on the Monday worksheet**

> **QUICK TIP**
> If you link to a Web page you must be connected to the Internet to test the link.

2. **Click the Insert Hyperlink button 🔗 on the Standard toolbar, then click Existing File or Web Page, if it is not already selected**
   The Insert Hyperlink dialog box opens. See Figure F-15. The icons under Link to on the left side of the dialog box let you specify the type of location you want the link to jump to: an existing file or Web page, a place in the same document, a new document, or an e-mail address. Because you want the link to display a document that has been created, the first icon, Existing File or Web Page, is correct.

3. **Click the Look in list arrow, navigate to the location where your Data Files are stored if necessary, then click Pay Rate Classifications.xls in the file list**
   The filename you selected appears in the Address text box. This is the document users see when they click this hyperlink. You can also specify the ScreenTip that users see when they hold the pointer over the hyperlink.

4. **Click ScreenTip, type Click here to see MediaLoft pay rate classifications, click OK, edit the Text to display text box to show Hourly Pay Rate, then click OK again**
   Cell N5 now contains underlined blue text, indicating that it is a hyperlink. After you create a hyperlink, you should check it to make sure that it jumps to the correct destination.

> **QUICK TIP**
> To remove a hyperlink or change its target, right-click it, then click Remove Hyperlink or Edit Hyperlink.

5. **Move the pointer over the Hourly Pay Rate text, view the ScreenTip, then click once**
   Notice that when you move the pointer over the text, the pointer changes to 🖑, indicating that it is a hyperlink, and the ScreenTip appears. After you click, the Pay Rate Classifications worksheet appears. See Figure F-16. The Web toolbar appears beneath the Standard and Formatting toolbars.

> **QUICK TIP**
> To print an entire workbook, click File on the menu bar, click Print, click to select the Entire workbook option button, then click OK.

6. **Click the Back button 🔙 on the Web toolbar, save the workbook, then print the worksheet**

Clues to Use

Finding and replacing data and formats

You can easily change worksheet data by using the Find and Replace feature. Click Edit on the menu bar, click Replace, enter the text you want to find, press [Tab], then enter the text with which you want to replace it. Use the Find Next, Find All, Replace, and Replace All buttons to find and replace any or all occurrences of the specified text. You can specify a data format for your search criteria by clicking the Options button, clicking the Format list arrow, and selecting a format.

FIGURE F-15: Insert Hyperlink dialog box

Locations a hyperlink can jump to

Click here to browse to hyperlink target

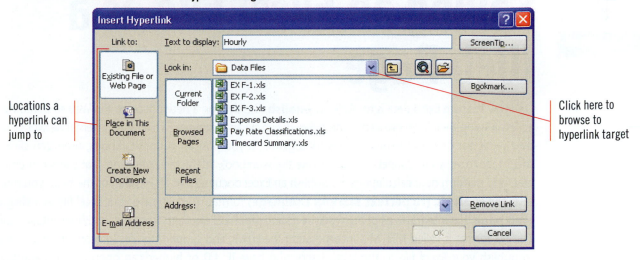

FIGURE F-16: Target document

Back button

Web toolbar

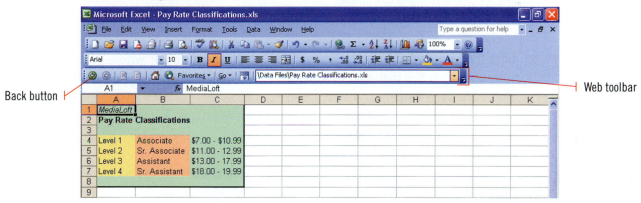

Clues to Use

Using research services

You can access resources online and locally on your computer using the Research task pane. To open the Research task pane, click Tools on the menu bar, then click Research. The Search for text box allows you to specify a research topic. The task pane also has a drop-down list of the resources available to search for your topic. You can insert the information you find into your worksheet by moving your cursor over the information you want to insert, clicking the list arrow on the right, then clicking Insert, Copy, or Look Up. The research services feature will expand as more companies develop databases that are specifically designed for use in the Research task pane.

UNIT
F
Excel 2003

Saving an Excel File as a Web Page

One way to share Excel data is to place, or **publish**, the data on a network or on the Web so that others can access it using their Web browsers. The network can be an **intranet**, which is an internal network site used by a particular group of people who work together. If you post an entire workbook, users can click work-sheet tabs to view each sheet. You can make the workbook interactive, meaning that users can enter, for-mat, and perform data calculations. To publish an Excel document to an intranet or the Web, you must first save it in an **HTML (Hypertext Markup Language)** format. You can save your Excel file as a **single file Web page** that integrates all of the worksheets and graphical elements from the workbook into a single file. This file format is called MHTML. Incorporating the HTML and supporting files into one file makes it easier to publish your Excel file to the Web. Users who have IE 4.0 or higher can open a Web page saved in MHTML format. Jim asks you to save the entire Timecard Summary workbook in MHT format so he can publish it on the MediaLoft intranet for managers to view.

STEPS

1. **Click File on the menu bar, then click Save as Web Page**
   The Save As dialog box opens. By default, the Entire Workbook option button is selected. You want the title bar of the Web page to be more descriptive than the filename.

2. **Click Change Title**
   The Set Page Title dialog box opens.

3. **Type MediaLoft Houston Timecard Summary, then click OK**
   The new title appears in the Page title area.

QUICK TIP

To avoid problems when publishing your pages to a Web server, it is best to use lowercase char-acters, omit special characters and spaces, and limit your filename to eight characters.

4. **Click the Save in list arrow to navigate to the drive and folder where your Data Files are stored, change the filename to timesum, then click the Save as type list arrow and click Single File Web Page**
   The Save as type list box indicates that the workbook is to be saved as a Single File Web Page, which is in MHTML or MHT format. See Figure F-17.

5. **Click Save**
   A dialog box appears, indicating that the custom views you saved earlier will not be part of the HTML file.

6. **Click Yes**
   Excel saves the workbook as an MHT file in the folder location you specified in the Save As dialog box. The MHT file is open on your screen.

7. **Click File on the menu bar, click Web Page Preview, then if necessary maximize the browser window**
   The workbook opens in your default Web browser, showing you what it would look like if you opened the workbook on an intranet or on the Web. See Figure F-18.

8. **Click the Summary Sheet tab, then print the worksheet using your browser**

9. **Close the Web browser window, then close the timesum.mht workbook and the Pay Rate Classifications.xls workbook**

Clues to Use

Converting Excel files to other file types

You can use the Save As option on the File menu to save a work-book in a format that can be opened in earlier versions of Excel or in other spreadsheet programs. You can also use the Save As option to convert an Excel file to other file types such as XML, TXT (text file type), and CSV (comma-delimited file type).

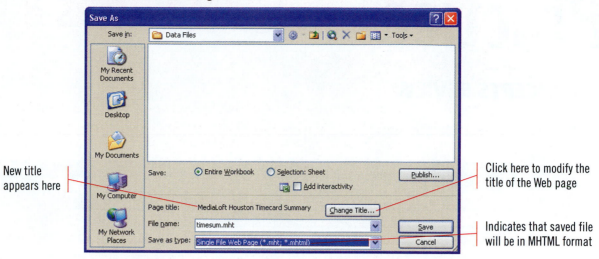

New title appears here

Click here to modify the title of the Web page

Indicates that saved file will be in MHTML format

FIGURE F-18: Workbook in Web page preview

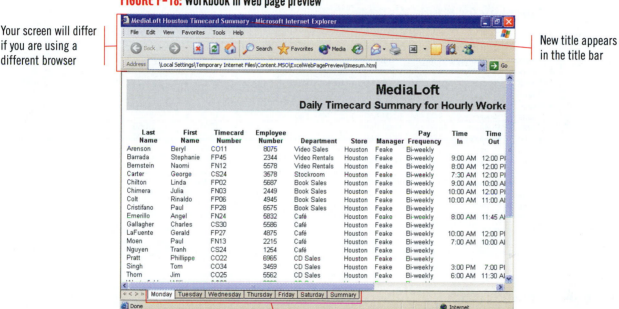

Your screen will differ if you are using a different browser

New title appears in the title bar

Sheet tabs allow users to view other sheets in their browser

Excel 2003

Clues to Use

Holding Web discussions

You can attach a discussion comment to an Excel worksheet that you are going to save as an HTML document. This allows people viewing your worksheet on the Web to review and reply to your comments. To insert a discussion comment in Excel, click Tools on the menu bar, point to Online Collaboration, then click Web Discussions. This displays the Web Discussions toolbar. See Figure F-19. You can add comments that others can view on the Web by clicking the Insert Discussion about the Workbook button on the Web Discussions Toolbar. Your comments, which are stored on a discussion server, appear with the worksheet when it is saved and published as a Web document. People viewing your worksheet on the Web can reply by clicking the Discuss button on the Standard Buttons toolbar.

in Internet Explorer to display the Discussions toolbar. Then they can click the Insert Discussion about the Workbook button. (*Note*: You must specify a discussion server to use this feature.)

FIGURE F-19: Web Discussion toolbar

Web Discussion toolbar

Click here to insert discussion about the workbook

Practice

▼ CONCEPTS REVIEW

FIGURE F-20

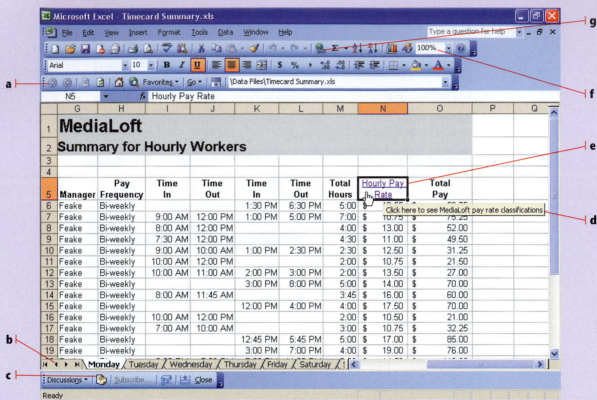

1. Which element points to a ScreenTip for a hyperlink?
2. Which element points to the Zoom box?
3. Which element points to a hyperlink?
4. Which element points to the Back button of the Web toolbar?
5. Which element do you click to insert a hyperlink into a worksheet?
6. Which element do you right-click to get a menu of the worksheets?
7. Which element do you click to insert a comment that can be viewed by others on the Web?

Match each term with the statement that best describes it.

8. Dashed line
9. Hyperlink
10. 3-D reference
11. ![image]
12. ![image]

a. Inserts a picture into header or footer
b. A navigational tool for use between worksheets or workbooks
c. Indicates a page break
d. Formats a picture in a header or footer
e. Uses values from different worksheets or workbooks

Select the best answer from the list of choices.

13. You can save frequently used display and print settings by using the _____ feature.
    - **a.** IITML
    - **b.** Custom Views
    - **c.** View menu
    - **d.** Save command

14. You can group several workbooks in a _____ so they can be opened together rather than individually.
    - **a.** Workgroup
    - **b.** Consolidated workbook
    - **c.** Workspace
    - **d.** Work unit

15. You can specify data formats in the Find and Replace dialog box by clicking the _____ button.
    - **a.** Options
    - **b.** Format
    - **c.** Data
    - **d.** Tools

16. You can group worksheets by pressing and holding _____ while clicking the sheet tabs that you want to group.
    - **a.** [Alt]
    - **b.** [Spacebar]
    - **c.** [Ctrl]
    - **d.** [F6]

▼ SKILLS REVIEW

1. **Freeze columns and rows.**
   a. Start Excel, open the Data File EX F-2.xls from the drive and folder where your Data Files are stored, then save it as **San Francisco Budget**.
   b. Activate the 2005 sheet if necessary, then freeze columns A and B and rows 1 through 3 for improved viewing. (*Hint*: Click cell C4 prior to issuing the Freeze Panes command.)
   c. Scroll until columns A and B and F through H are visible.
   d. Press **[Ctrl][Home]** to return to cell C4.
   e. Unfreeze the panes.
   f. Split the 2005 sheet into two horizontal panes. (*Hint*: Drag the Horizontal split box.) Remove the split by double-clicking over the split, then save your work.

2. **Insert and delete worksheets.**
   a. With the 2005 sheet active, use the sheet shortcut menu to insert a new sheet to its left.
   b. Delete the 2004 sheet, rename the new sheet 2007, and position it to the right of the 2006 sheet.
   c. Add a custom footer to the 2005 sheet with your name on the left side and the page number on the right side.
   d. Add a custom header with the worksheet name on the left side.
   e. Save and preview the 2005 sheet, compare your results to Figure F-21, then print it.

3. **Consolidate data with 3-D references.**
   a. In cell C22, enter a reference to cell G7.
   b. In cell C23, enter a reference to cell G18.
   c. Activate the 2006 worksheet.
   d. In cell C4, enter a reference to cell C4 on the 2005 worksheet.
   e. In the 2006 worksheet, copy the contents of cell C4 into cells C5:C6.
   f. Preview the 2006 worksheet, then use the Setup button to add your name to the left side of the footer.
   g. Print the 2006 worksheet, then save your work.

FIGURE F-21

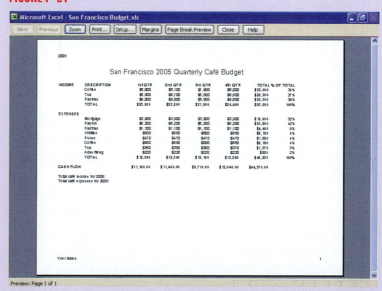

4. Hide and protect worksheet areas.

  a. On the 2005 sheet, unlock the expense data in the range C10:F17.

  b. On the 2005 sheet, hide the percent of total formulas in the range H4:H18 and the cash flow formulas in the range C20:G20.

  c. Protect the sheet without using a password.

  d. To make sure the other cells are locked, attempt to make an entry in cell D4. You should see the error message displayed in Figure F-22.

  e. Change the first quarter mortgage expense to $4000.

  f. Verify the formulas in column H and row 20 are hidden.

  g. Unprotect the worksheet.

  h. Save the workbook.

FIGURE F-22

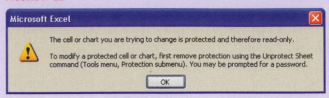

5. Save custom views of a worksheet.

  a. Set the zoom on the 2005 worksheet to fit the worksheet data to the screen.

  b. Make this a new view called **Entire 2005 Budget**.

  c. Use the Zoom box to change the magnification percentage of the worksheet to 200%. Save the worksheet at 200% as a new view called **200**.

  d. Use the Custom Views dialog box to delete the 200 view.

  e. Use the Custom Views dialog box to return to Generic view.

  f. Save the workbook.

6. Control page breaks and page numbering.

  a. Insert a page break above cell A9.

  b. Save the view as **Halves**.

  c. View the worksheet in Page Break Preview and modify the page break so it occurs after row ten. (*Hint*: Drag the page break line.)

  d. Return to the Halves view.

  e. Save the workbook.

7. Create a hyperlink between Excel files.

  a. On the 2005 worksheet, make cell A9 a hyperlink to the file **Expense Details.xls**.

  b. Test the link, then print the Expense Details worksheet.

  c. Edit the hyperlink in cell A9, adding a ScreenTip that reads **Expense Assumptions**.

  d. On the 2006 worksheet, enter the text **Based on 2005 budget** in cell A2.

  e. Make the text in cell A2 a hyperlink to cell A1 in the 2005 worksheet. (*Hint*: Use the Place in This Document button and note the cell reference in the Type the cell reference text box.)

  f. Test the hyperlink.

  g. Save the workbook and protect it with the password **pass**. (*Hint*: Use lowercase letters for the password.)

  h. Close and reopen the workbook to test the password. (*Hint*: If you cannot open the workbook, check that you are using lowercase letters.)

  i. Remove the password and save the workbook again.

8. Save an Excel file as a Web page.

  a. If you have access to a Web discussion server, attach a discussion comment to the 2005 worksheet with your name and the date you reviewed the budget. (If you don't have access to a discussion server, proceed to Step b.)

  b. Save the entire budget workbook as a Web page in MHT format with a title that reads **Our Budget** and the file named **sfbudget**.

  c. Preview the Web page in your browser. If your browser doesn't open automatically, check your taskbar.

  d. Test the worksheet tabs in the browser to make sure they work.

  e. Print the 2005 worksheet from your browser.

  f. Close your browser.

  g. Return to Excel, close the .mht document and the Expense Details.xls workbook, then exit Excel.

▼ INDEPENDENT CHALLENGE 1

As a new employee at SoftSales, a computer software retailer, you are responsible for tracking the sales of different product lines and determining which computer operating system generates the most software sales each month. Although sales figures vary from month to month, the format in which data is entered does not. You decide to create a worksheet tracking sales across platforms by month. Use a separate worksheet for each month and create data for three months. Use your own data for the number of software packages sold in the Windows and Macintosh columns for each product.

a. Start Excel, create a new workbook, then save it as **Software Sales Summary.xls** in the drive and folder where your Data Files are stored.

b. Add a fourth sheet by clicking Insert on the menu bar, then clicking Worksheet.

c. Drag the fourth sheet to the right of Sheet3.

d. Group the worksheets by clicking Sheet1, then press and hold [Shift] while clicking Sheet4.

e. With the worksheets grouped, use Table F-3 as a guide to enter the row and column labels that need to appear on each of the four sheets.

f. Rename Sheet1 to **January** by right-clicking the sheet name and entering the new name. Rename Sheet2 to **February**, Sheet3 to **March**, and Sheet4 to **Summary**.

g. Enter your own data, and formulas for the totals in the January, February, and March sheets.

h. Use the AutoSum function on the Summary sheet to total the information in all three monthly sheets.

i. Hide the Summary worksheet. (*Hint*: Select the Sheet command on the Format menu and choose Hide.)

j. Unhide the Summary worksheet. (*Hint*: Select the Sheet command on the Format menu and choose Unhide, then click OK.)

TABLE F-3

	Windows	Macintosh	Total
Games Software			
Combat Flight Simulator			
Safari			
NASCAR Racing			
Total			
Business Software			
Word Processing			
Spreadsheet			
Presentation			
Graphics			
Page Layout			
Total			
Utilities Products			
Antivirus			
File Recovery			
Total			

k. Group the worksheets again by clicking the January sheet then pressing and holding [Shift] while clicking the Summary sheet. Add headers to all four worksheets that include your name on the left, the sheet name in the center, and the date on the right.

l. Format the worksheet appropriately.

m. Save the workbook, preview and print the four worksheets, then exit Excel.

▼ INDEPENDENT CHALLENGE 2

You own PC Assist, a software training company located in Montreal, Canada. You have added several new entries to the August check register and are ready to enter September's check activity. Because the sheet for August includes much of the same information you need for September, you decide to copy it. Then you edit the new sheet to fit your needs for the September check activity. You use sheet referencing to enter the beginning balance and beginning check number. Using your own data, you complete five checks for the September register.

a. Start Excel, open the file EX F-3.xls from the drive and folder where your Data Files are stored, then save it as **Update to Check Register**. The expense amounts in the worksheet includes all taxes.

b. Delete Sheet2 and Sheet3, then create a worksheet for September by copying the August sheet and renaming it. If necessary, move the September sheet before the August sheet.

c. With the September sheet active, delete the data in the range A6:E24.

▼ INDEPENDENT CHALLENGE 2 (CONTINUED)

d. To update the balance at the beginning of the month, use sheet referencing from the last balance entry in the August sheet.

e. Generate the first check number. (*Hint*: Use a formula that references the last check number in August and adds one.)

f. Enter data for five checks using September 2006 dates. For the check number, use the number above it and add 1. Delete the balances in the range F11:F24.

g. Use the Find and Replace dialog box to change the beginning balance for August from **22000** to **27000**, formatted as a number with two decimal places. (*Hint*: The Options >> button allows you to change the data format.)

Advanced Challenge Exercise

- Add a new worksheet to the workbook and name it **Statistics**.
- Enter labels for August and September statistics into the Statistics worksheet using the table below as a guide.

August Statistics	
Number of Checks	
Average Check Amount	
Number of Classroom Expenses	
September Statistics	
Number of Checks	
Average Check Amount	
Number of Classroom Expenses	

- Use 3-D references and the appropriate statistical functions to enter the number of checks, average check amount, and the number of classroom expenses for the months of August and September. (*Hint*: Use the Insert Function dialog box to enter the COUNT function for the number of checks, the AVERAGE function for the check averages, and the COUNTIF function with the criteria **Classroom** for the number of classroom expenses.)
- Format the statistical information appropriately, add your name to the statistics worksheet footer, save the workbook, preview the worksheet, then print it in landscape orientation on a single page.

h. Add your name to the September sheet footer. Save the workbook, then preview and print the September worksheet. Close the workbook and exit Excel.

▼ INDEPENDENT CHALLENGE 3

You have decided to create a spreadsheet to track the long-distance phone calls made by you and your two roommates each month. You create a workbook with a separate sheet for each person and track the following information for each long-distance call: date of call, time of call, call minutes, city called, state called, area code, phone number, and call charge. Then you total the charges for each person and create a summary sheet of all three roommates' charges for the month. You are not sure what programs your roommates will be using to view the information so you also save the summary information in a text format.

a. Start Excel, create a new workbook, then save it as **Monthly Long Distance** in the drive and folder where your Data Files are stored.

b. Create a sheet for the first roommate. Enter column headings to track each call, then create two copies of the sheet and label the tabs.

c. Use your own data, entering at least three long-distance calls for each roommate.

d. Group the worksheets and create totals for minutes and charges on each roommate's sheet.

e. Create a summary sheet that shows each name and uses cell references to display the total minutes and total charges for each person.

f. On the summary sheet, create a hyperlink from each person's name to cell A1 of their respective worksheet. Enter your name on all worksheet footers, save the workbook, then print the four worksheets.

g. Create a workbook with the same type of information for the two people in the apartment next door. Save it as **Next Door.xls**. Enter your name on all worksheet footers, save the workbook, then print the three worksheets.

h. Arrange the two open workbooks in a tiled display on your screen. (*Hint*: Select the Arrange option on the Window menu.)

▼ INDEPENDENT CHALLENGE 3 (CONTINUED)

i. Use linking to create a 3-D reference that displays the neighbors' totals on your summary sheet so your roommates can compare their expenses with the neighbors'.

j. Create a workspace that includes the workbooks Monthly Long Distance and Next Door in the tiled layout. Name the workspace **Phonebill.xlw**. (*Hint*: Save Workspace is an option on the File menu.)

k. Hide the Next Door.xls workbook. (*Hint*: Hide is an option on the Window menu.)

l. Unhide the Next Door.xls workbook. (*Hint*: Unhide is an option on the Window menu.)

m. Change the workbook properties of the Next Door.xls workbook to Read-only.

n. Save the Summary sheet as a text file named Monthly Long Distance.txt. (*Hint*: Use the Save As command on the File menu.)

o. Close any open files and exit Excel.

▼ INDEPENDENT CHALLENGE 4

The creative director at WebProductions, a Web design company, is considering purchasing digital cameras for the New York and Montreal offices. You have been asked to research this purchase by comparing features and current prices in U.S. and Canadian currencies. You investigate online vendors and prepare a worksheet containing the following information about each camera: Manufacturer, Model, Zoom Lens Magnification, Megapixel Rating, Max Resolution, and Price in both U.S. and Canadian currencies. Your worksheet information will be protected but, because currency rates flucuate, the Canadian prices are unlocked. You use an online currency converter to calculate the price information in Canadian currency.

a. Find features and pricing (in U.S. dollars) for five digital cameras using the search engine of your choice. Also, search for a currency converter site, then convert the U.S. prices you found from the online vendors into Canadian currency.

b. Start Excel, create a new workbook, then save it as **Camera Research** in the drive and folder where your Data Files are stored, then enter the column headings shown in the table below.

Manufacturer	Model	Zoom Lens Magnification	Megapixel Rating	Max Resolution	Price $USD	Price $CAD

c. Enter the information you found on the Web into the worksheet. Some of the entries may include ranges of values.

d. Enter the information from the table into your Camera Research workbook. Name the worksheet **Online Vendors.**

e. Add a custom header that displays the sheet name centered on the printout.

f. Add a custom footer that includes your name on the left side of the printout.

g. Make the cells in the Manufacturer column hyperlinks to the manufacturer's Web site.

h. Use the Research task pane and the English (U.S. or Canada) thesaurus to find a synonym for **manufacturer**. Use the insert option in the Research task pane to replace the Manufacturer label in your worksheet with one of the listed synonyms.

i. Unlock the price information in the Canadian price column. Protect the worksheet without using a password. Save the workbook.

j. Save the workbook with the name **camera** in MHTML format for management's use and preview it in your Web browser.

k. Print the worksheet from your browser.

l. Exit your browser and return to the workbook in MHTML format.

Advanced Challenge Exercise

- Unprotect the worksheet, insert the company name, **WebProductions**, in cell A10 and create an e-mail link to it using your e-mail address.
- Insert a subject of **Digital Cameras** in the subject area.
- Add a ScreenTip of **Contact Us**.
- Preview the worksheet, then print it in landscape orientation on one page.

m. Close the workbook and exit Excel.

▼ VISUAL WORKSHOP

Create the worksheet shown in Figure F-23, then save it as **Martinez**. Enter your name in the footer, save the workbook and print the worksheet. Save the workbook as a Single File Web page (MHTML) using the name **martinez**. Preview the worksheet in your Web browser, then print the sheet from the browser. Notice that the text in cell A1 is a hyperlink to the Our History worksheet; the graphic is from the Clip Gallery. If you don't have this graphic, substitute a graphic of your choice.

FIGURE F-23

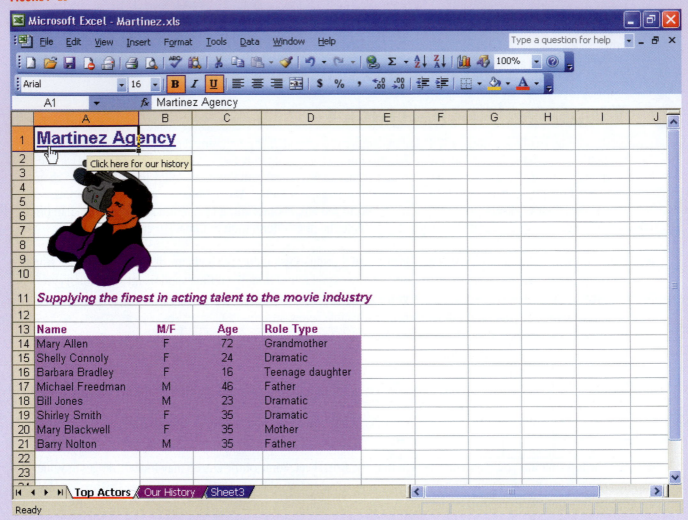

Automating Worksheet Tasks

OBJECTIVES

Plan a macro
Record a macro
Run a macro
Edit a macro
Use shortcut keys with macros
Use the Personal Macro Workbook
Add a macro as a menu item
Create a toolbar for macros

If you have a SAM user profile, you may have access to hands-on instruction, practice, and assessment of the skills covered in this unit. Log in to your SAM account and go to your assignments page to see what your instructor has assigned.

A **macro** is a set of instructions that performs tasks in the order you specify. You create macros to automate frequently performed Excel tasks. For example, if you usually enter your name and date in a worksheet footer, you can record the keystrokes in an Excel macro that enters the text and inserts the current date automatically when you run the macro. In this unit, you will plan and design a simple macro, then record and run it. Then you will edit the macro and explore ways to make it more easily available as you work. ▨ Jim Fernandez, the office manager for MediaLoft, wants you to create a macro for the Accounting Department. The macro needs to automatically insert text that identifies the worksheet as an Accounting Department document.

Planning a Macro

You create macros for tasks that you perform frequently. For example, you can create a macro to enter and format text or to save and print a worksheet. To create a macro, you record the series of actions or write the instructions in a special programming language. Because the sequence of actions is important, you need to plan the macro carefully before you record it. ▰▰▰ Jim wants you to create a macro for the Accounting Department that inserts the text "Accounting Department" in the upper-left corner of any worksheet. You work with him to plan the macro using the following guidelines:

DETAILS

- ## Assign the macro a descriptive name.
  The first character of a macro name must be a letter; the remaining characters can be letters, numbers, or underscores. Spaces are not allowed in macro names; use underscores in place of spaces. (Press [Shift][–] to enter an underscore character.) Jim wants you to name the macro "DeptStamp." See Table G-1 for a list of macros Jim might create to automate other tasks.

- ## Write out the steps the macro will perform.
  This planning helps eliminate careless errors. Jim writes a description of the macro he wants, as shown in Figure G-1.

- ## Decide how you will perform the actions you want to record.
  You can use the mouse, the keyboard, or a combination of the two. Jim wants you to use both the mouse and the keyboard.

- ## Practice the steps you want Excel to record, and write them down.
  Jim has written down the sequence of actions he wants you to include in the macro.

- ## Decide where to store the description of the macro and the macro itself.
  Macros can be stored in an active workbook, in a new workbook, or in the Personal Macro Workbook, a special workbook used only for macro storage. Jim asks you to store the macro in a new workbook.

TABLE G-1: Possible macros and their descriptive names

description of macro	descriptive name
Enter a frequently used proper name, such as Jim Fernandez	JimFernandez
Enter a frequently used company name, such as MediaLoft	Company_Name
Print the active worksheet on a single page, in landscape orientation	FitToLand
Add a footer to a worksheet	FooterStamp
Show a generic view of a worksheet using the default print and display settings	GenericView

Macro to create stamp with the department name

Name:	DeptStamp
Description:	Adds a stamp to the top left of the worksheet, identifying it as an Accounting Department worksheet
Steps:	1. Position the cell pointer in cell A1.
	2. Type Accounting Department, then click the Enter button.
	3. Click Format on the menu bar, then click Cells.
	4. Click the Font tab, under Font style, click Bold, under Underline, click Single, and under Color, click Red, then click OK.

Excel 2003

Clues to Use

Macros and viruses

When you open an Excel workbook that has macros, you may see a message asking you if you want to enable or disable them. If you know your workbook came from a trusted source, click Enable macros. If you are not sure of the workbook's source, click Disable macros, because a macro may contain a **virus**, a destructive software program that can damage your computer files. If you disable the macros in a workbook, you will not be able to use them. For more information about macro security and security levels, type "About macro security" in the Type a question for help text box.

Recording a Macro

The easiest way to create a macro is to record it using the Excel Macro Recorder. You turn the Macro Recorder on, name the macro, enter the keystrokes and select the commands you want the macro to perform, then stop the recorder. As you record the macro, Excel automatically translates each action into program code you can later view and modify. You can take as long as you want to record the macro; a recorded macro contains only your actions, not the amount of time you took to record it. Jim wants you to create a macro that enters a department "stamp" in cell A1 of the active worksheet. You create this macro by recording your actions.

STEPS

1. **Start Excel, save the new blank workbook as My Excel Macros in the drive and folder where your Data Files are stored**
   You are ready to start recording the macro.

2. **Click Tools on the menu bar, point to Macro, then click Record New Macro**
   The Record Macro dialog box opens. See Figure G-2. The default name Macro1 is selected. You can either assign this name or enter a new name. This dialog box also lets you assign a shortcut key for running the macro and assign a storage location for the macro.

3. **Type DeptStamp in the Macro name text box**

4. **If the Store macro in list box does not display This Workbook, click the list arrow and select This Workbook**

5. **If the Description text box does not contain your name, select the existing name, type your own name, then click OK**
   The dialog box closes. A small Stop Recording toolbar appears containing the Stop Recording button, and the word "Recording" appears on the status bar. Take your time performing the steps below. Excel records every keystroke, menu selection, and mouse action that you make.

   TROUBLE
   If the Stop Recording toolbar is not displayed, click View, point to Toolbars, then click Stop Recording.

6. **Press [Ctrl][Home]**
   When you begin an Excel session, macros record absolute cell references. By beginning the recording in cell A1, you ensure that the macro includes the instruction to select cell A1 as the first step, in cases where A1 is not already selected.

7. **Type Accounting Department in cell A1, then click the Enter button ✔ on the formula bar**

8. **Click Format on the menu bar, then click Cells**

9. **Click the Font tab, in the Font style list box click Bold, click the Underline list arrow and click Single, then click the Color list arrow and click the red color (third row, first color on the left)**
   See Figure G-3.

   TROUBLE
   If your results differ from Figure G-4, clear the contents of cell A1, then slowly and carefully repeat Steps 2 through 10. When prompted to replace the existing macro at the end of Step 5, click Yes.

10. **Click OK, click on the Stop Recording toolbar, click cell D1 to deselect cell A1, then save the workbook**
    Compare your results with Figure G-4.

FIGURE G-2: Record Macro dialog box

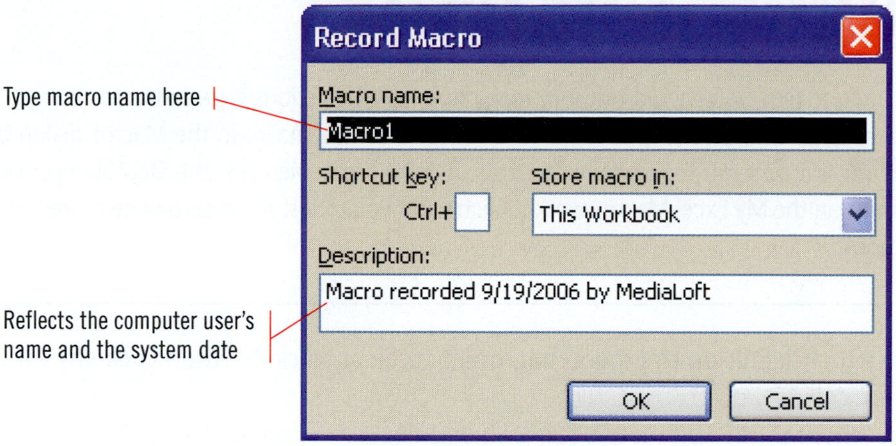

Type macro name here

Reflects the computer user's name and the system date

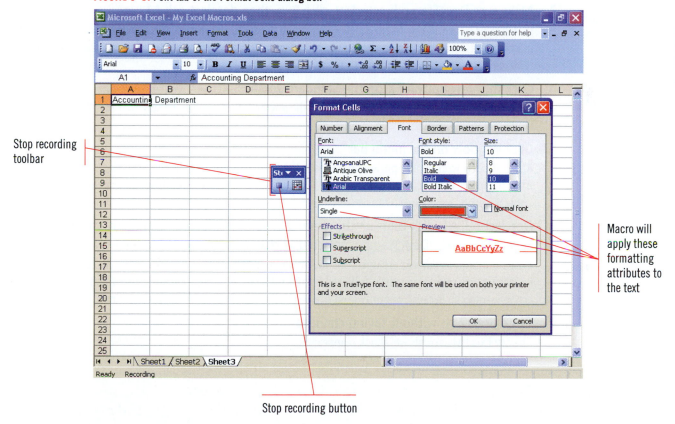

FIGURE G-3: Font tab of the Format Cells dialog box

Stop recording toolbar

Macro will apply these formatting attributes to the text

Stop recording button

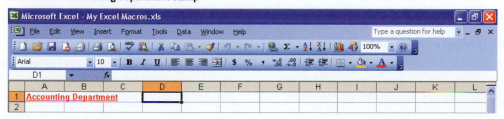

FIGURE G-4: Accounting Department stamp

Running a Macro

Once you record a macro, you should test it to make sure that the actions it performs are correct. To test a macro, you **run**, or play, it. One way to run a macro is to select the macro in the Macros dialog box, then click Run. Jim asks you to clear the contents of cell A1 and then test the DeptStamp macro. After you run the macro in the My Excel Macros workbook, he asks you to test the macro once more from a newly opened workbook.

STEPS

1. **Click cell A1, click Edit on the menu bar, point to Clear, click All, then click any other cell to deselect cell A1**

   When you delete only the contents of a cell, any formatting still remains in the cell. By using the Clear All option on the Edit menu, you can be sure that the cell is free of contents and formatting.

   QUICK TIP
   To delete a macro, select the macro name in the Macro dialog box, click Delete, then click Yes to confirm the action.

2. **Click Tools on the menu bar, point to Macro, then click Macros**

   The Macro dialog box, shown in Figure G-5, lists all the macros contained in the open workbooks. If other people have used your computer, other macros may be listed.

3. **Make sure DeptStamp is selected, click Run, then deselect cell A1**

   Watch your screen as the macro quickly plays back the steps you recorded in the previous lesson. When the macro is finished, your screen should look like Figure G-6. As long as the workbook containing the macro remains open, you can run the macro in any open workbook.

   QUICK TIP
   To stop a macro while it is running, press [Esc] then click End.

4. **Click the New button on the Standard toolbar**

   Because the new workbook automatically fills the screen, it is difficult to be sure that the My Excel Macros.xls workbook is still open.

5. **Click Window on the menu bar**

   A list of open workbooks appears underneath the menu options. The active workbook name (in this case, Book2) appears with a check mark to its left. The My Excel Macros.xls workbook appears on the menu, so you know it's open. See Figure G-7.

6. **Deselect cell A1, click Tools on the menu bar, point to Macro, click Macros, make sure 'My Excel Macros.xls'!DeptStamp is selected, click Run, then deselect cell A1**

   When multiple workbooks are open, the macro name in the Macro dialog box includes the workbook name between single quotation marks, followed by an exclamation point, indicating that the macro is outside the active workbook. Because you only used this workbook to test the macro, you don't need to save it.

7. **Close Book2.xls without saving changes**

   The My Excel Macros.xls workbook reappears.

Clues to Use

Setting macro security levels

If you get a security error message when attempting to open a workbook containing a macro, the security level may be set too high. You can enable macros by changing the security level for workbooks. Click the Tools menu, point to the Macro option, click Security, then set the security level to Medium. You must save, then close and reopen the workbook to activate the new security level.

FIGURE G-5: Macro dialog box

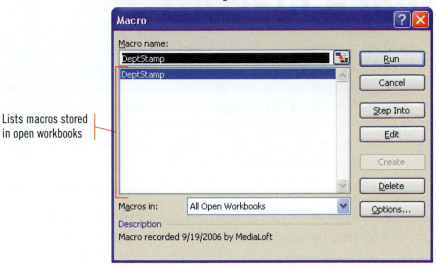

Lists macros stored in open workbooks

FIGURE G-6: Result of running DeptStamp macro

DeptStamp macro inserts formatted text in cell A1

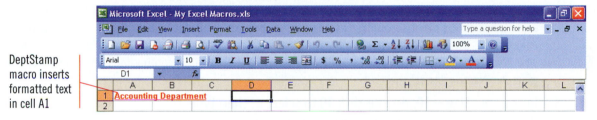

FIGURE G-7: Window menu listing open workbooks

Check mark indicates active workbook

Indicates this workbook is still open

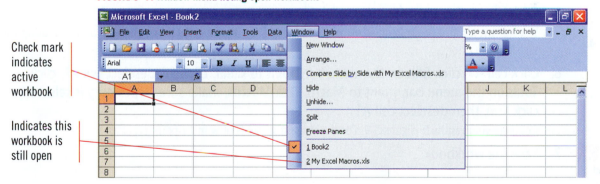

Clues to Use

Adding a digital signature to a macro

If the macro security level in Excel is set to High, only macros that are digitally signed from trusted sources can run. To sign a macro with a trusted digital signature, you need a valid certificate issued by a certificate authority. To digitally sign a macro with a certificate you have obtained, make sure the workbook containing it is open, then click the Tools menu, point to Macro, click Visual Basic Editor, select the macro in the module you want to sign in the Project Explorer (it will be in Module 1 unless you named the module), click the Tools menu, click Digital Signature, click Choose, select the certificate, then click OK twice.

Editing a Macro

When you use the Macro Recorder to create a macro, the program instructions, called **program code**, are recorded automatically in the **Visual Basic for Applications (VBA)** programming language. Each macro is stored as a **module**, or program code container, attached to the workbook. After you record a macro, you might need to change it. If you have a lot of changes to make, it might be best to rerecord the macro. But if you need to make only minor adjustments, you can edit the macro code directly using the **Visual Basic Editor**, a program that lets you display and edit your macro code. Jim wants you to modify his macro to change the point size of the department stamp to 14.

STEPS

TROUBLE

If the Properties window does not appear, click the Properties Window button on the Visual Basic Editor toolbar.

1. **Make sure the My Excel Macros.xls workbook is open, click Tools on the menu bar, point to Macro, click Macros, make sure DeptStamp is selected, then click Edit**

   The Visual Basic Editor starts, showing the DeptStamp macro steps in a numbered module window (in this case, Module1).

2. **If necessary, maximize the window titled My Excel Macros.xls – [Module1(Code)], then examine the steps in the macro, comparing your screen to Figure G-8**

   The name of the macro and the date it was recorded appear at the top of the module window. Below that, Excel has translated your keystrokes and commands into macro code. When you open and make selections in a dialog box during macro recording, Excel automatically stores all the dialog box settings in the macro code. For example, the line .FontStyle = "Bold" was generated when you clicked Bold in the Format Cells dialog box. You also see lines of code that you didn't generate directly while recording the DeptStamp macro; for example, .Name = "Arial".

3. **In the line .Size = 10, double-click 10 to select it, then type 14**

   Because Module1 is attached to the workbook and not stored as a separate file, any changes to the module are saved automatically when you save the workbook.

4. **In the Visual Basic Editor, click File on the menu bar, click Print, click OK to print the module, then review the printout**

QUICK TIP

You can return to Excel without closing the module by clicking the View Microsoft Excel button on the Visual Basic Editor toolbar.

5. **Click File on the menu bar, then click Close and Return to Microsoft Excel**

   You want to rerun the DeptStamp macro to make sure the macro reflects the change you made using the Visual Basic Editor.

6. **Click cell A1, click Edit on the menu bar, point to Clear, click All, deselect cell A1, click Tools on the menu bar, point to Macro, click Macros, make sure DeptStamp is selected, click Run, then deselect cell A1**

   Compare your results to Figure G-9. The department stamp is now in 14-point type.

QUICK TIP

Another way to start the Visual Basic Editor is to click Tools on the menu bar, point to Macro, then click Visual Basic Editor, or press [Alt][F11].

7. **Save the workbook**

FIGURE G-8: Visual Basic Editor showing Module1

Project Explorer with open module selected

Properties window showing properties for selected objects

Font size line

Properties Window button

Comments appear in green preceded by an apostrophe

Code window

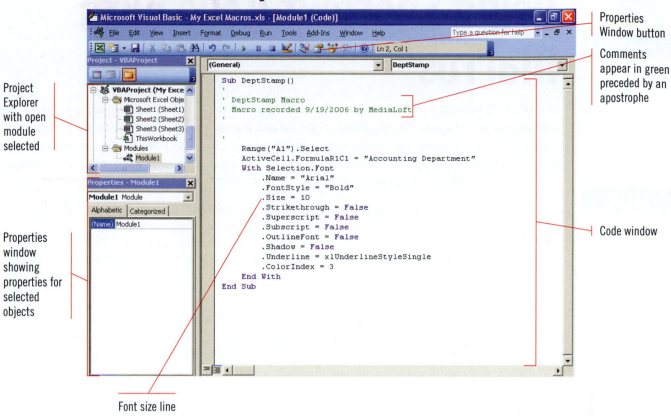

FIGURE G-9: Result of running edited DeptStamp macro

Font size enlarged to 14 point

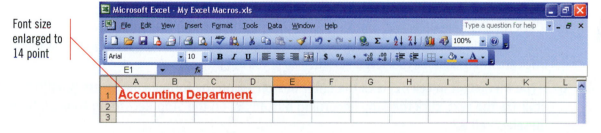

Using Shortcut Keys with Macros

In addition to running a macro from the Macro dialog box, you can run a macro by using a shortcut key combination you assign to it. Using shortcut keys reduces the number of actions you need to take to run a macro. You assign shortcut key combinations in the Record Macro dialog box. ▨ Jim also wants you to create a macro called CompanyName to enter the company name into a worksheet. You will assign a shortcut key combination to run the macro.

STEPS

1. **Click cell B2**

   You will record the macro in cell B2. You want the macro to enter the company name anywhere in a worksheet. Therefore, you do not begin the macro with an instruction to position the cell pointer, as you did in the DeptStamp macro.

2. **Click Tools on the menu bar, point to Macro, then click Record New Macro**

   The Record Macro dialog box opens. Notice the option Shortcut key: Ctrl+ followed by a blank box. You can type a letter (A–Z) in the Shortcut key text box to assign the key combination of [Ctrl] plus that letter to run the macro. You use the key combination [Ctrl][Shift] plus a letter to avoid overriding any of the Excel [Ctrl] [letter] shortcut keys, such as [Ctrl][C] for Copy.

3. **With the default macro name selected, type CompanyName, click the Shortcut key text box, press and hold [Shift], type C, then, if necessary, replace the name in the Description box with your name**

   Compare your screen with Figure G-10. You are ready to record the CompanyName macro.

4. **Click OK to close the dialog box**

   By default, Excel records absolute cell references in macros. Beginning the macro in cell B2 causes the macro code to begin with a statement to select cell B2. Because you want to be able to run this macro in any active cell, you need to instruct Excel to record relative cell references while recording the macro.

5. **Click the Relative Reference button ▣ on the Stop Recording toolbar**

   The Relative Reference button is now selected. See Figure G-11. This button is a toggle and retains the relative reference setting until you click it again to turn it off or you exit Excel.

6. **Type MediaLoft in cell B2, click the Enter button ✔ on the formula bar, press [Ctrl][I] to italicize the text, click the Stop Recording button ▣ on the Stop Recording toolbar, then deselect cell B2**

   MediaLoft appears in italics in cell B2. You are ready to run the macro in cell A5 using the shortcut key combination.

7. **Click cell A5, press and hold [Ctrl][Shift], type C, then deselect the cell**

   The company name appears in cell A5. See Figure G-12. Because the macro played back in the selected cell (A5) instead of the cell where it was recorded (B2), you know that the macro recorded relative cell references.

8. **Save the workbook**

FIGURE G-10: Record Macro dialog box with shortcut key assigned

Shortcut to run macro

FIGURE G-11: Stop Recording toolbar with Relative Reference button selected

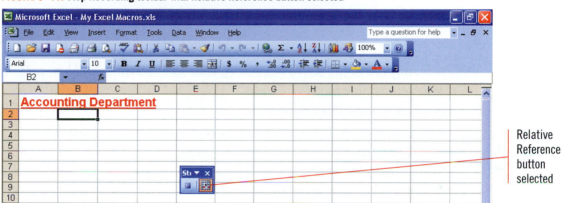

Relative
Reference
button
selected

FIGURE G-12: Result of running the CompanyName macro

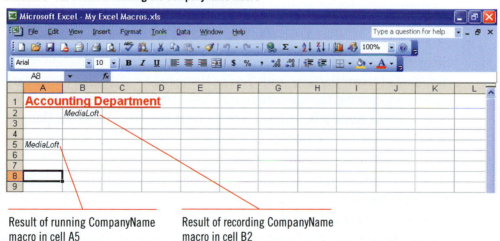

Result of running CompanyName
macro in cell A5

Result of recording CompanyName
macro in cell B2

Clues to Use

Running a macro from a hotspot on your worksheet

You can create a **hotspot** on your worksheet that runs a macro when you click it. To create a hotspot, first add an AutoShape to the worksheet: click AutoShapes on the Drawing toolbar, point to a shape category, and then click a shape. Drag across a worksheet area to create a shape, then type to add a label to the button, such as "Click to run Name macro." Right-click the button and click Assign Macro on the shortcut menu to choose the macro the button runs.

Using the Personal Macro Workbook

You can store commonly used macros in a **Personal Macro Workbook**. The Personal Macro Workbook is always available, unless you specify otherwise, and gives you access to all the macros it contains, regardless of which workbooks are open. The Personal Macro Workbook file is automatically created the first time you choose to store a macro in it. You can add additional macros to the Personal Macro Workbook by saving them there. By default, the Personal.xls workbook opens each time you start Excel, but you don't see it because Excel designates it as a hidden file. Jim often likes to add a footer to his worksheets identifying his department, the workbook name, the worksheet name, his name, and the current date. He wants you to create a macro that automatically inserts this footer. Because he wants to use this macro in future worksheets, he asks you to store this macro in the Personal Macro Workbook.

STEPS

1. **From any cell in the active worksheet, click Tools on the menu bar, point to Macro, then click Record New Macro**

   The Record Macro dialog box opens.

2. **Type FooterStamp in the Macro name text box, click the Shortcut key text box, press and hold [Shift], type F, then click the Store macro in list arrow**

   You have named the macro FooterStamp and assigned it the shortcut combination [Ctrl][Shift][F]. Notice that This Workbook is selected by default, indicating that Excel automatically stores macros in the active workbook. See Figure G-13. You also can choose to store the macro in a new workbook or in the Personal Macro Workbook.

3. **Click Personal Macro Workbook, replace the existing name in the Description text box with your own name, if necessary, then click OK**

   The recorder is on, and you are ready to record the macro keystrokes. If you are prompted to replace an existing macro named FooterStamp, click Yes.

4. **Click File on the menu bar, click Page Setup, click the Header/Footer tab (make sure to do this even if it is already active), click Custom Footer, in the Left section box, type Accounting; click the Center section box, click the File Name button 📄, press [Spacebar], type /, press [Spacebar], click the Tab Name button 📄 to insert the sheet name; click the Right section box, type your name followed by a comma, press [Spacebar], click the Date button 📅, then click OK to return to the Header/Footer tab**

   The footer stamp is set up, as shown in Figure G-14.

5. **Click OK to return to the worksheet, then click the Stop Recording button 📄 on the Stop Recording toolbar**

   You want to ensure that the macro can set the footer stamp in any active worksheet.

6. **Activate Sheet2, in cell A1 type FooterStamp macro test, press [Enter], press and hold [Ctrl][Shift], then type F**

   The FooterStamp macro plays back the sequence of commands.

7. **Preview the worksheet to verify that the new footer is inserted, then close the Preview window**

8. **Save the workbook, then print the worksheet**

Excel 2003

FIGURE G-13: Record Macro dialog box showing macro storage options

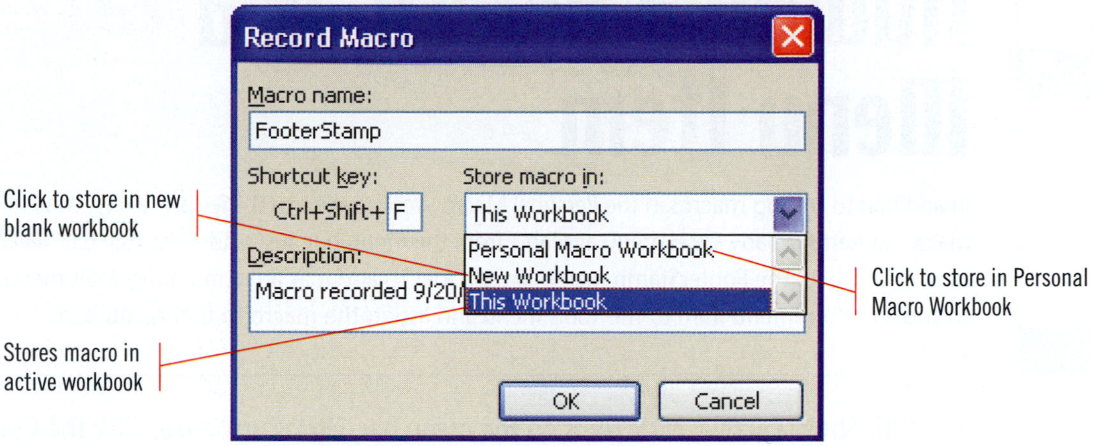

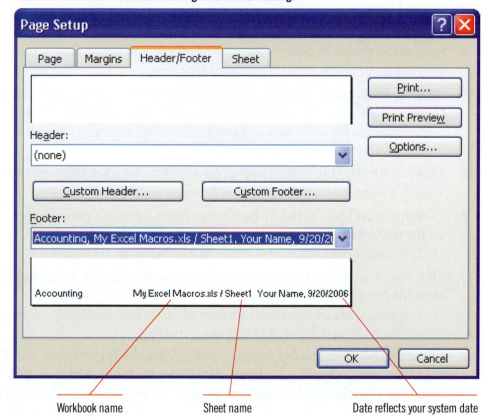

Click to store in new blank workbook

Stores macro in active workbook

Click to store in Personal Macro Workbook

FIGURE G-14: Header/Footer tab showing custom footer settings

Workbook name

Sheet name

Date reflects your system date

Clues to Use

Working with the Personal Macro Workbook

Once you use the Personal Macro Workbook, it opens automatically each time you start Excel so you can add macros to it. By default, the Personal Macro Workbook is hidden as a precautionary measure so you don't accidentally delete anything from it. If you need to delete a macro from the Personal Macro Workbook, click Unhide on the Window menu, click PERSONAL.XLS, then click OK. To hide the Personal Macro Workbook, click Hide on the Window menu when the workbook is active.

Adding a Macro as a Menu Item

In addition to storing macros in the Personal Macro Workbook so that they are always available, you can add macros as items on any Excel menu available from the menu bar, just under the title bar. To increase the availability of the FooterStamp macro, Jim decides to add it as an item on the Tools menu. He wants you to add a custom menu item to the Tools menu and assign the macro to that menu item.

STEPS

1. **With Sheet2 active, click Tools on the menu bar, click Customize, click the Commands tab, then under Categories, click Macros**

   See Figure G-15.

2. **Click Custom Menu Item under Commands, drag the selection over Tools on the menu bar (the menu opens), then point just under the last menu option, but do not release the mouse button**

   Compare your screen to Figure G-16.

3. **Release the mouse button**

   Now, Custom Menu Item is the last item on the Tools menu.

4. **With the Tools menu still open, right-click Custom Menu Item, select the text in the Name box (&Custom Menu Item), type Footer Stamp, then click Assign Macro**

   Unlike a macro name, the name of a custom menu item can have spaces between words like all standard menu items. The Assign Macro dialog box opens.

5. **Click PERSONAL.XLS!FooterStamp under Macro name, click OK, then click Close**

   You have assigned the FooterStamp macro to the new menu command.

6. **Click the Sheet3 tab, in cell A1 type macro menu item test, press [Enter], then click Tools on the menu bar**

   The Tools menu appears with the new menu option at the bottom. See Figure G-17.

7. **Click Footer Stamp, preview the worksheet to verify that the footer was inserted, then close the Print Preview window**

   The Print Preview window appears with the footer stamp. Because others using your computer might be confused by the macro on the menu, it's a good idea to remove it.

8. **Click Tools on the menu bar, click Customize, click the Toolbars tab, click Worksheet Menu Bar to highlight it, click Reset, click OK to confirm, click Close, click Tools on the menu bar to make sure that the custom item has been deleted, then save the workbook**

Clues to Use

Adding a custom menu

You can create a custom menu on an existing toolbar and assign macros to it. To do this, click Tools on the menu bar, click Customize, click the Commands tab, click New Menu in the Categories list, then drag the New Menu from the Commands box to the toolbar. To name the new menu, right-click, then enter a name in the Name box. You can drag Custom Menu Items from the Commands tab of the Customize dialog box to the menu and then right-click each menu item to assign macros to them.

FIGURE G-15: Commands tab of the Customize dialog box

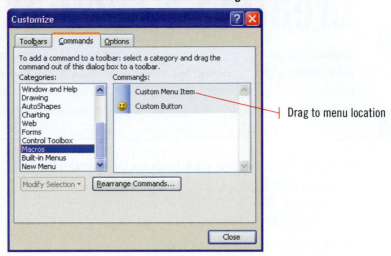

Drag to menu location

FIGURE G-16: Tools menu showing placement of the Custom Menu Item

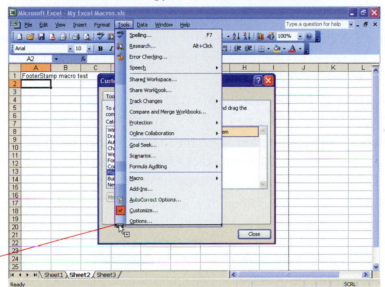

Pointer and line showing location at which to drop menu item

FIGURE G-17: Tools menu with new Footer Stamp item

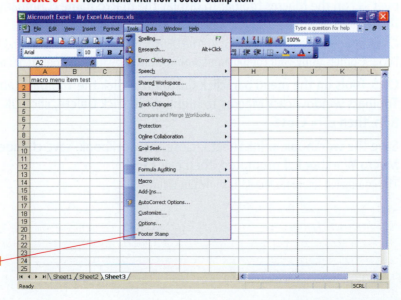

Added menu item

Creating a Toolbar for Macros

Toolbars contain buttons that let you single-click to issue commands you use frequently. You can create your own custom toolbars to organize commands so that you can find and use them quickly. Once you create a toolbar, you can add buttons to it so you can run macros by simply clicking the buttons. ▨▨▨▨ Jim asks you to create a custom toolbar called Macros that contains buttons to run two of his macros.

STEPS

1. **With Sheet3 active, click Tools on the menu bar, click Customize, click the Toolbars tab, then click New**

   The New Toolbar dialog box opens, as shown in Figure G-18. Under Toolbar name, a default name of Custom 1 is selected.

2. **Type Macros, then click OK**

   Excel adds the new toolbar named Macros to the bottom of the Toolbars list, and a small, empty toolbar named Macros opens. See Figure G-19. You cannot see the entire toolbar name. A new toolbar starts out small and expands to fit the buttons you assign to it.

3. **Click the Commands tab in the Customize dialog box, click Macros in the Categories list, then drag the Custom button ☺ over the new Macros toolbar and release the mouse button**

   The Macros toolbar now contains one button. You want the toolbar to contain two macros, so you need to add one more button.

4. **Drag the ☺ button over the Macros toolbar again**

   With the two buttons in place, you are ready to customize the buttons and assign macros to them.

5. **Right-click the left button ☺ on the Macros toolbar, select &Custom Button in the Name box, type Department Stamp, click Assign Macro, click DeptStamp, then click OK**

   With the first toolbar button customized, you are ready to customize the second button.

6. **With the Customize dialog box open, right-click the right button ☺ on the Macros toolbar, edit the name to read Company Name, click Change Button Image, click the ♟ image (seventh row, first column), right-click ♟, click Assign Macro, click CompanyName to select it, click OK, then click Close to close the Customize dialog box**

   The Macros toolbar appears with the two customized macro buttons.

7. **Move the mouse pointer over ☺ on the Macros toolbar to display the macro name (Department Stamp), then click to run the macro, click cell B2, move the mouse pointer over ♟ on the Macros toolbar to display the macro name (Company Name), click to run that macro, then deselect the cell**

   Compare your screen with Figure G-20. The DeptStamp macro automatically replaces the contents of cell A1. Because others using your computer might be confused by the new toolbar, it's a good idea to remove it.

8. **Click Tools on the menu bar, click Customize, click the Toolbars tab if necessary, in the Toolbars window click Macros to highlight it, click Delete, click OK to confirm the deletion, then click Close**

9. **Save the workbook, print Sheet3, close the workbook, save changes to the Personal Macro Workbook if prompted, then exit Excel**

   The completed figure for Sheet1 is shown in Figure G-12.

> **QUICK TIP**
>
> Toolbars you create or customize are available to all workbooks on your computer. You can ensure that a custom toolbar is visible in a specific workbook by attaching the toolbar to the workbook using the Toolbars tab in the Customize dialog box: click the Attach button, click the toolbar, then click Copy.

FIGURE G-18: New Toolbar dialog box

Type toolbar name here

FIGURE G-19: Customize dialog box with new Macros toolbar

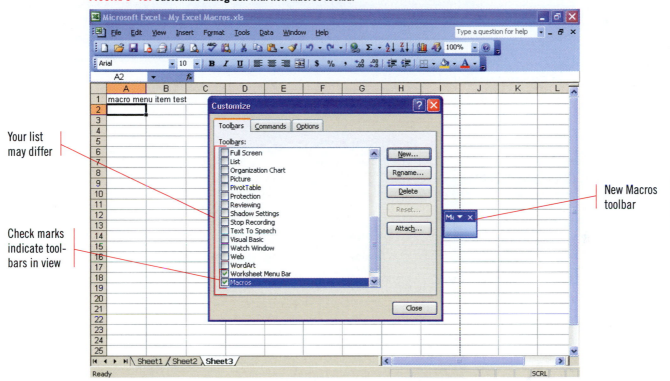

Your list may differ

Check marks indicate tool-bars in view

New Macros toolbar

FIGURE G-20: Worksheet showing Macros toolbar with two customized buttons

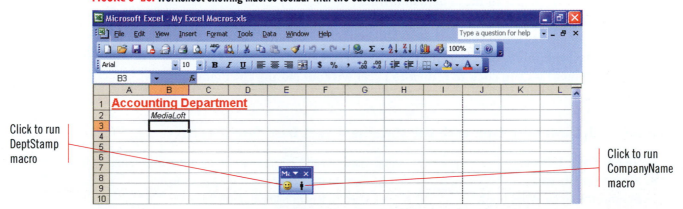

Click to run DeptStamp macro

Click to run CompanyName macro

Clues to Use

Organizing macros

You can organize your workbooks containing macros by placing them in folders with names that describe the macro tasks. To rename a folder, right-click the folder, click Rename on the shortcut menu, then enter the new name.

Practice

▼ CONCEPTS REVIEW

FIGURE G-21

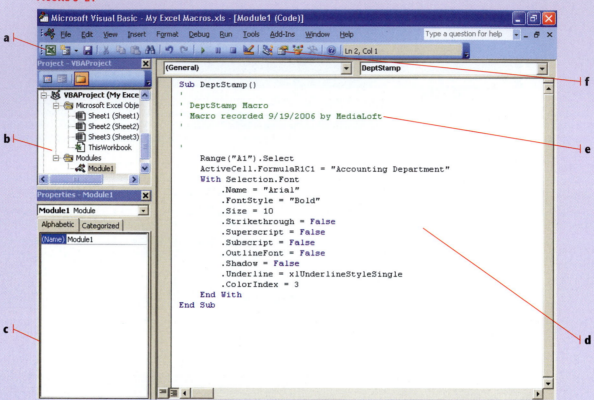

1. Which element points to a comment in the Visual Basic code?
2. Which element points to the Code window?
3. Which element points to the Properties Window button?
4. Which element points to the Project Explorer?
5. Which element points to the Properties window?
6. Which element do you click to return to Excel without closing the module?

Match each term or button with the statement that best describes it.

7. **Visual Basic Editor**
8. **Macro comments**
9. **Personal Macro Workbook**
10. 😊
11. ▦

a. Used to add a custom button on a macros toolbar code
b. Used to store commonly used macros
c. Used to record relative cell references
d. Used to make changes to macro code
e. Statements that appear in green explaining the macro

Select the best answer from the list of choices.

12. **Which of the following is the best candidate for a macro?**
    a. One-button or one-keystroke commands.
    b. Nonsequential tasks.
    c. Seldom-used commands or tasks.
    d. Often-used sequences of commands or actions.

13. **You can open the Visual Basic Editor by clicking the _____ button in the Macro dialog box.**
    a. Edit
    b. Visual Basic Editor
    c. Modules
    d. Programs

14. **Commonly used macros should be stored in:**
    a. The Common Macro Workbook.
    b. The Personal Macro Workbook.
    c. The Master Macro Workbook.
    d. The Custom Macro Workbook.

15. **Which of the following is *not* true about editing a macro?**
    a. A macro cannot be edited and must be recorded again.
    b. You edit macros using the Visual Basic Editor.
    c. You can type changes directly in the existing program code.
    d. You can make more than one editing change in a macro.

16. **Why is it important to plan a macro?**
    a. Macros won't be stored if they contain errors.
    b. Macros can't be deleted.
    c. It is impossible to edit a macro.
    d. Planning helps prevent careless errors from being introduced into the macro.

17. **Macros are recorded with relative references:**
    a. Only if relative references are chosen while recording the macro.
    b. In all cases.
    c. Only if the Relative Reference button is selected.
    d. Only if the Absolute Reference button is not selected.

18. **You can run macros:**
    a. From the Macro dialog box.
    b. From shortcut key combinations.
    c. From custom menu commands.
    d. Using all of the above.

19. **To change the security level for workbooks on your computer you must:**
    a. Click Tools, then click Security.
    b. Click Edit, then click Security.
    c. Click Edit, point to Tools, then click Security.
    d. Click Tools, point to Macros, then click Security.

▼ SKILLS REVIEW

1. **Plan a macro.**
   a. You need to plan a macro that enters and formats your name, address, and telephone number in a worksheet.
   b. Write out the steps the macro will perform.
   c. Write out how the macro could be used in a workbook.

2. Record a macro.

   a. Start Excel, open a new workbook, then save it as **Macros** in the drive and folder where your Data Files are stored. You want to record a macro that enters and formats your name, address, and telephone number in a worksheet.

   b. Name the macro **MyAddress**, store it in the current workbook, and make sure your name appears as the person who recorded the macro.

   c. Record the macro, entering your name in cell A1, your street address in cell A2, your city, state, and ZIP code in cell A3, and your telephone number in cell A4.

   d. Format the information in 12-point Arial bold.

   e. Resize column A to fit the information entirely in that column.

   f. Add a border and make the text blue.

   g. Stop the recorder and save the workbook.

3. Run a macro.

   a. Clear cell entries and formats in the range affected by the macro.

   b. Check the security level for workbooks on your computer. (*Hint*: Click the Tools menu, point to Macro, then click Security.)

   c. Run the MyAddress macro to place your name and address information in cell A1.

   d. On the worksheet, clear all the cell entries and formats generated by running the MyAddress macro.

   e. Save the workbook.

4. Edit a macro.

   a. Open the MyAddress macro in the Visual Basic Editor.

   b. Locate the line of code that defines the font size, then change the size to 16 point.

   c. Edit an existing comment line to describe this macro's function.

   d. Save and print the module, then use the Close and Return to Microsoft Excel option on the File menu to return to Excel.

   e. Test the macro on Sheet1.

   f. Save the workbook.

5. Use shortcut keys with macros.

   a. Record a macro called **NameStamp** in the current workbook that enters your full name in italics in the selected cell of a worksheet. (*Hint*: You need to record a relative cell reference).

   b. Assign your macro the shortcut key combination [Ctrl][Shift][N] and store it in the current workbook, using your name as the creator.

   c. After you record the macro, clear the cell containing your name that you used to record the macro.

   d. Use the shortcut key combination to run the MyName macro.

   e. Save the workbook.

6. Use the Personal Macro Workbook.

   a. Using Sheet1, record a new macro called **FitToLand** and store it in the Personal Macro workbook. The macro should set the print orientation to landscape, with content scaled to fit on one page. If you are prompted to replace the existing FitToLand macro, click Yes.

   b. After you record the macro, activate Sheet2, and enter test data in row 1 that exceeds one page width.

   c. In the Page Setup dialog box, make sure the orientation is set to portrait and the scaling is 100% of normal size.

   d. Run the macro.

   e. Preview Sheet2 and verify that it's in Landscape view and that the test data fits on one page.

   f. Save the workbook.

7. Add a macro as a menu item.

   a. On the Commands tab in the Customize dialog box, specify that you want to use the Macros category to create a Custom Menu Item placing the Custom Menu Item at the bottom of the Tools menu.

   b. Rename the Custom Menu Item **Fit to Landscape**.

   c. Assign the macro PERSONAL.XLS!FitToLand to the command.

   d. Go to Sheet3 and make sure the orientation is set to portrait and the scaling is 100% of normal size. Enter test data in column A that exceeds one page in length.

   e. Run the Fit to Landscape macro from the Tools menu.

    f. Preview the worksheet and verify that it is in landscape view and that the test data fits on one page.

    g. Reset the Worksheet Menu bar.

    h. Verify that the Fit to Landscape command has been removed from the Tools menu.

    i. Save the workbook.

8. Create a toolbar for macros.

    a. With the Macros.xls workbook still open, use the Toolbars tab of the Customize dialog box to create a new custom toolbar, titled **My Info**.

    b. Display the Macros category on the Commands tab of the Customize dialog box, then drag the Custom Button to the My Info toolbar.

    c. Drag the Custom Button to the My Info toolbar a second time to create another button.

    d. Rename the first button **My Address**, and assign the MyAddress macro to it.

    e. Rename the second button **My Name**, and assign the NameStamp macro to it.

    f. Change the second button image to one of your choice.

    g. On Sheet3, clear the existing cell data. Test the first macro button on the My Info toolbar. Select cell A7 and test the second macro button on the My Info toolbar.

    h. Use the Toolbars tab of the Customize dialog box to delete the toolbar named My Info.

    i. Save the workbook, print Sheet3, close the workbook, then exit Excel.

▼ INDEPENDENT CHALLENGE 1

As a computer-support employee of Boston Accounting Solutions, you need to develop ways to help your fellow employees work more efficiently. Employees have asked for Excel macros that can do the following:

- Delete the current row and insert a blank row.
- Delete the current column and insert a blank column.
- Place the department name of Accounting in a 12-point font in red in cell A1 (the width of A1 should be increased if necessary).

    a. Plan and write the steps necessary for each macro.

    b. Start Excel, save a blank workbook as **Excel Utility Macros** in the drive and folder where your Data Files are stored.

    c. Create a macro for each employee request described above, name them DeleteRow, DeleteColumn, and DepartmentName, then save them in the Excel Utility Macros.xls workbook.

    d. Add comment lines to each macro containing your name and describing the function of the macro, then return to Excel.

    e. Use the Commands tab of the Customize dialog box to add three Custom Menu items to the Tools menu. Right-click each Custom Menu item to name the new menu items DeleteRow, DeleteColumn, and DepartmentName. Assign the macros you created in Step c to the new menu items.

    f. Use the Toolbars tab of the Customize dialog box to create a new toolbar called **Helpers**.

    g. Use the Commands tab of the Customize dialog box to drag three Custom buttons to the Helpers toolbar.

    h. Right-click each toolbar button to name them DeleteRow, DeleteColumn, and DepartmentName. Assign the macros created in step c to the new toolbar buttons.

    i. Right-click each toolbar button to change the button images.

    j. Test each macro by using the Run command, the menu command, and the new toolbar button.

    k. Delete the new toolbar, then reset the Worksheet Menu Bar on the toolbars tab of the Customize dialog box.

    l. Save the workbook, print the module containing the program code for all three macros, then close the workbook and exit Excel.

▼ INDEPENDENT CHALLENGE 2

You are an analyst in the Atlantic Bank Loan Department. Every quarter, you produce a number of single-page quarterly budget worksheets. Your manager has informed you that certain worksheets need to contain a footer stamp indicating that the worksheet was produced in the loan department. The footer should also show the current page number out of the total number of pages, (for example, 1 of 5) and the workbook filename. It's tedious to add the footer stamp to the numerous worksheets you produce. You want to record a macro to do this.

a. Plan and write the steps to create the macro described above.

b. Start Excel, save a blank workbook as **Footer Stamp** in the drive and folder where your Data Files are stored.

c. Create the macro using the plan from Step a, name it **footerstamp**, assign it the shortcut key combination [Ctrl][Shift][H], and store it in the current workbook.

d. Edit the macro to add a descriptive comment line with your name.

e. Add the footerstamp macro to the Tools menu.

f. Create a toolbar titled **Stamp**, then add a button to the toolbar to run the macro.

g. Enter the text **Testing Footer** in cell A1. Test the macro using the shortcut key combination, then delete the footer. Test the macro using the menu command on the Tools menu, then delete the footer again. Test the new button on the Stamp toolbar.

h. Delete the new toolbar, then reset the Worksheet Menu Bar.

i. Save the workbook, print the module for the macro, close the module and the workbook, then exit Excel.

j. Create a folder named **Macros** in the drive and folder where your Data Files are stored then drag a copy of the Footer Stamp.xls file into the Macros folder.

k. Rename the folder **Footer Macros**.

l. Close the workbook, then exit Excel.

▼ INDEPENDENT CHALLENGE 3

You are an administrative assistant at the Sydney, Australia, branch of Computers Inc. A major part of your job is to create spreadsheets that project sales results in different markets. It seems that you are constantly changing the print settings so that workbooks print in landscape orientation and are scaled to fit on one page. You have decided that it's time to create a macro to streamline this process.

a. Plan and write the steps necessary to create the macro.

b. Start Excel, create a new workbook, then save it as **Computers Inc Macro** in the drive and folder where your Data Files are stored.

c. Create a macro that changes the page orientation to landscape and scales the worksheet to fit on one page. Name the macro **LandFit**, assign it the shortcut key combination [Ctrl][Shift][L], and store it in the current workbook.

d. Add the macro to the Tools menu.

e. Go to Sheet2 and enter the text **Testing Macro** in cell A1 and enter your name in cell A2. Enter test data in column A that exceeds one page in length. Test the macro using the new menu command.

f. Reset the Worksheet Menu Bar and go to Sheet3.

FIGURE G-22

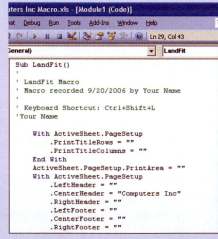

g. Edit the macro to include the company name, **Computers Inc**, in the center header and add your name as a comment. Use Figure G-22 as a guide. Enter test data in row 1 that exceeds one page in width. Test the macro using the shortcut key combination, making sure the header was added.

h. Add a custom menu to the standard toolbar and name it **Macros**. Add a custom menu item to the new Macros menu, name the menu option **Page Orientation**, and assign the LandFit macro to it.

i. On Sheet3, delete the header and change the page orientation to portrait, then test the macro using the new menu.

▼ INDEPENDENT CHALLENGE 3 (CONTINUED)

j. Reset the standard toolbar.

k. Print the module for the macro.

Advanced Challenge Exercise

- Use the Help feature in Excel to research how digital certificates, used to sign a macro, are obtained and copy your findings into Sheet1.
- Use the Help feature to find the difference between class 2 and class 3 digital certificates and copy your findings into Sheet1.
- Use the Help feature to find the steps to digitally sign a file and copy the steps into Sheet1. Print Sheet1.

l. Save and close the workbook, then exit Excel.

▼ INDEPENDENT CHALLENGE 4

PC Assist, a software training company, has decided to begin purchasing its branch office supplies through online vendors. One of the products the company needs to purchase is toner for the Hewlett-Packard LaserJet 3100 printers in the offices. You have been asked to research vendors and prices on the Web. You want to create a workbook to hold office supply vendor information that you can use for various products. You want to add a macro to this workbook to find the lowest price of the product, format the information, and add a descriptive footer to the worksheet.

Using the search engine of your choice, find three online suppliers of toner for the company's printers and note their prices.

a. Start Excel, create a new workbook, then save it as **Office Supplies**.

b. Complete the table below with three online suppliers of office products you found in your search.

c. Enter three vendors and their prices from your table into your worksheet. Enter the Product name **Toner** in the cell next to Office Product.

d. Create a macro named **Toner** in the Office Supplies.xls workbook that can be activated by the [Ctrl][Shift][T] key combination. The macro should do the following:

Office Product	
Vendor	Price
Lowest Price	

- Find the lowest price for the office product and insert it to the right of the Lowest Price label.
- Boldface the Lowest Price text and the cell to its right that will contain the lowest value.
- Place a thick box border around all the information.
- Fill the information area with a light turquoise color.
- Add a footer with the company name **PC Assist** on the left and the workbook name on the right.

e. Clear all the formatting, the footer, and the lowest price from the worksheet.

f. Test the macro using the key combination [Ctrl][Shift][T].

g. Enter your name in cell A15, save your workbook, then print the results of the macro. Open the macro in the Visual Basic Editor, enter your name as a comment, then print the macro code.

Advanced Challenge Exercise

- Return to Excel and create a macro named **Toner_Average** that does the following:
  - Inserts a label **Average Price** under the Lowest Price label.
  - Finds the average toner price, inserts it under the lowest price, and formats it as a number with two decimal places.
  - Boldfaces the Average Price label and the average toner price.
- Delete the average toner price that was inserted by recording the Toner_Average macro. Do not delete the Average Price label.
- Make the Average Price label a hotspot that runs the macro when clicked. Run the Toner_Average macro using the hotspot.
- In the Visual Basic code for the Toner_Average macro, enter your name as a comment, then print the macro code.

h. Print the worksheet. Save and close the workbook, then exit Excel.

▼ VISUAL WORKSHOP

Create the macro shown in Figure G-23. (*Hint*: Enter the months using the default font size, then change the size to the size shown.) Test the macro, save the workbook as **Accounting Macro**, and then print the module.

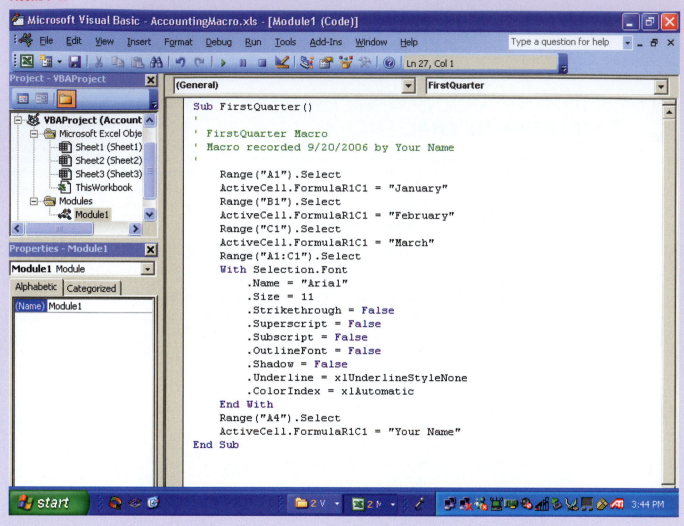

UNIT
H
Excel 2003

Using Lists

OBJECTIVES

Plan a list
Create a list
Add records with the data form
Find records
Delete records
Sort a list on one field
Sort a list on multiple fields
Print a list

If you have a SAM user profile, you may have access to hands-on instruction, practice, and assessment of the skills covered in this unit. Log in to your SAM account and go to your assignments page to see what your instructor has assigned.

In addition to using Excel's spreadsheet features, you can also use Excel as a database. A **database** is an organized collection of related information, such as a telephone book, a card catalog, or a roster of company employees. A worksheet used as a database contains rows and columns of similarly structured data and is called a **list**. Using an Excel list, you can organize and manage worksheet information so that you can quickly find data for projects, reports, and charts. In this unit, you'll learn how to plan and create a list; add, change, find, and delete information in a list; and then sort and print a list. MediaLoft uses lists to analyze new customer information. MediaLoft marketing director Jim Fernandez has asked you to help him build and manage a list of new customers as part of the ongoing strategy to focus on the company's advertising expenses.

Planning a List

When planning a list, consider what information the list needs to contain and how you want to work with the data, now and in the future. As you plan a list, you should understand its most important components. A list is organized into rows called records. A **record** contains data about an object or person. Records are composed of fields. **Fields** are columns in the list; each field describes a characteristic about the record, such as a customer's last name or street address. Each field has a **field name**, a column label that describes the field. To plan your list, use the steps below. See Table H-1 for additional planning guidelines. If your list contains more records than can fit on one worksheet (that is, more than 65,536 records), you should consider using database software rather than spreadsheet software. ▓▓▓▓ Jim has asked you to compile a list of new customers. Before entering the data into an Excel worksheet, you plan the list using the following guidelines.

DETAILS

- ### Identify the purpose of the list
  Determine the kind of information the list should contain. Jim wants to use the list to identify how new customers found out about MediaLoft.

- ### Plan the structure of the list
  Determine the fields that make up a record. Jim has customer cards that contain information about each new customer. Figure H-1 shows a typical card. Each record will contain data for one customer. The fields in each record correspond to the descriptive information on the cards.

- ### Write down the names of the fields
  Field names appear in the first row of a list. Field names can be up to 255 characters long (the maximum column width), although shorter names are easier to see in the cells. Field names describe each piece of information. Jim's list will contain nine field names, each one corresponding to the nine pieces of information on each card.

- ### Determine any special number formatting required in the list
  Most lists contain both text and numbers. When planning a list, consider whether any fields require specific number formatting. For example, some zip codes begin with zero. Because Excel automatically drops a leading zero when entering numeric data, you must format zip code fields using a special format to display the full zip code. Jim's list includes a zip code field that needs this format.

FIGURE H-1: Customer record and corresponding field names

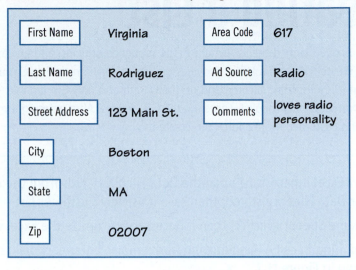

TABLE H-1: Guidelines for planning a list

worksheet structure guidelines	row and column content guidelines
Lists can be created from any contiguous range of cells on your worksheet	Plan and design your list so that all rows have similar items in the same column
A list should not have any blank rows or columns	Do not insert extra spaces at the beginning of a cell because that can affect sorting and searching
Data defined by your list can be used independently of data outside of the list on the worksheet	Instead of blank rows or columns between your labels and your data, use formatting to make column labels stand out from the data
Data can be organized on a worksheet using multiple lists to define sets of related data	Use the same format for all cells below the field name in a column

Creating a List

Once you have planned the list structure, the sequence of fields, and any appropriate formatting, you are ready to create the list. Table H-2 provides guidelines for naming fields. You then select the range and tell Excel that it is a list using a command on the Data menu. Jim asks you to build a list with his customer information. You begin by entering the field names. After entering the field names, you enter the corresponding customer information, then create the list.

STEPS

1. **Start Excel if necessary, open the Data File EX H-1.xls from the drive and folder where your Data Files are stored, then save it as New Customer List**

2. **Rename Sheet1 Practice, then if necessary maximize the Excel window**

> **QUICK TIP**
>
> If the field name you plan to use is wider than the data in the column, you can turn on Wrap Text on the Alignment tab in the Format Cells dialog box to stack the heading in the cell. You can also press [Alt][Enter] to force a line break while entering field names.

3. **Beginning in cell A1 and moving horizontally, enter each field name in a separate cell, as shown in Figure H-2**

   Field names are usually in the first row of the list. Don't worry if your field names are wider than the cells; you will fix this later.

4. **Select the field headings in range A1:I1, then click the Bold button B on the Formatting toolbar; with range A1:I1 still selected, click the Borders list arrow, then click the Thick Bottom Border (second column, second row)**

5. **Enter the information from Figure H-3 in the rows immediately below the field names, without leaving any blank rows**

   The data appears in columns organized by field name. The leading zeroes are dropped in the zip code column.

6. **Select column F, click Format on the menu bar, click Cells, on the Number tab under Category click Special, from the Type list click Zip Code, then click OK**

   The zip codes now have leading zeroes.

7. **Select the range A1:I4, click Format on the menu bar, point to Column, then click AutoFit Selection**

   Resizing the column widths this way is faster than double-clicking the column divider lines between each pair of columns.

> **QUICK TIP**
>
> If the List toolbar doesn't appear, click View on the menu bar, point to Toolbars, then click List.

8. **With A1:I4 selected, click Data on the menu bar, point to List, click Create List, make sure My list has headers is checked, click OK, then press [Ctrl][Home] to return to cell A1**

   The List toolbar appears and the list now has a blue border. See Figure H-4. **AutoFilter list arrows**, which let you display portions of your data, appear next to each column header. The blank last row of the list is the insert row, ready for new list data to be added.

TABLE H-2: Guidelines for naming fields

guideline	explanation
Use text to name fields	Numbers can be interpreted as parts of formulas
Do not use duplicate field names	Duplicate field names can cause Excel to enter and sort information incorrectly
Use descriptive names	Avoid names that might be confused with cell addresses, such as Q4

FIGURE H-2: Field names entered and formatted in row 1

FIGURE H-3: Cards with customer information

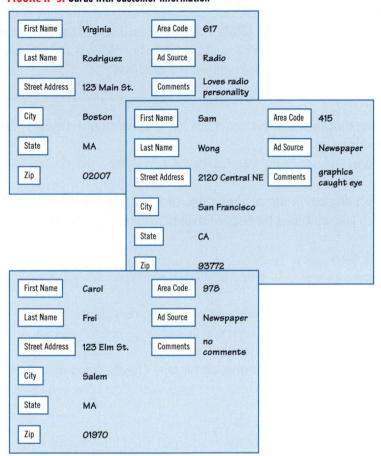

FIGURE H-4: List with three records

AutoFilter drop-down arrow

Blue border defines the list

Insert row

List toolbar (your toolbar location might differ)

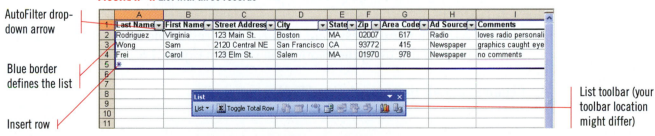

Adding Records with the Data Form

You can add records to a list by typing data directly into the last row of the list, which is called the **insert row**. Typing information in this row automatically adds the data to the list and expands the list's boundaries. You can also use a data form as a quick, easy method of data entry. A **data form** is a dialog box that displays one record at a time. You have entered all the customer records Jim had on his cards, but he receives the names of two additional customers. You decide to add the new customer information to the list using both methods: the data form and the insert row.

STEPS

1. **Make sure the New Customer List file is open, then activate Sheet2 and rename it Working List**

   Working List contains the nearly completed customer list.

   > **QUICK TIP**
   > You can also open a data form by clicking List on the List toolbar and then clicking Form.

2. **Select any cell in the customer list, click Data on the menu bar, then click Form**

   A data form containing the first record appears, as shown in Figure H-5.

3. **Click New**

   A blank data form appears with the insertion point in the first field.

   > **TROUBLE**
   > If you accidentally press [↑] or [↓] while in a data form and find that you displayed the wrong record, press [↑] or [↓] until you return to the desired record.

4. **Type Chavez in the Last Name box, then press [Tab]**

   The insertion point moves to the next field.

5. **Enter the rest of the information for Jane Chavez, using the information shown in Figure H-6**

   Press [Tab] to move the insertion point to the next field, or click in the next field box to move the insertion point there.

6. **Click Close to add Jane Chavez's record, then if necessary scroll down to view the end of the list**

   The record that you added with the data form appears at the end of the list.

   > **QUICK TIP**
   > Excel automatically extends formatting and formulas in lists.

7. **Click cell A47, enter Ross, press [Tab], then enter the rest of the information for Cathy Ross in the insert row using the information shown in Figure H-6**

8. **Return to cell A1, then save the workbook**

FIGURE H-5: Data form showing first record in the list

Current record number

Working List		1 of 44
Last Name:	Rodriguez	New
First Name:	Virginia	Delete
Street Address:	123 Main St.	Restore
City:	Boston	
State:	MA	Find Prev
Zip:	2007	Find Next
Area Code:	617	Criteria
Ad Source:	Radio	
Comments :	loves radio personality	Close

Total number of records

Click to open a blank data
form for adding a record

FIGURE H-6: Information for two new records

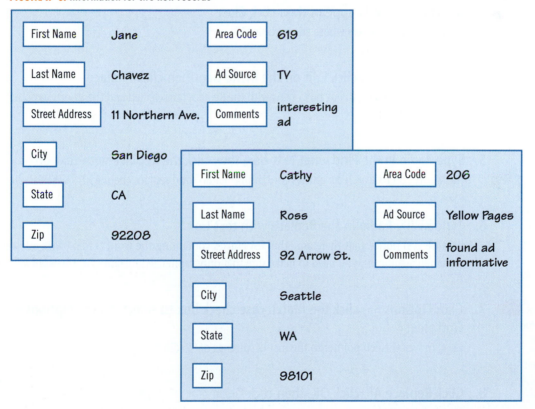

First Name	Jane	Area Code	619
Last Name	Chavez	Ad Source	TV
Street Address	11 Northern Ave.	Comments	interesting ad
City	San Diego		
State	CA		
Zip	92208		

First Name	Cathy	Area Code	206
Last Name	Ross	Ad Source	Yellow Pages
Street Address	92 Arrow St.	Comments	found ad informative
City	Seattle		
State	WA		
Zip	98101		

Finding Records

From time to time, you need to locate specific records in your list. You can use the Excel Find command on the Edit menu or the data form to search your list. You can also use the Replace command on the Edit menu to locate and replace existing entries or portions of entries with specified information. Jim wants to be more specific about the radio ad source, so he asks you to replace "Radio" with "KWIN Radio." He also wants to know how many of the new customers originated from the company's TV ads. You begin by searching for those records with the ad source "TV."

STEPS

1. Click cell A1 if necessary, click Data on the menu bar, click Form, then click Criteria

The data form changes so that all fields are blank and "Criteria" appears in the upper-right corner. See Figure H-7. In this dialog box, you enter criteria that specify the records you want to find. You want to search for records whose Ad Source field contains the label "TV."

2. Click in the Ad Source text box, type TV, then click Find Next

Excel displays the first record for a customer who learned about the company through its TV ads. See Figure H-8.

3. Click Find Next and examine the Ad Source field for each found record until no more matching records appear, then click Close

There are six customers whose ad source is TV.

4. Return to cell A1, click Edit on the menu bar, then click Replace

The Find and Replace dialog box opens with the Replace tab selected and the insertion point in the Find what box. See Figure H-9.

5. Type Radio in the Find what text box, then click the Replace with text box

Jim wants you to search for entries containing "Radio" and replace them with "KWIN Radio."

6. Type KWIN Radio in the Replace with text box

Because you notice that there are other list entries containing the word "radio" with a lowercase "r" (in the Comments column), you need to make sure that only capitalized instances of the word are replaced.

7. Click Options >>, click the Match case check box to select it, click Options <<, then click Find Next

Excel moves the cell pointer to the first occurrence of "Radio."

8. Click Replace All, click OK, then click Close

The dialog box closes. Excel made seven replacements. Note that in the Comments column, each instance of the word "radio" remains unchanged.

9. Make sure there are no entries in the Ad Source column that read "Radio," then save the workbook

FIGURE H-7: Criteria data form

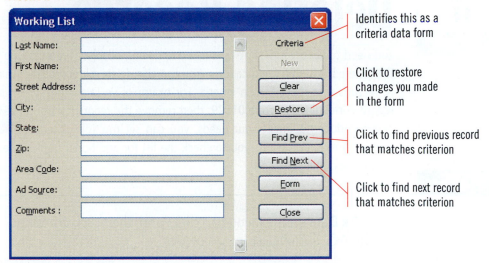

Identifies this as a
criteria data form

Click to restore
changes you made
in the form

Click to find previous record
that matches criterion

Click to find next record
that matches criterion

FIGURE H-8: Finding a record using the data form

Record number of
the displayed record

FIGURE H-9: Find and Replace dialog box

Type Radio here

Type KWIN Radio here

Click to replace all
occurrences of
item in the Find
what text box

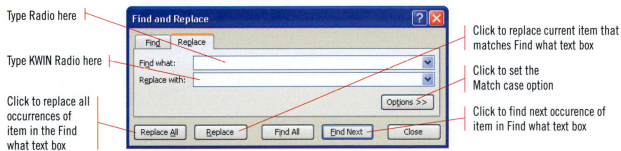

Click to replace current item that
matches Find what text box

Click to set the
Match case option

Click to find next occurence of
item in Find what text box

Clues to Use

Using wildcards to fine-tune your search

You can use special symbols called **wildcards** when defining search criteria in the data form or Replace dialog box. The question mark (?) wildcard stands for any single character. For example, if you do not know whether a customer's last name is Paulsen or Paulson, you can specify Pauls?n as the search criteria to locate

both options. The asterisk (*) wildcard stands for any group of characters. For example, if you specify Jan* as the search criteria in the First Name field, Excel locates all records with first names beginning with Jan (for instance, Jan, Janet, and Janice).

Deleting Records

You need to keep your list up to date by removing obsolete records. One way to remove records is to use the Delete button on the data form. You can also delete all records that share something in common—that is, records that meet certain criteria. For example, you can specify a criterion for Excel to find the next record containing zip code 01879, then remove the record by using the Delete button. If specifying one criterion does not meet your needs, you can set multiple criteria. 🖌️ Jim notices two entries for Carolyn Smith, and wants you to check the list for additional duplicate entries. You use the data form to delete the duplicate record.

STEPS

1. Click Data on the menu bar, click Form, then click Criteria

The Criteria data form opens.

QUICK TIP

You can use the data form to edit records by finding the desired record and editing the data in the appropriate box.

2. Type Smith in the Last Name text box, press [Tab] to move the insertion point to the First Name text box, type Carolyn, then click Find Next

Excel displays the first record for a customer whose name is Carolyn Smith. You decide to leave the initial entry for Carolyn Smith (record 5 of 46) and delete the second one, once you confirm that it is a duplicate.

3. Click Find Next

The duplicate record for Carolyn Smith, number 40, appears as shown in Figure H-10. You are ready to delete the duplicate entry.

QUICK TIP

Clicking Restore on the data form undoes your changes when you are adding a new record, as long as you click it before you press [Enter] or click Close. Restore cannot restore deleted record(s).

4. Click Delete, then click OK to confirm the deletion

The duplicate record for Carolyn Smith is deleted, and all the other records move up one row. The data form now shows the record for Manuel Julio.

5. Click Close to return to the worksheet, if necessary scroll down until rows 41–46 are visible, then read the entry in row 41

Notice that the duplicate entry for Carolyn Smith is gone and that Manuel Julio moved up a row and is now in row 41. You also notice a record for K. C. Splint in row 43, which is a duplicate entry.

6. Return to cell A1, and read the record information for K. C. Splint in row 8

After confirming the duplicate entry, you decide to delete the row.

7. Click cell A8, click List on the List toolbar, then point to Delete

The delete options are displayed. See Figure H-11.

8. Click Row

The duplicate record for K. C. Splint is deleted and the other records move up to fill in the gap.

9. Save the workbook

FIGURE H-10: Data form showing duplicate record for Carolyn Smith

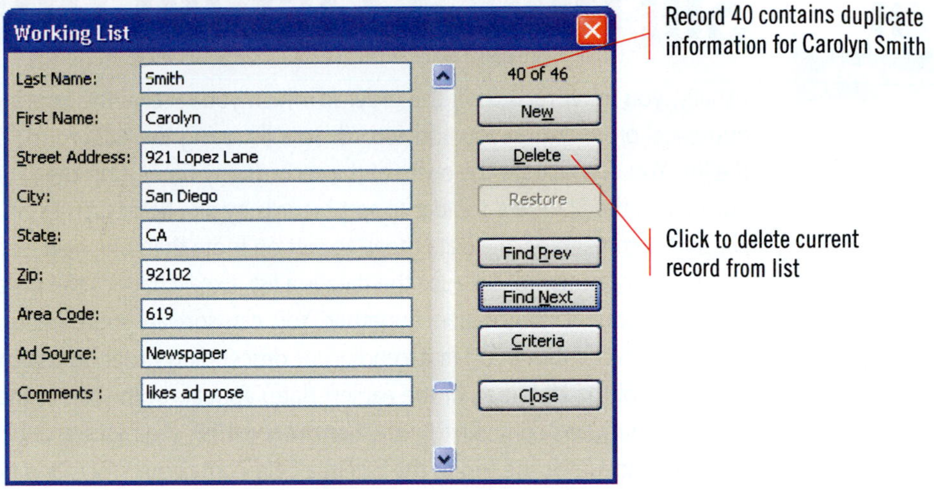

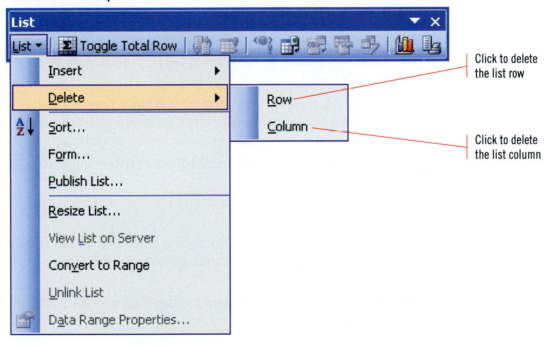

Record 40 contains duplicate information for Carolyn Smith

Click to delete current record from list

FIGURE H-11: Delete options

Click to delete the list row

Click to delete the list column

Clues to Use

Deleting records using the worksheet

When you delete a record using the data form, you cannot undo your deletion. When you delete a record by deleting its row in the worksheet, however, you can immediately retrieve it. To do so, you can either use the Undo command on the Edit menu, click the Undo button on the Standard toolbar, or press [Ctrl][Z].

Sorting a List on One Field

Usually, you enter records in the order in which you receive the information, rather than in alphabetical or numerical order. When you add records to a list using the data form, Excel adds the records to the end of the list. You can change the order of the records any time using the Excel **sort** feature. You can use the sort buttons on the Standard toolbar to sort records by one field, such as zip code or last name. You can also use the Sort command on the Data menu to sort on more than one field, such as zip code and then, within each zip code, by last name. Because the data is a list, Excel changes the order of the records while keeping each record, or row of information, together. You can sort an entire list or any portion of a list, and you can arrange sorted information in ascending or descending order. In **ascending order**, the lowest value (the beginning of the alphabet, or the earliest date) appears at the top of the list. In a field containing labels and numbers, numbers come first. In **descending order**, the highest value (the end of the alphabet or the latest date) appears at the top of the list. In a field containing labels and numbers, labels come first. Table H-3 provides examples of ascending and descending sorts. Because Jim wants to be able to return the records to their original order following any sorts, he wants you to create a new field called Entry Order. You then perform several single field sorts on the list.

STEPS

QUICK TIP

Before you sort records, consider making a backup copy of your list or create a field that numbers the records so you can return them to their original order, if necessary.

1. **Click cell J1, enter the column heading Entry Order, then format cell J1 with a thick bottom border**

   The AutoCorrect options button appears after you enter the label because the list is expanded to include the new column.

2. **Type 1 in cell J2, press [Enter], type 2 in cell J3, press [Enter], select cells J2:J3, then drag the fill handle to cell J45**

3. **Return to cell A1, then scroll to bring column J into view**

   The records are numbered as shown in Figure H-12. You are now ready to sort the list in ascending order by last name. You must position the cell pointer within the column you want to sort before issuing the sort command.

QUICK TIP

If your sort does not perform as you intended, press [Ctrl][Z] immediately to undo the sort.

4. **Return to cell A1 if necessary, then click the Sort Ascending button [A↓] on the Standard toolbar**

   Excel rearranges the records in ascending order by last name, as shown in Figure H-13. You can also sort the list in descending order by any field.

5. **Click cell G5, then click the Sort Descending button [Z↓] on the Standard toolbar**

   Excel sorts the list, placing those records with higher-digit area codes at the top. You are now ready to return the list to its original entry order.

6. **Click cell J1, click [A↓] on the Standard toolbar, then save the workbook**

   The list returns to its original order.

TABLE H-3: Sort order options and examples

option	alphabetic	numeric	date	alphanumeric
Ascending	A, B, C	7, 8, 9	1/1, 2/1, 3/1	12A, 99B, DX8, QT7
Descending	C, B, A	9, 8, 7	3/1, 2/1, 1/1	QT7, DX8, 99B, 12A

FIGURE H-12: List with Entry Order field added

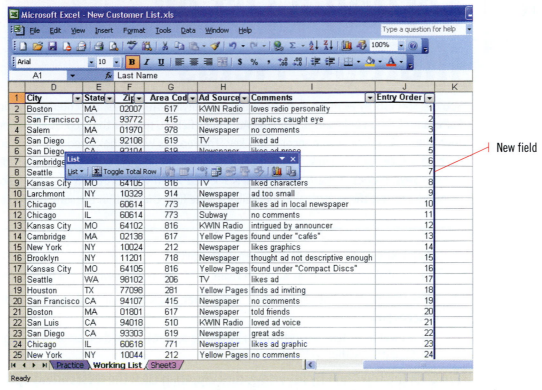

New field

FIGURE H-13: List sorted alphabetically by Last Name field

Record for Jane Chavez is kept together in the sorted list

Clues to Use

Sorting records using the AutoFilter

You can sort a list in ascending or descending order on one field using the AutoFilter list arrows next to the field name. Click the AutoFilter list arrow, then click Sort Ascending or Sort Descending to sort the list in the desired order. You may need to scroll up to the top of the list to see the sort commands.

UNIT H

Excel 2003

Sorting a List on Multiple Fields

You can sort lists by as many as three fields by specifying **sort keys**, the criteria on which the sort is based. For example, you could sort first on the Ad Source field to reorder the records according to ad source, and then specify Last Name as a second sort key. The records would be sorted by Ad Source, and then within each ad source, by last name. You can enter up to three column headings in the Sort dialog box to specify the sort keys. It doesn't matter which cell is selected when you sort using the Sort dialog box. Jim wants you to sort the records alphabetically by state first, then within the state by zip code.

STEPS

QUICK TIP

You can include capitalization as a sort criterion by clicking Options in the Sort dialog box, then selecting the Case sensitive box. When you choose this option, lowercase entries precede uppercase entries.

1. **Click List on the List toolbar, then click Sort**

   The Sort dialog box opens, as shown in Figure H-14. You want to sort the list by state and then by zip code.

2. **Click the Sort by list arrow, click State, then click the Ascending option button to select it, if necessary**

   The list will be sorted alphabetically in ascending order (A–Z) by the State field. A second sort criterion will sort the entries within each state grouping.

3. **Click the top Then by list arrow, click Zip, then click the Descending option button**

   You could also sort by a third key by selecting a field in the bottom Then by list box.

4. **Click OK to perform the sort, return to cell A1, then scroll through the list to see the result of the sort**

   The list is sorted alphabetically by state in ascending order, then within each state by zip code in descending order. Compare your results with Figure H-15.

5. **Save the workbook**

FIGURE H-14: Sort dialog box

First sort field
Second sort field
Third sort field
Fields on which the sort will be based

FIGURE H-15: List sorted by two fields

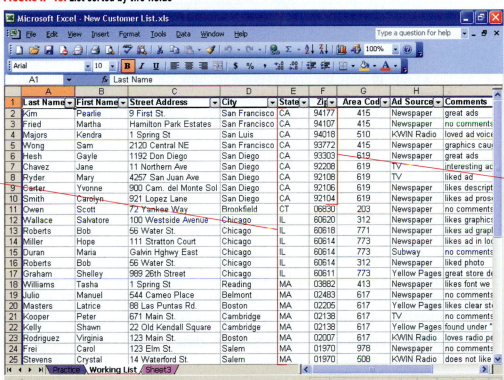

First sort by state in ascending order

Second sort by zip code in descending order

Excel 2003

Clues to Use

Specifying a custom sort order

You can identify a custom sort order for the field selected in the Sort by box. Click Options in the Sort dialog box, click the First key sort order list arrow, then click the desired custom order. Commonly used custom sort orders are days of the week (Sun, Mon, Tues, Wed, etc.) and months (Jan, Feb, Mar, etc.); alphabetic sorts do not sort these items properly.

Printing a List

If a list is small enough to fit on one page, you can print it as you would any other Excel worksheet. If you have more columns than can fit on a portrait-oriented page, you can set the page orientation to landscape. Because lists often have more rows than can fit on a page, you can define the first row of the list (containing the field names) as the **print title**, which prints at the top of every page. Most lists do not have any descriptive information above the field names on the worksheet. To augment the information contained in the field names, you can use headers and footers to add identifying text, such as the list title or report date. If you want to exclude any fields from your list report, you can hide the selected columns from view so that they do not print. Jim has finished updating his list and would like you to print it. You begin by previewing the list.

STEPS

1. **Click the Print Preview button on the Standard toolbar**

   The status bar reads Preview: Page 1 of 2. You want all the field names in the list to fit on a single page, but you need two pages to fit all the data.

2. **In the Print Preview window, click Setup, click the Page tab if necessary, click the Landscape option button under Orientation, click the Fit to option button under Scaling, double-click the tall box and type 2, click OK, then click Next**

   The list still does not fit on a single page. Because the records on page 2 appear without column headings, you want to set up the first row of the list, which contains the field names, as a repeating print title.

   > **QUICK TIP**
   >
   > If you open the Page Setup dialog box from the Print Preview window, you cannot set print titles. You must choose Page Setup from the File menu to assign print titles.

3. **Click Close to close the Print Preview window, click File on the menu bar, click Page Setup, click the Sheet tab, click the Rows to repeat at top text box under Print titles, click any cell in row 1, compare your Page Setup dialog box to Figure H-16, then click OK**

   When you select row 1 as a print title, Excel automatically inserts an absolute reference to a beginning row to repeat at the top of each page—in this case, the print title to repeat beginning and ending with row 1.

4. **Click , click Next to view the second page, then click Zoom**

   Setting up a print title to repeat row 1 causes the field names to appear at the top of each printed page.

5. **Click Setup, click the Header/Footer tab, click Custom Header, click the Left section box and enter your name, then click the Center section box and enter MediaLoft -, press [Spacebar], then click the Filename button**

6. **Select the header information in the Center section box, click the Font button , change the font size to 14 and the style to Bold, click OK, click OK again to return to the Header/Footer tab, click OK to preview the list, then click Close**

   > **QUICK TIP**
   >
   > To print more than one worksheet, select each sheet tab while holding down [Shift] or [Ctrl], then click the Print button .

7. **Save the workbook, print the worksheet, close the workbook, then exit Excel**

   Compare your printed worksheet with Figure H-17.

Indicates that row 1 will appear at the top of each printed page

Indicates which columns will appear at the left of each printed page

Turns gridline display on or off

Displays row and column headings on printout

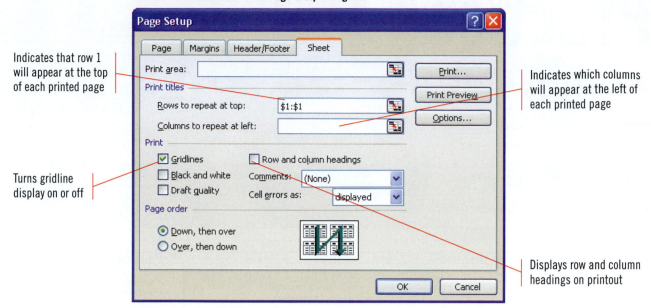

FIGURE H-17: Completed list

Clues to Use

Setting a print area

There are times when you want to print only part of a worksheet. To do this, select any worksheet range, then click File on the menu bar and click Print. In the Print dialog box, choose Selection under Print what, then click OK. If you want to print a selected area repeatedly, it's best to define a **print area**, which prints when you click the Print button on the Standard toolbar. To set a print area, click View on the menu bar, then click Page Break Preview. In the preview window, select the area you want to print. (If you see a Welcome dialog box,

click OK.) Right-click the area, then select Set Print Area. The print area becomes outlined in a blue border. You can drag the border to extend the print area or add nonadjacent cells to it by selecting them, right-clicking them, then selecting Add to Print Area. When printing a print area that is part of a list, you must select Active sheet, rather than List, in the Print what section of the Print dialog box. To clear a print area, click File on the menu bar, point to Print Area, then click Clear Print Area.

Practice

▼ CONCEPTS REVIEW

FIGURE H-18

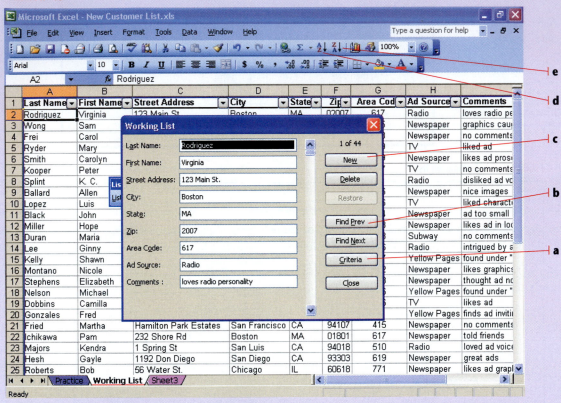

1. Which element do you click to sort a list in ascending order?
2. Which element do you click to sort a list in descending order?
3. Which element do you click to open a blank data form?
4. Which element do you click to search for records by specifying data in a field?
5. Which element do you click to find an earlier occurrence of a record that matches specified criteria?

Match each term with the statement that best describes it.

6. **Data form**   **a.** Arrange records in a particular sequence
7. **Record**   **b.** Organized collection of related information in Excel
8. **List**   **c.** Row in an Excel list
9. **Field name**   **d.** Used for entering data into a list
10. **Sort**   **e.** Label positioned at the top of the column identifying data

Select the best answer from the list of choices.

11. **Which of the following Excel sorting options do you use to sort a list of employee names in order from Z to A?**
    a. Absolute
    b. Ascending
    c. Alphabetic
    d. Descending

12. **Which of the following series appears in descending order?**
    a. 4, 5, 6, A, B, C
    b. 8, 6, 4, C, B, A
    c. 8, 7, 6, 5, 6, 7
    d. C, B, A, 6, 5, 4

13. **What color is the border that encloses a list on a worksheet?**
    a. Red
    b. Blue
    c. Green
    d. Yellow

14. **When printing a list on multiple pages, you can define a print title containing repeating row(s) to:**
    a. Include appropriate fields in the printout.
    b. Include the header in list reports.
    c. Include field names at the top of each printed page.
    d. Exclude from the printout all rows under the first row.

▼ SKILLS REVIEW

1. **Create a list.**
   a. Create a new workbook, then save it as **Employee List** in the drive and folder where your Data Files are stored.
   b. Enter the field names and records shown in the following table:
   c. Apply bold formatting to the field names and center the field names in the columns.
   d. Adjust the column widths to make the data readable.

Last Name	First Name	Years Employed	Position	Full/Part Time	Training?
Lenon	Sarah	5	Video Sales	F	Y
Marino	Donato	3	CD Sales	P	N
Khederian	Jay	4	Video Sales	F	Y
Jones	Cathy	1	Video Sales	F	N
Rabinowicz	Miriam	2	CD Sales	P	Y

   e. Select the field names and the records, then create a list from the selected range. Adjust the column widths, if necessary, to display the field names.
   f. Enter your name in the worksheet footer, then save and print the list.

2. **Add records with the data form.**
   a. Click any record in the list.
   b. Open the data form and add a new record for **Danielle Gitano**, a one-year employee in book sales. Danielle works full time and has not completed training.
   c. Use the insert row to add a new record for **George Worthen**. George works full time, has worked at the company five years in book sales, and has completed training.
   d. Use the insert row to add a new record for **Valerie Atkins**. Valerie works full time, has worked at the company three years in video sales, and has completed training.
   e. Save the file.

3. **Find and delete records.**

   a. Use the Find command to find the record for **Cathy Jones**.

   b. Delete the record.

   c. Use the Find command to find the record for **Valerie Atkins**.

   d. Delete the record.

   e. Save the file.

4. **Sort a list on one field.**

   a. Sort the list in descending order by years employed.

   b. Sort the list alphabetically in descending order by training.

   c. Sort the list alphabetically in ascending order by position.

   d. Sort the list alphabetically in ascending order by last name.

   e. Save the file.

5. **Sort a list on multiple fields.**

   a. Sort the list first in ascending order by years employed and then alphabetically in descending order by last name.

   b. Check the list to make sure the records appear in the correct order.

   c. Sort the list alphabetically in ascending order, first by whether or not the employees have completed training and then by last name.

   d. Check the list to make sure the records appear in the correct order.

   e. Save the file.

6. **Print a list.**

   a. Add a header that reads **Employee Information** in the center, then format the header in bold.

   b. Add the file name to the center section of the footer.

   c. Use the Margins tab in the Page Setup dialog box to add top and bottom margins of one inch.

   d. Select all of the information in the worksheet and change the font size to 16.

   e. Use the Sheet tab of the Page Setup dialog box to add column A as a print title that repeats at the left of each printed page.

   f. Save the workbook, then print the list.

   g. Close the workbook, then exit Excel.

▼ INDEPENDENT CHALLENGE 1

You own Personalize IT, an advertising firm located in New Zealand. The firm sells specialty items imprinted with the customer's name and/or logo such as hats, pens, mugs, and T-shirts. Plan and build a list of order information with eight records using the items sold. Your list should contain at least five different customers. (Some customers may place more than one order.)

a. Prepare a list plan that states your goal, outlines the data you need, and identifies the list elements.

b. Sketch a sample list on a piece of paper, indicating how the list should be built. Which of the data fields should be formatted as labels? As values?

c. Start Excel, create a new workbook, then save it as **Personalize IT** in the drive and folder where your Data Files are stored. Build the list by first entering **Personalize IT** as the worksheet title in cell A1, then enter the following field names in the designated cells:

d. Enter eight data records using your own data.

e. Select the range A2:E10 and create a list. Adjust the column widths as necessary.

f. Enter **Subtotal** in cell F2, **Total** in cell G2, **Tax** in cell H2, and **.125** in cell I2 (the 12.5% Goods and Services tax). Make sure the new items are added to the list range.

g. Enter formulas to calculate the subtotal (Quantity*Cost) in cell F3 and the total (including tax) in cell G3. Copy the formulas down the columns.

h. Format the Cost, Subtotal, and Total columns as currency. Adjust the column widths as necessary.

i. Add a new record to your list using the data form. Add another record using the insert row.

Cell	Field name
A2	Customer Last
B2	Customer First
C2	Item
D2	Quantity
E2	Cost

▼ INDEPENDENT CHALLENGE 1 (CONTINUED)

j. Sort the list in ascending order by Item using the Sort Ascending button on the Standard toolbar.

k. Enter your name in the worksheet footer, then save the workbook.

l. Preview the worksheet, print the worksheet on one page, close the workbook, then exit Excel.

▼ INDEPENDENT CHALLENGE 2

You are taking a class titled Television Shows: Past and Present at a local community college. The instructor has given you an Excel list of television programs from the '60s and '70s. She has included fields tracking the following information: the number of years the show was a favorite, favorite character, the show's length in minutes, least favorite character, and comments about the show. The instructor has included data for each show in the list. She has asked you to add a field (column label) and one record (a show of your choosing) to the list. Because the list should cover only 30-minute shows, you need to delete any records for shows longer than 30 minutes. Also, your instructor wants you to sort and format the list as needed before printing. Feel free to change any of the list data to suit your tastes and opinions.

a. Start Excel, open the file EX H-2.xls from the drive and folder where your Data Files are stored, then save it as **Television Shows of the Past**.

b. Add a field called **Rating** in column G. The list formatting should be extended to include the new column and your worksheet should look like Figure H-19. Complete the Rating field for each record with a value of 1–5 with 5 being the highest, that reflects the rating you would give the television show.

c. Use the data form to add one record for a 30-minute show to the list. Make sure to enter information in every field.

d. Use the data form to delete any records having show lengths other than 30. (*Hint*: Use the comparison operator <> in the Show Length field to find records not equal to 30.)

FIGURE H-19

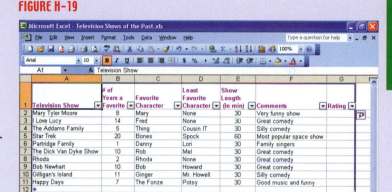

e. Make any formatting changes to the list as needed and save the list.

f. Sort the list in ascending order by show name.

g. Enter your name in the worksheet footer, save the workbook, then print the list.

h. Sort the list again, this time in descending order by the number of years the show was a favorite.

i. Add a centered header that reads **Television Shows of the Past: '60s and '70s**.

j. Save the workbook, preview it, then print the list.

Advanced Challenge Exercise

■ Use the Page Break Preview view to create a print area that prints only the first two columns, Television Show, and # of Years a Favorite. Print the print area. (*Hint*: You must change the "Print what" setting in the Print dialog box from List to Active sheet.)

■ Add the third column, Favorite Character, to the print area using the shortcut menu option, then print the print area.

k. Save the workbook, close the workbook, then exit Excel.

▼ INDEPENDENT CHALLENGE 3

You are the assistant manager at Nite Owl Video in Brisbane, Australia. You have assembled an Excel list of the most popular Australian films your store rents, along with information about the Australian Film Institute (AFI) award they won, the release dates, and the film genres. Your customers have suggested that you prepare an in-store handout listing the films with the information sorted in different ways.

a. Start Excel, open the file EX H-3.xls from the drive and folder where your Data Files are stored, then save it as **Best Films**.

b. Sort the list in ascending order by Genre. Sort the list again in ascending order by Film Name.

FIGURE H-20

c. Sort the list again using two fields, this time in descending order by Release Year, then in ascending order by Genre.

d. Enter your name in the worksheet footer, then save the workbook.

e. Use the data form to add a record to the list with the following information: Film Name: Fellowship of the Ring; Release Year: 2002; Genre: Drama; AFI Award: Best Foreign Film.

f. Use the data form to find and delete the record for the film *Passion*.

g. Use AutoFilter to display only dramas. (*Hint*: Click the AutoFilter list arrow in the Genre column and select Drama.) Compare your list to Figure H-20.

h. Redisplay all films. (*Hint*: Click the AutoFilter list arrow in the Genre column and select All.)

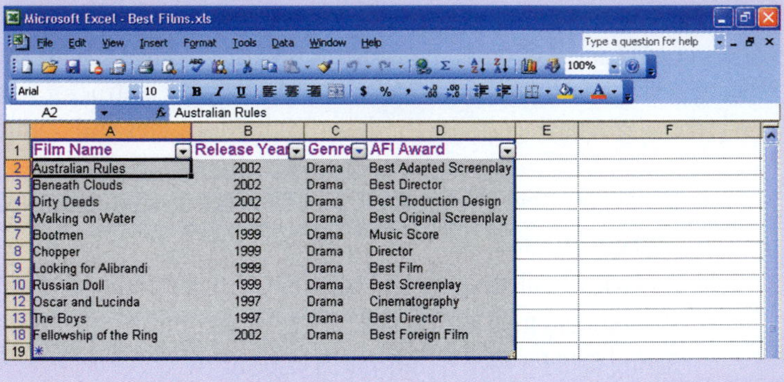

Advanced Challenge Exercise

■ Create your own sort order of: Drama, Comedy, Thriller, Suspense for the Genre column. (*Hint*: You must create a custom list using Options on the Tools menu and the Custom Lists tab.)

■ Sort the list in ascending order on the Genre field using your custom sort order. You need to clear all sort fields except the first key sort field in the Sort dialog box.

i. Save the workbook, print the list, close the workbook, then exit Excel.

▼ INDEPENDENT CHALLENGE 4

Your local newspaper has decided to start publishing the top-selling MP3 titles. They want to list the best-selling titles in the genres of Pop, Hip Hop, Country, and Classical. You have been asked to research the bestselling MP3 music along with price information. You create a list to hold the information about the top two titles for each genre. Using AutoFilter, you then display titles by the type of music and sort the list.

a. Go to the search engine of your choice and research the top selling MP3 titles in the categories of Pop, Country, Hip Hop, and Classical.

b. Complete the table below with the MP3 title information you found in your search.

Title	Artist	Genre	Price

c. Start Excel, enter your name in the worksheet footer of the new workbook, then save the workbook as **MP3 Titles**.

d. Use your table to enter the top two titles for each of the four music categories, along with the artist and price information, into your Excel worksheet. Save the workbook.

e. Create a list that contains the MP3 information.

f. Use AutoFilter to display only the Pop titles. (*Hint*: Click the AutoFilter arrow in the Genre column and select Pop.)

g. Use AutoFilter to display all the records. (*Hint*: Click the AutoFilter arrow in the Genre column and select All.)

h. Use the data form to delete both Pop records.

i. Use the AutoFilter to sort the list in ascending order by price. (*Hint*: Click the AutoFilter arrow in the Price column and select Sort Ascending.)

j. Save the workbook, print the list, close the workbook, then exit Excel.

▼ VISUAL WORKSHOP

Create the worksheet shown in Figure H-21. Save the workbook as **Famous Jazz Performers** in the drive and folder where your Data Files are stored. Once you've entered the field names and records, sort the list using two fields. The first sort should be in ascending order by Contribution to Jazz, and the second sort should be in ascending order by Last Name. Change the page setup so that the list is printed in landscape orientation on one page and centered on the page horizontally. Add a header that is centered, formatted in bold with a size of 16, and reads Famous Jazz Performers. Enter your name in the worksheet footer. Save the workbook, preview and print the list, close the workbook, then exit Excel.

FIGURE H-21

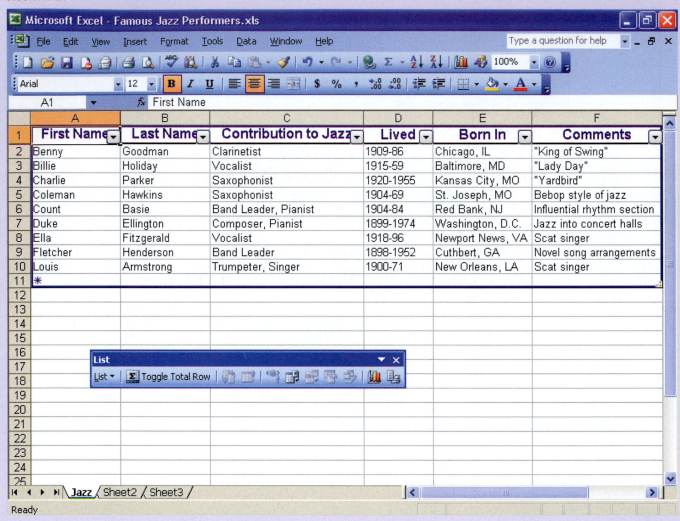

Integrating Word and Excel

OBJECTIVES

As you have learned, you use Word to create documents that contain primarily text and you use Excel to create workbooks that contain primarily values and charts. Sometimes, the documents you create in Word need to include values and charts from an Excel worksheet. You can use the integration capabilities of Office 2003 to insert information from an Excel worksheet into Word as a linked or embedded object. You can also create a hyperlink from a Word document to an Excel worksheet or from an Excel worksheet to a Word document. You are working as an assistant to Karen Rosen, the director of Human Resources at MediaLoft. Karen has asked you to explore new ways to integrate Word and Excel by creating a set of linked invoices and letters and a fact sheet.

UNIT
D
Integration

Project 1: Linked Invoices and Letters for Silver Screen Catering

MediaLoft has recently created a subsidiary focusing on food services for the film industry, called Silver Screen Catering. You offer to help the manager create a thank-you letter to accompany invoices e-mailed to film companies that have used Silver Screen's services. To save time, you decide to link each invoice with its accompanying letter so that you can quickly and easily update the letter when the invoice changes.

ACTIVITY

Creating the Letter in Word

STEPS

You create a letterhead and enter the text for the letter. The completed letter appears in Figure D-1.

1. Start Word, click the Styles and Formatting button 🔡 on the Formatting toolbar, right-click Normal, click Modify, select the Arial font and a font size of 13, click OK, then close the task pane and save the document as Letter 1 for Marlin Productions
The font for all text entered in the Normal style changes to 13-point Arial.

QUICK TIP

To show the Drawing toolbar, click View on the menu bar, point to Toolbars, then click Drawing.

2. Click the Insert WordArt button 📄 on the Drawing toolbar, click OK, type Silver Screen Catering, click the Font list arrow in the Edit WordArt Text dialog box, click Comic Sans MS, or another font if necessary, then click OK

3. Click the WordArt object to select it, click the WordArt Shape button 🅰 on the WordArt toolbar, select the Double Wave 2 shape (the last shape in the third row), click the Format WordArt button 🎨 on the WordArt toolbar, click the Colors and Lines tab if necessary, click the Fill Color list arrow, select the Blue color (second row, third from right), click the Line Color list arrow, then click No Line

4. Click the Size tab, select the contents of the Height text box, type .5, change the width to 3.5, click the Layout tab, click the Square wrapping style, click the Right option button in the Horizontal alignment section, then click OK

5. Double-click in the left margin at the same level as the WordArt, type the address as shown in Figure D-1, then select the text and change its font size to 10 point

6. Press [Enter] three times after the Web site address, click the Line button ⬉ on the Drawing toolbar, press and hold [Shift], then draw a horizontal line immediately below the address and above the drawing canvas that extends from the left margin to the right margin, as shown in Figure D-1
You press [Shift] so that the line remains straight. You click above the drawing canvas so that you can format the line on its own, rather than as part of a drawing on the drawing canvas. You use the drawing canvas when you want to combine two or more pictures or drawn objects into one drawing.

7. With the line still selected, click the Line Style button ☰ on the Drawing toolbar, click More Lines, click the Weight up arrow until 4.5 pt appears, click the Line Color list arrow, select the Gray-25% color box, then click OK

8. Click below the line, press [Enter] three times, drag the line back up so that it appears just under the letterhead as shown in Figure D-1, click the last paragraph mark, click the Style list arrow on the Formatting toolbar, then click Normal

9. Click Insert on the menu bar, click Date and Time, select the date format that corresponds to April 6, 2006, click OK, press [Enter] twice, type the text for the letter as shown in Figure D-1, then save the document
You insert the total price and discount where indicated after you've created the invoice in Excel.

Use font
size 10

320 Hansen Avenue
North Vancouver, BC V7J 1E4
Phone: (604) 555-1122

Silver Screen Catering

Current Date

Allison Young
Production Coordinator
Marlin Productions
17 East Main Street
Vancouver, BC V7P 3A8

Dear Ms. Young,

Thank you for choosing Silver Screen Catering to feed the cast and crew
of *Fish Fry* while on location in Vancouver. I hope the final days of shooting
in the studio went well.

Enclosed is our invoice in the amount of for the total cost of the catering
services we provided at various locations on 12 days between May 1 and
May 14. As we discussed, I have included a 15% discount of on the Snack
packs. Please click here to view the complete invoice.

Thank you again, Ms. Young, for choosing Silver Screen Catering to
supply hot meals, cold meals, snacks, and beverages on location for
Marlin Productions. I hope you consider using our services for your next
production that requires location shooting.

Sincerely,

Your Name
Account Manager

Total price is
inserted here

Hyperlink to
Excel file is
inserted here

Discount is
inserted here

ACTIVITY

Creating the Invoice in Excel

You first copy the letterhead from Word and paste it into a new Excel worksheet, and then you create and enhance the invoice in Excel and perform the required calculations. Finally, you link the Excel worksheet to the letter in Word.

STEPS

> **QUICK TIP**
> Use the arrow keys to position the WordArt object precisely.

1. Click the Show/Hide button ¶ on the Standard toolbar if necessary, select the address at the top of the letter to one paragraph mark below the line, click the Copy button 📋 on the Standard toolbar, start Excel, close the Getting Started task pane, click the Paste button 📋 on the Standard toolbar, then click and drag the WordArt object to the left so that it starts in the left half of cell E1

2. Click cell A9, enter and enhance the labels for cells A9 to H29 to match Figure D-2, then save the workbook as Invoice 1 for Marlin Productions

3. Select cells B20 to F20, click the Merge and Center button 🔳 on the Formatting toolbar, select cells G21 to H29, then click the Currency Style button $ on the Formatting toolbar
   Only the cells containing values and the blank cells are formatted in Currency style. The cells containing labels are not affected.

4. Click cell H21, enter the formula =A21*G21, press [Enter], click cell H21 again, drag the corner handle of cell H21 down to cell H24 to copy the formula, then widen the column
   You multiply the quantity by the unit price to determine the total amount due for each set of items.

5. Click cell H26, double-click the AutoSum button Σ on the Standard toolbar, verify that $8,500.00 appears in cell H26, click cell H27, enter the formula =H24*.15, press [Enter], enter the formula =(H26-H27)*.07 in cell H28, then press [Enter]
   You calculate the 15% discount on the total Snack pack amount due in cell H24 and then calculate 7% tax on the subtotal less the discount. Verify that $574.00 appears in cell H28.

6. In cell H29, enter the formula to subtract the discount from the sum of cells H26 and H28, press [Enter], verify that $8,774.00 appears in cell H29, select cells A9 to D12, click the Borders button list arrow 🔲▾ on the Formatting toolbar, click the Thick Box Border (last column, last row), apply the same border style to cells A14 to D17, add a Top and Bottom Border to cell H26, add a Top and Double Bottom Border to cell H29, then save the workbook
   The completed worksheet appears as shown in Figure D-3.

7. Click cell H29, click the Copy button 📋, switch to Word, then click after the first occurrence of the word of in the second paragraph of the letter

8. Click Edit on the menu bar, click Paste Special, click the Paste link option button, click Unformatted Text, click OK, then delete any extra spaces around the pasted amount
   You use the Paste Special command to paste the price as a link. You do not use the Paste button because it only places the data in the document without allowing for automatic updating. The value in cell H29 of the invoice ($8,774.00) appears.

9. Switch to Excel, click cell H27, click 📋, switch to Word, click after 15% discount of in the second paragraph, paste the value as a link (Unformatted Text), delete any extra spaces around the pasted amount, then save the document in Word
   The copied amounts appear in the Word letter as shown in Figure D-4.

FIGURE D-2: Worksheet labels and values

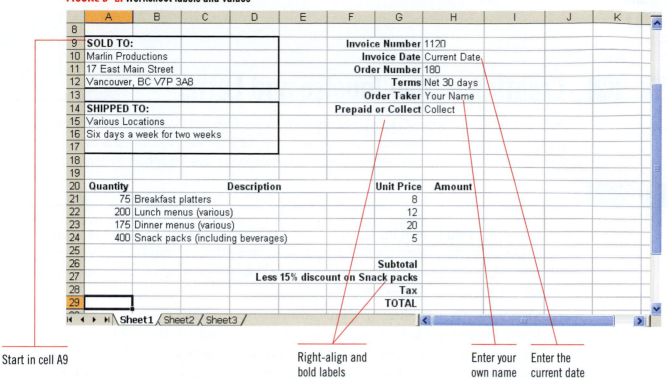

Start in cell A9

Right-align and bold labels

Enter your own name

Enter the current date

FIGURE D-3: Invoice data calculated and formatted

	A	B	C	D	E	F	G	H	I	J	K
8											
9	**SOLD TO:**					Invoice Number		1120			
10	Marlin Productions					Invoice Date		Current Date			
11	17 East Main Street					Order Number		180			
12	Vancouver, BC V7P 3A8					Terms		Net 30 days			
13						Order Taker		Your Name			
14	**SHIPPED TO:**					Prepaid or Collect		Collect			
15	Various Locations										
16	Six days a week for two weeks										
17											
18											
19											
20	**Quantity**		**Description**				**Unit Price**	**Amount**			
21	75	Breakfast platters					$ 8.00	$ 600.00			
22	200	Lunch menus (various)					$ 12.00	$ 2,400.00			
23	175	Dinner menus (various)					$ 20.00	$ 3,500.00			
24	400	Snack packs (including beverages)					$ 5.00	$ 2,000.00			
25											
26							Subtotal	$ 8,500.00			
27					Less 15% discount on Snack packs			$ 300.00			
28							Tax	$ 574.00			
29							TOTAL	$ 8,774.00			

Sheet1 / Sheet2 / Sheet3 /

FIGURE D-4: Amounts copied to Word

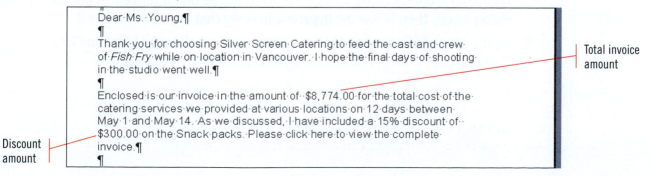

Dear Ms. Young,¶
¶
Thank you for choosing Silver Screen Catering to feed the cast and crew of *Fish Fry* while on location in Vancouver. I hope the final days of shooting in the studio went well.¶
¶
Enclosed is our invoice in the amount of $8,774.00 for the total cost of the catering services we provided at various locations on 12 days between May 1 and May 14. As we discussed, I have included a 15% discount of $300.00 on the Snack packs. Please click here to view the complete invoice.¶
¶

Total invoice amount

Discount amount

ACTIVITY

Creating a New Invoice and Letter

To further assist Silver Screen Catering, you create a hyperlink from text in Word to the invoice in Excel and print a copy of the invoice and letter. Then, you save both the Word letter and the Excel invoice under new names and change some of the values in the Excel invoice and update the links in the Word document so that they relate to a new version of the Excel invoice.

STEPS

1. Select the word here in the last sentence of the second paragraph, click the Insert Hyperlink button 🖳 on the Standard toolbar, verify that Existing File or Web Page is selected, navigate to the location where your Data Files are stored, then click the file-name Invoice 1 for Marlin Productions.xls

2. Click ScreenTip in the Insert Hyperlink dialog box, type This link opens Invoice 1 for Marlin Productions in Excel., as shown in Figure D-5, click OK, then click OK
   The word "here" is made into a hyperlink that, when clicked, opens the invoice in Excel.

3. Move your cursor over here, read the ScreenTip that appears, press [Ctrl] and click the hyperlink, type Thank you for your business! in cell A35 when the workbook opens in Excel, format it with italics, center it across cells A35 to H35, click File on the menu bar, click Page Setup, click the Margins tab, change the Right margin to .5, select the Horizontally check box, then click OK

4. Print a copy of the worksheet, save the workbook and leave it open, switch to Word, print a copy of the letter, then save the letter and leave it open

5. Save the letter as Letter 2 for Marlin Productions, switch to Excel, save the invoice as Invoice 2 for Marlin Productions, change selected values and text to update the invoice as shown in Figure D-6, then save the workbook
   The new total in cell H29 should be $10,539.50.

TROUBLE

If the invoice and discount amounts updated automatically in the letter, skip to Step 7 after switching to Word

6. Switch to Word, click Edit on the menu bar, click Links, click Change Source, click Invoice2 for Marlin Productions in the list of files, click Open, click the next entry in the Links dialog box, click Change Source, click Invoice 2 for Marlin Productions, click Open, click Update Now, then click OK

7. Verify that $10,539.50 and $450.00 appear in the letter as the invoice amount and discount, then change the text 12 days between May 1 and May 14 to 21 days between June 1 and June 21

8. Right-click here at the end of the second paragraph, click Edit Hyperlink, click Invoice 2 for Marlin Productions.xls, change the ScreenTip so that it references Invoice 2, close the dialog boxes, then follow the hyperlink to verify that it goes to Invoice 2

9. Print a copy of Invoice 2 and Letter 2, then save and close the letter and invoice
   The new versions of the letter and invoice appear as shown in Figure D-7 and D-8.

FIGURE D-5: Set Hyperlink ScreenTip dialog box

FIGURE D-6: Data for Invoice 2

Change "two" to "three"

Change these quantities

New invoice number

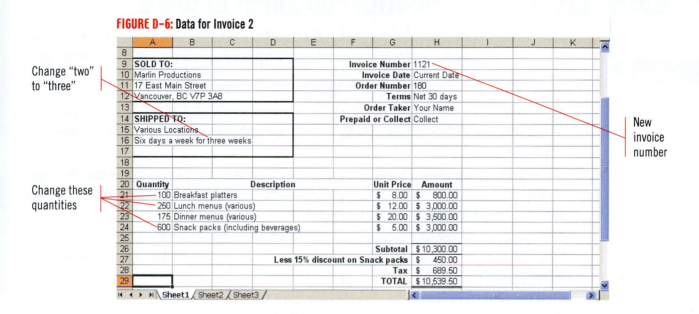

FIGURE D-7: Letter 2 for Marlin Productions

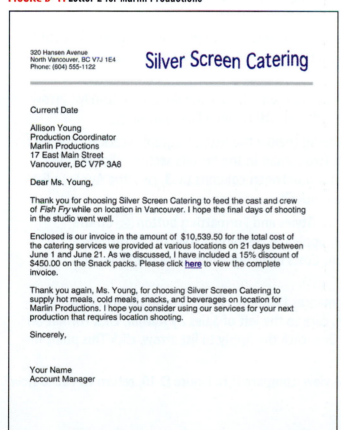

FIGURE D-8: Invoice 2 for Marlin Productions

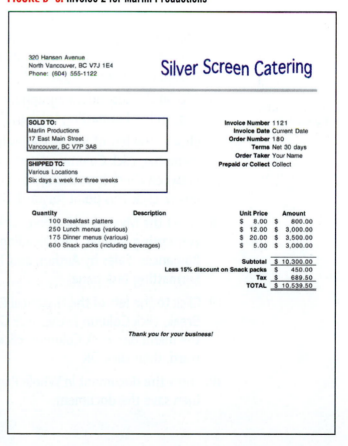

Project 2: Fact Sheet for Wessex Books

The editor of Wessex Books in England has sent you an e-mail asking if MediaLoft would be interested in sponsoring a book tour for some of the authors from Wessex Books. Before approaching management with the idea, you create a fact sheet about Wessex Books from the information provided by the editor. You create the fact sheet in Word, include a chart created in Excel, and embed an Excel worksheet.

ACTIVITY

Creating the Information Sheet in Word

You create a heading for the fact sheet that consists of a WordArt object that you've enhanced with an attractive texture and 3-D style. You then turn on columns and format selected headings with the Heading 1 style.

STEPS

1. Start Word, open the file INT D-1.doc from the drive and folder where your Data Files are stored, change all four margins to .6", then save the document as Fact Sheet for Wessex Books.doc

2. Show the Drawing toolbar if necessary, click the Insert WordArt button ⬛ on the Drawing toolbar, click OK, type Wessex Books, click OK, click the WordArt object to select it, click the WordArt Shape button ⬛ on the WordArt toolbar, then select the Can Up shape

3. Click the Format WordArt button ⬛ on the WordArt toolbar, click the Colors and Lines tab, click the Fill Color list arrow, click Fill Effects, click the Texture tab, select the Blue tissue paper texture, then click OK

4. Click the Line Color list arrow, click No Line, click the Layout tab, click Square, click the Center option button, click OK, click the 3-D Style button ⬛ on the Drawing toolbar, then select 3-D Style 7

   A small yellow handle appears at the bottom of the WordArt object because you changed the Layout from In Line with Text (the default setting) to the Square wrapping option.

TROUBLE
If necessary, use the sizing handles to modify the size of the WordArt object so that it matches Figure D-9.

5. Click and drag the yellow handle on the WordArt shape up as far as it goes, click at the left margin below the object, then press [Enter] twice to add more space below the object, as shown in Figure D-9

6. Click at the second paragraph mark above the text, click the Borders button list arrow ⬛ on the Formatting toolbar, then click the Horizontal Line button ⬛

7. Click to the left of the Mysteries heading (below the first paragraph), click Format on the menu bar, click Columns, select the Two format in the Presets section, click the Line Between check box, change the spacing between columns to .3, click the Apply to list arrow, click This point forward, then click OK

8. Select the Mysteries heading, click the Styles and Formatting button ⬛ on the Formatting toolbar, click Heading 1, apply the Heading 1 style to the Historical Romances, Sales by Author, and Tour Costs headings, then close the Styles and Formatting task pane

9. Click to the left of the Historical Romances heading, click Insert on the menu bar, click Break, click Column break, click OK, click to the left of Sales by Author, click Format on the menu bar, click Columns, click One, click the Apply to list arrow, click This point forward, then click OK

10. Show the document in Whole Page view, compare it to Figure D-10, return to 100% view, then save the document

FIGURE D-9: Modified WordArt object

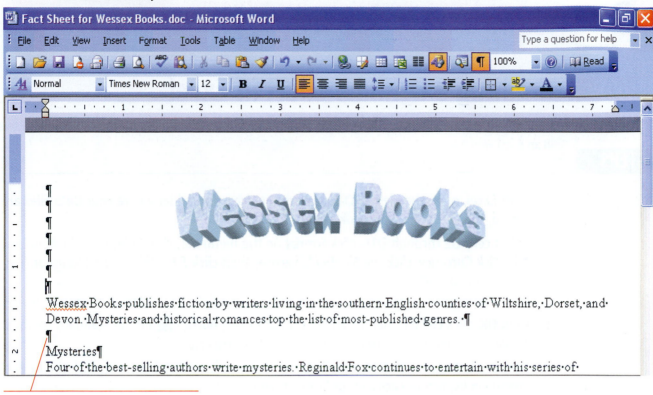

If paragraph marks are not visible, click the
Show/Hide ¶ button on the Standard toolbar

FIGURE D-10: Document shown in Whole Page view

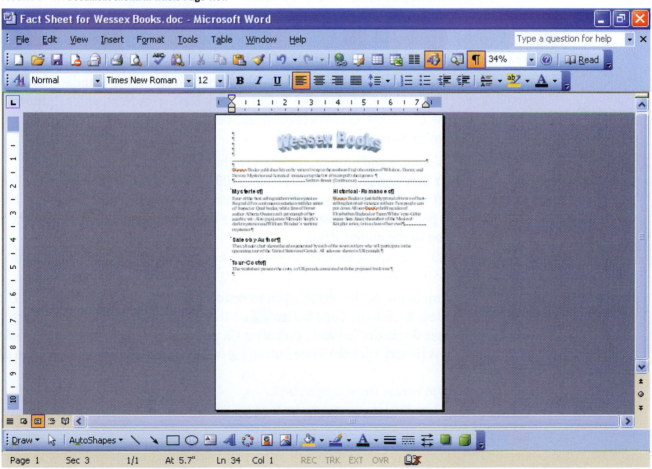

ACTIVITY

Creating a Cylinder Chart in Excel

The fact sheet refers to a chart in the paragraph under Author Sales. You create the chart from data entered in an Excel workbook.

STEPS

1. Start Excel, open the file **INT D-2.xls** from the drive and folder where your Data Files are stored, then save the workbook as **Data for Wessex Books**

2. Select cells **D2** through **D16**, click **Format** on the menu bar, click **Cells**, click the **Number tab**, click **Currency**, click the **Symbol list arrow**, then click **£ English (United Kingdom)** as shown in Figure D-11

   In the Currency area of the Format Cells dialog box, you can select from hundreds of currency types.

3. Click **OK**, click cell **B1**, then click the **Sort Ascending button** on the Standard toolbar

   The data is organized in alphabetical order by each author's last name.

4. Select cells **A1** through **D16**, click **Data** on the menu bar, click **Subtotals**, click the **At each change in list arrow**, click **Author Name**, then click **OK**

   The Subtotals list shows the total sales generated by each of the seven authors. For example, Reginald Fox generated sales of £43,000.

5. Click the **2** at the top of the outline detail as shown in Figure D-12

   The Subtotals list collapses to show just the rows that contain totals.

6. Click cell **B4**, type **Reginald Fox**, click cell **B6**, type **Sara Jones**, then relabel the remaining cells so that only the first and last name of each author is listed

7. Select cells **B4** through **D23**, click the **Chart Wizard button** on the Standard toolbar, scroll down the list of chart types, click **Cylinder**, click **Next**, click **Next**, enter **Author Revenues** as the chart title, click the **Legend tab**, click the **Show Legend check box** to deselect it, then click **Finish**

TROUBLE

Depending on how you move and size the chart, your z-axis values may change to show values in increments of 5,000 instead of 10,000.

8. Use your mouse to size and position the chart so that it extends from cell **A28 to D45**, right-click the z-axis (contains the values from 10,000 to 50,000), click **Format Axis**, click **Currency**, select the **£ English (United Kingdom)** currency, click the **Font tab**, change the font size to **10 point**, click **OK**, change the font size of the x-axis labels to **10 point**, then click **3** at the top of the outline detail

   With the Subtotals list expanded, the chart shows both individual entries and subtotals. The comparison between authors is no longer valid.

9. Click **2** at the top of the outline detail again to restore the chart, save the workbook, click the chart to select it, click the **Copy button** on the Standard toolbar, switch to **Fact Sheet for Wessex Books.doc** in Word, click after **UK pounds.** in the paragraph under Sales by Author, press **[Enter]**, click the **Paste button** on the Standard toolbar, then save the document

   The chart appears in Word as shown in Figure D-13.

FIGURE D-11: Currency style selected

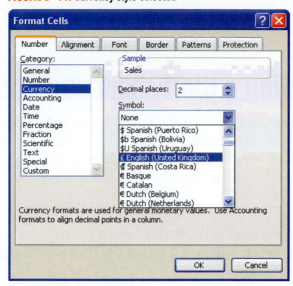

FIGURE D-12: Subtotals list collapsed to level 2

Click 2 to collapse the Subtotals list to level 2

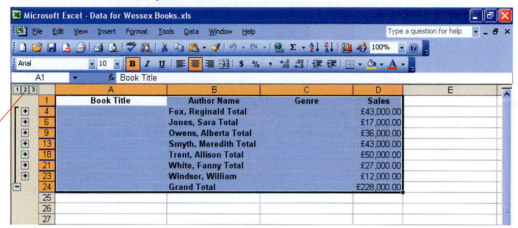

FIGURE D-13: Cylinder chart shown in Word

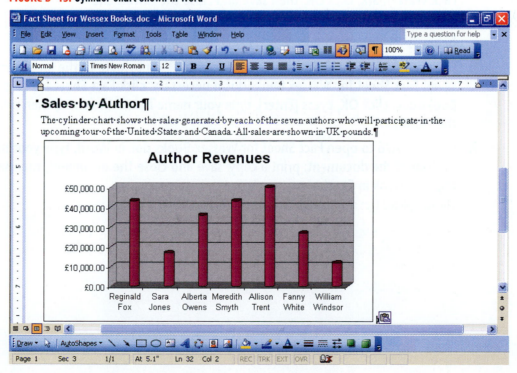

ACTIVITY

Embedding a Worksheet and Create a Link

The fact sheet refers to a worksheet in the paragraph under Tour Costs. You embed an Excel worksheet in Word so that you can use Excel features to work with the data. You then add an attractive theme to the fact sheet and insert a link from the Excel workbook to the fact sheet in Word. First, you reduce the size of the cylinder chart.

STEPS

1. Right-click the chart in Word, click Format Picture, click the Size tab, select the contents of the Height text box, type 2.5, click OK, then click the Center button ≣ on the Formatting toolbar

2. Click after tour. in the paragraph under the Tour Costs heading, press [Enter] twice, click Insert on the menu bar, click Object, scroll down the list of object types, click Microsoft Excel Worksheet, click OK, then enter the data shown in Figure D-14 into the worksheet

3. Click cell E2, enter the formula =C2*D2, copy the formula to cells E3 to E6, click cell E7, click the AutoSum button Σ on the Standard toolbar twice, select cells D2 through E7, then change the number format to £ English (United Kingdom)

4. Select cells A1 through E1, apply Bold and centering, then drag the lower-right corner handle of the worksheet window up and to the left so only the data appears in the worksheet, as shown in Figure D-15

5. Click outside the worksheet to return to Word, double-click the worksheet to open it for editing, change the Accommodation cost to £2,000, then click outside the worksheet
   Verify that the updated total is £27,500.00.

> **TROUBLE**
> Select a different theme if Watermark is not available.

6. Click Format on the menu bar, click Theme, scroll to the bottom of the list of themes, click Watermark, click OK, then save and close the document

7. Show Data for Wessex Books.xls in Excel, click cell A26, type the text The chart shown below is included in the Wessex Books fact sheet. Click here to open., then press [Enter]

8. Click cell A26, click the Insert Hyperlink button 🌐, navigate to the location where you saved Fact Sheet for Wessex Books.doc if necessary, click Fact Sheet for Wessex Books.doc, click OK, press [Enter], type your name below the chart, then print a copy of the workbook

9. Click cell A26 to open Fact Sheet for Wessex Books.doc in Word, type your name at the bottom of the document, print a copy, save and close the document, then save and close the workbook in Excel
   The completed fact sheet appears as shown in Figure D-16.

FIGURE D-14: Data for the embedded worksheet

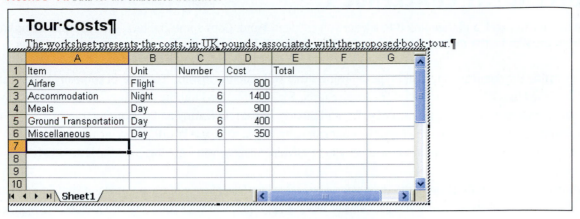

FIGURE D-15: Worksheet resized

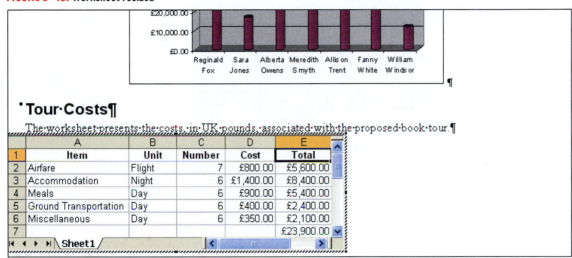

FIGURE D-16: Completed fact sheet

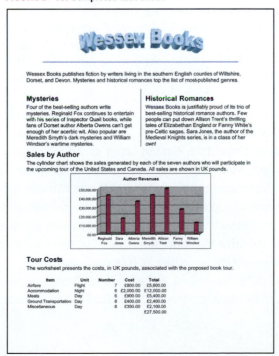

▼ INDEPENDENT CHALLENGE 1

Create an invoice in Excel, and then link it to a letter you create in Word. Copy some graphics, such as a picture or WordArt objects, from the Word letter to Excel, then copy some values in Excel, and paste them as links into the Word letter.

a. Determine the company name and type of business that will send the invoice. The type of company you select determines the kinds of items you list on the invoice form. For example, a ski touring company called Winter Pathways could list items such as skis, boots, and poles, and services such as ski waxing and ski-touring lessons.

b. In Word, create an attractive letterhead for your company. If you wish, use WordArt and include a picture.

c. Write and format a letter similar to the letter you created for Silver Screen Catering. Save the letter as **My Confirmation Letter**.

d. Set up an invoice in Excel similar to the invoice you created for Silver Screen Catering. Include your company letterhead on the invoice. Make sure you list items or services appropriate to your company and include the required calculations. Include a 15% discount on one of the items and charge 7% tax on the subtotal value.

e. Save the workbook as **My Invoice**, then copy the total amount and discount values and paste them as links in the appropriate locations in the Word document.

f. Include your name on both the letter and the invoice, print copies, then save the letter and invoice.

g. Change some values in the invoice, save it as **Revised Invoice** and print a copy, then update the links in the letter, save the letter as **Revised Confirmation Letter**, then print a copy.

▼ INDEPENDENT CHALLENGE 2

Create a fact sheet in Word for a company of your choice. Include references in the fact sheet to a chart and to an embedded worksheet. Use the fact sheet you created for Wessex Books as your guide. Include an attractively formatted WordArt object and format headings with a heading style. Format some of the text in columns, and apply a theme. In Excel, create a list that you can then convert into a Subtotals list that is sorted according to similar items in a specific column. Collapse the Subtotals list to level 2, create a chart based on the collapsed Subtotals list, then copy the chart to an appropriate area in the Word document. In Word, insert an embedded worksheet, entering data appropriate to the company covered by the fact sheet. Save the fact sheet as **My Fact Sheet**, and save the workbook as **My Fact Sheet**. Include your name on the document and on the workbook, then print a copy of each.

▼ INDEPENDENT CHALLENGE 3

As part of a research project for an educational consultant, you have compiled a list of the average scores obtained by Grade 7 students in Vancouver, British Columbia, and four neighboring suburbs in a provincewide mathematics exam. In Word, you write a short description of the test and the scores and include an embedded worksheet showing the average scores for each district in each subject. You use a Subtotals list to calculate the average scores earned by students located in five districts of the highest-scoring region, and then you display the data in a 3-D bar chart. The completed document appears in Figure D-17.

a. Start a new document in Word, set the top and bottom margins at .5" and the left and right margins at .8", then save the document as **Mathematics Study Results**.

b. As shown in Figure D-17, create and format the WordArt object, center it, then enter and format the text without including the chart and worksheet object. Note that you need to select the Cork texture (column 1 in the bottom row of the texture selections), the Deflate Bottom shape, and the 3-D Style 3 for the WordArt object. You also need to insert a horizontal line, apply the Heading 1 style to the headings, apply columns to selected text, and apply the Pixel theme. (*Hint*: Use a different theme if Pixel is not available. The font styles and sizes of another theme will not match Figure D-17 exactly.)

c. Open the file INT D-3.xls from the drive and folder where your Data Files are stored, save it as **Mathematics Study**.

d. Select cells A3 through C38, then sort the worksheet alphabetically by district.

e. Click Data on the menu bar, click Subtotals, then in the Subtotals dialog box, select District in the At each change in text box and Average in the Use Function text box, click District Score in the Add Subtotal to list, then click OK.

f. Collapse the Subtotals list to level 2, remove the word **Average** from the labels in column A, apply the Number style to the values in column C, then create a 3-D bar chart that appears as shown in the completed document in Figure D-17.

g. Enter your name below the chart, save the Excel workbook and print a copy, then copy the bar chart and paste it into the Word document as shown in Figure D-17.

h. In Word, insert an embedded worksheet as shown in Figure D-17, type your name at the bottom of the document, save the document, then print a copy.

FIGURE D-17

Overview

The Ministry of Education initiated the 2005 British Columbia Assessment of Mathematics to assess and report upon the achievement levels of Grade 7 students throughout the province.

Test Results

The results of the assessment are presented in the table below as average scores for each of the content areas assessed. The table compares the average scores attained by students in five regions of British Columbia.

Subject Area	Lower Mainland	Vancouver Island	North Coast	Caribou Interior	Rocky Mountains
Decimals	75	65	62	60	62
Fractions	72	58	68	62	58
Ratios	68	55	52	45	54
Integers	68	62	66	60	61
Geometry	62	73	68	72	75
Measuring	77	66	73	66	66

The column chart displayed below compares the scores earned by students in the five districts in the Lower Mainland. North Vancouver students earned the highest scores.

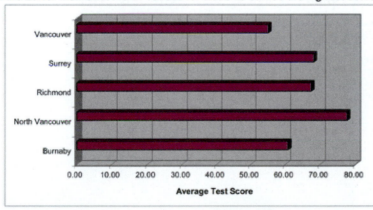

Test Implications

The scores in all areas except Geometry are consistently higher for students in the Lower Mainland. Only the score for Decimals is significantly higher – by an average of 10 points.

Action Plan

In September, 2007, BC School Districts will implement a new Geometry course for Grade 7 students. All teachers of Grade 7 Mathematics will attend a two-day seminar in the Spring of 2006 to prepare for the new course.

▼ VISUAL WORKSHOP

Create the Word document shown in Figure D-18. Create the worksheet as an embedded Excel worksheet. Note that you need to enhance the WordArt object with the Deflate Bottom shape, the Nightfall preset gradient fill, and Shadow Style 5. Search for **jazz band** to find the clip art picture or insert a clip art picture of your choice. Insert a Horizontal Line border just beneath the WordArt, and apply the Sumi Painting theme. Save the document as **Jazz Band Tour Information**. Include your name at the bottom of the Word document, then print a copy. Change the airfare cost to $600 and the hotel cost to $75 per night, then enter the updated total cost in the sentence above the embedded worksheet. Save the document as **Updated Jazz Band Tour Information**, then print a copy.

FIGURE D-18

Jasper Teen Jazz Band

Florida Bound!

In 2006, the Jasper Teen Jazz Band will embark on a five-day, four-concert tour of sunny Florida! The band will perform three solo concerts and then participate in a massed jazz band at a grand finale concert hosted by Epcot Center at Disney World! Each band member should bring both the casual and the concert uniform, along with two pairs of casual pants, three shirts, five pairs of socks and underwear, a bathing suit, and personal toiletries. The tour will be fully chaperoned with three assistants in addition to the band leader.

The table shown below breaks down costs for the tour. Please make sure your teen has sufficient funds for the extra meals, attractions, and spending money. The total cost for the tour is $1,295.

Expense	Unit	Unit Cost	Number	Total
Airfare from Edmonton	Ticket	$ 450.00	1	$ 450.00
Hotel	Night	$ 50.00	5	$ 250.00
Meals (prepaid)	Meal	$ 10.00	12	$ 120.00
Meals (extra)	Meal	$ 15.00	3	$ 45.00
Entrance Fees	Attraction	$ 60.00	3	$ 180.00
Spending Money	Day	$ 50.00	5	$ 250.00
			Total Cost	$ 1,295.00

Modifying the Database Structure

OBJECTIVES

Examine relational databases

Create related tables

Create one-to-many relationships

Create Lookup fields

Modify Text fields

Modify Number and Currency fields

Modify Date/Time fields

Modify field validation properties

If you have a SAM user profile, you may have access to hands-on instruction, practice, and assessment of the skills covered in this unit. Log in to your SAM account and go to your assignments page to see what your instructor has assigned.

In this unit, you will add a new table to an existing database and link the tables in one-to-many relationships to create a relational database. You will work with fields that have different data types, including Text, Number, Currency, Date/Time, and Yes/No to define the data stored by the database. You will also modify several field properties to format and validate data. Working with Fred Ames, the new coordinator of training at MediaLoft, you created an Access database to track the internal training courses attended by MediaLoft employees. Courses include hands-on computer classes, business seminars, and self-improvement workshops. The database consists of multiple tables that you will link together to create a relational database.

Examining Relational Databases

The purpose of a relational database is to organize and store data in a way that minimizes redundant data yet maximizes the flexibility by which that data may be queried and analyzed. To accomplish these goals, a relational database uses related tables of data rather than a single large table. The Training Department at MediaLoft has attempted to track information about their internal course offerings using a single Access table called Attendance Log, shown in Figure E-1. You see a data redundancy problem because some records duplicate the employee and course information. Therefore, you study the principles of relational database design in order to help the Training Department reorganize these fields into a correctly designed relational database.

DETAILS

To redesign a list into a properly structured relational database, follow these principles:

- **Design each table to contain fields that describe only one subject**

  Currently, the Attendance Log table in Figure E-1 contains three subjects: courses, employees, and attendance data. Putting multiple subjects in a single table creates redundant data. For example, the employee's name must be reentered every time that employee attends a different course. Redundant data causes extra data entry work, a higher rate of data entry inconsistencies and errors, and larger physical storage requirements. Moreover, it limits the user's ability to search for, analyze, and report on the data. These problems are minimized by implementing a properly designed relational database.

- **Identify a primary key field or key field combination for each table**

  A **primary key field** is a field that contains unique information for each record. An Employee Identification or Social Security Number field often serves this purpose in an Employees table. Although using the employee's last name as the primary key field might work in a small database, it is generally a poor choice because it does not accommodate two employees that have the same last name. A **key field combination** is the use of more than one field to uniquely identify each record.

- **Build one-to-many relationships between the tables of your database using a field common to each table**

  To tie the information from one table to another, a field must be common to each table. This common field will be the primary key field on the "one" side of the relationship and the **foreign key field** in the "many" side of the relationship. The primary key field contains a unique entry for each record, but the foreign key field contains the same value in "many" records to create a one-to-many relationship between the tables. Table E-1 describes common examples of one-to-many relationships. Note that the linking field doesn't need to have the same name in both the "one" and "many" tables.

  The new design for the fields of the training database is shown in Figure E-2. One employee may enroll in many courses so the Employees and Enrollments tables have a one-to-many relationship based on the linking EmployeeNo and SSN fields. One course may have many enrollments, so the Courses and Enrollments tables have a one-to-many relationship based on the common CourseID fields.

Clues to Use

Many-to-many relationships

As you are designing your database, you may find that two tables have a **many-to-many** relationship. To join them, you must establish a third table called a **junction table**, which contains two foreign key fields to serve on the "many" side of separate one-to-many relationships with the two original tables. The Employees and Courses tables have a many-to-many relationship because one employee can take many courses and one course may have many employees enrolled in it. The Enrollments table serves as the junction table to link the three tables together.

FIGURE E-1: Attendance Log as a single table

	CourseID	Description	Hours	Prereq	Cost	Last	First	Department	Attended	Passed
▶	Comp1	Computer Concepts	12		$200	Colletti	Shayla	CD	01/29/2006	☑
	Excel1	Introduction to Excel	12	Comp1	$200	Colletti	Shayla	CD	02/12/2006	☑
	Excel2	Intermediate Excel	12	Excel1	$200	Colletti	Shayla	CD	03/07/2006	☑
	ExcelLab	Excel Case Problems	12	Excel2	$200	Colletti	Shayla	CD	03/14/2006	☐
	Internet1	Internet Fundamentals	12	Comp1	$200	Colletti	Shayla	CD	03/14/2006	☑
	Netscape1	Introduction to Netscape	12	Internet1	$200	Colletti	Shayla	CD	04/04/2006	☑
	Outlook1	Introduction to Outlook	12	Comp1	$200	Colletti	Shayla	CD	04/01/2006	☑
	Retail1	Introduction to Retailing	16		$100	Colletti	Shayla	CD	05/07/2006	☑
	Retail2	Store Management	16	Retail1	$100	Colletti	Shayla	CD	05/14/2006	☑
	Word2	Intermediate Word	12	Word1	$200	Colletti	Shayla	CD	02/14/2006	☑
	Word1	Introduction to Word	12	Comp1	$200	Colletti	Shayla	CD	01/18/2006	☑
	Comp1	Computer Concepts	12		$200	Lee	Nancy	Video	01/29/2006	☑
	Access1	Introduction to Access	12	Comp1	$300	Lee	Nancy	Video	02/12/2006	☑
	Internet1	Internet Fundamentals	12	Comp1	$200	Lee	Nancy	Video	03/14/2006	☑
	Netscape1	Introduction to Netscape	12	Internet1	$200	Lee	Nancy	Video	04/04/2006	☑

Duplicate course descriptions

Duplicate employee names

Fields that describe the course

Fields that describe the employee

Fields that describe the enrollment of an employee in a course

FIGURE E-2: Attendance log data split into three related tables

	EmployeeNo	Last	First	Department
▶	115-77-4444	Colletti	Shayla	CD
	134-70-3883	Lee	Nancy	Video
	173-48-5873	Shimada	Jeff	Operations
	222-33-4400	Alber	Lauren	Accounting
	234-56-7800	Rath	Maria	Book
	321-00-8888	Fernandez	Jim	Accounting
	333-33-8887	Dumont	David	Training
	333-44-0099	Hayashi	Jayne	Book
	345-88-0098	Rollo	Miguel	Book

Employees table

	CourseID	Description	Hours	Prereq	Cost
▶	Access1	Introduction to Access	12	Comp1	$300
	Access2	Intermediate Access	24	Access1	$400
	AccessLab	Access Case Problems	12	Access2	$200
	Comp1	Computer Concepts	12		$200
	Excel1	Introduction to Excel	12	Comp1	$200
	Excel2	Intermediate Excel	12	Excel1	$200
	ExcelLab	Excel Case Problems	12	Excel2	$200
	IE1	Introduction to Internet Explorer	12	Internet1	$200
	IE2	Intermediate Internet Explorer	12	Netscape1	$200
	Internet1	Internet Fundamentals	12	Comp1	$200
	Netscape1	Introduction to Netscape	12	Internet1	$200

Courses table

One-to-many link (one employee can enroll many times)

One-to-many link (one course may have many enrollments)

	LogNo	SSN	CourseID	Attended	Passed
▶	1	115-77-4444	Comp1	01/29/2006	☑
	3	134-70-3883	Comp1	01/29/2006	☑
	4	173-48-5873	Comp1	01/29/2006	☑
	5	222-33-4400	Comp1	01/29/2006	☑
	6	234-56-7800	Comp1	01/29/2006	☑
	7	321-00-8888	Comp1	01/29/2006	☑
	8	333-33-8887	Comp1	01/29/2006	☑
	9	333-44-0099	Comp1	01/29/2006	☑
	10	345-88-0098	Comp1	01/29/2006	☑

Enrollments table

TABLE E-1: Common one-to-many relationships

table on "one" side	table on "many" side	linking field	description
Products	Sales	ProductID	A ProductID field must have a unique entry in a Products table, but may be listed many times in a Sales table as many copies of that item are sold
Customers	Sales	CustomerID	A CustomerID field must have a unique entry in a Customers table, but will be listed many times in a Sales table as multiple sales are recorded for the same customer
Employees	Promotions	EmployeeID	An EmployeeID field must have a unique entry in an Employees table, but will be listed many times in a Promotions table as the employee is promoted over time

Creating Related Tables

Once you have developed a valid relational database design, you are ready to define the tables in Access. All characteristics of a table, including field names, data types, field descriptions, field properties, lookup properties, and primary key field designations, are defined in **Table Design View**. Using the new database design, you create the Enrollments table.

1. **Start Access, then open the Training-E.mdb database from the drive and folder where your Data Files are stored**

   The Courses and Employees tables already exist in the database. You need to create the Enrollments table.

2. **Click Tables on the Objects bar (if it is not already selected), then click the New button in the Training-E database window**

   The New Table dialog box opens. There are several ways to create a new table. To name and define the fields for a new table, use Table Design View.

3. **Click Design View in the New Table dialog box, then click OK**

   Field names should be as short as possible, but long enough to be descriptive. The field name entered in Table Design View is used as the default name for the field in all later queries, forms, reports, and Web pages.

QUICK TIP

When specifying field data types, you can type the first letter of the data type to quickly select it.

4. **Type LogNo, press [Enter], click the Data Type list arrow, click AutoNumber, then press [Enter] twice to move to the next row**

   The LogNo field contains a unique number used to identify each record in the Enrollments table (each occurrence of an employee taking a course). The AutoNumber data type, which automatically sequences each new record with the next available integer, works well for this field. Text is the most common data type, but fields that contain dates should have a Date/Time data type, and fields that contain only a value of Yes or No should be defined with a Yes/No data type.

5. **Type the other field names, data types, and descriptions as shown in Figure E-3**

   Field descriptions entered in Table Design View are optional, but are helpful in that they provide further information about the field.

6. **Click LogNo in the Field Name column, then click the Primary Key button on the Table Design toolbar**

   A **key symbol** appears to the left of LogNo to indicate that this field is defined as the primary key field for this table.

7. **Click the Save button on the Table Design toolbar, type Enrollments in the Table Name text box, click OK, then close the table**

   The Enrollments table is now displayed as a table object in the Training-E database window as shown in Figure E-4.

FIGURE E-3: Table Design View for the new Enrollments table

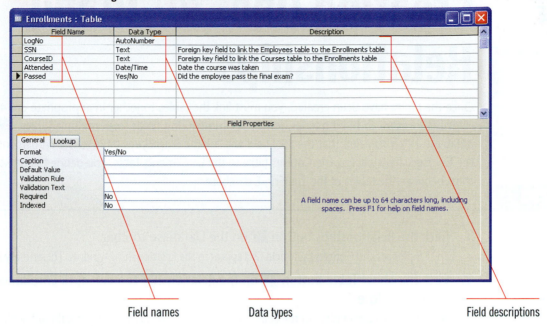

Field names   Data types   Field descriptions

FIGURE E-4: Enrollments table in the Training-E database window

New button

Enrollments table

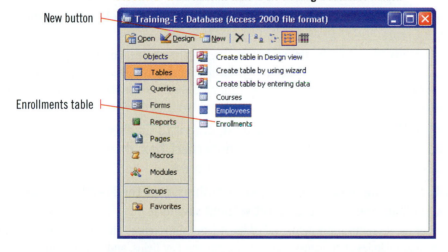

Clues to Use

Creating foreign key fields

A foreign key field in the "many" table must be given the same data type (Text or Number) as the primary key it is related to in the "one" table. An exception to this rule is when the primary key field in the "one" table is given an AutoNumber data type. In this case, the linking foreign key field in the "many" table must have a Number data type. Also note that linking fields must have the same value for the Field Size property. To change the field size property for the linking fields after the tables have been related, you must delete the relationship in the Relationships window, change the Field Size property for both fields in Table Design View, and then relink the tables in the Relationships window.

Creating One-to-Many Relationships

Once the tables have been created, you must link the tables together in appropriate one-to-many relationships before you can build queries, forms, or reports using fields from multiple tables. Your initial database sketch revealed that the SSN field will link the Employees table to the Enrollments table, and that the CourseID field will link the Courses table to the Enrollments table. You define the one-to-many relationships between the tables of the Training-E database.

STEPS

1. **Click the Relationships button on the Database toolbar**

   The Employees and Courses table field lists appear in the Relationships window. The primary key fields are bold.

   > **QUICK TIP**
   > Drag the table's title bar to move the field list.

2. **Click the Show Table button on the Relationship toolbar, click Enrollments, click Add, then click Close**

   With all three tables visible in the Relationships window, you're ready to link them together.

   > **QUICK TIP**
   > Drag the bottom border of the field list to display all of the fields.

3. **Scroll the Employees table field list, click EmployeeNo in the Employees table field list, then drag it to the SSN field in the Enrollments table field list**

   Dragging a field from one table to another in the Relationships window links the two tables with the selected fields and opens the Edit Relationships dialog box as shown in Figure E-5. Referential integrity helps ensure data accuracy.

4. **Click the Enforce Referential Integrity check box in the Edit Relationships dialog box, then click Create**

   The **one-to-many line** shows the linkage between the EmployeeNo field of the Employees table and the SSN field of the Enrollments table. The "one" side of the relationship is the unique EmployeeNo value for each record in the Employees table. The "many" side of the relationship is identified by an infinity symbol pointing to the SSN field in the Enrollments table. The CourseID field will link the Courses table to the Enrollments table.

   > **TROUBLE**
   > Right-click a relationship line, then click Delete if you need to delete a relationship and start over.

5. **Click CourseID in the Courses table field list, drag it to CourseID in the Enrollments table field list, click the Enforce Referential Integrity check box, then click Create**

   The finished Relationships window should look like Figure E-6.

   > **QUICK TIP**
   > Add your name as a label to the Report Header section in Report Design View if you want your name on the printout.

6. **Click File on the menu bar, click Print Relationships, click the Print button on the Print Preview toolbar, then close the report without saving it**

   A printout of the Relationships window, called the Relationships report, shows how your relational database is designed and includes table names, field names, primary key fields, and one-to-many relationships. This printout is very helpful as you later create queries, forms, and reports that use fields from multiple tables.

7. **Close the Relationships window, then click Yes when prompted to save changes to the layout**

FIGURE E-5: Edit Relationships dialog box

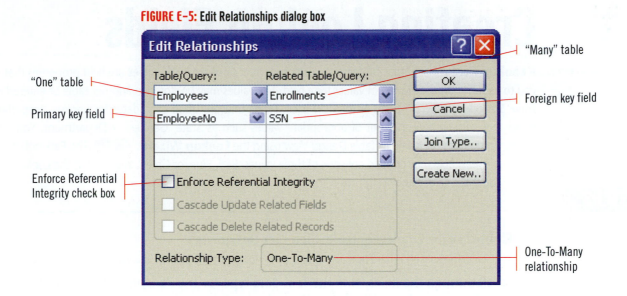

"One" table

Primary key field

Enforce Referential Integrity check box

"Many" table

Foreign key field

One-To-Many relationship

FIGURE E-6: Final Relationships window

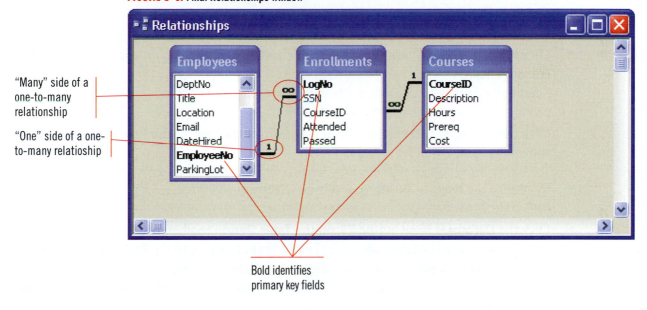

"Many" side of a one-to-many relationship

"One" side of a one-to-many relatioship

Bold identifies primary key fields

Clues to Use

Enforcing referential integrity

Referential integrity is a set of rules that help ensure that no orphan records are entered or created in the database. An **orphan record** is a record in the "many" table that doesn't have a matching entry in the linking field of the "one" table. (For example, an orphan record in the Training database would be a record in the Enrollments table that contains an SSN entry that has no match in the EmployeeNo field of the Employees table, or a record in the Enrollments table that contains a CourseID entry that has no match in the Courses table.) Referential integrity prevents the user from creating orphan records in multiple ways. By enforcing referential integrity you may not enter a value in a foreign key field of the "many" table that does not have a match in the linking field of the "one" table. Referential integrity also prevents you from deleting a record in the "one" table if a matching entry exists in the foreign key field of the "many" table. You should enforce referential integrity on all one-to-many relationships if possible. Unfortunately, if you are working with a database that already contains orphan records, you will not be able to enforce this powerful set of rules.

Creating Lookup Fields

A **Lookup field** is a field that contains Lookup properties. **Lookup properties** are field properties that allow you to supply a drop-down list of values for a field. The values may be stored in another table or entered in the **Row Source** Lookup property of the field itself. Fields that are good candidates for Lookup properties are those that contain a defined set of appropriate values such as State, Gender, or Department. You can set Lookup properties for a field in Table Design View using the **Lookup Wizard**. The ParkingLot field in the Employees table may contain only one of three values: Red, Blue, or Green. You will use the Lookup Wizard to provide these values as a list for this field.

STEPS

1. **Right-click the Employees table, then click Design View**

   You access the Lookup Wizard from the Data Type list for the field for which you want to apply Lookup properties.

2. **Scroll through the fields, click the Text data type for the ParkingLot field, click the Data Type list arrow, then click Lookup Wizard**

   The Lookup Wizard starts and prompts you for information about where the lookup column will get its values.

3. **Click the I will type in the values that I want option button, click Next, click the first cell in the Col1 column, type Red, press [Tab], type Blue, press [Tab], then type Green as shown in Figure E-7**

   These values will populate the lookup value list for the ParkingLot field.

4. **Click Next, then click Finish to accept the default label of ParkingLot and to complete the Lookup Wizard**

   Note that the data type for the ParkingLot field is still Text. The Lookup Wizard is a process for setting Lookup property values for a field, and is not a data type itself.

5. **Click the Lookup tab to observe the new Lookup properties for the ParkingLot field as shown in Figure E-8**

   The Lookup Wizard helped you enter the correct Lookup properties for the ParkingLot field, but you can always enter or edit them directly if you know what values you want to use for each property. The Row Source Lookup property stores the values that are provided in the drop-down list for a Lookup field.

6. **Click the Datasheet View button ⊞ on the Table Design toolbar, click Yes when prompted to save the table, press [Tab] eight times to move to the ParkingLot field, click the ParkingLot list arrow as shown in Figure E-9, then click Blue**

   The ParkingLot field now presents a list of values from which you can select when making an entry in this field.

7. **Close the Employees datasheet**

FIGURE E-7: Entering a Lookup list of values

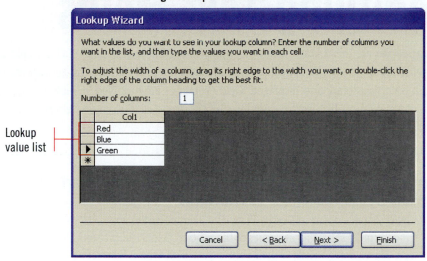

Lookup value list

FIGURE E-8: Viewing Lookup properties

ParkingLot field is selected

Data type is Text

Lookup tab

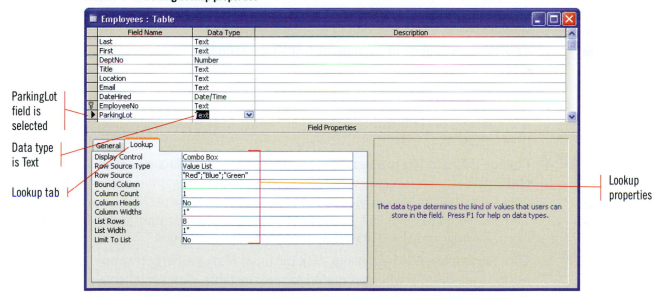

Lookup properties

FIGURE E-9: Using a Lookup field in a datasheet

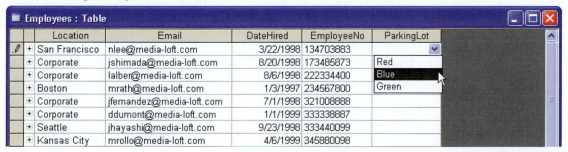

Modifying Text Fields

Field properties are the characteristics that apply to each field in a table, such as Field Size, Default Value, or Caption. These properties help ensure database accuracy and clarity because they are used to restrict the way data is entered, stored, and displayed. Field properties are modified in Table Design View. See Table E-2 for more information on Text field properties.  You decide to make field property changes to several Text fields in the Employees table.

STEPS

1. **If not already selected, click Tables on the Objects bar, right-click the Employees table, then click Design View on the shortcut menu**

   The Employees table opens in Design View. The field properties appear in the lower half of the Table Design View window and display the properties of the selected field. Field properties change depending on the field's data type. For example, when a field with a Text data type is selected, the Field Size property is visible. However, when a field with a Date/Time data type is selected, Access controls the Field Size property, so that property is not displayed. Many field properties are optional, but if they require an entry, Access provides a default value.

2. **Press [↓] to move through each field while viewing the field properties in the lower half of the window**

   A small black triangle in the **field selector button** to the left of the field indicates which field is currently selected.

3. **Click the Last field name, double-click 50 in the Field Size property text box, then type 30**

   Fifty is the default value for the Field Size property for a Text field, but you do not anticipate last name field values to be greater than 30. In general, making the Field Size property for Text fields as small as needed to accommodate the longest entry helps the database be more efficient. Changing the Field Size property for a field that stored two-letter state abbreviations to 2 would also help data accuracy because it would prevent typos such as TXX.

   QUICK TIP
   Press [F6] to move between field names and field properties in Table Design View.

4. **Change the Field Size property to 30 for the following field names: First, Title, Location, and Email**

   Changing the Field Size property to 30 for each of these text fields in this table will accommodate the longest entry you anticipate for each field. The **Input Mask** property provides a visual guide for users as they enter data. It also helps determine what types of values can be entered into a field.

   TROUBLE
   If the Input Mask Wizard is not installed on your computer, you can install it now or complete this step by typing 000-00-0000;;_ directly into the Input Mask property for the EmployeeNo field.

5. **Click the EmployeeNo field name, click the Input Mask property text box, click the Build button [...], click Yes when prompted to save the table, click Yes when alerted that some data may be lost (a result of changing the Field Size property from 50 to 30 in the previous steps, but because the entries are less than 30 characters, no data is actually lost), click Social Security Number, then click Finish**

   Table Design View of the Employees table should look like Figure E-10. Notice that the EmployeeNo field is selected and the new Input Mask property is entered. The EmployeeNo field is also the primary key field for the Employees table as evidenced by the key symbol beside the field name.

6. **Click the Save button 🖫 on the Table Design toolbar, click the Datasheet View button 🖩 on the Table Design toolbar, press [Tab] enough times to move to the EmployeeNo field for the first record, then type 115774444**

   The SSN Input Mask property creates an easy-to-use visual guide to facilitate accurate data entry.

7. **Close the Employees table**

FIGURE E-10: Changing Text field properties

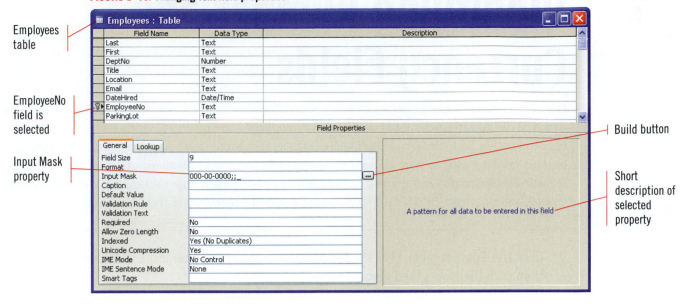

Employees table

EmployeeNo field is selected

Input Mask property

Build button

Short description of selected property

A pattern for all data to be entered in this field

TABLE E-2: Common Text field properties

property	description	sample field	sample property entry
Field Size	Controls how many characters can be entered into the field	State	2
Format	Controls how information will be displayed and printed	State	> (forces all characters to display in uppercase)
Input Mask	Provides a pattern for data to be entered	Phone	(999) 000-0000;1;_
Caption	A label used to describe the field in the first row of a datasheet, form, or report. If the Caption property is not entered, the field name itself is used to label the field.	Emp#	Employee Number
Default Value	Value that is automatically entered in the given field for new records	City	Kansas City
Required	Determines if an entry is required for this field	LastName	Yes

---

Clues to Use

Input Mask property

The Input Mask property provides a pattern for data to be entered using three parts separated by semicolons. The first part provides a pattern for what type of data can be entered. For example, 9 represents an optional number, 0 a required number, ? an optional letter, and L a required letter. The second part determines whether all displayed characters (such as dashes in a phone number) are stored in the field. For the second part of the input mask, a 0 entry stores all characters such as 555-7722, and a 1 entry stores only the entered data, 5557722. The third part of the input mask determines which character Access uses to guide the user through the mask. Common choices are the asterisk (*), underscore (_), or pound sign (#).

Modifying Number and Currency Fields

Even though some of the properties for Number and Currency fields are the same as for Text fields, each data type has its own specific list of valid properties. Numeric and Currency fields have very similar properties because they both contain numbers. Currency fields are used to store values that represent money, and Number fields are used to store values that represent all other types of numeric values such as quantities, numeric measurements, and numeric scores.  The Courses table contains both a Number field (Hours), and a Currency field (Cost). You decide to modify the properties of these two fields.

STEPS

1. **Click the Courses table, click the Design button ⬚ in the Training-E database window, then click the Hours field name**

   The Field Size property for a Number field defaults to Long Integer. See Table E-3 for more information on the options for the Field Size property of a Number field including Long Integer. Access controls the size of Currency fields to control the way numbers are rounded in calculations, so the Field Size property isn't available for Currency fields.

2. **Click Long Integer in the Field Size property text box, click the Field Size list arrow, then click Byte**

   Choosing a Byte value for the Field Size property allows entries from 0 to 255, so it greatly restricts the possible values and the storage requirements for the Hours field.

3. **Click the Cost field name, click Auto in the Decimal Places property text box, click the Decimal Places list arrow, then click 0**

   Your screen should look like Figure E-11. Because all of MediaLoft's courses are priced at a round dollar value, there is no need to display cents in the Cost field.

4. **Click the Save button ⬚ on the Table Design toolbar, then click the Datasheet View button ⬚ on the Table Design toolbar**

   Because none of the entries in the Hours field is greater than 255, the maximum value allowed by a Number field with a Byte Field Size, you won't lose any data. You want to test the new property changes.

5. **Press [Tab] twice to move to the Hours field for the first record, type 1000, then press [Tab]**

   Because 1000 is larger than the Byte Field Size property will allow (0–255), you are cautioned with an Access error message indicating that the value isn't valid for this field.

6. **Click OK, press [Esc] to remove the inappropriate entry in the Hours field, then press [Tab] twice to move to the Cost field**

   The Cost field is set to display zero digits after the decimal point.

7. **Type 199.75 in the Cost field of the first record, press [Enter], then click $200 in the Access1 record's Cost field**

   Even though the Decimal Places property for the Cost field dictates that entries in the field are formatted to display zero digits after the decimal point, 199.75 is the actual value stored in the field. Modifying the Decimal Places does not change the actual data. Rather, the Decimal Places property only changes the way the data is displayed.

8. **Click the Undo button ⬚ on the Table Datasheet toolbar to restore the Cost entry to $200, then close the Courses table**

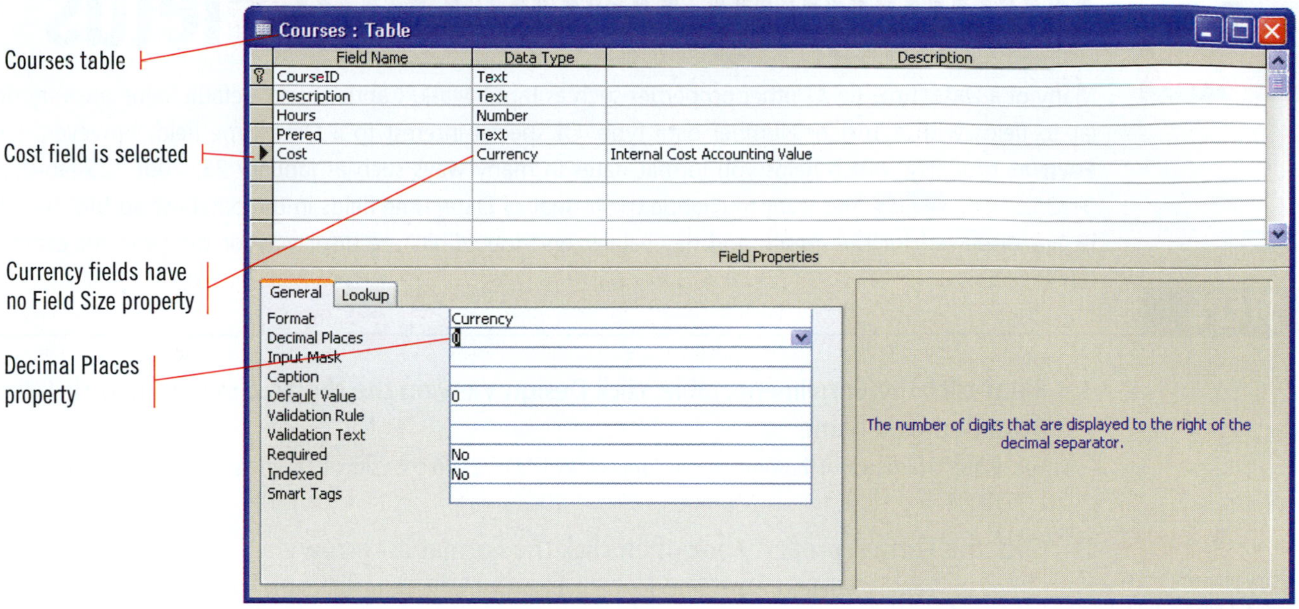

Courses table

Cost field is selected

Currency fields have no Field Size property

Decimal Places property

The number of digits that are displayed to the right of the decimal separator.

TABLE E-3: Common Number field properties

property	description
Field Size	Determines the largest number that can be entered in the field, as well as the type of data (e.g., integer or fraction)
	Byte stores numbers from 0 to 255 (no fractions)
	Integer stores numbers from −32,768 to 32,767 (no fractions)
	Long Integer stores numbers from −2,147,483,648 to 2,147,483,647 (no fractions)
	Single stores numbers (including fractions with six digits to the right of the decimal point) times 10 to the −38th to +38th power
	Double stores numbers (including fractions with over 10 digits to the right of the decimal point) in the range of 10 to the −324th to +324th power
Decimal Places	The number of digits displayed to the right of the decimal point

Modifying Date/Time Fields

Many of a Date/Time field's other properties such as Input Mask, Caption, and Default Value are very similar to fields with a Text or Number data type. Of special interest to a Date/Time field, however, is the **Format** property, which helps you format dates in many ways such as January 25, 2006; 25-Jan-06; or 01/25/2006. You want to change the format of Date/Time fields in the database so that two digits are displayed for the month and day values, and four digits are displayed for the year, for example, 05/31/2006.

STEPS

1. **Right-click the Enrollments table, click Design View on the shortcut menu, then click the Attended field name**

   You want the dates of Enrollments to appear as 01/17/2006 instead of the default presentation of dates, 1/17/2006.

2. **Click the Format property box, then click the Format list arrow**

   Although several predefined Date/Time formats are available, none matches the format you want. To define a custom format, enter symbols that represent how you want the date to appear.

3. **Type mm/dd/yyyy then press [Enter]**

   The updated Format property for the Attended field shown in Figure E-12 forces the date to appear with two digits for the month, two digits for the day, and four digits for the year. The parts of the date are separated by forward slashes.

4. **Click the Save button 🔲 on the Table Design toolbar**

   The Property Update Options button 🥢 appears to the left of the property and provides options that help you apply the property change you made to other places that the field appears, such as forms or reports. At this point, however, you haven't built any forms or reports in this database so you don't need to use this feature.

5. **Click the Datasheet View button 🔲 on the Table Design toolbar**

   You want to test the new Format property for the Attended field so you'll add a new record to see how it works.

6. **Press [Tab] to move to the SSN field, type 115774444, press [Tab], type Comp1, press [Tab], type 1/25/06, press [Tab], then press [Spacebar]**

   Your screen should look like Figure E-13. The new record is entered into the Enrollments table. The Format property for the Attended field makes the entry appear as 01/25/2006 as desired.

FIGURE E-12: Changing Date/Time field properties

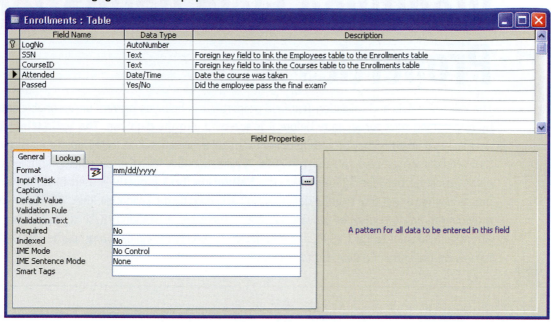

FIGURE E-13: Testing the Format property for the Attended field

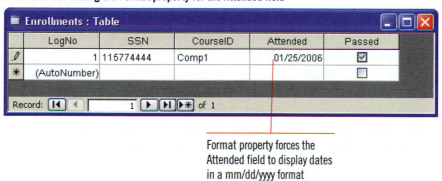

Format property forces the
Attended field to display dates
in a mm/dd/yyyy format

Clues to Use

Smart Tags

The Property Update Options button ⚡ is an Access Smart Tag. **Smart Tags** are buttons that automatically appear under certain conditions. They provide a small menu of options to help you work with the task at hand. Access provides two Smart Tags: the **AutoCorrect Options button** ⚡, which helps you correct typos (or when it appears as the Property Update Options, apply property changes to other areas of the database where a field is used), and the **Error Indicator button** ⬇, which helps identify potential design errors. For example, if you were working in Form Design View and added a text box to the form but did not correctly bind it to an underlying field, the Error Indicator button would appear by that text box to alert you to the problem.

Modifying Field Validation Properties

The Validation Rule and Validation Text field properties can help you prevent unreasonable entries for a field by establishing rules for an entry before it is accepted into the database. The **Validation Rule** property determines if an entry may be accepted. For example, a Validation Rule for a Date/Time field might indicate that valid dates must be on or after 1/1/2006. A Validation Rule for a Currency field might indicate that valid entries must be between $0 and $200. The **Validation Text** property is used to display an explanatory message when a user tries to enter data that isn't accepted by the Validation Rule. MediaLoft started providing in-house courses on January 17, 2004. Therefore, it wouldn't make sense to enter a date in the Attended field prior to 1/17/2004, and you decide to modify the validation properties of the Attended field to prevent the entry of dates prior to 1/17/2004.

STEPS

1. **Click the Design View button** on the Table Datasheet toolbar, click the Attended field, **click the Validation Rule property box**, then type >=1/17/2004

   This entry forces all dates in the Attended field to be greater than or equal to 1/17/2004. See Table E-4 for more examples of Validation Rule expressions. The Validation Text property provides a helpful message to the user in the event that the entry in the field isn't within the rule entered in the Validation Rule property.

2. **Click the Validation Text box**, then type Date must be on or after 1/17/2004

   The Design View of the Enrollments table should now look like Figure E-14. Once again, Access modified a property to include additional syntax by changing the entry in the Validation Rule property to >=#1/17/2004#. Pound signs (#) are used to surround date criteria.

3. **Click the Save button** on the Table Design toolbar, then click Yes when asked to test the existing data with new data integrity rules

   Because there are no dates in the Attended field earlier than 1/17/2004, there are no date errors in the current data, and the table is saved. You now want to test the Validation Rule and Validation Text properties as they work when entering data in the datasheet.

QUICK TIP

Access assumes that years entered with two digits from 30 to 99 refer to the years 1930 through 1999, and 00 to 29 refers to the years 2000 through 2029. To enter a year before 1930 or after 2029, enter all four digits of the year.

4. **Click the Datasheet View button** on the Table Design toolbar, press [Tab] three times to move to Attended field, type 1/1/02, then press [Tab]

   Because you tried to enter a date that was not true for the Validation Rule property for the Attended field, a dialog box opens and displays the Validation Text entry as shown in Figure E-15.

5. **Click OK to close the validation message**

   You now know that the Validation Rule and Validation Text properties work properly.

6. **Press [Esc] to reject the invalid date entry in the Attended field**

7. **Close the Enrollments table, then close the Training-E.mdb database and exit Access**

FIGURE E-14: Using the validation properties

Attended field is selected

Validation Rule property

Validation Text property

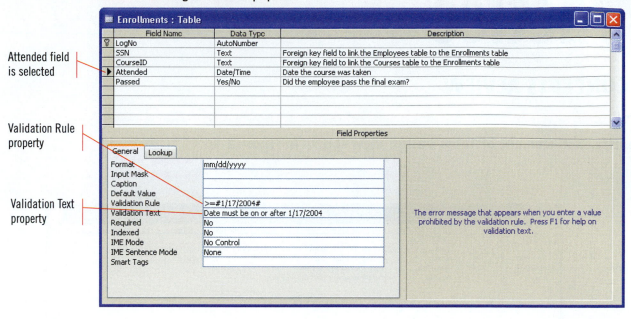

FIGURE E-15: Validation Text message

Validation Text

TABLE E-4: Validation Rule expressions

data type	validation rule expression	description
Number or Currency	>0	The number must be positive
Number or Currency	>10 And <100	The number must be between 10 and 100
Number or Currency	10 Or 20 Or 30	The number must be 10, 20, or 30
Text	"IA" Or "NE" Or "MO"	The entry must be IA, NE, or MO
Date/Time	>=#1/1/93#	The date must be on or after 1/1/1993
Date/Time	>#1/1/05# And <#1/1/06#	The date must be between 1/1/2005 and 1/1/2006

Practice

▼ CONCEPTS REVIEW

Identify each element of Table Design View shown in Figure E-16.

FIGURE E-16

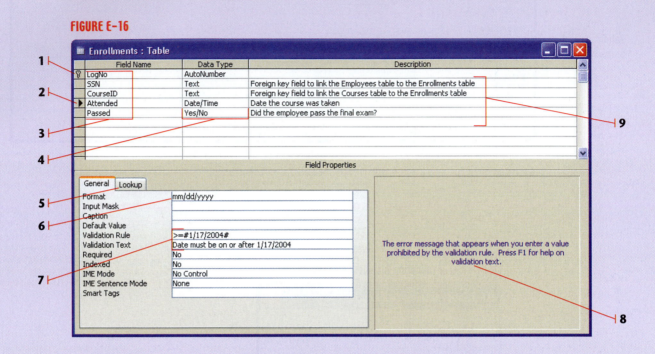

Match each term with the statement that best describes it.

10. **Primary key field**
11. **Validation properties**
12. **Table Design View**
13. **Row Source**
14. **Relational database**
15. **Input Mask**
16. **Lookup properties**

a. Several tables linked together in one-to-many relationships
b. Field that holds unique information for each record in the table
c. Field properties that help you prevent unreasonable data entries for a field
d. Field properties that allow you to supply a drop down of values for a field
e. Field property that provides a visual guide as you enter data
f. Lookup property that determines where the Lookup field gets its list of values
g. Access window where all characteristics of a table, such as field names and field properties, are defined

Select the best answer from the list of choices.

17. **Which of the following problems most clearly indicates that you need to redesign your database?**
    a. There is duplicated data in the field of several records of a table.
    b. Referential integrity is enforced on table relationships.
    c. Not all fields have Validation Rule properties.
    d. The Input Mask Wizard has not been used.

18. **Which of the following is *not* defined in Table Design View?**
    a. The primary key field
    b. Duplicate data
    c. Field Size properties
    d. Field data types

19. **What is the purpose of enforcing referential integrity?**
    a. To prevent orphan records from being entered
    b. To prevent incorrect entries in the primary key field
    c. To require an entry for each field of each record
    d. To force the application of meaningful validation rules

20. **To create a many-to-many relationship between two tables, you must create:**
    a. Foreign key fields in each table.
    b. Combination primary key fields in each table.
    c. A one-to-many relationship between the two tables with referential integrity enforced.
    d. A junction table.

▼ SKILLS REVIEW

1. **Examine relational databases.**
    a. Write down the fields needed to create an Access relational database to manage the membership information that a philanthropic club, community service organization, or special interest group might track.
    b. Identify those fields that contain duplicate values if all of the fields were stored in a single table.
    c. Group the fields into subject matter tables, and then identify the primary key field for each table.
    d. Pretend that your database will contain two tables: Members and Zipcodes. If you did not identify these two tables earlier, regroup the fields within these two table names, and then identify the primary key field for each table, the foreign key field in the Members table, and how the tables would be related using a one-to-many relationship.

2. **Create related tables.**
    a. Start Access, then click the Create a new file link at the bottom of the Open section of the Getting Started task pane.
    b. Click the Blank database link in the New File task pane. Navigate to the folder where your Data Files are stored, type **Membership-E** in the File name box, then click Create.
    c. Create a new table using Table Design View with the following field names and data types:
       FirstName, Text
       LastName, Text
       Street, Text
       Zip, Text
       Birthdate, Date/Time
       Dues, Currency
       MemberNo, Text
       MemberType, Text
       CharterMember, Yes/No
    d. Specify MemberNo as the primary key field, save the table with the name **Members**, then close it.

e. Create a new table using Table Design View with the following field names and data types:

Zip, Text

City, Text

State, Text

f. Identify Zip as the primary key field, save the table as **Zipcodes**, then close it.

g. Create a new table using Table Design View with the following field names and data types:

ActivityNo, AutoNumber

MemberNo, Text

ActivityDate, Date/Time

Hours, Number

h. Identify ActivityNo as the primary key field, save the table as **Activities**, then close it.

3. **Create one-to-many relationships.**

a. Open the Relationships window, double-click Activities, double-click Members, then double-click Zipcodes to add all three tables to the Relationships window. Close the Show Table dialog box.

b. Resize all field lists so that all fields are visible, then drag the Zip field from the Zipcodes table to the Zip field in the Members table to create a one-to-many relationship between the Zipcodes table and Members table using the common Zip field.

c. Enforce referential integrity for this relationship.

d. Drag the MemberNo field from the Members table to the MemberNo field in the Activities table to create a one-to-many relationship between the Members and the Activities table using the common MemberNo field.

e. Enforce referential integrity for this relationship.

f. Click File on the menu bar, click Print Relationships to create a report of the Relationships window, add your name as a label to the Report Header section if desired, and then print the report.

g. Close the Relationships report without saving the report, and then close the Relationships window. Save the changes to the Relationships window if prompted.

4. **Create Lookup fields.**

a. Open the Members table in Design View, then start the Lookup Wizard for the MemberType field.

b. Select the option that allows you to enter your own values, enter **Active**, **Inactive**, and **Senior** as the values for the lookup column, and then accept the rest of the Lookup Wizard defaults.

c. Save the table. In Datasheet View, tab to the MemberType field and click the list arrow to make sure the three values were entered properly for the Lookup field.

d. Press Esc twice to remove any edits to the first record of the Members table, then close the Members table.

5. **Modify Text fields.**

a. Open the Zipcodes table in Design View.

b. Change the Field Size property of the State field to **2**.

c. Use the Input Mask Wizard to create an Input Mask property for the Zip field. Choose the Zip Code Input Mask. Accept the other default options provided by the Input Mask Wizard. (*Note*: If the Input Mask Wizard is not installed on your computer, type **00000\-9999;;_** for the Input Mask property for the Zip field.)

d. Save the Zipcodes table, then close it.

e. Open the Members table in Design View.

f. Change the Field Size property of the FirstName, LastName, and Street fields to **30**. Save the changes to the table.

g. Use the Input Mask Wizard to create the Input Mask property for the Zip field. Choose the Zip Code input mask. Accept the other default options provided by the Input Mask Wizard. (*Note*: If the Input Mask Wizard is not installed on your computer, type **00000\-9999;;_** for the Input Mask property for the Zip field.)

h. Save the changes, then close the Members table.

6. Modify Number and Currency fields.

  a. Open the Members table in Design View.

  b. Change the Decimal Places property of the Dues field to **0**. Save the table then close the Members table.

  c. Open the Activities table in Design View.

  d. Change the Field Size property of the Hours field to **Byte**. Save the table then close the Activities table.

7. Modify Date/Time fields.

  a. Open the Members table in Design View.

  b. Change the Format property of the Birthdate field to **mm/dd/yyyy**.

  c. Save the table, then close the Members table.

  d. Open the Activities table in Design View.

  e. Change the Format property of the ActivityDate field to **mm/dd/yyyy**.

  f. Save the table, then close the Activities table.

8. Modify field validation properties.

  a. Open the Zipcodes table in Design View.

  b. Click the State field name, click the Validation Rule text box, then type **=IA OR KS OR MO**.

  c. Click the Validation Text box, then type **State must be IA, KS, or MO**. Note that Access automatically added quotation marks to the criteria in the Validation Rule property.

  d. Save the changes then open the Zipcodes table in Datasheet View.

  e. Test the Validation Text and Validation Rule properties by entering a new record with the Zip value of **661112222**, a City value of **Blue Valley**, and a State value of **MN**. Click OK when prompted with the Validation Text message, edit the State value to be **IA**, then close the Zipcodes table.

  f. Close the Membership-E.mdb database and then exit Access.

▼ INDEPENDENT CHALLENGE 1

As the manager of a music store's instrument rental program, you have decided to create a database to track instrument rentals to schoolchildren. The fields you need to track are organized with four tables: Instruments, Rentals, Customers, and Schools.

  a. Start Access, then create a new blank database called **Music Store-E** in the folder where your Data Files are stored.

  b. Use Table Design View to create the four tables in the Music Store-E database using the information in Table E-5. The primary key field for each table is identified with bold text.

  c. Enter **>1/1/04** as the Validation Rule property to the RentalDate field of the Rentals table. This change will only allow dates later than 1/1/04 to be entered into this field.

  d. Enter **Dates must be after 1/1/2004** as the Validation Text property to the RentalDate field of the Rentals table. Note that Access added pound signs (#) to the date criteria entered in the Validation Rule as soon as you entered the Validation Text property.

  e. Save and close the Rentals table.

TABLE E-5: Fields for tables

table	field name	data type
Customers	FirstName	Text
	LastName	Text
	Street	Text
	City	Text
	State	Text
	Zip	Text
	CustNo	Text
	SchoolNo	Text
Instruments	Description	Text
	SerialNo	Text
	MonthlyFee	Currency
Schools	SchoolName	Text
	SchoolNo	Text
Rentals	**RentalNo**	AutoNumber
	CustNo	Text
	SerialNo	Text
	RentalDate	Date/Time

▼ INDEPENDENT CHALLENGE 1 (CONTINUED)

f. Open the Relationships window, add all four tables to the window in the arrangement shown in Figure E-17, and create one-to-many relationships as shown. Be sure to enforce referential integrity on each relationship.

FIGURE E-17

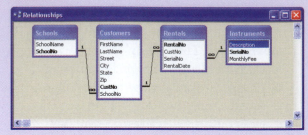

g. Preview the Relationships report, then print the report making sure that all fields of each table are visible. (If you need your name on the printout, add your name as a label to the Report Header.)

h. Close the Relationships report without saving it. Close the Relationships window, then save the layout if prompted.

i. Close the Music Store-E.mdb database, then exit Access.

▼ INDEPENDENT CHALLENGE 2

You want to document the books you've read by creating and storing the information in a relational database. You will design the database on paper by identifying the tables, field names, data types, and relationships between the tables.

a. On paper, create three balanced columns by drawing two vertical lines from the top to the bottom of the paper. At the top of the first column write **Table**. At the top of the second column write **Field Name**, and at the top of the third column write **Data Type**.

b. In the middle column, list all of the fields that need to be tracked to record information about the books you've read. You want to track information including the book title, category (such as Biography, Mystery, or Science Fiction), rating (a numeric value from 1–10 that indicates how much you liked the book), date you read the book, author's first name, and author's last name.

c. In the first column, identify the table where this field would be found. (*Hint*: You like to read multiple books from the same author, so you will need to separate the author information into a separate table to avoid duplicate author name entries in the Books table.)

d. Identify the primary key field for each table by circling it. You may have to add a new field to each table if you do not have an existing field that would naturally serve as the primary key field. (*Hint*: Each book has an ISBN—International Standard Book Number—that is a unique number assigned to every book. To uniquely identify each author, use an AuthorNo field. Do not use the AuthorLastName field as the primary key field for the Authors table because it would not uniquely identify authors who have the same last names.)

e. In a third column, identify the appropriate data type for each field.

f. Once all of the field names, table names, and data types are identified for each field, reorder the fields so that the fields for each table are listed together.

g. On a new piece of paper, sketch the field lists for each table as they would appear in the Relationships window of Access. Circle the primary key fields for each table. Include the one-to-many link lines as well as the "one" and "infinity" symbols to identify the "one" and "many" side of the one-to-many relationship. (*Note*: When building a one-to-many relationship between two tables, one field must be common to both tables. To create a common field, you may need to go back to your field lists in Step f and add a foreign key field to the table on the "many" side of the relationship in order to link the tables.)

▼ INDEPENDENT CHALLENGE 3

You want to create a database that documents blood bank donations by the employees of your company. You will design the database on paper including the tables, field names, data types, and relationships. You want to track information such as employee name, employee Social Security number, employee department, employee blood type, date of donation, and the hospital that is earmarked to receive the donation. Also, you'll want to track basic hospital information, such as the hospital name and address.

a. Complete Steps a through g as described in Independent Challenge 2 using the new case information. In this case, you should identify three tables: Employees, Donations, and Hospitals. When creating your field lists for each table, don't forget to always separate personal names into at least two fields, FirstName and LastName, so that you can easily sort, filter, and find data based on either part of a person's name.

b. To help determine how you should create the relationships between the tables, note that one employee can make several donations. One hospital can receive many donations.

Advanced Challenge Exercise

■ Build the database you designed in Access with the name **BloodDrive-E.mdb**. Don't forget to enforce referential integrity on the two one-to-many relationships in this database.

■ Print the Relationships report with your name added as a label to the Report Header section. Close the Relationships report without saving it, and then close the Relationships window and save the layout changes.

■ Add Lookup properties to the blood type field to provide only valid blood type entries of **A-**, **A+**, **B-**, **B+**, **O-**, **O+**, **AB-**, and **AB+** for this field.

■ Close BloodDrive-E.mdb, then exit Access.

▼ INDEPENDENT CHALLENGE 4

You are on the staff of an economic development team whose goal is to encourage tourism in the Baltic Sea region. You have created an Access database called Baltic-E to track important fields of information for the countries in that region and will use the Internet to find information about the area and enter it into existing forms.

a. Start Access, then open the **Baltic-E.mdb** database from the drive and folder where your Data Files are stored.

b. Connect to the Internet, and then go to www.google.com, www.lycos.com, or any general search engine to conduct research for your database. Your goal is to find three upcoming events for Munich, Germany, and to print the Web page(s) that provide this information.

c. Open the Cities form, find the Munich record, and enter three more events for Munich into the Events fields. EventID is an AutoNumber field, so it will automatically increment as you enter the EventName and EventDate information.

d. Open the Cities table in Design View, and then add a field called **MemberStatus** with a Text data type and a Field Size property of **11**. This field will be used to document the city's status with your economic development team.

e. Use the Lookup Wizard to provide the values **Active**, **Inactive**, and **No Interest** for the MemberStatus field. Save the Cities table.

Advanced Challenge Exercise

■ Open the Cities table in Datasheet View. Click the expand button to the left of the Munich, Germany, record to see the related records in the Events subdatasheet. Close the Cities table.

■ Using the Report Wizard, create a report based on all four fields in the Baltic Area Festivals query. View the data by Cities, do not add any more grouping levels, and then sort the records by EventDate.

■ Use a Stepped layout, a Portrait orientation, and a Corporate style.

■ Title the report **Baltic Area Events**, and then apply additional formatting embellishments as desired.

■ In Report Design View, add your name as a label to the Report Header section. Save, print, then close the report.

f. Close the Baltic-E.mdb database and then exit Access.

▼ VISUAL WORKSHOP

Open the **Training-E.mdb** database, and create a new table called **Vendors** using the Table Design View shown in Figure E-18 to determine field names and data types. Make the following property changes: Change the Field Size property of the VState field to **2**, the VZip field to **9**, and VPhone field to **10**. Change the Field size property of the VendorName, VStreet, and VCity fields to **30**. Be sure to specify that the VendorID field is the primary key field. Enter one record into the datasheet with your last name in the VendorName field and print the datasheet.

FIGURE E-18

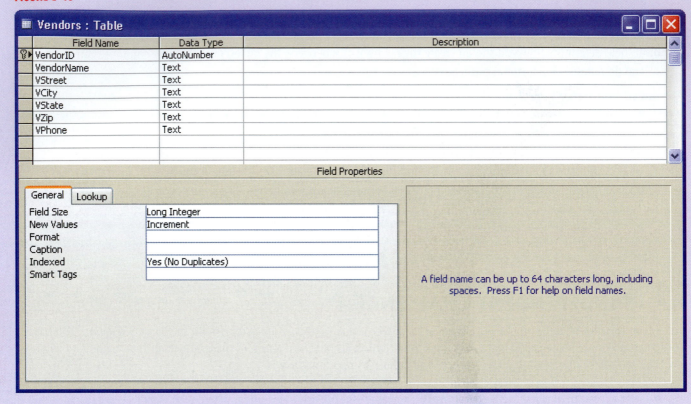

UNIT
F
Access 2003

Creating Multiple Table Queries

OBJECTIVES

Build select queries
Sort a query on multiple fields
Develop AND criteria
Develop OR criteria
Create calculated fields
Build summary queries
Build crosstab queries
Build PivotTables and PivotCharts

If you have a SAM user profile, you may have access to hands-on instruction, practice, and assessment of the skills covered in this unit. Log in to your SAM account and go to your assignments page to see what your instructor has assigned.

Queries are database objects that organize fields from one or more tables into a single datasheet. A **select query**, the most common type of query, retrieves fields from related tables and displays records in a datasheet. Select queries are used to select only certain records from a database, and can also sort records, calculate new fields of data, or calculate statistics such as the sum or average of a given field. You can also present data selected by a query in Query PivotTable View or Query PivotChart View. These views display information about summarized groups of records in a crosstabular report or graph. The MediaLoft Training database has been updated so that all three tables (Employees, Enrollments, and Courses) contain data. You help Fred Ames, the coordinator of training, create queries to analyze this information.

Building Select Queries

You can create select queries by using the **Simple Query Wizard** or by building the query in Query Design View. Creating a select query with the Simple Query Wizard is fast and easy, but learning how to use **Query Design View** gives you more flexibility and options regarding the information that you want to select as well as how you want that data presented. When you open (also called "**run**") a query, the fields and records that you have selected for the query are presented as a datasheet in **Query Datasheet View**. Query Datasheet View does not present a duplicate copy of the data stored in the tables. Rather, it displays table data in a new arrangement, sometimes called a **logical view** of the data. If you make any changes to data using a query datasheet, the changes are actually made to the underlying table just as if you were working directly in a table datasheet.  Fred asks you to create a query to answer the question, "Who is taking what courses?" You select fields from several tables using Query Design View to display a single datasheet that answers this question.

STEPS

1. **Start Access, then open the Training-F.mdb database from the drive and folder where your Data Files are stored**

2. **Click Queries on the Objects bar, then double-click Create query in Design view**
   The Show Table dialog box opens and lists all the tables in the database. You use the Show Table dialog box to add the tables that contain the fields you want to view in the final query datasheet.

TROUBLE

If you add a table to Query Design View twice by mistake, click the title bar of the extra field list, then press [Delete].

3. **Click Employees, click Add, double-click Enrollments, double-click Courses, then click Close**
   The upper part of Query Design View displays the fields for each of the three selected tables in three small windows called **field lists**. The name of the table associated with each field list is shown in the field list title bar. Primary key fields are bold. To rearrange the field lists in Query Design View, drag the title bar of a field list to move it, or drag the edge of a field list to resize it. Relationships between tables are displayed with **one-to-many join lines** that connect the linking fields, as shown in Figure F-1. The fields that you want the query to display are identified in the **query design grid**, the columns in the lower part of Query Design View.

QUICK TIP

When you drag a field to the query design grid, the existing fields move to the right to accommodate the new field.

4. **Drag the First field in the Employees table field list to the first column of the query design grid**
   The order in which the fields are placed in the query design grid is the order they appear in the datasheet.

5. **Double-click the Last field in the Employees field list, double-click the Registration field in the Enrollments field list, double-click the Description field in the Courses field list, then double-click the Hours field in the Courses field list**
   Query Design View should look like Figure F-2. You may delete a field from the query design grid by clicking the field selector above the field name and pressing [Delete]. Deleting a field from the query design grid removes it from the logical view of this query's datasheet, but does not delete the field from the database. A field is defined and the field's contents are stored in a table object only.

6. **Using the ▼ pointer, click the Hours field selector to select that column of the query design grid, press [Delete], then click the Datasheet View button 🖼 on the Query Design toolbar**
   The resulting datasheet looks like Figure F-3. The datasheet shows the four fields selected in Query Design View, First and Last from the Employees table, Registration from the Enrollments table, and Description from the Classes table. The datasheet displays 153 records that represent the number of times a MediaLoft employee has enrolled in a class. Megan Burik appears in 11 records because she has enrolled in 11 classes.

FIGURE F-1: Query Design View with multiple tables

Field lists

Primary key fields

One-to-many join lines

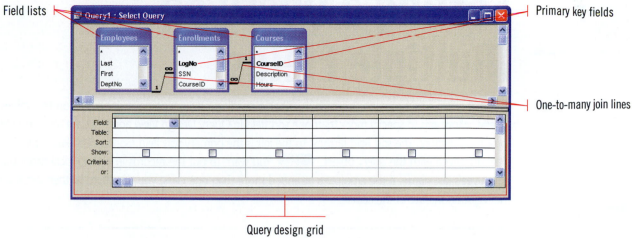

Query design grid

FIGURE F-2: Query Design View with five fields in the query design grid

Datasheet View button

Resize bar

Field selector

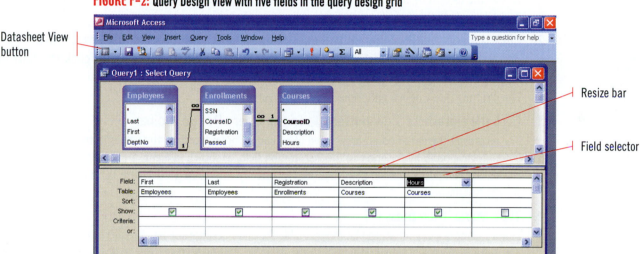

FIGURE F-3: Query datasheet showing related information from three tables

Field from the Courses table

Fields from the Employees table

Field from the Enrollments table

153 records

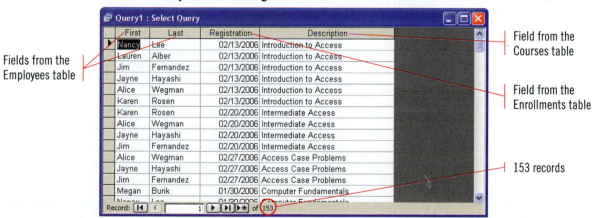

Clues to Use

Resizing Query Design View

Drag the resize bar up or down to provide more room for the upper (field lists) or lower (query design grid) panes of Query Design View. By dragging the resize bar down, you may have enough room to resize each field list so that you can see all of the field names for each table.

Sorting a Query on Multiple Fields

Sorting refers to reorganizing records in either ascending or descending order based on the values in a field. Queries allow you to specify more than one sort field in Query Design View and evaluate the sort fields from left to right. Therefore, the sort field farthest to the left is the primary sort field. Sort orders defined in Query Design View are saved with the query object. You want to put the records in alphabetical order based on the employee's last name. If the employee attended more than one class, you decide to further sort the records by the registration date of the course.

STEPS

1. **Click the Design View button ☑ on the Query Datasheet toolbar**

   To sort the records by name then by registration date, the Last field must be the primary sort field, and the Registration field the secondary sort field.

QUICK TIP

You can resize the columns of a datasheet by pointing to the right column border that separates the field names, then dragging ◄► left or right to resize the columns. Double-click ◄► to automatically adjust the column width to fit the widest entry.

2. **Click the Last field Sort cell in the query design grid, click the Sort list arrow, click Ascending, click the Registration field Sort cell in the query design grid, click the Sort list arrow, then click Ascending**

   The resulting query design grid should look like Figure F-4.

3. **Click the Datasheet View button ▦ on the Query Design toolbar**

   The records of the datasheet are now listed in ascending order based on the values in the Last field, then in chronological order by the entry in the Registration field, as shown in Figure F-5. Maria Abbott attended six classes, but you notice that her name has been incorrectly entered in the database as "Marie." Fix this error in the query datasheet.

4. **Type Maria, then press [▼]**

   Maria's name is pulled from the Employees table six times because she has attended six classes. But because her name is physically stored only once in the database, editing Maria's name in any view changes all other views that use that value as well.

5. **Double-click Fundamentals in the Description field of the third record, type Concepts, then press [▼] to observe the automatic change to Record 8**

   All occurrences of Computer Fundamentals have now been updated to Computer Concepts. A change made to data through a query datasheet automatically updates all other occurrences of that field value. When a query object is saved, it saves **Structured Query Language (SQL)** statements. You can view or work with SQL using Access query objects.

6. **Click the View button list arrow ☑▾ on the Query Datasheet toolbar, then click SQL View**

   The SQL statements determine what fields are selected, how the tables are joined, and how the resulting records will be sorted. Fortunately, you do not have to be able to write or understand SQL to use Access. The easy-to-use Query Design View gives you a way to select and sort data from underlying tables without being an SQL programmer.

7. **Close the SQL window, click Yes when prompted to save the changes, type Employee Registrations in the Query Name text box, then click OK**

   The query is now saved and listed as a query object in the Training-F database window.

FIGURE F-4: Specifying multiple sort orders in Query Design View

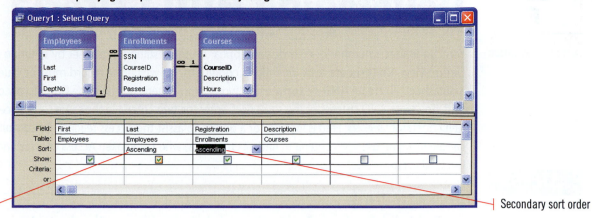

Primary sort order

Secondary sort order

FIGURE F-5: Records sorted by Last, then Registration

Primary sort field

Secondary sort field

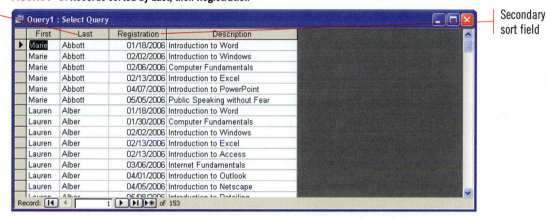

Clues to Use

Specifying a sort order different from the field order in the datasheet

If you had several different employees with the same last name and needed to include a secondary sort on first name but still wanted to display the fields in a first name, last name order, you could use the solution shown in Figure F-6. You can add a field to the query design grid twice and use the Show check box to sort the fields in one order (Last, First, Registration), yet display the fields in the resulting datasheet in another order (First, Last, Registration).

FIGURE F-6: Sorting on a field that is not displayed

Last field is used in query design grid twice

Show check box is unchecked

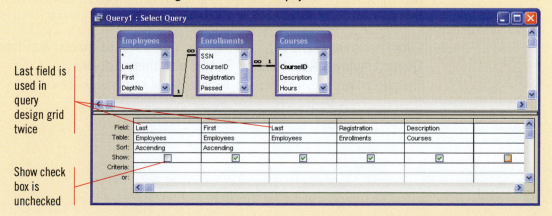

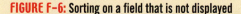

Developing AND Criteria

You can limit the number of records that appear on the resulting datasheet by entering criteria into Query Design View. **Criteria** are tests, or limiting conditions, for which the record must be true to be selected for a datasheet. To create **AND criteria** enter two or more criteria on the same Criteria row of the query design grid. To create AND criteria for the *same field*, enter the two criteria in the same Criteria cell separated by the AND operator. Fred is looking for a person to assist the Access teacher. To compile a list of potential candidates, you use AND criteria to find all employees who have taken Access courses and who have passed the final exam.

STEPS

1. **Right-click Employee Registrations, click Design View on the shortcut menu, click the View button list arrow on the Query Design toolbar, then click Design View**

   You decide to modify the Employee Registrations query because it already contains most of the data you need. The only additional field you need is the Passed field.

2. **Double-click the Passed field in the Enrollments field list**

   MediaLoft offers several Access courses, so the criteria to find these records must specify that the word "Access" is anywhere in the Description field. You use the asterisk (∗), a **wildcard character** that represents any combination of characters, to create this criterion.

3. **Click the Description field Criteria cell, type *access*, then click the Datasheet View button on the Query Design toolbar**

   The resulting datasheet, as shown in Figure F-7, lists thirteen records that match the criteria. The resulting records all contain the word "access" in some part of the Description field, but because of the placement of the asterisks, it doesn't matter *where* (beginning, middle, or end) Access was found.

4. **Click the Design View button on the Query Datasheet toolbar, click the Passed field Criteria cell, then type yes**

   You added the criterion to display only those records where the Passed field equals Yes as shown in Figure F-8. Access assists you with **criteria syntax**, rules by which criteria need to be entered. Access automatically adds quotation marks around text criteria in Text fields and pound signs (#) around date criteria in Date/Time fields. The criteria in Number, Currency, and Yes/No fields are not surrounded by any characters. In addition, notice that Access added the **Like operator** to the Description field criteria because the wildcard asterisk character was used. See Table F-1 for more information on common Access comparison operators and criteria syntax.

5. **Click on the Query Design toolbar to view the resulting records**

   Criteria added to the same line of the query design grid are AND criteria. When entered on the same line, each criterion must be true for the record to appear in the resulting datasheet. Only nine records contain "access" in the Description field and "yes" in the Passed field.

6. **Click File on the menu bar, click Save As, type Potential Access Assistants in the Save Query 'Employee Registrations' To text box, then click OK**

   The query is saved with the new name, Potential Access Assistants, as a new object in the Training-F database.

7. **Close the Potential Access Assistants datasheet**

FIGURE F-7: Datasheet for Access records

All records contain "Access" somewhere in the Description field

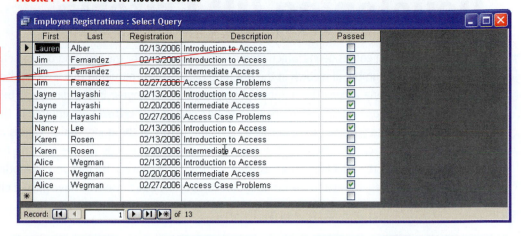

FIGURE F-8: AND criteria

AND criteria are entered on the same row

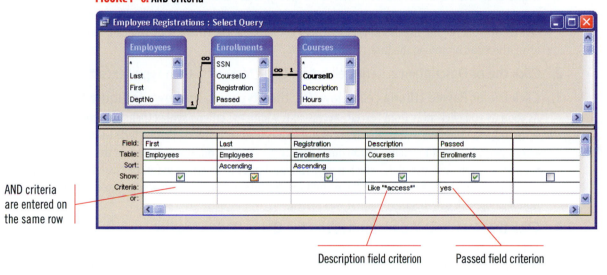

Description field criterion   Passed field criterion

TABLE F-1: Common comparison operators

operator	description	example	result
>	Greater than	>50	Value exceeds 50
>=	Greater than or equal to	>=50	Value is 50 or greater
<	Less than	<50	Value is less than 50
<=	Less than or equal to	<=50	Value is 50 or less
<>	Not equal to	<>50	Value is any number other than 50
Between...And	Finds values between two numbers or dates	Between #2/2/01# And #2/2/06#	Dates between 2/2/2001 and 2/2/2006, inclusive
In	Finds a value that is one of a list	In ("IA","KS","NE")	Value equals IA or KS or NE
Null	Finds records that have no entry in a particular field	Null	No value has been entered in a field
Is Not Null	Finds records that have any entry in a particular field	Is Not Null	Any value has been entered in a field
Like	Finds records that match the criterion	Like "A*"	Value starts with A
Not	Finds records that do not match the criterion	Not 2	Numbers other than 2

Developing OR Criteria

In a query, all criteria entries define which records will be selected for the resulting datasheet. Whereas AND criteria *narrow* the number of records in the resulting datasheet by requiring that a record be true for multiple criteria, OR criteria *expand* the number of records that will appear in the datasheet because a record needs to be true *for only one* of the criteria rows to be selected. **OR criteria** are entered in the query design grid on different lines (criteria rows). Because each criteria row of the query design grid is evaluated separately, the more OR criteria entries in the query grid, the more records will be selected for the resulting datasheet. Fred is looking for an assistant for the Excel courses. He asks you to modify the Potential Access Assistants query to expand the number of records to include those who have passed either the Access or the Excel courses.

STEPS

1. **Right-click the Potential Access Assistants query, then click Design View on the shortcut menu**

   To add OR criteria, you have to enter criteria in the next available "or" row of the query design grid. By default, the query grid displays nine "or" rows for additional OR criteria, but you can add even more rows using the Rows option on the Insert menu.

2. **Click the or Description criteria cell below Like "*access*", then type *excel***

3. **Click the or Passed criteria cell below Yes, then type yes, as shown in Figure F-9**

   As soon as you click away from *excel*, Access adds additional criteria syntax including quotation marks to surround text criteria as well as the Like operator that is used with criteria that include wildcard asterisk characters. Now, if a record matches *either criteria* row of the criteria grid, it is included in the query's datasheet. Each row is evaluated separately, which is why you must put the Yes criterion for the Passed field in both rows of the query design grid. Otherwise, the second row would specify all records where "excel" is in the description regardless of whether the final test was passed.

4. **Click the Datasheet View button on the Query Design toolbar**

   The resulting datasheet displays 28 records, as shown in Figure F-10. All of the records have course Descriptions that contain the word Access or Excel as well as Yes in the Passed field. Also, notice that the sort order (Last, then Registration) is still in effect.

   > **QUICK TIP**
   > To rename an object from the database window, right-click it, then choose Rename on the shortcut menu.

5. **Click File on the menu bar, click Save As, click between Access and Assistants, type or Excel, press [Spacebar], then click OK**

   The Potential Access or Excel Assistants query is saved as a new query object.

6. **Close the Potential Access or Excel Assistants query**

   The Training-F database displays the three queries you created in addition to the two queries that were previously created and stored in the database. Use the Details button on the database window toolbar to view more information about each query.

   > **QUICK TIP**
   > When using Details View, click the column headings to sort the objects based on that column.

7. **Click the Details button on the database window toolbar to view the date that the queries were created as well as the date that the queries were last modified, then click the List button to return to the default database window view**

FIGURE F-9: OR criteria

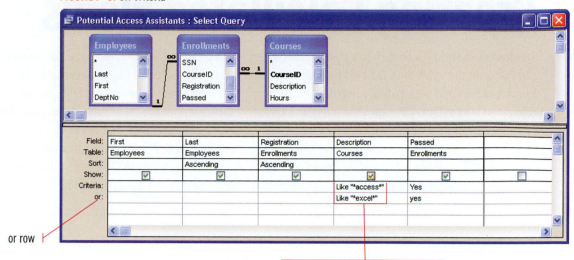

or row

OR criteria are entered on different rows

FIGURE F-10: OR criteria adds more records to the datasheet

First	Last	Registration	Description	Passed
Maria	Abbott	02/13/2006	Introduction to Excel	☑
Lauren	Alber	02/13/2006	Introduction to Excel	☑
Sandie	Blackwell	02/13/2006	Introduction to Excel	☑
Megan	Burik	02/13/2006	Introduction to Excel	☑
Megan	Burik	03/06/2006	Intermediate Excel	☑
Jim	Fernandez	02/13/2006	Introduction to Access	☑
Jim	Fernandez	02/13/2006	Introduction to Excel	☑
Jim	Fernandez	02/27/2006	Access Case Problems	☑
Jayne	Hayashi	02/13/2006	Introduction to Access	☑
Jayne	Hayashi	02/20/2006	Intermediate Access	☑
Jayne	Hayashi	02/27/2006	Access Case Problems	☑
Cynthia	Hayman	02/13/2006	Introduction to Excel	☑
Cynthia	Hayman	03/06/2006	Intermediate Excel	☑
John	Kim	02/13/2006	Introduction to Excel	☑
John	Kim	03/06/2006	Intermediate Excel	☑
John	Kim	03/15/2006	Excel Case Problems	☑

Record: 1 of 28

Passed field is always checked (Yes)

Excel or Access records were found

28 records found

Clues to Use

Using wildcard characters in query criteria

To search for a pattern, a wildcard character is used to represent any character in the criteria entry. Use a ? (question mark) to search for any single character and an * (asterisk) to search for any number of characters. Wildcard characters are often used with the Like operator. For example, the criterion Like "10/*/06" would find all dates in October of 2006, and the criterion Like "F*" would find all entries that start with the letter F.

Creating Calculated Fields

A **calculated field** is a field of data that can be created based on the values of other fields. For example, you can calculate the value for a Tax field by multiplying the value of the Sales field by a percentage. To create a calculated field and automatically populate every record with the correct value for that field, define the new calculated field in Query Design View using an expression that describes the calculation. An **expression** is a combination of field names, operators (such as +, –, /, and *), and functions that result in a single value. See Table F-2 for more information on arithmetic operators and Table F-3 for more information on functions.  Fred has asked you to report on the hourly cost of each course. To create this information, you'll create a calculated field called HourlyRate that is defined by dividing the Cost field by the Hours field.

STEPS

1. Click Queries on the Objects bar, double-click Create query in Design view, click Courses in the Show Table dialog box, click Add, then click Close

   The Courses field list is in the upper pane of the query design window.

2. Double-click the Description field, double-click the Hours field, then double-click the Cost field

   A calculated field is created in the Field cell of the design grid by entering a new descriptive field name followed by a colon, then an expression. Field names used in an expression are surrounded by square brackets.

   > **QUICK TIP**
   > Right-click an expression, then click Zoom to use the Zoom dialog box for long entries.

3. Click the blank Field cell of the fourth column, type HourlyRate:[Cost]/[Hours], then drag the ✛ mouse pointer on the right edge of the fourth column selector to the right to display the entire entry, as shown in Figure F-11

   > **QUICK TIP**
   > You do not need to show the fields used in the expression (in this case, Hours and Cost) in the query, but displaying them helps you determine if the expression is calculating correctly.

4. Click the Datasheet View button 🔲 on the Query Design toolbar

   The HourlyRate field calculates correctly, but you do not want to view more than two digits to the right of the decimal point. You can format fields in Query Design View.

5. Click the Design View button 🖌 on the Query Datasheet toolbar, right-click the HourlyRate field in the query design grid, then click Properties on the shortcut menu

   The Field Properties dialog box opens. Because the HourlyRate field represents dollars per hour, you want to format the field with a dollar sign and two digits to the right of the decimal point as provided by the Currency format.

6. Click the Format box, click the Format list arrow, click Currency, close the property sheet, then click 🔲 to display the records

   The data shown in the HourlyRate field is now formatted appropriately.

7. Press [Tab] twice, type 300 in the Introduction to Access Cost field, then press [Enter]

   The resulting datasheet is shown in Figure F-12. The HourlyRate field recalculated as soon as the Cost field was updated. It is extremely important to create calculated fields in queries rather than define them as new fields in Table Design View because calculated fields always display current data.

8. Click the Save button 🔲 on the Query Datasheet toolbar, type Hourly Rates in the Save As dialog box, click OK, then close the datasheet

   The query is saved as an object in the database.

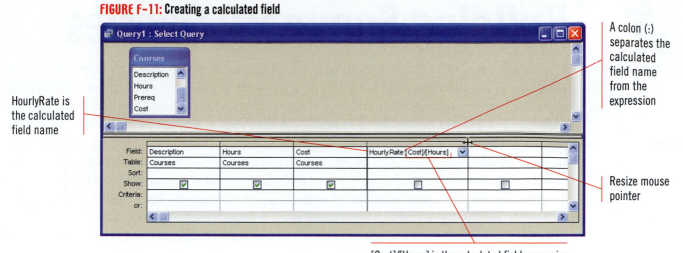

FIGURE F-11: Creating a calculated field

HourlyRate is the calculated field name

A colon (:) separates the calculated field name from the expression

Resize mouse pointer

[Cost]/[Hours] is the calculated field expression

FIGURE F-12: Formatting and testing the calculated field

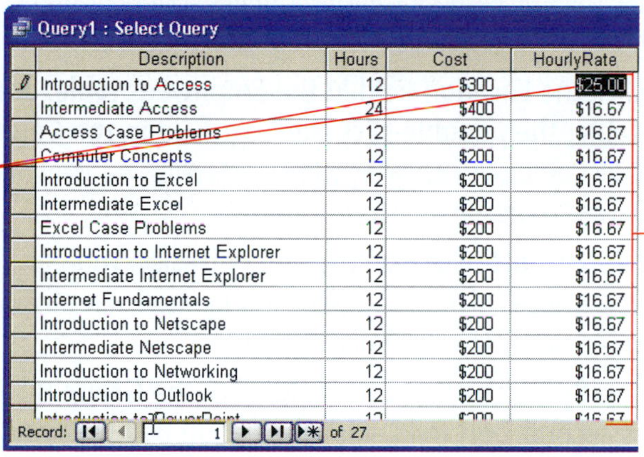

Updated Cost field automatically updates the calculated HourlyRate field

Currency format

TABLE F-2: Arithmetic operators

operator	description
+	Addition
–	Subtraction
*	Multiplication
/	Division
^	Exponentiation

TABLE F-3: Common functions

function	sample expression and description
DATE	DATE()-[BirthDate] Calculates the number of days between today and the date in the BirthDate field
PMT	PMT([Rate],[Term],[Loan]) Calculates the monthly payment on a loan where the Rate field contains the monthly interest rate, the Term field contains the number of monthly payments, and the Loan field contains the total amount financed
LEFT	LEFT([LastName],2) Returns the first two characters of the entry in the LastName field
RIGHT	RIGHT([Partno],3) Returns the last three characters of the entry in the Partno field
LEN	LEN([Description]) Returns the number of characters in the Description field

Building Summary Queries

A **summary query** calculates statistics about groups of records. To create a summary query, you use the **Total row** in the query design grid to specify how you want to group and calculate the statistics using aggregate functions. **Aggregate functions** calculate a statistic such as a subtotal, count, or average on a given field in a group of records. Some aggregate functions such as Sum can be used only on fields with Number or Currency data types, but others such as Min, Max, or Count can be used on Text fields, too. Table F-4 provides more information on aggregate functions. A key difference between the statistics displayed by a summary query and those displayed by calculated fields is that summary queries provide calculations that describe a *group of records*, whereas calculated fields provide a new field of information for *each record*. The Accounting Department wants to know the total training cost per location. They also want to know how many employees from each location have attended training classes. You will build a summary query to provide these statistics.

STEPS

1. **Click** Queries **on the Objects bar, then double-click** Create query in Design view

2. **Double-click** Courses, **double-click** Enrollments, **double-click** Employees, **then click** Close **in the Show Table dialog box**

   Even though you won't explicitly use fields from the Enrollments table, you need this table in your query to tie the fields from the Courses and Employees tables together.

3. **Double-click the** Location field **in the Employees table, double-click the** Cost field **in the Courses table, then double-click the** Cost field **in the Courses table again**

   You added the Cost field to the query grid twice because you want to compute two different summary statistics (subtotal and count) on the data in this field.

4. **Click the** Totals button Σ **on the Query Design toolbar**

   The Total row is added to the query grid below the Table row. You want to calculate statistics for each location, so the Location field is the Group By field.

5. **Click** Group By **for the first Cost field, click the** Group By list arrow, **click** Sum, **click** Group By **for the second Cost field, click the** Group By list arrow, **then click** Count

   The Totals row tells the query to group the records by the Location field, then sum and count the values in the Cost field as shown in Figure F-13.

6. **Click the** Datasheet View button **on the Query Design toolbar**

   The Boston location had $1,500 of internal charges for the 8 classes its employees attended, as shown in Figure F-14. By counting the Cost field in addition to summing it, you know how many records were combined to reach the total figure of $1,500 for the SumOfCost column. You can sort and filter summary queries, but you cannot enter or edit data in a summary query because each record represents the summary of several records.

7. **Click the** Save button **on the Query Datasheet toolbar, type** Internal Costs - Your Initials, **click** OK, **click the** Print button **, then close the datasheet**

   The name of the query is automatically placed in the header of the datasheet printout. Therefore, one way to uniquely identify a printout is to include your name or initials in the query name.

FIGURE F-13: Summary Query Design View

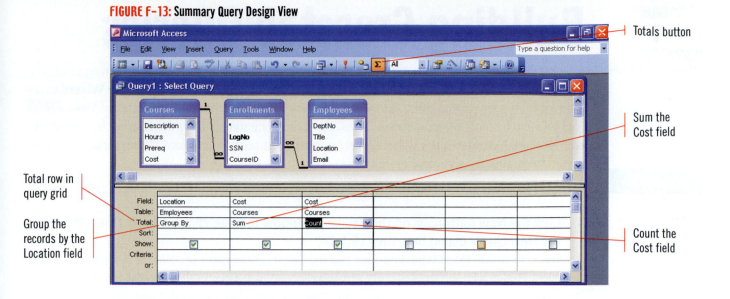

Totals button

Total row in query grid

Group the records by the Location field

Sum the Cost field

Count the Cost field

FIGURE F-14: Summarized records

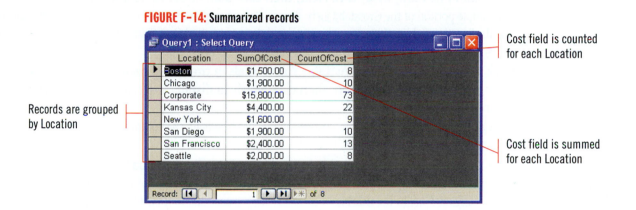

Cost field is counted for each Location

Records are grouped by Location

Cost field is summed for each Location

TABLE F-4: Aggregate functions

aggregate function	used to find the
Sum	Total of values in a field
Avg	Average of values in a field
Min	Minimum value in the field
Max	Maximum value in the field
Count	Number of values in a field (not counting null values)
StDev	Standard deviation of values in a field
Var	Variance of values in a field
First	Field value from the first record in a table or query
Last	Field value from the last record in a table or query

Building Crosstab Queries

A **crosstab query** calculates a statistic such as a sum or average by grouping records according to a field in the column heading as well as a field in the row heading. You can use the **Crosstab Query Wizard** to create a crosstab query or you can build the crosstab query from scratch using Query Design View. Fred asks you to continue your analysis of costs by location by summarizing the costs for each course for each location. A crosstab query will work well for this request because you want to summarize information by two fields, Location and (course) Description.

STEPS

TROUBLE

The "Create query by using wizard" shortcut in the database window creates a select query. You must click to use the other query wizards.

1. **Click the New button on the database window toolbar, click Crosstab Query Wizard in the New Query dialog box, then click OK**

   The first Crosstab Query Wizard question asks you which table or query contains the fields for the crosstab query. The fields for this crosstab query were previously saved in a query called Crosstab Fields.

2. **Click the Queries option button in the View section, click Crosstab Fields in the list of available queries, then click Next**

   The next questions organize how the fields are displayed in the crosstab query datasheet.

3. **Double-click Description to select it as the row-heading field, click Next, click Location for the column heading field, click Next, then click Sum in the Functions list**

   The Sample portion of the Crosstab Query Wizard dialog box presents the Description field as the row heading, the Location field as the column heading, and the summarized Cost field within the body of the crosstab query, as shown in Figure F-15.

4. **Click Next, type Location Crosstab - Your Initials in the query name text box, click the View the Query option button, then click Finish to display the crosstab query, as shown in Figure F-16**

   You can modify a crosstab query to change the row heading field, the column-heading field, or the calculation statistic in Query Design View.

QUICK TIP

Click the Query Type button list arrow on the Query Design toolbar, then click Crosstab Query to change any select query into a crosstab query.

5. **Click the Design View button on the Query Datasheet toolbar**

   Note that the Query Type button on the Query Design toolbar displays the crosstab icon and the words "Crosstab Query" are in the title bar of the query itself (versus the more common "Select Query"). The Total row shows that the datasheet is grouped by both the Description and the Location fields. The **Crosstab row** specifies that the Description field will be used as a Row Heading, and that the Location field will be used as a Column Heading.

6. **Click Sum in the Cost field Total cell, click the Sum list arrow, then click Count, as shown in Figure F-17**

   By changing the Sum aggregate function to Count, your crosstab query will now count the number of courses taken for each course description for each location rather than subtotaling the costs.

7. **Click the Datasheet View button on the Query Design toolbar, then click the Print button**

8. **Click the Save button, then close the crosstab query**

   Crosstab queries appear with a crosstab icon to the left of the query name in the database window.

Clues to Use

Query Wizards

The **Find Duplicates Query Wizard** is used to determine whether a table contains duplicate values in one or more fields. The **Find Unmatched Query Wizard** is used to find records in one table that do not have related records in another table. To use the Find Duplicates, Find Unmatched, or Crosstab Query Wizards, you must click the Queries button on the Objects bar, then click the New button on the database window toolbar. You access the Simple Query Wizard, which creates a select query, in the same way, or by clicking the "Create query by using wizard" option in the database window.

FIGURE F-15: Crosstab Query Wizard

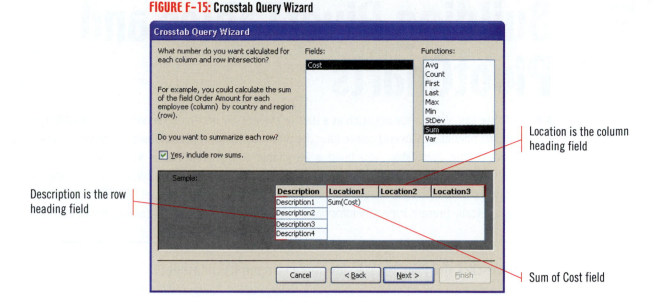

Location is the column heading field

Description is the row heading field

Sum of Cost field

FIGURE F-16: Crosstab datasheet

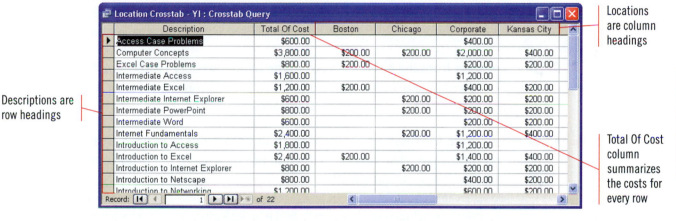

Locations are column headings

Descriptions are row headings

Total Of Cost column summarizes the costs for every row

FIGURE F-17: Query Design View of a crosstab query

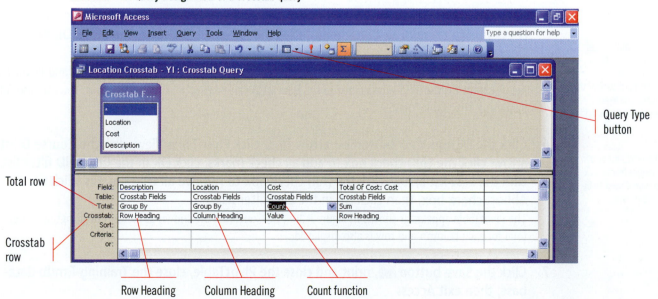

Query Type button

Total row

Crosstab row

Row Heading

Column Heading

Count function

Building PivotTables and PivotCharts

A **PivotTable** calculates a statistic such as a sum or average by grouping records like a crosstab query with the additional benefit of allowing you to filter the presented data. A **PivotChart** is a graphical presentation of the data in the PivotTable. You build a PivotTable using **PivotTable View**. Similarly, you design PivotCharts in **PivotChart View**. The PivotChart and PivotTable Views are bound to one another so that when a change is made in one view, the other is automatically updated as well.  You use PivotChart View to graphically present summary information about the courses taken by employees at each location.

STEPS

1. **Double-click the PivotTable Fields query to open its datasheet**

   You can view data of any existing table, query, or form in PivotTable and PivotChart views.

> **TROUBLE**
> If the Chart Field List does not appear, click the Field List button 🗔 to toggle it on.

2. **Click the Design View button list arrow 📉▾, then click PivotChart View**

   The PivotChart View and Chart Field List appear, as shown in Figure F-18. In PivotChart View, you drag a field from the Chart Field List to a **drop area**, a position on the chart where you want the field to appear. The fields in the **Chart Field List** are the fields in the underlying object, in this case, the PivotTable Fields query. The relationship between drop areas on a PivotChart, PivotTable, and crosstab query are summarized in Table F-5.

> **TROUBLE**
> To remove a field, drag it out of the PivotChart window.

3. **Drag Location from the Chart Field List to the Drop Category Fields Here drop area**

   When you successfully drag a field to a drop area, the drop area displays a blue border. Location field values will appear on the x-axis, also called the **category axis**.

> **TROUBLE**
> If you cannot see the Series drop area, drag the title bar of the Chart Field List.

4. **Drag Cost from the Chart Field List to the Drop Data Fields Here drop area, drag Last to the Drop Filter Fields Here drop area, then drag CourseID to the Drop Series Fields Here drop area, as shown in Figure F-19**

   Cost field values are now displayed as bars on the chart, and are measured by the numbers displayed on the y-axis, also called the **value axis**. The CourseID field is in the legend, also called the **series**, position for the chart. The Last field is in the filter position for the chart. PivotChart and PivotTable Views are used to present data as well as to analyze data. For example, you can use PivotChart fields to filter for only those records you want to analyze.

> **QUICK TIP**
> Click the Show Legend button 🗔 on the Formatting (PivotTable/PivotChart) toolbar to display the legend below the Series field.

5. **Click the Field List button 🗔 to toggle it off, click the CourseID list arrow, click the (All) check box to remove all check marks, click the Access1 check box, then click OK in the CourseID filter list**

   The PivotChart is filtered to display only the records for the Access courses. All PivotTable and PivotChart fields (except for the field summarized in the Data area) can be used to filter information. You can also filter data using PivotTable View.

> **QUICK TIP**
> The field's list arrow changes from black to blue if used to filter the data.

6. **Click the Design View button list arrow 📉▾, click PivotTable View, click the CourseID list arrow, click the (All) check box to add all check marks, click OK in the CourseID filter list, click the Last list arrow, click the (All) check box to remove all check marks, click the Abbott check box, then click OK in the Last filter list**

   The PivotTable appears as shown in Figure F-20. The CourseIDs are shown as column headings, and a grand total for each column and row is also displayed.

7. **Click the Save button 🖫, print and close the PivotTable, close the Training-F.mdb database, then exit Access**

FIGURE F-18: PivotChart drop areas

Field List button

Filter field area

Data field area

Scale depends on the size of the window

Category field area

Chart Field List

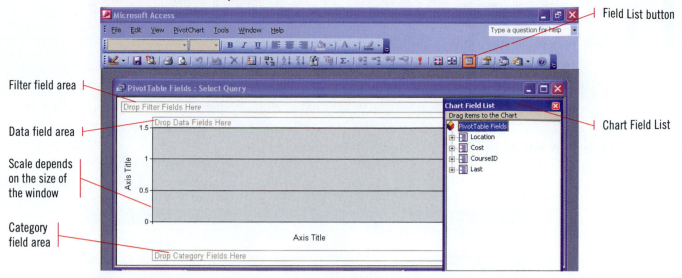

FIGURE F-19: PivotChart View

Last field in the Filter area

Cost field in the Data area

Value axis, y-axis

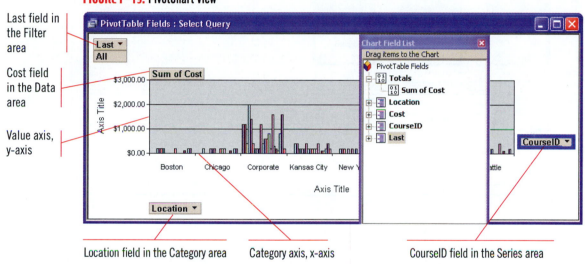

Location field in the Category area

Category axis, x-axis

CourseID field in the Series area

FIGURE F-20: PivotTable View

Field list arrows

Grand Total column

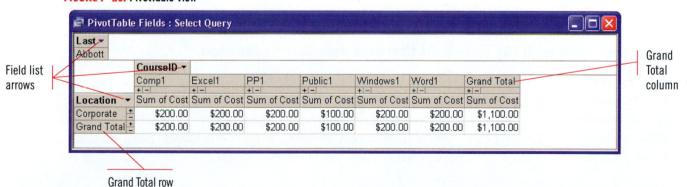

Grand Total row

TABLE F-5: PivotTable and PivotChart drop areas

drop area on PivotTable	drop area on PivotChart	crosstab query field position
Filter Field	Filter Field	(NA)
Row Field	Category Field	Row Heading
Column Field	Series Field	Column Heading
Totals or Detail Field	Data Field	Value

Access 2003

Practice

▼ CONCEPTS REVIEW

Identify each element of the Query Design View shown in Figure F-21.

FIGURE F-21

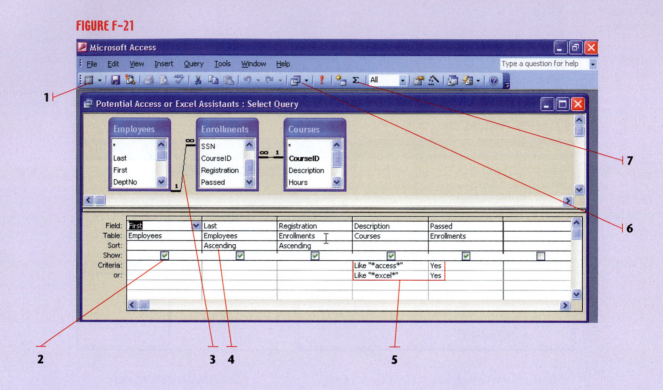

Match each term with the statement that best describes its function.

8. Select query   **a.** Placing the records of a datasheet in a certain order

9. Wildcard character   **b.** Asterisk (*) or question mark (?) used in query criteria

10. AND criteria   **c.** Retrieves fields from related tables and displays records in a datasheet

11. Sorting   **d.** Entered on more than one row of the query design grid

12. OR criteria   **e.** Entered on one row of the query design grid

Select the best answer from the list of choices.

13. The query datasheet can best be described as a:
  a. Duplication of the data in the underlying table's datasheet.
  b. Logical view of the selected data from an underlying table's datasheet.
  c. Separate file of data.
  d. Second copy of the data in the underlying tables.

14. Queries may *not* be used to:
  a. Set the primary key field for a table.
  b. Calculate new fields of data.
  c. Enter or update data.
  d. Sort records.

15. When you update data in a table that is also displayed in a query datasheet:
  a. You must also update the data in the query datasheet.
  b. You must relink the query to the table in order for the data to refresh.
  c. The data is automatically updated in the query.
  d. You have the choice whether or not you want to update the data in the query.

16. Which of the following is *not* an aggregate function available to a summary query?
  a. Subtotal
  b. Avg
  c. Count
  d. Max

17. The order in which records in a query are sorted is determined by:
  a. The order in which the fields are defined in the underlying table.
  b. The alphabetic order of the field names.
  c. The importance of the information in the field.
  d. The left-to-right position of the fields in the query design grid that contain a sort order choice.

18. The presentation of data in a crosstab query is most similar to:
  a. Report Print Preview.
  b. PivotTable View.
  c. Table Datasheet View.
  d. PivotChart View.

19. SQL stands for:
  a. Standard Query Limits.
  b. Saved Query Links.
  c. Simple Query Layout.
  d. Structured Query Language.

20. In a crosstab query, which field is the most likely candidate for the Value position?
  a. FName
  b. Department
  c. Country
  d. Cost

▼ SKILLS REVIEW

1. **Build select queries.**
   a. Start Access and open the **Membership-F.mdb** database from the drive and folder where your Data Files are stored.
   b. Create a new select query in Query Design View using the Members and Zipcodes tables.
   c. Add the following fields to the query design grid in this order:
      FirstName, LastName, and Street from the Members table
      City, State, and Zip from the Zipcodes table
   d. In Datasheet View, replace the LastName value in the first record with your last name.
   e. Save the query as **Address List**, print the datasheet, then close the query.

2. **Sort a query on multiple fields.**
   a. Open the Address List query in Query Design View.
   b. Drag the FirstName field from the Members field list to the right of the LastName field in the query design grid to make the first three fields in the query design grid FirstName, LastName, and FirstName.
   c. Add the ascending sort criteria to the second and third fields in the query design grid, and uncheck the Show check box in the third column. The query is now sorted in ascending order by LastName, then by FirstName, but the order of the fields in the resulting datasheet will still appear as FirstName, LastName.
   d. Use Save As to save the query as **Sorted Address List**, view the datasheet, print the datasheet, then close the query.

3. **Develop AND criteria.**
   a. Open the Address List in Design View.
   b. Type **M*** (the asterisk is a wildcard) in the LastName field criteria cell to choose all people whose last name starts with M. Access assists you with the syntax for this type of criterion and enters Like "M*" in the cell when you click elsewhere in the query design grid.
   c. Enter **KS** as AND criteria for the State field. Be sure to enter the criteria on the same line in the query design grid as the Like "M*" criteria.
   d. View the datasheet. It should select only those people from Kansas with a last name that starts with the letter M.
   e. Enter a new value in the City field of the first record to uniquely identify the printout.
   f. Use Save As to save the query as **Kansas M Members**, print, then close the datasheet.

4. **Develop OR criteria.**
   a. Open the Kansas M Members query in Query Design View.
   b. Enter **M*** in the second criteria row (the or row) of the LastName field.
   c. Enter IA as the criterion in the second criteria row (the or row) of the State field so that those people from IA with a last name that starts with the letter M are added to this query.
   d. Use Save As to save the query as **Kansas or Iowa M Members**, view and print the datasheet, then close the query.

5. **Build calculated fields.**
   a. Create a new select query using Query Design View using only the Members table.
   b. Add the following fields to the query design grid in this order: FirstName, LastName, Birthday.
   c. Create a calculated field called Age in the fourth column of the query design grid by entering the expression:
      Age: (Date()-[Birthday])/365 to determine the number of years old each person is based on the information in the Birthday field.
   d. Sort the query in descending order on the calculated Age field, then view the datasheet.
   e. Return to Query Design View, open the Property sheet for the Age field, then format the Age field with a Standard format and **0** in the Decimal Places property text box.
   f. Save the query with the name **Age Calculation**, view the datasheet, print the datasheet, then close the query.

6. **Build summary queries.**
   a. Create a new select query in Query Design View using the Members and Activities tables.
   b. Add the following fields: FirstName and LastName from the Members table, Hours from the Activities table.
   c. Add the Total row to the query design grid, then change the function for the Hours field from Group By to Sum.
   d. Sort in descending order by Hours.
   e. Save the query as **Total Hours - Your Initials**, view the datasheet, print the datasheet, then close the query.

7. **Build crosstab queries.**

   a. Create a select query with the City and State fields from the Zipcodes table, and the Dues field from the Members table. Save the query as **Crosstab Fields**, then close the query.

   b. Click the New button in the database window, click Crosstab Query Wizard in the New Query dialog box, click OK, then base the crosstab query on the Crosstab Fields query.

   c. Select City as the row heading, State as the column heading, and sum the Dues field within the crosstab datasheet.

   d. Name the query **Dues Crosstab - Your Initials**, then click Finish.

   e. View, print, then close the datasheet.

8. **Build PivotTables and PivotCharts.**

   a. Create a select query with the State field from the Zipcodes table, and the CharterMember and Dues fields from the Members table. Save it as **Dues Analysis - Your Initials**.

   b. Switch to PivotChart View, open the Chart Field List if it is not already visible, drag the State field to the Drop Category Fields Here drop area, the CharterMember field to the Drop Series Fields Here drop area, and the Dues field to the Drop Data Fields Here drop area.

   c. Use the State field to display only the data for the records where the State field value is equal to KS or MO as shown in Figure F-22.

   d. Switch to PivotTable View, then print it.

   e. Save the changes to the **Dues Analysis - Your Initials** query, close it, close the Membership-F.mdb database, then exit Access.

FIGURE F-22

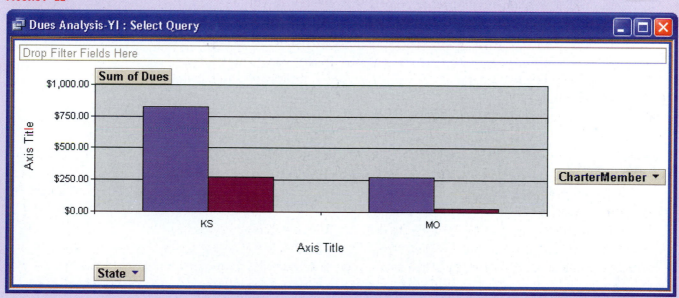

Access 2003

▼ INDEPENDENT CHALLENGE 1

As the manager of a music store's instrument rental program, you have created a database to track instrument rentals to schoolchildren. Now that several rentals have been made, you want to query the database for several different datasheet print-outs to analyze school information.

a. Start Access and open the **Music Store-F.mdb** database from the drive and folder where your Data Files are stored.

b. In Query Design View, create a query with the following fields in the following order:

SchoolName field from the Schools table

RentalDate field from the Rentals table

Description field from the Instruments table

(*Hint*: You need to add the Customers table to this query to make the connection between the Schools table and the Rentals table even though you don't use any fields from the Customers table.)

c. Sort ascending by SchoolName, then ascending by RentalDate.

d. Save the query as **School Rentals**, view the datasheet, replace the current entry in the first record with your elementary school name, then print the datasheet.

e. Modify the School Rentals query by deleting the Description field. Then, use the Totals button to group the records by SchoolName and to Count the RentalDate field. Print the datasheet and use Save As to save the query as **School Count**. Close the datasheet.

f. Use the Crosstab Query Wizard to create a crosstab query based on the School Rentals query. Use Description as the row heading and SchoolName as the column heading. Count the RentalDate field.

g. Save the query as **School Crosstab**, then view, print, and close it.

h. Modify the School Rentals query so that only those schools with the word Elementary in the SchoolName field are displayed. (*Hint*: You have to use wildcard characters in the criteria.)

i. Use Save As to save the query as **Elementary Rentals**, then view, print, and close the datasheet.

j. Close the Music Store-F.mdb database, then exit Access.

▼ INDEPENDENT CHALLENGE 2

As the manager of a music store's instrument rental program, you have created a database to track instrument rentals to schoolchildren. The database has already been used to answer several basic questions, and now that you've shown how easy it is to get the answers using queries, more and more questions are being asked. You will use queries to analyze customer and rental information.

a. Start Access and open the **Music Store-F.mdb** database from the drive and folder where your Data Files are stored.

b. In Query Design View, create a query with the following fields in the following order:

Description and MonthlyFee fields from Instruments table

Zip and City fields from the Customers table

(*Hint*: You will need to add the Rentals table to this query to make the connection between the Customers table and the Instruments table even though you don't need any fields from the Rentals table in this query's datasheet.)

c. Add the Zip field to the first column of the query grid and specify an Ascending sort order for this field. Uncheck the Show check box for the first Zip field so that it will not appear in the datasheet.

d. Specify an Ascending sort order for the Description field.

e. Save the query as **Zip Analysis**.

f. View the datasheet, replace Des Moines with the name of your hometown in the first record's City field, then print and close the datasheet.

g. Modify the Zip Analysis query by adding criteria to find the records where the Description is equal to **viola**.

h. Use Save As to save this query as **Violas**.

Advanced Challenge Exercise

- On a piece of paper, write down how many records the Violas query contains.
- Modify the Violas query with AND criteria that further specify that the City must be **Ankeny**.
- Save this query as **Violas in Ankeny**. On the paper, note how many records the Violas in Ankeny query contains. Briefly explain how AND criteria affected this number.
- Modify the Violas in Ankeny query with OR criteria that find all violas or violins, regardless of where they are located.
- Use Save As to save this query as **Violas or Violins**. On the paper, note how many records the Violas and Violins query contains. Briefly explain how OR criteria affected this number.
- Using the Crosstab Query Wizard, create a crosstab query based on the School Analysis query that uses the Description field for the row headings, the SchoolName field for the column headings, and that Counts the RentalNo field.
- Save the crosstab query as **Crosstab Rentals - Your Initials**, preview the datasheet, then print the datasheet in landscape orientation so that it fits on one page.

i. Close the Music Store-F.mdb database, then exit Access.

▼ INDEPENDENT CHALLENGE 3

As the manager of a music store's instrument rental program, you have created a database to track instrument rentals to schoolchildren. Now that several rentals have been made, you want to query the database to analyze customer and rental information.

   a. Start Access and open the **Music Store-F.mdb** database from the drive and folder where your Data Files are stored.

   b. In Query Design View, create a query with the following fields in the following order:

       FirstName and LastName from the Customers table

       Description and MonthlyFee from the Instruments table

       (*Hint*: You need to add the Rentals table to this query to make the connection between the Customers table and the Instruments table even though you don't need any fields from the Rentals table in this query's datasheet.)

   c. Sort the records in ascending order by the LastName field.

   d. Save the query as **Customer Rentals - Your Initials**, view the datasheet, enter your own last name in the first record's LastName field, then print the datasheet.

   e. In Query Design View, modify the Customer Rentals query by deleting the FirstName and LastName fields. Then, click the Totals button to group the records by Description and to Sum the MonthlyFee field.

   f. Add another MonthlyFee field as a third column to the query design grid, and use the Count function to find the count of rentals within that group.

   g. Sort the records in ascending order by the Description field.

   h. Use Save As to save the query as **Monthly Instrument Income - Your Initials**.

   i. View, print, then close the datasheet.

Advanced Challenge Exercise

- Open the Customer Rentals - Your Initials query in Design View, click the Show Table button on the Query Design toolbar to add the Schools table to the query, then add the SchoolName field as the fifth field in the query design grid.
- Display PivotChart View, then create the PivotChart shown in Figure F-23. The Description field has been used as a filter to show only MonthlyFee data for cellos and violins.
- Click the Show Legend button on the Formatting (PivotTable/PivotChart) toolbar to show the legend box under the Description field in the Series field drop area.
- Print the PivotChart, save and close the Customer Rentals - Your Initials query.

FIGURE F-23

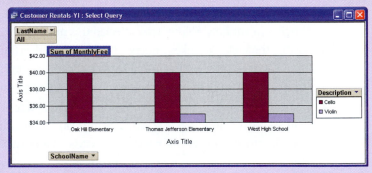

   j. Close the Music Store-F database, then exit Access.

▼ INDEPENDENT CHALLENGE 4

You are on the staff of an economic development team whose goal is to encourage tourism in the Baltic Sea region. You have created an Access database called Baltic-F to track important fields of information for the countries in that region, and are using the Internet to find information about the area that you then enter into existing forms.

a. Start Access and open the **Baltic-F.mdb** database from the drive and folder where your Data Files are stored.

b. Connect to the Internet, then go to www.google.com, www.about.com, or any general search engine to conduct some research for your database. Your goal is to find three upcoming events for Stockholm, Sweden, then print the Web page(s).

c. Open the Cities table datasheet, click the expand button for the Stockholm record to show a subdatasheet of related records from the Events table, and enter the three events you found for Stockholm into the subdatasheet. EventID is an AutoNumber field, so it will automatically increment as you enter the EventName and EventDate information.

d. Using Query Design View, create a select query with the following fields in the following order:
Country and City from the Cities table
EventName and EventDate from the Events table

e. Save the query with the name **Event Info**, then close it.

Advanced Challenge Exercise

■ Use PivotTable View to organize the Event Info information by putting Country in the Filter Fields drop area, City in the Column Fields drop area, EventDate in the Row Fields drop area, and EventName in the Detail Fields drop area.

■ Filter for only the data in Sweden, then print the PivotTable.

f. Save and close the Event Info query, close the Baltic-F.mdb database, then exit Access.

▼ VISUAL WORKSHOP

Open the **Training-F.mdb** database from the drive and folder where your Data Files are stored. In Query Design View create a new select query with the Location field from the Employees table, the Cost and CourseID fields from the Courses table, and the Passed field from the Enrollments table. Display the query in PivotChart View, then create it as shown in Figure F-24. Filter the data for CourseIDs Access1 and Access2 and for the Passed value of Yes. Click the Show Legend button on the Formatting (PivotTable/PivotChart) toolbar to display the legend below the Location field in the Series field area. Save the query with the name **Access PivotChart – Your Initials**, then print it.

FIGURE F-24

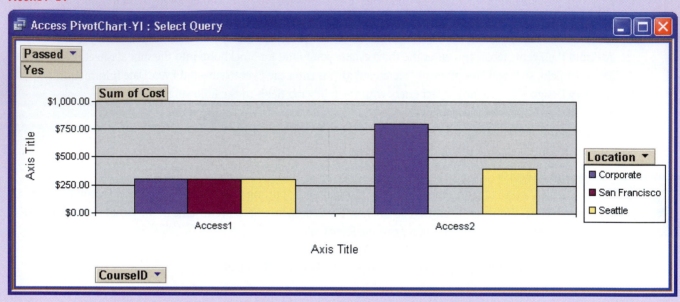

UNIT G — Access 2003

Developing Forms and Subforms

OBJECTIVES

Understand the form/subform relationship

Create subforms using the Form Wizard

Create subforms using queries

Modify subforms

Add a combo box for data entry

Add a combo box to find records

Add option groups

Add command buttons

Add ActiveX controls

If you have a SAM user profile, you may have access to hands-on instruction, practice, and assessment of the skills covered in this unit. Log in to your SAM account and go to your assignments page to see what your instructor has assigned.

A **form** is a database object designed to make data easy to find, enter, and edit. Forms are created by using **controls** such as labels, text boxes, combo boxes, and command buttons, which make data easier to find, enter, and manipulate than working with data in a datasheet. A form that contains a **subform** allows you to work with related records in an easy-to-use screen arrangement. For example, a form/subform combination would allow you to display customer data as well as all of the orders placed by that customer at the same time. Fred Ames wants to improve the usability of the forms in the MediaLoft training database. You will build and improve forms by working with subforms, combo boxes, option groups, command buttons, and ActiveX controls.

Understanding the Form/Subform Relationship

A **subform** is actually a form within a form. The form that contains the subform is called the **main form**. You add a subform to a main form using a subform control. The subform shows records that are related to the record currently displayed in the main form. Therefore, a form/subform combination is often used to display the records of two tables that are related in a one-to-many relationship. Sometimes a one-to-many relationship is called a **parent/child relationship**, because the "parent" record in the main form is linked to many "child" records displayed in the subform. Well-designed forms/subforms encourage fast, accurate data entry, and shield the data entry person from the complexity of underlying tables and relationships. Creating forms with subforms requires careful planning, so you study form/subform guidelines before creating the forms in Access.

DETAILS

To plan a form/subform:

- **Sketch the layout of the form/subform on paper, identifying which fields belong in the main form and which belong in the subform**

  The sketch in Figure G-1 displays employee information in the main form and enrollment information in the subform to accommodate the one-to-many relationship between the Employees and Enrollments tables. Figure G-2 displays course information in the main form and employee enrollment information in the subform to accommodate the one-to-many relationship between the Courses and Enrollments tables.

- **Decide whether to use the Form Wizard to create the form/subform in one process or whether to create each form separately**

  This decision determines each form's Record Source property value. The **Record Source property** identifies the recordset for the form and may be a table name, a query name, or a Structured Query Language (SQL) statement. Recall that the **recordset** is the data—the fields and records—that will appear on the form. Although building a form/subform using the Form Wizard is fast and easy, this process will insert an SQL statement for the Record Source property value of the form if either the form or subform is based on fields from multiple tables. While the initial form will function well using an SQL statement for the Record Source property, modifying that form's recordset depends upon your SQL skills. For example, later you might want to add a new field to the form or use criteria to limit the number of records that the form displays. Both of these tasks require modifying the recordset.

  If you create the form and subform separately, basing each form on an individual query object, the Record Source property value is the name of the query. Later, if you want to modify the recordset for either form, you simply modify the query that defines the recordset in Query Design View, a relatively simple task compared to that of editing SQL.

  To create each form on an individual query object, you must first build the queries, then build the forms, and then link the subform to the main form. This is obviously a much longer process than building the form /subform combination in one step via the Form Wizard. If you anticipate that you may want to change the recordset for either the form or subform later, however, the extra work may be worth it.

  You decide to use the Form Wizard and then create separate queries and forms to build two form/subform combinations so that you can compare the two processes.

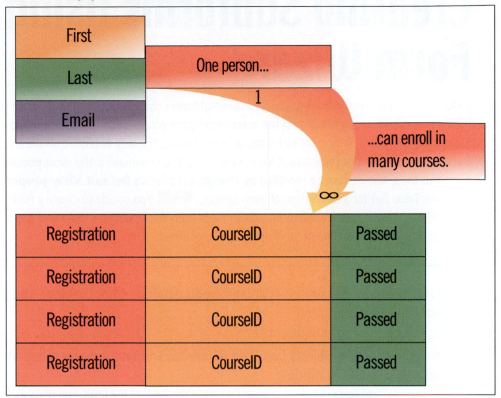

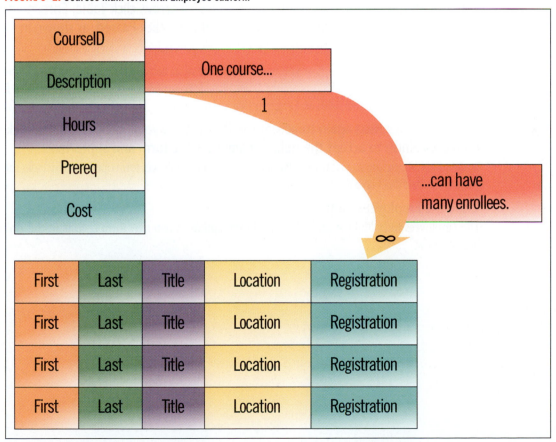

Creating Subforms Using the Form Wizard

When you use the Form Wizard to create a form/subform combination, you create both the main form and subform and position the subform in the main form in one process. The Form Wizard also asks you to choose a layout for each form. A form **layout** is the general way that the data and controls are arranged on the form. Columnar is the most popular layout for a main form, and Datasheet is the most popular layout for a subform, but these choices can be modified by changing the form's **Default View property** in Form Design View. See Table G-1 for a description of form layouts.  You decide to create a form/subform using the Form Wizard. The main form will display three fields from the Employees table and the subform will display three fields from the Enrollments table as previously planned.

STEPS

1. **Start Access, then open the Training-G.mdb database from the drive and folder where your Data Files are stored**

   The Training-G.mdb database opens.

2. **Click Forms on the Objects bar, then double-click Create form by using wizard in the Training-G database window**

   The Form Wizard appears and prompts you to select the fields of the form. You need six fields that are stored in three different tables for the final form/subform.

3. **Click the Tables/Queries list arrow, click Table: Employees, double-click First, double-click Last, double-click Email, click the Tables/Queries list arrow, click Table: Enrollments, double-click Registration, double-click CourseID, then double-click Passed, as shown in Figure G-3**

4. **Click Next**

   This Form Wizard question asks how you want to view the data. Because the Employees and Enrollments tables are linked in a one-to-many relationship, the Form Wizard recognizes the opportunity to create a form/subform combination for the selected fields and suggests that arrangement.

   QUICK TIP

   Use the Standard style when saving a database to a floppy disk. The other styles contain graphics that increase the storage requirements of the form.

5. **Click Next, click Next again to accept the Datasheet layout, click Standard, click Next, then click Finish to accept the default names for the form and subform**

   By default, subforms are created with a Datasheet layout. The Employees form opens and includes the Enrollments subform in Datasheet layout, as shown in Figure G-4.

6. **Close the Employees form**

   The Employees form and the Enrollments subform appear as two new form objects in the Training-G database window.

FIGURE G-3: Form Wizard

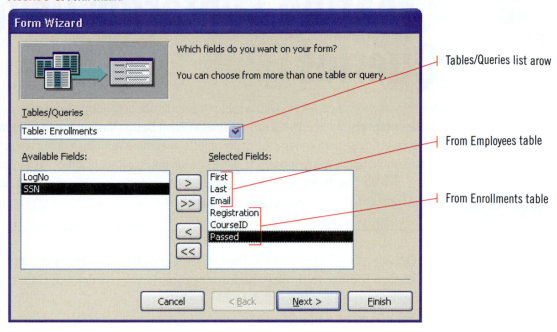

Tables/Queries list arow

From Employees table

From Enrollments table

FIGURE G-4: Employees main form with Enrollments subform

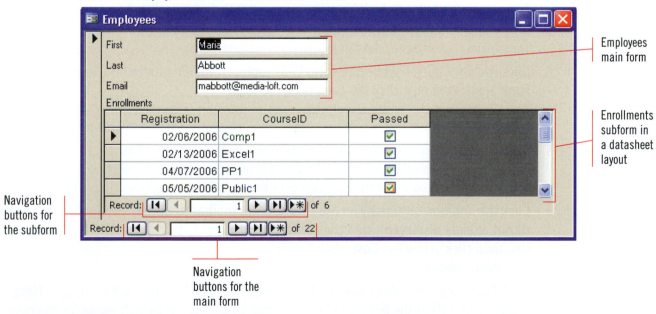

Employees main form

Enrollments subform in a datasheet layout

Navigation buttons for the subform

Navigation buttons for the main form

TABLE G-1: Form layouts

layout	description
Columnar	Each field appears on a separate row with a label to its left
Tabular	Each field appears as an individual column and each record is presented as a row
Datasheet	Fields and records are displayed as they appear in a table or query datasheet
PivotTable	Fields are organized in a PivotTable arrangement
PivotChart	Fields are organized in a PivotChart arrangement

Creating Subforms Using Queries

Another way to create a form with a subform is to create both forms separately, basing them on individual queries, and then link the two forms together in Form Design View of the main form. Although creating the forms by building them on separate query objects takes more work than doing the same thing using the Form Wizard, the advantage is being able to easily change the recordset of either form by modifying the underlying query.  You decide to create the second form/subform that you previously designed without the help of the Form Wizard. You start by building the subform.

1. **Double-click Create form in Design view, click the Properties button �",on the Form Design toolbar to display the form's property sheet, click the Data tab, click the Record Source list arrow, then click Employee Info**

   The field list for the Employee Info query opens, showing you the fields you can choose for the subform.

2. **Click 🖳 to toggle off the property sheet, double-click the Employee Info field list title bar to select all fields in the list, then drag the selected fields to the form as shown in Figure G-5**

   Now that the subform's fields are selected, you decide to change the Default View property of the subform to Datasheet to match how most subform layouts are organized.

3. **Double-click the Form Selector button to reopen the form's property sheet, click the Format tab, click the Default View list arrow, click Datasheet, click 🖳 to toggle off the property sheet, then click the Datasheet View button 🔲 on the Form Design toolbar**

   The subform displays the selected data in a datasheet presentation.

4. **Click the Save button 💾 on the Form View toolbar, type Employee Info Subform in the Form Name text box, click OK, then close the form**

   With the Employee Info Subform saved, you're ready to connect it to the main form. The Course Info form has already been created to serve as the main form. Now you need to add the Employee Info Subform to it.

5. **Right-click Course Info, then click Design View on the shortcut menu**

   In the upper portion of the form, the Course Info form displays fields from the Course Info query. The Employee Info Subform will be related to the Course Info main form through the common CourseID field.

6. **Click the Toolbox button 🛠 on the Form Design toolbar to display the Toolbox toolbar (if not already displayed), click the Subform/Subreport button 🔳 on the Toolbox toolbar, then click below the Cost label**

   The SubForm Wizard appears.

7. **Click Employee Info Subform in the Use an existing form list box, click Next, click Next to accept CourseID as the linking field, click Finish to accept the default name for the new subform control, click the Form View button 🔳 on the Form Design toolbar, then resize the subform and columns in Form Design View and Form View as shown in Figure G-6**

   The first of 27 courses, Access1, is displayed in the main form. The six employees who completed that course are displayed in the subform.

8. **Save and close the form**

FIGURE G-5: Creating the Employee Info Subform

Field List button

Form Selector button

Toolbox button

Properties button

Employee Info field list

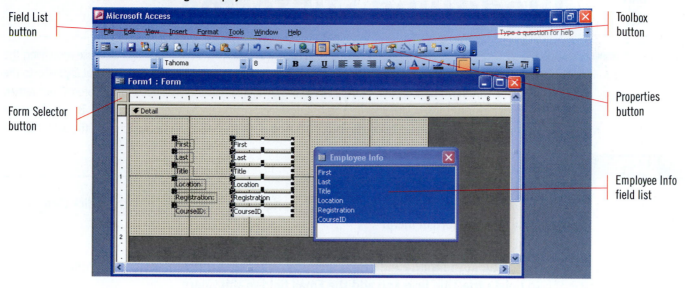

FIGURE G-6: Courses Info main form with Employee Info Subform

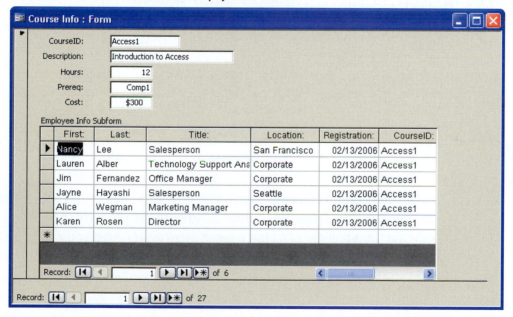

Access 2003

Clues to Use

Linking the form and subform

If the form and subform do not appear to be correctly linked, examine the subform's property sheet, paying special attention to the **Link Child Fields** and **Link Master Fields** properties on the Data tab.

These properties tell you which field serves as the link between the main form and subform. The field specified for this property should be present in both queries that underlie the main form and subform.

Modifying Subforms

When you build a form/subform on query objects it is easy to modify the recordset later because modifying the query that is used in the form's Record Source property automatically modifies the recordset that is passed to the form. You have decided that you don't need the Title field in the Employee Info Subform, but rather, would like to display the Email field in that position. Because the Employee Info Subform is based on the Employee Info query, you can modify the Employee Info query in Query Design View to change the fields that are available to the Employee Info Subform.

STEPS

1. **Click the Queries button on the Objects bar, right-click Employee Info, then click Design View on the shortcut menu**

   The Employee Info query opens in Query Design View.

2. **Click Title in the third Field cell in the query grid, click the Title list arrow, then click Email to delete the Title field and add the Email field to this query**

   The Employee Info query should look like Figure G-7.

3. **Click the Save button 🖫 on the Query Design toolbar, then close the query**

   With the Employee Info query modified, the recordset sent to the Employee Info Subform is also automatically modified because the Record Source property of the Employee Info Subform is the Employee Info query.

4. **Click the Forms button on the Objects bar, right-click Employee Info Subform, then click Design View on the shortcut menu**

   Notice that the Title field now displays an **error indicator**, a small green triangle in the upper-left corner of the Title text box. You already know the reason for this error—the Title field is no longer part of the Employee Info query upon which this form is based. If you did not know the cause of the error, however, you could use the Error Checking Options button to get more information.

TROUBLE
Point to the Error Checking Options button to display the list arrow.

5. **Click the Title text box, then click the Error Checking Options list arrow ◈ as shown in Figure G-8**

   The shortcut menu indicates that no field named Title exists in the Field List, and that you could remedy this by either changing the control's Control Source property or the form's Record Source property. You want the text box to display the contents of the Email field, so you'll modify its Control Source property to make this change.

6. **Click Edit the Control's Control Source Property, click the Control Source list arrow, click Email, then click the Properties button 🖆 to close the property sheet**

   Now the text box is bound to a field that is part of the recordset defined by the Employee Info query, so the error indicator has disappeared. The label to the left of the field needs to be modified to describe the new data.

7. **Click the Title label to select it, double-click Title, type Email, then press [Enter]**

   Your form should look like Figure G-9. Both the text box and label are modified to display information about the Email field versus the Title field.

8. **Save and close the Employee Info Subform, then double-click the Course Info form to open it in Form View**

   The Email field information now appears in the subform.

FIGURE G-7: Changing the Employee Info query

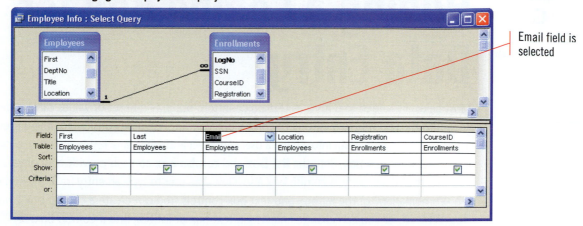

Email field is selected

FIGURE G-8: Using the Error Checking Options button

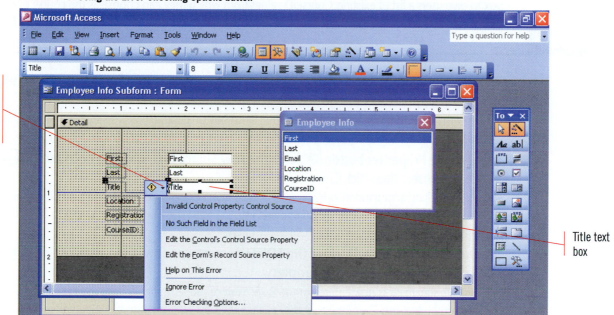

Error Checking Options button list arrow

Title text box

FIGURE G-9: Modifying the subform text box and label

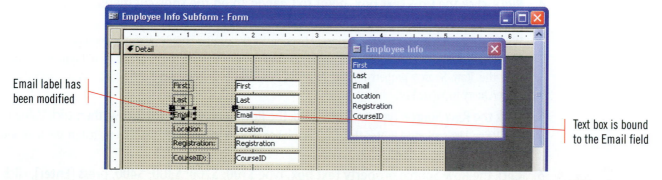

Email label has been modified

Text box is bound to the Email field

Clues to Use

Error checking options

Access 2003 will check several types of common errors for you in Form and Report Design View. When it finds an error, Access will display the Error Checking Options button to help you resolve the error. The types of errors that Access will check and the ability to turn this feature on and off are found on the Error Checking tab of the Options dialog box. To open the Options dialog box, click Options on the Tools menu.

Adding a Combo Box for Data Entry

Most fields are added to a form as text box controls, but if a finite set of values can be identified for a field, changing the text box to a list box or combo box control should be considered. If you provide the user with a combo box to enter data into a field, a user can select and enter data faster and more accurately than entering data using a text box. Both the **list box** and **combo box** controls provide a list of values from which the user can choose an entry. A combo box also allows the user to type an entry from the keyboard; therefore, it is a "combination" of the list box and text box controls. You can create a combo box by using the **Combo Box Wizard**, or you can change an existing text box or list box into a combo box. You decide to change the Prereq text box (which specifies if a prerequisite course is required) from a text box into a combo box to give users a list of existing CourseID values from which they can choose as the course prerequisite. You also decide to change the Cost text box to a combo box to provide users a list of valid entries for that field.

1. **Click the Design View button , right-click the Prereq text box in the Detail section of the form, point to Change To, then click Combo Box**

   Now that the control has been changed from a text box to a combo box, you are ready to populate the combo box list with values from the CourseID and Description fields from the Courses table.

   > **QUICK TIP**
   > The title bar of the property sheet identifies the name of the control that you are currently working with.

2. **Click the Properties button , click the Row Source box, click the Build button , double-click Courses, then click Close**

   The SQL Statement window opens and displays a query design grid and a field list you can use to select the fields you want to display in the combo box list. You want the values in the CourseID field to appear in the combo box list, so you'll add this field to the query.

3. **Double-click CourseID, close the SQL Statement window, then click Yes when prompted to save the changes to the property**

   An SQL statement is now entered in the **Row Source** property that defines the values that are presented in the combo box list. Your final step is to change the Cost text box into a combo box as well. MediaLoft has only four internal charges for its classes, $100, $200, $300, and $400. You want to display these values in the list of a combo box.

4. **Right-click the Cost text box, point to Change To on the shortcut menu, then click Combo Box**

   With the combo box in place you are ready to populate the combo box list with the appropriate values, $100, $200, $300, and $400. Because these values do not exist in a field in the database, you'll type them directly into the Row Source property. First, however, you must change the Row Source Type property from Table/Query to Value List.

5. **Click the Row Source Type text box, click the Row Source Type list arrow, then click Value List**

   The Value List option indicates that the combo box gets its values from the list entered in the Row Source property.

   > **TROUBLE**
   > Enter semicolons (;) between the values in the Row Source property.

6. **Click the Row Source property text box, type $100; $200; $300; $400, press [Enter], click the Limit to List property list arrow, then click Yes as shown in Figure G-10**

   Because you changed the **Limit to List** property to "Yes," the user cannot enter a new entry in this combo box from the keyboard. In other words, the text box part of the combo box has been disabled and the user must select a value from the list.

7. **Click to toggle off the property sheet, click the Save button , click the Form View button , click the Cost combo box list arrow, then click $400**

   The updated form with two combo boxes should look like Figure G-11.

FIGURE G-10: Modifying the Cost combo box

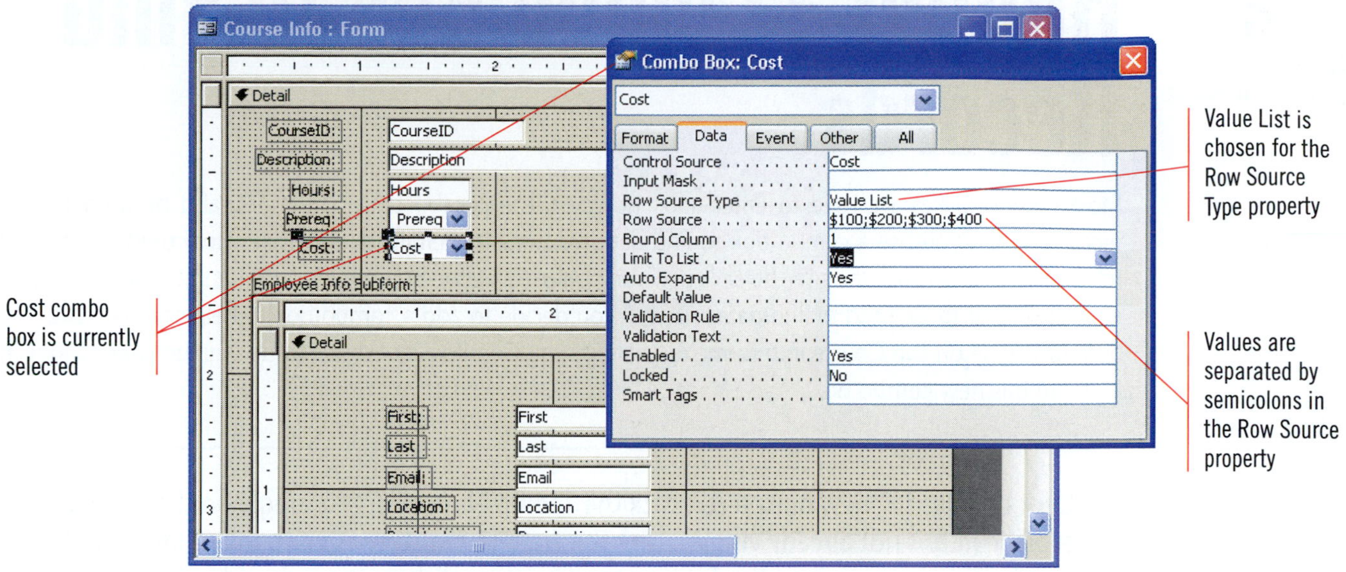

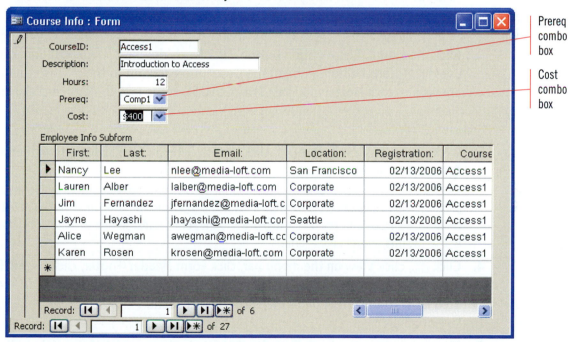

Cost combo box is currently selected

Value List is chosen for the Row Source Type property

Values are separated by semicolons in the Row Source property

FIGURE G-11: Two new combo boxes for data entry

Prereq combo box

Cost combo box

Clues to Use

Choosing between a combo box and a list box

The list box and combo box controls are very similar, but the combo box is more popular for at least two reasons. While both provide a list of values from which the user can choose to make an entry in a field, the combo box also allows the user to make a unique entry from the keyboard. More importantly, however, most users like the drop-down list behavior of the combo box. A list box also provides a list of values, though it displays the list of values from which the user scrolls and selects a choice (the list box has no drop-down action). Some users refer to the combo box as a drop-down list because of the drop-down action.

Adding a Combo Box to Find Records

Most combo boxes are used to enter data; however, the combo box control can also be used to find records. When you use a combo box to find data, you must carefully identify it as a tool used to find and retrieve records so that the user doesn't become confused between the behavior of combo boxes used to enter data and those used to find data. You decide to add a combo box to help quickly locate the desired course on the Course Info form. You will use the Combo Box Wizard to help guide your actions in building this new combo box.

STEPS

TROUBLE

If the Combo Box Wizard does not appear, delete the combo box control, make sure that the Control Wizards button on the Toolbox toolbar is selected, then try to add the combo box again.

1. **Click the Design View button, click the Toolbox button to toggle on the Toolbox toolbar (if it is not already visible), click the Field List button to toggle it off, click the Combo Box button on the Toolbox toolbar, then click on the right side of the main form**

   The Combo Box Wizard opens as shown in Figure G-12. The first question prompts you for the behavior of the combo box. The first option corresponds to how you created the Prereq combo box. The Prereq combo box enters data into the Prereq field by looking up CourseID values from the CourseID field in the Courses table. The second option corresponds to how you created the Cost combo box. The Cost combo box enters data into the Cost field by using a series of values that you entered into the combo box's Value List property. The third option corresponds to what you want to do now—use the combo box to find a record.

2. **Click the Find a record option button, click Next, double-click Description, click Next, use ✥ to drag the right edge of the Description column to the right so that all entries are visible, click Next, type FIND THIS COURSE in the label box, then click Finish**

   The new combo box appears in Form Design View as shown in Figure G-13. You test the combo box in Form View.

3. **Click the Form View button, click the FIND THIS COURSE list arrow, then click Computer Concepts**

   The selection for this combo box determines which record is displayed in the main form. In this case, it displays the Computer Concepts course, which is the fourth record. Now that you've added and tested the combo box successfully, you decide to move it to the Form Header section so that it is in a more logical position as the first control on the form.

4. **Click ⬚, click View on the menu bar, click Form Header/Footer, click the FIND THIS COURSE combo box to select it, then use ✋ to move the new combo box and its associated label to the left edge of the Form Header section**

   Save and test your form.

5. **Move and resize the FIND THIS COURSE combo box and label as needed, click the Save button, click ⬚, click the FIND THIS COURSE list arrow, then click Internet Fundamentals**

   The new placement of the combo box should look like Figure G-14.

FIGURE G-12: Combo Box Wizard

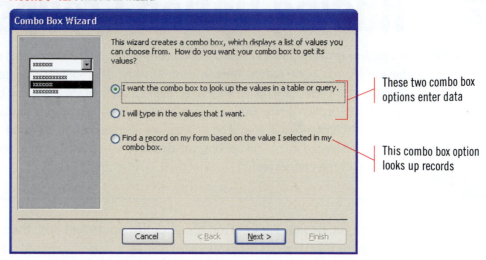

These two combo box options enter data

This combo box option looks up records

FIGURE G-13: New combo box used to find data

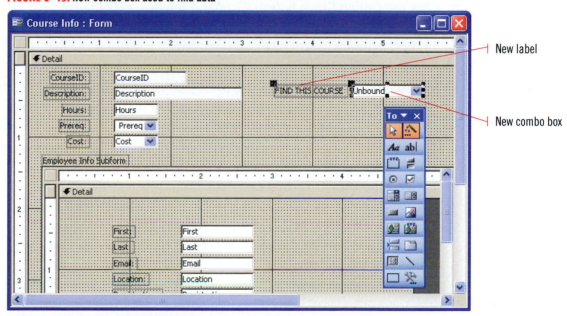

New label

New combo box

FIGURE G-14: Final placement of combo box used to find data

Form Header section

New combo box

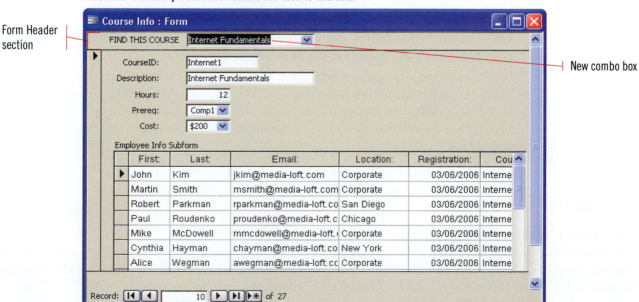

Adding Option Groups

An **option group** is a special type of bound control that is often used when only a few values are available for a field. You place **option button** controls within the option group to determine the value that is selected in the field. Each option button represents a different value that can be entered into the field that is bound to the option group. Option buttons within an option group are mutually exclusive; only one can be chosen at a time. ▰▰▰ MediaLoft's classes are offered in 6-, 8-, 12-, and 16-hour formats. Because this represents a limited number of options, you decide to use an option group control for the Hours field to further simplify the Courses form.

STEPS

1. **Click the Design View button ⬒, click the Hours text box, then press [Delete]**

   Both the Hours text box and its associated label are deleted. You will add the Hours field back to the form as an option group.

2. **Click the Option Group button ⬚ on the Toolbox, click the Field List button ⬚ to toggle it on, then drag the Hours field from the field list to the top of the right side of the form**

   The **Option Group Wizard** guides you as you develop an option group. The first question asks about label names for the option buttons.

3. **Type 6 hrs, press [Tab], type 8 hrs, press [Tab], type 12 hrs, press [Tab], type 16 hrs, click Next, click the No, I don't want a default option button, then click Next**

   The next question prompts you for the actual values associated with each option button.

4. **Type 6, press [Tab], type 8, press [Tab], type 12, press [Tab], then type 16 as shown in Figure G-15**

   The rest of the Option Group Wizard questions confirm what field the option group is bound to, the style you want to use for your option buttons, and how you want to label the option group.

5. **Click Next, click Next to accept Hours as the field that the value is stored in, click Next to accept Option buttons controls in an Etched style, then click Finish to accept Hours as the caption for the option group**

   An option group can contain option buttons, check boxes, or toggle button controls. The most common choice, however, is option buttons in an etched style. The Control Source property of the option group identifies the field it is bound to. The **Option Value property** of each option button identifies what value will be placed in the field when that option button is clicked. The new option group and option button controls are shown in Figure G-16.

6. **Click the Form View button ⬚, use the FIND THIS COURSE list arrow to find the Access Case Problems class, then click the 16 hrs option button**

   Your screen should look like Figure G-17. You changed the Access Case Problems course from 12 to 16 hrs. To add more option buttons to this option group at a later time, work in Form Design View and use the Option Button button ⬚ on the Toolbox toolbar to add the new option button to the option group. Modify the value represented by that option button by opening the option button's property sheet and modifying the Option Value property.

Clues to Use

Protecting data

You may not want to allow all users who view a form to change all the data that appears on that form. You can design forms to limit access to certain fields by changing the Enabled and Locked properties of a control. The **Enabled property** specifies whether a control can have the focus in Form View. The **Locked property** specifies whether you can edit data in a control in Form View.

FIGURE G-15: Option Group Wizard

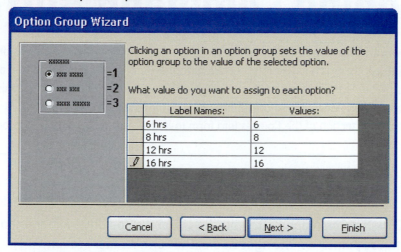

FIGURE G-16: Working with an option group in Form Design View

New option group

Option buttons

Option Group button

Option Button button

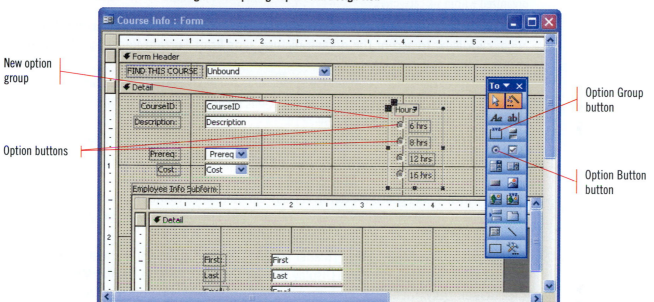

FIGURE G-17: Using an option group

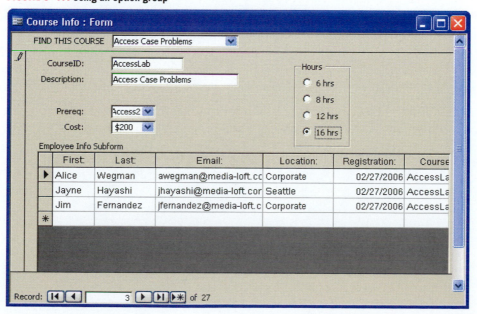

Adding Command Buttons

A **command button** is used to initiate a common action in Form View such as printing the current record, opening another form, or closing the current form. Command buttons are often added to the Form Header or Form Footer sections as the first or last controls on a form. **Sections** determine where controls appear and print. See Table G-2 for more information on form sections. ▧▧▧ You add a command button to the Form Header section of the Courses Info form to help users print the current record.

STEPS

1. **Click the Design View button** ▨

   You will add the new command button to the right side of the Form Header section.

2. **Click the Command Button button** ▨ **on the Toolbox toolbar, then click with the** ⁺▢ **mouse pointer on the right side of the Form Header section**

   The Command Button Wizard opens, listing over 30 of the most popular actions for the command button, organized within six categories.

3. **Click Record Operations in the Categories list, click Print Record in the Actions list, click Next, click Next to accept the default picture, type Print Current Record as the button name, then click Finish**

   Your screen should look similar to Figure G-18. By default, the Print button ▨ on the Standard toolbar prints every record using the form layout, which creates a long printout. Therefore, adding a command button to print only the current record is very useful.

4. **Click the Form View button** ▨ **to view the new command button, double-click Lee in the first record of the subform, type your last name, then click the Print Record button** ▨ **in the Form Header section**

   Only the current record prints. You can also modify the form so that controls in certain form sections, such as the Form Header, appear on the screen but do not print. The **Display When** property of the Form Header determines when the controls in that section appear on screen and print.

QUICK TIP

Double-click the menu bar to immediately display all options for that menu.

5. **Click** ▨**, double-click the Form Header section to open its property sheet, click the Format tab, click Always for the Display When property, click the Display When list arrow, click Screen Only, then click the Properties button** ▨ **to toggle off the property sheet**

   Now the Print Record button will appear on the screen when you are working in the form, but will not appear on printouts.

TROUBLE

If your printout is still too wide for one sheet of paper, drag the right edge of the form to the left in Form Design View.

6. **Click the Save button** ▨**, click** ▨**, then click the Print Preview button** ▨ **to confirm that the Print button no longer appears on the printout**

   Using either the Print button ▨ or the Print Preview button ▨ on the Form View toolbar will print or preview all records. Now, though, the Form Header section will not appear on the printout whether you are printing all of the records or only one using the Print Record command button you placed on the form.

7. **Click the Close button** Close**, then return to Form View**

   The final Courses Info form should look like Figure G-19.

8. **Close the Courses Info form**

FIGURE G-18: Adding a command button

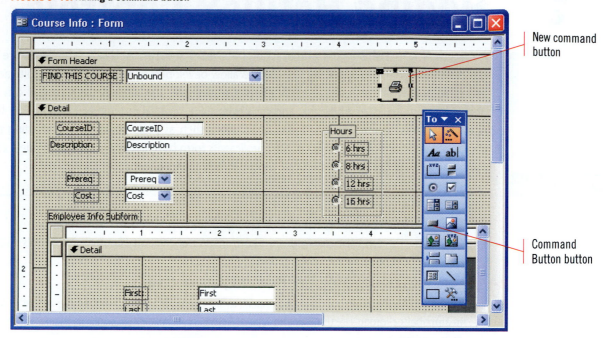

New command button

Command Button button

FIGURE G-19: Final Courses Info form

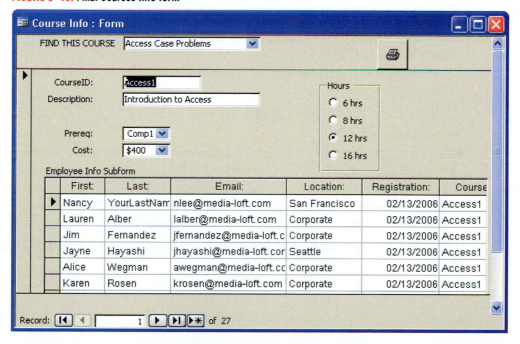

TABLE G-2: Form sections

section	description
Detail	Appears once for every record
Form Header	Appears at the top of the form and often contains command buttons or a label with the title of the form
Form Footer	Appears at the bottom of the form and often contains command buttons or a label with instructions on how to use the form
Page Header	Appears at the top of a printed form with information such as page numbers or dates
Page Footer	Appears at the bottom of a printed form with information such as page numbers or dates

Adding ActiveX Controls

An **ActiveX control** is a control that follows ActiveX standards. **ActiveX standards** are programming standards that were developed by Microsoft to allow developers to more easily share software components and functionality across multiple applications. For example, the same ActiveX control can be used in an Access form, in an Excel workbook, and on a Web page opened in Internet Explorer. The functionality of ActiveX controls covers a wide range of applications such as multimedia players, charting programs, and encryption software. ▰▰▰▰▰ Users of the Enrollments form have asked if you can provide a calendar on the form. You will use the Calendar ActiveX control to add the calendar that they request.

STEPS

1. **Right-click Attendance, then click Design View on the shortcut menu**

   Right now, the form lists six fields in a horizontal arrangement. The ActiveX controls will be placed just below the text boxes in the Detail section.

QUICK TIP

ActiveX controls are also available by clicking the More Controls button on the Toolbox toolbar.

2. **Click Insert on the menu bar, then click ActiveX Control**

   The Insert ActiveX Control dialog box opens as shown in Figure G-20, listing the available ActiveX controls in alphabetical order. The number and type of ActiveX controls will depend on the other programs loaded on your computer.

3. **Press C to move to the ActiveX Controls that start with the letter "C," click Calendar Control 11.0, then click OK**

   The Calendar control is added to the Detail section.

TROUBLE

The Spreadsheet control may be inserted below the Calendar control.

4. **Use the 🖐 mouse pointer to move the calendar control just below the text boxes as shown in Figure G-21**

   The **Calendar control** appears with the current date chosen. You can use the Calendar control to find or display a date.

5. **Click the Form View button 🖼, click the Year list arrow, click 2006, click the Month list arrow, then click Feb**

   Using the Calendar control, you can quickly find out what day of the week a particular class started on as shown in Figure G-22. In this case, you determine that the class currently displayed on 2/13/2006 started on a Monday. With additional programming skills, you could connect the Attended text box to the ActiveX Calendar control so that the date clicked in the control was inserted as the value for the Attended field. For now, however, you will use the calendar control for reference purposes.

6. **Click the Save button 🖫, close the Attendance form, close the Training-G.mdb database, then exit Access**

FIGURE G-20: Insert ActiveX Control dialog box

Your list depends on the programs installed on your computer

FIGURE G-21: ActiveX Calendar control in Form Design View

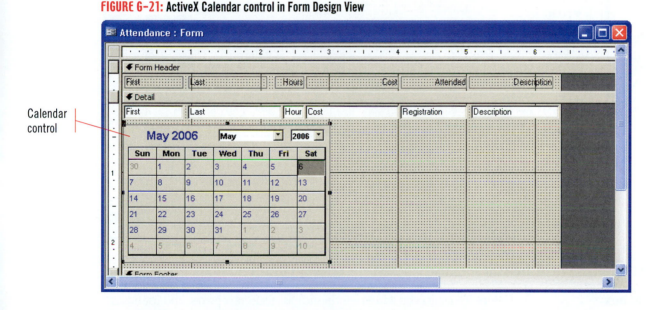

Calendar control

FIGURE G-22: Using the ActiveX Calendar control

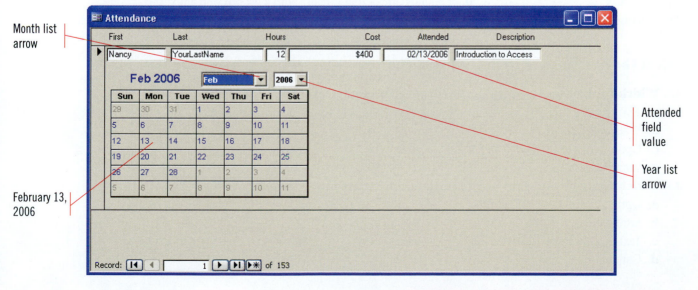

Month list arrow

Attended field value

Year list arrow

February 13, 2006

Access 2003

Practice

▼ CONCEPTS REVIEW

Identify each element of the Form Design View shown in Figure G-23.

FIGURE G-23

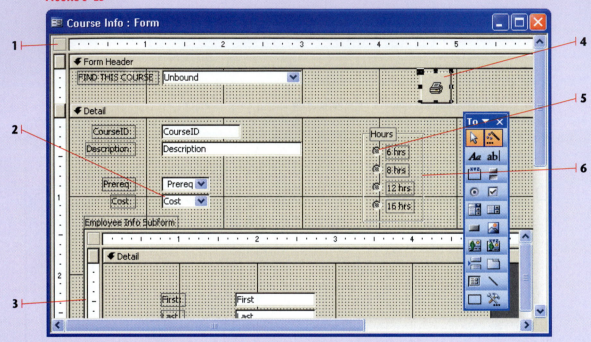

Match each term with the statement that best describes its function.

7. **Combo box**
8. **Command button**
9. **Subform**
10. **Controls**
11. **Option group**

a. Elements you add to a form such as labels, text boxes, and list boxes
b. A control that shows records that are related to one record shown in the main form
c. An unbound control that executes an action when it is clicked
d. A bound control that is really both a list box and a text box
e. A bound control that displays a few mutually exclusive entries for a field

Select the best answer from the list of choices.

12. **Which control would work best to display three choices for a field?**
    a. Text box
    b. Label
    c. Option group
    d. Command button

13. **Which control would you use to initiate a print action?**
    a. Option group
    b. List box
    c. Text box
    d. Command button

14. **Which control would you use to display a drop-down list of 50 states?**
    a. Check box
    b. Field label
    c. List box
    d. Combo box

15. **To view linked records within a form, use a:**
    a. Subform.
    b. List box.
    c. Design template.
    d. Link control.

16. **Which of the following defines what fields and records appear on a form?**
    a. Recordset
    b. Toolbox
    c. Property sheet
    d. ActiveX control

17. **Which is a popular layout for a main form?**
    a. Datasheet
    b. PivotTable
    c. Columnar
    d. Global

18. **Which is a popular layout for a subform?**
    a. Datasheet
    b. PivotTable
    c. Columnar
    d. Global

19. **Which of the following is true of ActiveX controls?**
    a. They always display data from the recordset.
    b. They can be used in many applications.
    c. They are quite limited in scope and functionality.
    d. They are added to a form in Form View.

20. **Which form section would most likely contain a command button?**
    a. Form Header
    b. Page Header
    c. Detail
    d. Page Footer

▼ SKILLS REVIEW

1. **Understand the form/subform relationship.**
    a. Start Access and open the **Membership-G.mdb** database from the drive and folder where your Data Files are stored.
    b. Click the Relationships button on the Database toolbar.
    c. Double-click File on the menu bar, then click Print Relationships.
    d. The Relationships for Membership-G appears as a report in Print Preview. In Report Design View, insert your name as a label in the Report Header section, then print the report.
    e. Close the Relationships report window without saving the report, and then close the Relationships window.
    f. Based on the one-to-many relationships defined in the Membership-G database, sketch two form/subform combinations that you could create.

2. **Create subforms using the Form Wizard.**

   a. Start the Form Wizard.

   b. Select all of the fields from both the Activities and the Members tables.

   c. View the data by Members, then verify that the Form with subform(s) option button is selected.

   d. Accept a Datasheet layout for the subform, a Standard style, name the form **Member Info**, and accept the default title of **Activities Subform** for the subform. View the Member Info form in Form View.

   e. Find the record for Lois Market and enter your own first and last names into the FirstName and LastName text boxes.

   f. Click File on the menu bar, then click Print. Click the Selected Record(s) option button in the Print dialog box to print only the record that contains your name.

   g. Save, then close the Member Info form.

3. **Create subforms using queries.**

   a. Open the Zips in the IA or MO query in Design View, then add the criteria to find only those records from **IA** or **MO** in the State field. View the datasheet to make sure that you have entered the criteria correctly, then save and close the query.

   b. Using either the Form Wizard or Form Design View, build a columnar form based on the Zips in the IA or MO query using all fields in the query. Name the form **IA or MO**.

   c. Open the IA or MO form in Design View, and add a subform control using the Subform Wizard below the three text boxes in the Detail section of the form.

   d. Use the Subform Wizard to specify that the subform will use an existing query, click Next, then select all of the fields in the Dues query for the subform.

   e. Allow the Subform Wizard to link the form and subform so that they show Dues for each record in IA or MO using Zip.

   f. Accept Dues subform as the subform's name, and then display the form in Form View.

   g. Resize the IA or MO form and Dues Subform as necessary to display all of the information clearly. Be sure to resize the datasheet columns so that all of the information in the subform is clearly visible.

   h. Find the record for Zip 64105, enter your last name in the LastName field of the first record, and print only that record.

   i. Click File on the menu bar, click Save As, name the main form **Zips**, then save and close the form and subform.

4. **Modify subforms.**

   a. Open the Zips in the IA or MO query in Query Design View.

   b. Delete the criteria that specifies that only the records with State values of IA or MO appear in the recordset.

   c. Use Save As to save the modified query as **All Zips**, then close the query.

   d. Open the Zips form in Form Design View.

   e. Open the property sheet for the form. Click the Data tab, then change the Record Source property from Zips in IA or MO to **All Zips**.

   f. Close the property sheet, save the form, view the form in Form View, then navigate to the record that displays Zip 64145 for Shawnee, Kansas.

   g. Change the city to the name of your hometown, print only this record, then close the Zips form.

5. **Add a combo box for data entry.**

   a. Open the Members form in Design View, then right-click the Zip text box and change it to a combo box control.

   b. In the property sheet of the new combo box, click the Row Source property, then click the Build button.

   c. Select the Zipcodes table only for the query, and then double-click the Zip field to add it as the only column of the query grid.

   d. Close the SQL Statement window, and save the changes.

   e. Close the property sheet, then save and view the form in Form View.

   f. Navigate to the second record, then change the Zip to **64105** using the new combo box.

6. **Add a combo box to find records.**

   a. In Form Design View, open the Form Header section of the Members form.

   b. Use the Combo Box Wizard to add a new combo box to the left side of the Form Header section that finds records in the form based on a value you specify.

   c. Select the FirstName and LastName fields, make sure that each column is wide enough to view all values, and label the combo box **Find this Member**.

   d. Save the Members form, then view it in Form View.

   e. Use the Find this Member combo box to find your own record, then print it.

7. Add option groups.

   a. Open the Members form in Design View, then delete the Dues text box and label.

   b. Add the Dues field back to the form as an option group using the Option Group Wizard and below the Birthday text box.

   c. Enter **$25** and **$50** as the label names, then accept $25 as the default choice.

   d. Change the values to **25** and **50** to correspond with the labels.

   e. Store the value in the Dues field, choose Option buttons with an Etched style, type the caption **Annual Dues**, then click Finish.

   f. Save the Members form, display it in Form View, use the combo box to find the record with your name, then change the Annual Dues to **$25**.

8. Add command buttons.

   a. Open the Members form in Design View.

   b. Use the Command Button Wizard to add a command button to the right side of the Form Header section.

   c. Choose the Print Record action from the Record Operations category.

   d. Display the text **Print Current Record** on the button, then name the button **Print**.

   e. Save the form, display it in Form View, then use the combo box to find the record for Christine Collins. The final form should look similar to Figure G-24.

   f. Navigate to the record with your own name, change the month and day of the Birthday entry to your own, then print the record using the new Print Current Record command button.

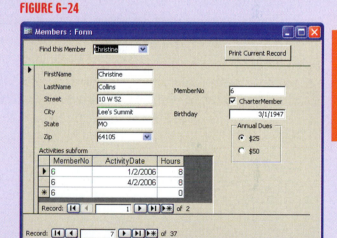

FIGURE G-24

   g. Save, then close the Members form.

9. Add ActiveX Controls.

   a. Open the Member Info form in Design View, then add a Microsoft Office Spreadsheet 11.0 ActiveX control to the Detail section of the main form.

   b. Resize the spreadsheet control so that about three columns and four rows are visible, then move it just below the CharterMember check box. Move the Activities subform down about 1" so that everything fits on the form.

   c. Save the Member Info form, then view it in Form View. The spreadsheet ActiveX control will be used to calculate the value of the time donated to various activities.

   d. Navigate to the record with your last name. In cell A1 of the spreadsheet, type **8**, the total number of hours you have contributed based on the information in the subform.

   e. In Cell A2 of the spreadsheet, type **12**, the value of one hour of work, to determine your contributions to this club.

   f. In Cell A3 of the spreadsheet, type **=A1*A2**, then press [Enter] to calculate the total value of the hours of time you have donated.

   g. Click File on the menu bar, click Print, then choose the Selected Record(s) option button to print only this record.

   h. Save and close the Member Info form, close the Membership-G.mdb database, then exit Access.

Access 2003

▼ INDEPENDENT CHALLENGE 1

As the manager of a music store's instrument rental program, you have created a database to track instrument rentals to schoolchildren. Now that several rentals have been made, you wish to create a form/subform to facilitate the user's ability to enter a new rental record.

   a. Start Access, then open the database **Music Store-G.mdb** from the drive and folder where your Data Files are stored.

   b. Using the Form Wizard, create a new form based on all of the fields in the Customers and Rentals tables.

   c. View the data by Customers, choose a Datasheet layout for the subform and a Standard style, then accept the default form titles of **Customers** for the main form and **Rentals Subform** for the subform.

   d. Add another record to the rental subform for Raquel Bacon by typing **888335** as the SerialNo entry and **5/1/06** as the RentalDate entry.

   e. Close the Customers form.

   f. You want to add the Description field to the subform information. To do this, start a new query in Query Design View to serve as the record source for the subform.

   g. Add the Rentals and Instruments tables to the query, then close the Show Table dialog box.

   h. Add all of the fields from the Rentals table and the Description field from the Instruments table to the query, save the query with the name **Rental Description**, view the query datasheet, then close it.

   i. Open the Rentals Subform in Design View, then change the Record Source property of the form from Rentals to **Rental Description**.

   j. Open the subform's field list, then drag the Description field to just below the RentalDate text box in the Detail section. The field may not line up perfectly with the others but because the Default View of this form is set to Datasheet, this form will appear as a datasheet regardless of the organization of the controls in Form Design View.

   k. Close the property sheet, save, then close the Rentals Subform.

   l. Open the Customers form. It now contains a new Description field in the subform. Enter your first and last name in the first record of the main form, then use the Selected Records option in the Print dialog box to print only that record. (*Hint*: To open the Print dialog box, click File on the menu bar, then click Print.)

   m. Close the Customers form, close the Music Store-G.mdb database, then exit Access.

▼ INDEPENDENT CHALLENGE 2

As the manager of a music store's instrument rental program, you have created a database to track instrument rentals to schoolchildren. You add command buttons to a form to make it easier to use.

a. Start Access then open the database **Music Store-G.mdb** from the drive and folder where your Data Files are stored.

b. Using the Form Wizard, create a form/subform using all the fields of both the Customers and Schools tables.

c. View the data by Schools, use a Datasheet layout for the subform, then choose a Standard style.

d. Accept the default names of **Schools** for the main form and **Customers Subform** for the subform.

e. Resize the subform columns to view all of the data in Form View. Use Form Design View to resize the subform as necessary to display all columns.

f. In Form Design View, open the Form Header section, then drag the top edge of the Detail section down about 0.5" to provide room in the Form Header section for a command button.

g. In Form Design View, add a command button to the middle of the Form Header using the Command Button Wizard. The action should print the current record and display the text **Print School Record**. Name the button **Print**.

Advanced Challenge Exercise

- Add a second command button to the left side of the Form Header section using the Command Button Wizard. The action should add a new record and display the text **Add New School**. Name the button **Add**.
- Add a third command button to the right side of the Form Header section using the Command Button Wizard. The action should close the form and display the text **Close**. Name the button **Close**.
- Select all three command buttons, then use the Top option on the Align submenu of the Format menu to align the top edges of all three controls.
- Open the property sheet for the Form Header and give the Display When property the **Screen Only** value. Close the property sheet, then save the Schools form.
- Display the form in Form View, click the Add New School button, add the name of your high school to the SchoolName field, allow the SchoolNo to increment automatically, then add the information of a friend as the first record within the subform. Note that the CustNo and SchoolNo fields in the subform will be entered automatically.

h. Use the Print School Record button to print only this new school record.

i. Close the Schools form, close the Music Store-G.mdb database, then exit Access.

▼ INDEPENDENT CHALLENGE 3

As the manager of a music store's instrument rental program, you have created a database to track instrument rentals to schoolchildren. Now that the users are becoming accustomed to forms, you add a combo box and option group to make the forms easier to use.

   a. Start Access, then open the database **Music Store-G.mdb**.

   b. Using the Form Wizard, create a form/subform using all the fields of both the Instruments and Rentals tables.

   c. View the data by Instruments, use a Datasheet layout for the subform, and choose a Standard style.

   d. Enter the name **Instruments Main Form** for the main form and **Rentals** for the subform.

   e. In Form Design View of the Instruments Main Form, delete the MonthlyFee text box and label.

   f. Add the MonthlyFee field as an option group to the right side of the main form using the Option Group Wizard.

   g. Enter the Label Names as **$35**, **$40**, **$45**, and **$50**. Do not specify a default option. The corresponding values for the option buttons should be **35**, **40**, **45**, and **50**.

   h. Store the value in the MonthlyFee field. Use Option buttons with an Etched style.

   i. Caption the option group **Monthly Fee**, save the form, then view it in Form View. Resize and move controls as necessary to see all the fields clearly. Move through each of the 30 instrument records in the main form. For those instruments that do not display a $35, $40, or $45 monthly fee value, click the $45 option button. Save and close the Instruments Main Form.

Advanced Challenge Exercise

   ■ In Table Design View of the Instruments table, add a field named **Condition** with a Text data type. This field will record the condition of the instrument as Excellent, Good, Poor, or Fair.

   ■ Start the Lookup Wizard for the Condition field, and choose the "I will type in the values that I want" option button.

   ■ Enter **Excellent**, **Good**, **Fair**, and **Poor** as the four possible values, and accept the name **Condition** as the label for the lookup column. Save and close the Instruments table.

   ■ In Form Design View of the Instruments Main Form, drag the Condition field from the field list area just below the SerialNo text box. On a piece of paper, explain why the Condition field was automatically added as a combo box control rather than a text box control.

   ■ Right-click the Condition combo box and change it into a list box. Resize and move the Condition list box as well as the Rentals subform so that both controls fit on the form without overlapping.

   ■ Save the form then display it in Form View. Move through the records, selecting Excellent as the Condition value choice for the first two records and Good for the third and fourth records. On your paper, comment on the differences between the combo box control and list box control as perceived by the user of the form.

   j. Print only the fourth record (Cello, 1234570) by clicking File on the menu bar, clicking Print, then choosing the Selected Records option button before clicking OK in the Print dialog box.

   k. Close the Instruments Main Form, close the Music Store-G.mdb database, and then exit Access.

INDEPENDENT CHALLENGE 4

You are in the process of organizing your family's photo library. After reviewing the general template sample databases, but not finding any good matches to use for your project, you decide to browse the template gallery featured at the Microsoft Web site to determine if there is a sample database that you can download and use or modify for this purpose.

a. Connect to the Internet, then go to the home page for Access, www.microsoft.com/access.

b. Search for a link to database templates in the Templates Gallery. (You may be able to access templates directly at http://officeupdate.microsoft.com/templategallery/.)

c. Once you are at the Template Gallery, search for database templates.

d. Scroll through the list of available database templates, select the Photograph database, Genealogy database, or any other database template that interests you, then download the template. You may be prompted to accept an end-user license agreement for templates. Read the agreement, then click Accept if you understand and accept the agreement.

e. A file is downloaded to your computer, which you need to double-click to open.

f. Follow the prompts to extract the database.

g. Open the database, explore the objects in the database, enter several records, then print one of them.

h. Close the database, then exit Access.

▼ VISUAL WORKSHOP

Open the **Training-G.mdb** database. Use the Form Wizard to create a new form, as shown in Figure G-25. The First, Last, and Location fields are from the Employees table, the Description field is from the Courses table, and the Registration and Passed fields are from the Enrollments table. View the form by Employees, choose a Datasheet layout for the subform, and choose a Standard style. Name the form **Employee Basic Info**, then name the subform **Test Results**. Add command buttons to the Form Header to print the current record as well as to close the form. Add your name as a label to the Form Header section, then print the first record.

FIGURE G-25

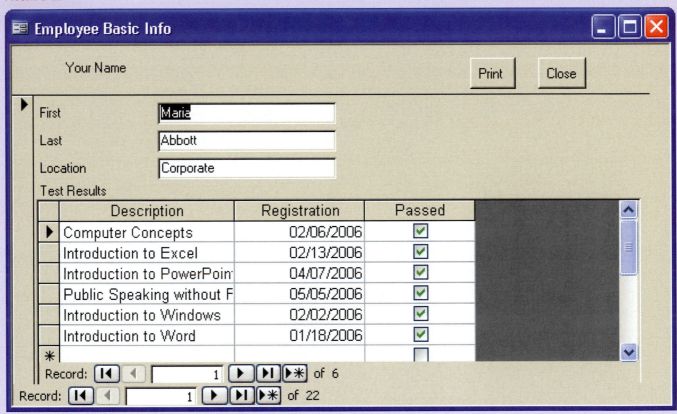

Sharing Information and Improving Reports

OBJECTIVES

Import data
Apply conditional formatting
Add lines
Use the Format Painter and AutoFormats
Create a dynamic Web page
Export data
Compact and repair a database
Back up a database

If you have a SAM user profile, you may have access to hands-on instruction, practice, and assessment of the skills covered in this unit. Log in to your SAM account and go to your assignments page to see what your instructor has assigned.

Although you can print data in forms and datasheets, **reports** give you more control over how data is printed and greater flexibility in presenting summary information. To create a report, you use bound controls such as text boxes to display data, and unbound controls such as lines, graphics, and labels to clarify the data. Another way to share Access information with other people is to export Access data to file formats that others can read such as Excel spreadsheets or Web pages. You will export Access data to various file formats to electronically share Access data with others. You will also create paper reports that use conditional formatting, colors, and lines to clarify the information. Finally, you will learn how to compact, repair, and back up the Training database.

Importing Data

Importing brings data from an external file, such as an Excel spreadsheet or another database, into an existing Access database. The Access import process copies the data from the original source and pastes the data in the Access database. See Table H-1 for more information on the types of data that Access can import. The Accounting Department has requested a quarterly electronic update of data currently stored in the Training-H database. You will create a new database for the Accounting Department, and then import historical cost and attendance information from the Training-H database into it. In addition, you will import data currently stored in an Excel spreadsheet into the new Accounting database.

STEPS

TROUBLE
You can't import from the Training-H database if it is opened in another Access window.

1. **Start Access, click the Create a new file link in the Getting Started task pane, click the Blank database link in the New File task pane, navigate to the drive and folder where your Data Files are stored, type Accounting in the File name text box, then click Create**
   The Accounting database window appears, but no objects are currently in the database.

2. **Click File, point to Get External Data, click Import, navigate to the drive and folder where your Data Files are stored, then double-click Training-H.mdb**
   The Import Objects dialog box opens, as shown in Figure H-1. Any object in the Training-H database can be imported into the Accounting database.

3. **Click the Tables tab (if not already selected), click 1QTR-2006, click Courses, click the Queries tab, click Accounting Info, click the Reports tab, click Accounting Report, then click OK**
   The four selected objects are imported from the Training-H database into the Accounting database.

4. **Click Queries on the Objects bar, then click Tables on the Objects bar to confirm that all four objects were imported successfully**
   The MediaLoft Accounting Department stores department codes in an Excel workbook that also needs to be imported into this database.

5. **Click File on the menu bar, point to Get External Data, click Import, click the Files of type list arrow, click Microsoft Excel, then double-click Deptcodes.xls**
   The Import Spreadsheet Wizard presents the data that you want to import, and then guides you through the rest of the import process.

6. **Make sure the First Row Contains Column Headings check box is checked as shown in Figure H-2, then click Next**
   The column headings in the first row will be the field names when the data is imported as a table into the Accounting database.

7. **Make sure the In a New Table option button is selected, click Next, click Next to accept the default field options, click the Choose my own primary key option button, make sure Code is displayed in the primary key list box, click Next, type Codes in the Import to Table box, click Finish, then click OK**
   The Deptcodes spreadsheet is imported as a table named Codes into the Accounting database.

8. **Explore the imported objects, close all open objects, then close the Accounting database**

FIGURE H-1: Import Objects dialog box

Tables tab is selected

Table objects in Training-H database

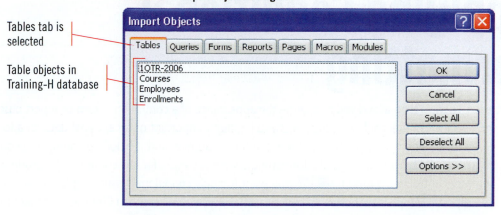

FIGURE H-2: Import Spreadsheet Wizard

Column headings will be field names

Data to import from the spreadsheet

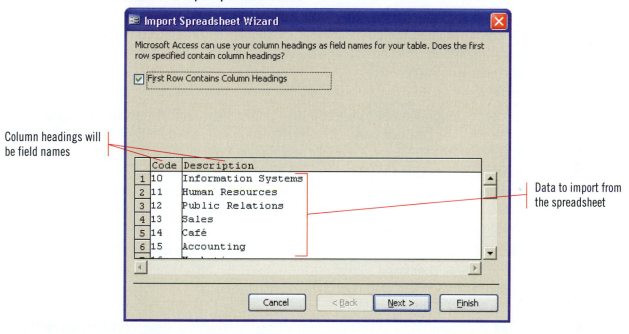

TABLE H-1: Data sources Microsoft Access can import

data source	version or format supported	data source	version or format supported
Microsoft Access database	2.0, 7.0/95, 8.0/97, 9.0/2000, and 10.0/2002	Microsoft Exchange	All versions
Microsoft Access project	9.0/2000, 10.0/2002	Delimited text files	All character sets
dBASE	III, IV, 5, and 7	Fixed-width text files	All character sets
Paradox, Paradox for Windows	3.x, 4.x, 5.0, and 8.0	HTML	1.0 (if a list) 2.0, 3.x (if a table or list)
Microsoft Excel	3.0, 4.0, 5.0, 7.0/95, 8.0/97, 9.0/2000, and 10.0/2002	XML documents	All versions
Lotus 1-2-3	.wks, .wk1, .wk3, and .wk4	SQL tables, Microsoft Visual FoxPro, and other data sources that support ODBC protocol	**Open Database Connectivity (ODBC)** is a protocol for accessing data in Structured Query Language (SQL) database servers

Applying Conditional Formatting

Conditional formatting allows you to change the appearance of a control on a form or report based on criteria you specify. Conditional formatting helps you highlight important or exceptional data on a form or report. When formatting several controls at the same time, you may find it helpful to group the controls. When you **group controls** it means that a formatting choice you make for any control in the group will be applied to every control in the group. You want to apply conditional formatting to the Attendance by Location report to emphasize those employees that have received more than 200 hours of training. You also want to apply other report formatting techniques such grouping controls and hiding duplicate values.

STEPS

1. Open the Training-H.mdb database, click Reports on the Objects bar, double-click Location Report, then press [Page Down] and use the Zoom In pointer to preview each page of the report

   The records are grouped by Location and the Hours field is subtotaled for each Location.

2. Click the Design View button on the Print Preview toolbar to switch to Report Design View, click the Last text box in the Detail section, press and hold [Shift], click the First text box in the Detail section, click the Title text box, release [Shift], click Format on the menu bar, then click Group

   Group selection handles surround the group of three text boxes, so when you click on *any* control in a group, you select *every* control in the group. Clicking a control within a *selected group* still selects just that single control.

3. Click the Properties button, click the Format tab, click No in the Hide Duplicates property, click the Hide Duplicates list arrow, click Yes, then click to toggle off the property sheet

   With the **Hide Duplicates** property set to Yes, the First, Last, and Title values will print only once per employee rather than once for each record in the Detail section. This change will help distinguish the records for each employee within each location.

4. Click the =Sum([Hours]) text box in the Location Footer section, click Format on the menu bar, then click Conditional Formatting

   The Conditional Formatting dialog box opens.

5. Click the between list arrow, click greater than, press [Tab], type 200, click the Bold button for Condition 1, click the Fill/Back Color button list arrow for Condition 1, then click the yellow box

   The Conditional Formatting dialog box should look like Figure H-3.

6. Click OK in the Conditional Formatting dialog box, click the Save button, click the Print Preview button, then zoom and position the report as shown in Figure H-4

   Conditional formatting made the Kansas City subtotal appear bold and with a yellow fill color because the value is greater than 200. Default formatting was applied to the subtotal for the New York group because it was not greater than 200.

7. Click the Design View button, click the Label button on the Toolbox toolbar, click the right side of the Report Header section, then type your name

8. Save, print, then close the Location Report

FIGURE H-3: Conditional Formatting dialog box

Default formatting

Condition 1 formatting

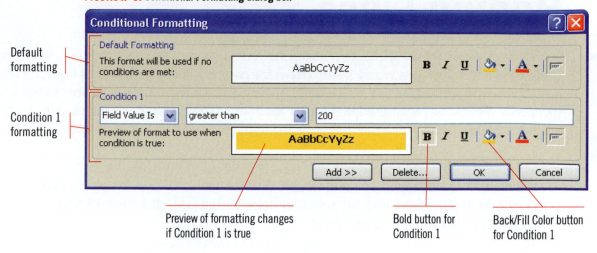

Preview of formatting changes if Condition 1 is true

Bold button for Condition 1

Back/Fill Color button for Condition 1

FIGURE H-4: Location Report with conditional formatting

Duplicate values are hidden

Condition 1 formatting applied

Default formatting applied

Page 5

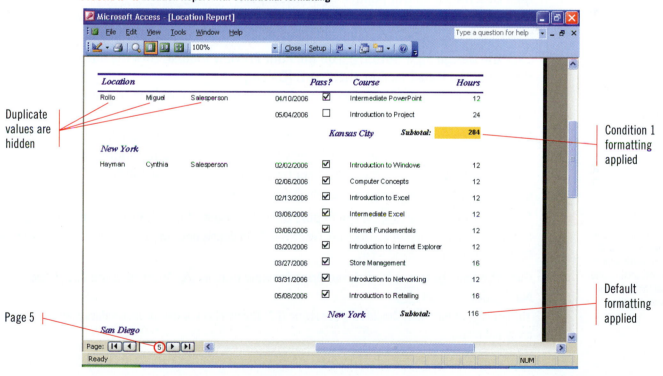

Adding Lines

Unbound controls such as labels, lines, and rectangles are used to enhance the clarity of a report. When you create a report with the Report Wizard, it often creates line controls at the top or bottom of the report sections to visually separate the sections on the report. You can add, delete, or modify these lines to best suit your needs. ![palette] The Personnel Department has asked you to create a report that lists all of the course registrations, and to subtotal each course by hours and costs. You use line controls to clarify the subtotals.

STEPS

1. **Double-click Create report by using wizard, click the Tables/Queries list arrow, click Query: All Registrations, click the Select All Fields button ⟩⟩, click Next, click by Employees, click Next, then click Next**

   After determining the grouping field(s), the Report Wizard prompts for the sort field(s).

2. **Click the first sort field list arrow, click Registration to sort the detail records by the registration date of the class, then click the Summary Options button**

   The Summary Options dialog box allows you to include the sum, average, minimum, or maximum value of fields in various sections of the report.

3. **Click the Hours Sum check box, click the Cost Sum check box, click OK, click Next, click the Outline 2 Layout option button, click the Landscape Orientation option button, click Next, click the Formal style, click Next, type Registration Report as the report title, click Finish, then click the Zoom Out pointer ⊖ on the report**

   The wizard created several line and rectangle controls identified in Figure H-5. You want to delete the line between each detail record.

4. **Click the Design View button ✎ on the Print Preview toolbar, click the line control near the top of the Detail section, then press [Delete]**

   You also want to add double lines below the calculations in the Report Footer section to indicate that they are grand totals.

5. **Click the Line button ＼ on the Toolbox toolbar, press and hold [Shift], drag a line from the bottom-left edge of the =Sum([Hours]) text box to the bottom-right edge of the =Sum([Cost]) text box in the Report Footer section, then release [Shift]**

   Copying and pasting lines creates an exact duplicate of the line.

6. **Click the Copy button 📋 on the Report Design toolbar, then click the Paste button 📋**

   Design View of the report should look like Figure H-6. Short double lines under the calculations in the Report Footer section indicate grand totals.

7. **Click the Save button 💾, click the Print Preview button 🔍, then click the Last Page Navigation button ▶️**

   The last page of the report should look like Figure H-7. The two lines under the final values indicate that they are grand totals.

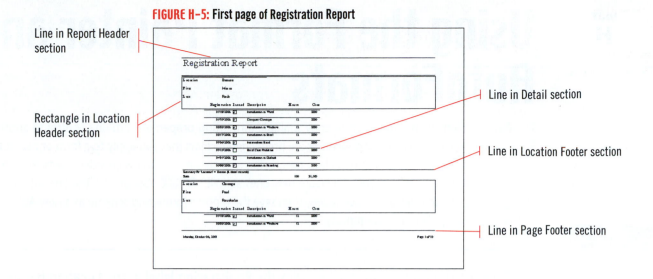

FIGURE H-5: First page of Registration Report

Line in Report Header section

Rectangle in Location Header section

Line in Detail section

Line in Location Footer section

Line in Page Footer section

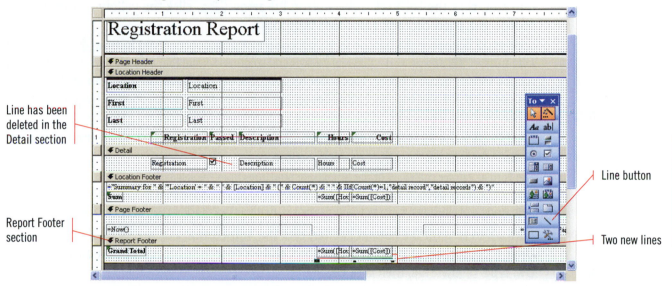

FIGURE H-6: Registration Report in Design View

Line has been deleted in the Detail section

Line button

Report Footer section

Two new lines

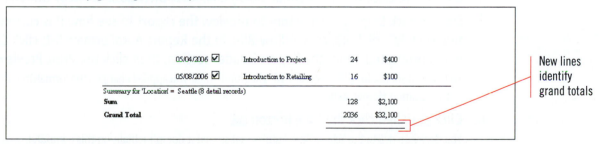

FIGURE H-7: Last page of Registration Report

| 05/04/2006 ☑ | Introduction to Project | 24 | $400 |
| 05/08/2006 ☑ | Introduction to Retailing | 16 | $100 |

Summary for 'Location' = Seattle (8 detail records)

| **Sum** | | 128 | $2,100 |
| **Grand Total** | | 2036 | $32,100 |

New lines identify grand totals

Clues to Use

Line troubles

Sometimes lines are difficult to find in Report Design View because they are placed against the edge of a section or the edge of other controls. To find lines that are positioned next to the edge of a section, drag the section bar to expand it to expose the line. To draw a perfectly horizontal line, hold [Shift] down while creating or resizing it. Also note that it is easy to accidentally widen a line beyond the report margins, thus creating extra unwanted pages in your printout. To fix this problem, narrow any controls that extend beyond the margins of the printout and drag the right edge of the report to the left. Because the default left and right margins for an 8.5" x 11" sheet of paper are 1" each, a report in portrait orientation must be no wider than 6.5" and a report in landscape orientation must be no wider than 9".

Using the Format Painter and AutoFormats

The **Format Painter** is a tool used to copy multiple formatting properties from one control to another in Form or Report Design View. **AutoFormats** are predefined formats that you apply to a form or report to set all of the formatting enhancements such as font, color, and alignment. Access provides several AutoFormats that you can use or modify, or you can create new ones as well. You will use the Format Painter to change the characteristics of selected labels, then save the report's formatting scheme as a new AutoFormat so that you can apply it to other reports.

STEPS

1. **Click the Design View button** , **click the Registration label in the Location Header section, click the Font/Fore Color button list arrow** , **click the blue box in the second row, click the Fill/Back Color button list arrow** , **click the yellow box in the fourth row, then click the Align Left button**

   Some of the buttons on the Formatting (Form/Report) toolbar such as the **Bold button** **B** and the **Align Left button** appear with a different background color to indicate that they are applied to the selected control. Others, such as the **Font/Fore Color button** and **Fill/Back Color button** , display the last color that was selected. The Format Painter can help you apply multiple formats from one control to another very quickly.

2. **Double-click the Format Painter button** **on the Report Design toolbar, then click each of the labels in the Location Header section**

   The Format Painter copied all of the formatting properties from the Registration label and pasted those formats to the other labels in the Location Header section, as shown in Figure H-8. You decide to save this set of formatting embellishments as a new AutoFormat so that you can quickly apply them to another report.

   <blockquote>QUICK TIP
You can also press [Esc] to release the Format Painter.</blockquote>

3. **Click** **to turn off the Format Painter, click the AutoFormat button** **on the Report Design toolbar, click Customize, click the Create a new AutoFormat option button, click OK, type Yellow-Blue, then click OK**

   The AutoFormat dialog box should look like Figure H-9.

4. **Click OK to close the AutoFormat dialog box, save, then close the Registration Report**

   <blockquote>TROUBLE
Resize the Email text box in Report Design view as needed.</blockquote>

5. **Double-click Employee Directory to preview the report to see how it is currently formatted, click** , **click** , **click Yellow-Blue in the Report AutoFormats list, click OK, click OK when prompted about the Report Header section, then click the Print Preview button**

   Your screen should look like Figure H-10. The AutoFormat you applied changed the formatting properties of labels in the Location Header section.

6. **Click** , **then click the Save button**

   You decide to delete the Yellow-Blue AutoFormat so that it doesn't remain on this computer.

7. **Click** , **click Yellow-Blue, click Customize, click the Delete 'Yellow-Blue' option button, click OK, then click Close**

8. **Click the Label button** **on the Toolbox toolbar, click the right side of the Report Header section, type your name, save, print, then close the Employee Directory report**

FIGURE H-8: Using the Format Painter

Format Painter button

Bold button

Align Left button

AutoFormat button

Fill/Back Color button

Font/Fore Color button

Labels have been formatted the same way

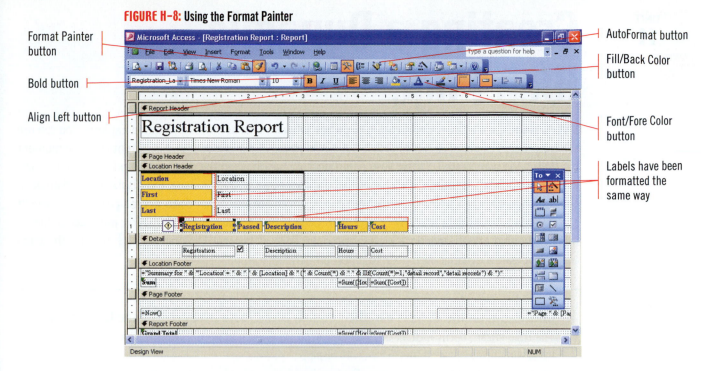

FIGURE H-9: Creating a new AutoFormat

New AutoFormat

Sample of new AutoFormat

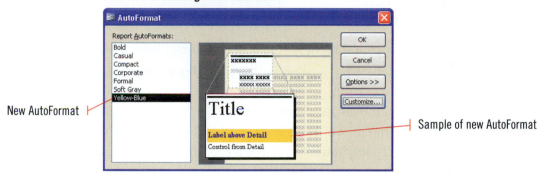

FIGURE H-10: Applying the Yellow-Blue AutoFormat to the Employee Directory report

Yellow-Blue AutoFormat changed the controls in the Location Header section

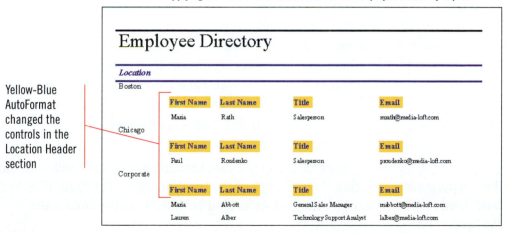

Clues to Use

Creating summary reports

Sometimes you may not want to show all the details of a report, but rather only the summary information that is calculated in the Group Footer section. You can accomplish this by deleting all controls in the Detail section. Calculated controls in a Group Footer section will still calculate properly even if the individual records used within the calculation are not displayed using the Detail section.

Creating a Dynamic Web Page

A **Web page** is a file that is viewed using **browser** software such as Microsoft Internet Explorer. You can use the export capabilities of Access to create static Web pages displaying data that is current as of the moment the Web page was created. **Static** Web pages do not change when the database is updated. You can also use Access to create **dynamic** Web pages that are connected to the database and display up-to-date data. Use the page object to create dynamic Web pages, which are also called **data access pages**. The benefit of converting Access data into any type of Web page is that it makes the information more accessible by merely opening a Web page in a browser program such as Internet Explorer. 🎨 You use the page object to create a dynamic Web page to report employee information.

STEPS

1. **Click Pages on the Objects bar, then double-click Create data access page by using wizard**
   The Page Wizard opens with an interface similar to the Form and Report Wizards. First, you need to determine what fields you want the Web page to display.

2. **Click the Tables/Queries list arrow, click Table: Employees, click the Select All button >> , then click Next**
   Web pages, like reports, can be used to group and sort records.

3. **Double-click Location to specify it as a grouping field, click Next, then click Next**

4. **Type Employees by Location for the title, click the Open the page option button, then click Finish**
   The Web page opens in **Page View**, a special view within Access that allows you to see how your Web page will appear when opened in Internet Explorer. You modify the structure of a data access page in **Page Design View**.

   > **TROUBLE**
   > If the Web page opens in Design View, click the Page View button 🔳 to switch to Page View.

5. **Click the Expand button + to the left of the Location label to show the fields within that group**
   Your page should look like Figure H-11. On a data access page, the **navigation bars** at the bottom of the Web page not only allow you to move from record to record, they contain buttons to edit, sort, and filter the data. Page View shows you how the Web page will appear from within Internet Explorer.

6. **Click the Save button 🖫 on the Page View toolbar, type einfo as the filename, navigate to the drive and folder where your Data Files are stored, then click Save**
   To view the Web page in Internet Explorer, use the **Web Page Preview** view, which opens the page in Internet Explorer.

   > **TROUBLE**
   > If presented with a message about the connection string, read the message, then click OK.

7. **Click the View button list arrow 🖌· , then click Web Page Preview**
   Internet Explorer loads and presents the Web page.

8. **Click the Next button ▶ twice on the Employees-Location navigation toolbar to move to the Corporate location, click + to the left of the Location label, click 8/20/1998 in the DateHired text box, then click the Sort Ascending button 🔼 on the Employees Navigation bar**
   The Web page should look like Figure H-12.

   > **TROUBLE**
   > Web pages created through the page object in Access require Internet Explorer version 5.0 or later.

9. **Close Internet Explorer, then close the Employees by Location page**

FIGURE H-11: Employees by Location Web page in Page View

Grouping field

Collapse button

Sorting field

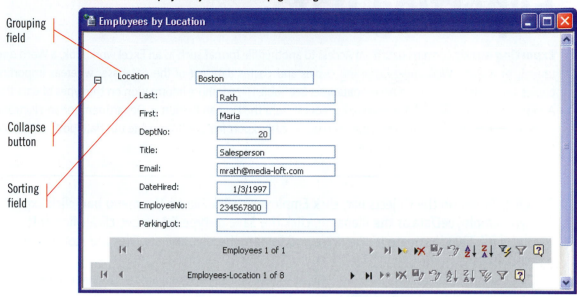

FIGURE H-12: einfo.htm dynamic Web page in Internet Explorer

Internet Explorer

Path to the Web page

DateHired text box

Sort Ascending button on Employees Navigation bar

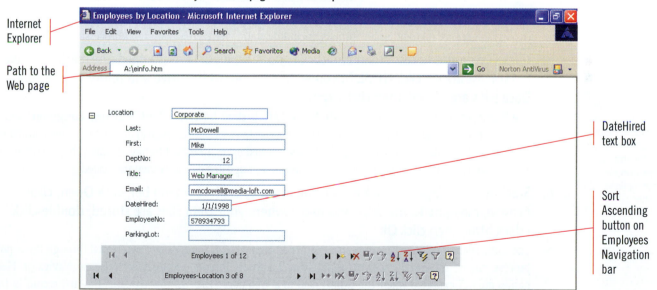

Exporting Data

Exporting quickly converts data from Access to another file format such as an Excel workbook, a Word document, or a static Web page. Exporting copies and pastes data *out of* the database, whereas importing copies and pastes data *into* an Access database. See Table H-2 for more information on the types of data that Access can export.  You received a request from the Human Resources Department for an electronic copy of the data in the Employees table. You use Access export features to provide this data both as an Excel spreadsheet and as a static Web page.

1. **Click Tables on the Objects bar, click Employees, click File on the menu bar, click Export, type EmployeeData as the filename, click the Save as type list arrow, click Microsoft Excel 97-2003, navigate to the drive and folder where your Data Files are stored, then click Export**

   The export process creates the EmployeeData.xls Excel workbook that contains the Employees data.

2. **Click the Start button ⊞ start on the taskbar, point to All Programs, point to Microsoft Office, click Microsoft Office Excel 2003, click the Open button 📂 on the Excel Standard toolbar, navigate to the drive and folder where your Data Files are stored, double-click EmployeeData.xls, then close the task pane if it is open**

   The EmployeeData spreadsheet opens. All of the data has been successfully exported, but some of it is hidden because the columns are too narrow.

3. **Click the Select All button (a blank box above Row 1 and to the left of Column A), double-click the ↔ pointer on the line that separates column heading A and B, then click anywhere on the data**

   With the columns widened, you can clearly see all the data that was exported, as shown in Figure H-13. Field names are exported to Row 1 and the record for the first employee is in Row 2.

4. **Click the Save button 🖫, click File on the menu bar, then click Exit**

   Exporting Access data to other file formats, including static Web pages, is a similar process.

5. **Click File on the Access menu bar, click Export, type edata as the filename, click the Save as type list arrow, click HTML Documents, navigate to the drive and folder where your Data Files are stored, then click Export**

   The Employees table is saved as an HTML file. **HTML** is short for **HyperText Markup Language**, which defines a set of tags that, when inserted into a text file, give browser software such as Internet Explorer instructions on how to display the file as a Web page. Web pages created using the export feature are *static*; they do not retain any connection to the database and will not display new or updated data after they are created.

6. **Start Internet Explorer, click File on the Internet Explorer menu bar, click Open, click Browse, navigate to the drive and folder where your Data Files are stored, double-click edata.html, then click OK**

   The static edata.html Web page appears as shown in Figure H-14. Static Web pages created through the export process can be successfully viewed using either Microsoft Internet Explorer or Netscape Navigator. Field names are not exported when you export data to a Web page. The first row contains the first record in the database for Megan Burik.

7. **Close Internet Explorer**

FIGURE H-13: EmployeeData.xls spreadsheet

Excel

EmployeeData.xls

Select All button

Field names

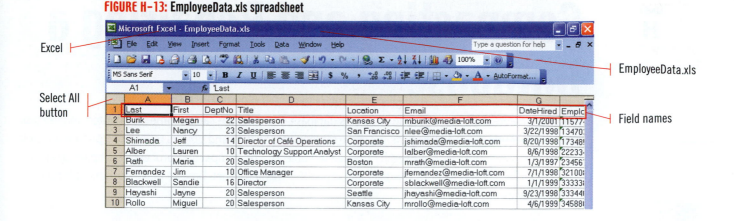

FIGURE H-14: edata.html static Web page

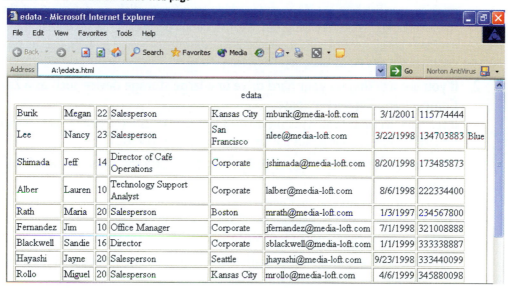

TABLE H-2: Data formats Microsoft Access can export

application	version or format supported	application	version or format supported
Microsoft Access database	2.0, 7.0/95, 8.0/97, 9.0/2000, and 10.0/2002	Lotus 1-2-3	.wk2, .wk1, and .wk3
Microsoft Access project	9.0/2000, 10.0/2002	Delimited text files	All character sets
dBASE	III, IV, 5, and 7	Fixed-width text files	All character sets
Paradox, Paradox for Windows	3.x, 4.x, 5.0, and 8.0	HTML	1.0 (if a list), 2.0, 3.x, and 4.x (if a table or list)
Microsoft Excel	3.0, 4.0, 5.0, 7.0/95, 8.0/97, 9.0/2000, and 10.0/2002	SQL tables, Microsoft Visual FoxPro, and other data sources that support ODBC protocol	Visual FoxPro 3.0, 5.0, and 6.x
Microsoft Active Server Pages	All	XML documents	All

Compacting and Repairing a Database

When you delete data and objects in an Access database, the database can become fragmented and use disk space inefficiently. **Compacting** the database reorganizes the data and objects to improve performance by reusing the space formerly occupied by the deleted objects. The compacting process also repairs damaged databases. You want to compact and repair the Training-H database to make sure that it is running as efficiently as possible.

STEPS

1. **Click Tools on the menu bar, then point to Database Utilities**

    The **Compact and Repair Database** option on the Database Utilities menu allows you to compact and repair an open database, but *if you are working on a floppy disk, do not compact the database*. The compaction process creates a temporary file that is just as large as the database itself. If the floppy disk does not have enough space to build the temporary file, it will not be able to finish the compaction process, and you may corrupt your database beyond repair.

2. **If you are working on your hard drive or a large storage device such as a Zip drive, click Compact and Repair Database**

    If you want to compact and repair the database on a regular basis, you can use the **Compact on Close** feature, which compacts and repairs the database every time it is closed.

3. **Click Tools on the menu bar, click Options, then click the General tab of the Options dialog box**

    The Options dialog box with the Compact on Close option is shown in Figure H-15. By default, the Compact on Close option is not checked for new databases. More information on the default options that you can modify in the Options dialog box is shown in Table H-3.

4. **If you are working on your hard drive or a large storage device such as a Zip drive, click the Compact on Close check box, then click OK**

    The next time you exit the database, Access will automatically compact and repair it before closing the database.

Clues to Use

Object dependencies

Before you delete objects in a database, you may want to view dependencies between database objects. **Object dependencies** identify which objects rely on other objects in your database. For example, a report's record source might depend on the XYZ query, and the XYZ query might depend on one or more tables. Viewing object dependencies helps you avoid deleting an object that affects others. It also helps identify those objects that if deleted, would not affect anything else. This information helps you compact and maintain the database as efficiently as possible. You open the **Object Dependencies task pane** to view object dependencies. Click View on the menu bar, point to Toolbars, then click Task Pane. Click the Task Pane list arrow, then click Object Dependencies. Click the object you want to examine in the database window, click the Show dependency information for the selected object link in the task pane, and then click OK if prompted.

General tab

Compact on Close

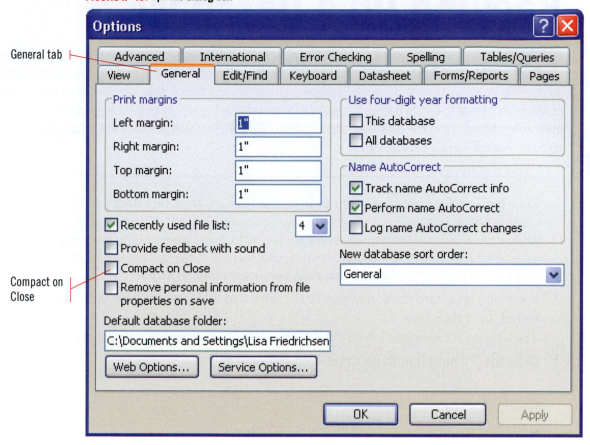

TABLE H-3: Default settings in the Options dialog box

tab	description
View	Determines what items are displayed on the screen such, as the status bar, Startup task pane, new object shortcuts, hidden objects, and system objects; also determines whether an object is opened with a single- or double-click
General	Stores the default print margins, determines the way dates are formatted (with two or four digits), sets the default database folder, and contains default settings for Web, AutoCorrect, and other database features
Edit/Find	Sets the defaults for find/replace, filter by form, and delete confirmation messages
Keyboard	Establishes the default behavior for keystrokes used to enter and edit data
Datasheet	Sets the default color, font, gridlines, cell effects, and other datasheet options
Forms/Reports	Identifies the default form and report templates and other default form and report options
Pages	Sets default page colors and styles and default page folders
Advanced	Stores the default Dynamic Data Exchange (DDE), file format, record locking, and other database-level default options
International	Identifies the defaults for direction of text, alignment, and cursor movement
Error Checking	Identifies which rules are flagged as errors and what color is used for the error indicator
Spelling	Determines which dictionaries are used for the spell check feature, which spell check rules are used, and which AutoCorrect options are applied
Tables/Queries	Stores the default field type and properties for new fields in Table Design View, as well as the default screen elements and query options for Query Design View

Access 2003

UNIT
H
Access 2003

Backing Up a Database

If hardware is stolen or destroyed, a recent **backup**, an up-to-date copy of the data files, can minimize the impact of that loss to the business. A good time to back up a database is right after it has been compacted. You can use Windows Explorer to copy individual database files and floppy disks, use backup software such as Microsoft Backup to create backup schedules to automate the backup process, or back up the database from within Access using the Back Up Database utility. Now that the database is compacted and repaired, you will make a backup copy of it.

STEPS

1. **Click Tools on the menu bar, point to Database Utilities, then click Back Up Database**

   The Save Backup As dialog box appears and the backup database is given a default name that includes the database name and the current date as shown in Figure H-16. If you wanted to give the backup a different name, you could change it now. If you are working on a floppy disk, you probably won't have room to save the backup. *If working on a floppy disk, read, but do not complete Step 2.*

2. **If working on a hard drive, navigate to the drive and folder where your Data Files are stored, then click Save**

   A backup copy of the database is saved and you return to the database window in the Training-H database.

3. **Close the Training-H.mdb database, then exit Access**

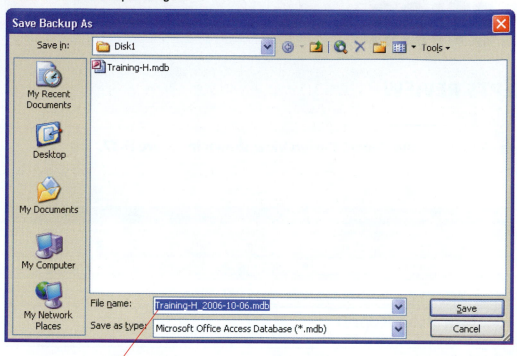

Default backup filename
(your date will differ)

Access 2003

Clues to Use

Backing up an entire folder to floppy disks

If your Data Files are stored in one folder on the hard drive and you want to create a backup to floppy disks, you can do that in one process using Windows Explorer. First, locate the folder that stores your Data Files in the Folders list within Windows Explorer. Right-click the folder, click Send To on the shortcut menu, then click 3½ Floppy (A:). Insert a blank floppy disk into drive A when prompted. If all of the Data Files will not fit on one floppy disk, you will be prompted to insert another floppy disk. One file, however, cannot be larger than a single floppy disk for this backup method to work. If one file is larger than the storage space of a floppy disk, approximately 1.44 MB, you must use backup software such as Microsoft Backup or compression software such as WinZip to compress the files before copying them to a floppy. You can also use a larger storage device such as a Zip, Jaz, or a network drive that accommodates files larger than 1.44 MB. A final option for backing up large files is to upload them to a Web site or attach them to an e-mail that you can access later.

Practice

▼ CONCEPTS REVIEW

Identify each element of the Report Design View shown in Figure H-17.

FIGURE H-17

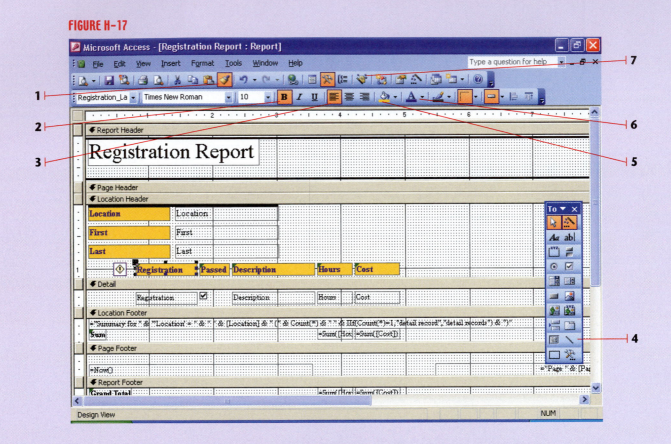

Match each term with the statement that best describes its function.

8. Exporting

9. Compacting

10. Backup

11. Format Painter

12. Importing

a. An up-to-date copy of data files

b. A process to quickly copy data from an external source into an Access database

c. A process that rearranges the data and objects of a database to improve performance and to decrease storage requirements

d. A process to quickly copy data from an Access database to an external file

e. Used to copy formatting properties from one control to another

Select the best answer from the list of choices.

13. Which control would you use to visually separate groups of records on a report?
    a. Option group
    b. Image
    c. Bound Object Frame
    d. Line

14. Which wizard would you use to create a dynamic Web page?
    a. Page Wizard
    b. Table Wizard
    c. HTML Wizard
    d. Web Wizard

15. What feature allows you to apply the formatting characteristics of one control to another?
    a. AutoContent Wizard
    b. AutoFormat
    c. Report Layout Wizard
    d. Format Painter

16. Which of the following file types cannot be imported into Access?
    a. Excel
    b. Lotus 1-2-3
    c. Lotus Notes
    d. HTML

17. If you want to apply the same formatting characteristics to several controls at once, you might consider _____ them.
    a. AutoFormatting
    b. AutoPainting
    c. Grouping
    d. Exporting

18. Which feature compacts and repairs the database every time it is closed?
    a. Compact on Close
    b. Conversion Wizard
    c. Backup Wizard
    d. Repair Wizard

19. Which Access feature would you use to create a static Web page?
    a. Web page Wizard
    b. Export
    c. Mailto: HTML
    d. Conversion Wizard

20. What feature allows you to change the appearance of a control on a form or report based on criteria you specify?
    a. AutoFormat
    b. Behavioral formatting
    c. Event-driven formatting
    d. Conditional formatting

▼ SKILLS REVIEW

1. **Import data.**
   a. Open the **Membership-H.mdb** database from the drive and folder where your Data Files are stored.
   b. Import the data in the **Prospects.xls** Excel spreadsheet as a table named **Prospects**. The first row contains the column headings, and ContactID should be set as the primary key field.
   c. Open the Prospects table in Datasheet View.
   d. Add your personal information as a new record using **10** as the entry for the ContactID field.
   e. Print the datasheet in landscape orientation, then close the datasheet.

2. **Apply conditional formatting.**
   a. Using the Report Wizard, create a report based on the Member Activity Log using all of the fields in that query.
   b. View the data by Activities, group by MemberNo, sort ascending by ActivityDate, and Sum the Hours field.
   c. Use the Outline 1 Layout, Portrait Orientation, Compact style, type **Member Activity Log** as the report title, then preview the report.
   d. In Report Design View, select the =Sum([Hours]) calculated field in the MemberNo Footer section and use Conditional Formatting to change the text to bold italic, and the Font/Fore color to blue if the field value is greater than or equal to **10**.
   e. Add a label to the Report Footer section with the text **Created by Your Name**.
   f. Group all of the controls in the Report Footer section, then apply italics to the group.
   g. Save, preview, then print the last page of the report.

3. **Add lines.**
   a. Open the Member Activity Log report in Design View, then delete one of the lines above and below the labels in the MemberNo Header section. (*Hint*: There are two lines both above and below the labels in the MemberNo Header section—delete one of them in each position.)
   b. Format the two remaining lines in the MemberNo Header section bright blue. (*Hint*: Use the Line/Border color button on the Formatting (Form/Report) toolbar.)
   c. Delete the text box with the ="Summary for …" calculation and the line at the top of the MemberNo Footer section.
   d. Draw two short horizontal lines just below the =Sum([Hours]) calculation in the Report Footer section to draw attention to this grand total. (*Hint*: Press and hold [Shift] while creating the line for it to be perfectly horizontal.)
   e. Save the report, then print the last page.

4. **Use the Format Painter and AutoFormats.**
   a. Open the Member Activity Log report in Design View.
   b. Format the MemberNo label in the MemberNo Header section with a bold Arial Narrow 11-point font. Be careful to format the MemberNo label and not the MemberNo text box.
   c. Use the Format Painter to copy that format to the five other labels in the MemberNo Header section (ActivityDate, FirstName, LastName, Dues, and Hours). Be careful to format the labels and not the text boxes in the MemberNo Header section.
   d. Change the color of the Member Activity Log label in the Report Header section to red.
   e. Create a new AutoFormat named **RedTitle** based on the Member Activity Log report.
   f. Add a label with your name to the Report Header section, print the first page of the Member Activity Log report, then save it.
   g. In Design View, apply the Corporate AutoFormat. (*Hint*: Click the report selector button in the upper-left corner of the report to select the entire report before applying an AutoFormat. If an individual section or control is selected when you apply an AutoFormat, it will be applied to only that section or control.)
   h. Use the Customize button in the AutoFormat dialog box to delete the RedTitle style.
   i. Preview, then print the first page of the Member Activity Log report. Save, then close the report.

5. **Create a dynamic Web page.**
   a. Use the Page Wizard to create a Web page based on all of the fields in the Members table.
   b. Group the information by Zip, do not add any sorting orders, title the page **Zip Code Groups**, then open it in Page View.

▼ SKILLS REVIEW (CONTINUED)

   c. Navigate to the 50266 zip code, then expand the records to show the information for Kristen Larson. Enter your first and last name into the page, as shown in Figure H-18, then save and print that page.

   d. Save the data access page with the name **zip.htm** to the drive and folder where your Data Files are stored, then close the page.

FIGURE H-18

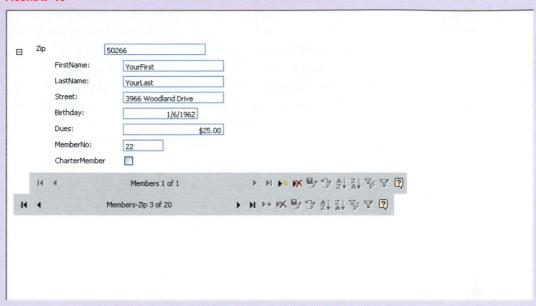

6. Export data.

   a. Export the Members table as an HTML Document with the name **members.html** to the drive and folder where your Data Files are stored.

   b. Start Internet Explorer, click File on the menu bar, click Open, then click Browse. Find and then double-click the **members.html** Web page, click OK to view it in Internet Explorer, then click Print on the Standard Buttons toolbar to print that page.

   c. Close Internet Explorer, then return to the Membership-H database window.

7. Compact and repair a database.

   a. If working on a hard drive, compact and repair the database.

   b. If working on a hard drive, set the Compact on Close option so that the database automatically compacts and repairs itself every time it is closed.

8. Back up a database.

   a. If working on a hard drive, back up the database with the default filename using the Tools menu. Store the backup in the drive and folder where your Data Files are stored.

   b. Close the Membership-H.mdb database, then exit Access.

▼ INDEPENDENT CHALLENGE 1

As the manager of a music store's instrument rental program, you created a database to track instrument rentals to schoolchildren. Now that several instruments have been purchased, you often need to print a report listing instruments in inventory. You create a single instrument inventory report based on a parameter query that prompts the user for the type of instrument to be displayed on the report. You conditionally format the report to highlight instruments in poor condition.

a. Start Access, then open the database **Music Store-H.mdb**.

b. Use the Report Wizard to create a report based on the Instruments by Type query. Select all of the fields, group by the Description field, sort in ascending order by the SerialNo field, use a Stepped Layout, use a Portrait Orientation, apply a Corporate style, and title the report **Instruments in Inventory**.

c. Preview the report and type **Cello** when prompted for the type of instrument.

d. Open the report in Design View, then add a label with your name to the Report Header.

e. Select the Condition text box in the Detail section, then use conditional formatting so that when the field value is equal to **Poor**, the text is bold italic, and the Font/Fore Color is red.

f. Save, then preview the report. Enter **Violin** when prompted for the type of instrument.

g. Print the report, then close the Instruments in Inventory report.

h. If working on the hard drive, check the Compact on Close option.

i. Close the Music Store-H.mdb database, then exit Access.

▼ INDEPENDENT CHALLENGE 2

As the manager of a music store's instrument rental program, you have created a database to track instrument rentals to schoolchildren. Now that several instruments have been rented, you need to create a conditionally formatted report that lists which schools have a large number of rentals.

a. Start Access, then open the database **Music Store-H.mdb**.

b. Use the Report Wizard to create a report with the following fields from the following tables:
Schools: SchoolName
Instruments: Description, MonthlyFee
Rentals: RentalDate

c. View the data by Schools, do not add any additional grouping levels, sort in ascending order by RentalDate, and Sum the MonthlyFee field.

d. Use an Outline 1 Layout, Portrait Orientation, Casual style, and title the report **School Summary Report**.

e. Open the report in Design View, then click the =Sum([MonthlyFee]) control in the SchoolNo Footer section.

f. Use Conditional Formatting to specify that the field be Bold and have a bright yellow Fill/Back Color if the sum is greater than or equal to 200.

g. Add a label to the Report Header section with your name, then save the report.

h. Print the first page of the report.

i. Close the School Summary Report, close the Music Store-H.mdb database, then exit Access.

▼ INDEPENDENT CHALLENGE 3

As the manager of a music store's instrument rental program, you have created a database to track instrument rentals to schoolchildren. You need to build both static and dynamic Web pages for this database.

a. Start Access, then open the database **Music Store-H.mdb**.

b. Use the Page Wizard to create a data access page with the SchoolName field from the Schools table, the RentalDate field from the Rentals table, and all of the fields in the Instruments table.

c. Group the records by SchoolName, sort them in ascending order by RentalDate, title the page **School Rentals**, then display it in Page View.

d. In Design View, click in the Click here and type title text prompt, then type your name.

e. Save the page as **school.htm** in the folder where your Data Files are stored, then display it in Web Page Preview.

f. Find the record for the Thomas Jefferson Elementary school, then click the Expand button.

Advanced Challenge Exercise

- Double-click Excellent in the Condition field for the first instrument, then click the Filter by Selection button in the upper navigation bar to find all instruments rented to this school in excellent condition
- Navigate to the second instrument with an Excellent condition for the Thomas Jefferson Elementary school, then print that page.

g. Close Internet Explorer, close the Music Store-H.mdb database, then exit Access.

▼ INDEPENDENT CHALLENGE 4

You are on the staff of an economic development team whose goal is to encourage tourism in the Baltic Sea region. You have created an Access database called Baltic-H to track important fields of information for the countries in that region, and are using the Internet to find information about the area.

a. Start Access and open the **Baltic-H.mdb** database from the drive and folder where your Data Files are stored.

b. Connect to the Internet, then go to www.yahoo.com, www.about.com, or any general search engine to conduct some research for your database. Your goal is to find three upcoming events for Warsaw, Poland, then print the Web page(s).

c. Open the datasheet for the Cities table, then expand the subdatasheet for Warsaw, Poland. Enter the three events for Warsaw in the subdatasheet, then close the Cities table.

d. Use the Report Wizard to build a report based on all of the fields in the Cities table except the CityID, and the EventName and EventDate from the Events table.

e. View the data by Cities, do not add any more grouping levels, sort the records in ascending order by EventDate, use a Block Layout and Portrait Orientation, apply a Bold style, and title the report Baltic Events.

f. Preview the report.

g. In Report Design View, add your name as a label to the Report Header section, then save, print, and close the Baltic Events report.

Advanced Challenge Exercise

- Use Save As to save the report with the name **Baltic Events - Blue**.
- In Report Design View, group and then format the labels in the Page Header section so that all of the text for each label is clearly visible.
- Modify the color of the lines at the top and the bottom of the Page Header section to be bright blue. Modify the text color of the labels in the Report Header section to be bright blue.
- Save, print, and close the Baltic Events - Blue report.

h. Close the Baltic-H.mdb database, then exit Access.

▼ VISUAL WORKSHOP

Open the **Training-H.mdb** database and use the Report Wizard to create the report shown in Figure H-19. Select the First, Last, and Location fields from the Employees table, and the Description and Hours fields from the Courses table. View the data by Employees, do not add any more grouping levels, sort in ascending order by Description, and Sum the Hours. Use the Stepped, Portrait, and Soft Gray style options. Title the report **Employee Education Report**. In Report Design View enter your name as a label in the Report Header section and widen the Description field to display all values clearly. Delete the long calculated field and the Sum label in the EmployeeNo Footer section, and add conditional formatting so that the =Sum([Hours]) field displays in bold with a bright yellow background if the value is greater than or equal to 100. Add a subtotal line above the =Sum([Hours]) field in the EmployeeNo Footer section, and two lines to indicate a grand total below the =Sum([Hours]) field in the Report Footer section. Make other changes as necessary so that the last page of your report looks like Figure H-19.

FIGURE H-19

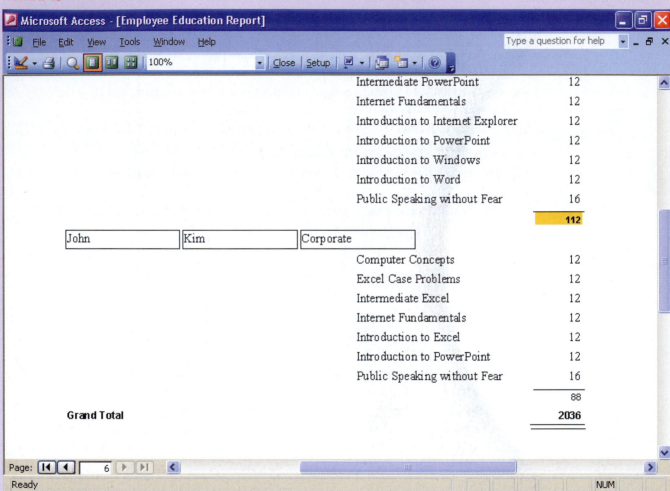

Integrating Word, Excel, and Access

OBJECTIVES

As you have learned, many businesses maintain Access databases that contain names, addresses, and other useful information about customers, suppliers, employees, and inventory. You can combine information stored in a database with Word to produce form letters, labels, and catalogs: instead of creating a data source in Word, you select an Access database as the data source. You can also include in a merged document charts and spreadsheets that you've created from Access data and analyzed in Excel.  Karen Rosen, the director of human resources at MediaLoft, asks you to learn how to set up and run mail merges in Word using a data source from Access and spreadsheet data from Excel. You need to use the three programs to produce form letters for an upcoming conference and to create a sheet of labels for a collection of CDs.

Project 1: Form Letters for the Technology Plus Conference

MediaLoft's Human Resources Department is working with the organizers of the Technology Plus Conference in Chicago to coordinate the registration of employees from all of the MediaLoft outlets. You need to merge the database that lists conference participants with a form letter you create in Word. The form letter also needs to include a chart created in Excel from data stored in the Access database.

ACTIVITY

Setting Up the Conference Database

You create the Participants and Workshops tables from the data you have for six participants. You use the Table Wizard to create the Participants table, and then create the Workshops table in Datasheet View.

STEPS

1. Start Access, click **Create a new file** in the Open section of the Getting Started task pane, click **Blank database** under New in the New File task pane, locate the drive and folder where your Data Files are stored, type **Conference Database** in the File name box, click **Create**, then double-click **Create table by using wizard**

2. Click **Contacts** in the Sample Tables list, click the **Select Single Field button** ⟩ to select the ContactID field, click **Rename Field**, type **ID**, click **OK**, select **FirstName, LastName,** and **Dear**, select **Address** and rename it **Address1**, select **City** and rename it **Address2**, select **Country/Region** and rename it **Country**, then select **Title** and rename it **Track**

> **QUICK TIP**
> Double-click the column dividers to make the columns automatically fit the text.

3. Click **Next**, name the table **Participants**, click **Next**, click **Finish**, enter the records and format the column widths as shown in Figure E-1, then close and save the **Participants** table

4. Double-click **Create table in Design view**, type **ID**, click the **Primary Key button** 🔑 on the Table Design toolbar, press **[Tab]**, click the **Data Type list arrow**, click **AutoNumber**, click the **Save button** 💾, type **Workshops**, click **OK**, then enter the field names as shown in Figure E-2

5. Switch to **Datasheet View**, click **Yes** to save the table, enter the records in the Workshops table and format the column widths as shown in Figure E-3, then close and save the table

6. Click **Tools** on the menu bar, click **Relationships**, add the **Participants** and **Workshops** tables to the Relationships window, close the Show Table dialog box, click **Track** in the Participants table, drag **Track** from the Participants table over **Track** in the Workshops table, click **Create**, then close and save the Relationships window

   The two tables are related by the Track field. A "track" is a pair of related workshops.

7. Click **Queries** in the Objects bar, double-click **Create query by using wizard**, click the **Select All Fields button** ⟩⟩ to add all the fields from the Participants table, click the **Tables/Queries list arrow**, click **Table: Workshops**, then add the **Workshop1, Time1, Workshop2,** and **Time2** fields

8. Click **Next**, name the query **Conference Letter**, click **Finish**, then scroll right to see the workshops that Dena Martelli will attend and compare your screen to Figure E-4

   As shown in Figure E-4, Dena Martelli from Italy will attend the workshops in Track A: XML Made Easy, at 0900 hours, and Introduction to Open Source Language, at 1300 hours.

9. Close the Conference Letter query

FIGURE E-1: Records for the Participants table

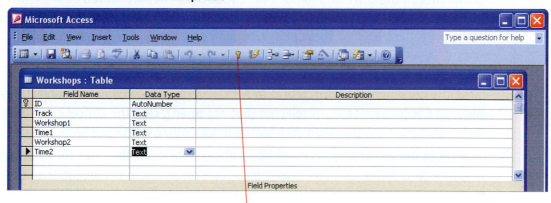

Participants : Table

ID	First Name	Last Name	Dear	Address1	Address2	Country	Track
1	Dena	Martelli	Ms. Martelli	Via del pastini 110	Roma 00186	Italy	A
2	Michael	Banks	Mr. Banks	52 Rushton Lane	London SE6 4JD	United Kingdom	B
3	Monique	Menton	Ms. Menton	18 rue Jacob	18790 Paris	France	C
4	Sean	Kelly	Mr. Kelly	200 Limerick Drive	Castleknock Dublin 16	Ireland	C
5	Hans	Schultz	Mr. Schultz	Markt 38	53441 Bonn	Germany	B
6	Bridget	O'Brian	Ms. O'Brian	101 Shamrock Lane	Dublin 10	Ireland	A

Record: 7 of 7

FIGURE E-2: Field names for the Workshops table

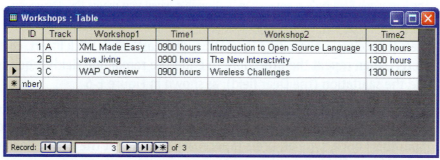

Workshops : Table

Field Name	Data Type	Description
ID	AutoNumber	
Track	Text	
Workshop1	Text	
Time1	Text	
Workshop2	Text	
Time2	Text	

Field Properties

Primary Key button

FIGURE E-3: Records for the Workshops table

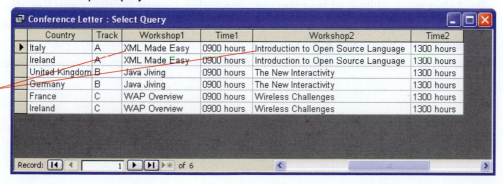

Workshops : Table

ID	Track	Workshop1	Time1	Workshop2	Time2
1	A	XML Made Easy	0900 hours	Introduction to Open Source Language	1300 hours
2	B	Java Jiving	0900 hours	The New Interactivity	1300 hours
3	C	WAP Overview	0900 hours	Wireless Challenges	1300 hours

Record: 3 of 3

FIGURE E-4: Completed query

Conference Letter : Select Query

Country	Track	Workshop1	Time1	Workshop2	Time2
Italy	A	XML Made Easy	0900 hours	Introduction to Open Source Language	1300 hours
Ireland	A	XML Made Easy	0900 hours	Introduction to Open Source Language	1300 hours
United Kingdom	B	Java Jiving	0900 hours	The New Interactivity	1300 hours
Germany	B	Java Jiving	0900 hours	The New Interactivity	1300 hours
France	C	WAP Overview	0900 hours	Wireless Challenges	1300 hours
Ireland	C	WAP Overview	0900 hours	Wireless Challenges	1300 hours

Workshops that Dena Martelli will attend

Record: 1 of 6

ACTIVITY

Creating the Form Letter

You use the OfficeLinks feature to merge the records in the Conference Letter query table with a form letter you create in Word. Your first task is to enter the text required for the form letter.

STEPS

TROUBLE

If a message appears advising you that the database is in exclusive mode, close the database, open it again, click Enable macros if prompted, then repeat Step 2.

1. Start Word, set the Top and Bottom margins at .7, enter and format the text required for the form letter as shown in Figure E-5, then save the document as Technology Plus Conference in the drive and folder where your Data Files are stored

   Make sure you enter the current date and your name where indicated. As you work through the steps required for the merge, you insert fields that contain information from the database, such as the name and address of each participant and information about the workshops they will attend. In the next activity, you insert the pie chart referenced in the letter.

2. Close the document in Word, return to Access, verify that no database objects are open and that Conference Letter is selected (but not open), click the OfficeLinks list arrow 📧▾ on the Database toolbar, then click Merge It with Microsoft Office Word

3. Click OK to use an existing Microsoft Word document, locate the drive and folder where you saved the form letter, click Technology Plus Conference.doc in the file list, then click Open

   In a few moments, Word opens with the Mail Merge task pane open.

4. Maximize the Word window if necessary, verify that Use an existing list is selected in the Mail Merge task pane, then click Next: Write your letter at the bottom of the task pane

5. Click one line below the current date in the letter, press [Enter], click More items in the Mail Merge task pane, click FirstName, click Insert, then click Close

   The FirstName field code is entered, indicating that when you merge the documents, the first name of each participant is inserted in place of the field code.

6. Press [Spacebar] once, click More items, click LastName, click Insert, click Close, press [Enter], then repeat the procedure to enter the remaining fields required for the address and the salutation (the Dear field), as shown in Figure E-6

7. Scroll down to the second paragraph, click after workshops:, press [Enter] twice, click More items in the Mail Merge task pane, click Workshop1, click Insert, click Close, press [Spacebar] once, type at, press [Spacebar], then insert the Time1 field and close the Insert Merge Field dialog box

8. Press [Enter], enter the Workshop2 field, press [Spacebar], type at, press [Spacebar], then enter the Time2 field

9. Select the two lines of text you just typed, click Format on the menu bar, click Bullets and Numbering, click the bullet style shown in Figure E-7, click OK, save the document, and leave both Word and Access open

   Before you complete the merge, you need to create the pie chart, which you do in the next activity.

FIGURE E-5: Text for the form letter

Technology Plus Conference
802 Markham Road, London NE5 4GD

Current Date

Dear

Welcome to the Technology Plus Conference, held this year in Dublin, Ireland. The conference starts on September 21 at 0800 hours with a keynote speech by Dame Edna Janzen, author of the best-selling book *The Challenge of 21ˢᵗ Century Technology*.

This letter confirms your participation in the following workshops:

With over 7,000 people attending the conference this year, we are truly an international event! The pie chart shown below displays the breakdown of participants by country.

Thank you for your participation in the Technology Plus Conference. If you have any questions, please call me at 44 01 555-4324.

Sincerely,

Your Name
Conference Organizer

FIGURE E-6: Form fields inserted for the address and salutation

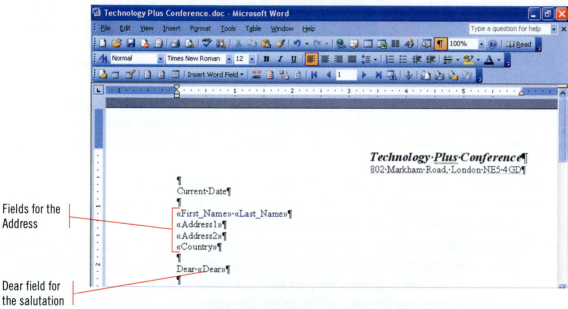

Fields for the Address

Dear field for the salutation

FIGURE E-7: Bullets and Numbering dialog box

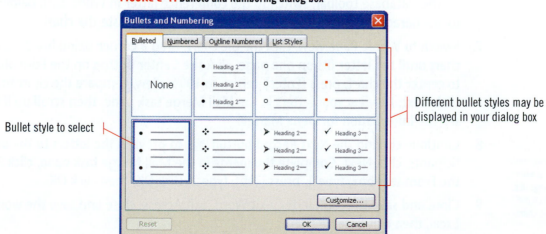

Bullet style to select

Different bullet styles may be displayed in your dialog box

UNIT
E
Integration

ACTIVITY

Creating the Pie Chart

The form letter needs to include a pie chart that shows the breakdown of participants by country. First, you create a query showing the participants' last names and countries, and then you analyze the data and create a pie chart in Excel. Finally, you can copy the chart to the Word letter.

STEPS

1. Return to Access, double-click **Create query by using wizard**, click the **Tables/Queries list arrow**, click **Table: Participants**, click **FirstName**, click the **Select Single Field button** `>`, add the **LastName** and **Country** fields, click **Next**, name the query **Countries**, then click **Finish**

2. Close the query table, click the **OfficeLinks list arrow** 🖳▾ on the Database toolbar, then click **Analyze It with Microsoft Office Excel**

   A workbook called Countries.xls opens in Excel.

3. Select cells **C1** to **C7** in the Excel worksheet, click **Data** on the menu bar, click **PivotTable and PivotChart Report**, click **Next** to create a PivotTable, click **Finish**, click **Country** in the PivotTable Field List, then as shown in Figure E-8, drag **Country** first to the **Drop Row Fields Here** section of the PivotTable, then drag it to the **Drop Data Items Here** section

   The resulting PivotTable appears as shown in Figure E-9. You use the PivotTable command to count the number of times each country appears. In the PivotTable shown in Figure E-9, Ireland is counted twice because two of the records in the original table contained Ireland in the Country field.

4. Click the **Chart Wizard button** 📊 on the PivotTable toolbar, click **Chart** on the menu bar, click **Chart Type**, click **Pie**, click **OK**, right-click the **Count of Country button** above the pie chart, click **Hide PivotChart Field Buttons**, click the gray area surrounding the pie chart, then press **[Delete]**

5. Click **Chart** on the menu bar, click **Chart Options**, type **Participant Countries** as the chart title, click the **Legend tab**, click the **Show Legend check box** to deselect it, click the **Data Labels tab**, click the **Category name check box**, then click **OK**

6. Right-click **Participant Countries** at the top of the chart, click **Format Chart Title**, click the **Font tab**, select the **18 point font size**, click **OK**, right-click any data label (e.g., **France**), click **Format Data Labels**, change the font size to **18 point**, click **OK**, click anywhere in the white area surrounding the pie chart to select the entire chart, click the **Copy button** 📋 on the Database toolbar, switch to the conference letter in Word, click below the second to last paragraph, press **[Enter]**, then press **[Ctrl][V]** to paste the chart

7. Switch to **Whole Page view**, click the pie chart, drag a corner sizing handle to reduce the chart until the letter fits on one page, click the **Center button** on the Formatting toolbar to center the chart, press **[Enter]**, return to **100% view**, compare the chart to Figure E-10, click **Next: Preview your letters** in the Mail Merge task pane, then scroll up if necessary to see the information for **Dena Martelli**

QUICK TIP

Before printing, verify that the entire letter fits on one page. If it doesn't, reduce the size of the pie chart.

8. Continue clicking the **Next Record button** `>>` to preview the letters to the other five participants, click **Next: Complete the merge** in the Mail Merge task pane, click **Print**, click the **From text box**, type **1**, press **[Tab]**, type **2**, click **OK**, then click **OK**

9. Close and save the form letter, exit Word, exit Access, close and save the workbook in Excel, then exit Excel

FIGURE E-8: Country field dragged to the PivotTable in Excel

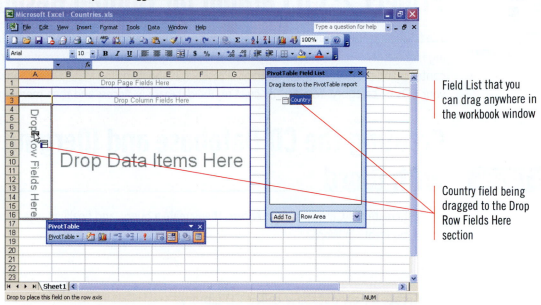

Field List that you can drag anywhere in the workbook window

Country field being dragged to the Drop Row Fields Here section

FIGURE E-9: Completed PivotTable in Excel

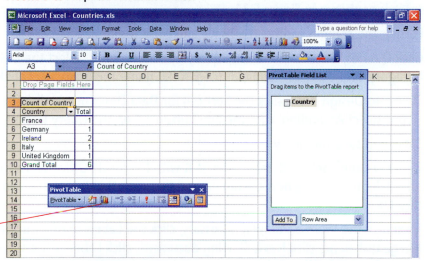

Chart Wizard button on the PivotTable toolbar

FIGURE E-10: Pie chart sized and positioned

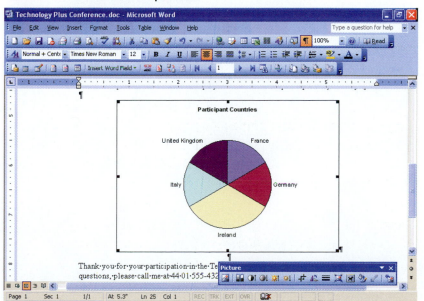

UNIT
E
Integration

Project 2: CD Catalog for Human Resources

The MediaLoft Human Resources Department has accumulated stacks of CDs containing data, images, training film files, and sound files. You've been asked to organize these CDs by creating a database that lists their contents and producing labels for the CD cases. You also want to create a chart showing the breakdown of your CDs by category. You start by creating the database in Access and then merging it with Word.

Creating the CD Database and Merging It with Word

ACTIVITY

You first create the CD database in Access, then create a query, and finally merge the data in the query with labels you create in Word.

STEPS

1. Create a new database called CD Library

2. Create a table called CD List that includes a primary key and contains the field names and records as shown in Figure E-11

3. Format the column widths, then save and close the table

4. Click Queries, double-click Create query by using wizard, select the Data Description, Category, and Date Burned fields, click Next, name the query CD Labels, then click Finish

5. Switch to Design View, click the Sort cell for Data Description, click the Sort cell list arrow, select Ascending, click the Run button [icon] on the Query Design toolbar

6. Close and save the query

TROUBLE
If a message appears advising you that the database is in exclusive mode, close the database, open it again, click Enable macros if prompted, then repeat Step 4.

7. With CD Labels selected, select Merge It with Microsoft Office Word from the OfficeLinks list, click the Create a new document and then link the data to it option button, then click OK

8. Maximize the Word window if necessary, click the Labels option button in the Mail Merge task pane, click Next: Starting document, click Label options, select 5824 – CD Label, then click OK

   The CD label you selected produces a 4.5" × 4.5" label. You can also select other labels, such as CD-Spine and CD-Case.

FIGURE E-11: Fields and records for the CD List table

ID	Data Description	Category	File Type	Date Burned
1	Department Web Site Backup	Web Site	HTML	3/3/2005
2	Staff Photos: 2000 - 2005	Images	JPEG	3/15/2005
3	Company Picnic Photos: 2004	Images	JPEG	7/10/2005
4	Supervisory Skills Training Program	Program	EXE	6/5/2004
5	Interviewing Techniques Manual	Document	DOC	12/10/2005
6	Department Financial Records	Document	XLS	5/10/2005
7	Project Management Training Program	Program	EXE	12/22/2005
8	Personnel Records: 2004	Database	MDB	12/31/2004
9	Personnel Records: 2005	Database	MDB	12/31/2005
10	2004 Sales Conference Photos	Images	JPEG	9/13/2004
11	2005 Sales Conference Photos	Images	JPEG	9/15/2005
12	Office Procedures Training Manual	Document	DOC	4/10/2004
13	Photocopy Records: 2002 - 2005	Database	MDB	1/10/2005
14	Company Orientation Manual	Document	DOC	10/10/2005
15	Change Management Training Program	Program	EXE	1/11/2005

CD List : Table

Record: 16 of 16

Integration

ACTIVITY

Completing the Merge

STEPS

You need to insert a clip art picture on the CD label and complete the merge.

1. Click **Next: Select recipients** at the bottom of the Mail Merge task pane, verify that **Use an existing list** is selected, click **Next: Arrange your labels**, click **More items**, click **Insert**, then click **Close**

   The Data Description field is inserted.

2. Press **[Enter]**, insert the **Category field**, close the Insert Merge Field dialog box, press **[Enter]** twice, insert the **Date Burned field**, then click **Close**

3. Click **View**, point to **Toolbars**, click **Tables and Borders**, click the **Alignment list arrow** on the Tables and Borders toolbar, click the **Align Top Center button**, then close the Tables and Borders toolbar

4. Click the **Data Description field** at the top of the label, click **Format** on the menu bar, click **Paragraph**, change the **Before Spacing** to **42 point**, click **OK**, format the field labels as shown in Figure E-12, type your name in the document header, then save the document as **CD Labels**

5. Press **[Enter]** three times after the Date Burned field, display the **Drawing toolbar**, click the **Insert Clip Art button** on the Drawing toolbar, click the **Search for text box** in the Clip Art task pane, type **CD**, press **[Enter]**, scroll down through the results, then insert the picture shown in Figure E-13 or a similar picture

6. Size and position the clip art picture so that it appears similar to Figure E-13

7. Close the Clip Art task pane, click **Tools** on the menu bar, point to **Letters and Mailings**, click **Mail Merge** to open the Mail Merge task pane again, click the small triangle at the bottom of the task pane to scroll if necessary, then click **Update all labels**

   You can also scroll down the Word document to see that a second label has been inserted on the page. When the merged labels are printed, two labels appear on each page.

8. Click **Next: Preview your labels**, click the **Next Record button** continuously to examine each of the CD labels and verify that the correct data appears on each label, click **Next: Complete the merge**, click **Print**, enter **1** in the From text box, enter **2** in the To text box, click **OK**, click **OK**, save the document, then close the document and exit Word

FIGURE E-12: Formatted fields for CD label

24 point, bold

18 point, bold

12 point

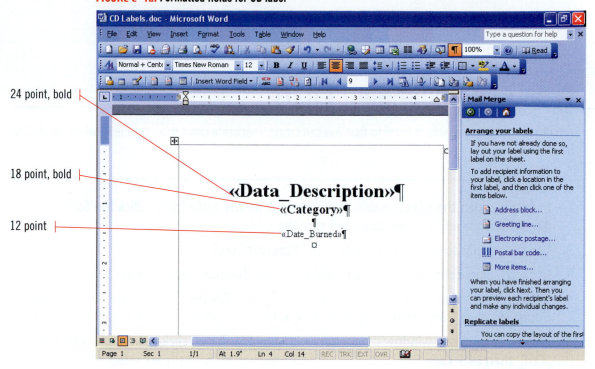

FIGURE E-13: Clip art inserted on the CD label

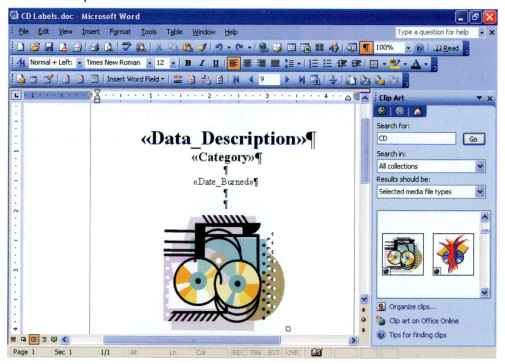

ACTIVITY

Creating a Doughnut Chart

You display the CD List table in Excel so that you can create a separate chart showing the breakdown of CDs by category.

STEPS

1. In Access, open the CD List table, click Category on the table frame, click the Sort Ascending button , then close and save the table

2. Use OfficeLinks to analyze the table with Microsoft Excel

3. In Excel, select cells A1 through E16, click Data on the menu bar, then click Subtotals

4. Click the At each change in list arrow, click Category, click the Use function list arrow, click Count, deselect the Date Burned check box, select the Category check box, then click OK

5. Maximize the Excel window if necessary, click any blank cell, click cell C5, press and hold [Ctrl], then click cells C10, C15, C19, and C21 so that all five cells are selected

6. Click the Chart Wizard button , click Doughnut in the list of chart types, then click Next

7. Click the Columns option button if necessary, click the Series tab, click the Collapse Dialog Box button next to the Category Labels text box to collapse the Chart Wizard dialog box, press and hold [Ctrl], click cells C4, C6, C11, C16, and C20, then click the Expand Dialog Box button

8. Click Next, click the Titles tab if necessary, type Breakdown of CD Categories in the Chart title text box, click the Data Labels tab, click the Value check box, click Finish, size and position the chart as shown in Figure E-14

9. Click the purple wedge in the doughnut chart (represents Web Sites) one time, click the wedge again to select it, right-click the selected wedge, click Format data point, click the Light Purple color (5th row, 2nd from right), then click OK

10. Add your name to the workbook, save and print the workbook, then close all files and exit all programs

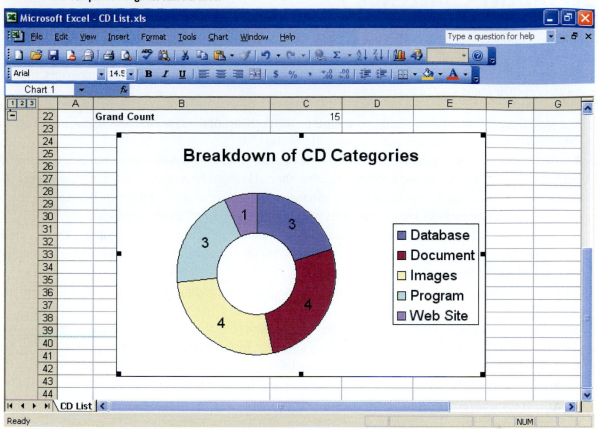

Integration

▼ INDEPENDENT CHALLENGE 1

Create a database to list participants in a conference, course, or special event of your choice. The database can be similar to the database you created in the Technology Plus Conference project. For example, you could create a database containing information about members of a sports team or about participants in a packaged tour. Merge the database with a form letter you create in Word, and then create a chart in Excel that graphically displays a specific characteristic about the participants, such as their best time in a race, or their home state or province.

a. Select a special event that involves multiple participants. Each participant needs to receive a welcome letter. Then identify one characteristic of the participants that you'd like to chart.

b. Determine the information required for the tables in the database. One table should contain information about the participants, such as their names and addresses, and the other table should contain information related to the special event, such as the tours that the participants have selected or the number of races each athlete has run. Both tables must contain one common field. Refer to the tables you created for Portfolio Project 1 for ideas.

c. Create a database called **Special Event Database** in the location where your Data Files are stored, then create a **Participants** table that includes at least eight fields, including the characteristic you wish to chart (e.g., home state or best time). Make sure you create a primary key.

d. Create the second table and give it an appropriate name. Make sure that you include one field that also appears in the Participants table.

e. Create a relationship between the two tables based on the common field, then create a query that merges the two tables.

f. Merge the query table in Word, and then create a form letter that includes at least three appropriate fields from the query table. Make sure to include your name in the form letter.

g. In Access, create a query that lists all the participants along with the special characteristic you plan to chart.

h. Analyze the query table in Excel, and then create a pie chart that shows the breakdown of participants according to the special characteristic. You can use the PivotTable feature to count the number of times that each category appears. Display data and/or percentage labels as desired.

i. Copy the pie chart into the letter in Word. Make sure you include appropriate text to introduce the chart, then format the chart and the letter so everything fits on one page.

j. Complete the merge, print two of the letters, then save the Word document as **Form Letter for Special Event**.

k. Save and close all files, and exit all programs.

▼ INDEPENDENT CHALLENGE 2

Create a database that contains information about your personal collection of CDs, DVDs, photographs, or a collection of your choice. Look through the list of labels available in the Label Options dialog box to find a label appropriate for the items in your collection. Create a database called **My Collection** in the drive and folder where your Data Files are stored. (*Hint*: If you are saving your work to floppy disks, you may need to save this database on a separate disk.) Set up a table that includes fields to differentiate the various records in terms of genre, category, or type, as appropriate. If your table lists all your DVDs, for example, you could include fields for Title, Genre, Date, and even Price. Merge the table in Word by following the steps in the Mail Merge task pane to select a label, insert fields, and format the label. Complete the merge and print two labels. Switch back to Access, sort one of the fields in the table alphabetically, then analyze it in Excel, and create a chart that shows the breakdown of items by genre (or other appropriate category). Add your name to the Excel worksheet, then print the chart and worksheet. Save and close all open files, and exit all programs.

▼ INDEPENDENT CHALLENGE 3

You own a small software company that creates digital puzzles for children and adults. You've decided to classify and then analyze the types of customers who have bought your puzzles in the past month in terms of age, occupation, and geographical location. Follow the instructions provided to create the Customer Analysis document shown in Figure E-15.

a. Open the file Digital Puzzles.mdb from the drive and folder where your Data Files are stored.

b. Sort the records in the Customer List table by Occupation in ascending order, analyze the table with Excel, and then create a cone chart that shows the breakdown of customers by occupation. You need to calculate the number of customers in each occupation category (for example, Child, Consultant, etc.). Remove the legend from the chart.

▼ INDEPENDENT CHALLENGE 3 (CONTINUED)

c. In Word, enter and format just the text shown in Figure E-15 (do *not* include the table), then save the document as **Digital Puzzles Customer Analysis** in the drive and folder where your Data Files are stored.

d. In Access, click the OfficeLinks button list arrow, then click Publish It with Microsoft Word. The table appears in a new file called Customer List.rtf.

e. Select the table, copy it, paste it below the first paragraph of text in the Digital Puzzles Customer Analysis document, select the table in Word, click Table on the menu bar, click Table AutoFormat, select Table List 7 from the list of table styles, click Apply, select and delete column 1 (contains the ID field), then adjust column widths, as shown in Figure E-15.

f. Copy the cone chart from Excel and paste it in the Word document as shown in Figure E-15. Resize the chart so that it fits on page 1 of the document.

g. Add a picture from the Clip Art task pane (search for **puzzle**), as shown in Figure E-15. Make sure you format the clip art object's layout as Tight and Right.

h. Format the page attractively in Word, add your name to the document, print a copy, save and close all files, then exit all programs.

FIGURE E-15: Completed customer analysis

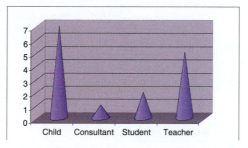

Digital Puzzles

We have analyzed the types of customers who have bought our puzzles during the month of September in terms of age, occupation, and geographical location. The following table shows the breakdown of customers for September 2006.

Last Name	First Name	Age	Occupation	State or Province	Product
Ralston	Harry	13	Child	Georgia	Math Puzzles
Washington	Marla	15	Child	Delaware	Art Puzzles
Amin	Afsaneh	11	Child	California	Brain Teasers
Lu	Cecilia	16	Child	Texas	Space Puzzles
Takashi	Hiromi	12	Child	California	Space Puzzles
Townsend	Patty	13	Child	Iowa	Science Puzzles
Ali	Manjit	12	Child	Florida	Jigsaw Puzzles
Quigley	Grace	36	Consultant	New York	Jigsaw Puzzles
Bennet	Elinor	18	Student	Oregon	Science Puzzles
Harrison	Tom	18	Student	Alberta	Space Puzzles
Merton	Charles	33	Teacher	New York	Art Puzzles
Rogers	Sean	29	Teacher	Wisconsin	Jigsaw Puzzles
Malfoy	Lucinda	31	Teacher	Nova Scotia	Science Puzzles
Trelawney	Sybil	48	Teacher	Ontario	Math Puzzles
Yaretz	Wilson	42	Teacher	Montana	Math Puzzles

As shown in the cone chart illustrated below, our single biggest occupation group is children under the age of 16. To continue serving this ever-growing market, Digital Puzzles plans to develop a marketing strategy in consultation with contacts at the local school boards. This plan will also bring us into more intensive contact with our second largest occupation group – teachers.

▼ VISUAL WORKSHOP

Create a database in the drive and folder where your Data Files are stored called **Northeast Computers**, then create a table called **Northeast Sales**, as shown in Figure E-16, that includes a primary key. Select the Currency format for the data type for the Software and Accessories fields. Analyze the table in Excel, and then create a bar chart in Excel, as shown in Figure E-17. (*Hint*: Before you create the chart in Excel, select cells C2 through D7, click Format on the menu bar, click Cells, click the Number tab, click Currency in the Category list, then reduce the number of decimal places to 0.) To create the chart in Excel, select cells B1 through D7, then click the Chart Wizard button and select Bar. You need to resize the chart and make sure that the font size of the y-axis labels and legend labels is 10 point and the font size of the x-axis labels is 8 point. To change the font size of a set of labels (for example, the y-axis labels), right-click one of the labels, click Format Axis, click the Font tab, then select the required font size. Add your name to the Excel worksheet, save and print the worksheet, save and close all files, then exit all programs.

FIGURE E-16

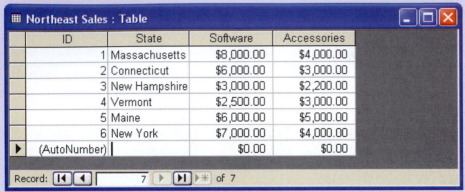

FIGURE E-17

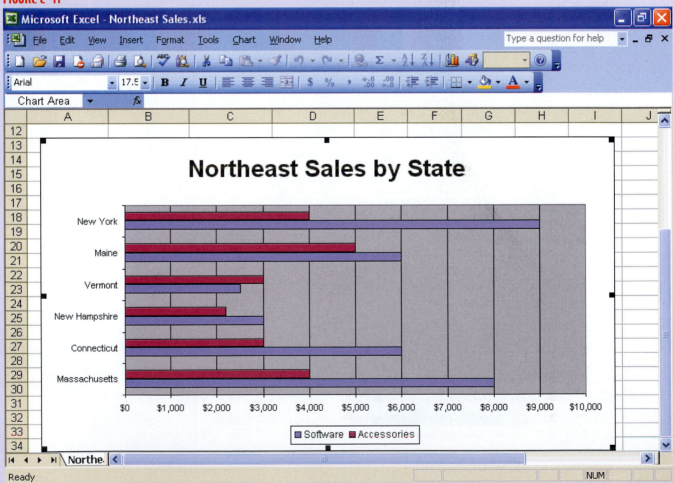

UNIT
E

PowerPoint 2003

Customizing a Presentation

OBJECTIVES

Understand PowerPoint masters

Format master text

Change master text indents

Adjust text objects

Use advanced drawing tools

Use advanced formatting tools

Insert and format WordArt

Create a template

If you have a SAM user profile, you may have access to hands-on instruction, practice, and assessment of the skills covered in this unit. Log in to your SAM account and go to your assignments page to see what your instructor has assigned.

Design features such as text spacing and color are some of the most important qualities of a professional-looking presentation. It is important to make design elements consistent throughout a presentation to hold the reader's attention and to avoid confusion. PowerPoint helps you achieve the look you want by providing ways of customizing and enhancing your slides, notes pages, and handouts. Maria Abbott is MediaLoft's general sales manager. You are her assistant, and you have been working on a marketing presentation for a new Internet product that you will give later in the month. After receiving some initial feedback from a couple of coworkers, you revise the presentation by customizing the slide format and enhancing the graphics. You then create a presentation template so you and other coworkers at MediaLoft can create additional presentations with a similar look.

Understanding
PowerPoint Masters

Each presentation in PowerPoint uses **Master views** to store information about the design template. This information includes font styles, text placeholder position and size, and color scheme. Design elements that you place in Slide Master view appear on every slide in the presentation. For example, you could insert a company logo in the upper-right corner of the slide master and that logo would then appear on every slide in your presentation. There are three Master views: Slide Master view, Handout Master view, and Notes Master view. Changes made to the slide master are reflected on all the slides, changes made to the notes master are reflected in the Notes Page view, and changes made to the handout master are reflected when you print your presentation using one of the Handout print options. Slide Master view actually has two master slides: one for the slide master and one for the title master. These two masters are called a **slide-title master pair**. Table E-1 describes the Slide Master View toolbar buttons. You want to make a few changes and add an optional design template to the presentation, so you open your presentation and examine the slide master.

STEPS

QUICK TIP

You can press and hold [Shift] and click the Normal View button 🔲 to display the slide master.

1. **Start PowerPoint, open the presentation PPT E-1.ppt from the drive and folder where your Data Files are stored, then save the presentation as eMediaE**
   The title slide of the presentation appears.

QUICK TIP

A slide master is preserved by default when you insert, paste, or drag a design template into Slide Master view or when you add a new design template in Slide Master view. A preserved slide master is identified by a push pin icon.

2. **Click View, point to Master, then click Slide Master**
   The presentation's Slide Master view appears, showing the title master in the Slide pane. The slide-title master pair appears as thumbnails to the left of the Slide pane. The title master controls the title, subtitle, and footer placeholders for any slide in the presentation with the Title Slide layout. You can add more than one design template to the same presentation.

3. **Click the Slide Design button 📝Design on the Formatting toolbar, scroll down through the design templates, click the Compass design template list arrow in the Slide Design task pane in the Available For Use section, then click Add Design**
   There are now two slide-title master pairs to the left of the Slide pane indicating that there are two design templates available in this presentation. You can apply a different template for different audiences or situations. You can also use multiple templates in one presentation at the same time.

QUICK TIP

Click the second slide master thumbnail to display the title master.

4. **Click the first slide master thumbnail**
   The slide master for the first presentation design template appears. It contains a **Master title placeholder** and a **Master text placeholder**, as shown in Figure E-1. These placeholders control the format for each title text object and body text object for each slide in the presentation that doesn't have the Title Slide layout. Figure E-2 shows Slide 6 of the presentation. Examine Figures E-1 and E-2 to better understand the relationship between the slide master and the slide.

   - The Master title placeholder, labeled "Title Area for AutoLayouts", indicates the position of the title text object and its font size, style, and color. Compare this to the slide title shown in Figure E-2.
   - The Master text placeholder, labeled "Object Area for AutoLayouts", determines the characteristics of the body text objects on all the slides in the presentation. Compare the colors and fonts of each bullet level in the body text objects of both figures.
   - You can resize and move Master title and text placeholders as you would any placeholder in PowerPoint.
   - The slide master can contain background objects, such as AutoShapes, clip art, or pictures, that appear on every slide in the presentation behind the text and objects on the slides.

FIGURE E-1: Slide Master

Slide master slide

Icon indicates animation effects

Title master slide

Push pin icon indicates that the template design is preserved

Bullet levels

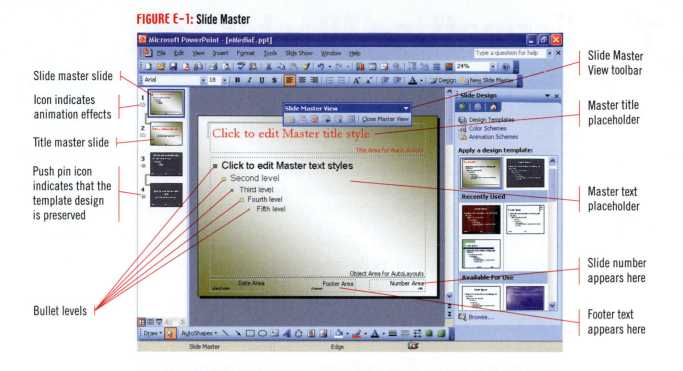

Slide Master View toolbar

Master title placeholder

Master text placeholder

Slide number appears here

Footer text appears here

FIGURE E-2: Slide 6 in Normal view

Bullets

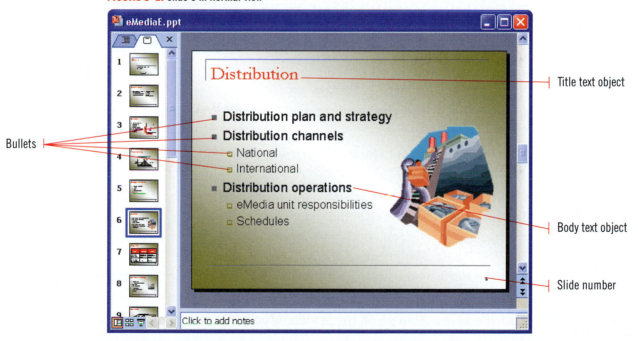

Title text object

Body text object

Slide number

TABLE E-1: Slide Master View toolbar buttons

button	button name	function
	Insert New Slide Master	Inserts a new blank slide master thumbnail below the current slide-title master pair
	Insert New Title Master	Inserts a new blank title master thumbnail below the current slide-title master pair
	Delete Master	Deletes a slide master thumbnail or a title master thumbnail from the presentation
	Preserve Master	Prevents a slide-title master pair from being accidentally deleted
	Rename Master	Provides a text box in which a new master name can be typed
	Master Layout	Opens the Master Layout dialog box; Master placeholders can be deleted and restored

Formatting Master Text

To ensure that you don't use a mixture of fonts and styles throughout the presentation, you can format text in a Master view. Changes made in a Master view are applied to the whole presentation. For example, if your presentation is part of a marketing campaign for a travel tour to the Middle East, you may decide to switch the title text font of the entire presentation from the standard Times New Roman font to a script font. You format text in the Master view the same way you format text in any of the other PowerPoint views. You can change text color, style, size, and bullet type in the Master view. When you change a bullet type, you can use a character bullet symbol from a font, a picture bullet from the Clip Organizer, or an image that you scan in. You decide to make a few formatting changes to the Master text placeholder of your presentation.

STEPS

1. **Make sure the slide master for the first presentation design template appears in the Slide pane, click Window on the menu bar, then click Arrange All**
   This ensures that your screen matches the figures in this book.

2. **Click Click to edit Master text styles in the first line of text in the Master text placeholder**
   Clicking I anywhere in a Master view selects the entire line of text.

3. **Click the Bold button B on the Formatting toolbar, then click the Shadow button S on the Formatting toolbar**
   The first line of text becomes bold with a shadow; it is now more prominent on the slide.

4. **Right-click Second level in the Master text placeholder, then click Bullets and Numbering on the shortcut menu**
   The Bullets and Numbering dialog box opens. Notice that there is also a Numbered tab that you can use to create sequentially numbered or lettered bullets.

5. **Click Customize, click the Font list arrow, then click Wingdings 3**
   The available bullet choices change.

6. **Click the scroll arrows to locate the arrow symbol shown in Figure E-3, click the arrow symbol, then click OK**

7. **Click the Color list arrow, click the red color (fourth from the left in the top row), click OK, then click a blank area of the slide**
   A red arrow replaces the second-level bullet. The second-level bullet is more visible now that the bullet symbol is changed and formatted.

8. **Click the Normal View button, then click the Slide 5 thumbnail in the Slides tab**
   Compare your screen to Figure E-4.

9. **Click the Save button on the Standard toolbar to save your changes**

FIGURE E-3: Symbol dialog box

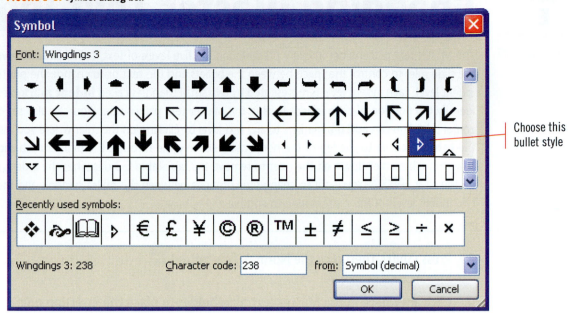

Choose this bullet style

FIGURE E-4: Slide 5 with modified text and bullet styles

First-level text is bold and shadowed

New bullet in second-level text

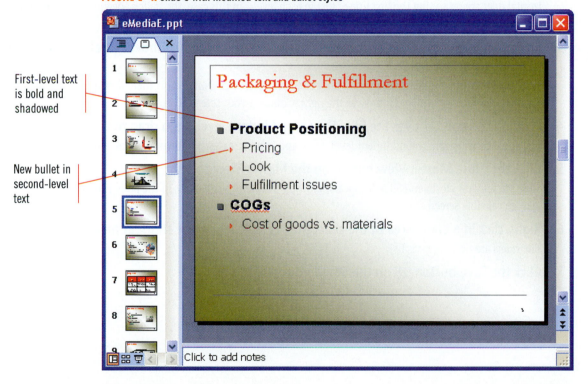

Clues to Use

Exceptions to the slide master

If you change the format of text on a slide and then apply a different template to the presentation, the slide that you formatted retains the text formatting changes you made. These format changes that differ from the slide master are known as exceptions. Exceptions can only be changed on the individual slides where they occur. For example, you might change the font and size of a particular text object on a slide to make it stand out and then decide later to add a different template to your presentation. The text you formatted before you applied the template is an exception and it is unaffected by the new template. Another way to override the slide master is to remove the master graphics on one or more slides. You might want to do this to get a clearer view of your slide text. Click Format on the menu bar, click Background, then click the Omit background graphics from master check box to select it.

Changing Master Text Indents

The Master text placeholder in every presentation has five levels of text, called **indent levels**. You can use the slide ruler to control the space between the bullets and the text or to change the position of the whole indent level. Each indent level is represented by two small triangles called **indent markers** on the ruler that identify the position of each indent level in the Master text placeholder. You can also set tabs on the horizontal ruler. You can add tab markers to any text level by clicking on the ruler where you want the tab. Click the **tab indicator** to the left of the horizontal ruler to cycle through the different tab alignment options. Drag the tab marker down off the ruler to remove the tab. Table E-2 describes the indent and tab markers on the ruler. You want to change the distance between the bullet symbols and the text in the first two indent levels of the presentation to emphasize the bullets.

STEPS

1. **Press [Shift], then click the Normal View button**
   Slide Master view appears.

2. **Click anywhere in the Master text placeholder to place the insertion point, click View on the menu bar, then click Ruler**
   The horizontal and vertical slide rulers for the Master text placeholder appear. The indent markers on the horizontal ruler are set so that the first line of text in each level—in this case, the bullet—begins to the left of subsequent lines of text. This is called a **hanging indent**.

3. **Position the pointer over the left indent marker of the first indent level, then drag to the ½" mark on the ruler**
   The space between the first-indent level bullet and text increases. Notice also that all of the indent markers for the other four indent levels move to the right. Compare your screen to Figure E-5.

4. **Position the pointer over the of the second indent level, then drag to the 1⅛" mark**
   The space between the second indent level bullet and text increases as shown in Figure E-6.

5. **Click the Close Master View button on the Master View toolbar**
   Slide Master view closes and Slide 5 appears, showing the increased indents in the body text object. The rulers take up valuable screen area.

6. **Right–click in a blank area of the slide, then click Ruler on the shortcut menu**
   The rulers are no longer visible.

7. **Click the Save button on the Standard toolbar**

TABLE E-2: Indent and Tab Markers

symbol	name	function
▽	**First line indent marker**	Controls the position of the first line of text in an indent level
⌂	**Left indent marker**	Controls the position of subsequent lines of text in an indent level
L	**Left tab stop**	Aligns tab text on the left
⅃	**Right tab stop**	Aligns tab text on the right
⊥	**Center tab stop**	Aligns tab text in the center
⊥·	**Decimal tab stop**	Aligns tab text on a decimal point

FIGURE E-5: Slide Master with first-level, left indent marker moved

Tab indicator

First-line indent marker of the first indent level

Left-indent marker of the first indent level

First-level indent increases

Vertical ruler

Horizontal ruler

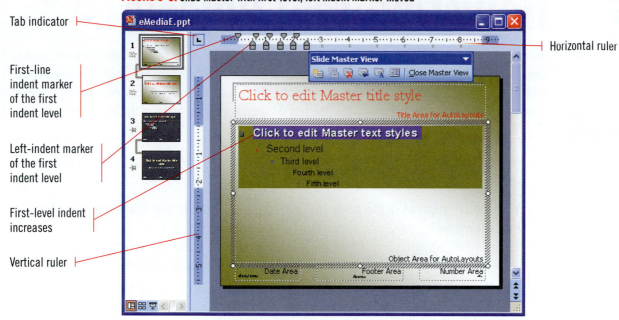

FIGURE E-6: Slide Master with second-level, left indent marker moved

Left-indent marker of the second indent level

Second-level indent increases

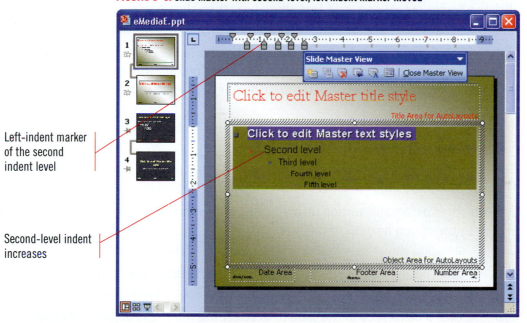

Clues to Use

Restoring the master layout

If a master placeholder is missing or deleted from a master view, you can click the Master Layout button ⊞ on the Slide Master View toolbar to reapply the placeholder. Clicking the Master Layout button opens the Master Layout dialog box, as shown in Figure E-7. Click the placeholder check box to reapply the placeholder. Each master view has its own Master Layout dialog box.

FIGURE E-7: Master Layout dialog box

Adjusting Text Objects

You have complete control over the placement of your text on PowerPoint slides. With the **text anchor** feature, you can adjust text position within text objects or shapes to achieve the best look. If you want your text to fill more or less of the slide, you can adjust the spacing between lines of text, called **leading** (rhymes with "wedding"). You decide to adjust the text position and line spacing of the text object on Slide 11.

1. **Click the Slide 11 thumbnail in the Slides tab**

   Slide 11 appears in the slide pane.

2. **Press [Shift], right-click the body text object, then click Format Placeholder on the shortcut menu**

   Pressing [Shift] when clicking a text object ensures that the entire text object is selected. The Format AutoShape dialog box opens. The text would look better centered in the text box.

> **TROUBLE**
>
> If the Format AutoShape dialog box prevents you from seeing the slide, drag it out of the way.

3. **Click the Text Box tab, click the Text anchor point list arrow, click Middle Centered, then click Preview**

   Compare your Format AutoShape dialog box to Figure E-8. The text moves to the middle center of the text object. To make it easier to select, resize the text object.

4. **Click the Resize AutoShape to fit text check box, then click Preview**

   The text object shrinks to fit the text. The text object would look better with a fill color behind the text.

> **QUICK TIP**
>
> You can also drag the Transparency scroll box to the desired percentage.

5. **Click the Colors and Lines tab, click the Color list arrow in the Fill section, click the teal color (second from right in row below Automatic Fill Color button, labeled Follow Accent and Hyperlink Scheme Color), click the Transparency up arrow until 60% appears, then click OK**

   The text object is filled with a teal color. The bulleted lines are a little too close together.

6. **Click Format on the menu bar, then click Line Spacing**

   The Line Spacing dialog box opens. Line spacing can be measured in lines or points. Change the measurement method to points when you need a more precise line spacing measurement.

7. **Click the After paragraph section up arrow four times so that 0.2 appears, click Preview, then drag the dialog box out of the way**

   The space, or leading, after each paragraph bulleted item increases. The text is easier to read.

8. **Click the Line spacing section up arrow until 2 appears, then click Preview**

   Compare your Line Spacing dialog box to Figure E-9. The line spacing between the text lines increases.

9. **Click OK, click a blank area of the slide to deselect the main text object, then save your changes**

   Compare your screen to Figure E-10.

Changing margins around text in shapes

You can also use the Text Anchor Point command to change the margins around a text object to form a shape that suits the text better. Right-click the shape, click Format Placeholder, click the Text Box tab, then adjust the Internal margin settings. Click Preview to see your changes before you apply them to the shape.

FIGURE E-8: Format AutoShape dialog box

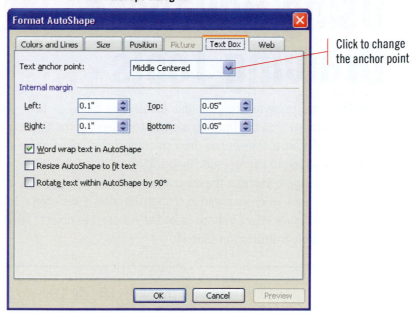

Click to change the anchor point

FIGURE E-9: Line Spacing dialog box

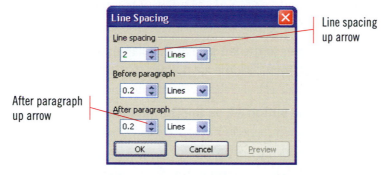

Line spacing up arrow

After paragraph up arrow

FIGURE E-10: Slide showing formatted body text object

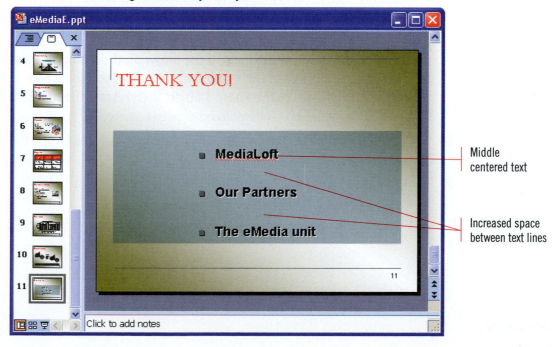

Middle centered text

Increased space between text lines

Using Advanced Drawing Tools

PowerPoint has powerful tools on the AutoShapes menu to help you draw all types of shapes. The AutoShapes menu is on the Drawing toolbar. For example, the Curve tool allows you to create a free-form curved line, the Arc tool helps you draw smooth, curved lines and pie-shaped wedges, and the Connector line tool allows you to connect AutoShape objects with a line. Once you have drawn a shape, you can format and rearrange it to create the effect you want. As you work with different objects in PowerPoint there may be an occasion when you need to change the order of the objects to achieve a desired result. The Order command moves an object in front of or behind another object. The Connector line tool works great to complete a diagram on Slide 10.

STEPS

1. **Click the Slide 10 thumbnail in the Slides tab, click the AutoShapes menu button on the Drawing toolbar, point to Connectors, then click the Straight Arrow Connector button**
   The pointer changes to +.

2. **Move the + pointer to the right side of the Phase 2 object until it changes to ⬦ and blue dots appear around the object, then click the blue dot on the right side of the Phase 2 object**
   See Figure E-11. The blue dots are anchor points for the connector arrow.

3. **Move the + pointer to the left side of the diamond object when you see the left blue dot inside the pointer, then click the ⬦ pointer to place the right side of the connector arrow**
   A red circle appears at either end of the connector arrow, indicating that the arrow connects the two objects.

4. **Click the Line Style button ≡ on the Drawing toolbar, then click the 2¼ pt line style**
   The line style of the arrow connector changes to a thicker weight.

5. **Click the Arrow Style button ⬄ on the Drawing toolbar, click More Arrows, then click the Colors and Lines tab in the Format AutoShape dialog box**
   The arrow would look better with a more distinct shape.

6. **Click the End size list arrow in the Arrows section, click the Arrow R Size 8 button (second button, last row), then click OK**
   The style of the arrow on the connector line changes to a more distinct style.

7. **Place the + pointer over the head of the arrow on the diamond shape, drag the connector arrow to the left side of the Phase 3 object, when you see a blue dot inside the ⬦ pointer on the left side of the Phase 3 object then release the mouse button**
   The arrow connector crosses over the diamond shape and connects the Phase 2 and Phase 3 objects.

8. **Click the Draw menu button on the Drawing toolbar, point to Order, then click Send to Back**
   The arrow connector line moves behind the diamond shape.

9. **Click in a blank area of the slide, then save the presentation**
   Compare your screen to Figure E-12.

FIGURE E-11: Slide showing Connector anchor points

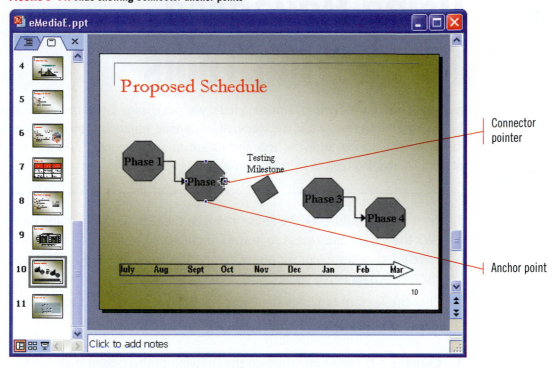

Connector
pointer

Anchor point

FIGURE E-12: Slide showing formatted connector arrow

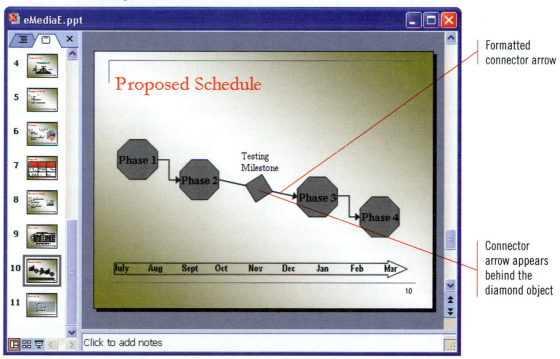

Formatted
connector arrow

Connector
arrow appears
behind the
diamond object

Clues to Use

Drawing a freeform shape

A freeform shape can consist of straight lines, freehand (or curved) lines, or a combination of the two. To draw a freeform shape, click the AutoShapes menu button, point to Lines, then click the Freeform button 🕝. Drag the pointer to draw the desired shape (the pointer changes to a pencil as you draw), then double-click when you are done. To draw a straight line with the Freeform tool, click where you want to begin the line, drag the pointer, then double-click to deactivate the Freeform tool. To edit a freeform object, right-click the object, then click Edit Points on the shortcut menu.

UNIT

E

PowerPoint 2003

Using Advanced Formatting Tools

With the PowerPoint advanced formatting tools, you can change formatting attributes such as fill texture, 3-D effects, and shadow for text and shapes. If you like the attributes of an object, you can use the Format Painter to pick up the attributes and apply them to another object. ⬛ You decide to use the advanced formatting tools to enhance the diagram Slide 10.

STEPS

1. **Press [Shift], right-click the Phase 1 object, click Format AutoShape on the shortcut menu, click the Colors and Lines tab in the Format AutoShape dialog box if it is not already selected, click the Color list arrow in the Fill section, then click Fill Effects**
   The Fill Effects dialog box opens.

QUICK TIP

The name of the texture appears below the samples.

2. **Click the Texture tab, click the Paper bag thumbnail (second square in the fifth row), click OK, then click OK again**
   The paper bag texture fills the shape.

QUICK TIP

When you click ⬛, you can click one of the 3-D styles on the shortcut menu. The default 3-D style is Style 1, the first style in the first row.

3. **Click the 3-D Style button ⬛ on the Drawing toolbar, then click 3-D Settings**
   The 3-D Settings toolbar appears.

4. **Click the Depth button ⬛ on the 3-D Settings toolbar, then click 36 pt**
   A 3-D effect is applied and the depth of the 3-D effect lengthens from the default of 0 points to 36 points.

5. **Click the Direction button ⬛ on the 3-D Settings toolbar, click the middle effect in the top row, as shown in Figure E-13, then click the Close button ✖ on the 3-D Settings toolbar**
   The 3-D effect changes to the bottom of the object.

6. **With the Phase 1 object still selected, click the Font Color list arrow ⬛ on the Drawing toolbar, then click the white color (labeled Follow Background Scheme Color)**
   The other four objects would look better if they matched the formatted Phase 1 object.

7. **Double-click the Format Painter button ⬛ on the Standard toolbar, click each of the other four objects, then click ⬛ to turn off the Format Painter**
   Now all the objects on the slide have the same fill and 3D effects. When you use the Format Painter tool, it "picks up" the attributes of the object that is selected and copies them to the next object that you click. If you click the Format Painter button only once, it pastes the attributes of the selected object to the next object you select, then turns off automatically.

8. **Click in a blank area of the slide, then save your changes**
   Compare your screen to Figure E-14.

9. **Press [Home] to view Slide 1, click the Slide Show button ⬛, then view the presentation**

FIGURE E-13: Slide showing formatted 3-D object

Depth button

Direction button

Formatted object

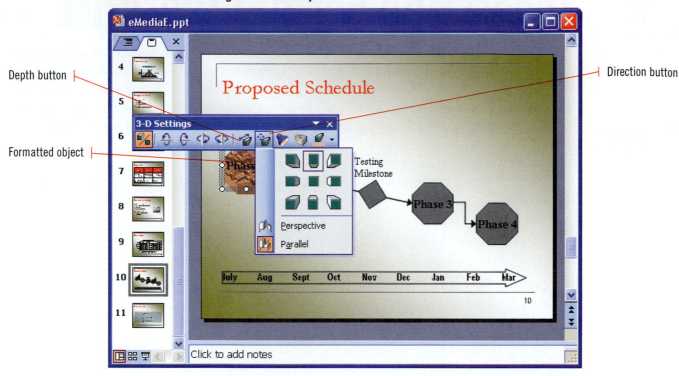

FIGURE E-14: Slide showing formatted objects

Font formatted

3-D depth and direction

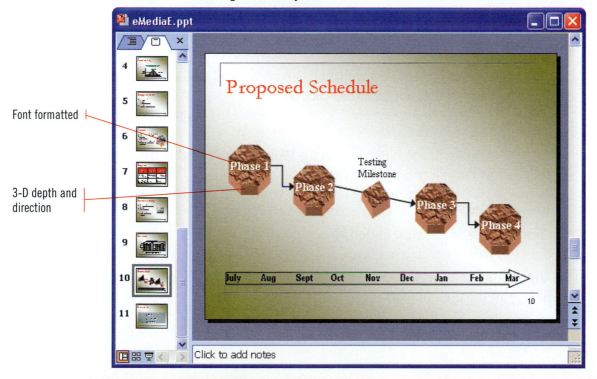

Clues to Use

Applying a color scheme to another presentation

If you develop a custom color scheme that you like, you can use the Format Painter tool to apply it to another presentation. To apply a color scheme from one presentation to another, open each presentation in Slide Sorter view, then use the Arrange All command on the Windows menu to arrange the Presentation windows side by side. Select a slide in the presentation with the color scheme you want to copy, double-click the Format Painter button on the Standard toolbar, then click each slide that you want to change in the other presentation.

Insert and Format WordArt

When you want to be artistic with text in PowerPoint, you can insert and format WordArt. Using WordArt you can apply a number of special effects to text, such as a predefined shape, a special shadow, or a stretched effect. A WordArt object is a drawn object and can be changed and formatted like any object that you create using the AutoShapes menu button. ██████ Use WordArt to create a simple logo for the new eMedia product. Because you want every slide to display the new WordArt object, you put the object on the Slide Master.

STEPS

1. **Click the Slide 2 thumbnail in the Slides tab, press [Shift], then click the Normal View button** ⊞

   Slide Master view appears.

2. **Click the Insert WordArt button** 🔷 **on the Drawing toolbar**

   The WordArt Gallery dialog box opens displaying all of the WordArt styles.

3. **Click the style shown in Figure E-15, then click OK**

   The Edit WordArt Text dialog box opens. The default font for the text is Times New Roman 36 pt.

4. **Type eMedia, then click OK**

   The WordArt object appears in the shape you selected using the default font in the middle of the slide. The WordArt toolbar, which you can use to format the WordArt object, also appears.

5. **Click the Format WordArt button** 🔷 **on the WordArt toolbar**

   The Format WordArt dialog box opens. The Colors and Lines tab is selected.

6. **Click the Color list arrow, click Fill Effects, click the Color 1 list arrow, click the red color (labeled Follow Title Text Scheme Color), then click OK**

TROUBLE

If you can't choose the exact position settings listed in this step, select settings that are close.

7. **Click the Position tab, click the Horizontal up arrow until 8.46 appears, click the Vertical down arrow until 0.26 appears, then click OK**

   The WordArt object moves to the upper-right corner of the slide and changes color. The object would look a little better with a different shape.

8. **Click the WordArt Shape button** 🔷 **on the WordArt toolbar, click the Triangle Down shape shown in Figure E-16, then click** ⊞

   The new WordArt object appears in the upper-right corner of the slide. Because you inserted the WordArt object on the slide master slide, the object appears on every slide in the presentation, except the title slide.

9. **Click the Slide Sorter View button** 🔡

   Figure E-17 shows the final presentation.

10. **Add your name to Slide 1 and as a footer to the notes and handouts, save your changes, then print the presentation as handouts (4 per page)**

FIGURE E-15: WordArt Gallery dialog box

Click this
WordArt style

FIGURE E-16: WordArt Shape button

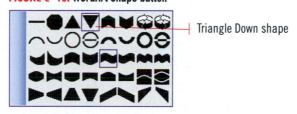

Triangle Down shape

FIGURE E-17: Completed presentation in Slide Sorter view

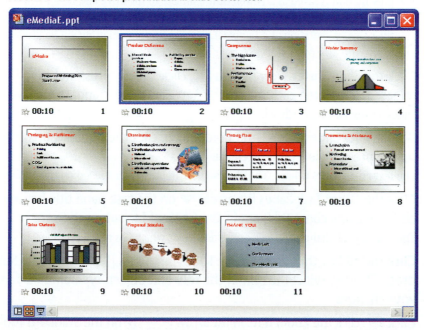

Creating a Template

You are not limited to using the standard templates PowerPoint provides or the ones you find on the Web. You can create your own template from scratch using a blank presentation, or you can modify any existing PowerPoint template or presentation that you have access to. For example, you might want to use your company's color as a slide background or incorporate your company's logo on the slides of a presentation. If you modify an existing template, you can keep, change, or delete any color, graphic, or font as necessary. When you are finished with your template, you can save it as a special template file in PowerPoint, which adds the .pot extension to the file. You can then use your customized template as a basis for new presentations. You are finished customizing your presentation for now. You want to save the presentation as a template so you and others can use this template for future company presentations.

STEPS

1. **Click the Slide 2 thumbnail in the Slides tab**

   Slide 2 appears in the Slide pane.

2. **Click File, click Save As to open the Save As dialog box, click the Save as type list arrow, click the down scroll arrow, then click Design Template (*.pot)**

   Because this is a template, PowerPoint automatically opens the Templates folder on your hard drive as shown in Figure E-18. Templates saved in this folder appear in the Slide Design task pane in PowerPoint.

3. **Click the Save in list arrow, locate the drive and folder where your Data Files are stored, drag to select the filename (currently eMediaE.pot) in the File name list box, type eMedia Template, then click Save**

   The presentation is saved as a PowerPoint template to the drive and folder where your Data Files are stored, and it appears in the PowerPoint window. Notice the .pot extension on the filename in the title bar, which identifies this presentation as a template. Because this presentation will be used as a template for other presentations, the slide content is no longer needed.

4. **Click the Slide Sorter View button, click Slide 3, press and hold [Shift], click Slide 11, release [Shift], then click the Cut button on the Standard toolbar**

   Slides 3 through 11 are deleted.

5. **Double-click Slide 2, press and hold [Shift], click the title text box, click both body text boxes, press [Delete], then release [Shift]**

   The text on Slide 2 is deleted. The placeholders are no longer needed on this slide.

6. **Click the Other Task Panes list arrow ▼ on the task pane title bar, click Slide Layout, then click the Blank content layout in the Content Layouts section**

   The slide layout changes to the Blank slide layout, which has no placeholders.

7. **Click the Slide 1 thumbnail in the Slides tab, press [Shift], click the Subtitle text object, press [Delete], select the text in the title text object, type eMedia Template, then save your changes**

8. **Click, click the Zoom button list arrow [100%] on the Standard toolbar, then click 100%**

   Figure E-19 shows the final template presentation in Slide Sorter view.

9. **Save your changes, print the template presentation as handouts (2 per page), close the presentation, then exit PowerPoint**

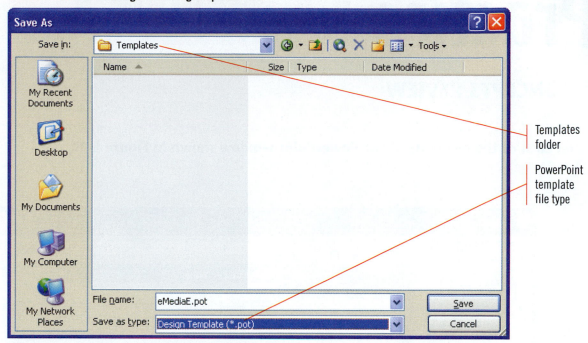

Templates folder

PowerPoint template file type

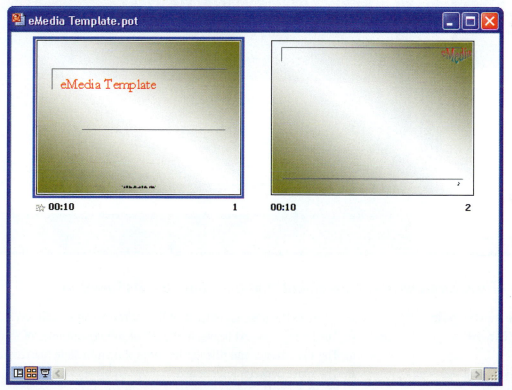

Clues to Use

Applying a template from another presentation

When you apply a design template from another presentation, you automatically apply the master layouts, fonts, and colors over the existing presentation's design template. To apply a template from another presentation, open the Slide Design task pane, then click the Browse hyperlink at the bottom of the pane. In the Apply Design Template dialog box, click All PowerPoint Files in the Files of type list box, then use the Look in list arrow to navigate to the presentation whose design you want to apply. (It does not have to be a template.) Click the presentation or template name, then click Apply.

PowerPoint 2003

Practice

▼ CONCEPTS REVIEW

Label each of the elements of the PowerPoint window shown in Figure E-20.

FIGURE E-20

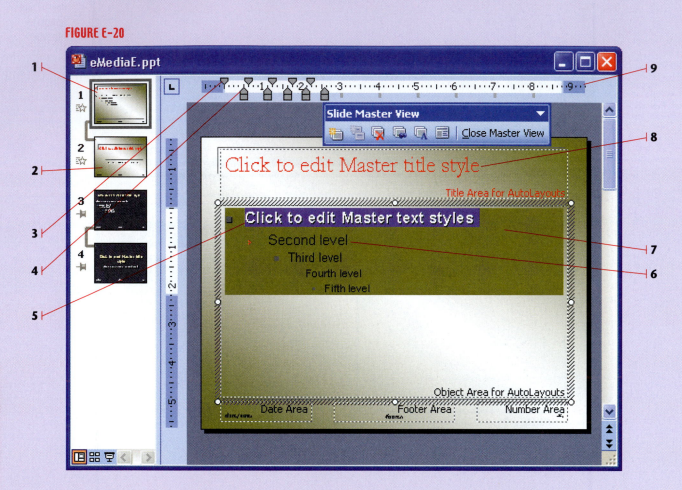

Match each of the terms with the statement that best describes its function.

10. **Slide-title master pair**
11. **First line indent marker**
12. **Indent levels**
13. **Exception**
14. **Leading**
15. **Hanging indent**

a. Controls the position of the first line of text in an indent level
b. The first line of text begins to the left of subsequent lines of text
c. The slide master and title master slides shown in Slide Master view
d. The space between lines of text
e. The five levels of text in a master text placeholder
f. A format change that is different from the slide master

Select the best answer from the list of choices.

16. What does the Slide Master view do in PowerPoint?
    a. Places figures that are used on the slides of the presentation.
    b. Stores information about the design template, text placeholders, and the color scheme.
    c. Saves a presentation to the Web.
    d. Previews a presentation before printing.

17. A background item on the slide master:
    a. Changes all views of your presentation.
    b. Is visible when you print handouts.
    c. Is a simple way to place an object on every slide of your presentation.
    d. Does not affect the slides of your presentation.

18. The small triangles that represent the position of each indent level in a text placeholder are:
    a. Indent markers.
    b. Indent levels.
    c. Ruler marks.
    d. Tabs.

19. Text anchor allows you to adjust the:
    a. Vertical space between lines of text.
    b. The distance between text objects.
    c. The diagonal space between letters.
    d. Text position within a text object.

20. The Format Painter button:
    a. Allows you to change the type of AutoShape.
    b. Is the feature you use to paint objects in PowerPoint.
    c. Changes the order of AutoShapes on a slide.
    d. Picks up and applies formatting attributes from one object or slide to another.

21. In PowerPoint, tabs:
    a. Have symbols for top and bottom tabs.
    b. Determine the location of margins.
    c. Can be aligned on the left, right, or center of a character or on a decimal.
    d. Can be only left- or center-aligned.

▼ SKILLS REVIEW

1. Format Master text.
    a. Start PowerPoint and open the presentation PPT E-2.ppt, then save it as **BookSource Report** to the drive and folder where your Data Files are stored.
    b. Go to Slide 2, switch to Slide Master view, then make the first-level bulleted item in the Master text placeholder bold.
    c. Change the bullet symbol of the first-level bullet to a character bullet. In Wingdings, select Character code 38, the seventh bullet from the left in the first row.
    d. Use the Bullets and Numbering dialog box to set the size of the bullet to 75% of the text.
    e. Change the bullet color to the yellow color (far-right color).
    f. Change the bullet symbol color of the second indent level to dark blue (third from left).
    g. Take the shadow attribute off the second-level bulleted item and change its font to Arial.
    h. Save the presentation.

2. Change Master text indents.

   a. Display the rulers.

   b. Move the left indent marker of the first-level bullet to just beyond the ½" mark and the second-level bullet to 1⅛".

   c. Hide the rulers, then save the presentation. Compare your screen to Figure E-21.

   d. Switch to Normal view.

FIGURE E-21

3. Adjust text objects.

   a. Press [Shift], right-click anywhere in the body text object on Slide 2, then click Format Placeholder on the shortcut menu.

   b. Click the Text Box tab.

   c. Set the text anchor point to Top Centered.

   d. Adjust the internal margin on the left and right sides to 0.5 and preview your change.

   e. Select the Resize AutoShape to fit text check box, preview it, and click OK.

   f. Select the entire text object. (*Hint*: Press [Shift] while clicking the object.)

   g. Change the line spacing to 0.75 lines, preview it, then click OK.

   h. Move the text object up and to the left about ½".

   i. Save your changes.

4. Use advanced drawing tools.

   a. Go to Slide 4.

   b. Use the Elbow Connector to connect the left corner of the Warehouse diamond to the top corner of the Regional Warehouse diamond.

   c. Use the Straight Connector to connect the right side of the Regional Warehouse diamond to the left side of the Individual Stores diamond.

   d. Use the Elbow Connector to connect the top corner of the Individual Stores diamond to the right corner of the Warehouse diamond.

   e. Select all three of the connector lines, make them 3 points wide, then deselect them.

   f. Change the dash style of the connector line connecting the Regional Warehouse diamond to the Individual Stores diamond to the Square Dot, dashed line style.

   g. Change the arrow style of the two elbow connector lines to Arrow Style 10.

   h. Deselect all objects, then save your changes.

5. Use advanced formatting tools.

   a. Go to Slide 1.

   b. Select the entire text object in the lower-right corner of the slide.

   c. Use the Texture tab in the Fill Effects dialog box to apply the White Marble texture to the object. (*Hint*: Read the description of the selected texture in the box under the textures.)

   d. Change the font to 20 pt. Arial.

   e. Double-click the Format Painter to pick up the format of the selected text box on the title slide and apply it to each of the diamond objects on Slide 4, then deselect the Format Painter and all objects.

   f. Use the 3-D Style button to apply 3-D Style 7 to the objects on Slide 4.

   g. Click the 3-D Color list arrow on the 3-D Settings toolbar, then click the blue color (Follow Accent Scheme Color).

   h. Deselect all objects, close the 3-D Settings toolbar, then save your changes.

6. Insert and format WordArt.

  a. Go to Slide 5.

  b. Create a new slide, then apply the Blank slide layout to the new slide.

  c. Create a WordArt object. In the WordArt Gallery dialog box, select the fifth style in the third column.

  d. Type the text, **Moving Toward Excellence**.

  e. Drag the bottom right sizing handle of the WordArt object at least an inch.

  f. Change the shape of the WordArt object to the Curve Down shape.

  g. Drag the WordArt object to the middle of the slide, then save your changes.

  h. View the presentation in Slide Sorter view.

  i. Add your name to the notes and handouts footer, print the presentation as Handouts, six slides per page.

7. Create a template.

  a. Open the Save As dialog box, then save the presentation as a Design Template (*.pot), named **BookSource Template** to the drive and folder where your Data Files are stored.

  b. Delete Slides 3, 4, 5, and 6, delete all the text in the text objects on Slide 2, then delete the clip art on Slide 2.

  c. Go to Slide 1, delete the text in the Subtitle text object, then type **BookSource Template** in the title text object in place of the current text.

  d. Save the presentation template, then print the presentation as handouts, two slides per page.

  e. Close the presentation and exit PowerPoint.

▼ INDEPENDENT CHALLENGE 1

You are the finance director at ZIPPO Records in Los Angeles, CA. ZIPPO Records specializes in alternative music, Rap, and Hip Hop. As a growing record company, your business is looking for investment capital to expand its business markets and increase sales. It is your responsibility to develop the outline and basic look for a standard presentation that the president can present to various investors.

You will complete an outline and choose a custom background for the presentation. You'll need to create a presentation consisting of at least six slides. Assume the following about ZIPPO Records:

- ZIPPO Records has been in business for 12 years.
- ZIPPO Records currently has 32 recording contracts. ZIPPO wants to double that during the next two years.
- ZIPPO Records has five superstar recording groups, including the groups Jam It and The Skunk.

  a. Open the file PPT E-3.ppt from the drive and folder where your Data Files are stored, then save it as **ZIPPO** to the location where your Data Files are stored.

  b. Enter text into the title and main text placeholders of the slides.

  c. Format the Master text placeholder by changing master text indents and bullet styles.

  d. Add clip art and format the presentation using PowerPoint formatting tools.

  e. Use advanced drawing and formatting tools to create a unique look.

  f. Create one slide that has at least two AutoShapes connected by connectors.

  g. Include WordArt in one slide.

  h. Add your name to the notes and handouts footer, save the presentation, then print the slides of your final presentation as handouts in pure black and white.

  i. View the presentation in Slide Show view, then close the presentation and exit PowerPoint.

▼ INDEPENDENT CHALLENGE 2

You are the owner of Down Under Catering in Brisbane, Queensland, Australia. You have built your business on private parties, wedding receptions, and special events over the last five years. To expand, you decide to cater to the business community by offering executive meals and business luncheons. Use PowerPoint to develop a presentation that you can use to gain corporate catering accounts.

Create an outline and modify the look of a presentation. You will create your own material to complete the slides of the presentation. Assume the following about Down Under:

- Down Under Catering has 15 full-time employees and 20 part-time or on-call staff.
- Down Under Catering handles catering jobs up to 500 people.
- Down Under Catering is a full-service catering business providing cost estimates, setup, complete preparation, service personnel, and cleanup.

   a. Open the file PPT E-4.ppt from the drive and folder where your Data Files are stored, then save it as **DUCatering**.

   b. Switch to the Outline tab and create a presentation outline. Add your name to the notes and handout footer.

   c. Customize your presentation by formatting the Slide Master.

   d. Search PowerPoint clip art and add a koala bear to both the slide master and the title master. Format the clip art as necessary.

   e. Use the PowerPoint advanced drawing and formatting tools to give your presentation a unique look. Be sure to use 3-D effects, and Fill Effects.

   f. Switch to the last slide and change the text anchor and line spacing to create the best look.

   g. Add and format a WordArt object.

   h. Add transitions and animation effects.

   i. Save and print the presentation as handouts, two slides per page.

   j. View the presentation in Slide Show view.

Advanced Challenge Exercise

- Save this presentation as a template, name the template **Catering Template**, then save it to the drive and folder where your Data Files are stored.
- Delete all the slides except the first slide and the last slide.
- Add two additional design templates (title-master pairs) to the template.
- Print the slides of your final template.

   k. Close the presentation template and exit PowerPoint.

▼ INDEPENDENT CHALLENGE 3

You are a computer game designer for eNetGames, an Internet interactive game developer. One of your jobs is to develop new interactive game concepts and present the information at a company meeting. Develop a 10- to 15-slide presentation that promotes two of the new interactive games concepts you've developed. Use PowerPoint clip art and shapes to enhance your slides. Use a PowerPoint template, design one of your own, or copy one from another presentation. Use the following game ideas in your presentation or create two of your own.

- **Space Raiders** is an interactive game that puts you in one of four different futuristic situations, where you are a space law enforcement officer trying to prevent an evil villain from destroying Earth.
- **SUB Command** is an adventure game in which you are a submarine commander during the Cold War trying to prevent a nuclear holocaust between the United States and the Soviet Union. Assume that there are four different game scenarios.

Create your own information, but assume the following:

- The product is designed for adults and children ages 13 and up.
- The cost of product development is estimated to be $300,000.
- Development time is three months.

   a. Open a new presentation and save it as **eNetGames** to the drive and folder where your Data Files are stored.

   b. Plan the story line of how the software was developed using five or more slides. Plan the beginning and ending slides. What do you want your audience to know about the product idea?

c. Use clip art and shapes to enhance the presentation. Change the bullet and text formatting in the Master text and title placeholders to fit the subject matter.

d. Use advanced drawing and formatting tools to create a unique look.

e. Add your name to the notes and handouts footer, then save the presentation.

Advanced Challenge Exercise

- Open the Slide Design task pane, click Browse at the bottom of the task pane, then locate where your Data Files are stored for this unit.
- Locate the file eMedia Template.pot, then click Apply.
- Click Yes in the dialog box that opens to place all of the templates in the presentation.
- Go to the Slide Master view, locate the eMedia logo on the slide master slide, then delete it.

f. Print the final presentation as handouts in pure black and white.

g. View the presentation Slide Show view, close the presentation, and exit PowerPoint.

▼ INDEPENDENT CHALLENGE 4

You are the travel coordinator for Mediaquest Inc., a large graphic multimedia development company in Seattle, WA. One of the benefits Mediaquest offers its employees is the option to vacation at a destination planned by the company. Your job is to find a reasonable vacation spot and then negotiate with travel companies for reduced group rates that are charged to Mediaquest employees if they choose to utilize the benefit. Once you negotiate a contract with a travel organization, you create a brief presentation that outlines the vacation benefit packages for the employees.

Plan and create an 8- to 10-slide presentation that details the vacation package for the current year. Develop your own content, but assume the following:

- The vacation package is a 7-day Alaskan cruise or a 7-day Mexican cruise.
- Air travel originates from the Seattle/Tacoma Airport (SeaTac).
- Cruises can be booked on one of two different cruise lines.
- The price is 30% off the listed price based on double occupancy.
- Mediaquest employees can book a cruise anytime during the current year.

You'll need to find the following information on the Web:

- Price and schedule information. (*Hint*: Remember the price you list in the presentation is 30% lower than the listed price you find on the Internet.)
- A list of ships with a brief description of at least one ship from each cruise line.
- Ports of call for one Mexican cruise and one Alaskan cruise.

a. Open a new presentation, and save it as **Mediaquest** to the location where your Data Files are stored.

b. Add your name as the footer on all slides and handouts.

c. Connect to the Internet, then use a search engine to locate Web sites that have information on Mexican and Alaskan cruises.

d. Review at least two Web sites that contain information about Mexican cruises and Alaskan cruises. Print the Home pages of the Web sites you use to gather data for your presentation.

e. Decide on two cruise lines to use in your presentation, then create slides that present the information.

f. Use clip art and shapes to enhance the presentation. Change the bullet and text formatting in the Master text and title placeholders to fit the subject matter.

g. Apply a template to the presentation and customize the slide background appropriately.

h. Use advanced drawing and formatting tools to create a unique look.

i. Use text formatting as necessary to make text visible and help emphasize important points.

j. Spell check the presentation, view the final presentation in Slide Show view, then save the final version.

k. Print the slides and handouts, then close the presentation and exit PowerPoint.

PowerPoint 2003

▼ VISUAL WORKSHOP

Create two slides that look like the examples in Figures E-22 and E-23. Be sure to use connector lines. Add your name to the handout footer, then save the presentation as **Product**. Print the Slide view of the presentation. Submit the final presentation as printed handouts.

FIGURE E-22

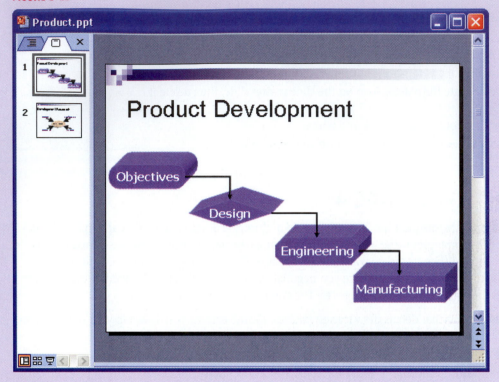

FIGURE E-23

UNIT F
PowerPoint 2003

Enhancing Charts

OBJECTIVES

Insert data from a file into a datasheet
Format a datasheet
Change the chart type
Change chart options
Work with chart elements
Animate charts and add sound
Embed an organization chart
Modify an organization chart

A PowerPoint presentation is first and foremost a visual communication tool. Slides that deliver information with relevant graphics have a more lasting impact than slides with plain text. Graphs and charts often communicate information more effectively than words alone. Microsoft Graph and Microsoft Organization Chart are built-in PowerPoint programs that allow you to easily create and embed graphs and charts in your presentation. In this unit, you update the data and enhance the appearance of a Microsoft Graph chart and then you create and format an organization chart showing the management structure of the eMedia division.

Inserting Data from a File into a Datasheet

With Microsoft Graph, you can enter your own data into a datasheet using the keyboard, or you can import existing data from a spreadsheet file that was created in a program like Microsoft Excel. The Accounting Department just gave you an updated sales projection spreadsheet in an Excel file. You need to insert this updated data into the chart on Slide 11 of the eMedia presentation. To do this, you open Microsoft Graph and import the data from Excel into the presentation.

STEPS

1. **Start PowerPoint, open the presentation PPT F-1.ppt from the drive and folder where your Data Files are stored, then save the presentation as eMediaF**

2. **Click View on the menu bar, click Task Pane, click Window on the menu bar, then click Arrange All**

   Your screen now matches the figures in this book.

3. **Click the Slide 11 thumbnail in the Slides tab, then double-click the chart object on the slide in the Slide pane**

   When you double-click an embedded object in PowerPoint, the object opens in the program in which the object was created. The Graph chart and datasheet open and the Graph menu bar and toolbars are now displayed. You can replace the data in the Graph datasheet with data that is in an Excel worksheet.

4. **Click the Dept. cell in the datasheet (first cell, first column)**

   Clicking a cell identifies where the imported data begins in the datasheet.

   TROUBLE

   If you don't see 📥 on the Standard toolbar, click a Toolbar Options button 📄 on a toolbar to locate buttons that are not visible on your toolbar.

5. **Click the Import File button 📥 on the Graph Standard toolbar**

   The Import File dialog box opens.

6. **Navigate to the drive and folder where your Data Files are stored, click PPT F-2.xls, then click Open**

   Excel files have an .xls file extension. The Import Data Options dialog box opens. Because you want to import the entire sheet and overwrite the existing cells, all the options are correctly specified.

7. **Click OK**

   The chart changes to reflect the new data you imported into the datasheet. Compare your screen to Figure F-1. Notice the column headings, the gray boxes along the top of the datasheet, now show lettered headings. The row headings, the gray boxes along the left side of the datasheet, now show numbered headings. Spreadsheets identify columns with letters and rows with numbers.

   QUICK TIP

   To include data that you've previously excluded, double-click the control box again.

8. **Double-click the column D column heading**

   The data in column D is grayed out, indicating that it is excluded from the datasheet and will not appear in the chart. See Figure F-2.

9. **Click the Save button 💾 on the Graph Standard toolbar**

FIGURE F-1: Datasheet showing imported data

Import File button

Column heading

Row heading

Imported data

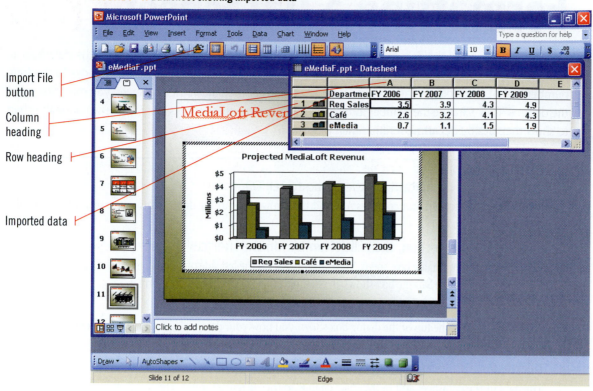

FIGURE F-2: Datasheet showing excluded column

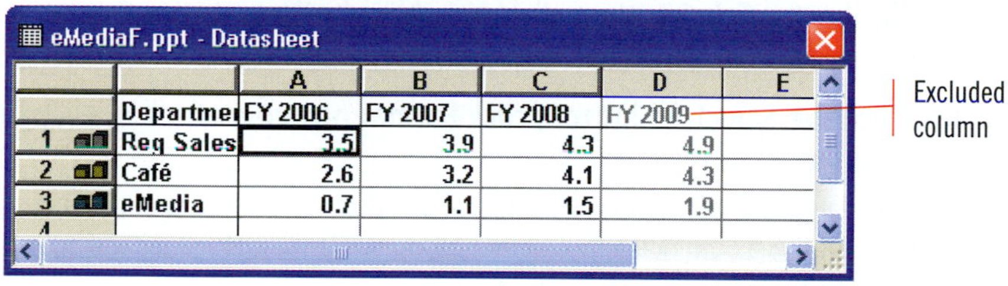

Excluded column

PowerPoint 2003

Clues to Use

Data series and data series markers

Each column or row of data in the datasheet is called a data series. Each data series has corresponding data series markers in the chart, which are graphical representations such as bars, columns, or pie wedges. Figure F-3 shows how each number in the eMedia data series appears in the chart. Notice the correlation between the data in the third row of the datasheet and the data series markers in the chart.

FIGURE F-3: Graph chart and datasheet

eMedia data series

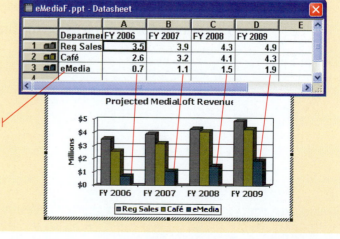

Formatting a Datasheet

Once you've imported the data from another file, it can be helpful to modify and format the datasheet to make your data easier to view and use. With Graph, you can make simple formatting changes to the font, number format, and column size in your datasheet. To format the data in the datasheet, you must first select the data.  Change the number format to show the sales numbers as currency, then change the chart to show the sales by department rather than by year.

1. **Click cell A1 in the datasheet, then drag to cell D3**

   You selected the cells in four columns A-D and three rows 1-3. All the data in this group of continuous cells, or range, is selected.

2. **Right-click the selection, then click Number on the shortcut menu**

   The Format Number dialog box opens. The Category list on the left side of the dialog box indicates the available format categories. The Sample box shows an example of the currently selected format.

3. **Click Currency in the Category list**

   The Sample box at the top of the dialog box shows you how your data will appear in the currency format with a dollar sign and two decimal places. See Figure F-4.

> **QUICK TIP**
>
> To quickly change the number format to Currency, click the Currency Style button $ on the Graph Formatting toolbar.

4. **Click OK**

   The data in the datasheet and in the chart change to the currency format. The numbers represent millions of dollars, so the number of digits after the decimal place needs to be adjusted.

5. **Click Format on the menu bar, click Number, click the Decimal places down arrow once to display 1, click OK, then click anywhere in the datasheet**

   The datasheet columns can be adjusted to better fit the data.

> **QUICK TIP**
>
> To quickly adjust the column width to fit the widest cell of data in a column, double-click the border to the right of the column heading box.

6. **Click the Select All button, click Format on the menu bar, click Column Width, then click Best Fit**

   The datasheet looks better with the columns containing the numbers narrowed and the first column wide enough to accommodate the column heading. The Best Fit command automatically resizes the selected column widths to fit the widest label in each column.

7. **Click any cell in the datasheet, then click the By Column button ⊞ on the Graph Standard toolbar**

   The chart is more helpful showing the sales figures along the Value axis, in a series by column. The icons now appear in the column headings in the datasheet to indicate that the fiscal year in the columns is now graphed in the chart. The column headings now appear in the legend. Compare your datasheet to Figure F-5.

8. **Click the Close button ⊠ in the datasheet**

   The datasheet closes, but Graph is still open.

9. **Click the Save button ⊟ on the Graph Standard toolbar**

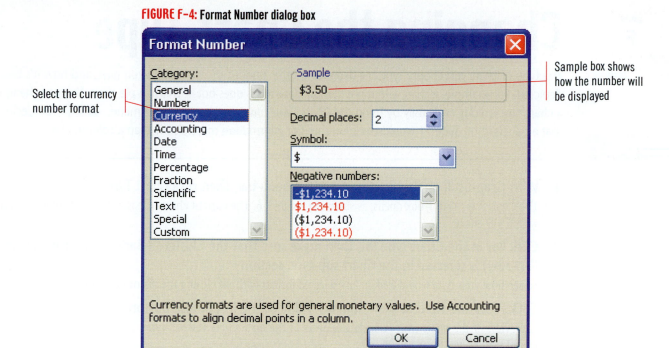

FIGURE F-4: Format Number dialog box

Select the currency number format

Sample box shows how the number will be displayed

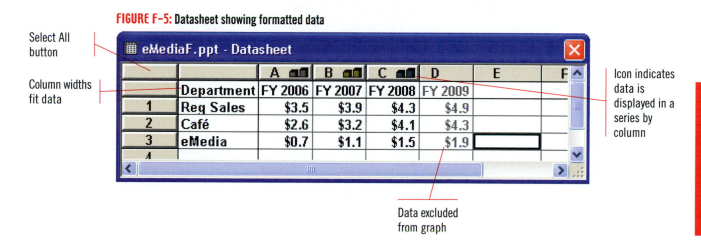

FIGURE F-5: Datasheet showing formatted data

Select All button

Column widths fit data

Icon indicates data is displayed in a series by column

Data excluded from graph

Clues to Use

Formatting datasheets and charts

You can format data in both datasheets and in charts created by Graph. Sometimes it's easier to view the numbers in the datasheet after they have been formatted; other times, you may want to manipulate the numbers after they have been placed into a chart to get a better picture. After you've formatted the data in the datasheet, the formatting changes will be reflected in the chart; however, formatting changes made to the data in the chart will not be reflected in the datasheet.

Changing the Chart Type

The type of chart you choose typically depends on the amount of information you have and how it's best depicted. For example, a chart with more than six data series does not fit well in a pie chart. You can change a chart type quickly and easily by using the Chart Type command on the Chart menu. You decide that a bar chart on Slide 11 would communicate the information more clearly than a column chart.

1. **With Graph still open, click Chart on the menu bar, then click Chart Type**

   The Chart Type dialog box opens, as shown in Figure F-6. The current chart type is a clustered column chart with a 3-D effect.

2. **Click Bar in the Chart type list, then make sure that the Clustered Bar subtype (first chart, first row) is selected in the Chart sub-type section**

   To see how your data would look in any selected format without closing the dialog box, you can preview it.

3. **Click Press and Hold to View Sample and hold the left mouse button**

   A preview of the chart with your data appears in the area where the sub-types had been listed. This chart would look better if it were 3-D.

4. **Release the left mouse button, then click the Clustered Bar with a 3-D visual effect sub-type in the Chart sub-type section (first chart, second row)**

   The box below the sub-type section shows that you have selected a clustered bar with a 3-D visual effect.

5. **Click Press and Hold to View Sample and hold the left mouse button**

   The preview shows a 3-D version of the column chart.

6. **Release the left mouse button, then click OK**

   The chart type changes to the 3-D bar chart. Compare your screen with Figure F-7.

7. **Click the Save button on the Graph Standard toolbar**

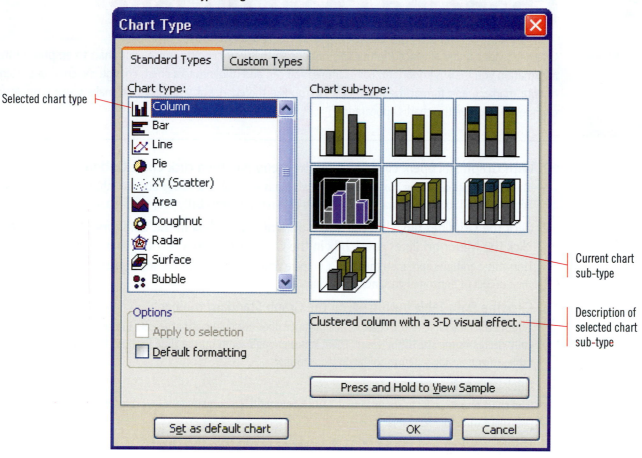

Selected chart type

Current chart sub-type

Description of selected chart sub-type

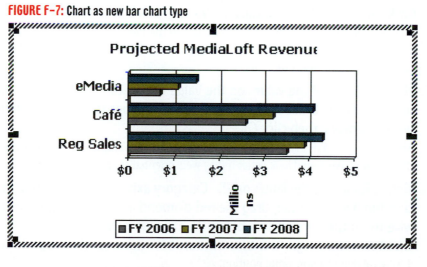

Clues to Use

Customized chart types

There are two ways to create customized chart types: you can use PowerPoint custom types or customize your own. To use PowerPoint custom types, click the Custom Types tab in the Chart Type dialog box. You will see more chart types such as Floating Bars and Area Blocks. To customize your own, click any chart series element (such as a bar) in the chart window, click Format on the menu bar, then click Selected Data Series to open the Format Chart dialog box. Use the Patterns, Shape, Data Labels, or Options tabs to customize the color, shape, or appearance of the selected element. You can reuse the chart type you have created through customization. To make your customized chart a type in the Chart Type dialog box, click the User-defined option button, click Add, then assign a name to it and click OK. To use it later, click the User-defined option button in the Chart Type dialog box and then click the name of the chart you added.

Changing Chart Options

Graph provides many advanced formatting options so that you can customize your chart to emphasize the information you think is important. For example, you can add gridlines to a chart, change the color or pattern of data markers, and format the axes. You like the chart but you decide to make some formatting changes to improve the chart's appearance.

STEPS

1. **With Graph still open, click Chart on the menu bar, then click Chart Options**

   The Chart Options dialog box opens. The Titles tab is selected. The dialog box has tabs for Axes, Gridlines, Legend, Data Labels, and Data Table. Gridlines help separate and clarify data series markers.

QUICK TIP

To quickly add major gridlines, click the Category Axis Gridlines button on the Standard toolbar.

2. **Click the Gridlines tab, click the Major gridlines check box in the Category (X) axis section, click the Minor gridlines check box in the Category (X) axis section, then click OK**

   Horizontal gridlines appear on the chart. Compare your screen to Figure F-8. Adding minor gridlines increases the number of horizontal gridlines in the chart.

3. **Click the Data Table button on the Graph Standard toolbar**

   Adding the data table to the chart in this instance does not help clarify the data in the chart and it dramatically decreases the size of the chart. There is not enough room on the slide for both the chart and the data table, so you decide to return to the previous format.

4. **Click again**

   The chart returns to its previous format. Data labels, which place data numbers directly on the chart, take up less space than the data table.

TROUBLE

If the incorrect dialog box opens, you double-clicked the wrong chart element or double-clicked too slowly. Close the dialog box, then double-click the correct chart element.

5. **Double-click one of the FY 2008 data series markers in the chart**

   The Format Data Series dialog box opens.

6. **Click the Data Labels tab, click the Value check box to select it, then click OK**

   The FY 2008 values from the datasheet appear to the right of the columns, as shown in Figure F-9. Adding data labels to one of the data series makes the series easier to identify. You can also change the way the numbers appear on the horizontal axis.

7. **Right-click one of the values on the Value axis, click Format Axis on the shortcut menu to open the Format Axis dialog box, click the Number tab, click the Decimal places up arrow until 1 appears, then click OK**

   After the Format Axis dialog box closes, the values on the Value axis display one decimal point. The labels on the Category axis would look better if they were oriented at an angle.

8. **Right-click any of the labels on the Category axis, click Format Axis on the shortcut menu, click the Alignment tab, drag the red diamond in the Orientation section counterclockwise to set the Degrees text box to 15, then click OK**

   The labels on the Category axis are oriented at a 15-degree angle. The Category axis title would look better if it were rotated to a horizontal position.

9. **Right-click the Millions axis title, click Format Axis Title on the shortcut menu, click the Alignment tab if it is not already selected, drag the red diamond in the Orientation section clockwise to set the Degrees text box to 0, then click OK**

10. **Click a blank area of the slide twice, then save your presentation**

    Compare your screen to Figure F-10.

FIGURE F-8: Chart with new gridlines

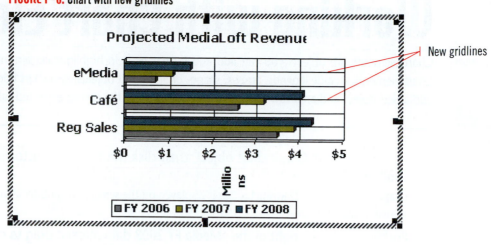

New gridlines

FIGURE F-9: Chart showing data labels

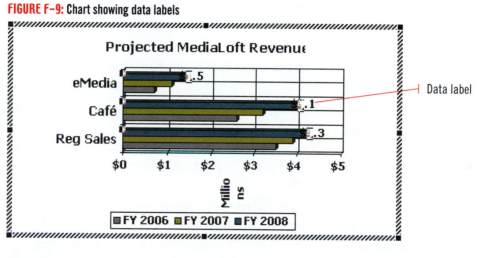

Data label

FIGURE F-10: Modified chart

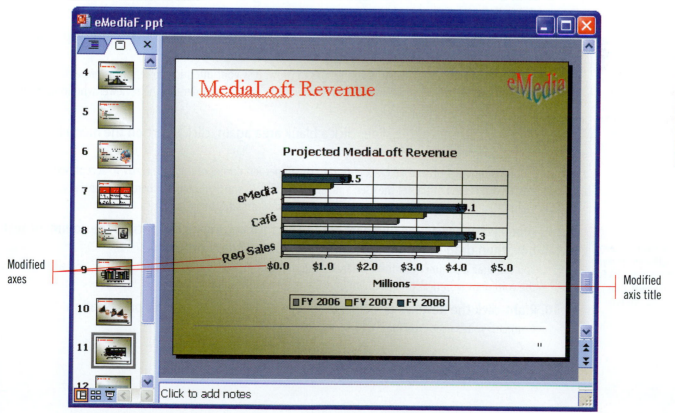

Modified axes

Modified axis title

Working with Chart Elements

Chart elements are objects you can add and format to help highlight certain information in your chart. Chart elements include legends, arrows, shapes or lines, text objects, and chart titles. You decide to add a text object and an arrow object to draw attention to the strong expected sales in the café in 2008.

1. **Double-click the Graph chart object, then click the Text Box button ▦ on the Drawing toolbar**

   Graph opens and the Drawing toolbar is displayed on the screen. The pointer changes to ╂ when it is positioned in the chart area.

2. **Position ╂ to the right of the eMedia FY 2008 data marker, drag to create a text box, then type Exceeds Goal!**

   The default size of the text, 8 point, is too small, so you change the color and size of the text to make it easier to read.

3. **Drag I over the text to select it, click the Font Size list arrow ⬚ 8 ▾ on the Formatting toolbar, then click 18**

4. **Click the Font Color list arrow 🅰 ▾ on the Drawing toolbar, click the Red color, then click a blank area of the chart**

   If the text object is not where you want it, position the pointer over the edge of the text object, then drag it to another position in the chart. Compare your screen to Figure F-11. Arrows can help connect text objects to data markers in a chart.

5. **Click the Arrow button ➘ on the Drawing toolbar, position ╂ under the word "Goal," then drag an arrow from the text object to the end of the Café FY 2008 data marker**

   Arrows can be formatted so they are more prominent, or fit a design theme.

6. **Click the Arrow Style button ⇄ on the Drawing toolbar, click More Arrows, then click the Color list arrow in the Line section**

7. **Click the Red color (first column, third row), click the Weight up arrow until 2 pt appears, then click OK**

   You are satisfied with the way the chart looks for now. It is your intention to send this presentation out for review when you complete your work, so you decide to write a comment to the reviewer who looks over the sales numbers in this chart.

8. **Click a blank area of the slide, click a blank area again, click Insert on the menu bar, then click Comment**

   A new comment icon and text box appear in the upper-left corner of the slide ready to accept text. The comment icon has the initials of the user, you, and a number. Comments are numbered sequentially; this is comment 1. The Reviewing toolbar also appears below the Standard toolbar.

9. **Type Please review the numbers in this chart for accuracy, click outside the comment text box, then drag the comment icon to the right of the chart title**

   You can drag a comment icon anywhere on the slide as well as edit the comment. Usually, you want to place the comment icon near the slide item on which you are commenting.

10. **Right-click the Reviewing toolbar, click Reviewing, then save your presentation**

    Compare your screen to Figure F-12.

FIGURE F-11: Chart showing new text object

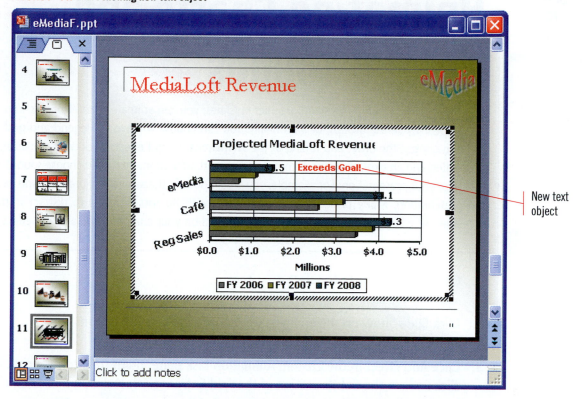

New text object

FIGURE F-12: Chart showing added chart elements and comment icon

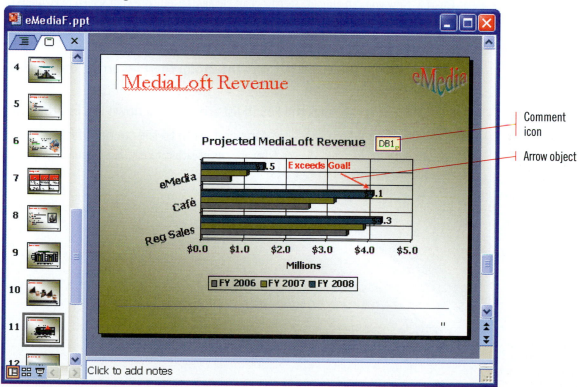

Comment icon

Arrow object

Clues to Use

Moving and sizing chart elements

To move a chart element, such as an arrow or the legend, you must first select the object to view its sizing handles, then drag the object to its new location. Make sure that the pointer is over the object's border when you drag it, not over a sizing handle. To change the size of a chart element, click the object to view its sizing handles, then drag a sizing handle.

Animating Charts and Adding Sounds

Just as you can animate bullets and graphics on slides, you can animate chart elements. You can have chart bars appear by series, groups, or individually. You can choose to have the legend and grid animated. You can also control the order and timing of the animations. Sound effects, including applause, a drum roll, a typewriter, and an explosion, can accompany the chart animation. Be sure to choose sounds that are appropriate for your presentation. For example, you would not use the screeching brakes sound in a serious financial presentation. Many presentations are effective with no sound effects to distract from the speaker's message.  You decide to animate the elements on your chart and add a sound effect.

STEPS

1. **Click the chart once to select it**
   Make sure you do not double-click the chart.

2. **Click Slide Show on the menu bar, then click Custom Animation**
   The Custom Animation task pane opens.

3. **Click Add Effect in the Custom Animation task pane, point to Entrance, click More Effects, click Fade in the Subtle section of the Add Entrance Effect dialog box, then click OK**
   The Fade animation effect is added to the chart, and the chart is added to the Effects list in the task pane as Chart 2. Now you can animate specific chart elements. Compare your screen to Figure F-13.

4. **Click the Chart 2 list arrow in the task pane, then click Effect Options**
   The Fade dialog box opens.

5. **Click the Chart Animation tab, click the Group chart list arrow, then click By element in category**

6. **Click the Effect tab, click the Sound list arrow, scroll down the list, then click Push**

7. **Click OK, then watch the Slide pane and listen to the sound effect**
   The chart grid appears first, then each bar appears in each category, accompanied by the Push sound. Compare your screen to Figure F-14.

FIGURE F-13: Screen showing Custom Animation task pane

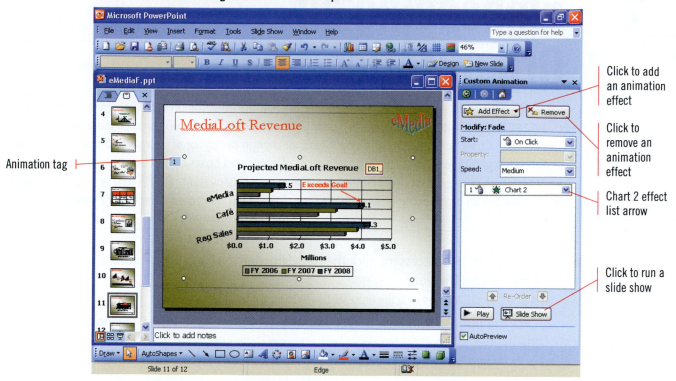

Animation tag

Click to add an animation effect

Click to remove an animation effect

Chart 2 effect list arrow

Click to run a slide show

FIGURE F-14: Slide showing animated Graph chart

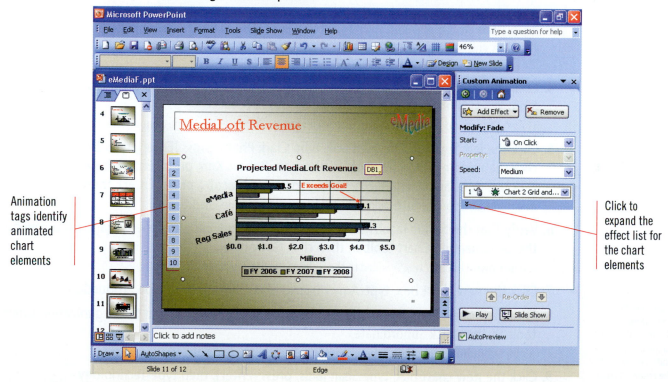

Animation tags identify animated chart elements

Click to expand the effect list for the chart elements

Clues to Use

Adding voice narrations

If your computer has a sound card and a microphone, you can record a voice narration that plays with your slide show. To record a narration, click Slide Show on the menu bar, then click Record Narration. If you want the recording to be linked to the presentation, click the Link narrations in check box. If you do not select this option, the recording will be embedded in the presentation. If the Record Narration command is not available, then you do not have the necessary hardware.

Embedding an Organization Chart

When you need to illustrate a hierarchical structure, such as the organization of a company or group, you can create and embed an organization chart in your presentation. To do so, you can click the Insert Diagram or Organization Chart button on the Drawing toolbar or change the layout of your slide to one of the Content layouts. An organization chart is made up of a series of connected boxes called chart boxes in which you can enter text, such as the names and job titles of people in your organization. ▓▓▓ You now turn your attention to creating an organization chart showing the management structure for the eMedia group.

STEPS

TROUBLE

If the text you type doesn't appear as the slide title, click in the title placeholder, then type it again.

1. **Go to Slide 11 if necessary, click the New Slide button** 🔲 **on the Formatting toolbar, then type eMedia Division**

   A new Slide 12 appears with the title eMedia Division.

2. **Click the Insert Diagram or Organization Chart button** 🔁 **on the Drawing toolbar**

   The Diagram Gallery dialog box opens. In the Diagram Gallery dialog box, you have the option to insert one of six diagrams. See Table F-1 for information on how to use the different diagrams. The Organization Chart option is selected.

3. **Click OK**

   An organization chart appears on the slide with the Organization Chart toolbar. See Figure F-15. The default organization chart contains four placeholder chart boxes. The chart box at the top of the window is a Manager chart box and the three chart boxes below it are Subordinate chart boxes. To enter text in a chart box, select the chart box and then type.

4. **Click the Manager chart box (top chart box) if it is not already selected, type Recina Sipin, press [Enter], then type Manager**

   The text is entered into the text box. The spell checker identifies the name as not in the dictionary.

5. **Click the left Subordinate chart box, type Clark Pham, press [Enter], type Development, click the middle Subordinate chart box, type Robert Koo, press [Enter], type Marketing, click the right Subordinate chart box, type Sarina Jacobs, press [Enter], then type Sales**

   Additional chart boxes can be added to the default organization chart.

6. **Verify that the Sarina Jacobs chart box is still selected, click the Insert Shape list arrow on the Organization Chart toolbar, then click Coworker**

   A new Coworker chart box is added to the right of the Sarina Jacobs chart box.

QUICK TIP

Each chart box you add automatically decreases the size of all the chart boxes and their text so that the entire organization chart will fit on the slide.

7. **Click the new chart box, type Amy Hilliard, press [Enter], then type Production**

8. **Click the Robert Koo chart box, click the Insert Shape list arrow on the Organization Chart toolbar, then click Subordinate**

   A new Subordinate chart box appears under the Robert Koo chart box.

9. **Click the new chart box, type Sean Janis, press [Enter], then type Technology**

10. **Click a blank area of the slide to deselect the chart, then save your changes**

    Compare your screen to Figure F-16.

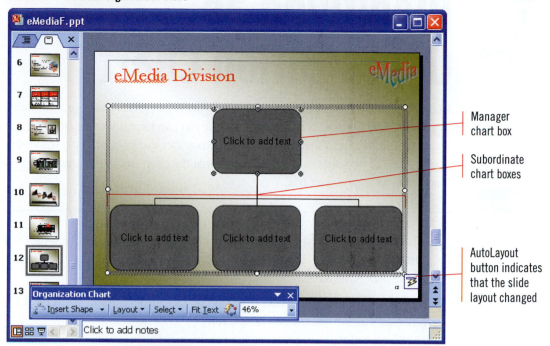

Manager chart box

Subordinate chart boxes

AutoLayout button indicates that the slide layout changed

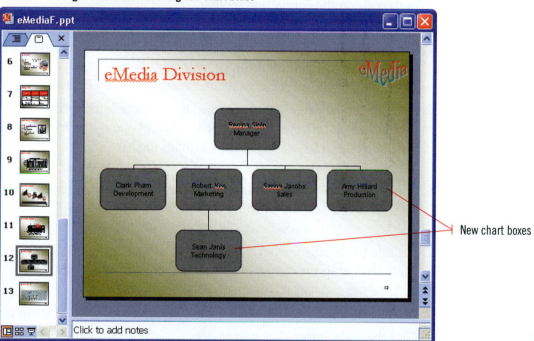

New chart boxes

TABLE F-1: Diagram Gallery dialog box

diagram icon	diagram name	diagram used to show
	Organization Chart	hierarchical relationships
	Cycle Diagram	a process with a continuous cycle
	Radial Diagram	relationships with a core element
	Pyramid Diagram	foundational relationships
	Venn Diagram	overlap between elements
	Target Diagram	steps toward a goal

UNIT
F
PowerPoint 2003

Modifying an Organization Chart

After you add all the chart boxes you need for your organization chart, you can format the chart boxes and connecting lines. Attributes of a chart box that you can format include fill color, line color, line style, font size, color, and type and shadow style. Chart boxes can also be rearranged within the organization chart as desired. 🎨 To enhance the slide, you format the chart boxes and connecting lines of the organization chart and rearrange a chart box.

STEPS

1. Click the Recina Sipin chart box, click the Select button on the Organization Chart toolbar, then click Branch

   All the chart boxes are selected and ready to be formatted.

2. Click the Fill Color list arrow 🎨 on the Drawing toolbar, then click the olive green color (labeled Follow Accent Scheme Color)

   The fill color of the chart boxes changes to olive green.

3. Click the Font list arrow on the Formatting toolbar, click Arial Black, then click the Shadow button ⓢ on the Formatting toolbar

   Compare your screen to Figure F-17.

4. Click the Shadow Style button 🔲 on the Drawing toolbar, then click Shadow Style 6 (second style in the second row)

   A shadow is applied to each chart box. A darker shadow might make the chart boxes stand out more on the slide.

5. Click 🔲, click Shadow Settings to open the Shadow Settings toolbar, click the Shadow Color list arrow 🔲, click the teal color (Follow Accent and Hyperlink Scheme Color), then click the Close button ❌ on the Shadow Settings toolbar

   Thicker connecting lines between the chart boxes would look better.

6. Click Select on the Organization Chart toolbar, click All Connecting Lines, click the Line Style button ☰ on the Drawing toolbar, then click 3 pt

   The connector lines are now thicker. You can move chart boxes within the chart.

   > **QUICK TIP**
   > Only chart boxes at the end of a branch can be moved to another position in the organization chart.

7. Position the mouse pointer over the edge of the Sean Janis chart box so that it changes to ⚓, then drag the chart box on top of the Clark Pham chart box

   Compare your organization chart to Figure F-18.

8. Click the Slide Show button 🖵 to view Slide 12, then press [Esc] to end the slide show

9. Click the Slide Sorter View button 🔠

   Compare your screen to Figure F-19. Slides 11 and 12 are the only slides you modified in this unit.

10. Click the Normal View button 🖼, add your name to Slide 1 and as a footer to the notes and handouts, save your presentation, print the presentation as handouts (6 slides per page), then close the presentation and exit PowerPoint

FIGURE F-17: Organization chart showing formatted chart boxes

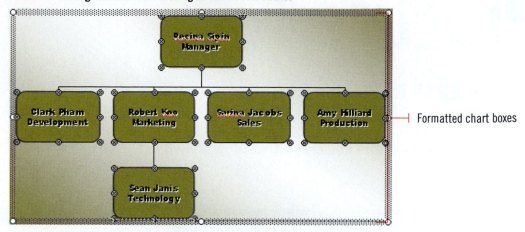

Formatted chart boxes

FIGURE F-18: Organization chart showing rearranged chart box

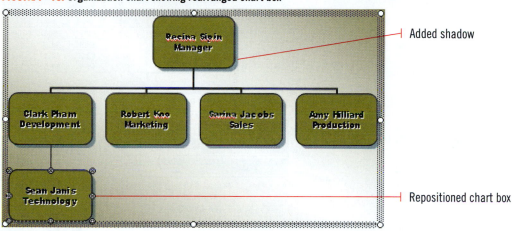

Added shadow

Repositioned chart box

FIGURE F-19: Final presentation in Slide Sorter view

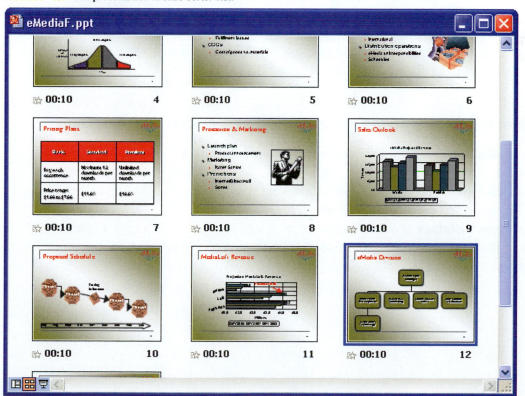

Practice

▼ CONCEPTS REVIEW

Label each element of the PowerPoint window shown in Figure F-20.

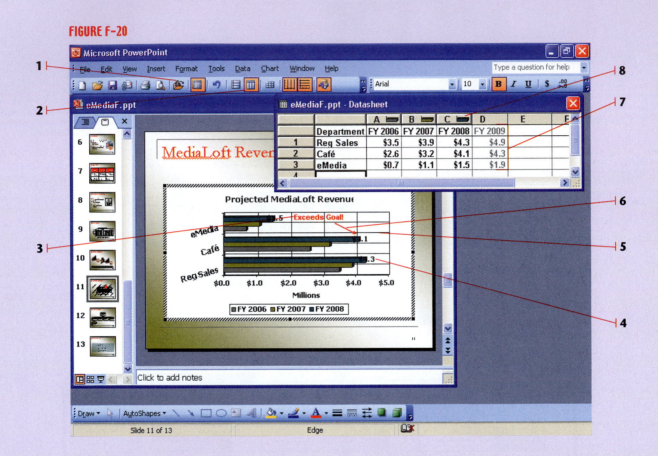

FIGURE F-20

Match each of the terms with the statement that best describes its function.

9. The type of diagram you would use to show relationships with a core element

10. Lines that separate and clarify data series markers

11. A group of connected cells in a datasheet

12. Graphical representation of a data series

13. The type of diagram you would use to show foundational relationships

    a. Pyramid
    b. Gridlines
    c. Data series markers
    d. Radial
    e. Range

Select the best answer from the list of choices.

14. **What does it mean when data is grayed out in the datasheet?**
    a. The data is excluded from the datasheet.
    b. The data is excluded from the chart.
    c. The data has been accidentally deleted.
    d. The data appears only in the chart.

15. **What is a data series?**
    a. A graphical representation of a data series marker.
    b. A range of data.
    c. All of the data elements in a chart.
    d. A column or row of data.

16. **Which of the following is not true about chart types?**
    a. A chart with eight data series would fit well in a pie chart.
    b. The type of chart you choose usually depends on the amount of data.
    c. You can create a custom chart type using the Custom Types tab in the Chart Type dialog box.
    d. Examples of custom chart types include area blocks, floating bars, and outdoor bars.

17. **Which is not true about animation sound effects?**
    a. Most presentations are ineffective without some sort of animation sound.
    b. A sound effect can distract from the speaker's message.
    c. Animation sound effects include a drum roll and an explosion.
    d. A sound effect can accompany a chart animation.

18. **What is the chart or diagram called that is made up of connected chart boxes?**
    a. Venn diagram.
    b. Organization chart.
    c. Graph chart.
    d. Target diagram.

19. **Based on what you know of organization charts, which of the following data would best fit in an organization chart?**
    a. Spreadsheet data.
    b. A company's annual financial numbers.
    c. A company's database mailing list.
    d. A company's division structure.

20. **What do chart gridlines help you do?**
    a. Combine data series markers.
    b. Separate and clarify data series markers.
    c. See chart elements, such as text or lines.
    d. Change the chart type.

▼ SKILLS REVIEW

1. **Insert data from a file into a datasheet.**
    a. Start PowerPoint, open the presentation PPT F-3.ppt, then save it as **London Publishing** to the drive and folder where your Data Files are stored.
    b. Select Slide 3, then open Microsoft Graph.
    c. Click the upper-left cell in the datasheet, then import Sheet1 of the Excel file PPT F-4 .xls from the drive and folder where your Data Files are stored into the Graph datasheet.
    d. Exclude the Mystery column from the chart, then save the chart.

2. **Format a datasheet.**
    a. Select the range of cells from cell A1 to cell D5.
    b. Format the datasheet numbers with Currency format.

    c. Change the format of the datasheet numbers so that they have no decimal places. (*Hint*: Click the Decrease Decimal button on the Standard toolbar twice.)

    d. Adjust the column width for all the columns to Best Fit. Compare your datasheet with Figure F-21.

    e. Close the datasheet.

    f. Save the chart.

3. Change the chart's type.

    a. Change the chart type to a clustered 3-D column chart.

    b. Change the chart to a line chart with markers displayed at each data value, preview it, then accept it.

    c. Save the chart.

4. Change chart options.

    a. Show major gridlines on both the x and the y axes.

    b. Add a title to the y axis that reads **Thousands**.

    c. Save your changes.

5. Work with chart elements.

    a. Add a text box object in the upper-right corner of the chart for Liverpool Fiction sales.

    b. Add the text **A Record!** to the text box.

    c. Change the font size of the text to 22 point and the font to Times New Roman.

    d. Change the color of the text to blue.

    e. Add a blue arrow pointing from the text box to the appropriate data point.

    f. Format the arrow line as 3 point.

    g. Compare your chart with Figure F-22 and adjust the text box and arrow positions as necessary.

    h. Click a blank area of the slide, then save your changes.

6. Animate charts and add sounds.

    a. Animate the chart with the Entrance Fade effect.

    b. Animate the chart elements so they are introduced by series.

    c. Add the Arrow sound effect to the animation.

    d. In the Custom Animation task pane, click the Speed list arrow and change the speed to Fast.

    e. Preview the animation.

    f. Check the animation in Slide Show view, then save the presentation.

7. Embed an organization chart.

    a. Select Slide 4.

    b. Add an organization chart to the slide.

    c. At the top level, type **Sarah Wiley** as **Division Manager**.

    d. In the Subordinate chart boxes, type the following names and titles:

        Janice Britt, Distribution Manager

        Robert Sarhi, Purchasing Manager

        Evelyn Storey, Circulation Manager

FIGURE F-21

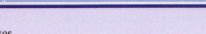

London Publishing.ppt - Datasheet

	2005 Fiscal Year	Fiction	Non-Fiction	Children's	Mystery
1	Victoria	$250	$230	$260	$250
2	Waterloo	$180	$200	$240	$300
3	Paddington	$120	$130	$115	$120
4	Euston	$130	$150	$110	$90
5	Liverpool	$320	$229	$100	$140

FIGURE F-22

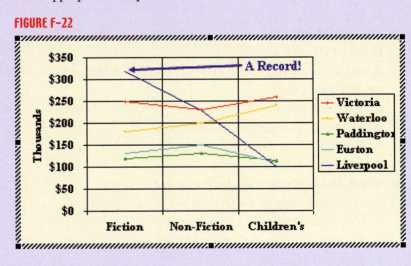

   e. Change the fill color for all the chart boxes to a light blue color.

   f. Change the line color for all the chart boxes to a dark purple color, then save your changes.

8. Modify an organization chart.

   a. Add an assistant chart box to the Sarah Wiley chart box.

   b. Drag the organization chart sizing handles to make the chart as big as possible.

   c. Enter **Kris Courter** as her **Special Assistant**.

   d. Add two Subordinate boxes to the Evelyn Storey chart box, and enter the following:

      Perry Jones, Purchase Orders

      Lynette Groshem, Financial Assistant

   e. Drag the Perry Jones chart box and the Lynette Groshem chart box so they are under the Robert Sarhi chart box.

   f. Select the Sarah Wiley chart box and change the font to 16 point.

   g. Format all the other chart boxes using the formatting characteristics from the Sarah Wiley chart box. (*Hint*: Use the Format Painter button.)

   h. Format the connecting lines to 3 point.

   i. Select Slide 1, then view the presentation in Slide Show view.

   j. Reduce the font size for all the text in the chart to 12 point. (*Hint:* Select the chart, then click the Decrease Font Size button on the Formatting toolbar twice.)

   k. Add your name to the notes and handouts footer.

   l. Save your changes, print the presentation as handouts (3 slides per page), then close the presentation and exit PowerPoint.

▼ INDEPENDENT CHALLENGE 1

You work for Ryers Associates, a business consulting company that helps small- and medium-sized businesses organize or restructure themselves to be more efficient and profitable. You are one of six senior consultants who works directly with clients. To prepare for an upcoming meeting with executives at ComSystems, a mobile phone communications company, you create a brief presentation outlining Ryers' typical investigative and reporting techniques, past results versus the competition, and the company's business philosophy.

The following is a sample of the type of work you perform as part of your duties at Ryers: You usually investigate a client's business practices for two weeks and analyze all relevant records. Once the initial investigation stage is complete, you submit a client recommendation report to your boss that describes the known problem areas, the consequences of the problems, the reasons for the problems, the recommended solutions, the anticipated results for each solution, the anticipated cost to the client for each solution, and Ryers' final professional recommendation. After your boss approves the client recommendation report, you prepare a full report for the client. If the client approves the plan, you develop a maintenance schedule (usually one year or less) to make sure the plan is implemented correctly.

   a. Open the file PPT F-5.ppt from the drive and folder where your Data Files are stored, then save it as **Ryers Presentation**.

   b. Think about the results you want to see, the information you need, and how you want to communicate the message. Sketch how you want your presentation to look.

   c. Create charts on Slides 3 and 4 using one of the charts available in the Diagram Gallery. Use the information provided in this Independent Challenge to show the various stages of investigation and reporting.

   d. Create a Graph chart on Slide 5 that shows how Ryers compares with two competitors. For example, you might illustrate the satisfaction level of Ryers clients compared to its competitors' clients or Ryers' consumer rating.

   e. Format the chart and add additional chart elements using the skills learned in this unit.

Advanced Challenge Exercise

   ■ Change the chart type of the chart on Slide 5 to a cylinder with a 3-D Column with a cylindrical shape sub-type.

   ■ Open the Format Axis dialog box for the Value axis, open the Scale tab, then change the Major unit from the default setting.

   ■ Change the Maximum scale on the Scale tab to a number that displays the values on the chart well.

PowerPoint 2003

f. Format the text on the slides. Modify the master views to achieve the look you want.

g. Spell check and save your presentation.

h. Add your name as a footer to the slides and handouts, print the slides of the presentation, then submit your presentation plan and printouts.

i. View the presentation in Slide Show view, close the presentation, and exit PowerPoint.

▼ INDEPENDENT CHALLENGE 2

This year, you have been selected by your peers to receive a national teaching award for the educational program that you created for disabled children in your home state of Vermont. In accepting this award, you have the opportunity to give a presentation describing your program's results since its introduction. You will give the presentation at an educator's convention in Washington, DC.

Plan and create a slide presentation describing your results. Create your own data, but assume the following:

- Over the last three years, 3,548 children in 251 classrooms throughout Vermont have participated in your program.
- Children enrolled in your program have shown at least a 7% improvement in skills for every year the program has been in effect.
- Children ages 4 through 12 have participated in the program.
- Money to fund the program comes from the National Education Association (NEA) and the State of Vermont Public School Department. The money goes to each participating school district in the state.
- Funding per child is $2,867 per school year. Funding per child in a regular classroom is $3,950 per year.

a. Think about the results you want to see, the information you need to create the slide presentation, and how your message should be communicated.

b. Create a presentation using a chart from the Diagram Gallery to build some of your slides. Think about how you can effectively show information in a chart.

c. Format the charts using PowerPoint's formatting features.

d. Use clip art, shapes, and a shaded background to enhance the presentation. Change the bullet and text formatting in the Master text and title placeholders to fit the subject matter.

e. Spell check and save the presentation as **Award** to the drive and folder where your Data Files are stored.

f. Add your name as a footer to the slides and handouts, then print the final slide presentation.

g. View the presentation in Slide Show view, close the presentation, and exit PowerPoint.

▼ INDEPENDENT CHALLENGE 3

MedTech Industries is a large company that develops and produces technical medical equipment and machines for operating and emergency rooms throughout the United States. You are the business manager, and one of your assignments is to prepare a presentation for the stockholders on the profitability and efficiency of each division in the company.

Plan and create a slide presentation that shows all the divisions and divisional managers of the company. Also, graphically show how each division performed in relation to its previous year's performance. Create your own content, but assume the following:

- The company has seven divisions: Administration, Accounting, Sales and Marketing, Research and Development, Product Testing, Product Development, and Manufacturing.
- Three divisions increased productivity by at least 15%.
- The presentation will be given in a boardroom using a projector.

a. Think about the results you want to see, the information you need to create the slide presentation, what type of message you want to communicate, and the target audience.

b. Use Outline view to create the content of your presentation.

c. Create a Graph chart, then insert the Excel file PPT F-6.xls into the datasheet.

▼ INDEPENDENT CHALLENGE 3 (CONTINUED)

Advanced Challenge Exercise

- Add one of the following entrance animation effects for the Graph chart: Blinds, Box, Diamond, or Fade.
- Change the effect options of the animation effect in the Chart Animation tab so that the data series markers of the chart appear by element, by category.
- In the Chart Animation tab deselect the Animate grid and legend check box.
- On the Custom Animation task pane change the Direction to Vertical and the Speed to Fast.

d. Create organization charts to help present the information you want to communicate.

e. Use clip art, pictures, or a shaded background to enhance the presentation, and format the content.

f. Save the presentation as **MedTech Industries** to the drive and folder where your Data Files are stored.

g. Add your name as a footer to the slides and handouts, then print the final slide presentation.

h. View the presentation in Slide Show view, close the presentation and exit PowerPoint.

▼ INDEPENDENT CHALLENGE 4

You are a PC game analyst for Potus Inc., a computer software research company. One of your responsibilities every quarter is to create a brief presentation that identifies the top three computer games based on industry and consumer reviews. In your presentation, you include charts that help define the data you compile.

Develop your own content, but assume the following:

- Each game has at least one defined mission or task.
- Consumer satisfaction of each game is identified on a scale of 1.0 to 10.0.
- There are three categories of games: Adventure, Action, and Strategy.

You'll need to find the following information on the Web:

- Consumer or industry reviews of three PC computer games.
- A description of each game, including the story line of the game or individual mission.
- The price of each game.

a. Open a new presentation, and save it as **3 Qrtr Review** to the drive and folder where your Data Files are stored.

b. Add your name as the footer on all slides and handouts.

c. Connect to the Internet, then use a search engine to locate Web sites that have information on PC computer games.

d. Review at least two Web sites that contain information about computer games. Print the Home pages of the Web sites you use to gather data for your presentation.

e. Using PowerPoint, create an outline of your presentation. It should contain between eight and 10 slides, including a title slide.

f. Include at least one chart that identifies consumer satisfaction numbers that you develop.

g. Create a diagram or organization chart that briefly explains the story line of one of the games.

h. Create a table that lists the price of each game.

i. Enhance the presentation with clip art or other graphics, an appropriate template and/or background, or other items that improve the look of the presentation.

j. Change the master views, if necessary, to fit your presentation.

k. Spell check, save the presentation, then view the presentation in Slide Show view.

l. Print the slides of the presentation as handouts (4 slides per page).

m. Close the presentation and exit PowerPoint.

▼ VISUAL WORKSHOP

Create two slides that look like the examples in Figures F-23 and F-24. Save the presentation as **Eastern Products**. Add your name as a footer on the slides, then save and print the presentation slides.

FIGURE F-23

FIGURE F-24

Working with Embedded and Linked Objects and Hyperlinks

OBJECTIVES

Embed a picture

Embed an Excel chart

Link an Excel worksheet

Update a linked Excel worksheet

Insert an animated GIF file

Insert a sound

Insert a hyperlink

Create a photo album

SAM

If you have a SAM user profile, you may have access to hands-on instruction, practice, and assessment of the skills covered in this unit. Log in to your SAM account and go to your assignments page to see what your instructor has assigned.

PowerPoint offers many ways to add graphic elements to a presentation. In this unit, you will learn how to embed and link objects. Embedded and linked objects are created in another program and then either stored in or linked to the PowerPoint presentation. In this unit, Maria Abbott asks you to create a brief presentation that outlines MediaLoft's Video Department using embedded and linked objects. She will use the slide presentation you create in a company meeting next week at MediaLoft's headquarters.

Embedding a Picture

You can embed more than 20 types of pictures, including JPEG File Interchange Format (**.jpg**), Windows Bitmap (**.bmp**), and Graphics Interchange Format (**.gif**) using the Insert Picture command. Frequently, a presentation's color scheme will not match the colors in pictures, especially photographs. In order to make the picture look good in the presentation, you may need to adjust the slide's color scheme, recolor the picture, or change the presentation's template. ███████ You want to embed a photograph on Slide 2 of the presentation you are working on for Maria. After you embed the picture you adjust the slide's color scheme to make the photograph look better.

STEPS

1. **Start PowerPoint, open the presentation PPT G-1.ppt from the drive and folder where your Data Files are stored, save the presentation as Video Report, click View on the menu bar, click Task Pane, click Window on the menu bar, then click Arrange All**

2. **Click Slide 2 in the Slides tab, click the Insert Picture button 🖼 on the Drawing toolbar, select the file PPT G-2.jpg from the drive and folder where your Data Files are stored, then click Insert**

   A picture with a travel theme appears in the center of the slide and the Picture toolbar opens.

   > **TROUBLE**
   > If the Picture tool-bar is in the way, move the toolbar to another part of the screen.

3. **Resize and drag the picture to match Figure G-1**

   A different slide background color would provide a better contrast for this picture.

4. **Click the Slide Design button 🖉 Design on the Formatting toolbar, then click the Color Schemes hyperlink in the Slide Design task pane**

   The Slide Design task pane opens, showing the available color schemes. There are nine standard color schemes from which to choose.

5. **Click each color scheme list arrow, then click Apply to Selected Slides to preview each of the color schemes for Slide 2**

   You can evaluate each color scheme as it is applied to the presentation. The color scheme in the first row and first column matches best with the picture colors.

   > **TROUBLE**
   > If you click Apply to All Slides by mistake, click the Undo button 🔄 ▾, then repeat Step 6.

6. **Click the blue color scheme list arrow (first row, first column), then click Apply to Selected Slides**

   Make sure you do not click Apply to All Slides or click the color scheme box, which is the same as applying the color scheme to all of the slides. The color scheme for Slide 2 changes to a blue background.

7. **Click a blank area of the slide, compare your screen to Figure G-2, then click the Save button 🖫 on the Standard toolbar**

FIGURE G-1: Slide showing embedded picture

Sizing handle

Notes entered in the notes pane

FIGURE G-2: Slide showing new color scheme

New slide title color

New slide background color

New bullet color

Clues to Use

Exporting a presentation

Sometimes it's helpful to use a word processing program like Word to create detailed speaker's notes or handouts. You might also want to create a Word document based on the outline of your PowerPoint presentation. To export a presentation to Word, click File on the menu bar, point to Send to, then click Microsoft Office Word. The Send to Microsoft Office Word dialog box opens and provides you with a number of document layout options from which to choose. Select a layout, click OK, and a new Word document opens with your embedded presentation or outline, using the layout you selected. To include text you enter in the notes pane of your slides, select one of the Notes layouts. If you want to export just the text of your presentation, you can save it as an outline in rich text format (.rtf format). You can view RTF documents in any word processing program. To do this, click File on the menu bar, click Save As, click Outline/RTF in the Save as type list box, then click Save.

Embedding an Excel Chart

When a chart is the best way to present information on a slide, you can create a chart using Microsoft Graph from within PowerPoint; however, for large amounts of data, it's easier to create a chart using a spreadsheet program like Excel. Then you can embed the chart file in your PowerPoint presentation and edit it using Excel tools. Excel is the chart file's **source program**, the program in which the file was created. PowerPoint is the **destination program**, the file into which the chart is embedded. ▧▧▧ Maria created an Excel chart showing MediaLoft's quarterly video sales. She wants you to include this chart in the presentation, so you embed it in a new slide.

STEPS

1. Click Slide 3 in the Slides tab, click the New Slide button 🔲 on the Formatting toolbar, then click the Title Only layout in the Slide Layout task pane
   The new Slide 4 is selected and appears in the Slide pane.

2. Type Quarterly Sales in the title placeholder

3. Click Insert on the menu bar, click Object, click the Create from file option button in the Insert Object dialog box, click Browse, locate the file PPT G-3.xls in the drive and folder where your Data Files are stored, click OK, then click OK in the Insert Object dialog box
   The chart containing the quarterly sales data appears on the slide. The text labels on the chart are too small to read. Because the chart is embedded, you can edit the chart using Excel formatting tools.

TROUBLE
If the Chart toolbar appears in the middle of your screen, drag it to the top of the screen.

4. Double-click the chart to open Microsoft Excel
   The Excel menu bar and Excel toolbars now appear on the screen.

5. Right-click the Chart Title, click Format Chart Title on the shortcut menu, click the Font tab in the Format Chart Title dialog box, click 28 in the Size list, then click OK
   The chart title is larger and more legible.

QUICK TIP
You can see if you selected the correct object on the graph because the name of the selected object appears in the Chart Objects box on the Chart toolbar.

6. Right-click the Value Axis Title, click Format Axis Title, click 24 in the Size list, click OK, click the Legend, then press [F4]
   The axis title and legend are now larger and easier to read. Pressing [F4] repeats the last formatting action in Excel.

7. Right-click the Value Axis, click Format Axis, click 22 in the Size list, click OK, click the Category Axis, then press [F4]
   Compare your screen to Figure G-3.

8. Double-click the chart area to the right of the chart title, click the Patterns tab in the Format Chart Area dialog box, click Fill Effects, click the Preset option button, click the Preset colors list arrow, scroll down, then click Silver

9. Click the Diagonal down option button in the Shading styles section, click OK, then click OK in the Format Chart Area dialog box
   The chart background becomes a shaded silver color.

10. Click outside the chart to exit Excel, click a blank area of the slide to deselect the chart object, then save the presentation
    Compare your screen to Figure G-4.

FIGURE G-3: Embedded chart with formatted text

Title text increased to 28 points

Formatted axis label

Formatted axes

Formatted legend

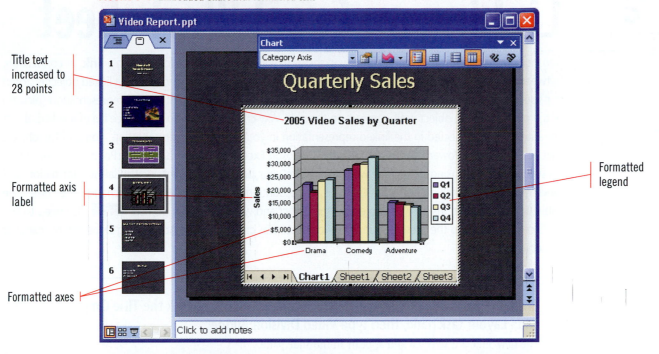

FIGURE G-4: Embedded chart with silver background

Silver chart background

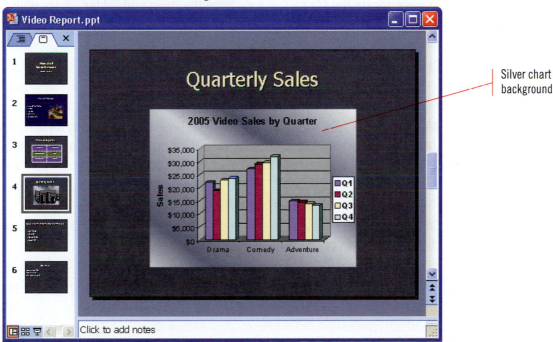

Clues to Use

Embedding a worksheet

You can embed all or part of an Excel worksheet in a PowerPoint slide. To embed an entire worksheet, go to the slide where you want to place the worksheet. Click Insert on the menu bar, then click Object. The Insert object dialog box opens. Click the Create from file option button, click Browse, locate and double-click the spreadsheet filename, then click OK. The worksheet is embedded in the slide. Double-click it to edit it using Excel commands as needed to work with the worksheet. To insert only a portion of a worksheet, open the Excel workbook and copy the cells you want to include in your presentation. Leave Excel and the source worksheet open, open the PowerPoint presentation, click Edit on the menu bar, then click Paste Special. To paste the cells as a worksheet object that you can edit in Excel, click Microsoft Excel Worksheet Object in the Paste Special dialog box, and then click OK.

Linking an Excel Worksheet

Another way to connect objects like Excel worksheets to your presentation is to establish a **link**, or connection, between the source file and the PowerPoint presentation. Unlike an embedded object, a linked object is stored in its source file, not on the slide, so when you link an object to a PowerPoint slide, a representation (picture) of the object, not the object itself, appears on the slide. Any changes made to the source file of a linked object are automatically reflected in the linked representation in your PowerPoint presentation. Some of the objects that you can link to PowerPoint include movies, Microsoft Excel worksheets, and PowerPoint slides from other presentations. Use linking when you want to be sure your presentation contains the latest information and when you want to include an object, such as an accounting spreadsheet, that may change over time. See Table G-1 for suggestions on when to embed an object and when to link an object. You need to link an Excel worksheet to the presentation. The worksheet was created by the Accounting Department manager earlier in the year.

STEPS

QUICK TIP

If you plan to do the steps in this unit again, be sure to make and use a copy of the Excel file PPT G-4.xls.

1. **Click the New Slide button** on the Formatting toolbar, **click the Title Only layout in the Slide Layout task pane, then type Video Division Budget**
   The new Slide 5 is selected and appears in the Slide pane.

2. **Click Insert on the menu bar, click Object, click the Create from file option button, click Browse, locate the file PPT G-4.xls from the drive and folder where your Data Files are stored, click OK, then click the Link check box to select it**
   Compare your screen to Figure G-5.

3. **Click OK in the Insert Object dialog box**
   A very small image of the linked worksheet appears on the slide. The worksheet would be easier to see if it were larger and had a background fill color.

4. **With the worksheet still selected, drag the bottom-right sizing handle down to the right toward the right edge of the slide, drag the bottom-left sizing handle down to the left toward the left edge of the slide, then position the worksheet vertically in the middle of the slide**
   The worksheet should be about as wide as the slide.

5. **Click the Fill Color list arrow** on the Drawing toolbar, **click the Automatic box, then click a blank area of the slide**
   A purple background fill color appears behind the worksheet, as shown in Figure G-6.

6. **Click the Save button** on the Standard toolbar, **then click the Close button** in the presentation title bar
   PowerPoint remains open but the Presentation window closes.

TABLE G-1: Embedding Versus Linking

situation	action
When you are the only user of an object and you want the object to be a part of your presentation	Embed
When you want to access the object in its source application, even if the original file is not available	Embed
When you want to update the object manually while working in PowerPoint	Embed
When you always want the latest information in your object	Link
When the object's source file is shared on a network or when other users have access to the file and can change it	Link
When you want to keep your presentation file size small	Link

POWERPOINT G-6 WORKING WITH EMBEDDED AND LINKED OBJECTS AND HYPERLINKS

FIGURE G-5: Insert Object dialog box ready to link an object

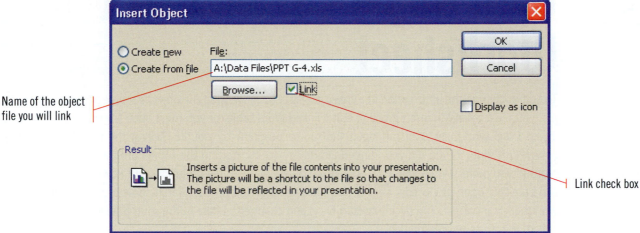

Name of the object file you will link

Link check box

FIGURE G-6: Linked worksheet with background fill color

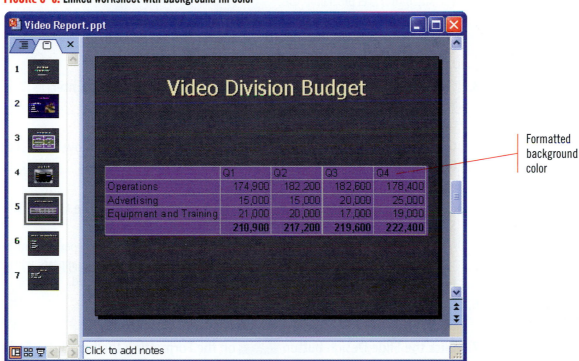

Formatted background color

Clues to Use

Linking objects using Paste Special

You can also link an object or selected information from another program to PowerPoint by copying and pasting. This technique is useful when you want to link part of a worksheet rather than the entire file. For example, you may want to link a worksheet from a Microsoft Excel workbook that contains both a worksheet and a chart. To link just the worksheet, open the Microsoft Excel workbook file that contains the worksheet, select the worksheet, then copy it to the Clipboard. Leaving Excel and the source worksheet open, open the PowerPoint presentation, click Edit on the menu bar, click Paste Special, click the Paste link option button, then click OK.

UNIT
G
PowerPoint 2003

Updating a Linked Excel Worksheet

To edit or change the information in a linked object, you must open the object's source program. For example, you must open Microsoft Word to edit a linked Word table, or you must open Microsoft Excel to edit a linked Excel worksheet. You can open the source program by double-clicking the linked object in the PowerPoint slide, as you did with embedded objects, or by starting the source program directly using any method you prefer. When you work on a linked object in its source program, your PowerPoint presentation can be either open or closed. ✎ You have just received an e-mail that some of the data in the Excel worksheet is incorrect. You decide to start Excel and change the data in the source file and then update the linked object in the presentation.

STEPS

1. **Click the Start button** 🏁 **start on the taskbar, point to All Programs, point to Microsoft Office, then click Microsoft Office Excel 2003**

   The Microsoft Excel program opens.

QUICK TIP

To edit or open a linked object in your presentation, the object's source program and source file must be available on your computer or network.

2. **Click File on the menu bar, click Open, select the file PPT G-4.xls from the drive and folder where your Data Files are stored, then click Open**

   The PPT G-4.xls worksheet opens.

3. **Click cell B3, type 22000, click cell C3, type 18000, then press [Enter]**

   The Q1 and Q2 totals are automatically recalculated. The Q1 total now reads 217,900 instead of 210,900 and the Q2 total reads 220,200 instead of 217,200.

4. **Click the Close button** ✖ **in the Microsoft Excel program window, then click Yes to save the changes**

   Microsoft Excel closes and the PowerPoint window opens.

QUICK TIP

The destination file can remain open when you update links. After you change the source file and switch back to the presentation file, the linked object is updated.

5. **Click in the PowerPoint program window to activate it, click the Open button** 📂 **on the Standard toolbar, click the file Video Report, then click Open**

   A Microsoft Office PowerPoint alert box opens, telling you that the Video Report presentation contains links and asking if you want to update them. See Figure G-7. This message appears whenever you open a PowerPoint presentation that contains linked objects that have been changed.

6. **Click Update Links**

   The worksheet in the presentation slide is now updated with the new data.

7. **Click the Slide Design button** 📐 Design **on the Formatting toolbar, click Window on the menu bar, click Arrange All, then click Slide 5 in the Slides tab**

   Compare your screen to Figure G-8. The linked Excel worksheet shows the new totals for Q1 and Q2. The changes you made in Excel were automatically entered in this linked copy when you updated the links.

8. **Click the Save button** 💾 **on the Standard toolbar**

FIGURE G-7: Alert box to update links

FIGURE G-8: Slide with updated, linked worksheet

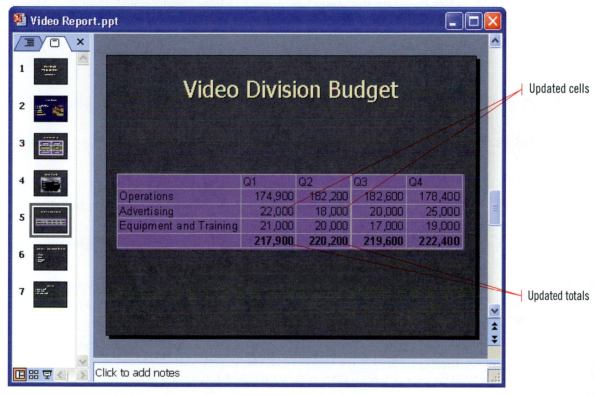

Updated cells

Updated totals

Clues to Use

Using the Links dialog box

You can use the Links dialog box to update a link, open a linked object's source program, change a linked object's source program, break a link, and determine if links are updated automatically or manually. To open the Links dialog box, click Edit on the menu bar, click Links, then click the link you want. The Links dialog box opens, as shown in Figure G-9. If the Manual option button is selected, the links in the target file will not be updated unless you select the link in this dialog box and click Update Now.

FIGURE G-9: Links dialog box

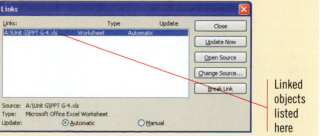

Linked objects listed here

Inserting an Animated GIF File

In your presentations, you may want to use special effects to illustrate a point or capture the attention of your audience. You can do this by inserting an animation or a movie. An **animation** contains multiple images that stream together or move when you run a slide show to give the illusion of motion. Animations are stored as Graphics Interchange Format (GIF) files. PowerPoint comes with a number of animated GIFs, which are stored in the Microsoft Clip Organizer. The **Clip Organizer** contains various drawings, photographs, clip art, sounds, animated GIFs, and movies that you can insert into your presentation. A **movie** is live action captured in digital format by a movie camera. You continue to develop your presentation by embedding an animated GIF file in a slide about international videos.

STEPS

1. Click Slide 6 in the Slides tab

2. Click Insert on the menu bar, point to Movies and Sounds, then click Movie from Clip Organizer

   The Clip Art task pane opens and displays all the animated GIFs available for you to use. If you don't want to view all the animation clips in the Clip Art task pane, you can narrow the results that it displays.

3. Type travel in the Search for text box, then click Go

   All the clips that have a travel attribute appear in the Clip Art task pane. The animation clip you want is near the bottom of the list.

TROUBLE

If you do not see the GIF file in Figure G-10, choose a different GIF or ask your instructor or technical support person for help.

4. Click the down scroll arrow until you see the GIF file of the bridge shown in Figure G-10, then click the GIF file image

   The animated GIF appears in the center of the slide and the Picture toolbar opens.

5. Resize the image so it is approximately the same height as the bulleted list, then drag the image so it's directly across from the bulleted list

   If a GIF image is too dark or too light, or if its colors don't match the color scheme, you can format the image using the commands on the Picture toolbar.

6. Click the Color button 📷 on the Picture toolbar, then click Grayscale

   The animated GIF's colors are changed to shades of gray, which makes the animation look a little better with the presentation's color scheme, but the animation looks too dark now.

7. Click 📷, click Automatic, then click the More Brightness button 🔆 once on the Picture toolbar

   The animated GIF changes back to color and is slightly brightened.

8. Click the Less Contrast button 🔅 on the Picture toolbar twice, then click in a blank area of the slide

   The animated GIF has less contrast. Compare your screen with Figure G-11. The animation won't begin unless you view it in Slide Show view.

QUICK TIP

An animated GIF file will also play if you publish the presentation as a Web page and view it in a browser such as Internet Explorer or Netscape Navigator.

9. Click the Slide Show button 🖥, watch the animation, press [Esc], then click the Save button 💾 on the Standard toolbar

FIGURE G-10: Clip Organizer showing animated GIF files

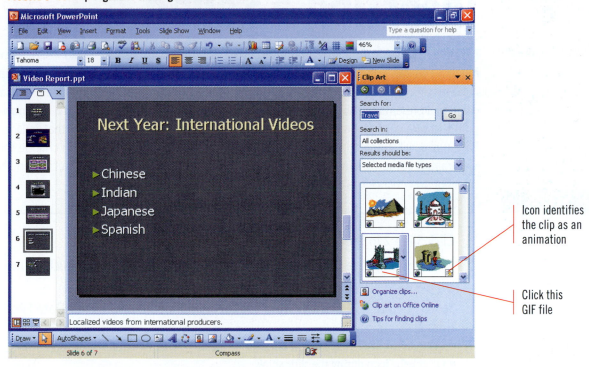

Icon identifies the clip as an animation

Click this GIF file

FIGURE G-11: Animated GIF in Normal view

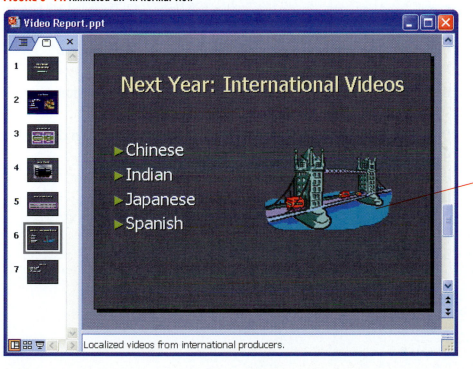

The GIF appears in Normal view but only plays in Slide Show view

Clues to Use

Inserting movies

You can insert movies from the Clip Organizer, the Microsoft Web site, or from disk files. To insert a movie from a disk, click Insert on the menu bar, point to Movies and Sounds, then click Movie from File. Navigate to the location of the movie you want, then insert it. If you're using the Clip Art task pane, search for the file you want, then insert it. After you insert a movie, you can edit it using the Picture toolbar. You can also open the Custom Animation task pane and apply an effect to the movie. From the Custom Animation task pane, you can indicate whether to continue the slide show or to stop playing the clip.

Inserting a Sound

PowerPoint allows you to insert sounds in your presentation just as you would insert animated GIF files or movies. You can add sounds to your presentation from files on a disk, the Microsoft Clip Organizer, the Internet, or a location on a network. Use sound to enhance the message of a slide. For example, if you are creating a presentation about a raft tour of the Colorado River, you might insert a rushing water sound on a slide showing a photograph of people rafting. If you try to insert a sound that is larger than 100 KB, PowerPoint will automatically link the sound file to your presentation. You can change this setting on the General tab in the Options dialog box. You insert a sound of a camera click on Slide 2 of the presentation to enhance the picture on the slide.

STEPS

1. **Click Slide 2 in the Slides tab**

2. **Click Insert on the menu bar, point to Movies and Sounds, then click Sound from File**
   The Insert Sound dialog box opens.

3. **Select the file PPT G-5.wav from the drive and folder where your Data Files are stored, then click OK**
   A dialog box opens asking if you want the sound to play automatically or if you want it to play only when you click the icon during the slide show.

> **TROUBLE**
> The sound icon you see may be different from the one illustrated in Figure G-12 depending on your sound card software.

4. **Click Automatically**
   A small sound icon appears on the slide, as shown in Figure G-12. The sound will play automatically during a slide show.

5. **Click Format on the menu bar, click Picture, then click the Size tab**
   The Size tab opens in the Format Picture dialog box.

6. **Double-click the number in the Height text box in the Scale section, type 150, then click OK**
   The sound icon enlarges to 150% of its original size.

7. **Drag the sound icon to the lower-right corner of the slide, then click the slide background to deselect the icon**
   Compare your screen to Figure G-13.

> **TROUBLE**
> If you do not hear a sound, your computer may not have a sound card installed. See your instructor or technical support person for help.

8. **Double-click the sound icon**
   The sound of the shutter on a camera clicking plays out of your computer's speakers.

9. **Click the Save button 🖫 on the Standard toolbar**

FIGURE G-12: Slide showing small sound icon

Sound icon

FIGURE G-13: Slide showing resized and repositioned sound icon

Resized and repositioned sound icon

Clues to Use

Playing music from a CD

You can play a CD audio track during your slide show. Click Insert on the menu bar, point to Movies and Sounds, then click Play CD Audio Track. The Insert CD Audio dialog box opens. Select the beginning and ending track number and the timing options you want. See Figure G-14. When you are finished in the Insert CD Audio dialog box, click OK. A CD icon appears on the slide. You can indicate if you want the CD to play automatically when you move to the slide or only when you click the CD icon during a slide show. The CD must be in the CD-ROM drive before you can play an audio track.

FIGURE G-14: Insert CD Audio dialog box

Inserting a Hyperlink

Often you will want to view a document that either won't fit on the slide or is too detailed for your presentation. In these cases, you can insert a hyperlink, a specially formatted word, phrase, graphic, or drawn object that you click during your slide show to "jump to," or display, another slide in your current presentation; another PowerPoint presentation; a Word, Excel, or Access file; or a Web page on the World Wide Web. Inserting a hyperlink is similar to linking because you can change the object in the source program after you click the hyperlink. You decide to add a hyperlink to the presentation to show a recent product review, which is in a Word document.

STEPS

1. **Click Slide 7 in the Slides tab**

2. **Select Video News on the slide, click the Insert Hyperlink button 🌐 on the Standard toolbar, then click Existing File or Web Page**

   The Insert Hyperlink dialog box opens. Compare your dialog box with Figure G-15. You want to hyperlink to another file.

3. **Select the file PPT G-6.doc from the drive and folder where your Data Files are stored, click OK, then click in a blank area of the slide**

   Now that you have made "Video News" a hyperlink to the file PPT G-6.doc, the text formatting changes to a light green color, the hyperlink color for this presentation's color scheme, and is underlined. It's important to test any hyperlink you create.

4. **Click the Slide Show button 🖵, point to Video News to see the pointer change to 👆, then click the Video News hyperlink**

   Microsoft Word opens, and the Word document containing the review appears on the screen, as shown in Figure G-16. The Web toolbar appears below the Formatting toolbar.

5. **Click the Back button 🔵 on the Web toolbar**

   The Reviews slide reappears in Slide Show view. The hyperlink is now light blue, the color for followed hyperlinks in this color scheme, indicating that the hyperlink has been used.

6. **Press [Esc] to end the slide show, right-click the Word program button on the taskbar, then click Close on the shortcut menu**

   The Word program closes.

7. **Click Slide 1 in the Slides tab, click the Slide Sorter View button 🔲, click in the Zoom box on the Standard toolbar, type 50, then press [Enter]**

   Compare your screen to Figure G-17.

8. **Click 🖵, advance through all of the slides, making sure you click the hyperlink on Slide 7, then click 🔵 to return to the slide show**

9. **Add your name to the notes and handouts footer, click File on the menu bar, click Print, click the Print what list arrow, click Notes Pages, then click OK**

10. **Save your changes, then close the presentation**

FIGURE G-15: Insert hyperlink dialog box

Click to link to a file

Your list might include different files

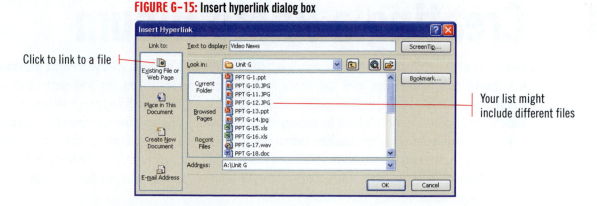

FIGURE G-16: Linked review in Word

Microsoft Word title bar

Web toolbar

Back button

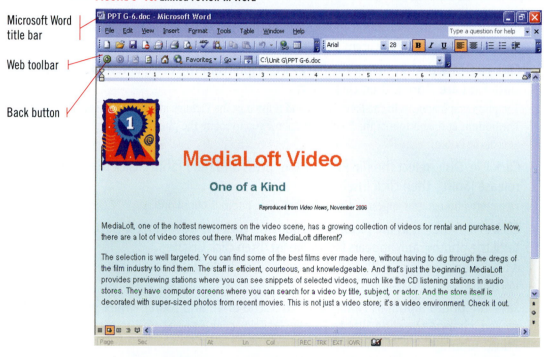

FIGURE G-17: Final presentation in Slide Sorter view

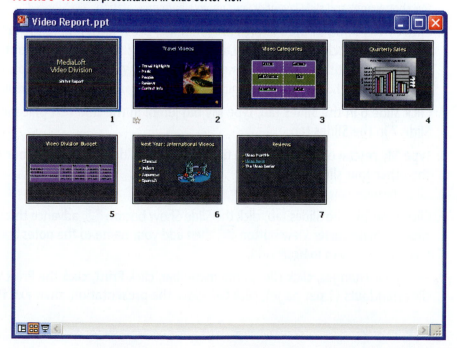

Creating a Photo Album

You can use PowerPoint to create a presentation using your favorite pictures. A **PowerPoint photo album** is a special presentation designed specifically to display photographs. You can add pictures to a photo album from your hard drive, digital camera, scanner, or Web camera. As with any presentation, you can customize the layout of a photo album by adding title text to slides, applying frames around the pictures, and applying a design template. You can also format the pictures of the photo album by adding a caption below the pictures, converting the pictures to black and white, rotating the pictures, and changing their brightness and contrast. You have a little extra time at the end of your day and you decide to use PowerPoint to create a photo album of a recent family ski trip.

STEPS

1. Click Insert on the menu bar, point to Picture, then click New Photo Album

   The Photo Album dialog box opens.

2. Click File/Disk button, select the file PPT G-7.jpg from the drive and folder where your Data Files are stored, then click Insert

   The photograph appears in the Preview box and is listed in the Pictures in album list as shown in Figure G-18. The buttons at the bottom of the Preview box allow you to rotate the photo, or change the contrast or brightness of the photo.

   TROUBLE

   If the files in the Insert New Picture dialog box are not sorted by File Name, select pictures PPT G-8, PPT G-9, PPT G-10, PPT G-11, and PPT G-12 in the list.

3. Click File/Disk, select the file PPT G-8.jpg, press and hold [Shift], click the file PPT G-12.jpg, release [Shift], then click Insert

   Five more photographs appear in the dialog box. One photo is out of order.

4. Click PPT G-12.jpg in the Pictures in album list, click the down arrow button below the list until the photograph appears last in the list, then click Create

   A new presentation appears. PowerPoint creates a title slide along with a slide for each photograph that you inserted.

   QUICK TIP

   If you want others to have access to your photo album on the Web, you can save the photo album presentation as a Web page.

5. Save the photo album as Family Ski Trip to the drive and folder where your Data Files are stored, change the slide title to Family Ski Trip, click Format on the menu bar, then click Photo Album

   The slide title changes and the Format Photo Album dialog box opens. You can use this dialog box to format the photographs and slide layout of your photo album presentation.

6. Click PPT G-7.jpg in the Pictures in album list, press and hold [Shift], click PPT G-12.jpg, release [Shift], click the Picture Layout list arrow in the Album Layout section, click 1 picture with title, click the Frame shape list arrow, click Corner Tabs, then click Update

   Notice that all of the slides now have a title text placeholder and all of the photographs have corner tabs.

7. Click Slide 6 in the Slides tab, type My big jump! in the title text placeholder, then click Slide 7 in the Slides tab

8. Type My rescue off the hill in the title text placeholder, then enter your own title text on the other four slides

   All of the slides now have a title.

9. Click Slide 1 in the Slides tab, click the Slide Show button 🖵, advance through the slides, click the Slide Sorter View button 🔡, then add your name to the notes and handouts header

   Compare your screen to Figure G-19.

10. Save your changes, click File on the menu bar, click Print, click the Print what list arrow, click Handouts (1 per page), click OK, close the presentation, then exit PowerPoint

FIGURE G-18: Photo Album dialog box

File/Disk button

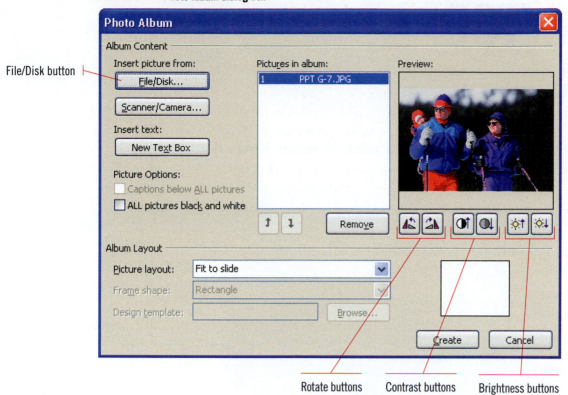

Rotate buttons   Contrast buttons   Brightness buttons

FIGURE G-19: Completed photo album presentation

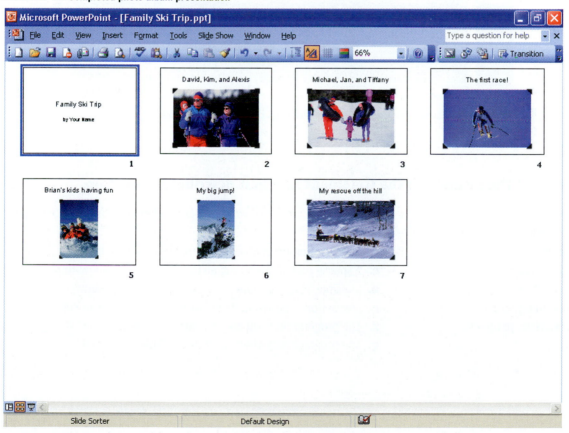

Practice

▼ CONCEPTS REVIEW

Label each element of the PowerPoint window shown in Figure G-20.

FIGURE G-20

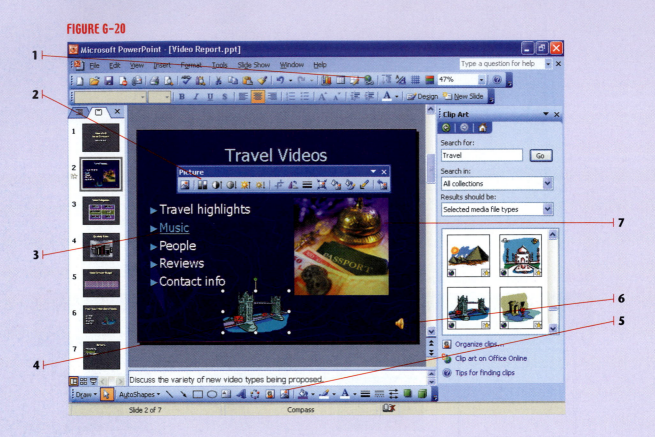

Match each of the terms with the statement that best describes its function.

8. **Movie**
9. **Hyperlink**
10. **Animation**
11. **Photo Album**
12. **Linked object**
13. **Source program**
14. **Destination program**

a. A specially formatted word or graphic that you can click to jump to another document

b. A representation of an object stored in its source file

c. A special presentation designed specifically to work with photographs

d. Multiple images that move when you run a slide show

e. Live action captured in digital format by a movie camera

f. The program that you use to create an embedded file

g. The program into which an embedded file is inserted

Select the best answer from the list of choices.

15. **Which statement about embedded objects is not true?**
    a. Embedded objects can be edited in their source program.
    b. Embedded objects always have the latest information.
    c. Embedded objects are not a part of the presentation.
    d. Embedded objects can be edited even if the original file is not available.

16. **Which statement about linked objects is true?**
    a. To edit a linked object, you must open its source file.
    b. A linked object substantially increases the size of your presentation file.
    c. You can access a linked object even when the source file is not available.
    d. A linked object is an independent object inserted directly on a slide.

17. **Which statement best describes a hyperlink?**
    a. A hyperlink is a type of animation.
    b. A hyperlink is a type of chart that you embed using Graph.
    c. A hyperlink is a portal button that you click on a slide when you want to search the Web.
    d. A hyperlink is a specially formatted word that you click to display a Web page.

18. **The best way to display your photographs using PowerPoint is to create**
    a. An animation.
    b. An embedded object.
    c. A photo album.
    d. A hyperlink.

▼ SKILLS REVIEW

1. **Embed a picture.**
    a. Start PowerPoint, open the presentation PPT G-13.ppt from the drive and folder where your Data Files are stored, then save it as **Marketing 2006**.
    b. Go to Slide 4 and insert the image PPT G-14.jpg.
    c. Resize the picture so it fits in the blank area of the slide, then use the arrow keys on the keyboard to adjust its position.
    d. Save your changes.

2. **Embed an Excel chart.**
    a. Insert a new slide after Slide 5 using the Blank slide layout.
    b. Embed the chart from the file PPT G-15.xls.
    c. Using Excel tools, enlarge the chart title text to 24 points and the Value and Category axes to 14 points.
    d. Change the Value axis title and Legend text to 18 points and reposition the legend so it is at the bottom of the chart (*Hint*: Click the Placement tab in the Format Legend dialog box.)
    e. Resize and reposition the chart so it is centered horizontally and vertically on the slide.
    f. Save your changes.

3. **Link an Excel worksheet.**
    a. Create a new slide after Slide 6 with the Title Only layout.
    b. Title the slide **Basic P & L**.
    c. Link the spreadsheet file PPT G-16.xls from the drive and folder where your Data Files are stored.
    d. Resize the object so that it fills the slide width.
    e. Reposition the object so it is centered vertically. (*Hint:* To center it more precisely, hold down [Alt] while you drag, or hold down [Ctrl] while you press the arrow keys.)
    f. Fill the spreadsheet object with light gray (the Follow Accent and Followed Hyperlink Scheme Color).
    g. Save and close the Marketing 2006 presentation.

4. **Update a linked Excel worksheet.**
   a. Start Excel, then open the worksheet PPT G-16.xls.
   b. Replace the value in cell B4 with **95,000**.
   c. In cell D7, enter **1,350,000**.
   d. Close Excel after saving your changes.
   e. Open the Marketing 2006.ppt presentation file in PowerPoint, updating the link as you do so.
   f. Go to Slide 7 and view your changes. Save the presentation.

5. **Insert an animated GIF file.**
   a. Go to Slide 8.
   b. Insert an animated GIF file of your choosing on the slide. Use the word **email** to search for an appropriate animated GIF.
   c. Resize and reposition the GIF file as necessary.
   d. Preview it in Slide Show view. Save the presentation.

6. **Insert a sound.**
   a. Go to Slide 2.
   b. Insert the sound file PPT G-17.wav from the drive and folder where your Data Files are stored. Set the sound to play when you click the sound icon.
   c. In the Format Picture dialog box, scale the sound icon to 125% of its original size.
   d. Drag the sound icon to the lower-right corner of the slide.
   e. Test the sound in Slide Show view. Save the presentation.

7. **Insert a hyperlink.**
   a. Go to Slide 7 in the presentation, then add a new slide with the Title and Text layout.
   b. Title the slide **Reviews**.
   c. In the first line of the main text placeholder, enter **Jeff Sanders, Web Cheese Review** and on the second line enter **Jorge Fonseca, Online Cheese Today**.
   d. Select the entire main text placeholder, and change its font size to 36 points.
   e. Resize the text placeholder to fit the text, then center it on the slide.
   f. Convert the Jeff Sanders bullet into a hyperlink to the file PPT G-18.doc.
   g. Click in the notes pane, then type **The hyperlink links to Jeff's cheese review of the 2006 Camembert**.
   h. Run the slide show and test the hyperlink.
   i. Use the Back button to return to the presentation.
   j. End the slide show.
   k. Exit Word.
   l. Run the spellchecker, view the presentation in Slide Show view, and evaluate your presentation. Make any necessary changes.
   m. Add your name as a footer to notes and handouts, print the slides as Notes Pages, then save and close the presentation.

8. **Create a photo album.**
   a. Create a new photo album, then insert the files PPT G-19.jpg, PPT G-20.jpg, PPT G-21.jpg, and PPT G-22.jpg from the drive and folder where your Data Files are stored.
   b. Make sure the pictures appear in descending order.
   c. Change the title on the title slide to **Jeff's Playoff Game**.
   d. Format the album layout to one picture with a title on each slide.
   e. Format the frame shape to Rounded Rectangle.
   f. Enter a title of your choosing on each slide with a photograph.
   g. Save the photo album as **Jeff's Playoff Game** to the drive and folder where your Data Files are stored.
   h. View the photo album in Slide Show view, then add your name to the notes and handouts header.
   i. Save your changes, print the photo album handouts, close the presentation, then exit PowerPoint.

▼ INDEPENDENT CHALLENGE 1

D & K Engineering is a mechanical and industrial design company that specializes in designing manufacturing plants in the United States and Canada. As the company financial analyst, you need to investigate and report on a possible contract to design and build a large manufacturing plant in Belize. The board of directors wants to make sure that they can make a minimum profit on the deal. It is your job to provide a recommendation to the board.

Create your own information using the basic presentation provided and assume the following about D & K Engineering:

- The new manufacturing plant in Belize will be 75,000 square feet in size. The projected cost for D & K Engineering to design and build the plant in Belize is about $280.00 per square foot based on a four-phase schedule: planning and design, site acquisition and preparation, underground construction, and above-ground construction.
- Factors that helped determine D & K Engineering's cost to build the plant include: D & K Engineering payroll for 45 people in Belize for 24 months; materials cost; hiring two Belizean construction companies to construct the plant; and travel expenses.
- Factor in a $1.5 million dollar profit margin for D & K Engineering above the cost of the building.

a. Open the file PPT G-23.ppt, then save it as **Belize Plant**.

b. Think about what results you want to see, what information you will need to create the slide presentation, and how your message should be communicated. In order for your presentation to be complete, it must include the following objects: (i) an embedded picture; (ii) an embedded Excel chart; and (iii) a sound from the Clip Organizer.

c. Use Microsoft Excel and PowerPoint to embed objects into your presentation. Use the assumptions previously listed to develop information that would be appropriate for a table.

d. Give each slide a title and add main text where appropriate.

e. Make the last slide in the presentation your recommendation to pursue the contract, based on the financial data you present.

f. Add your name as a footer to the notes and handouts, save your changes, then print the final slide presentation as handouts (two slides per page).

Advanced Challenge Exercise

- Click File on the menu bar, point to Send To, then click Microsoft Office Word.
- Click the Blank lines next to slides option button, then click **OK**.
- Save the Word document as **Belize Plant Proposal ACE**. then add your name to the document footer.

g. View the presentation in Slide Show view, then exit PowerPoint.

▼ INDEPENDENT CHALLENGE 2

You are the director of operations at The Templeton Group, a large investment banking company in Texas. Templeton is considering merging with Redding, Inc, a smaller investment company in Arizona, to form the 10th largest financial institution in the United States. As the director of operations, you need to present some financial projections regarding the merger to a special committee formed by Templeton to study the proposed merger.

Create your own information using the basic presentation provided on your Project Disk. Assume the following facts about the merger between Templeton and Redding:

- Templeton earned $7 million dollars in profit last year. Projected profit this year is $5 million dollars. Templeton's operating expenses run approximately $31 million dollars each year.
- Redding earned $3 million dollars in profit last year. Projected profit this year is $4 million dollars. Redding's operating expenses run approximately $22 million dollars each year.
- Templeton has a 19% share of the market without Redding. Redding has a 6% share of the market without Templeton. Combined, the companies would have a 25% share of the market.
- With the merger, the projected profit next year is $12 million dollars. Templeton would need to cut $7.6 million dollars from its annual operating costs and Redding would need to cut $2 million dollars from its annual operating costs.

a. Open the file PPT G-24.ppt from the drive and folder where your Data Files are stored, then save it as **T & R Merger**.

b. Think about what results you want to see, what information you will need to create the slide presentation, and how your message should be communicated. In order for your presentation to be complete, it must include the following objects: (i) a linked Excel worksheet; (ii) an embedded PowerPoint table, chart, or other object; and (iii) a hyperlink.

c. Use Microsoft Excel to link a worksheet to your presentation. Use the preceding assumptions to develop related information that would be appropriate for the worksheet. Use the profit and operating expense figures to create your own revenue figures. (Revenue minus operating expenses equals profit.)

d. Hyperlink to the file Redding, Inc.ppt. Choose the slide in the presentation where the hyperlink should be placed. You can use existing text or create a drawn or other object to use as the hyperlink.

e. Give each slide a title and add main text where appropriate. Create slides as necessary to make the presentation complete.

f. Add your name as a footer to the notes and the handouts, save your changes, then print the final slide presentation.

g. View the presentation in Slide Show view, then exit PowerPoint.

▼ INDEPENDENT CHALLENGE 3

You have just been promoted to the position of sales manager at Import Express, a U.S. company that exports goods and professional services to companies in Japan, South Korea, China, and the Philippines. One of your new responsibilities is to give a presentation at the biannual finance meeting showing how the sales department performed during the previous six-month period.

Plan and create a short slide presentation (six to eight slides) that illustrates the sales department's performance during the last six months. Identify the existing accounts (by country), then identify the new contracts acquired during the last six months. Create your own content, but assume the following:

- The majority of goods and services being exported are as follows: food products (such as rice, corn, and wheat); agriculture consulting; construction engineering; and industrial designing and engineering.
- The company gained five new accounts in China, South Korea, and the Philippines.
- The sales department showed a $4.2 million dollar profit for the first half of the year.
- Department expenses for the first half of the year were $3.5 million dollars.
- The presentation will be given in a boardroom using a projection machine.

a. Think about what results you want to see, what information you will need to create the slide presentation, and how your message should be communicated. In order for your presentation to be complete, it must include the following objects: (i) an embedded Excel chart; (ii) a sound from the Clip Organizer; (iii) an embedded picture; and (iv) an animated GIF file or embedded movie.

b. Use the movies provided for you in PowerPoint, or if you have access to another media source that does not infringe on copyright laws, choose an appropriate movie from that source to embed in your presentation.

c. Give each slide a title and add main text points where appropriate.

d. Add a template, background shading, or other enhancing objects to make your presentation look professional.

Advanced Challenge Exercise

- With your PowerPoint file open, open the Excel file PPT G-25.xls from the drive and folder where your Data Files are stored, then select and copy the data on Sheet 1.
- Display your open PowerPoint file, create a new slide, then use the Paste Special command to paste the object.
- Use the same operation to paste the data on Sheet 2 of the PPT G-25.xls file to a new slide in your presentation.

e. Save the presentation as **Imports** to the drive and folder where your Data Files are stored.

f. Add your name as a footer to the slides and notes and handouts, save your changes, then print the final slide presentation.

g. View the presentation in Slide Show view, then exit PowerPoint.

▼ INDEPENDENT CHALLENGE 4

You are the business manager for Partners Inc., a large nonprofit educational organization in Los Angeles, California. One of your duties is to purchase new and used computer equipment for the organization every three years. Partners Inc. has allotted some money in the budget this year to upgrade some of the computer equipment. Your job is to prepare a brief presentation, outlining the cost of purchasing new and used equipment and selling the old equipment, for the board of directors' next monthly meeting.

Develop your own content, but assume the following:

- Ten computer systems need to be sold.
- The old computers are configured as follows: Pentium III, 866 MHz, 64 MB RAM, 10 GB HDD, IDE CD-ROM with Sound and 4 MB Video, 56 K Modem 10/100 3Com Network Card, Windows 2000.

The 15 replacement computer systems need to be configured as follows: Pentium 4, 2.0 GHz - 2.5 GHz, 128 MB RAM, 50+GB HD, DVD CD-RW with Sound and 24 MB Video, 56 K Modem 10/100 3Com Network Card, Windows XP.

- Add $50.00 to the price of each purchased computer for tax and shipping.
- You are allowed to spend up to $1000.00 per new computer.

You'll need to find the following information on the Web:

- The average price of the old computer systems that need to be sold.
- The prices of the new computer systems.
- Auction Web sites where the old computers can be sold.

a. Open a new presentation, and save it as **Partners** to the drive and folder where your Data Files are stored.
b. Add your name as the footer on all slides and handouts.
c. Connect to the Internet, then use a search engine to locate Web sites that have information on used computer systems.
d. Think about what results you want to see, what information you will need to create the slide presentation, and how your message should be communicated. Review at least two Web sites that contain information about used computers. Print the pages of the Web sites you use to gather data for your presentation. (Remember to gather information on the old computers as well as the new computers.)
e. In order for your presentation to be complete, it must include the following objects: (i) an embedded picture; (ii) an embedded Excel worksheet or chart; (iii) a GIF animation or movie; and (iv) a sound.
f. Create an Excel worksheet that describes the difference between the purchase of the new systems and the sale of the old systems.
g. Give each slide a title and add main text where appropriate. Create slides as necessary to make the presentation complete.
h. Apply an appropriate slide design. Change the slide design colors as necessary.
i. Spell check the presentation, view the final presentation in Slide Show view, save the final version, then print the slides as handouts.
j. Close the presentation, exit PowerPoint, and disconnect from the Internet.

PowerPoint 2003

▼ VISUAL WORKSHOP

Create two slides that look like the examples in Figures G-21 and G-22. Save the presentation as **Expenses**. Add your name as a footer on the slides, then save and print the slides. Submit the final presentation output.

FIGURE G-21

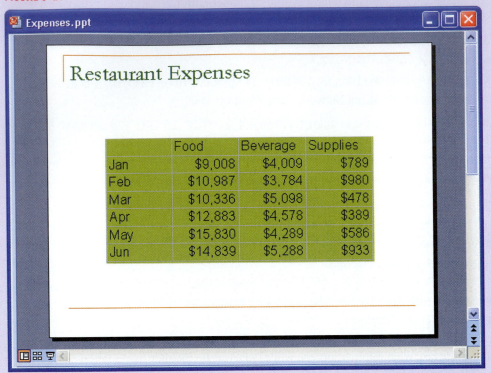

FIGURE G-22

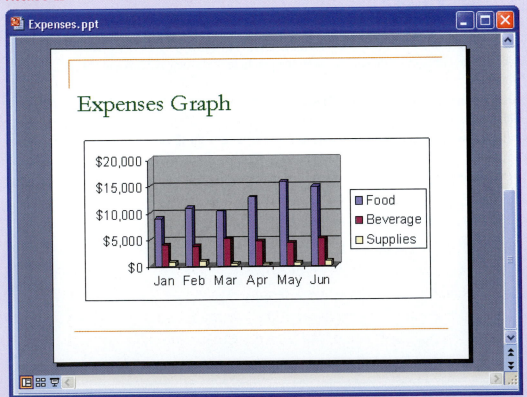

Using Advanced Features

OBJECTIVES

Send a presentation for review

Combine reviewed presentations

Set up a slide show

Create a custom show

Rehearse slide timings

Publish a presentation for the Web

Package a presentation

Broadcast a presentation

If you have a SAM user profile, you may have access to hands-on instruction, practice, and assessment of the skills covered in this unit. Log in to your SAM account and go to your assignments page to see what your instructor has assigned.

After your work on a presentation is complete, you have the option of sending the presentation over the Internet for others to review and send back to you. Reviewers can add comments as well as make changes to the presentation that you can review and accept or reject. Once you are finished changing the presentation, you need to produce the final output that you will use when you give your presentation. You can print the presentation, display it as a slide show using a computer or projector, publish it on the Web for others to view, or broadcast it live over the Web. ▨ You have finished creating the content for the MediaLoft Video Division presentation. Now you need to send it to your supervisor, Maria Abbott, and to the marketing manager, Alice Wegman, for review. After you incorporate the reviewer's comments and changes, you produce an on-screen slide show, and publish it for viewing on the World Wide Web.

Sending a Presentation for Review

When you finish creating a presentation, it is often helpful to have others look over the content for accuracy and clarity. You can use Microsoft Outlook or any other compatible 32-bit e-mail program to send a presentation out for review. When you send a presentation for review using Outlook, a review request e-mail message is created automatically that includes an attached copy of the presentation file. Reviewers can use any version of PowerPoint to make changes and insert comments on the slides of your presentation. Outlook automatically tracks changes made by multiple reviewers, so you don't have to keep track of which reviewer made which change. Changes to a presentation sent electronically are much easier to track and combine than changes marked on printed copies of the presentation. Use Outlook to send your presentation to Maria and Alice for their suggestions and comments.

STEPS

TROUBLE
If you don't have access to Microsoft Outlook, read the information in the Clues to Use to send your presentation for review using another program.

1. **Start PowerPoint, open the presentation PPT H-1.ppt from the drive and folder where your Data Files are stored, then save it as Final Status Report**

2. **Click File on the menu bar, point to Send To, then click Mail Recipient (for Review)**
   A Microsoft Outlook e-mail message window opens, as shown in Figure H-1. Notice that the subject line and some basic e-mail text are automatically entered in the Outlook window, and the presentation is attached.

3. **Click the To button [⊞ To...] in the message window**
   The Select Names dialog box opens. Use this dialog box to select all the people who you want to review the presentation.

TROUBLE
If your name does not appear in the list of names in the Select Names dialog box, type your e-mail address in the To: box. If necessary, ask your instructor for help.

4. **Click your name in the list of names, click the To button, then click OK**
   Your name and e-mail address appear in the To text box in the Outlook window.

5. **Click in the Outlook message window below the message text, then type If you could review this presentation and send it back to me by Friday, I would appreciate it. Thanks.**
   The new text appears below the original text. Compare your screen to Figure H-2.

QUICK TIP
If there are linked files in the presentation you are sending for review, you need to attach the linked files to your e-mail message or change the linked files to embedded objects.

6. **Click the Send button [⊞ Send] on the Outlook E-mail toolbar**
   Outlook sends the e-mail message with the attached presentation file (or places it in the Outlook Outbox). The Outlook window closes and you are returned to the PowerPoint presentation window. The Reviewing toolbar now appears below the Formatting toolbar, indicating that the presentation has been sent out for review.

7. **Start Microsoft Office Outlook, click the Mail icon [✉], click the Inbox folder in the Navigation Pane, then click the Send/Receive button [⊞ Send/Receive] on the Outlook toolbar**
   You may have to wait a short time before the message appears. The message you just sent to yourself appears in the Inbox message list. If the message is selected, it will appear in the Reading Pane.

8. **Click the Outlook Close button [✕] on the title bar**
   Outlook closes and the PowerPoint screen appears.

FIGURE H-1: Outlook window

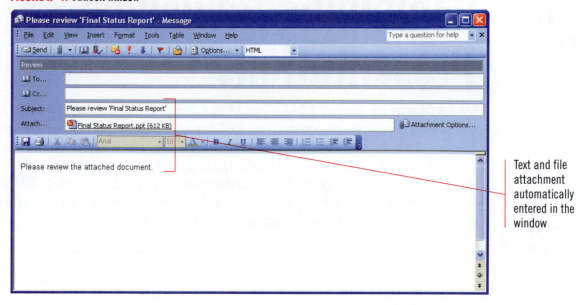

Text and file attachment automatically entered in the window

FIGURE H-2: Completed Outlook window

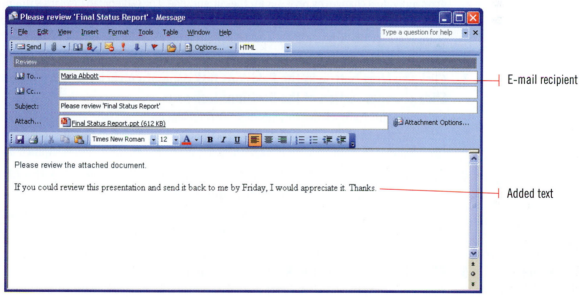

E-mail recipient

Added text

Clues to Use

Other ways to send a presentation for review

If you are not using Outlook as your e-mail program, you can still send a presentation out for review over the Web using another 32-bit e-mail program, as long as it is compatible with Messaging Application Programming Interface (MAPI). You can also use a Microsoft Exchange server, a network server, or a floppy disk. To send a presentation out for review using any of these methods, open the presentation, then use the Save As command to save it with a new name. In the Save As dialog box, click the Save as type list arrow, click Presentation for Review, then click Save. Open your e-mail program, create a new message, attach the presentation file to the message, then send the message.

Combining Reviewed Presentations

Once a reviewer has completed their review of your presentation and sends it back, you can combine the changes into your original presentation using the Compare and Merge Presentations command. You can apply individual changes, changes by slide, changes by reviewer, changes on the slide master, or changes to the entire presentation. You can continue to combine changes to your original presentation until you have applied all the changes, deleted all the changes markers, saved the presentation, or ended the review. 🎨 You sent out the Final Status Report presentation to your supervisor and another manager in MediaLoft to review. Now you want to combine the two reviewed versions with your original presentation.

STEPS

1. **Click Tools on the menu bar, then click Compare and Merge Presentations**

   The Choose Files to Merge with Current Presentation dialog box opens.

2. **Click the Look in list arrow, navigate to the drive and folder where your Data Files are stored, click PPT H-2.ppt, press [Ctrl], click PPT H-3, then click Merge**

   The two reviewed presentations are merged with your original presentation. The Revisions task pane opens on the right side of the screen. It is divided into two tabs: the List tab and the Gallery tab. The List tab displays individual changes by reviewer for the current slide. The Gallery tab displays a thumbnail of the current slide and shows what the slide would look like if all the suggested changes were made. Each reviewer's changes are identified by a different color marker on the slide. If more than one reviewer made a change on the same object, the change is identified by a white color marker. There are no revisions on Slide 1.

3. **Click the Next button in the Revisions task pane, then click the MA1 comment icon in the Slide changes section of the Revisions task pane**

   Slide 2 appears. The open item on this slide is a comment made by Maria Abbott as shown in Figure H-3. Each comment or reviewer change has a change description box that appears on the slide next to its corresponding color comment icon or reviewer marker. Since this is a comment, no action is required by you.

QUICK TIP

To undo one change or all the changes made on a slide, click the Unapply button list arrow 🔽 on the Reviewing toolbar, then select one of the options.

4. **Click the Next Item button 🔷 on the Reviewing toolbar, then click the All changes to Text 2 check box in the change description box**

   A check mark appears on the reviewer color marker, in the check boxes in the change description box, and on the reviewer color marker in the Revisions task pane, which indicates that all of the changes by Maria Abbott have been made to the slide.

5. **Click the 🔷 twice on the Reviewing toolbar**

   Slide 6 appears and a change description box opens. This is an animation setting change made by Alice Wegman, which you don't want to incorporate into the presentation, so you decide to move to the next change.

6. **Click the Delete Marker button ✖️▼ on the Reviewing toolbar, click the white reviewer marker on the slide, click the check boxes in the change description box as shown in Figure H-4, then review the changes in the body text box**

   The reviewer color marker is white, indicating that the marked change contains more than one reviewer's changes. Compare your screen to Figure H-4.

7. **Click the End Review button End Review... on the Reviewing toolbar, read the information in the dialog box, then click Yes to end the review**

   The Reviewing toolbar and Revisions task pane close and the color markers on the slide are deleted.

8. **Save your changes, click View on the menu bar, click Task Pane, click Window on the menu bar, then click Arrange All**

   Now your screen will match the rest of the figures in this book.

FIGURE H-3: Figure showing Revisions task pane

Next Item button

Reviewing toolbar

Comment color icon

Delete button

End Review button

Changes and comments for this slide appear here

Next button

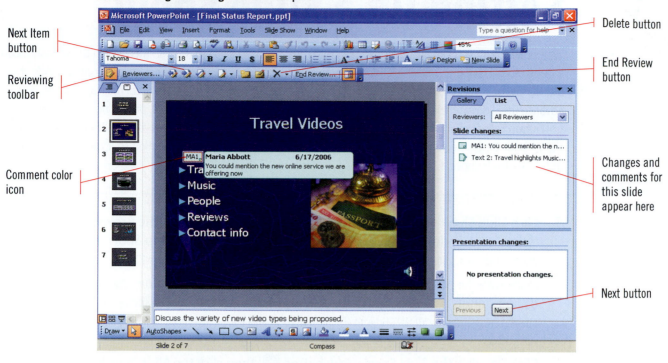

FIGURE H-4: Figure showing revised slide

Two reviewers made changes to this body text object

White color marker

Change description box

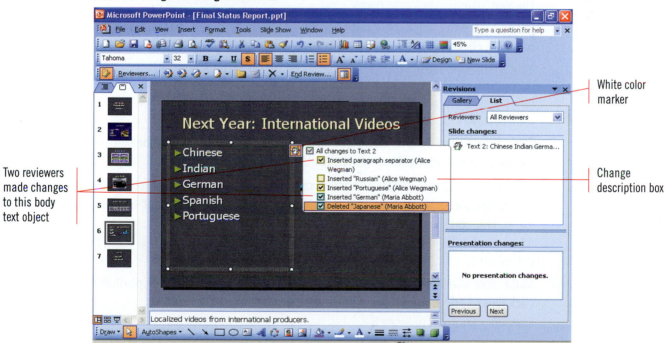

PowerPoint 2003

Clues to Use

Reviewing a presentation

To evaluate a presentation someone sends for your review, simply open the presentation in PowerPoint and make your changes. The Reviewing toolbar will automatically open when you open the presentation. When you are finished making changes, save the presentation. Next, click File on the menu bar, point to Send To, then click Original Sender to send the presentation back to its original owner using Outlook. If you want to edit the message in the e-mail before you send the presentation back, you can click the Reply with Changes button on the Reviewing toolbar.

Setting Up a Slide Show

With PowerPoint, you can create a slide show that runs automatically. Viewers can then watch the slide show on a stand-alone computer, called a kiosk, at a convention or trade show. You can create a self-running slide show that loops, or runs, through the entire show, without users touching the computer. You can also let viewers advance the slides at their own pace by pressing the Spacebar, clicking the mouse, or clicking an on-screen control button called an action button. A self-running slide show is also useful when you publish a presentation to the Web for others to view.   You prepare the Final Status Report presentation so it can be viewed at an upcoming trade show.

STEPS

1. Click Slide Show on the menu bar, click Set Up Show, then click the Browsed at a kiosk (full screen) option button in the Show type section of the Set Up Show dialog box

   The Set Up Show dialog box has options you can set to specify how the show will run.

2. Make sure the All option button is selected in the Show slides section, then make sure the Using timings, if present option button is selected in the Advance slides section

   These settings include all the slides in the presentation and have PowerPoint advance the slides at time intervals you set.

3. Click OK, click the Slide Sorter View button [image], then click the Slide Transition button [image] on the Slide Sorter toolbar

   The Slide Transition task pane opens.

4. In the task pane, click the Automatically after check box in the Advance slide section to select it, click the Automatically after up arrow until 00:08 appears, click Apply to All Slides, click Slide Show, view the show, let it start again, then press [Esc]

   PowerPoint advances the slides automatically at eight-second intervals, or faster if someone advances the slide manually. There may be times when you want users to advance slides by clicking a button that is actually a hyperlink to jump to the next slide.

5. Click Slide Show on the menu bar, click Set Up Show, click the Manually option button in the Advance slides section, then click OK

6. Double-click Slide 1, click Slide Show on the menu bar, point to Action Buttons, click Action Button: Forward or Next button [image], then drag the pointer to draw a button in the lower-left corner of Slide 1

   A new action button appears on the bottom of the slide and the Action Settings dialog box opens, as shown in Figure H-5.

7. Make sure the Hyperlink to option button is selected, click the Hyperlink to list arrow, click Next Slide if necessary, then click OK

   Compare your screen to Figure H-6.

8. With the action button selected, press [Ctrl][C] to copy it, click the Next Slide button [image], press [Ctrl][V] to paste the button on Slide 2, repeat for slides 3-7, then click the Slide 1 thumbnail in the Slides tab

9. View the slide show, click the action buttons to move from slide to slide, press [Esc] to end the slide show, then save your changes

   Make sure you wait for the animated objects to appear on the slides before you click the action buttons.

FIGURE H-5: Action Settings dialog box

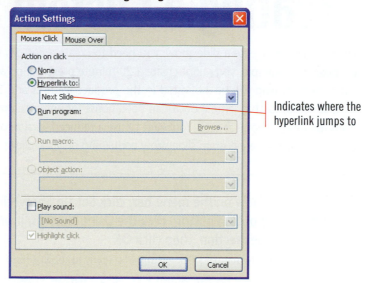

Indicates where the
hyperlink jumps to

FIGURE H-6: Slide 1 showing new action button

Action button

Your button
might be a
different
size

Clues to Use

Hiding a slide during a slide show

During a slide show, you can hide slides you don't want the audience to see. Hidden slides are not deleted from the presentation; they just don't appear during a slide show. The easiest way to hide a slide is to right-click the slide thumbnail in Normal view or Slide Sorter view, then click Hide Slide. When a slide is hidden, its slide number has a hide symbol—a gray box with a line through it—over it. To unhide the slide, right-click the slide thumbnail, then click Hide Slide. You can display a hidden slide during a slide show by right-clicking the slide prior to the hidden slide, pointing to By Title, then clicking the title of the hidden slide.

Creating a Custom Show

Often when you create a slide show, you need to create a custom version of it for a different audience or purpose. For example, you might create a 20-minute presentation about a new product to show to potential customers who will be interested in the product features and benefits. Then you could create a five-minute version of that same show for an open house for potential investors, selecting only appropriate slides from the longer show. You want to use a reduced version of the slide show in a marketing presentation, so you create a custom slide show containing only the slides appropriate for that audience.

STEPS

1. **Click Slide Show on the menu bar, click Set Up Show, click the Presented by a speaker (full screen) option button, click the Using timings, if present option button in the Advance slides section, then click OK**

   This turns off the manual kiosk settings you made in the last lesson.

2. **Click Slide Show on the menu bar, click Custom Shows, then click New in the Custom Shows dialog box**

   The Define Custom Show dialog box opens. The slides that are in your current presentation are listed in the Slides in presentation list box.

3. **Press and hold [Ctrl], click 2. Travel Videos, click 6. Next Year: International Videos, click 7. Reviews, release [Ctrl], then click Add**

   The three selected slides move to the Slides in custom show list box, indicating that they will be included in the new presentation. See Figure H-7.

4. **Click 3. Reviews in the Slides in custom show list, then click the Slide Order up arrow button one time to move it up one position in the list**

   You can arrange the slides in any order in your custom show using the Slide order up and down arrows.

5. **Drag to select the existing text in the Slide show name text box, type Marketing Presentation, then click OK**

   The Custom Shows dialog box lists your custom presentation. The custom show is not saved as a separate slide show on your disk even though you assigned it a new name. To view a custom slide show, you must first open the presentation you used to create the custom show in Slide Show view. You then can open the custom show from the Custom Shows dialog box.

6. **Click Show, view the Marketing Presentation slide show, then press [Esc] to end the custom show after you view the Next Year: International Videos slide**

   The slides in the custom show appear in the order you set: Slide 2, 7, then 6. After pressing [Esc] you return to the presentation in Normal view.

7. **Press [Ctrl][Home], then click the Slide Show button** 🖥

   Slide 1 appears and the text animation on the slide begins.

8. **Right-click anywhere on the screen, point to Custom Show, then click Marketing Presentation, as shown in Figure H-8**

   The Marketing Presentation custom show appears in Slide Show view.

9. **Press [Esc] after viewing the Next Year: International Videos slide, then save your changes**

FIGURE H-7: Define Custom Show dialog box

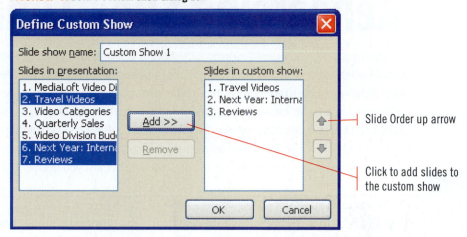

Slide Order up arrow

Click to add slides to the custom show

FIGURE H-8: Switching to the custom slide show

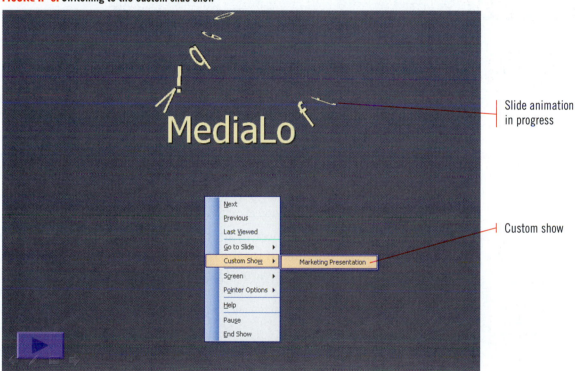

Slide animation in progress

Custom show

Clues to Use

Using action buttons to hyperlink to a custom slide show

You can use action buttons to switch from the "parent" show to the custom show. Click Slide Show on the menu bar, point to Action Buttons, then choose any action button. Drag the pointer to draw a button on the slide, then, in the Action Settings dialog box, select Custom Show in the Hyperlink to list box. Select the name of the custom show to which you want to hyperlink, then click OK. When you run the show, click the hyperlink button you created to run the custom show.

Rehearsing Slide Timings

Whether you are creating a self-running slide show or you're planning to talk about the slides as they appear, you should rehearse the slide timings, the amount of time each slide stays on the screen. If you assign slide timings to your slides without actually running through the presentation, you will probably discover that the timings do not allow enough time for each slide or point in your presentation. To set accurate slide timings, use the PowerPoint Rehearse Timings feature. As you run through your slide show, the Rehearsal toolbar shows you how long the slide stays on the screen. When enough time has passed, click the mouse to move to the next slide. 🎨 You decide to rehearse the slide timings of the presentation, but first you decide to modify Slide 2 a little more.

STEPS

1. **Click Slide 2 in the Slides tab, right-click the comment icon, then click Delete Comment**
   The reviewer comment is deleted.

2. **Click Travel in the title text object, click Tools on the menu bar, then click Thesaurus**
   The Research task pane opens displaying a list of synonyms for the word travel.

3. **Point to the word tour, click the tour list arrow, then click Insert**
   The word Tour replaces the word Travel and now appears in the title text object.

4. **Click the Slide Sorter View button ⊞, then click Slide 1**
   Before you complete the steps of this lesson, first read the steps and comments so you are aware of what happens during a slide show rehearsal.

5. **Click the Rehearse Timings button 🕮 on the Slide Sorter toolbar**
   Slide Show view opens, and Slide 1 appears. The Rehearsal toolbar appears in the upper-left corner of the screen, as shown in Figure H-9 and starts timing the slide. Be sure to leave enough time to present the contents of each slide thoroughly.

   TROUBLE
   Make sure you wait until the animations are finished on each slide before clicking the Next button.

6. **When you feel an appropriate amount of time has passed for the presenter to speak and for the audience to view the slide, click the Next button ⏩ on the Rehearsal toolbar or click your mouse anywhere on the screen**
   Slide 2 appears and the timing counter begins for this slide.

   TROUBLE
   If too much time has elapsed, click the Repeat button ↩ on the Rehearsal toolbar to restart the timer for that slide. You can also set the time for each slide by typing it in the Slide Time text box.

7. **Click ⏩ at an appropriate interval after Slide 2 appears, click ⏩ after viewing Slide 3, then continue setting timings for the rest of the slides in the presentation**
   At the end of the slide rehearsal, a Microsoft PowerPoint message box opens, it displays the total time for the slide show, and asks if you want to keep the slide timings. If you save the timings, the next time you run the slide show, the slides will appear automatically at the intervals you specified during the rehearsal.

8. **Click Yes to save the timings**
   Slide Sorter view appears showing the new slide timings, as shown in Figure H-10. Your timings will be different. When you run the slide show, it will run by itself, using the timings you rehearsed. The rehearsed timings override any previous timings you set.

   QUICK TIP
   To move to the next slide before your rehearsed slide timing has elapsed, click the slide to advance to the next slide.

9. **Click the Slide Show button 🖥, then view the presentation with your timings**

10. **Save your changes, add your name to the Notes and Handouts footer, click File on the menu bar, click Print, click the All option button, then print the Handouts (4 slides per page)**

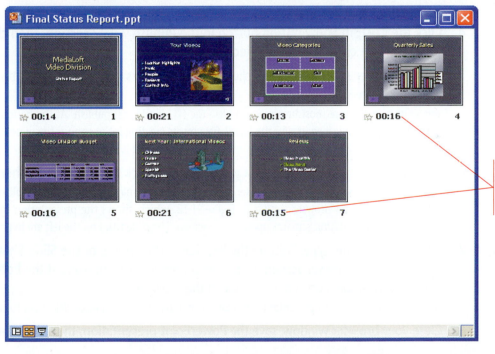

FIGURE H-9: Rehearsal toolbar in Slide Show view

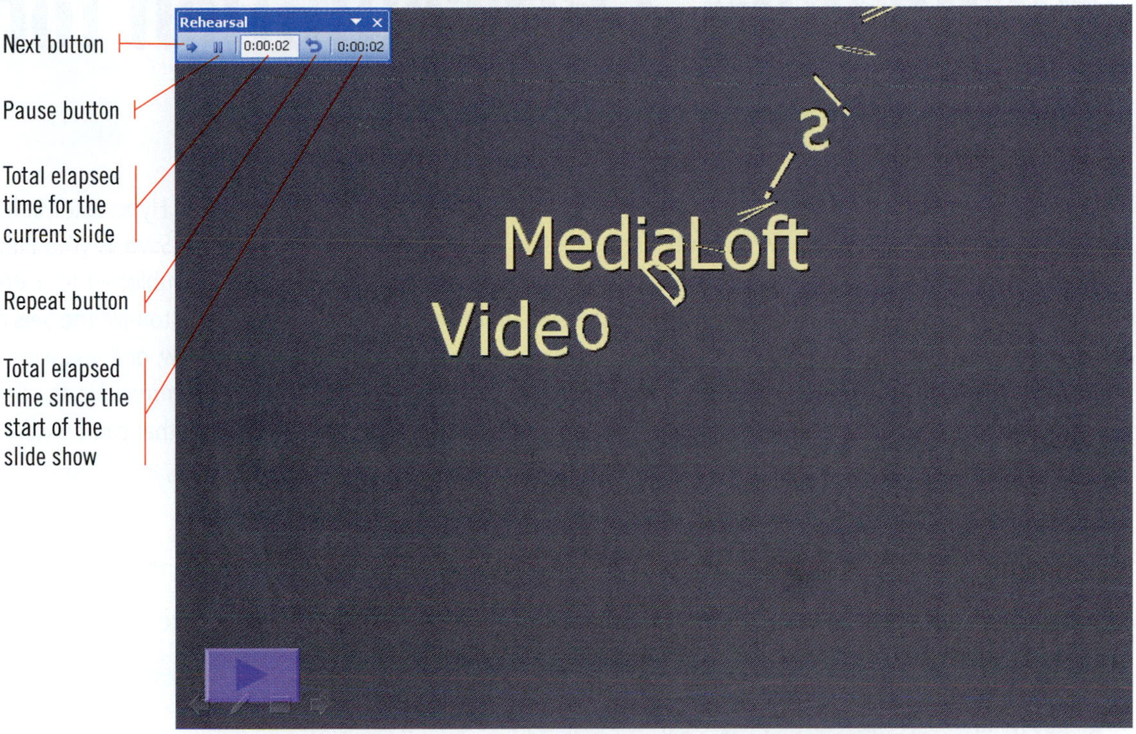

Next button
Pause button
Total elapsed time for the current slide
Repeat button
Total elapsed time since the start of the slide show
Rehearsal
0:00:02
0:00:02
MediaLoft
Video

FIGURE H-10: Final presentation in Slide Sorter view showing new slide timings

Final Status Report.ppt
MediaLoft Video Division
Tour Videos
Video Categories
Quarterly Sales
00:14
1
00:21
2
00:13
3
00:16
4
Video Division Budget
Next Year: International Videos
Reviews
00:16
5
00:21
6
00:15
7
Slide timings you rehearsed (your time will be different)

PowerPoint 2003

Clues to Use

Changing the page setup

When you need to customize the size and orientation of your presentation you can change its page setup. Click File on the menu bar, then click Page Setup to open the Page Setup dialog box. In the Page Setup dialog box, you can change the width and height of the slides to ten different settings, including On-screen Show, Letter Paper, and 35mm Slides. You can also set a custom slide size by determining the height and width of the slides. You can also change the orientation of the presentation. There is an orientation setting for the slides of the presentation and then another separate setting for the notes, handouts, and outline.

Publishing a Presentation for the Web

You can use PowerPoint to create presentations for viewing on the Web by saving the file in Hypertext Markup Language (HTML) format. To save the entire presentation, click File on the menu bar, click Save as Web Page, then click Save in the dialog box that opens. This creates a single file Web page. Once published to a Web server, others can view (but not change) the presentation over the Web. If you want to customize the version that you are saving as a Web page (for example, if you wanted to save only the custom show, or if you wanted to make adjustments to how the presentation will look as a Web page), click the Publish command in the Save As dialog box. You want to create a version of the Final Status Report presentation that can be viewed on the MediaLoft intranet page. You do not want to include the information on Slides 2, 3, 4, and 5, so you use the Publish feature to publish the Marketing custom show you created earlier.

STEPS

QUICK TIP

At this point, you can click Save in the dialog box to save a presentation in HTML format, but you can only save the whole presentation, and you don't get to choose which browser is supported.

1. Click **File** on the menu bar, click **Save as Web Page**, click the **Save in list arrow**, then select the drive and folder where your Data Files are stored
   The Save As dialog box opens.

2. Make sure the filename in the File name text box is selected, then type **webpres**

3. Click **Publish**
   The Publish as Web Page dialog box opens.

4. Click the **Custom Show option button** in the Publish what? section, then click the **Display speaker notes check box** to deselect it

QUICK TIP

To change the format of elements on the Web page, click Web Options in the Publish as Web Page dialog box.

5. In the Browser support section, click the **All browsers listed above (creates larger files) option button**
   You want to make sure most browsers can view the HTML file you publish. At the bottom of the dialog box, notice that the default filename for the HTML file you are creating is the same as the presentation filename, and that it will be saved to the same folder in which the presentation is stored. Compare your screen to Figure H-11.

6. Click the **Open published Web page in browser check box** to select it, then click **Publish**
   PowerPoint creates a copy of your presentation in HTML format and opens the published presentation in your default Internet browser similar to Figure H-12, which shows the presentation in Internet Explorer. Your original presentation remains open on the screen. The slide titles on the left are hyperlinks to each slide.

QUICK TIP

Once you publish a presentation and create the HTML files, you'll need to copy it to a Web server so others can open it from the Web.

7. Click the **slide title hyperlinks** on the left side of the screen, or the **Slide Show button** at the bottom of the browser screen, or the **Next** and **Previous buttons** at the bottom of the screen, to view each presentation slide in the browser
   Because each slide in this presentation has an action button, you can also click them to advance the slides.

8. Close your browser window, save the PowerPoint presentation, then close the presentation

FIGURE H-11: Publish as Web Page dialog box

FIGURE H-12: Custom show from Video Division presentation in Internet Explorer

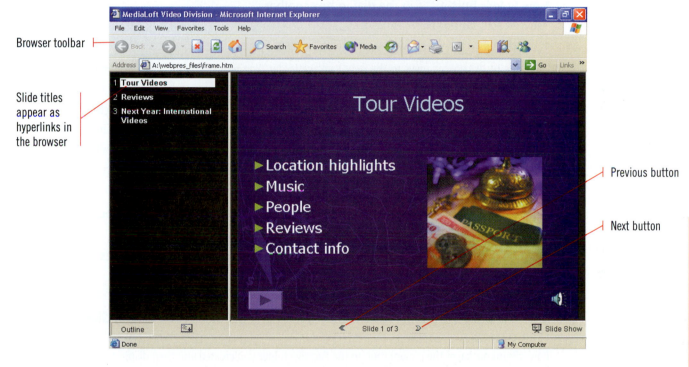

Browser toolbar

Slide titles appear as hyperlinks in the browser

Previous button

Next button

Clues to Use

Online meetings

If you are on a network, you can use Windows NetMeeting and PowerPoint to host or participate in meetings over an intranet or the Web. As the host of a meeting, you can share a presentation in real time with others who may be located in another office in your building or across the country. If you are the host of a meeting, you are required to have NetMeeting (a program automatically installed with Office), the shared document, and its application installed on your computer. As a participant in a meeting, all you are required to have installed on your computer is NetMeeting. As the host, you can schedule a meeting by clicking Tools on the menu bar, pointing to Online Collaboration, then clicking Schedule Meeting. Follow the steps in the dialog boxes to send an e-mail message to the person you are inviting to the meeting. To start an unscheduled online meeting from within the presentation you want to share, click Tools on the menu bar, point to Online Collaboration, then click Meet Now. Follow the steps in the dialog boxes to call participants to the meeting. If the participants accept your meeting invitation, the Online Meeting toolbar opens and the meeting begins.

Packaging a Presentation

When you need to distribute one or more presentations or present a slide show using another Windows computer, you can package your presentation to a CD or a network folder. To package everything you'll need to run a slide show on another computer (including your presentation, embedded and linked objects, and fonts), you'll use the Package for CD feature. If you are running Microsoft Windows XP or later and have the ability to create your own CDs, you can use the Package to CD feature to make a CD of your presentation. The PowerPoint Viewer is included by default with the presentation. The PowerPoint Viewer is a program that allows you to view a presentation in Slide Show view even if PowerPoint is not installed on the computer. 🎨 You package a presentation using the Package to CD feature so you can present it at an off-site meeting. You don't have the ability to create a CD, so you package the presentation to a new folder that you create on your computer's hard drive.

STEPS

TROUBLE

If you decide to place the Package folder in a different location, make sure the folders in the path name have a maximum of eight characters and contain no spaces.

1. **Open the presentation Video Division Report Offsite.ppt from the drive and folder where your Data Files are stored, click File on the menu bar, click Save As, then click the Create New Folder button 📁 in the dialog box toolbar**
   The New Folder dialog box opens.

2. **Type Package in the Name text box, then click OK**
   The Save in list box changes to the new Package folder. You will save your packaged presentation in this new folder.

3. **Type Video Division Report Packed Version in the File name list box, then click Save**
   If your original presentation is on your hard disk, you can place the packaged version directly on a floppy disk. If the presentation is too big for one disk, PowerPoint lets you save across multiple floppy disks.

4. **Click File on the menu bar, click Package for CD, then read the information in the dialog box**
   The Package for CD dialog box opens as shown in Figure H-13.

5. **Type Packed Report in the Name the CD text box, then click the Options button**
   The Options dialog box opens.

6. **Read the information in the dialog box, click the Embedded TrueType fonts check box, click OK, then click Copy to Folder**
   The Copy to Folder dialog box opens as shown in Figure H-14.

7. **Click the Browse button, locate and click the Package folder you created, click Select, then click OK**
   PowerPoint packages the presentation to the Package folder you created and then displays the Package for CD dialog box.

8. **Click the Close button, close the presentation, then exit PowerPoint**

9. **Open Windows Explorer, navigate to the Packed Report folder, then view the contents as shown in Figure H-15**
   All the files needed to run this presentation are in this folder.

FIGURE H-13: Package for CD dialog box

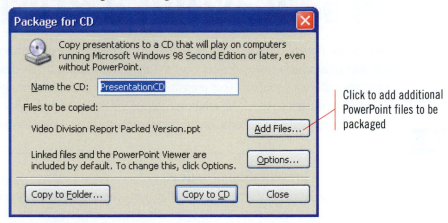

Click to add additional PowerPoint files to be packaged

FIGURE H-14: Copy to Folder dialog box

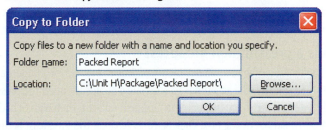

FIGURE H-15: Windows Explorer window showing Packed Report Folder

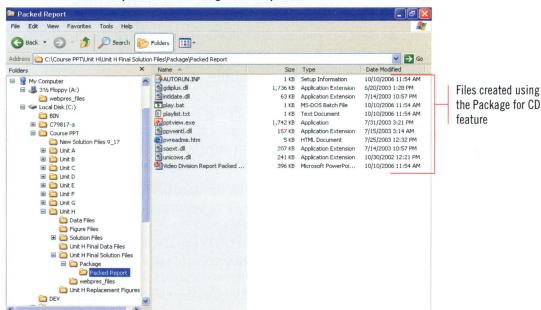

Files created using the Package for CD feature

Clues to Use

Using the Microsoft PowerPoint Viewer

The Microsoft PowerPoint Viewer is a program used to show a presentation on a computer that doesn't have PowerPoint installed. The PowerPoint Viewer is a free program distributed by Microsoft from the Office Web site. You can include the PowerPoint Viewer with your presentation by choosing the Viewer for Microsoft Windows in the Pack and Go Wizard. To view a presentation slide show using the PowerPoint Viewer, open the PowerPoint Viewer dialog box by double-clicking the pptview.exe. From the Microsoft PowerPoint Viewer dialog box, you can run a slide show, set Viewer options, and print a presentation. To show a packaged presentation using the PowerPoint Viewer, you must first unpackage the presentation. Locate the folder that contains the packaged presentation, then double-click the pngsetup icon. Extract the presentation to a folder. A message dialog box appears asking if you want to run a slide show; click Yes.

Broadcasting a Presentation

You can use PowerPoint as a communication tool to broadcast the presentation over an intranet or the Web. You can start an unscheduled broadcast at any time, or use NetMeeting to schedule a broadcast to take place at a specific date and time. If you want your presentation broadcast available for on-demand viewing, you can record and save it to a network server where others can access the broadcast and replay it at their convenience. In preparation for hosting a presentation broadcast next month, you learn the basics of broadcasting.

DETAILS

- ### Set up a presentation broadcast

  Using the PowerPoint broadcasting feature, you can set up a presentation broadcast for a small group of up to 10 computers that are all on the same intranet or have access to the Web. As the presenter, you will need PowerPoint 2003, Microsoft Internet Explorer 5.1 or later, Microsoft Outlook, or another e-mail program, a shared computer or server, and a connected video camera and microphone if you want to broadcast live video and audio. To broadcast a presentation to more than 10 computers at one time, you'll need to have access to a Windows Media Server or a third-party Windows Media Server provider.

- ### Schedule a presentation broadcast

  To give the members of your audience plenty of time to prepare for a presentation broadcast, you can schedule the broadcast for a specific date and time. To schedule a broadcast, open the presentation that you want to broadcast, click Slide Show on the menu bar, point to Online Broadcast, then click Schedule a Live Broadcast. In the Schedule Presentation Broadcast dialog box, click Settings to open the Broadcast Settings dialog box. Indicate your audio, video, and display preferences. Use the File Location section to enter your server or shared computer information. See Figure H-16. If you will be using a Windows Media Server or including audience feedback, click the Advanced tab, then enter the necessary information. Click OK, then click Schedule. A dialog box similar to an e-mail message box opens. Add participants' e-mail addresses to the To text box, change other settings in the dialog box as necessary, then click the Send button on the toolbar.

- ### Begin a presentation broadcast

  When you are ready to begin your presentation broadcast, you start by clicking Slide Show on the menu bar, pointing to Online Broadcast, then clicking Start Live Broadcast Now. If Outlook is your e-mail program, a message dialog box opens telling you that a program is trying to access your e-mail addresses; click Yes to continue. The Live Presentation Broadcast dialog box opens and lists the available presentations ready for broadcast. Select the presentation you want to broadcast, then click Broadcast.

  - If the broadcast has been previously scheduled and you are using a microphone or camera in your broadcast, the Broadcast Presentation dialog box opens. Complete the testing of the equipment, then click Start. The presentation broadcast begins.

  - If the broadcast is unscheduled, the Live Presentation Broadcast dialog box opens similar to Figure H-17. Click Settings, select the appropriate preferences for this broadcast, then click OK. Click Invite Audience and let the people you want to attend know that you are broadcasting. When you are ready to start the broadcast, click Start. If you are using audio and video, complete the testing of the equipment, then click Start.

- ### View a presentation broadcast

  The easiest way to participate in an online broadcast is to open the e-mail message that contains the broadcast invitation and click the Uniform Resource Locator (URL) for the broadcast. The lobby page of the online broadcast appears in your browser. At the scheduled broadcast time, the presentation appears on your screen. During the meeting, you are able to send e-mail messages to the presenter. Figure H-18 shows how your screen might look if you were participating in an online broadcast.

FIGURE H-16: Broadcast Settings dialog box

Indicate your audio and video preferences in this section

Enter server or shared file location here

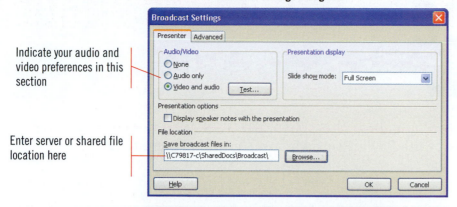

FIGURE H-17: Live Presentation Broadcast dialog box

Click to open the Broadcast Settings dialog box

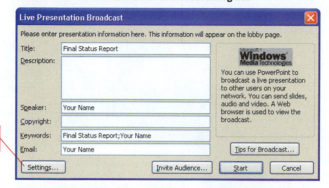

FIGURE H-18: Presentation broadcast in Internet Explorer

If the online broadcast includes live video, the video appears here

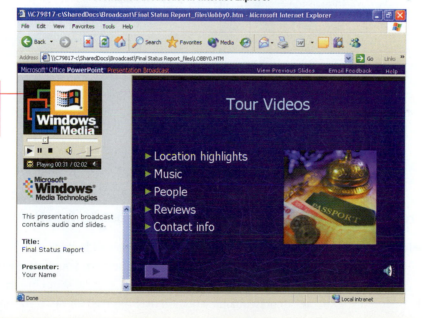

Clues to Use

Record and save a broadcast

If you don't want to broadcast your presentation live, you can record it and save it to a network server where others can access it at any time. Open the presentation you want to broadcast, click Slide Show on the menu bar, point to Online Broadcast, then click Record and Save a Broadcast. The Record Presentation Broadcast dialog box opens. Change the information as necessary. Click Settings, change any of the video, audio, and display preferences, then identify the server or shared computer where the broadcast files will be stored. Click Record, complete the equipment testing, then click Start. Record your broadcast. When you want others to view the recorded broadcast, you will need to send an e-mail and identify the link to the starting page of the broadcast. To view the broadcast, the audience member clicks Replay Broadcast on the start page of the presentation.

Practice

▼ CONCEPTS REVIEW

Label each of the elements of the PowerPoint window shown in Figure H-19.

FIGURE H-19

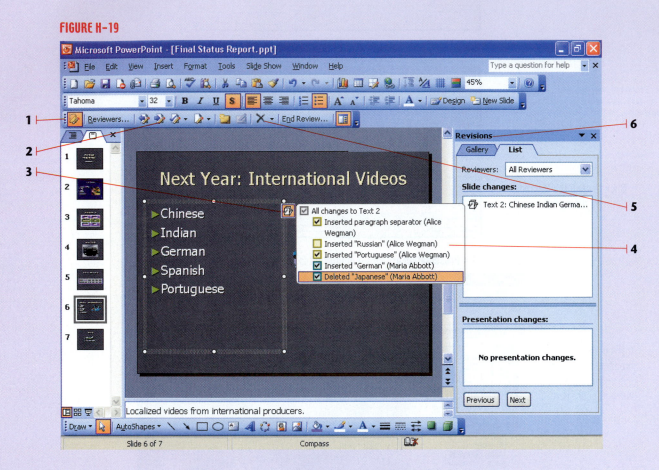

Match each of the terms with the statement that best describes its function.

7. **Online Collaboration**

8. **Custom show**

9. **Package to CD**

10. **Online Broadcast**

11. **Kiosk**

a. A stand-alone computer that runs a slide show

b. To host or participate in a Web meeting, you must use this feature

c. A special slide show created from selected slides in a presentation

d. To present a presentation over the Web for up to 10 computers, you need to use this feature

e. A feature that packages a presentation to take it to another computer

Select the best answer from the list of choices.

12. Which of the following statements about reviewing presentations is false?

    a. You can use any 32-bit e-mail program to send a presentation out for review.

    b. Reviewers must use PowerPoint 2003 to review presentations.

    c. Outlook automatically creates a review request e-mail message.

    d. Reviewers can make changes and add comments to a presentation.

13. How do you know that more than one reviewer made a change to the same item?

    a. The change is highlighted in yellow.

    b. Each reviewer's change is identified by a different color marker.

    c. A thumbnail of the changes automatically appears on the slide.

    d. A white color marker appears.

14. Which of the following statements about rehearsing your slide timings is true?

    a. Rehearsing the slides in your presentation gives each slide the same slide timing.

    b. During a rehearsal, you have no way of knowing how long the slide stays on the screen.

    c. If you give your slides random slide timings, you may not have enough time to adequately view each slide.

    d. If you rehearse your presentation, someone on another computer can set the slide timings.

15. How is a reviewer's change identified on the slide?

    a. A color marker

    b. A message box

    c. Reviewer's changes are italicized.

    d. The only place a reviewer's change is identified is in the Revisions task pane.

16. Which of the following statements about hiding slides is false?

    a. You know a slide is hidden if you see a hide symbol over the slide number in Slide Sorter view.

    b. Hidden slides don't appear during a slide show.

    c. Hidden slides are deleted if you save a presentation with a hidden slide.

    d. It's possible to view a hidden slide during a slide show.

17. How do you create a presentation so it can be viewed on the Web?

    a. Copy the presentation to a network server.

    b. Save the presentation as an HTML file.

    c. Import the presentation to a Web page.

    d. Open the presentation in a Web browser.

18. What does the Package for CD feature allow you to do?

    a. View a presentation on the Web.

    b. Create an online broadcast.

    c. Burn music CDs.

    d. Distribute a presentation for others to view.

19. What does the PowerPoint Viewer allow you to do?

    a. View a presentation on the Web.

    b. View and participate in an online meeting.

    c. View a presentation in Slide Show view on any compatible computer.

    d. View a presentation in all four views at the same time.

▼ SKILLS REVIEW

1. Send a presentation for review.

    a. Open the presentation PPT H-4.ppt and save it as **SF Series Proposal**.

    b. Click File on the menu bar, point to Sent To, then click Mail Recipient (for Review) to send the presentation via e-mail to yourself for review.

    c. Open Outlook, or your compatible e-mail program, make sure the e-mail message was received, then close your e-mail program.

2. Combine reviewed presentations.

    a. Compare and merge the presentation PPT H-5.ppt to SF Series Proposal.

    b. Click the Next Item button on the Reviewing toolbar to read all the comments, and accept all other suggested changes from the reviewer.

    c. End the review, then save your changes.

3. Set up a slide show.

    a. Set up a slide show that will be browsed at a kiosk, using slide timings.

    b. Set the slides to appear every five seconds.

    c. Run the slide show all the way through once, then stop it.

    d. Set the slide show to run manually, presented by a speaker.

    e. Put a Forward or Next action button, linked to the next slide, in the lower-right corner of Slide 1.

    f. Copy the action button, then paste it onto all of the slides except the last one.

    g. Select Slide 2 and place an Action Button: Back or Previous in the lower-left corner. Have it link to the previous slide. Resize the button so it is the same size as the button you created in Step e, and place it near the bottom of the slide, approximately one inch from the left side and bottom.

    h. Copy the Back button, then paste it on all of the slides except the first one.

    i. Run through the slide show from Slide 1 using the action buttons you inserted. Move forward and backward through the presentation, watching the animation effects as they appear.

    j. When you have finished viewing the slide show, save your changes.

4. Create a custom show.

    a. Create a custom show called **New Series** which includes Slides 3, 4, 5, 6, and 7.

    b. Move the two slides that discuss performances above the lecture slides.

    c. View the show from within the Custom Shows dialog box, using the action buttons to move among the slides and waiting for the graphics animations. Press [Esc] to end the slide show after viewing the Financing Lectures slide.

    d. Move to Slide 1, begin the slide show, then, when Slide 1 appears, go to the Custom Show.

    e. View the custom slide show, then return to slide view and save your changes.

5. Rehearse slide timings.

    a. Open the Rehearsal toolbar, set new slide timings, then save your new timings and review them.

    b. Add your name as a footer on notes and handouts, then save your changes.

    c. Print your New Series custom show as handouts (6 slides per page.)

    d. Print all the slides in the presentation as handouts (6 slides per page.)

6. Publish a presentation for the Web.

    a. Publish the entire SF Series Proposal presentation for the World Wide Web as **sfpropsl**. Do not include speaker notes, and make it viewable using all browsers listed.

    b. Open the mht file in your browser and navigate through the presentation.

    c. Close your browser, then close the presentation and PowerPoint.

7. Package a presentation.

    a. Create a new folder on your hard drive and name it **Pack2**.

    b. Save the **SF Series Proposal** presentation in the Pack2 folder you created.

    c. Open the Package for CD dialog box, then change the options so that Truetype fonts are embedded.

    d. Click the Copy to Folder button, then change the name of the folder to **SF Series Proposal**.

    e. Click the Browse button to locate the Pack2 folder, then click OK.

    f. Close the SF Series Proposal Packed presentation.

    g. View the contents of the **Pack2** folder using Windows Explorer.

▼ INDEPENDENT CHALLENGE 1

You work for Island Tours, an international tour company that provides specialty tours to destinations throughout Asia and the Pacific. You have to develop presentations that the sales force can use to highlight different tours at conferences and meetings. You will use some PowerPoint advanced slide show features such as slide builds and interactive settings to finish the presentation you started. Create at least two additional slides for the basic presentation provided on your Data Disk using your own information. Assume that Island Tours has a special (20% off regular price) on tours to Bora Bora and Tahiti during the spring of 2006. Also assume that Island Tours offers tour packages to the following countries: the Philippines, Japan, Australia, and New Zealand.

a. Open the presentation PPT H-6.ppt, then save it as **Pacific Islands** to the drive and folder where your Data Files are stored.

b. Merge the presentation PPT H-7.ppt to the Pacific Islands file. Accept all the suggested changes.

c. Use the assumptions provided to help you develop additional content for your presentation. Use pictures, movies, and sounds provided on the Office CD-ROM or from other media sources to complete your presentation.

d. Animate the entire chart object so that it dissolves in and has an appropriate sound effect play as it appears.

e. Create a custom version of the show that can be shown at a trade show kiosk.

f. Rehearse slide timings for the presentation.

g. View the presentation in Slide Show view.

h. Use the Package for CD feature to package your presentation.

i. Add your name as a footer on all notes and handouts. Print the final slide presentation and all related documents in the format of your choice.

▼ INDEPENDENT CHALLENGE 2

You work for BreakAway Travel Services, a travel service company. BreakAway Travel is a subsidiary of Globus Inc. Every October, BreakAway Travel needs to report to Globus Inc. on the past year's activity. Create your own information using the basic presentation provided in the Project File. Assume the following:

- BreakAway purchased major routes from Canada to Asia and the Far East from Canadian AirTours.
- BreakAway's average revenue runs about $12 million dollars per quarter.
- Twelve new tour packages to Eastern Europe were created this year. Two of the new tours are The Great Wall Tour and The Trans-Siberian Rail Tour.
- BreakAway increased its staff by 8% during the year.

a. Open the presentation PPT H-8.ppt, then save it as **Breakaway**.

b. Use the assumptions provided to help you develop additional content for your presentation on two separate slides. Use pictures, movies, or sounds provided on the Office CD-ROM or from other media sources to complete your presentation.

c. Rehearse slide timings.

d. Create a custom version of your show to run continuously at a conference kiosk, using the timings that you rehearsed.

e. Create a custom version of the show for a specific audience of your choice.

f. Publish the presentation in HTML format, save it as **Breakaway**, preview it in your browser, then close your browser.

Advanced Challenge Exercise

- Send your presentation to another student in your class for review using the Send To feature.
- Have the student review your presentation, add at least one comment and make at least one change, then send it back to you.
- Use the Compare and Merge Presentations feature to combine the presentations.

g. View the presentation in Slide Show view.

h. Add your name as a footer on all notes and handouts. Save the presentation, then print the final slide presentation and all related documents in the format of your choice.

▼ INDEPENDENT CHALLENGE 3

You are the assistant director of operations at Pacific Cargo Inc., an international marine shipping company based in San Francisco, California. Pacific Cargo handles 65% of all the trade between Asia, the Middle East, and the West Coast of the United States. You need to give a quarterly presentation to the company's operations committee which outlines the type and amount of trade Pacific Cargo handled during the previous quarter. Plan and create a 10- to 15-slide presentation that details the type of goods Pacific Cargo carried, how much was carried, which companies (foreign and domestic) purchased goods, which companies (foreign and domestic) sold goods, and how much revenue Pacific Cargo earned. You also need to identify the time it took to deliver the goods to their destinations and the delivery cost. Create your own content, but assume the following:

- Pacific Cargo hauled automobiles from Tokyo to San Francisco during the last quarter. A car-carrier ship can hold 184 cars or 166 pickup trucks.
- Pacific Cargo hauled large tractor equipment and parts made by Caterpillar Tractor and John Deere Tractor from the United States. One ship went to Brazil and one went to Kuwait.
- Typical household goods carried by Pacific Cargo include electronic equipment, appliances, toys, and furniture.
- The cost of hauling goods by ship is $3,380 per ton. Pacific Cargo owns five cargo ships that can operate simultaneously. All five ships were in operation during the last quarter.
- Pacific Cargo hauled a total of 980,000 tons during the last quarter.

a. Create a new presentation, then save it as **PC Report Q1**.

b. Use clip art or shapes to enhance your presentation.

c. Use the assumptions provided to help you develop the content for your presentation. Use movies and sounds provided on the Office CD-ROM or from other media sources to complete your presentation.

d. Use Excel to embed or link objects into your presentation. Use the preceding assumptions to develop related information that would be appropriate for a table or worksheet.

e. Set transitions and animations, and rehearse slide timings.

f. View the presentation in Slide Show view.

Advanced Challenge Exercise

- Open the Page Setup dialog box.
- Change the size of the slide to Letter Paper (8.5 × 11 in).
- Change the orientation to Portrait. See Figure H-20 for an example of a slide with Portrait orientation.
- Resize the objects on the slides as necessary.

g. Add your name as a footer on all notes and handouts. Print the final slide presentation and all related documents in the format of your choice.

FIGURE H-20

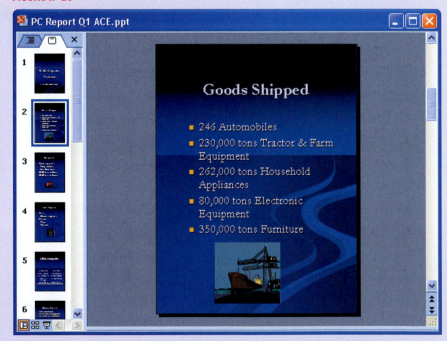

You are the sales manager for Música Internacional, an international music distributor of South American music located in Brasilia, Brazil. This year the M.I. music festival, which showcases different musical groups and styles from all over Central and South America, is being held in Brasilia. Your boss wants you to create a presentation that highlights the variety of musical groups and styles distributed by Música Internacional for the festival. There is wide international appeal for South and Central American music, especially in Europe and Asia. The music festival attracts thousands of artists, presenters, recording company representatives, promoters, and fans every year.

a. Open a new presentation, and save it as **Festival Pres**.

b. Add your name as the footer on all slides and handouts.

c. Connect to the Internet, then use a search engine to locate Web sites that have information on South American music. You'll need to find the names of at least five South American musical groups.

d. Think about what results you want to see, what information you need to create the slide presentation, and how your message should be communicated. Print the pages of the Web sites you use to gather data for your presentation.

e. In order for your presentation to be complete, it must include the following objects: (i) an embedded table; (ii) a GIF animation or movie; and (iii) sound.

f. Title each slide and add main text where appropriate. Create more slides to make the presentation complete.

g. Apply an appropriate slide design. Change the slide design colors as necessary. See Figure H-21 for an example of a slide.

h. Create a custom show that focuses on the interest in South American music in Europe and Asia.

i. Spell check the presentation, then view the final presentation in Slide Show view.

j. Save the final version, then print the slides and handouts.

k. Publish the presentation for the Web as **music**, then view the presentation using your Internet browser.

l. Close the presentation, exit PowerPoint, then disconnect from the Internet.

FIGURE H-21

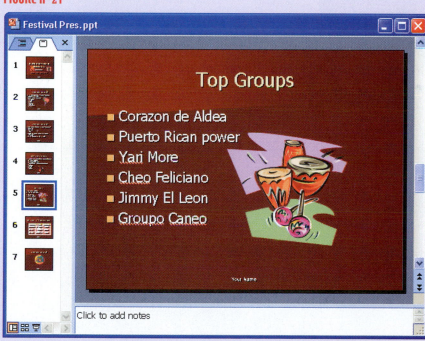

▼ VISUAL WORKSHOP

Create the slides shown in Figure H-22. Save the presentation as **Mountain Tours**. The clip art is in the Clip Organizer. Set transitions, animations, and slide timings. Insert forward and backward action buttons for the slides. View the presentation in Slide Show view. Print the presentation as handouts (3 slides per page).

FIGURE H-22

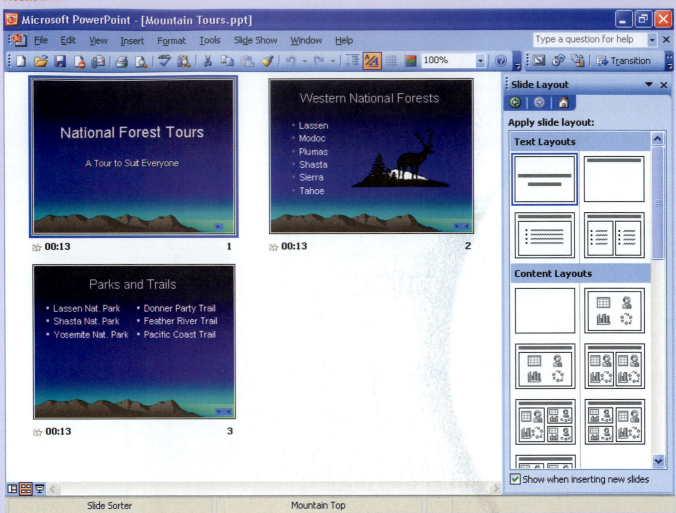

UNIT F
Integration

Integrating Word, Excel, Access, and PowerPoint

OBJECTIVES

You can include objects from most Microsoft Office applications in most other Microsoft Office applications. For example, you can publish an Access report in Word, transfer an Excel chart to PowerPoint, or insert a PowerPoint slide in a Word document. Usually you create documents containing objects from multiple applications when you want to present information in the form of reports and presentations. As a result, Word and PowerPoint are the applications in which you most often combine objects from multiple applications. Alice Wegman, MediaLoft's marketing manager, works with marketing data contained in all four Microsoft Office applications. She asks you to explore how to work with objects from multiple applications to create a report in Word and a presentation in PowerPoint.

Project 1: Online Marketing Report

MediaLoft is planning to acquire Literary Lane, a Seattle-based bookstore that focuses on selling only literary classics. Literary Lane is in the process of exploring ways to market its products online. Its owner has asked you to help her put together a report describing Literary Lane's online marketing efforts, so that she can then deliver the report to MediaLoft management. Some of the information for the report is contained in another Word file and in objects created in Excel, PowerPoint, and Access. You start by opening the report in Word and then embedding an Excel worksheet and inserting a linked chart.

ACTIVITY   Adding Objects from Excel

You need to embed an Excel worksheet on page 1 of the report and then insert a pie chart that is linked to its source file in Excel.

STEPS

TROUBLE
If paragraph marks are not visible, click the Show/Hide ¶ button ¶ on the Standard toolbar.

1. Start Word, open the file **INT F-1.doc** from the drive and folder where your Data Files are located, save it as **Literary Lane Report**, click **Edit** on the menu bar, click **Go To**, click **Bookmark** in the Go to what list box, click the **Enter bookmark name list arrow**, click **Worksheet**, click **Go To**, click **Close**, then delete the placeholder text **Excel Worksheet Here**, but not the ¶ mark following Here

   You use the Bookmark feature to jump to the location where you want to place the Excel worksheet.

2. Start Excel, create and format the worksheet shown in Figure F-1, save the workbook as **Literary Lane Data**, then close the workbook

3. In Word, click **Insert** on the menu bar, click **Object**, click the **Create from File tab**, click the **Browse button**, navigate to the location where you saved Literary Lane Data.xls, click **Literary Lane Data.xls** in the list of files to select it, click **Insert**, then click **OK**

   The Excel worksheet from the Excel file appears already formatted in Word. The Excel worksheet is inserted as an embedded object, which means that you can open and edit the worksheet using Excel toolbars, but any changes you make to the file in Word are not reflected in the original Excel file.

4. Go to Excel, open the file **Literary Lane Data.xls**, click the **Sheet2 tab** at the bottom of the Excel worksheet, then enter the labels and values and create the pie chart shown in Figure F-2

5. Click a white area of the pie chart to select it, click the **Copy button** 🖳 on the Standard toolbar, show **Literary Lane Report.doc** in Word, press **[Ctrl][G]** to open the Go To tab in the Find and Replace dialog box, select the **Pie bookmark**, click **Go To**, click **Close**, then delete the text **Pie Chart Here**, but not the ¶ following Here

6. Click **Edit** on the menu bar, click **Paste Special**, click the **Paste link option button**, then click **OK**

   The pie chart appears in the Word report. After pasting this chart into the report, you receive new data regarding advertising expenses for faxes.

7. Return to the pie chart in Excel, change the value in cell B3 to **5000** (the Faxes slice increases to 25%), save and close the Excel workbook, return to the report in Word, right-click the chart, then click **Update Link**

   The pie chart in Word is updated to reflect the change you made to the chart in Excel.

8. Right-click the pie chart in Word, click **Format Object**, click the **Size tab**, change the height to **2.5"**, click **OK**, click the **Outside Border button** 🖽 on the Formatting toolbar, compare the pie chart object in the Word report to Figure F-3, then save the document

FIGURE F-1: Worshheet data entered in Excel

Bold and center cells A2 and B2

Bold and right-align cell A8

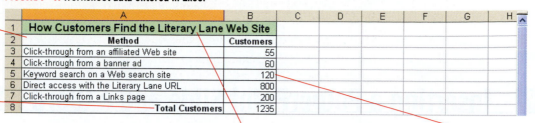

Enhance text with 12-point bold, use the Merge and Center feature to center the text over cells A1 and B1, and fill the cell with Light Green

Apply border lines to cells A1 through B8

FIGURE F-2: Pie chart created in Excel

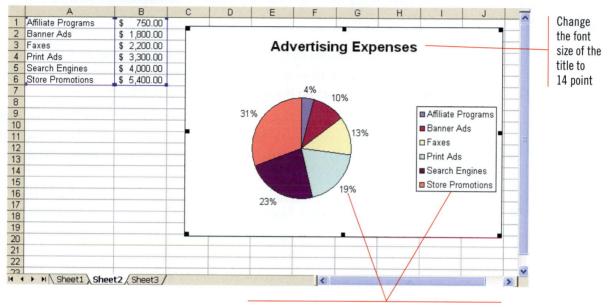

Change the font size of the title to 14 point

Change the font size of the labels and legend text to 10 point

FIGURE F-3: Updated pie chart formatted in Word

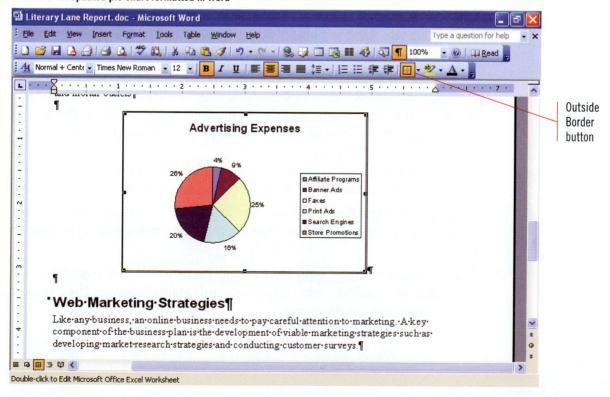

Outside Border button

Integration

ACTIVITY

Inserting a PowerPoint Slide and a Word File

The Literary Lane Report will be distributed at a meeting with MediaLoft executives where a PowerPoint presentation will also be delivered. To help participants visualize the connection between the printed report and the PowerPoint presentation, you use the theme from the PowerPoint presentation on the title page of the report. You then insert a Word file containing additional information for the report.

STEPS

1. Press **[Ctrl][Home]** to move to the beginning of the document, click **Insert** on the menu bar, click **Break**, click **OK** to insert a page break, press **[Ctrl][Home]** to move to the top of the document, click **Insert** on the menu bar, then click **Object**

2. Scroll down, select **Microsoft PowerPoint Slide** in the Object type list, then click **OK**

   A blank PowerPoint slide appears along with the PowerPoint toolbars. Although you modify the slide using PowerPoint tools, the slide is embedded in the Word document which means that it is not saved as a PowerPoint file.

3. Click in the **Click to add title text box**, type **Literary Lane Report**, click in the **Click to add subtitle text box**, type **Online Marketing Activities**, press **[Enter]**, then type **your name**

4. Click the **Slide Design button** 〔Design〕 on the Formatting toolbar in PowerPoint, click the **Pixel.pot** design to apply the Pixel slide design, click **Color Schemes** in the Slide Design task pane, then select the **Green** color scheme as shown in **Figure F-4**

5. Click the **Zoom control list arrow** on the Standard toolbar, click **Whole Page**, click below the embedded slide object, right-click the object, click **Format Object**, click the **Size tab**, type **6** in the Width text box in the Size and rotate area, then click **OK**

6. Click **Format** on the menu bar, click **Borders and Shading**, click **Box** in the Setting area on the Borders tab, select the border Style, Color, and Width shown in **Figure F-5**, click **OK**, then click to the right of the slide object to deselect it

   The PowerPoint slide appears in the Word report as shown in Figure F-6.

7. Press **[Ctrl][G]**, select the **Word** bookmark, click **Go To**, click **Close**, return to 100% view, delete the text **Word File Here** but leave the ¶ mark, click **Insert** on the menu bar, click **File**, navigate to the drive and folder where your Data Files are located if necessary, click **INT F-2.doc**, then click **Insert**

   The contents of the INT F-2.doc file appear in your current document. If you make changes to the text you inserted in this destination file, then the changes are not reflected in the INT F-2.doc source file.

8. Scroll up and delete the title **Market Research Methods** including the ¶, select the **Webographics heading**, click the **Style list arrow** on the Formatting toolbar, then click **Heading 3**

9. Repeat the procedure to apply the Heading 3 style to the Psychographics and Demographics headings, remove the two hard returns following the Demographics section, then save the document

FIGURE F-4: Selecting a custom color scheme

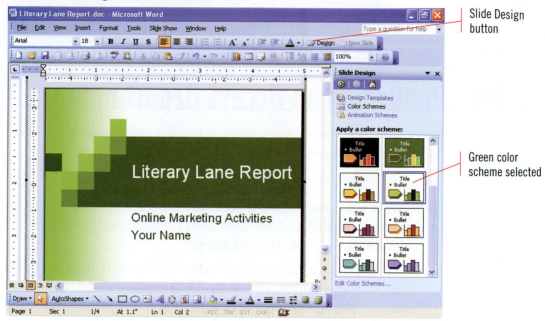

Slide Design button

Green color scheme selected

FIGURE F-5: Border options selected

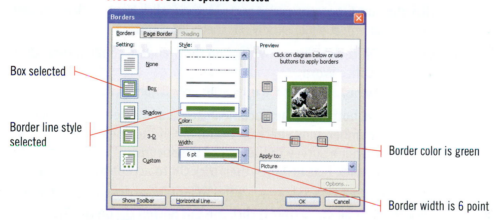

Box selected

Border line style selected

Border color is green

Border width is 6 point

FIGURE F-6: PowerPoint slide in Word

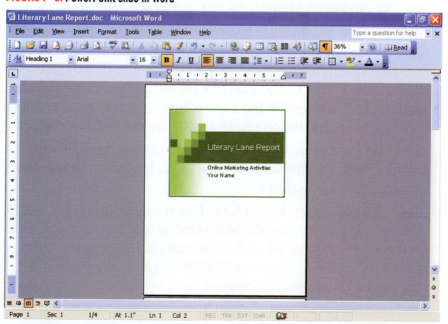

ACTIVITY

Publishing an Access Report in Word

Information related to online survey results for Literary Lane is contained in an Access database. You decide to create a report in Access and then to publish the Access report in Word.

STEPS

1. Press [Ctrl][G], use the Access bookmark, delete the text Access Report Data Here but not the ¶, start Microsoft Access, then open the file Literary Lane.mdb from the drive and folder where your Data Files are stored

2. Click Reports in the Objects bar, double-click Create report by using wizard, click the Tables/Queries list arrow, click Table: Online Survey, click Location in the list of available fields, click the Select Single Field button >, then select the Access Method, Purchase, and Rating fields

3. Click Next, click > to make Location a grouping level as shown in Figure F-7, click Next, click the Sort list arrow, click Access Method, click Next, click Align Left 2, click Next, click the Formal report style, click Next, then click Finish

4. Click the OfficeLinks list arrow 📝▾ on the Standard toolbar, then click Publish It with Microsoft Office Word

   In a few moments, a Word window opens with a new document named Online Survey.rtf.

QUICK TIP

By default, Word enters the number of columns equal to the maximum number of tab characters in any one line of text. The first column in the table is blank.

5. Move to the bottom of the document, select and delete the last line containing the date and page number, move back up to the top of the document, select all lines from the first line under Online Survey to the end of the document, click Table on the menu bar, point to Convert, click Text to Table, then click OK to accept the number of columns entered

6. Scroll up, click in the table, move the pointer over the top of column 1 to show the ⬇, click to select all of column 1, click the Cut button ✂ on the Standard toolbar, click the ⊞ at the upper-left corner of the table to select the entire table, move the pointer over any column division between the first and second columns to show the +‖+, then double-click to automatically resize the columns to fit the data

QUICK TIP

To show the Tables and Borders toolbar, click View on the menu bar, point to Toolbars, then click Tables and Borders.

7. With the table still selected, click Format on the menu bar, click Paragraph, set the Before and After spacing at 0 and the line spacing to Single, click OK, show the Tables and Borders toolbar, select row 1 of the table, click the Merge Cells button 🔲, click after Location, press [Delete], add a colon and a space, apply 15% gray shading to the row, then as shown in Figure F-8, repeat the process to similarly format each row containing a location

8. Select the table again, copy it, paste it into Literary Lane Report.doc, select the entire table in Word, click the Center button ≣ on the Formatting toolbar, then click away from the table to deselect it

TROUBLE

Delete hard returns if necessary to make the report fit onto four pages as shown in Figure F-9.

9. Click the Print Preview button 🔍 to view the document in the Print Preview screen, click the Multiple Pages button 🔳 on the toolbar, select 2 x 2 pages, compare the four pages of the report to Figure F-9, click Close, add your name to the footer, save the document, print a copy, close it, then close all other files and programs

   You don't need to save the Online Survey.rtf file.

FIGURE F-7: Location designated as a grouping level

FIGURE F-8: Table formatted

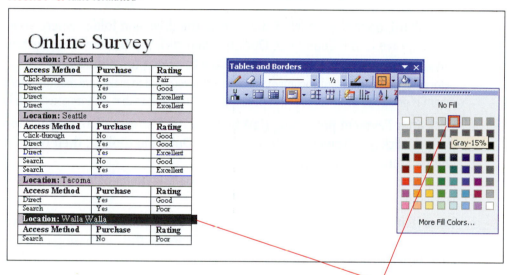

To fill cells with shading, click the Shading Color button list arrow, then click Gray-15%

FIGURE F-9: Completed report in Print Preview

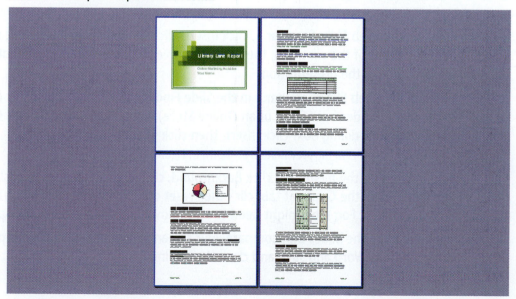

Project 2: E-Commerce Lecture Presentation

As part of several book promotions, MediaLoft plans to offer evening seminars on various topics of interest to local businesspeople in the Los Angeles store. You've been put in charge of helping the seminar facilitators create presentations for the seminars. The first presentation will be on the options available for creating a Web site in order to sell products and services online. The facilitator has provided some of the information for the presentation saved in Outline format in a Word document. You'll combine this information with other content from Access and Excel to create a presentation on e-commerce options.

ACTIVITY — Sending a Word Outline to PowerPoint

Some of the information for the presentation is included in a Word outline and some is included in slides of an existing presentation. You start by sending the Word outline to PowerPoint and then you insert slides from the existing presentation. You then format the presentation in PowerPoint.

STEPS

1. **Start Word, open the file INT F-3.doc from the drive and folder where your Data Files are located, save it as E-Commerce Options, then click the Outline View button ▣ in the lower-left corner of the document window to switch to Outline view**

   Before you can send a Word document to PowerPoint, you need to make sure that the information in the document is presented in an outline with headings and subheadings that are formatted with heading styles.

2. **Click after Payment processing (last bullet under Features of an Online Store), press [Enter], click the Promote button ➕ on the Outlining toolbar, then type Goals of an Online Store as shown in Figure F-10**

   You click the Promote button to move the text to level 1. When the outline is sent to PowerPoint, the text you just typed appears as a slide title.

3. **Press [Enter], click the Demote button ➡ on the Outlining toolbar to move to level 2, type Attract customers, press [Enter], type Expedite the purchasing process, press [Enter], then type Provide timely help**

   QUICK TIP
   You can also press [Tab] to move from level 1 to level 2 and [Shift][Tab] to move from level 2 back to level 1.

4. **Click File on the menu bar, point to Send To, click Microsoft Office PowerPoint, then when the outline appears in PowerPoint, save the presentation as E-Commerce Options**

5. **Click Insert on the menu bar, click Slides from Files, click Browse, navigate to the drive and folder where your Data Files for this book are stored, then double-click INT F-4.ppt**

   In the Slide Finder dialog box, you select the slides you want to insert into the active presentation.

6. **Click Slide 1. Web Skills Seminar 1, click Insert, click the newly inserted slide in the Slides bar (at the left of the window), then drag it above the current slide 1 so that it becomes the first slide in the presentation**

7. **Click Slide 1. Web Skills Seminar 1 in the Slide Finder dialog box to deselect it, click Slide 4 in the Slides bar (Goals of an Online Store), click Slide 2. Entry-Level Options in the Slide Finder dialog box, click Insert, then click Close**

   The new slide appears in the presentation as shown in Figure F-11.

8. **Click Format on the menu bar, click Background, click the Background fill list arrow, click Fill Effects, click the Gradient tab, click the Preset option button, click the Preset colors list arrow, select Fog (you might need to scroll down), click OK, then click Apply to All**

9. **Click Slide 1 in the Slides bar, compare your screen to Figure F-12, save the presentation, then return to Word and save and close the outline**

FIGURE F-10: Working in Outline view in Word

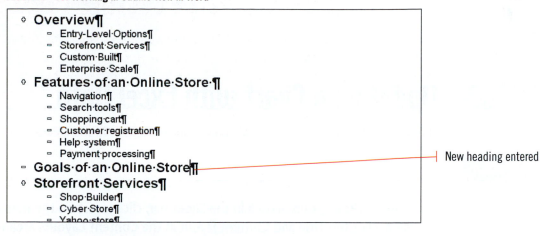

New heading entered

FIGURE F-11: Slide from another file inserted in the presentation

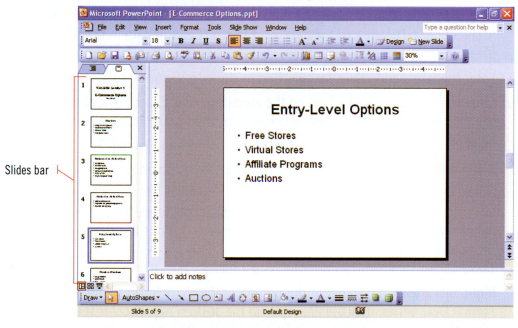

Slides bar

FIGURE F-12: Presentation formatted with the Fog preset gradient background

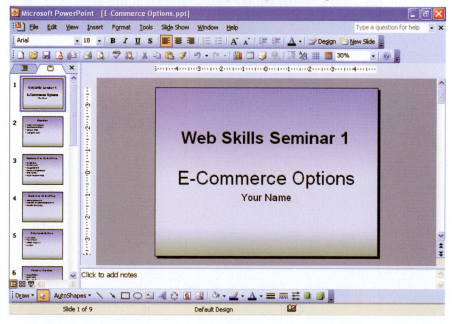

ACTIVITY

Updating a Chart with Excel Data

The presentation includes a chart that you will update from a file you create in Excel. You can then modify the appearance of the chart on the PowerPoint slide.

STEPS

1. In PowerPoint, click Slide 5 in the Slides bar, click Insert on the menu bar, click New Slide, click the Title and Content layout in the Content Layouts area of the Slide Layout task pane, then close the Slide Layout task pane

2. Click the Insert Chart button in the center of the new slide, click the gray rectangle in the upper-left corner of the datasheet to select all the data in the datasheet, then press [Delete]

3. Enter the labels and values for the chart as shown in Figure F-13

4. Close the datasheet, click Chart on the menu bar, click Chart Type, click Bar, click OK, click the Click to add title text in the slide title area, then type Most Valuable Features

5. Start Excel, then enter the labels and values as shown in Figure F-14

6. Select cells B1 through B6, click the Percent Style button on the Formatting toolbar, save the worksheet as E-Commerce Options Data, then close the workbook

7. In PowerPoint, double-click the chart, click Edit on the menu bar, click Import File, navigate to the location where you saved E-Commerce Options Data.xls, select the file, click Open, then click OK

   The data entered in the Excel file overrides the data originally entered in the datasheet for the chart.

8. Right-click the light blue bar at the bottom of the chart (representing Security), click Format Data Series, click the Pink color in the bottom row of color selections, then click OK

9. Fill the Favorites Lists bar (gray) with Orange and the Searching bar (black) with Lavender, click outside the chart to deselect it, then save the presentation

   The chart appears as shown in Figure F-15.

FIGURE F-13: Chart data in PowerPoint

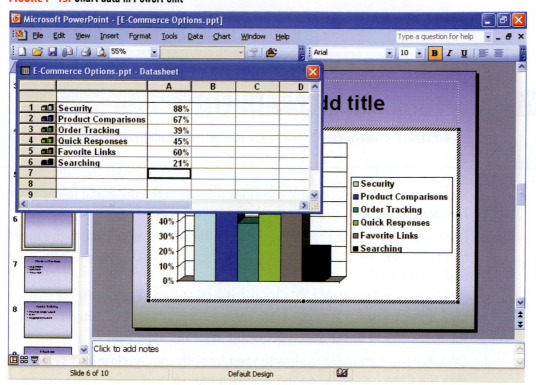

FIGURE F-14: Data entered in Excel

	A	B	C	D	E	F	G	H	I	J
1	Security	0.38								
2	Product Comparisons	0.24								
3	Order Tracking	0.15								
4	Quick Response	0.12								
5	Favorites Lists	0.09								
6	Searching	0.02								
7										
8										

FIGURE F-15: Completed bar chart and text box

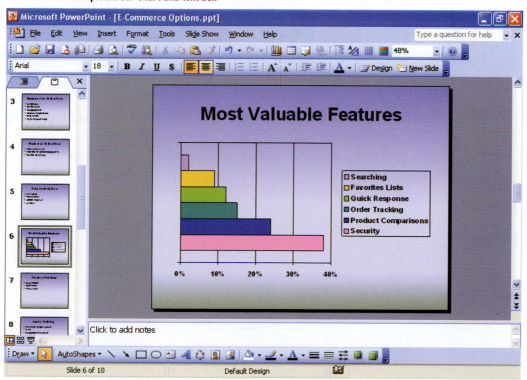

ACTIVITY	**Inserting an Access Query**

The presentation also needs to include a query created from data stored in an Access database.

STEPS

1. Start Access, open E-Commerce Options.mdb from the drive and folder where your Data Files are stored, then click Queries in the Objects bar

2. Double-click Create query by using wizard, click Company Name in the list of available fields, click the Select Single Field button ▶, then select the Location, Web Site Type, and Annual Online Sales fields

3. Click Next, click Next, click Finish, click the Design View button 📐 to switch to Design View, then as shown in Figure F-16, enter Los Angeles in the Criteria cell for Location and select Ascending as the Sort type for the Web Site Type field

4. Click the Run button ❗ to view the results of the query, close and save the query, then click the Copy button 📋 on the Standard toolbar

5. View the presentation in PowerPoint, click Slide 9, click Insert on the menu bar, click New Slide, enter Sample Company Revenues as the slide title, click the Title Only layout in the Text Layouts area of the Slide Layout task pane, close the Slide Layout task pane, click in a blank area of the slide, then click the Paste button 📋 on the Standard toolbar

6. Click the table to select it, click the shaded border, drag the table away from the Company Web Sites Query text, click Company Web Sites Query, click the shaded border surrounding the text, then press [Delete]

7. Click the table to select it, click the shaded border, click Format on the menu bar, click Table, click the Fill tab, click the Fill Color list arrow, click More Colors, click a Light Pink color, click OK, then click OK

8. With the table still selected, click the Font Size list arrow on the Formatting toolbar, click 18, then size, position, and format text in the table as shown in Figure F-17

   You can use the mouse to drag sizing handles to modify the size of the table.

9. Go to Slide 1 in the presentation, enter your name where indicated, click File on the menu bar, click Print, click the Print what list arrow, click Handouts, verify that 6 slides will print on each page, click OK, then save and close the presentation and close all open applications

FIGURE F-16: Query requirements

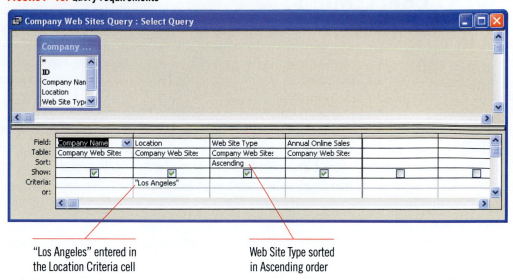

"Los Angeles" entered in
the Location Criteria cell

Web Site Type sorted
in Ascending order

FIGURE F-17: Access query table formatted in PowerPoint

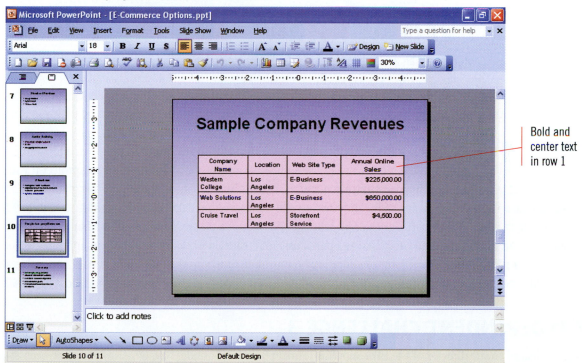

Bold and
center text
in row 1

▼ INDEPENDENT CHALLENGE 1

Create a multiple-page report in Word that includes objects from Excel, PowerPoint, and Access, and another Word file. Base the report on a business-oriented subject. For example, you could write a report that describes sales activities over the past six months related to a company of your choice, or you could write a report that proposes a change to a specific policy such as the employee dress code or the establishment of an employee recognition program. Follow the steps provided to create the report in Word and then to include objects for a variety of other applications.

a. Start Word, then type text for the report. Include placeholders for objects that you will insert from other applications. Your report should include space for an embedded worksheet from Excel, an embedded slide from PowerPoint, a linked chart from Excel, a report from Access, and a file from Word. In addition, include your name in the footer.

b. Save the report as **My Long Report**, start Excel, then create a worksheet containing data appropriate to a section of your report and a chart. You determine what kind of chart (for example, pie, line, etc.). Save the Excel workbook as **My Long Report Data**.

c. Embed the Excel worksheet in your Word report, then copy the chart to an appropriate place in the report and paste it as a link.

d. Embed a PowerPoint slide somewhere in the report. You can choose to include the slide as your title page or in another location. Enter appropriate text and apply a slide design.

e. Insert a Word file containing additional information for your report.

f. Start Access, create a database called **My Long Report**, create a table containing data relevant to your report, then create a query and a report that highlights some aspect of the data.

g. Publish the Access report in Word, convert the text to a table, enhance the table attractively, then copy it to an appropriate location in the report.

h. Print a copy of the report, save and close the report, then save and close all open documents and exit all programs.

▼ INDEPENDENT CHALLENGE 2

Create a lecture presentation on an academic or business-related subject of your choice.

a. Create an outline in Word of the slide titles and bulleted items for the presentation. Remember to work in Outline view and use the Promote and Demote buttons to designate levels. Text at level 1 is formatted with the Heading 1 style and appears as a slide title. Save the outline as **My Lecture Outline**.

b. Send the outline to PowerPoint, add your name to the first slide in the presentation, then add additional slides from another PowerPoint presentation (you can use a presentation you've created for another project if you wish). Save the current presentation as **My Lecture**, then apply a background fill. Use one of the preset gradient fills if you wish.

c. Create a chart on one of the slides and then update the chart from data you've entered in an Excel worksheet. Modify the data series in the chart. For example, change the color of a pie wedge to green or a bar to yellow.

d. Open an Access database you've created previously (or create a new one), then copy an appropriate query and paste it onto a slide in your PowerPoint presentation. Remove the title from the query and enhance the table attractively.

e. Print a copy of your presentation as a handout with nine slides to a page, then save and close all files.

▼ INDEPENDENT CHALLENGE 3

As the assistant to the director of the Lake Superior Tourism Board in Thunder Bay, Ontario, you have been asked to prepare a yearly progress report from data contained in a variety of sources. The completed report appears in Figure F-18.

a. Open the file INT F-5.doc from the drive and folder where your Data Files are located, then save it as **Tourism Board Report**. (Hint: If you are saving your work to floppy disks, you may need to save this file on a separate disk.)

b. As shown in Figure F-18, insert a PowerPoint slide as an embedded object and enter the text indicated (including your name). Apply the Mountain Top.pot slide design with the turquoise color scheme shown in Figure F-18. Change the width of the object to 3" and center it.

c. Replace the text Excel Worksheet with the worksheet in the file INT F-6.xls (located in the drive and folder where your Data Files are stored), inserted as an embedded object.

d. Replace the text Word File with the file in the file INT F-7.doc located in the drive and folder where your Data Files are stored.

e. Start Access, open the file Thunder Bay Sports.mdb from the drive and folder where your Data Files are stored, create a query that lists only events to be held in 2006, publish the query in Word, then copy the query to the report, replacing the text Access Query Here and format it as shown in Figure F-18. (*Hint*: Apply the Table Columns 2 Table AutoFormat.)

f. Delete hard returns and adjust margins as necessary to make your document resemble Figure F-18, type your name at the end of the report, print a copy of the document, then save and close the document and all other files.

Integration

FIGURE F-18

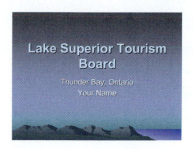

Lake Superior Tourism Board

Thunder Bay, Ontario
Your Name

Recreational Activities Committee Report – Josephine Daimler
- Josephine circulated a report on recreational activities appropriate for visitors to the Thunder Bay region. The report provided information about the following topics:
  - Summer 2006 committee meetings
  - Family canoe night in partnership with Jeremy Watson, owner of Thunder Bay Canoe Rentals
  - Shown below is a summary of the revenue generated by local tour outfitters in the 2005 and 2006 summer seasons.

Thunder Bay Tour Operators Revenue					
Superior Canoe Rentals	Muskeg Treks	Shining Waters Fishing	Lakeland Hikes	Lakehead Tours	Water World Paddling
Summer, 2005 $25,000.00	$28,000.00	$35,000.00	$48,500.00	$85,400.00	$38,400.00
Summer, 2006 $29,400.00	$32,700.00	$75,600.00	$82,900.00	$47,600.00	$36,500.00

Tourism Board Activities
- The luncheon held for tour outfitters on Tour Appreciation Day was a success
- The tourist board plans to host a Welcome to Thunder Bay event on July 31. Volunteers are requested to assist with tourist-centered activities.

Tourism Director's Report
- The Professional Development day on February 24 was successful. Tour outfitters learned how to use the new Tour Marketing Program accessible on the World Wide Web.
- A new hotel is under construction overlooking the lake. The hotel is slated to open on July 1 in time for Canada Day celebrations.
- The Bed and Breakfast Information Meeting held in May was fully attended. Bed and Breakfast operators from all over the western Ontario region enjoyed a spirited presentation by Martha Harris, the guru of the successful B & B business.

Committee Reports
T.B.S.A. (Thunder Bay Sports Association)
- On July 2 T.B.S.A. will sponsor a run event that includes a marathon, a 5K fun, and a 2K walk/run. The cost of the run will be $25.00 and includes a hat OR a T-shirt.
- Shown below are all the events sponsored by T.B.S.A. for summer 2006.

Event	Category	Commercial Sponsor	Year
Snowshoe Marathon	Individual	Tom Howe's Donuts	2006
Summer Marathon	Individual	Home Station	2006
Black Fly Trek	Individual	Muskeg Credit Union	2006
Fly Fishing Derby	Individual/Team	Lakeland Real Estate	2006

Prepared by Your Name

As the resident naturalist at the Maplewood Nature Preserve in North Vancouver, British Columbia, you are responsible for putting together presentations about the local wildlife for school and community groups. You need to create two slides that you can later use to integrate into other presentations. One slide contains a query table from Access and another slide contains a chart that needs to be updated with data from an Excel worksheet. The Daybreak preset gradient fill is used for the background on both slides. Open the Access database called Nature Preserve.mdb from the drive and folder where your Data Files are stored, create a query from the Bird Sightings table that includes only birds sighted on June 6, copy the Access query into a blank PowerPoint slide, then add the title and format the table as shown in Figure F-19. Insert a new slide, create the chart shown in Figure F-20, change the color of the black column to red and the lime green column to yellow, then update the chart with data from the Excel data file called INT F-8.xls. Type your name in the slide footer, save the presentation as **Nature Preserve**, print a copy of the slides, then close the files and exit all programs.

FIGURE F-19

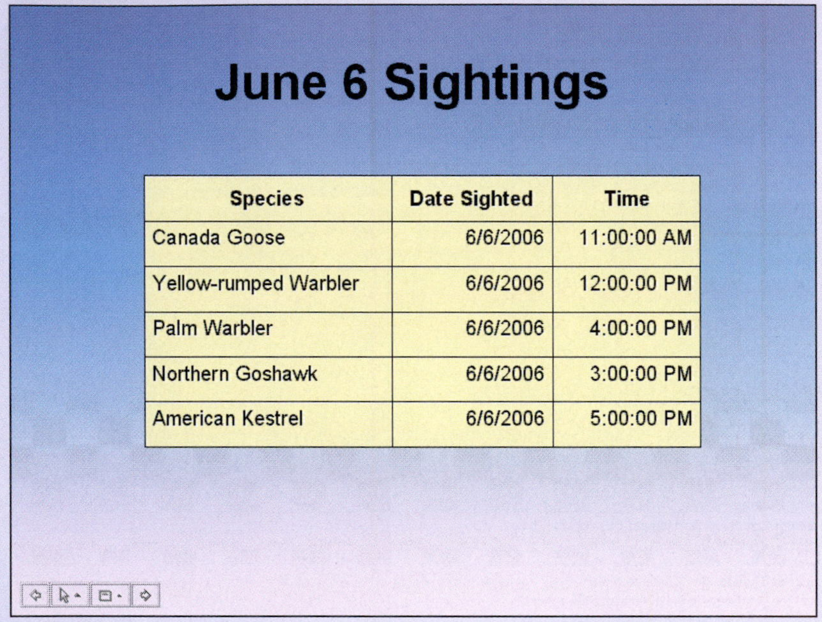

June 6 Sightings

Species	Date Sighted	Time
Canada Goose	6/6/2006	11:00:00 AM
Yellow-rumped Warbler	6/6/2006	12:00:00 PM
Palm Warbler	6/6/2006	4:00:00 PM
Northern Goshawk	6/6/2006	3:00:00 PM
American Kestrel	6/6/2006	5:00:00 PM

FIGURE F-20

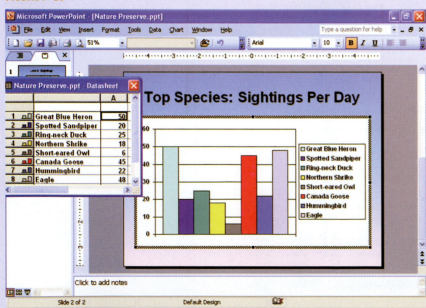

Getting Started with Publisher 2003

OBJECTIVES

Define desktop publishing software
Start Publisher and view the Publisher window
Create a publication using an existing design
Replace text in text boxes
Format text
Resize and move objects
Insert a picture
Save, preview, and print a publication
Close a publication and exit Publisher

Microsoft Publisher 2003 is a desktop publishing program that helps you transform your ideas into visually appealing publications and Web sites for your business, organization, or home. In this unit, you will learn how to use one of Publisher's existing designs to create a publication that includes text and graphics. Then, you will save and print your publication before closing it and exiting Publisher. You are the director of human resources at MediaLoft, a nationwide chain of bookstore cafés that sells books, CDs, and videos. You use Publisher to create a flyer announcing the MediaLoft summer barbecue for the San Francisco-based employees.

Defining Desktop Publishing Software

Desktop publishing programs let you integrate text, pictures, drawings, tables, and charts in one document, called a **publication**. You can design a publication from scratch, or you can customize an existing design. Figure A-1 shows three publications created using Publisher's premade designs. You want the flyer for the MediaLoft summer barbecue to be informative and eye-catching. You decide to create it using one of Publisher's designs. Figure A-2 shows the original design that you will customize to create the flyer. You first review Publisher's features.

DETAILS

- ### Create professionally designed publications

  Publisher includes more than 1000 premade designs for creating newsletters, flyers, calendars, and many other types of publications. The premade designs include sample text and graphics, a sample layout, and sample color palettes. You plan on using the BBQ flyer design to create the flyer.

- ### Create a set of publications with a common design

  Publisher includes more than 40 **design sets**, groups of sample publications with the same design theme. You could use a design set to ensure a consistent look for all the printed materials for your company.

- ### Change your publication's color scheme

  Publisher includes more than 50 preset color schemes that you can apply to the publications. Each color scheme contains five colors that work well together. You plan on using the Meadow color scheme in the flyer.

- ### Insert text and graphics created in other applications and insert clip art

  You can insert files created in other programs into your publications, such as text from a Word file. You can insert photos, scanned images, or images drawn using Publisher or another drawing program. The Clip Art task pane, which contains downloadable images from the Web and is included with Publisher and all Microsoft Office applications, contains thousands of pictures, sounds, and motion clips that you can also add to your publications. You can also use the **Catalog Merge** feature to insert records from a data source such as a spreadsheet or database to create publications with multiple records.

- ### Arrange text and graphics easily

  All elements of a publication are **objects**—boxes that contain text or frames that contain graphics that you can easily move, flip, resize, overlap, or color to control the overall appearance of a publication.

- ### Choose from preset font schemes and format text easily

  Fonts play a very important role in setting the mood and conveying the message of a publication. A **font** is the typeface or design of a set of characters, such as letters and numbers. Publisher includes 30 **font schemes**, or sets of fonts that look good together. You can also use Publisher's text-formatting features to enhance fonts by adding characteristics such as bold and italics. You choose the Punch font scheme.

- ### Print publications on a printer or prepare a publication for commercial printing

  Publisher's commercial printing technology supports process color, spot color and black-and-white printing, the four major color models (RGB, HSL, CMYK, and PANTONE), and automatic and manual color trapping.

- ### Publish to the Web

  You can create Web sites using Publisher's Web site premade designs or using the Web Site Wizard. Publisher includes hundreds of Web page backgrounds and animated GIF files. You can also convert an existing publication to a Web page or e-mail.

FIGURE A-1: Sample Publisher publications

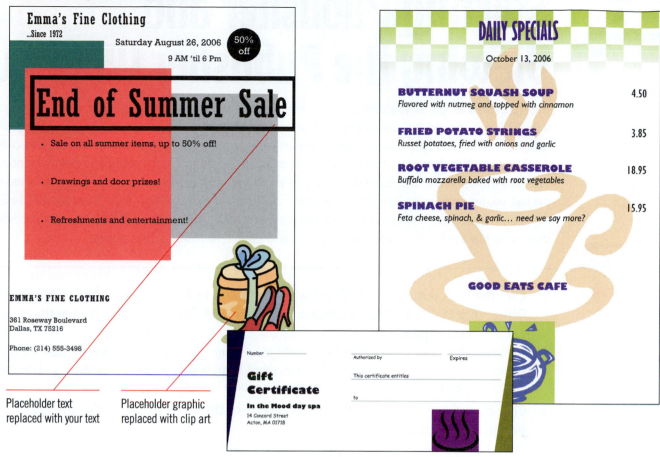

Placeholder text replaced with your text

Placeholder graphic replaced with clip art

FIGURE A-2: Your notes for modifying the flyer

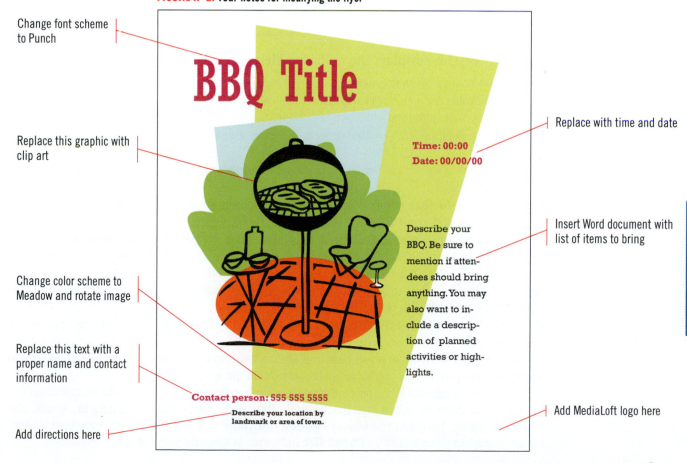

Change font scheme to Punch

Replace this graphic with clip art

Change color scheme to Meadow and rotate image

Replace this text with a proper name and contact information

Add directions here

Replace with time and date

Insert Word document with list of items to bring

Add MediaLoft logo here

Starting Publisher and Viewing the Publisher Window

You start Publisher just as you start any other Windows application—by using the Start menu. When you start Publisher, you see that the screen is divided into two panes. The left pane is called the **task pane**, which is a window that provides the most commonly used commands. Using the task pane, you can create a publication either from scratch or by choosing a premade design and customizing it to meet your needs. Table A-1 lists options in the New Publication task pane. The task pane displays different options based on the task you are performing. The right pane, called the **Publications Gallery**, displays thumbnails of existing designs from which you can choose if you don't want to start from scratch. You start Publisher, start a new blank publication, and take a look at the important elements of the program.

STEPS

TROUBLE
If Microsoft Office is not on your All Programs menu, ask your technical support person for assistance.

1. **Click the Start button** <kbd>start</kbd> **on the taskbar, point to All Programs, point to Microsoft Office, click Microsoft Office Publisher 2003, then click Publications for Print in the New Publication task pane**

   Publisher opens. You can see that the screen is divided into two panes, as shown in Figure A-3. The Publication Gallery on the right side of the screen shows **thumbnails**, or small representations, of the Quick Publications, the Publication Type listed first under Publications for Print.

2. **Click Blank Print Publication in the New section of the task pane, then click the Close button in the task pane**

   The task pane and the Publications Gallery close, and a blank one-page publication appears in the publication window, as shown in Figure A-4. Until you save a publication and give it a name, the temporary name is Publication1.

DETAILS

The Publisher window displays the following elements:

- The **title bar** contains the name of your publication and the program name.
- The **menu bar** lists the names of menus that contain Publisher commands. Clicking a menu name displays a list of related commands from which you can choose.
- When you start Publisher, four **toolbars** appear by default, although your screen may differ depending on past usage.
- The **Standard toolbar** includes buttons for the most commonly used commands, such as opening, saving, or printing a publication.
- The **Formatting toolbar** contains buttons for the most frequently used formatting commands, such as changing the font, and formatting and aligning text.
- The **Objects toolbar** includes buttons for selecting and creating text boxes, shapes, and picture frames, as well as buttons for working with other types of objects. The **Connect Text Boxes toolbar** gives you options for connecting overflow text from one part of your publication to another.
- The **publication window** includes the **publication page** or pages and a **desktop workspace** for storing text and graphics prior to placing them in your publication.
- The **vertical and horizontal rulers** help you to position, size, and align text and graphics precisely in your publications.
- The **vertical and horizontal scroll bars** work like scroll bars in any Windows program—you use them to display different parts of your publication in the publication window.
- The **status bar**, located below the publication window, displays the position and size of the selected object in a publication and shows the current page. You can use the **Page Navigation buttons** to jump to a specific page in your publication. You can use the **Object Position indicator** to position the pointer or an object containing text or graphics precisely, and the **Object Size indicator** to gauge the size of an object accurately.

FIGURE A-3: Publisher opening screen with task pane open

New Publication task pane

Click to close Publication Gallery

Click to open a blank publication

Your list of files will vary

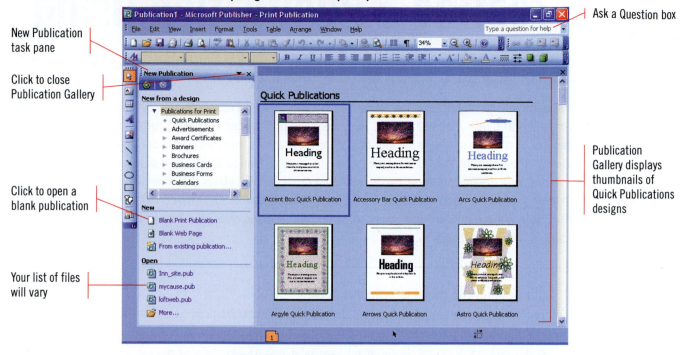

Ask a Question box

Publication Gallery displays thumbnails of Quick Publications designs

FIGURE A-4: Blank one-page publication

Title bar

Menu bar

Standard toolbar

Formatting toolbar

Objects toolbar

Your default display may differ depending on past usage

Vertical ruler

Scroll bars

Status bar

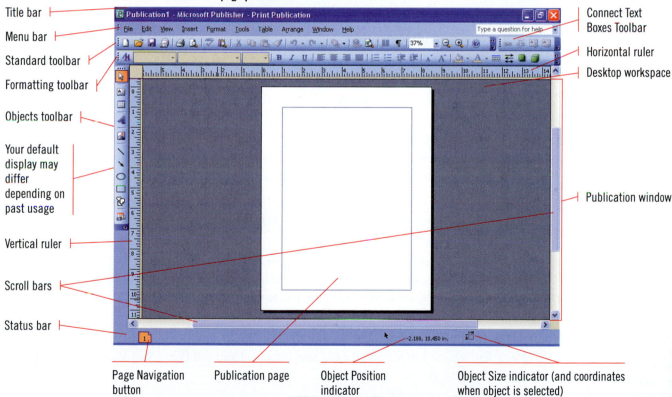

Connect Text Boxes Toolbar

Horizontal ruler

Desktop workspace

Publication window

Page Navigation button

Publication page

Object Position indicator

Object Size indicator (and coordinates when object is selected)

Publisher 2003

TABLE A-1: Task pane options available when starting a new publication

area of task pane	options available
New from a design	Click a publication type from the list, then click a design in the Publication Gallery
New	Start a blank publication or Web page from scratch or from an existing publication
Open	Open a publication that has been recently opened by clicking its name on the list, or click More to find a publication on your computer

Creating a Publication Using an Existing Design

Although you can always start from scratch, the easiest way to create a publication is to start from an existing design and then modify it to meet your needs and preferences. Publisher provides hundreds of premade designs all containing sample layouts, font schemes, graphics, and colors schemes. You can use the New by Design or the New by Publication Type options in the task pane to access these designs. Some of the objects in a premade design contain **wizards**, which ask you questions about the information you want to include in your publication, and then customize the object according to your answers. You start a new publication by using the New Publication task pane. You decide to create the flyer for the summer barbecue by starting with an existing design.

STEPS

1. **Click File on the menu bar, then click New**

    The task pane opens, displaying options for creating a new publication.

2. **Click Publications for Print if it isn't expanded under New from a design at the top of the task pane, click Flyers, then click Event in the expanded list of flyer types**

    The Publication Gallery displays thumbnails of Event Flyers, as shown in Figure A-5.

3. **Click the BBQ Flyer in the Publications Gallery**

    The BBQ flyer appears in the publication window. The task pane now displays options for modifying the layout of the flyer.

4. **Click Publication Designs in the task pane**

    The Publications Designs task pane displays flyers, with the BBQ flyer design selected. You can apply a new design at this point by clicking any one of the designs listed.

5. **Click Color Schemes in the task pane**

    The Apply a color scheme list appears in the task pane. Each color scheme includes five colors that work well together. Floral is the color scheme selected by default for the BBQ flyer design.

6. **Scroll through the alphabetical list of color schemes, then click Meadow**

    The Meadow color scheme is applied to the flyer in the publication window.

7. **Click Font Schemes in the task pane**

    A list of named font schemes appears in the task pane, showing 30 predefined sets of fonts that work well together. Font schemes make it possible to change the look of your publication quickly, assigning all text in major fonts to one style, and all text in a minor font to another style, ensuring that fonts are applied consistently throughout your publication.

8. **Scroll down the list of font schemes, then click Punch**

    The new font scheme that includes the Gill Sans Ultra Bold font and Comic Sans MS font is applied to the BBQ flyer. Compare your screen to Figure A-6.

9. **Click the Close button X in the task pane**

    The task pane closes, and the publication window expands to give you more room to work.

FIGURE A-5: Event flyers displayed in Publication Gallery

New Publication task pane

Types of publications listed here

Select this flyer

Publication Gallery displays thumbnails of event flyers

FIGURE A-6: BBQ flyer with Meadow color scheme and Punch font scheme

Font Schemes task pane

Click to choose a color scheme

Click to choose Punch font scheme

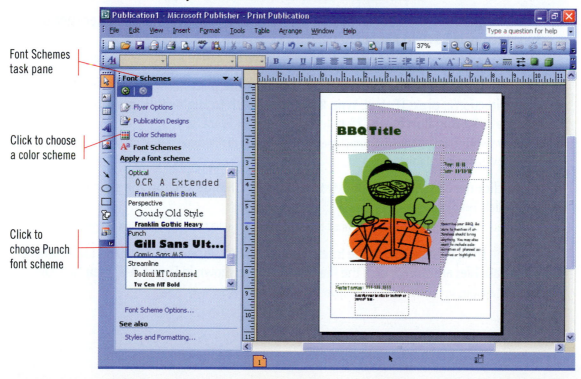

Clues to Use

Personal Stationery Sets

Publisher allows you to create coordinated stationery elements, including letterheads, address labels, and envelopes using the Personal Stationery Sets feature. To create Personal Stationery Sets, click Design Sets under the New from a design section of the New Publication task pane, then click Personal Stationery Sets. Choose a theme, such as Garden or Ambassador, then choose an item such as an envelope or letterhead. If you have updated the Personal Information Wizard, your address and business information is automatically filled in for you, creating an instant, professional set of stationery items.

Replacing Text in Text Boxes

In Publisher, every element in a publication is contained in a frame. A **frame** is an object that contains text or graphics. A **text box** is a frame that holds text. Before you can add text to a Publisher publication, you must first create a text box to hold the text. Once you create a text box, you can type text directly into it, or you can insert text from a Word document file into it. To enter or insert text in a text box, first you must select it. When you click a text box to select it, **sizing handles**, or handles appear around its edges. If you type or insert more text than fits in the text box, you may resize the text, resize the text box, or continue the text in another text box. You are ready to replace the placeholder text in the flyer with your own text. You type some of the text directly into the text boxes and insert text describing the summer barbecue from a Word file you created last week.

STEPS

QUICK TIP

The green circular handle at the top of the box is called a rotation handle. By dragging this handle, you can rotate the object freely or flip the object upside-down.

1. **Click in the center of the BBQ Title text box to select the placeholder text**
   The title placeholder text is selected and sizing handles appear around the text box, indicating that the box itself is also selected.

2. **Type Company BBQ, click 00:00 in the Time text box, then press [F9]**
   Pressing [F9] zooms in on the selected section of your publication, making it easier to see your work in detail. The [F9] key is a **toggle key**—press it once to zoom in, then press it again to zoom back out.

3. **Type Noon 'til ???, click 00/00/00 in the Date text box, then type Friday, July 14**

TROUBLE

Make sure you select the phone number, as well.

4. **Scroll down to see the Contact person text box, select the text in the Contact person text box, then type RSVP to Karen Rosen, ext. 213, by July 3**
   The text you type replaces the placeholder text and takes on the default formatting for the text box.

5. **Click the Describe your location text box to select the placeholder text in the frame, then type Directions:, press [Enter], type Route 101 North to Highway 1, press [Enter], then type Take Stinson Beach exit, 23 miles north of San Francisco**
   If you are writing long stories, it's sometimes easier to create the document in Word and then insert the file into a text frame in Publisher.

6. **Right-click the Describe your BBQ frame, point to Change Text on the shortcut menu, then click Text File**
   The Insert Text dialog box opens. You need to locate and then select the file you plan to insert.

7. **Click the Look in list arrow in the Insert Text dialog box, locate the drive and folder where your Data Files are stored, click the file PB A-1.doc as shown in Figure A-7, then click OK**
   The text appears in the document. Compare your flyer with Figure A-8.

FIGURE A-7: Insert Text dialog box

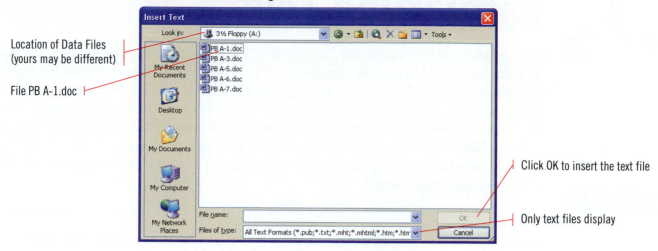

Location of Data Files
(yours may be different)

File PB A-1.doc

Click OK to insert the text file

Only text files display

FIGURE A-8: BBQ flyer with placeholder text replaced

Text you entered

Text inserted from Word file

Clues to Use

Creating text boxes

If you need additional text boxes in your publication, or if you are creating a publication from scratch, you can easily create a new text box. To create a text box, click the Text Box button on the Objects toolbar. The pointer changes to a crosshair pointer. Position the pointer where you want one corner of the text frame to appear, press and hold the mouse button, then drag diagonally to create a rectangular frame, as shown in Figure A-9. Release the mouse button when the text box is the size and shape that you want. Then, you can enter text in the text box by clicking in the frame and typing or inserting a Word file.

FIGURE A-9: Creating a text box

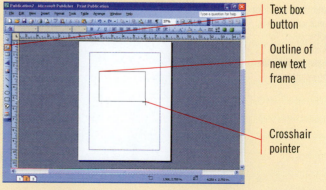

Text box button

Outline of new text frame

Crosshair pointer

Publisher 2003

Formatting Text

Once you enter text in your publication, you can select it and then apply formatting to enhance its appearance. You can format text using the Formatting toolbar, which includes buttons for boldfacing, italicizing, and underlining text, and for changing text alignment and text color. You can easily change the font style and the **font size**, the physical size of the characters measured in points, using the Font Size list arrow on the Formatting toolbar. Another formatting feature is AutoFit. **AutoFit** automatically sizes text to fit it in a text box. You format the text to make the flyer more attractive and readable. You use the AutoFit feature to resize text, you change the font in other text boxes from Comic Sans to Franklin Gothic Demi, then you remove bold formatting.

STEPS

1. **Click in the Company BBQ text box, press [F9] to zoom in, select the text, click Format on the menu bar, point to AutoFit Text, then click Best Fit**

   All the text in the Company BBQ text box is now bigger, as shown in Figure A-10. The font and font size of the selected text are displayed on the Formatting toolbar. The font is Gill Sans Ultra Bold and the font size is 58.8.

2. **Press [F9], then click in the For Friday's beach party text box**

3. **Press [Ctrl][A] to select all the text in the text box, press [F9] to zoom in, then click the Font list arrow ⬚ on the Formatting toolbar**

   The names of the fonts in the Font list are formatted in the font they represent, making it easier for you to choose among them.

   QUICK TIP

   Recently selected fonts may appear at the top of the font list as well as within the alphabetical list.

4. **Scroll through the list of fonts, then click Franklin Gothic Demi on the Font list, as shown in Figure A-11**

   The selected text changes to Franklin Gothic Demi.

5. **Click in the Directions text box, select the text, click the Font list arrow ⬚, click Franklin Gothic Demi, press [Ctrl][B] to turn off bolding, click the Font Color list arrow 🔺, then click the dark blue square**

   The text now appears in dark blue in Franklin Gothic Demi. The Font Color button now shows the color dark blue, indicating that you can click it to apply dark blue formatting to selected text.

   QUICK TIP

   Press [Ctrl][B] to quickly bold text after you select it.

6. **Press [F9], select the text in the Time text box, then click the Bold button B on the Formatting toolbar**

   The selected text is no longer boldface.

   QUICK TIP

   It is a good idea to limit the number of fonts you use in a publication. Too many fonts can make a publication look cluttered.

7. **Select the text in the Date text box, click B, select the text in the RSVP text box, then click B**

   The fonts are consistent, and the flyer looks professional.

FIGURE A-10: AutoFitting text in a frame

Font of selected text

Font size of selected text in text box

AutoFit command creates larger text in text box

Bold button

FIGURE A-11: Choosing a font

Font list arrow

Franklin Gothic Demi

All text in the text box is selected

Font Color list arrow

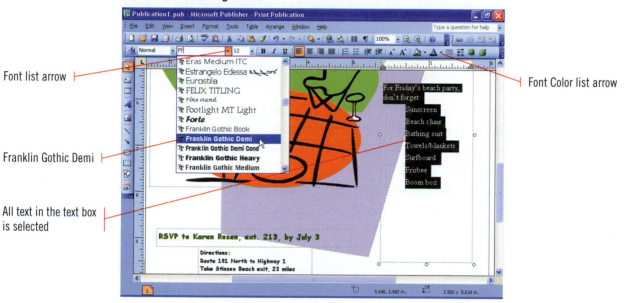

Clues to Use

Checking your publication

Before you finalize a publication, you should check it for spelling and design errors. To have Publisher check for spelling errors in your publication, click Tools on the menu bar, point to Spelling, then click Spelling. If there are words that Publisher does not recognize, the Check Spelling dialog box will open. In the Check Spelling dialog box, shown in Figure A-12, you can choose to ignore or change the words Publisher identifies as misspelled. You can also add a word to the dictionary. To check the spelling in every text box in your publication, make sure the Check all stories check box is selected in the Check Spelling dialog box. Design errors include text that runs off the page, overflow text, or graphics that are not scaled proportionally. To check for design errors, click Tools on the menu bar, then

click Design Checker. In the Design Checker task pane, to go to an item, click an item in the Select an item to fix list.

FIGURE A-12: Check Spelling dialog box

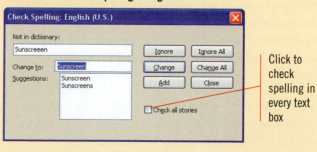

Click to check spelling in every text box

Resizing and Moving Objects

In the course of creating a publication, you might find it necessary to resize or move objects. For example, you might want to make a text box smaller because it contains too much white space, or you might want to move a picture closer to its caption. To move or resize an object, you must first select it. To resize an object, you drag a handle. To move an object, you click anywhere on the object (except on a handle) and drag it to a new location. 🎨 You resize the text boxes at the bottom of the flyer to align their right edges. You also decide to move the picture frame down and to the left so that it is even with the left margin.

STEPS

1. **Click the Directions text box to select it**
   Handles appear around the edges of the text box.

2. **Position the pointer over the middle-right handle**
   When you position the pointer over a handle, a Resize pointer appears. Depending on the handle, the pointer is either a horizontal, vertical, or diagonal resize pointer. See Table A-2 for a list of common pointer shapes. The rulers can be used as guides to align objects precisely as you resize and move them. A line moves along the ruler as you move the object to guide your placement.

3. **Drag the middle-right handle right to the 5" mark on the horizontal ruler, as shown in Figure A-13**
   The text automatically expands to fill the resized text box area.

4. **Click the BBQ graphic in the blue frame, then press [F9]**
   The pointer changes to the Move pointer ✛. You use this pointer to move any Publisher object.

5. **Click and drag the BBQ graphic down and to the left slightly so that its left edge is on the left margin, then release the mouse button**
   The handles still surround the graphic, with a green rotation handle at the top. You can adjust the angle of any object by dragging the rotation handle.

6. **Click the blue background object, then drag the rotation handle to the left ¼"**
   The blue picture frame is now less sharply angled. Compare your screen to Figure A-14.

Clues to use

Aligning objects

You can align objects with guides by hand or you can have Publisher align them for you. To align an object by hand, simply drag or resize the object using the mouse. The Object Position and Object Size indicators in the status bar can help you to place objects exactly. You can also use Publisher's Snap to and Nudge features to help you align objects precisely to guides. To turn on the Snap to feature, enable one or more of the Snap commands on the Arrange menu. Snap To Ruler Marks snaps an object to the closest ruler mark, Snap To Guides automatically snaps an object to the closest layout guide, and Snap To Objects snaps an object to the closest object.

Publisher's Nudge feature allows you to move or nudge an object one small increment at a time. To nudge an object, select the object, click Arrange on the menu bar, point to Nudge, then click Up, Down, Left, or Right. You can also nudge an object by pressing and holding [Alt] while pressing one of the arrow keys. To change the distance objects are nudged using the keyboard, click Tools on the menu bar, click Options, then click the Edit tab in the Options dialog box. Select the Arrow keys nudge objects by check box, then type the nudging distance.

FIGURE A-13: Resizing an object

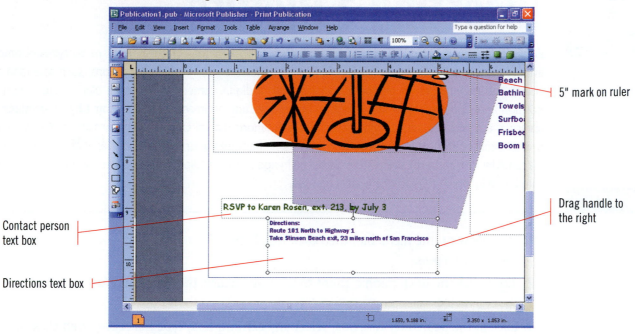

5" mark on ruler

Contact person text box

Drag handle to the right

Directions text box

FIGURE A-14: Moving and rotating an object

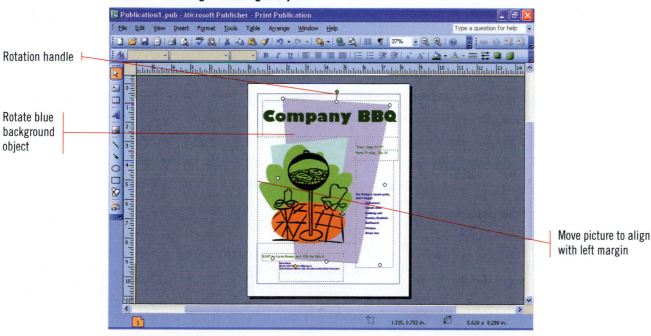

Rotation handle

Rotate blue background object

Move picture to align with left margin

TABLE A-2: Common pointer shapes

pointer shape	use to	pointer shape	use to
↖ ↔ ↗ ↕	Resize an object in the direction of the arrows		Drag selected text to a new location
+	Draw a frame		Insert overflow text
✛	Move an object to a new location		Rotate an object
⊣⊤⊢ ⌐⌙⌐⌐	Crop an object		

Inserting a Picture

Publications usually include both text and graphics. With Publisher, you can insert many types of graphic images into your publications, including clip art, images created in other applications (such as a logo or a chart), scanned images, or photographs taken with a digital camera. You insert a blank picture frame to position and size where your image will go before selecting an image. The Microsoft **Clip Organizer** is a library of art, pictures, sounds, video clips, and animations that all Office applications share. You can easily preview images from the Clip Organizer and insert them into your publications. You replace the placeholder clip art in the flyer with a barbecue image from the Clip Organizer. You also insert a blank picture frame in which to place the MediaLoft logo.

STEPS

QUICK TIP

To open the task pane, press [Ctrl][F1].

1. **Click View on the menu bar, then click Task Pane**
   The task pane opens.

2. **Right-click the BBQ graphic, point to Change Picture, then click Clip Art**
   The Clip Art task pane opens.

3. **Click in the Search for text box, select any existing text, type barbecue, then click Go**
   The Results window in the task pane appears, and images relating to barbecue appear. It may take a minute or two to display all the images.

TROUBLE

If you don't see the image shown in Figure A-15, click another image.

4. **Click the first barbecue image in the Results window**
   The new barbecue image replaces the placeholder barbecue image on the flyer, as shown in Figure A-15. Your search results may be different.

5. **Click the Picture Frame button 🖼 on the Objects toolbar, then click Empty Picture Frame**
   The pointer changes to the Drawing pointer ╈.

QUICK TIP

Use the Object Size indicator on the status bar to view the size of the frame as you draw it.

6. **Use the pointer to draw a blank picture frame in the lower-right corner of the page, approximately 1.750 × 1.750**

7. **Right-click the frame, point to Change Picture, then click From File**
   The Insert Picture dialog box opens. You use the existing MediaLoft logo.

8. **Click the Look in list arrow, locate the drive and folder where your Data Files are stored, click PB A-2.jpg, then click Insert**
   The MediaLoft logo is inserted in the frame and the frame size adjusts proportionally to fit the image.

9. **Close the task pane**

10. **Press [F9] to zoom in on the logo if necessary, drag the upper-left handle to resize the logo picture frame until it reaches 6" on the horizontal ruler and 8⅛" on the vertical ruler, as shown in Figure A-16, then release the mouse button**
    Congratulations, you have successfully completed the flyer!

Clues to Use

Considering image file size

To see the size of the graphic you are inserting, position the pointer over the image in the task pane and view the size in the ScreenTip that appears. Smaller file sizes make it easier to send files over e-mail or the Web, or to save your documents to a floppy disk.

FIGURE A-15: Clip Art search results

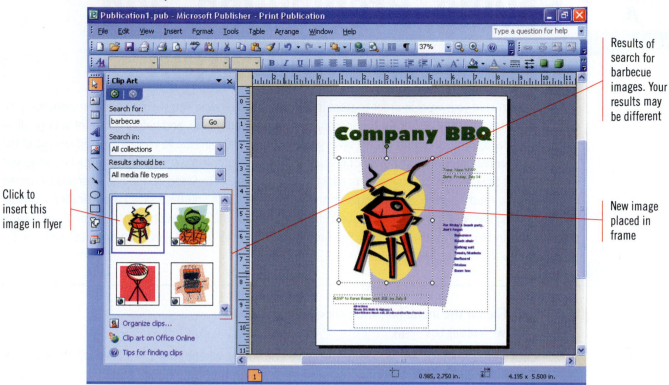

Results of search for barbecue images. Your results may be different

Click to insert this image in flyer

New image placed in frame

FIGURE A-16: Resizing MediaLoft's logo

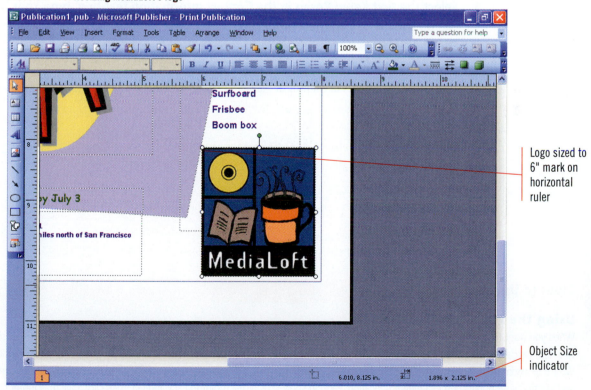

Logo sized to 6" mark on horizontal ruler

Object Size indicator

Saving, Previewing, and Printing a Publication

You need to save your work in order to store it permanently on a disk. You should save your work every 10 to 15 minutes, after any significant changes that you don't want to lose, and before you print your publication. By default, Publisher automatically saves your work every 10 minutes, so you can take advantage of the AutoRecover feature if you lose power or if you have a system problem. To save a file for the first time, you can use the Save or Save As command, or click the Save button on the Standard toolbar. After you've named the file, you must save any new changes to the publication. Once you have saved a publication, you can print it using the Print command. It's a good idea to proofread your publication before you print so that you can catch and fix any mistakes. You save the flyer, check it for mistakes, then print it so you can distribute it to the MediaLoft employees.

STEPS

QUICK TIP

After you've saved your publication for the first time, click the Save button on the Standard toolbar to quickly save changes to your publication.

1. **Click File on the menu bar, then click Save**
   The Save As dialog box opens.

2. **Click the Save in list arrow, locate the drive and folder where your Data Files are stored, type Picnic in the File name text box, compare your dialog box with Figure A-17, then click Save**

3. **Click View on the menu bar, point to Zoom, then click Whole Page**
   The zoom level adjusts so that the whole page fits in the publication window. When you change the zoom level, you can select a specific zoom percentage, or a specific area to view. You can also click the Zoom list arrow on the Standard toolbar to change the zoom level.

QUICK TIP

Press [Ctrl][P] to access the Print dialog box quickly. Click the Print button on the Standard toolbar to print the publication with the current settings.

4. **Select the text Karen Rosen in the Contact information text box, type Your Name, click File on the menu bar, then click Print**
   The Print dialog box opens, as shown in Figure A-18.

5. **Make sure the number of copies is 1, then click OK**
   Your publication prints in color or in black and white, depending on your printer. Figure A-19 shows a copy of the completed flyer.

Clues to Use

Using the Pack and Go Wizard

When you want to transfer your publication to another computer or to a commercial printing service, you can use the Pack and Go Wizard to assemble and compress all the files necessary for viewing and printing your publication in a different location. Packing your publication (that is, including the fonts and graphics that you used in your publication) ensures that it will look the same on another computer as it does on yours. If you're packing your publication to disks, Publisher automatically compresses and splits the files so they fit on multiple disks and includes a program to unpack the files on other computers. To use the Pack and Go Wizard, click File on the menu bar, point to Pack and Go, then click Take to Another Computer or Take to a Commercial Printing Service. You read the Wizard screens and make your selections, click Next after each choice, then click Finish when you have answered all of the Wizard's questions.

FIGURE A-17: Save As dialog box

Location of Data Files
(yours may differ)

Save in list arrow

File name text box

Click to Save

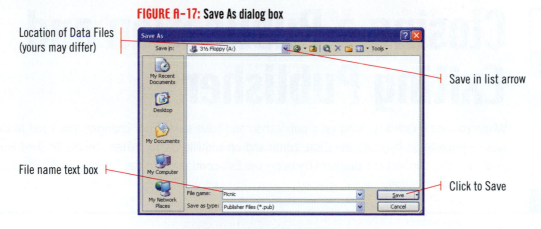

FIGURE A-18: Print dialog box

Click to set
printer properties

Click to change
default printer

Click to select how
many pages of the
publication to print

Click to change
number of copies

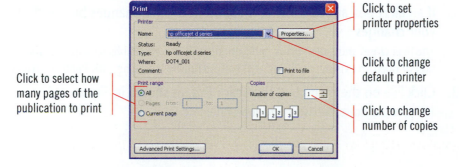

FIGURE A-19: Completed publication

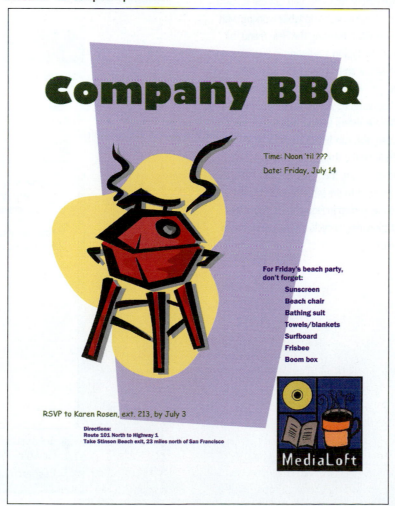

Closing a Publication and Exiting Publisher

When you are finished working on a publication and have saved your changes, you need to close it. You close a publication by using the Close command on the File menu. When you are finished working with Publisher, you can exit the program by using the Exit command on the File menu. 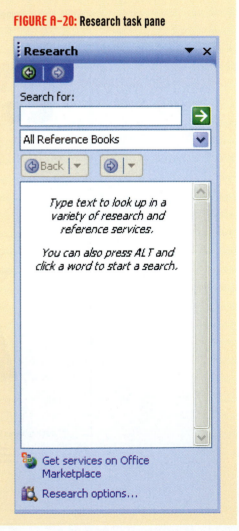 You close the flyer and exit Publisher.

STEPS

1. Click **File** on the menu bar, then click **Close**, as shown in Figure A-21

2. If an alert box appears asking if you want to save changes before closing, click **Yes** to save your changes

   The flyer closes and a new, blank publication appears in the Publisher window. You can create a new publication or open an existing publication. If you are finished working with Publisher, you can exit the program.

3. Click **File** on the menu bar, then click **Exit**, as shown in Figure A-22

   The program closes; Publisher is no longer running.

Clues to Use

Getting Help

Publisher includes an extensive Help system that you can use to learn about features and commands. You can get help while working with Publisher by using the Office Assistant, by using the Help menu, by using the Research task pane, or by typing a question in the Ask a Question box. The Office Assistant is an animated character that gives context-appropriate tips while you work. To get help from the Office Assistant, simply click the Office Assistant, then type your question. This unit assumes that the Office Assistant is hidden. If the Office Assistant appears on your screen, you can hide it by right-clicking the character and then clicking Hide on the shortcut menu. To access Help online, click Help on the menu bar, then click Microsoft Office Online. You must be able to connect to the Internet to access the Web site. The Research task pane, shown in Figure A-20, provides access to resources such as dictionaries, encyclopedias, business and financial sites, and news sources.

FIGURE A-20: Research task pane

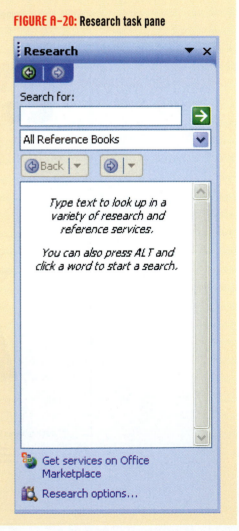

File menu

Click to close
a publication

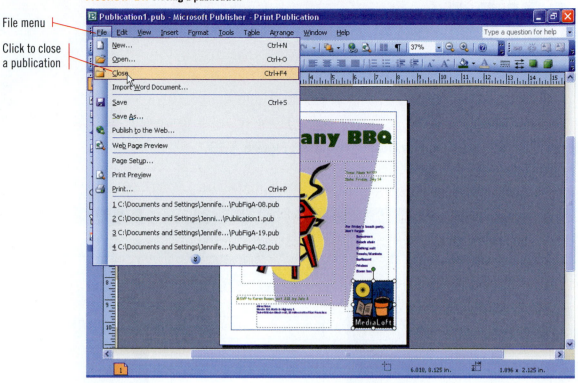

Click to close
publication
and exit
Publisher at
the same time

Click to exit
Publisher

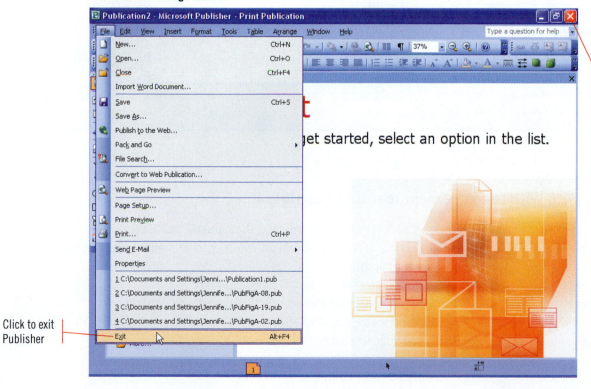

Publisher 2003

Practice

▼ CONCEPTS REVIEW

Label each element of the Publisher window shown in Figure A-23.

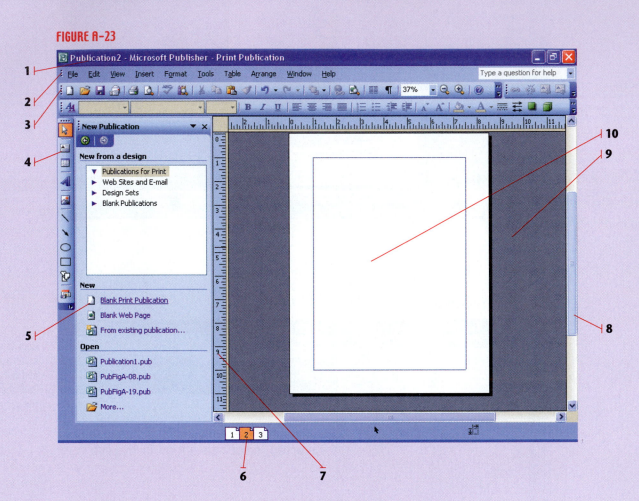

FIGURE A-23

Match each term with the statement that best describes it.

11. **AutoFit**
12. **Clip Organizer**
13. **Research task pane**
14. **Color scheme**
15. **Font scheme**

a. Preset colors used consistently throughout a publication
b. Library of art, pictures, sounds, video, and animations that all Office programs share
c. Feature that resizes text to fit in a text box
d. Preset fonts used consistently throughout a publication
e. Help source that connects you to online dictionaries, business sites, and other reference material

▼ SKILLS REVIEW

1. **Start Publisher and view the Publisher window.**
   a. Start Publisher and open a blank publication.
   b. Identify as many parts of the publication window as you can without referring to the unit material.

2. **Create a publication using an existing design.**
   a. Open the New Publication task pane if necessary.
   b. In the task pane, select the Borders House for Sale Flyer from the Sale Flyers category.
   c. Change the color scheme to Iris.
   d. Change the font scheme to Capital, which includes the font Perpetua Titling.

3. **Replace text in text boxes.**
   a. Close the task pane, zoom as needed, then type **$200,000** for the price.
   b. Select the Age of home text box, then type the following information, pressing [Enter] after each bullet except the last:
      - **Built in 1982**
      - **3 bedroom**
      - **2 1/2 baths**
      - **Hardwood floors**
      - **Eat-in kitchen**
      - **2 acres**
   c. Select the Special features text box, then insert into the text box the text file PB A-3.doc.
   d. Select the text in the Contact person frame, and replace the text with **Call your name for more information**.
   e. Fill in your information in the Business Name, Address, Phone, and E-mail text boxes.

4. **Format text.**
   a. Select the Business Name text box, then press [Ctrl][A] to select all of the text in the frame.
   b. Bold the text in that text box, then bold the fonts in the Address and Phone text boxes.
   c. Select the Directions text box, press [Ctrl][A], then format the text to AutoFit, Best Fit.
   d. Reduce the font size of the text in the price text box to 24 points.
   e. Change the text color of the Call your name text box to orange. (*Hint*: Use the Font Color button on the Formatting toolbar to choose another color in the scheme.)
   f. Change the Directions text to Perpetua and italics. Notice that the font size changes to fill the text box because you formatted the text earlier with AutoFit.

5. **Resize and move objects.**
   a. Drag the middle-left resizing handle of the House for Sale frame to the 1" mark on the horizontal ruler.
   b. Drag the middle-right sizing handle of the House for Sale frame to the 7½" mark on the horizontal ruler.
   c. Select the Directions text box and drag the upper-middle sizing handle up to the 5¾" mark on the vertical ruler. The text automatically resizes because you set it to AutoFit.
   d. Press [F9] to zoom back out and see more of your publication.

6. **Insert a picture.**
   a. Right-click the sky picture frame at the top of the flyer, then click Delete Object.
   b. Draw a blank picture frame to fill the space left by the sky graphic.
   c. Right-click the frame, point to Change Picture, then click From File.
   d. Insert the file PB A-4.jpg from the drive and folder where you store your Data Files, then resize the image, if necessary.
   e. Delete the logo placeholder at the top of the flyer.

7. **Save, preview, and print a publication.**
   a. Save the publication as **House** to the drive and folder where your Data Files are stored.
   b. Switch to Whole Page view to proof your publication and make any last-minute changes.
   c. Save your changes, then print your publication.

8. **Close a publication and exit Publisher.**
   a. Close the publication, then exit Publisher.

▼ INDEPENDENT CHALLENGE 1

FIGURE A-24

Your cat has just had kittens and you would like to place them in good homes. You decide to use a Publisher template to create a flyer to post at the local veterinary clinic.

a. Start Publisher, use the New Publication task pane, and select the Pets Available Flyer from the Sale Flyers category.

b. Using Figure A-24 as a guide, replace the placeholder text and format that text. Use the Crocus color scheme.

c. Replace the Describe text frame with the text file PB A-5.doc.

d. Replace the placeholder graphic with a cat of your choosing from the Media Gallery and size the image appropriately.

e. Replace the name Trey with **your name** in the Please call text box and in the tear-off Kittens frames.

f. Save the publication as **Kittens**.

g. Proof the flyer for mistakes, print and close the publication, then exit Publisher.

▼ INDEPENDENT CHALLENGE 2

You've volunteered to create a home page for your son's elementary school's Web site.

a. Start Publisher, then choose the Kid Stuff Services Web Site design from the Services Web Sites (click Web Sites and E-mail, click Web Sites, then click the Professional Services category in the New Publication task pane).

b. Choose Sunrise as the color scheme, and Casual as the font scheme.

c. Replace the placeholder text with the text in Table A-3. (*Hint*: Click No in the autoflow dialog box.)

d. Delete the placeholder graphic and caption, then increase the size of the Vision text box by dragging the right-middle sizing handle to the right to be even with the Home text box, then AutoFit the text.

e. Enter information into the Phone/Fax/E-mail text box at the bottom of the page.

f. Apply bold formatting to the subheadings Vision and Mission, and change the text color to Red. (*Hint*: Use the Font Color button.)

g. Delete the placeholder logo.

h. Save the publication as **Washington**. (*Hint*: You may need to insert a floppy disk, if necessary.)

TABLE A-3

placeholder text frame	replace with
Business Name	**Washington Elementary School**
Your business tag line here	**Making Education Count!**
This is the first page….	Text File PB A-6.doc (Click No to have Publisher fit the text.)
Frame below "To contact us"	**Your Name** **Washington Elementary School** **23 School Street** **Waverly, WA 98722**

Advanced Challenge Exercise

- Click Insert on the menu bar, point to Picture, then click WordArt.
- Choose a vertical style from the far-right column, then click OK.
- Type **Washington**, then click OK.
- Right-click the WordArt, then click Format WordArt.
- Change the line color to red using the Format WordArt dialog box, then click OK.
- Position the WordArt to the right of the contact information text boxes.

i. Proof your publication, print and close the publication, then exit Publisher.

▼ INDEPENDENT CHALLENGE 3

Create a calendar for next month using a Publisher template.

a. Start Publisher, click Publications for Print, click the Calendar category, then select a full-page calendar template from the New Publication task pane. (*Hint*: If Publisher prompts you to run a wizard to install this feature, click Yes.)

b. On the Calendar options task pane, choose the monthly option and change the date range from the beginning of next month to the end of next month. Do not include a schedule of events.

c. Choose a color and font scheme of your choice.

d. Replace the placeholder text with text of your own, making sure to include your name somewhere on the calendar. Format the text appropriately, and customize the logo if a logo placeholder is part of the template. Replace any clip art with appropriate images.

e. Save the publication as **Calendar**. Click No if asked to save the logo to the Primary Business personal information set.

f. Proofread and spell check your publication, print and close the publication, then exit Publisher.

▼ INDEPENDENT CHALLENGE 4

You own a small travel agency and have put together a six-day tour package to London. You plan to create a brochure providing information to prospective tour guests about the package. To complete the flyer, you will first need to do some research on the Internet about London.

a. Use a search engine such as Google (www.google.com) or AltaVista (www.altavista.com) and research the following information:
   1. Name and street address of 5-star hotel
   2. Name of art museum, with specific exhibit mentioned
   3. Name of another museum that is not art-related
   4. Names of two shopping districts or stores
   5. One nightlife activity (such as a cabaret, disco, or comedy club) providing the name of the locale
   6. Sightseeing activity of your choosing
   When you've gathered all your information, you are ready to create the flyer. To create the flyer:

b. Start Publisher. In the New Publication task pane, select the 3 Picture Product Flyer in the Sale Flyers category.

c. Replace the Product Title Placeholder text with **6 Days in London**. Replace the text in the Product Heading text box with **Theatre, museums, and more!**

d. In the text box directly below Theatre, museums, and more! replace the placeholder text with file PB A-7.doc. Click No in the autoflow dialog box, then resize the text box so the text fits. Change the font to 12-point Agency FB.

e. In the List feature here frame, replace the placeholder bullets with six bullets of your own, providing information on the items you researched. Use Step a. as a guide for creating the bullets.

f. Replace the three placeholder graphics on the flyer with clip art images from the Clip Organizer.

g. Include a logo at the bottom of the flyer for Cultural Excursions, Inc., using the Font Focus logo.

h. In the Contact person frame, replace the placeholder text with **Call your name for pricing and reservations**. Add a phone number.

i. Save the flyer as **London**, and don't save the logo if prompted.

Advanced Challenge Exercise

- Select the text 6 Days in London.
- Click Format on the menu bar, then click Font.
- Click the Shadow check box.
- Click the Small Caps check box.
- Click OK to close the dialog box.
- Click the Center button on the Formatting toolbar.

j. Check the spelling, print and close the publication, then exit Publisher.

Create the flyer shown in Figure A-25 using the Ascent Event Flyer design in the Event Flyer category. Use the Parrot color scheme and the Virtual font scheme. Replace the placeholder photo and graphics with the clip art shown. (*Hint*: Open the Insert Clip Art task pane, then search for Fish. If the images shown are not available, choose other ones.) Drag the green rotation handle to rotate the fish in the red and black rectangles 90 degrees to the right. To create the logo, select the placeholder logo, click the Logo Wizard button to open the Logo Designs task pane, then choose the Top Bar design. (*Hint*: To add the fish graphic to the logo at the bottom of the page, right-click the logo, click Ungroup, click Yes, then deselect all graphics. Right-click the graphic placeholder, point to Change Picture, click Clip Art to open the Clip Art task pane, then type **fish** in the Search text box.) Add your name to the Call frame. AutoFit the text in every frame except the Date, Time, and Call Your Name frames. Save the publication as **Grand Opening** in the drive and folder where your Data Files are stored, don't save the logo if prompted, then print a copy.

FIGURE A-25

Working with Text and Graphics

OBJECTIVES

Plan a publication

Create columns of text

Work with overflow text

Use guides

Create picture captions

Create headers and footers

Wrap text around objects

Layer and group objects

Merge information from a data source

Publisher provides you with a wide array of tools to help you work with text and graphics. In this unit, you will learn how to create a newsletter. You will place text in columns and learn how to manage text that doesn't all fit in one text box. Then, you will insert a caption for a picture and learn how to wrap text around that and other objects. You will learn how to insert headers and footers that appear on every page of your publication. You will also learn about layering and grouping objects and inserting information from a data source.  You produce a quarterly newsletter called *LoftLife* for MediaLoft employees. You start by planning the content of the newsletter. Then, you use the skills covered in this unit to create it.

Planning a Publication

Before creating a publication, you must first plan its design and content. Careful planning helps to ensure that your publication is both informative and eye-catching. Before you start working on the newsletter, you plan the next edition of the *LoftLife* newsletter. Figure B-1 shows your plan for the content, graphics, and layout.

Some of the factors you need to consider are as follows:

- ### What layout to use

  Choosing the layout is the first decision you need to make in planning a multipage publication. Either you can use one of the many sample designs that Publisher provides and customize it to meet your needs, or you can start from scratch. No matter which option you choose, you need to decide up front how many columns of text the publication will have, and how many pages it will be. You also need to decide how you want it to look when printed. For example, will the pages be folded or printed back to back? You use the same newsletter design for each issue of *LoftLife* so that all issues have the same look and feel. For this issue, you decide to change the layout of the inside pages of the newsletter from three columns to two. As in the last issue, the pages will be printed back to back.

- ### What text to include and how to present it

  Once you've chosen your layout, you need to decide on your content. Write a list of all the articles you plan on including, similar to the list you created in the first column of Figure B-1. Next, decide how you want to present your content. In a publication you can present text in two ways—either as a story or as a table. A **story**, also called an article, is composed of text, and is meant to be read from beginning to end. A **table** contains text or numbers in columns and rows. Use tables to organize information so that it is easy to read at a glance, such as the table of contents. You will also use a catalog merge to create a publication introducing new employees at MediaLoft. You list all the stories the *LoftLife* Editorial Board picked for this issue.

- ### Where to place your text

  Next, you have to plan where to place each story and table in the publication. Sometimes, all the text for a particular story won't fit in one text box and needs to continue into another text box in a different part of the publication. This type of text is called **overflow text**. In the plan in Figure B-1, you note that you need to use overflow text for The Common Review Date story on page 1, which you decide to continue on page 4.

- ### What pictures and captions to include

  Once you've settled on your stories, it's time to plan for graphics. A **picture caption** is a description that appears adjacent to a picture. When you add a picture or any object to your publication, you can choose to have Publisher wrap the text around that object or around the object's frame. **Wrapping** means that the text flows around the object rather than over it. You plan to wrap text around graphics for four stories in the newsletter.

- ### What content should appear on every page

  A **header** is information that appears at the top of every page in your publication. A **footer** is information that appears at the bottom of every page in your publication. You will put the Volume and Issue number in the header of the newsletter, and will add a footer containing page numbers. You will specify not to show the header and footer on page 1.

- ### What special effects to include

  Publisher gives you many tools to create special effects. For example, you can add a pull quote or sidebar. A **pull quote** is a quotation from an article that is pulled out and treated like a graphic. A **sidebar** is text that is set apart from the major text but in some way relates to that text. You can also create unique effects by layering objects on top of each other to add depth and dimension to your publication. Figure B-2 shows the first page of the completed newsletter.

FIGURE B-1: Your content, layout, and graphics plan for the March issue of *LoftLife*

Stories for March issue

Requires overflow text

Stories	Page	Contributor	Graphics
A Word from Our President	1	Leilani Ho	Insert pull-quote and wrap text around it; add Success graphic at end
Common Review Date	1, 4	Me	
LoftLife Needs You (sidebar)	1	Me	
Vision Service Plan	2	Jim Fernandez	Wrap text around Owl picture
401K Notes	2	John Kim	
Employee Advisory Resource	2	Me	
Slaves to Fashion	3	Elizabeth Reed	Wrap text around pull quote between columns
They Asked for What?	4	Elizabeth Reed	

FIGURE B-2: Printout of page 1 of the completed newsletter

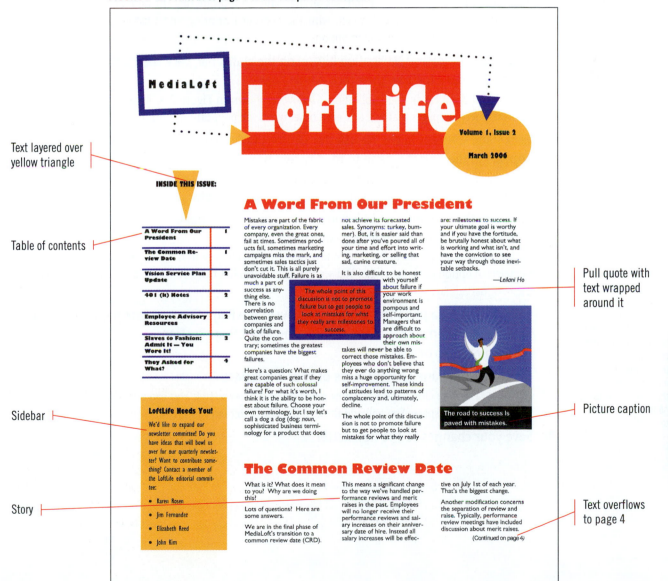

Text layered over yellow triangle

Table of contents

Sidebar

Story

Pull quote with text wrapped around it

Picture caption

Text overflows to page 4

MediaLoft

LoftLife

Volume 1, Issue 2

March 2006

INSIDE THIS ISSUE:

LoftLife Needs You!

We'd like to expand our newsletter committee! Do you have ideas that will bowl us over for our quarterly newsletter? Want to contribute something? Contact a member of the LoftLife editorial committee:

• Karen Rosen
• Jim Fernandez
• Elizabeth Reed
• John Kim

A Word From Our President

Mistakes are part of the fabric of every organization. Every company, even the great ones, fail at times. Sometimes products fail, sometimes marketing campaigns miss the mark, and sometimes sales tactics just don't cut it. This is all purely unavoidable stuff. Failure is as much a part of success as anything else. There is no correlation between great companies and lack of failure. Quite the contrary; sometimes the greatest companies have the biggest failures.

Here's a question: What makes great companies great if they are capable of such colossal failure? For what it's worth, I think it is the ability to be honest about failure. Choose your own terminology, but I say let's call a dog a dog (dog; *noun,* sophisticated business terminology for a product that does

not achieve its forecasted sales. Synonyms: turkey, bummer). But, it is easier said than done after you've poured all of your time and effort into writing, marketing, or selling that sad, canine creature.

It is also difficult to be honest with yourself about failure if your work environment is pompous and self-important. Managers that are difficult to approach about their own mistakes will never be able to correct those mistakes. Employees who don't believe that they ever do anything wrong miss a huge opportunity for self-improvement. These kinds of attitudes lead to patterns of complacency and, ultimately, decline.

The whole point of this discussion is not to promote failure but to get people to look at mistakes for what they really

> The whole point of this discussion is not to promote failure but to get people to look at mistakes for what they really are: milestones to success.

are: milestones to success. If your ultimate goal is worthy and if you have the fortitude, be brutally honest about what is working and what isn't, and have the conviction to see your way through those inevitable setbacks.

—Leilani Ho

The road to success is paved with mistakes.

The Common Review Date

What is it? What does it mean to you? Why are we doing this?

Lots of questions? Here are some answers.

We are in the final phase of MediaLoft's transition to a common review date (CRD).

This means a significant change to the way we've handled performance reviews and merit raises in the past. Employees will no longer receive their performance reviews and salary increases on their anniversary date of hire. Instead all salary increases will be effec-

tive on July 1st of each year. That's the biggest change.

Another modification concerns the separation of review and raise. Typically, performance review meetings have included discussion about merit raises.

(Continued on page 4)

Publisher 2003

Creating Columns of Text

Formatting text in columns can make text easier to read and more visually appealing. To create columns, you can either choose a Publisher design that includes columns, or you can format text into columns using options on the Newsletter Options task pane. You have been working on the newsletter for a few days. You used a Publisher sample design to create the newsletter, and then you replaced the placeholder text and graphics with the content for *LoftLife*. Today, you plan to finish the newsletter. You begin by opening the partially completed publication and changing the column format on the inside pages from three columns to two.

STEPS

TROUBLE

Click View on the menu bar, click Task pane, click the task pane list arrow, then click Newsletter Options to open the Newsletter Options task pane, if necessary.

1. **Start Publisher, then click the More link at the bottom of the New Publication task pane**

   The Open Publication dialog box opens.

2. **Click the Look in list arrow, locate the drive and folder where your Data Files are stored, click Loftlife.pub, then click Open**

   The newsletter opens with the first page displayed. Some graphic images are in the workspace, which you will use later in the unit. The Mobile newsletter sample design with a three-column format was used to create the publication. The Page Navigation buttons on the status bar indicate that the publication has four pages. The Newsletter Options task pane is open, with the two-sided printing and Customer address none options selected. You stick with these default options.

QUICK TIP

The task pane can be moved on the screen by dragging its title bar.

3. **Click the Page 2 Page Navigation button on the status bar, click the Zoom list arrow** `34%` **on the Standard toolbar, then click Whole Page**

   Pages 2 and 3 appear in the Publication window, as shown in Figure B-3. Pages 2 and 3 are a **two-page spread**. These are pages that will face each other when the publication is printed.

4. **Click Page Content in the Newsletter Options task pane, then make sure Left inside page appears in the Select a page to modify text box**

   Compare your Page Content task pane to Figure B-4. The options on the task pane apply to the left page because you have selected the Left inside page as the page to modify.

QUICK TIP

You can apply column-formatting changes quickly to the current page or to all pages of your publication. Position the pointer on the selected Columns on Left Page icon in the task pane, click the down arrow to open a shortcut menu, then click Apply to All Pages, or Apply to the Page.

5. **Click 2 in the Columns on Left Page section in the task pane**

   Publisher reformats the left inside page with two columns. At this point, you could continue to change the content by choosing from the options under Content for Left Page in the task pane, but you are happy with the selected option of three stories. You see that page 3 still has three columns, and that it looks odd next to the reformatted page 2.

6. **Click the Select a page to modify list arrow in the Page Content task pane, click Right inside page, then click 2 in the Columns on Right Page section**

   Page 3 now has two columns.

7. **Close the task pane to view more of your workspace**

   With the task pane closed, you can now see more of the newsletter. You can also see that there are graphic images in the workspace. You will add these to the newsletter later in the unit.

8. **Save your changes to the newsletter**

FIGURE B-3: Pages 2 and 3 of the newsletter

Zoom list arrow

Newsletter Options task pane

Page Navigation buttons

Pages 2 and 3 appear as facing pages

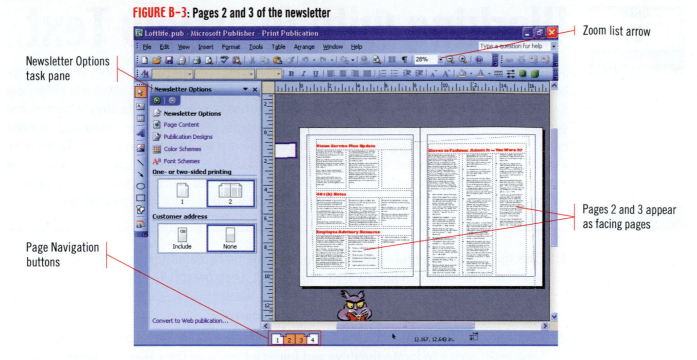

FIGURE B-4: Changing the number of columns with the Page Content task pane

Select a page to modify look in list arrow

Click here to reformat left page to two columns

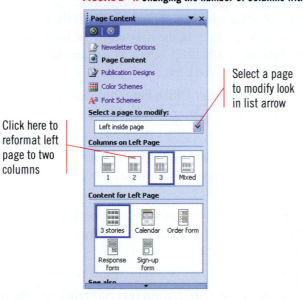

Clues to Use

Creating columns in existing text boxes

You can also change the number of columns of text in existing text boxes. Sometimes it is easier to read narrower columns. For example, you could turn one wide column of text into two or three more-readable columns. To create columns in an existing text box, right-click the text box, then click Format Text Box on the shortcut menu. Click the Text Box tab, click Columns to open the Columns dialog box, then specify the number of columns and the amount of spacing between the columns, as shown in Figure B-5.

FIGURE B-5: Columns dialog box

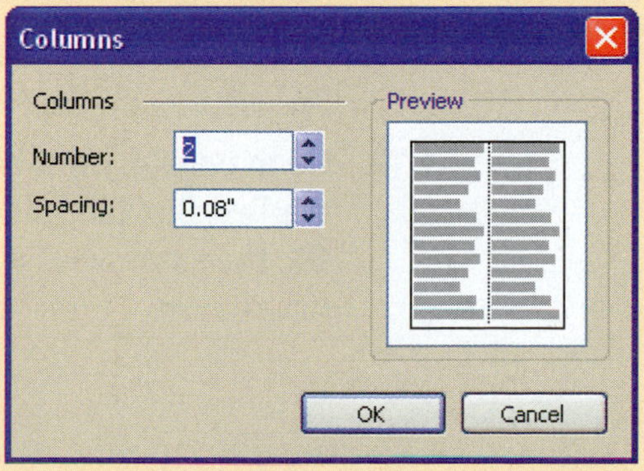

Working with Overflow Text

Sometimes there isn't enough room in a text box to hold all of the text for a particular story. When this happens, a Text in Overflow icon appears at the bottom of the text box to indicate that not all text in the story is visible. To display all the text, you either must enlarge the text box or continue the story in another text box on a different page of the publication. To continue a story in another text box, you connect that text box to the overflowing text box, and then "pour" the overflow text into the next text box. See Table B-1 for a description of the different text flow icons.  You asked one of your colleagues to write a 500-word article for the newsletter on MediaLoft's new annual review policy. You plan to begin this story on page 1 and continue it on page 4. You receive the article as a Word file and import it into the newsletter.

STEPS

QUICK TIP

Click [icon] to select the next frame.

1. **Click the Page 1 Page Navigation button, click the first column text box beneath the headline "The Common Review Date" to select it, then press [F9]**

   The Go to Next Text Box icon [icon] indicates that the selected frame is linked to the text box in the next column, as shown in Figure B-6. These text boxes are **connected**.

2. **Click Insert on the menu bar, click Text File to open the Insert Text dialog box, click the Look in list arrow to locate the drive and folder where your Data Files are stored, click PB B-1.doc, then click OK**

   Text from the Word document automatically pours into the three connected text boxes on page 1, but because there is too much text to fit in the three boxes, Publisher prompts you to use autoflow. When you use **autoflow**, Publisher automatically flows text from one existing empty text box to the next, asking for confirmation before it flows into each text box.

3. **Click No in the Microsoft Office Publisher dialog box**

   The Text in Overflow icon [icon] appears at the bottom of the third text box.

4. **Click the Create Text Box Link button [icon] on the Connect Text Box toolbar**

   The pointer changes to a pitcher [icon]. When you place the pointer over a text box that doesn't include the current story, the pitcher changes to [icon]. When you click an empty text box with the pitcher pointer, the overflow text flows into that text box.

QUICK TIP

You can press [Ctrl][G], enter a page number, then click OK to move to another page in your publication.

5. **Click the Page 4 Page Navigation button on the status bar, position the [icon] pointer in the first column text box under the headline "The Common Review Date (continued)", then click**

   Again, the text does not entirely fit in the text box, as shown in Figure B-7.

6. **Click [icon], click the second column text box, click [icon], then click the third column text box**

QUICK TIP

If you add pages to a publication, Publisher automatically updates the Continued on page numbers.

7. **Go to page 1, right-click the third column text box of the story, click Format Text Box on the shortcut menu, then click the Text Box tab**

   Figure B-8 shows options for continuing text. When a story continues on another page, continued notices provide cues that help the reader find the rest of the story.

8. **Click the Include "Continued on page..." check box to select it, then click OK**

   Publisher adds the text "(Continued on page 4)" to the bottom of the text box.

9. **Go to page 4, right-click the first column text box of the story, click Format Text Box, click the Text Box tab, click the Include "Continued from page..." check box to select it, click OK, then save your work**

   Publisher adds the text "(Continued from page 1)" to the top of the text box.

FIGURE B-6: Two connected text boxes

Go to Next Text Box icon

Page 1 Navigation button

First frame in story

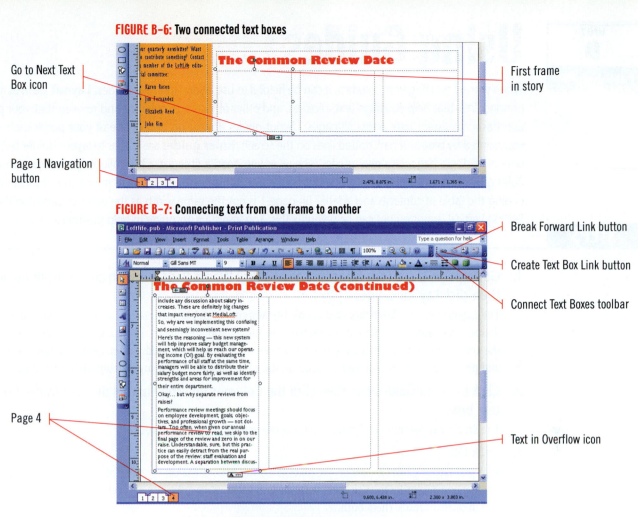

FIGURE B-7: Connecting text from one frame to another

Break Forward Link button

Create Text Box Link button

Connect Text Boxes toolbar

Page 4

Text in Overflow icon

FIGURE B-8: Format Text Box dialog box with Text Box tab displayed

Click to add Continued on page 4 message to page 1

Click to add Continued from page 1 message to page 4

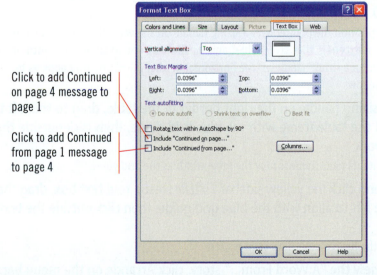

TABLE B-1: Text Flow icons

text flow icon	description
← ▬	Indicates that text box is connected to another text box and that text flows from that text box to this one. Click to move quickly to the previous frame.
▬ →	Indicates that text box is connected to another text box and that text flows to that text box. Click to move quickly to the next frame.
A •••	Indicates that text box is not connected to another text box and that there is more text that does not fit in the text frame.

Using Guides

When you are working with columns, it can be helpful to use layout and ruler guides. **Layout guides** are non-printing lines that help you align text, pictures, and other objects into columns and rows so that your publication has a consistent look across all pages. Layout guides appear on every page of your publication and are represented by blue and pink dotted lines on the screen. **Ruler guides** are similar to layout guides but appear only on a single page. Use ruler guides whenever you need a little extra help aligning an object on a page. Ruler guides are represented by green dotted lines on the screen. ![palette] You notice that the column containing the table of contents and sidebar on page 1 is not the same width as the other columns on the page. Setting vertical layout guides can help you fix this. You insert a ruler guide to help position a picture.

STEPS

1. **Go to page 1, click the Zoom list arrow, click Whole Page, click Arrange on the menu bar, then click Layout Guides**

   The Layout Guides dialog box opens with the Margin Guides tab selected, as shown in Figure B-9. Use this dialog box to adjust the margin guides, baseline guides, and grid guides. The margin guides appear in pink on the screen and outline the **margin**, or perimeter, of the page. The grid guides appear in blue on the screen and provide a perimeter for each column on the page. Baseline guides are horizontal, brown, dotted lines.

2. **Click the Grid Guides tab, then click the Columns up arrow until 4 displays in the Columns text box**

   The Preview shows blue grid guides dividing the page into four columns.

3. **Click OK**

   Four grid layout guides appear on the newsletter. You will now select the table of contents and the design element above it in order to align them with the grid guide. They are grouped together, so you just need to select one in order to resize them both.

4. **Select the table of contents table frame, then press [F9] to zoom in on that frame, as shown in Figure B-10**

   If you carefully position the pointer over a sizing handle on the vertical border of a column in the table, the pointer and a ScreenTip that says "Table" appear, allowing you to adjust the width of the column. If you place the pointer on a sizing handle on the horizontal border, the pointer appears to allow you to adjust the height of the row.

5. **Point to the sizing handle on the right border of the table, drag to the left to align the right edge of the table frame with the blue grid guide, then click outside the frame to check your work**

   The table of contents table frame is now the same width as the grid guide.

6. **Scroll down and click the yellow sidebar *LoftLife* Needs You! text box, drag the middle-right handle to the left to align with the blue grid guide, then click outside the text box to check your work**

   Both frames in the first column have been resized.

7. **Scroll up to view the "A Word From..." story, click Arrange on the menu bar, point to Ruler Guides, then click Add Horizontal Ruler Guide**

   A green horizontal line appears on the page near the top of the story.

8. **Place the pointer over the green line so the pointer changes to the Adjust pointer ⊥, press and hold [Shift], click and drag ⊥ to align with the 5½" mark on the vertical ruler, then release [Shift]**

   The ruler guide is now set as shown in Figure B-11. You will use this newly created ruler guide in the next lesson.

9. **Save your changes**

FIGURE B-9: Layout Guides dialog box

Margin Guides tab

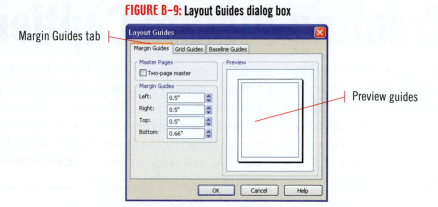

Preview guides

FIGURE B-10: Table of contents table frame

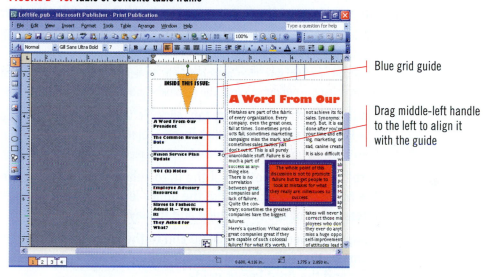

Blue grid guide

Drag middle-left handle to the left to align it with the guide

FIGURE B-11: Setting a ruler guide

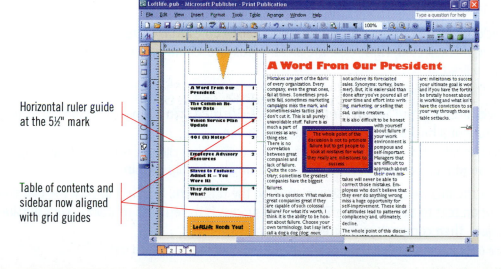

Horizontal ruler guide at the 5½" mark

Table of contents and sidebar now aligned with grid guides

Publisher 2003

Clues to Use

Using baseline guides

Baseline guides are used to align text across multiple columns. They are brown, dotted horizontal lines that appear spaced evenly throughout the publication, and indicate where text lines start. In order to make the last row of text align with the bottom margin, you need to set the baseline guides at a multiple of the space between the top and bottom margins. Since text is measured in points, it is helpful to use point sizes when setting the margin guides and baseline guides so that it is easy to adjust both to coordinate the text properly.

Creating Picture Captions

A **picture caption** is text that describes or elaborates on a picture. Captions can be located above, below, or next to a picture. You can create a picture caption by typing text in a text box that you create, or you can use Publisher's Design Gallery to choose one of the picture caption designs. The design collection includes objects such as picture captions, logos, and calendars. The designs are organized by category and design type. You can also create and save your own objects in the Design Gallery. You would like to add a motivational piece of clip art at the bottom of the president's article on page 1. You do this by using one of Publisher's preset picture captions in the Design Gallery and choosing an appropriate piece of clip art.

STEPS

1. On page 1, select the first column text box below the "A Word From Our President" text box

2. Click the Design Gallery Object button 🖼 on the Objects toolbar

   The Microsoft Office Publisher Design Gallery opens, as shown in Figure B-12. Each of the three tabs has a list of categories or design sets. The Categories list in the left pane shows the large variety of predesigned objects you can use to enhance your publication. The right pane shows thumbnails of selections in each category.

3. On the Objects by Category tab, click Picture Captions in the Categories list, click the Solid Bar Picture Caption, then click Insert Object

   The object, an image with "Caption describing picture or graphic" text appears on top of the article.

> **TROUBLE**
> If the Picture toolbar opens at any time, click the Close button.

4. Scroll to view the bottom of the third column of that story, then drag the object using the Move pointer ✛ so that the upper-left handle of the object is positioned at the intersection of the ruler guide and the layout guide, as shown in Figure B-13

5. Drag the lower-right handle up and to the left using the Resize pointer ↖ to resize the frame so that it is aligned with the bottom of the column at the 7⅞" mark on the vertical ruler and the right layout guide

   The Design Gallery provides a placeholder graphic as well as placeholder caption text. You can change it at any time.

6. Click the picture of the deer, notice the small handles that appear around the picture when it is selected, right-click the picture, point to Change Picture on the shortcut menu, then click Clip Art

   The Clip Art task pane opens.

> **TROUBLE**
> If you don't see this picture, click another image.

7. Type success in the Search for text box, click Go, then scroll down the results to display the picture of a businessman crossing the finish line

   The Clip Art task pane displays the results of your search. If you click the right side of any image, a menu appears with various options for working with the image in the Clip Organizer.

8. Click the picture of a businessman crossing the finish line to insert it, click the placeholder caption text to select it, type The road to success is paved with mistakes., click outside the object, then compare your screen to Figure B-14

   The placeholder picture and caption are replaced with a relevant image and text.

9. Close the Clip Art task pane, then save your changes

FIGURE B-12: Microsoft Publisher Design Gallery

Objects by Design tab

My Objects tab

Objects by Category tab

Categories of Publisher-designed objects

Insert Object button

FIGURE B-13: Positioning the object using guides

Upper-left handle positioned at intersection of ruler and layout guides

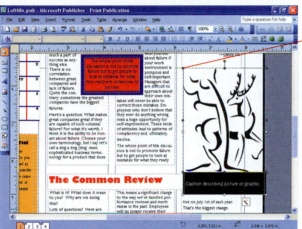

FIGURE B-14: Inserting clip art using the task pane

Click to insert this image into the newsletter

Search results for "success" (yours may differ)

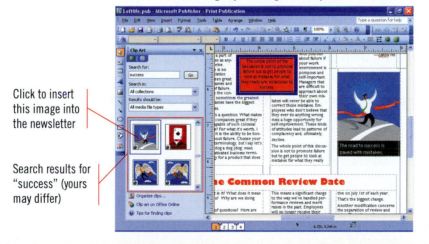

Publisher 2003

Clues to Use

Adding your own objects to the Design Gallery

You can add your own objects to the Design Gallery for use in future publications. For example, if you design your own pull quote that you intend to use in every edition of an annual publication, you would want to add this to the Design Gallery. Select the object you want to save, click Insert on the menu bar, and then click Add Selection to Design Gallery. In the Add Object dialog box, type a name for the object and type or choose a category, then click OK. This object then appears on the My Objects tab. To delete an object from the My Objects tab of the Design Gallery, right-click the object, click Delete This Object on the shortcut menu, then click Yes to confirm the deletion.

Creating Headers and Footers

A **header** is information that appears on the top of every page of a publication, such as the name of the publication. A **footer** is information that appears on the bottom of every page of a publication, such as a page number. When you create a header or footer in Publisher, you use the **master page**, also known as the **background**, which is a layer that appears behind every page in a publication. If you want certain objects or information to appear in the same place on every page of a publication, you must place them on the master page. The **foreground** sits on top of the background and consists of the objects that appear on a specific page of a publication. You add a header and a footer to your newsletter. You need to add a master page so that your margins are adjusted for left and right pages. Lastly, you make sure the header and footer do not appear on page 1.

STEPS

QUICK TIP
Click View on the menu bar, click Task Pane, click the Task Pane list arrow, then click Edit Master Pages to open the task pane, if necessary.

1. **Click View on the menu bar, click Header and Footer, then press [F9] to zoom out**

   The background right master page appears, and the Edit Master Pages task pane opens. At the moment, the page navigation button is an "R," indicating that there is only one master page, which by default is the right-hand one. Because this publication has two-page spreads, you need both a right and a left master page.

2. **Click in the header text box, type VOLUME 1 ISSUE 2, then click the Align Right button 📄 on the Formatting toolbar**

3. **Click in the footer text box, click Insert on the menu bar, click Page Numbers, click OK in the Page Numbers dialog box, press [F9], click to the left of the pound sign (#), type Page, then press [Spacebar]**

   The page number appears as shown in Figure B-15.

4. **Click the Master R list arrow on the Edit Master Pages task pane, click Change to Two-page, press [F9] to zoom out, then drag both header text boxes and each footer text box to the position shown in Figure B-16 if necessary**

   The Page Navigation buttons now indicate that there are both a left and right master page with the same information, both labeled "R." The information you added to the header and footer appears on both master pages.

QUICK TIP
Press [Ctrl][M] to toggle quickly between the foreground and the background.

5. **Press [Ctrl][M], then use the Page Navigation buttons to view all pages of your publication**

   You can see both headers and footers on each page.

6. **Go to page 1, click View on the menu bar, then click Ignore Master Page**

   The header and footer no longer appear on page 1 but still appear on pages 2-4 with pagination continuing from page 1.

FIGURE B-15: Completed left footer

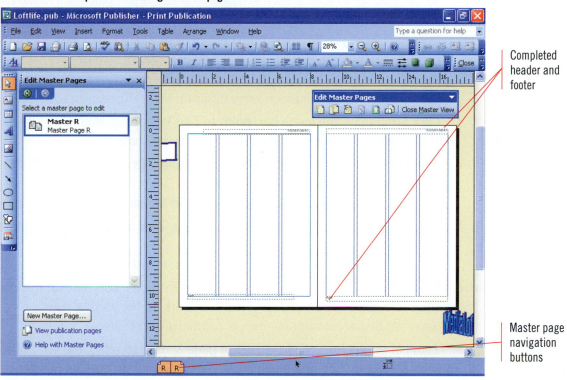

Pound sign indicates page number placeholder

FIGURE B-16: Completed left and right master pages

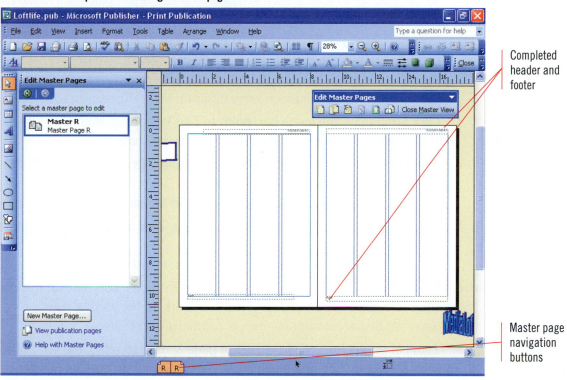

Completed header and footer

Master page navigation buttons

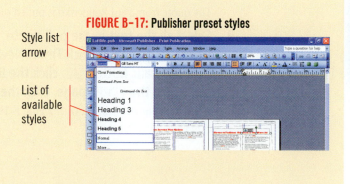
Publisher 2003

Wrapping Text Around Objects

To help make your stories more visually interesting, Publisher gives you the ability to wrap text around any object. **Wrapping** means that the text flows around the object rather than on top of or behind it. You can wrap text around pictures or around other text, such as pull quotes. A **pull quote** is a quotation from a story that is pulled out into its own frame and treated like a graphic. You can choose to wrap text around an object's frame or around the object itself. ▰ You are ready to add graphics to your stories on page 2 and 3. You collected graphics and placed them on the workspace. You plan to place an owl graphic in the Vision Service story on page 2, and will insert a pull quote into the Fashion story on page 3, then you wrap text around both objects.

STEPS

1. **Go to page 2, then zoom out to view the whole page, if necessary**
   You can store clip art in the desktop workspace for use in the publication. You should delete any unused clip art because it increases file size.

QUICK TIP
To manually adjust how close the text is to certain areas of the object, click the Text Wrapping button ▣ on the Picture toolbar, then click Edit Wrap Points. When you click this button, handles appear all around the object that you can use to resize the wrap.

2. **Drag the owl clip art located at the bottom of your desktop workspace so that it is centered between the two columns of text in the "Vision Service Plan Update" story, click Arrange on the menu bar, point to Order, then click Bring to Front**
   The text in the article automatically wraps around the square-shaped frame containing the owl.

3. **Click Arrange on the menu bar, point to Text Wrapping, then click Tight**
   The text now wraps tightly around the contours of the owl's body.

4. **Click Insert on the menu bar, click Design Gallery Object, then click Pull Quotes in the Categories list**
   The Design Gallery opens, with the Objects by Category tab and Pull Quotes selected, as shown in Figure B-18.

5. **Scroll down the Pull Quotes in the right pane, click the Bubbles Pull Quote design, then click Insert Object**
   The pull quote frame with placeholder text needs to be moved between the two columns of the story.

QUICK TIP
Don't place an object in the middle of a single column so that the object divides lines of text. It is difficult to read lines of text separated by a graphic.

6. **Drag the Pull Quote frame to the "Slaves to Fashion" story so that it is centered between the two columns approximately at the 4" mark on the vertical ruler**
   Notice that the text automatically wraps around the pull quote frame.

7. **Zoom in on the lower-right corner of page 3, drag to select the last bulleted item in the second column, beginning with In junior high..., including Paul Roudenko, then click the Copy button ▣ on the Standard toolbar**
   Text can be copied from one text box or frame to another.

8. **Scroll to view the Pull Quote frame, click to select the placeholder text, then click the Paste button ▣ on the Standard toolbar**
   The quote from Paul Roudenko is pulled out and highlighted in the pull quote on the page.

9. **Select all the text in the pull quote, click the Font list arrow** Gill Sans MT ▾ **on the Formatting toolbar, click Times New Roman, click the Font Size list arrow** 9 ▾ **, click 10, click the Italic button** *I* **, click the Bullets button** ▤ **on the Formatting toolbar, zoom out to see the whole page, click the desktop, then save your changes**
   Compare your publication with Figure B-19.

FIGURE B-18: Design Gallery with Pull Quotes category selected

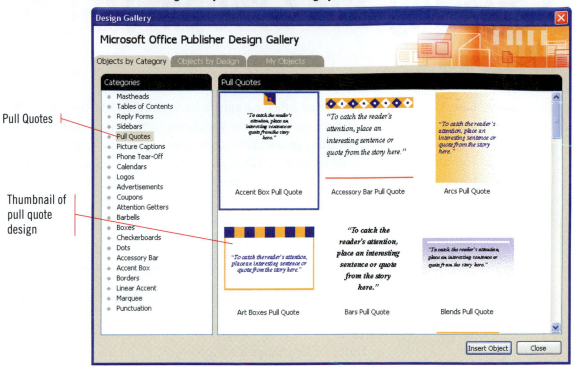

Pull Quotes

Thumbnail of
pull quote
design

FIGURE B-19: Wrapping text around clip art and pull quotes

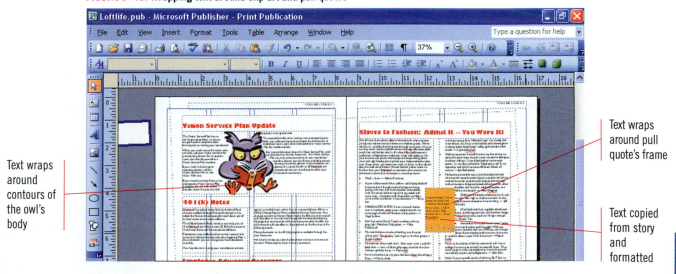

Text wraps
around
contours of
the owl's
body

Text wraps
around pull
quote's frame

Text copied
from story
and
formatted

Clues to Use

Rotating and flipping objects

You can create interesting effects in a publication by rotating or flipping text and objects. When you rotate an object, you change its angle in degrees relative to a baseline. For example, text that is rotated 90 degrees appears vertically rather than horizontally. To rotate an object in 90-degree increments, select the object, click Arrange on the menu bar, point to Rotate or Flip, then click the option you want. To rotate an object by dragging it, select the object, then point to the green rotation handle at the top of the frame. Drag the mouse in the direction you want to rotate. To rotate the object in 15-degree increments using the dragging method, press and hold [Shift] while dragging the rotation handle.

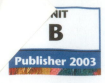
Layering and Grouping Objects

You can layer two or more objects on top of each other in a publication to create an interesting visual effect. When you layer objects, they appear on the page in the order you placed them, as if you had placed different pieces of paper on top of one another. You can change the layer order by using the Bring to Front, Send to Back, Bring Forward, or Send Backward commands. When you are happy with the arrangement of your layered objects, you can group them so you can work with the objects as a single object. Grouping objects allows you to move and resize the group rather than each object individually, saving time. 🎨 You want to improve the look of the MediaLoft contact information on page 4 of *LoftLife*. You decide to layer the logo on top of several different rectangle shapes to make it more attractive.

STEPS

QUICK TIP

AutoShapes provide you with a wide variety of shapes, connectors, callouts, and arrows. To access them click the AutoShapes button on the Objects toolbar.

1. **Go to page 4, then zoom in on the upper-left corner of the page and the desktop workspace to the left of the page**

   The MediaLoft logo is positioned above the yellow box, and an AutoShape graphic with a blue border is seen in the top left of the desktop workspace. An **AutoShape** is a predesigned shape provided with Publisher that you can use in your publications.

2. **Select the blue-bordered rectangle in the desktop workspace, then drag it to the publication page so that the upper-left corner is positioned at the 1" mark on both the horizontal and vertical rulers**

   Compare your screen to Figure B-20.

TROUBLE

Be sure to select the entire yellow rectangle and not one of the text boxes that appears on top of the rectangle. If you send the wrong frame to the back, click the Undo button on the Standard toolbar and repeat the step.

3. **Click the top-left corner of the yellow rectangle to select it, click Arrange on the menu bar, point to Order, then click Send to Back**

   The yellow rectangle is now positioned behind the blue-bordered rectangle. Once you perform an Order operation, that order button appears on the Standard toolbar with a list arrow.

4. **Click the logo, click the Bring to Front button 🔲 on the Standard toolbar, then drag the logo down so that it is centered in the blue-bordered rectangle**

   The logo is now on top of the blue-bordered rectangle, which is on top of the yellow rectangle.

5. **Verify that the logo is still selected, press and hold [Shift], then click the blue-bordered rectangle**

   Notice that both of the frames are selected and the Group Objects button 🔲 appears in the lower-right corner of the selection box. Clicking this button groups all the selected objects into one single object.

6. **Click the Group Objects button 🔲 beneath the objects**

   The objects are now grouped and you can move, resize, or format them as a whole, as shown in Figure B-21. The Group Objects button has changed to an Ungroup Objects button 🔲 now that the selected object is a group. You can click this button to ungroup the objects and work with them individually.

7. **Select Tel: (415) 555-2398 in the yellow rectangle, type your name, press [Enter], type Editor, then save your changes to the newsletter**

8. **Click the Spell check button 🔲 on the Standard toolbar, check all the stories in the publication, correct any misspelled words, then compare your newsletter to Figure B-22**

9. **Save any changes, print the file, then close the publication**

   You will now use Catalog Merge to create an additional page listing the new employees at MediaLoft.

FIGURE B-20: Working with three layers

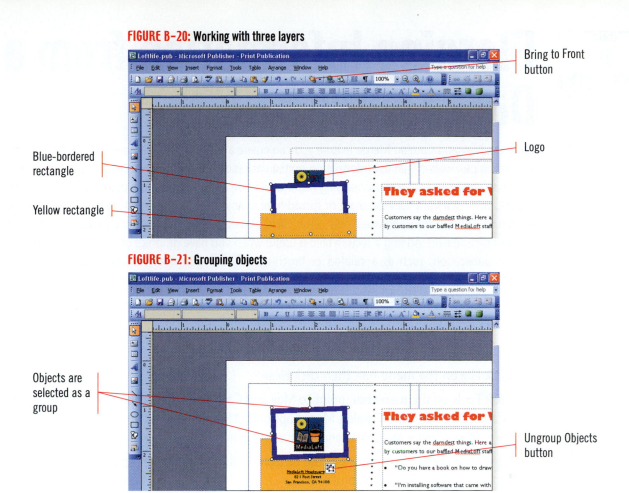

Bring to Front button

Logo

Blue-bordered rectangle

Yellow rectangle

FIGURE B-21: Grouping objects

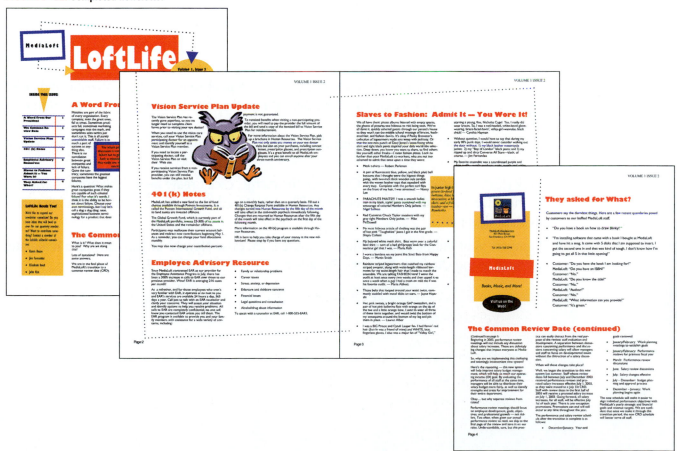

Objects are selected as a group

Ungroup Objects button

FIGURE B-22: Completed newsletter

Merging Information from a Data Source

Using the Mail and Catalog Merge feature you can create a brochure or add an additional page or pages to an existing publication that use information from a data source. Using the Mail and Catalog Wizard you can choose to create an address list or catalog file, then choose a source, such as a database or spreadsheet. You can add the fields from your database or spreadsheet in any order and position them to create the look you want, and you can choose to select only certain fields. When adding a field, you choose whether to add it as a text or picture field. Adding a picture field is useful when you have graphics or images you want to display in your publication, such as a catalog or brochure. You need to add a page listing the new MediaLoft employees to the newsletter. You will create a catalog merge using a new publication, then choose an Excel spreadsheet as your data source. You will work through the wizard to select appropriate options, then merge the data to a new publication.

STEPS

1. Click **File** on the menu bar, then click **New**

2. Click **Tools** on the menu bar, point to **Mail and Catalog Merge**, click **Mail and Catalog Merge Wizard**, then click the **Catalog Merge option button**, if necessary

   The Mail and Catalog Merge task pane opens, as shown in Figure B-23.

3. Click **Next: Select data source** at the bottom of the Mail and Catalog Merge task pane, click **Browse** in the Select data source section, navigate to the drive and folder where your Data Files are stored, click **PB B-2.xls**, then click **Open**

   The Select Table dialog box opens, displaying the Excel data sheets.

4. Click **OK**, click **OK** in the Catalog Records dialog box, then click **Next: Create your template** in the task pane

   Next you will choose and position the fields to create the merge template.

5. Click the **FirstName list arrow**, click **Insert as Text**, repeat to insert the LastName and Title fields, click the **Photo list arrow**, click **Insert as Picture**, then format, size, and position the fields as shown in Figure B-24

   The two name fields are formatted using 24-point Arial Black. The Title field is formatted using 16-point Arial Black.

6. Click **Next: Preview**, click **Next: Complete the merge**, click **Create new publication**, navigate to the drive and folder where your Data Files are stored, then save the merged publication as **New hires.pub**

7. Compare your finished publication to Figure B-25, close New hires.pub, close the template without saving changes, then exit Publisher

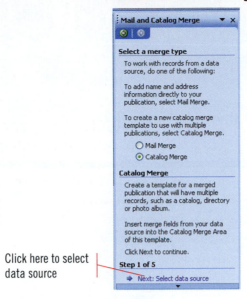

Click here to select data source

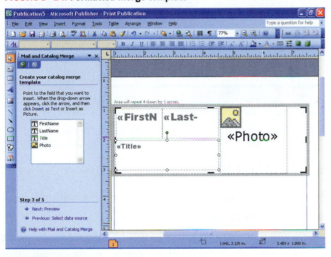

Clues to Use

Creating a drop cap

A **drop cap** is a specially formatted first letter of the first word of a paragraph. Usually, a drop cap is in a much larger font size than the paragraph text itself, and sometimes the drop cap is formatted in a different font. To create a drop cap, click anywhere in the paragraph where you want the drop cap to appear, click Format on the menu bar, click Drop Cap, click one of the available drop cap styles in the Drop Cap dialog box, shown in Figure B-26, then click OK. You can also use the options on the Custom Drop Cap tab to create your own drop cap style.

FIGURE B-26: Drop Cap dialog box

Practice

Label each element of the publication shown in Figure B-27.

FIGURE B-27

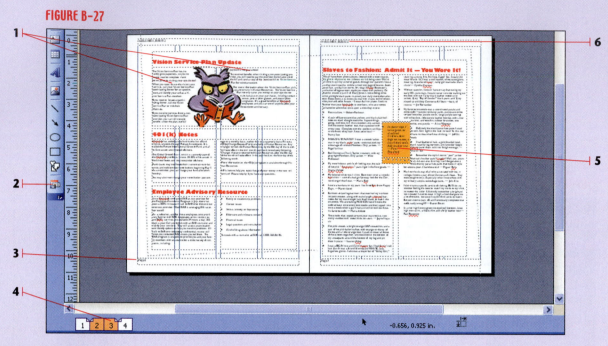

Match each term with the statement that best describes it.

7. **Master page**
8. **Data source**
9. **Ruler guides**
10. **Send to Back**
11. **Story**
12. **Wrapping**
13. **Autoflow**
14. **Header**

a. Also called an article, is composed of text and read from top to bottom
b. Feature that flows text from one text box to another
c. The layer where you place objects that you want to appear on every page
d. The flow of text around an object, such as a clip art image or pull quote
e. Command used to send an object behind a stack of objects
f. A file, such as a database or spreadsheet, that is a source for merged information
g. Information that appears at the top of every page of a publication
h. Nonprinting lines that can assist you in aligning objects on all pages

▼ SKILLS REVIEW

1. Create columns of text.

a. Start Publisher, open the file Rental.pub, then go to page 2 of the publication.
b. Right-click the text box beneath the heading Why Rent a Computer, change the number of columns in this text box to 2, with .14" of space in between, then close the Format Text dialog box.

2. Work with overflow text.

a. Select the empty text box in the second panel on page 2, insert the file PB B-3.doc into it, then click No when asked if you want to use autoflow.
b. Connect the text box containing PB B-3.doc to the empty text box in the third panel on page 2, then insert the overflow text into this connected text box.
c. Connect the text box in the third column of page 2 to the blue text box in the first column of page 1.
d. Go to page 2. Insert a Continued on notice at the end of the text box in the third panel on page 2, then insert a Continued from notice at the beginning of the text box in the first panel on page 1.

3. **Use guides.**
   a. Create grid guides for three columns.
   b. In the first panel on page 2, increase the width of the text box containing the double columns of text so that the right side of the text box is aligned with the blue layout guides, and the left side is ⅛" from the edge of the page.
   c. Drag the lower-middle handle of the text box up to the 5½" mark on the vertical ruler.

4. **Create picture captions.**
   a. In the Why Rent a Computer? panel, insert a picture caption below the text box. Choose the Thin Frame Picture design.
   b. Resize and move the picture so that its top edge is just below the text, and its bottom edge is at the 8" mark on the vertical ruler.
   c. Replace the placeholder graphic with a picture of a computer from the Clip Art task pane, then replace the placeholder caption text with **Don't buy — rent!**
   d. Change the font of the picture caption to 14-point Book Antiqua, bold, and center-aligned.

5. **Create headers and footers.**
   a. Insert a header at the top of the first column that contains this text: **Visit us at www.qcrental.com!** (*Hint*: Click View on the menu bar, then click Header and Footer.)
   b. Insert a footer at the bottom of the first column that contains this text: **Call Quality Computer today at (314) 555-4321!**
   c. Verify that the footer and header text is left-aligned, format the footer and header text in 10-point Book Antiqua and italic, then close Master Page view.

6. **Wrap text around objects.**
   a. Go to page 1, select the computer clip art from the bottom of the first column and move it up into the paragraph of text, so its top edge is at the 3" mark on the vertical ruler and its left edge is flush against the text box. Choose the square text wrapping option.
   b. Go to the story in the first panel of page 2, then insert a pull quote using the Blends Pull Quote design.
   c. Position the pull quote frame so that it is centered between the two columns of text in the first panel, with the top edge at the 3" mark on the vertical ruler.
   d. Replace the placeholder text with **As soon as you buy a system, it is outdated**. Drag the lower-middle handle up to the 4" mark on the vertical ruler, then format the text in 9-point Book Antiqua and italic.

7. **Layer and group objects.**
   a. In the workspace to the right of the brochure, create the Quality Computer logo by assembling the Quality Computer, Inc. text with the brown rectangle, the dot pattern, the black square, and the black-bordered shape. Use the logo at the top of page 1 as a model, using the brown rectangle in place of the blue.
   b. Use the Order buttons as necessary to complete this task. When the logo is assembled correctly, group the items and move the logo to just above the address on page 2.
   c. Go to page 1, create a ½" text box at the 5" mark on the vertical ruler in the middle panel that spans the column width, then type your name in center-aligned 14-point Book Antiqua font.
   d. Proofread and spell check all stories, save your changes, print and close the publication.

8. **Merge information from a data source.**
   a. In order to create a cover sheet that can be tri-folded with the mailing addresses on it, start a new blank publication.
   b. Choose the mail merge option, and use sheet 1 from PB B-4.xls from your Data Files as the data source.
   c. Create your publication.
   d. Click Address Block in the task pane, accept default settings in the Insert Address Block dialog box.
   e. Position the address block in the center of the page, and resize it to 2.00 × 1.00.
   f. Preview the publication, then complete the merge to a new publication. Save it as **Addresses**, then close the publication. Close the template without saving changes, then exit Publisher.

▼ INDEPENDENT CHALLENGE 1

You are a travel agent with Escape Travel. You are in charge of creating a brochure on vacations to Nova Scotia. You started the brochure a few days ago, you have received additional marketing text and are ready to add the finishing touches.

a. Start Publisher, open the file Nova Scotia.pub, then add layout guides for three columns.

b. On page 2, insert the Data File PB B-5.doc from where your Data Files are stored into the two empty columns. Do not use autoflow. (*Hint*: Connect the text boxes.)

c. Insert a picture caption under Nova Scotia in the third column of page 1. Choose a picture frame that you like and change the placeholder text to **Don't wait to get away!** Format the caption text in 11-point Arial Black. Replace the picture with a map of Nova Scotia from the Clip Art task pane. (*Hint*: Ungroup the picture and frame if necessary.)

d. Insert a right-aligned footer with the text **Call Escape Travel at (207) 555-4321 for more information**, then create a left-aligned header that contains your name.

Advanced Challenge Exercise

- Create a logo using a text box, AutoShape, and Clip Art image.
- Experiment with layering orders and grouping to position the logo to your liking.
- Place the logo in the second panel on page 1.

e. Proofread, spell check, save, and print the publication.

▼ INDEPENDENT CHALLENGE 2

You are the development director for the Wolf Pond Arts Academy. You have partially completed a brochure announcing the annual fundraiser. You need to finish placing objects in the publication and finish formatting it.

a. Start Publisher, and open the file **Fundraiser.pub**.

b. In the third panel on page 1, replace the text <name> in the two text boxes with **Warren Pond Arts Academy**.

c. In the leftmost panel on page 1, replace the text Back panel heading with **Live Onstage**. In the text box below this heading, insert two pieces of clip art that illustrate the paragraph text. Resize the graphics to appropriate sizes, and specify the text wrapping of your choice.

d. In the first panel on page 2, insert PB B-6.doc in the text box below **Our annual fundraising gala!**, increase the size of the text box by aligning the right edge with the layout guide, then format the text into two columns.

e. Insert any pull quote frame centered between the two columns of text. Use the Carla Davis quote from the paragraph, and format the text in 9-point Century, italic, and center-aligned. Reduce the size of the pull quote box to 1" tall by 1" wide.

Advanced Challenge Exercise

- Rotate one of the inserted clip art images using the green rotation handle.
- Edit the wrap points on one of the inserted clip art images.
- Insert a custom drop cap in both the Gala and Live Onstage stories.

f. In the top text box in the middle panel on page 1, replace the text <designer> with your name, proofread, spell check, make any other adjustments, save, print, and close the publication.

▼ INDEPENDENT CHALLENGE 3

You own a small novelty store and you need to create a two-page brochure to promote your new summer items. You use the Mail and Catalog Merge feature to create a Publisher catalog that uses an Excel spreadsheet. You will then format the template so that the fonts and positions are attractive and legible.

a. Start Publisher, open a new blank publication, then start the Mail and Catalog Merge Wizard.

b. Choose to create a catalog, then select PB B-7.xls from your Data Files as the data source.

c. In the Catalog Records dialog box, sort the items by price. (*Hint*: Click the Price column head.)

▼ INDEPENDENT CHALLENGE 3 (CONTINUED)

d. Insert all fields, making sure that the Photo field is inserted as a photo field.

e. Position and resize the text boxes and photo field in any order you wish.

f. Format the fonts and insert at least one filled AutoShape behind a text box.

g. Preview the catalog, merge it to a new publication, then save the publication as **Toy Catalog**.

h. Add a footer that includes your name, and add a WordArt title at the top of page 1.

i. Proofread and spell check, save the publication, print, close it, close the template without saving changes.

▼ INDEPENDENT CHALLENGE 4

You own a small bed and breakfast in a city of your choice, anywhere in the world. You decide to create a brochure to attract visitors to your inn. You first need to do some research on the Internet about your chosen city.

a. Log on to the Internet, go to a search engine site such as Google (www.google.com) and research the following information to include in your brochure:
- The name, address, and phone number of the bed and breakfast in your chosen city
- The price per night for a single and double room, using the local currency
- A description of the hotel with a picture
- Photos or pictures of the city or country in which your inn is located
- Three short articles about your hotel and the interesting tourist attractions that are nearby, written by you, based on your research. You should write these articles using Microsoft Word, then save them with the file names specified in the table below. (*Hint*: Replace "your city" with your city's name.)

TABLE B-2

story title	story description	word count	save as file
Welcome to your city	Describe the city, providing brief overview of key facts	100	City.doc
About the Inn	Describe the inn, its offerings, prices, and amenities	100	Inn.doc
What to do in your city	Describe the key tourist attractions in your chosen city	100	Attractions.doc

b. Open a new publication and choose the Borders Informational brochure from the New Publications task pane.

c. Type the name of your bed and breakfast in the top text box on the third panel of page 1. (*Hint*: If your name or another name appears as the Business Name in this panel, replace that with the name of your bed and breakfast.)

d. Replace the text in the Product/Service Information with a short phrase that summarizes the experience you want your guests to have (such as **A Home Away from Home**).

e. Replace the placeholder photo in the third column of page 1 with a picture of an inn.

f. In the bottom text box in the third column of page 1, replace the placeholder phone number with your inn's phone number. Insert your inn's address in the text box above the phone number.

g. On page 2, replace the Main Inside Heading placeholder text with the heading **Welcome to your city**, then replace the story placeholder text with the file City.doc that you created.

h. Replace the first Secondary Heading in column 2 of page 2 with the text **About Our Inn**, then replace the placeholder story text with your file Inn.doc.

i. Replace the second Secondary Heading with the title **Things to do in your city**, then replace the placeholder story text under the heading with your file Attractions.doc.

j. On page 1, replace the placeholder text for the Back Panel Heading with **Make your reservation today**, then replace the story placeholder text with the file PB B-8.doc. Insert the rate information for your inn into the story.

k. Replace all the placeholder photos with images relating to your city or inn and change captions as necessary.

l. On the second column of page 1, delete the placeholder logo, if necessary, then insert your name, the name, address, and phone number of the inn in the empty text box at the bottom of the page.

m. Save your publication as **Inn brochure**, then spell check, print, and close the publication.

▼ VISUAL WORKSHOP

Create the advertisement for the play shown in Figure B-28. Use the Floating Oval Event Flyer Wizard. Replace the placeholder clip art with the image of Romeo and Juliet, which is available in the Clip Art task pane. Group the four text boxes containing date, time, location, and contact information, and then move them into the position shown. Insert your name in the Contact text box. In the black rectangle at the bottom of the page, insert a text box with two columns and insert the text file PB B-9.doc. (*Hint*: Click inside the text box, press [Ctrl][A] to select all the text, then change the font color to white.) Insert a pull quote, choosing the Linear pull quote design from the Design Gallery and using the Fill Color button on the Formatting toolbar to add color to the frame. Save your publication with the name **Play flyer.pub**.

FIGURE B-28

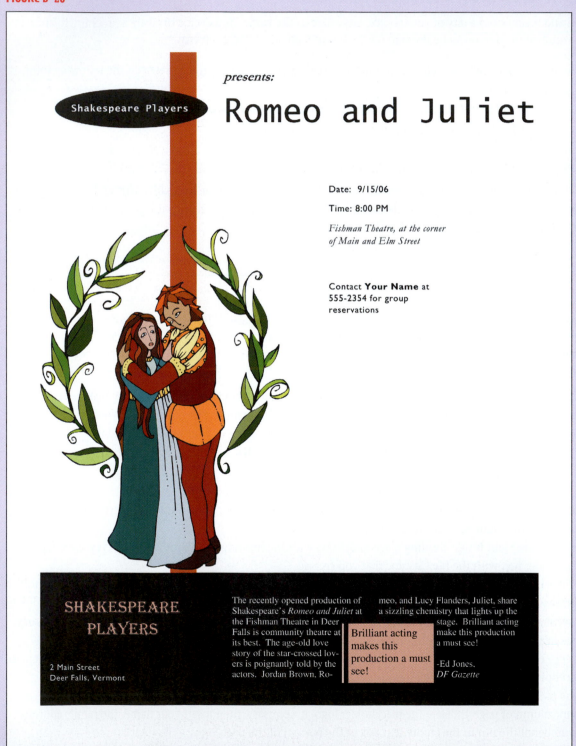

Creating a Web Publication

OBJECTIVES

Understand and plan Web publications
Create a new Web publication
Format a Web publication
Modify a Web form
Add form controls
Preview a Web publication
Convert a Web publication to a Web site
Send a publication as an e-mail

Publisher lets you create Web pages quickly and easily. You can start with a premade design and customize it to your needs. Publisher provides many tools that facilitate the development of Web pages. You can also convert an existing publication to a layout suitable for the Web.  You produce a quarterly newsletter called *LoftLife* for MediaLoft employees. You will use one of the Web site designs available from the New Publication task pane to create a two-page *LoftLife* Web site for the company intranet. You will also convert the most recent issue to a Web layout.

Understanding and Planning Web Publications

The **World Wide Web**, or simply the **Web**, is a collection of electronic documents available to people around the world through the **Internet**, a global computer network. **Web pages** are the documents that make up the Web. A group of associated Web pages is known as a **Web site**. Anyone with Internet access can create Web pages and Web sites and add them to the network. **Web browser** software allows anyone to view Web sites. All Web pages are written in a common programming language called **Hypertext Markup Language (HTML)**.

With Publisher, you can create a **Web publication**—a publication that you later convert to either a Web page or a Web site—without needing to know HTML.  You can use the Publisher skills you already possess to design and create the content, and then let Publisher create the HTML code for you. Figure C-1 shows how a Web page created with Publisher looks in a browser.

DETAILS

You can use Publisher to create the components of your Web publication. Following is an overview of these Web components:

- Planning a Web site is an important first step. A detailed outline of the entire site, also known as a **storyboard**, should include which pages link to each other and how, as well as where elements should appear on a page, and any special graphics you might need. You plan which features you will add to your Web site. Figure C-2 shows a sketch of your plan.

- A **hyperlink**, or simply a **link**, is specially formatted text or a graphic that a user can click to open an associated Web page. Links serve as the foundation of the Web. Almost all pages on the Web are connected to each other through a series of links, and each Web page can contain links to many different Web sites. You will place a welcome paragraph on the home page that describes the features of *LoftLife Online*, and then you will add a link to the feedback form on page 2.

- Much like its paper counterpart, a **Web form** can include areas for text input, such as name and address, and provide an easy way for a user to submit information. Unlike its paper counterpart, a Web form also can offer boxes that users click to submit information via the Web. Many organizations that do business online allow users to select products or services using a Web form. You will add a feedback form to *LoftLife Online*, where users can answer the Question of the Month and provide comments on the latest issue.

- When your Web site has multiple pages, it's important to provide users with an easy and consistent method of navigating between them. A **navigation bar** provides a set of links to the most important pages in a Web site, displayed in the same location on each page.

- When you create a Web publication using the New Publication task pane, Publisher can automatically create one or more navigation bars on the main pages and update them as you add or delete pages. You will insert navigation bars at the top and bottom of both pages, making it easier for viewers to jump quickly to where they want to go.

Clues to Use

Publishing a Web site

If you want to make your Web site available to all users of the Internet, you need to publish it, or store your Web site files on a Web server, known as a **host**. A Web server is always connected to the Web, making your pages available to anyone with Web access. If you already have an account with a commercial Internet service provider (ISP) or a school, room for your Web site on the Web server may be included with the account. Additionally, several Internet companies offer free space for Web pages on their servers; in exchange, they place an advertisement on each page in your Web site. All Web servers impose limits on the amount of data you can store; be sure to check these limits before publishing your Web site. A graphics-heavy site can quickly mushroom in size, so it is important to place graphics sparingly in your Web if your allotted space is small.

FIGURE C-1: Web page created using Publisher

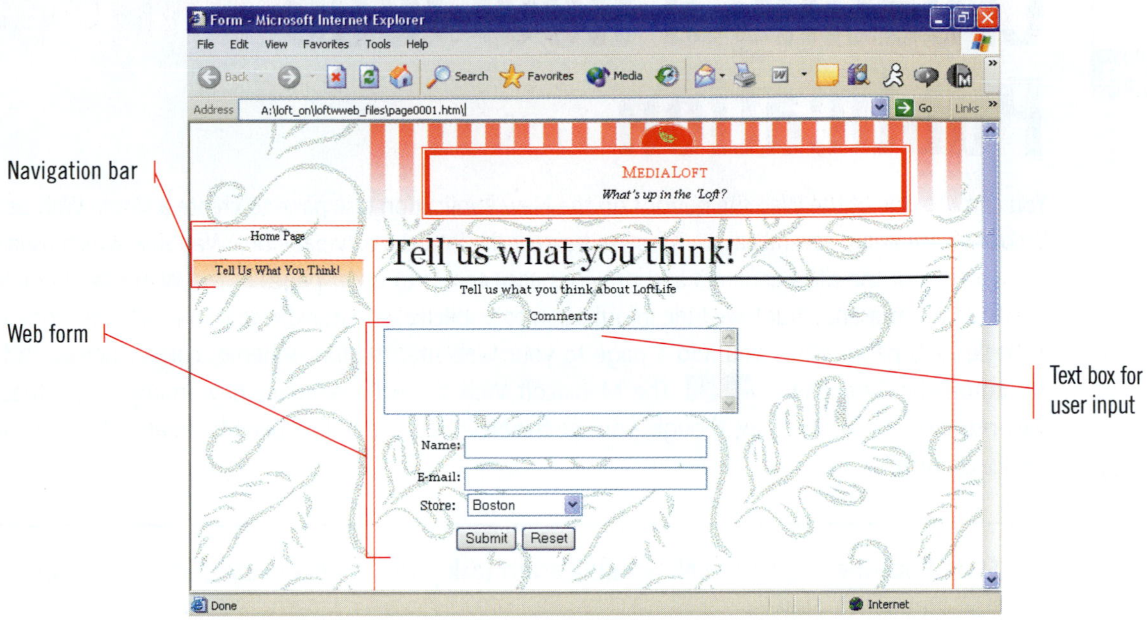

Navigation bar

Web form

Text box for user input

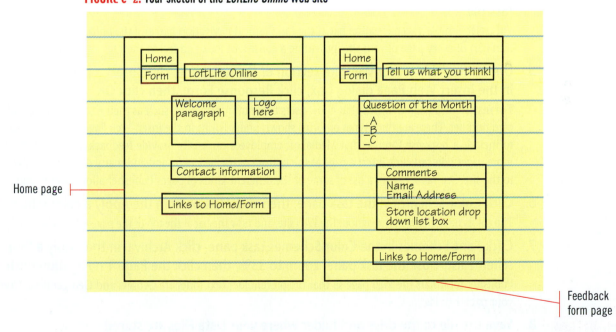

FIGURE C-2: Your sketch of the *LoftLife Online* Web site

Home page

Feedback form page

Creating a New Web Publication

You can use one of the Web site designs on the New Publication task pane to create a single Web page, or a Web site containing several pages. A **home page** is the introductory page of a Web site, which usually gives an overview of the site's contents and provides easy access to other pages in the Web site. If you want to create a Web presence but have little information to publicize, you may be able to fit all the information on a single Web page. When you add a page to your Web site, the font scheme, color scheme, and design are automatically applied. The MediaLoft Web site will eventually have many pages that link to past issues of *LoftLife*. For now, though, you use the New Publication task pane to create a home page and a feedback form.

STEPS

1. **Start Publisher, open the New Publication task pane, if necessary, click File on the menu bar, then click New**

2. **Click Web Sites and E-mail in the New from a design list**
   The Publication Gallery displays sample home page designs, as shown in Figure C-3.

TROUBLE
If a dialog box asks you to enter information about yourself in the wizard, click OK, then click Cancel.

3. **Scroll down the Publication Gallery, click the Mobile Easy Web Site design, then click OK in the Easy Web Site Builder dialog box**
   The Publication Gallery closes, and a new publication opens in the workspace with the Mobile Easy Web Site design. The Web Site Options task pane displays options for navigation bars, adding pages, and other formatting options. The navigation bar will contain links to all the pages in the Web Site.

4. **Verify that the Vertical and Bottom icon is selected in the Navigation bar section of the task pane**
   This selection places a navigation bar at the top (Vertical navigation bar) and the bottom (Horizontal navigation bar) of every page of your site, providing a consistent look and feel to the site.

5. **Under the Add to your Web site section of the task pane, click Insert a page, click Forms in the Insert Web Page dialog box, click Response Form, then click OK**
   Forms are Web page elements that allow users to input information, such as their name, address, and credit card number. There are three types of forms shown under Forms in the Insert Web Page dialog box. You want to include a response form so that MediaLoft employees can easily provide feedback about *LoftLife*. To add more pages you can click Insert a page at the bottom of the task pane and add many different kinds of pages to the site. See Table C-1 for a list of some of the different kinds of pages Publisher allows you to add.

6. **Click Color Schemes in the task pane, then click Harbor from the Apply a color scheme list**
   The colors have changed throughout the Web site, and now the bar at the top of the page is teal instead of purple.

7. **Click Font Schemes in the Color Schemes task pane, click Archival in the Apply a font scheme list, close the task pane, zoom to 33%, then click the Page 1 navigation button**
   Publisher reformats the Web page so that the placeholder text fonts are Georgia and Georgia Bold. Compare your page 1 to Figure C-4.

TROUBLE
Click No if asked to save the modified logo.

8. **Save the file to the drive and folder where your Data Files are stored**
   The file is saved in Publisher publication format with a .pub file extension.

FIGURE C-3: Web site designs in Publication Gallery

Web Sites and E-mail category selected

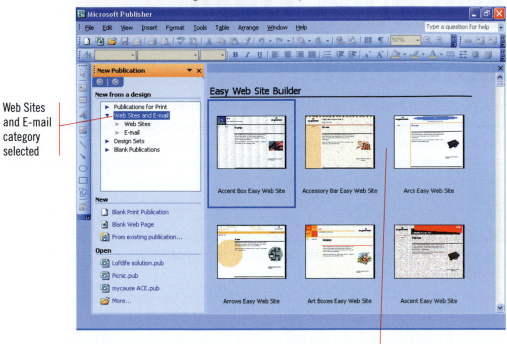

Web Site designs displayed here

FIGURE C-4: New home page with Harbor color scheme and Archival font scheme

Vertical navigation bar

Bottom navigation bar

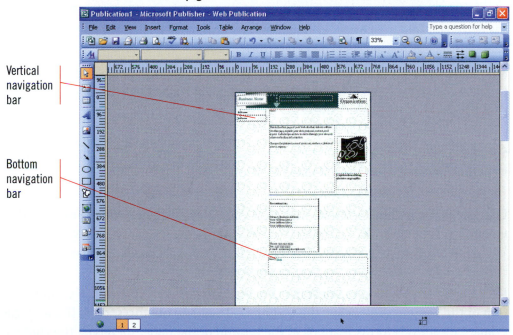

TABLE C-1: Some types of Web pages you can create using the Insert a page command from the task pane

web page type	useful for
FAQ	List of frequently asked questions about your organization
Calendar	List of upcoming important dates/events
Event	Information about an upcoming event
Special Offer	Details of a sale or discount
Photos	You can present photos with captions, links, or in a gallery
Related links	Descriptions and links for other relevant Web sites

Formatting a Web Publication

After you create a Web publication using a design from the task pane, you need to personalize the contents and adjust the formatting to your needs. In addition to the standard formatting options available for all publications, Publisher offers several tools specifically for use in Web publications. Table C-2 shows these special toolbar buttons and explains how to use them. You start customizing your Web publication by changing the default home page text and graphics.

STEPS

1. Zoom in as necessary, triple-click in the rectangle frame in the upper-left corner of the page to select the Business Name placeholder text, type MediaLoft, then click outside the frame

2. Click in the large Home frame above the text to select the placeholder text, type LoftLife Online, then resize the text to 36 pt

3. Select the text Your business tag line here. in the frame above LoftLife Online, then type What's up in the 'Loft?

4. Select the picture caption text box beneath the footprints, press [Delete], right-click the clip art of the footprints, point to Change Picture, click From File, select PB C-1.jpg from the drive and folder where your Data Files are stored, then click Insert
   The MediaLoft logo now appears in the picture frame.

5. Right-click to select both paragraphs of text, point to Change Text, click Text File, select the PB C-2.doc from the drive and folder where your Data Files are stored, click OK, then click the desktop to deselect the text box
   The new text now appears in the text box. Compare your screen with Figure C-5.

6. Select the text Feedback Form in the second paragraph you inserted, then click the Insert Hyperlink button on the Standard toolbar
   The Insert Hyperlink dialog box opens.

7. Click the Place in This Document icon, click Page 2. Form in the Select a place in this document list, then click OK
   The text "Feedback Form" now appears underlined and in color, indicating that it is now a link that viewers can click to open the page that contains the feedback form.

8. Click the pyramid image to select the Organization logo, press [Delete], scroll to the bottom of the content area, select the text box with phone numbers, press [Delete], click the Primary Business Address text box at the bottom of the page, then type the contact information and format the text for MediaLoft, as shown in Figure C-6

9. Save the publication

FIGURE C-5: Top section of home page completed

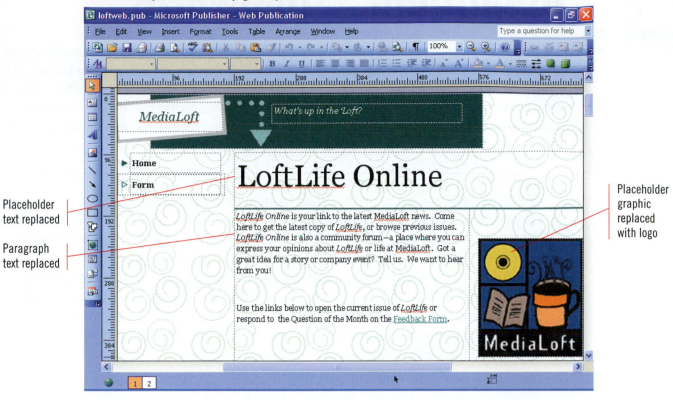

Placeholder text replaced

Paragraph text replaced

Placeholder graphic replaced with logo

FIGURE C-6: *LoftLife* contact information

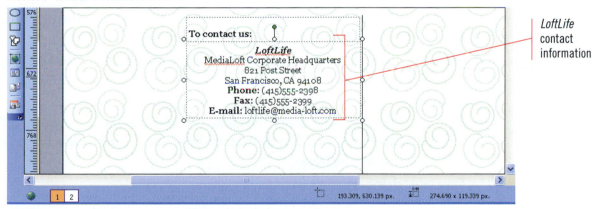

LoftLife contact information

TABLE C-2: Web page formatting options

option	button	description
Hot Spot		Formats a single graphic with links to multiple Web pages
Form Control		Inserts a form field for user input, such as a text box or check box
HTML Code Fragment		Allows advanced users to add additional HTML code to a specific part of a publication
Insert Hyperlink		Adds a hyperlink to the selected object
Web Page Preview		Opens the current Web page using your system's default Web browser

Modifying a Web Form

Including a form in a Web page is a great way to encourage users to interact with your site. Using forms, you can collect valuable information, such as customer names and addresses, or feedback on a product. The response form that you selected in the Web Options task pane contains four placeholder questions, a comments text area, and user contact information text boxes. You want to customize the response form you created from the task pane by changing the form headings and modifying one of the questions. You delete the other three questions and rearrange the remaining objects.

STEPS

1. **Click the Page 2 Navigation button, then zoom in on the top of the page**
   The publication's second page contains the feedback form you selected in the Web Page Options task pane. Notice that some of the text fields at the top reflect formatting changes that you made to corresponding fields on the home page.

2. **Click Response Form, type Tell us what you think!, resize the text to 28 pt, select the Ask readers text box, press [Delete], click Response form title, type We want to know., click Type a description, then type Answer the question below and use the comments area to tell us your opinions about LoftLife.**
   Compare your screen with Figure C-7.

3. **Click Question 1, type Which job perk is most important to you?, click Answer A, type Summer hours, click Answer B, type Free beverages, click Answer C, then type Telecommuting policy**
   The question and three choices are complete. You can select multiple objects by dragging the mouse diagonally to create a rectangular shape around the objects. This is called dragging a selection rectangle.

4. **Drag a selection rectangle around the third question and its three answers and the fourth question and its three answers to select all eight objects, then press [Delete]**
   You deleted two of the placeholder questions and answer options.

5. **Drag a selection rectangle around the second question and its three answers, then press [Delete]**
   One question remains on the form.

6. **Drag a selection rectangle around the Comments label and the Comments multiline text box to select both objects, then drag them up until they are just below Telecommuting policy**
   Compare your screen with Figure C-8.

7. **Save your changes**

> **TROUBLE**
> Be sure to include all parts of each object when dragging a selection rectangle. If your selection box doesn't include all the desired objects or you select too many objects, press [Shift], then click the additional or extraneous objects.

FIGURE C-7: Form Page with new heading text

Reflects changes made to home page

Replaced heading text

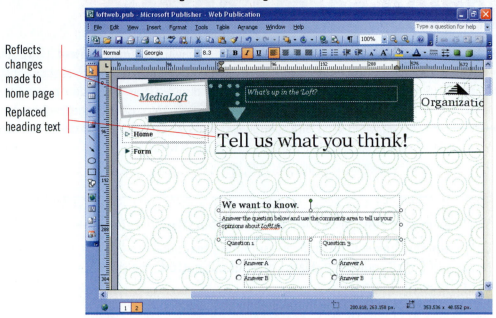

FIGURE C-8: Form page with modified question and comments fields moved

Modified question

Comments label and text boxes moved

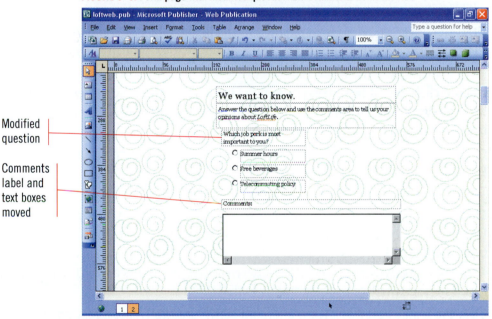

Publisher 2003

Clues to Use

Adding multimedia components to a Web publication

In addition to including text and graphics in your Web sites, Publisher allows you to add multimedia elements to make the site more eye-catching and to make more information available to your viewers. The Web Site Options task pane lets you select a background fill as well as sound for your site, which plays on the user's browser when the page opens. To insert and format a sound, click the Page Content link on the Web Site Options task pane, click Background fill and sound, click Background sound to open the Web Page Options dialog box, then type a sound file location in the Background sound File name text box. You can choose to have the sound continuously loop or play as many times as you specify.

You can add simple animation to a site by inserting an animated GIF. GIF stand for graphics interchange file, and is a standard format for displaying images on Web pages. An animated GIF is a short animation encoded in the same format, which plays repeatedly when it opens in a browser. To add GIFs to your Web publication, click Insert on the menu bar, point to Picture, click From File, then type the name and location of the .gif file you want to add. Some .gif files are available in the Clip Organizer.

You can also add video and other objects by selecting Object on the Insert menu, clicking the Create from File option button, then specifying the object's location in the dialog box.

Adding Form Controls

Each item in a form, such as a text box or a check box, is known as a **form control**. HTML allows Web pages to use seven different types of form controls to collect information from users, as shown in Table C-3. Each control is usually associated with a text box, which can display a label or question, or provide guidance to the user about the type of information to be collected. ⬛ You customize the feedback form further by modifying the contact information form controls and labels. You delete some of the default controls and labels to make it less cluttered, and leave the controls and labels for a name and an e-mail address. You also add a drop-down list for users to provide their store location.

STEPS

1. Scroll down as necessary, click the Phone text box, then type Name:

2. Delete the text box control and corresponding text label for Address, then drag the Name and E-mail controls and label, the Submit button, and the Reset button to the positions shown in Figure C-9

   You deleted and rearranged the controls to better meet your needs.

3. Click the Form Control button 🖾 on the Objects toolbar, then click List Box

   A list box appears showing three items.

4. Drag the lower-middle resizing handle of the list box up so that only Item One appears, then drag the list box to just below the E-mail: text box control

   You modified the list box to show only one item at a time.

5. Double-click the list box, make sure Item One is selected in the Appearance section of the List Box Properties dialog box, click Modify, type Boston in the Item text box, click the not selected option button, then click OK

6. Click Item Two, click Modify, type Chicago, click OK, click Item Three, click Modify, type Houston, then click OK

   The List Box Properties dialog box shows three items: Boston, Chicago, and Houston.

7. Click Add, type Park City in the Item text box, click OK, click Add, type New York, click OK, click Add, type San Diego, click OK, click Add, type San Francisco, click OK, click Add, type Seattle, click OK, then click OK

   The list box displays the text "Boston." MediaLoft employees who use this form will be able to click the arrow next to the text and select the city where they work.

QUICK TIP

Click the label, press and hold [Shift], click the text box control, click the Group Objects button 🖾, then move them together as a group.

8. Click the E-mail text label, press and hold [Ctrl], drag to create a text box to the left of the list box you just created that is a copy of the E-mail label above, select the text in the copied E-mail label, then type Store:

   The list box now has a Store label next to it. Compare your screen with Figure C-10.

9. Double-click the Submit button, click Form Properties, click the Save the data in a file on my Web server option button, click OK twice, then save your publication

   All data entered by users will be stored in a file on the MediaLoft Web server.

FIGURE C-9: Form page with deleted and moved controls and labels

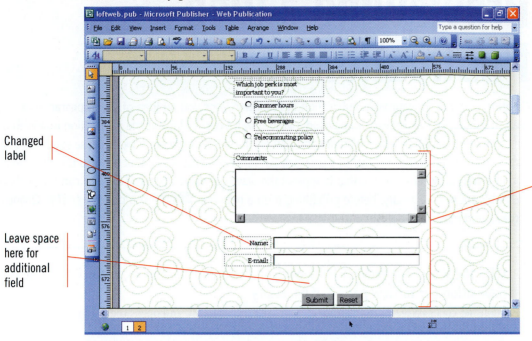

Changed label

Leave space here for additional field

Move these labels, controls, and buttons to these positions

FIGURE C-10: Completed form

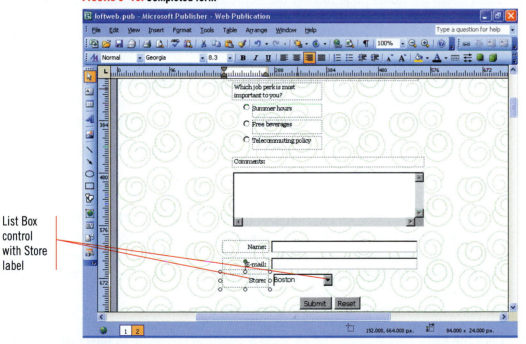

List Box control with Store label

TABLE C-3: Web page form controls

control name	uses
Textbox	Short input, such as a name or e-mail address
Text Area	Longer input, such as comments
Checkbox	A question or option that the user can select, such as not being added to a mailing list
Option Button	A list of choices, of which the user should pick a limited number
List Box	A drop-down menu providing a list of choices
Submit Button	A command button, used to submit information entered in the form
Reset Button	A command button, used to clear information from a form

UNIT
C
Publisher 2003

Previewing a Web Publication

Creating and editing your Web publication in Publisher gives you an idea of the appearance of your final Web site. However, whenever you develop a Web site, it's best to look at the publication in a Web browser before actually turning it into a Web site and making it available on a network. Because some aspects of the publication can appear differently in a browser, Publisher provides a tool that lets you preview the publication in a Web browser to ensure that it appears the way you want. Upon review, you can make changes to the publication, if necessary, before publishing it on a network. You preview *LoftLife Online* in your browser and make final adjustments.

STEPS

1. **Click the Web Page Preview button** **on the Standard toolbar, then click Home on the navigation bar to view page 1, if necessary**
    Publisher creates a temporary version of your Web site in HTML and opens the file in your Web browser, as shown in Figure C-11.

2. **Scroll down the home page to view the entire contents, click Form on the navigation bar to open the second page, then scroll to view all the contents of page 2**
    You notice that you need to reposition and adjust the size of some of the text boxes containing the information on page 2. Both pages contain large gaps between the elements at the top and the bottom.

3. **Click the Microsoft Publisher program button on the taskbar to return to Publisher, drag the center-right sizing handle on the question text box to the right so that the question fits on one line, then delete the placeholder logo at the top of the page**

4. **Click the Page 1 Navigation button of the publication, click the Zoom list arrow on the Standard toolbar, then click 50%**
    You can now view all of the page contents.

5. **Resize the imported text box so that its bottom line is at 384 on the vertical ruler, delete the vertical black line, select the green line and two contact information text boxes, drag them so that the green horizontal line is at 442 on the vertical ruler, then drag the bottom green horizontal line and the navigation bar so that the line is at 656 on the vertical ruler**
    The entire contents of the home page are now closer to the top of the page.

6. **Click the Page 2 Navigation button, drag a selection rectangle to select all the objects from the We want to know text box to the Submit and Reset buttons, drag the selected items so that the top of the We want to know text box is at 192 on the vertical ruler, then drag the bottom green line and the navigation bar so that the green line is at 724 on the vertical ruler**

7. **Save your publication, then click the Web Page Preview button**
    The form page appears with all the elements consolidated, as shown in Figure C-12.

8. **Test the links on the navigation bar to view the home page, then close the browser**

FIGURE C-11: Preview of home page in browser

Your path will vary

FIGURE C-12: Preview of form page with lower objects moved up

Lower objects now closer to top of the page

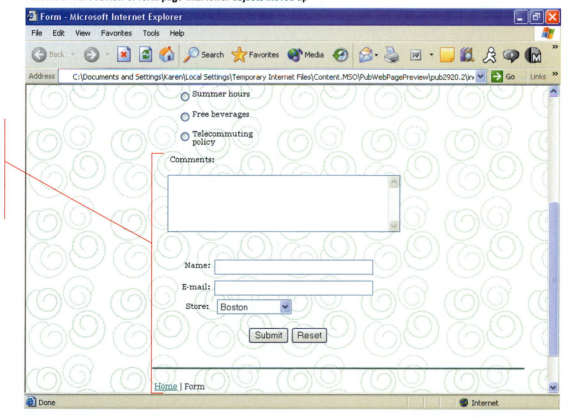

Converting a Web Publication to a Web Site

In your work on the Web site so far, you have edited and saved the publication in the Publisher file format (which has the file extension .pub). When you are satisfied with the publication's appearance and layout, you need to convert the publication to HTML format (which has the file extension .htm). The HTML document you produce can then be published on a network (either the Internet or an intranet) and displayed by Web browsers. You are satisfied with the preview of your Web site in the Web browser and are ready to convert the publication to an HTML document.

STEPS

1. **If necessary, click the Microsoft Publisher program button on the taskbar to return to Publisher**

2. **Click File on the menu bar, then click Publish to the Web**

   The Publish to the Web dialog box opens, as shown in Figure C-13.

3. **Navigate to the drive and folder where your Data Files are stored, click the Create New Folder button, type loft_on in the Name text box, click OK, select index.htm in the Name text box, type loftweb, then click Save**

   A separate folder is created just for this Web site so that all the files, including the graphics for the top and bottom page borders, are grouped together.

4. **Click File on the menu bar, click Close, start Internet Explorer (or your default browser), click File on the Internet Explorer menu bar, click Open, click Browse, open the loft_on folder where you saved the .HTML file, click loftweb.htm, click Open, then click OK**

   The *LoftLine Online* Web page, now saved as an HTML file, appears in your default Web browser.

5. **Click the Form link on the navigation bar**

   The second page of the Web site opens, as shown in Figure C-14.

6. **Type your name in the Name text box, click File on the menu bar, click Print, click Print, click the Home link on the navigation bar, click File on the menu bar, click Print, then click Print**

   You printed both the home page and the form page of your Web site.

7. **Click File on the Internet Explorer menu bar, then click Close**

   You exited the browser, but Publisher is still open.

FIGURE C-13: Publish to the Web dialog box

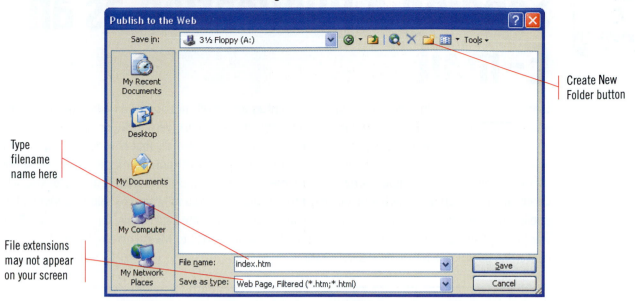

Type filename name here

File extensions may not appear on your screen

Create New Folder button

FIGURE C-14: Feedback form page in Web browser

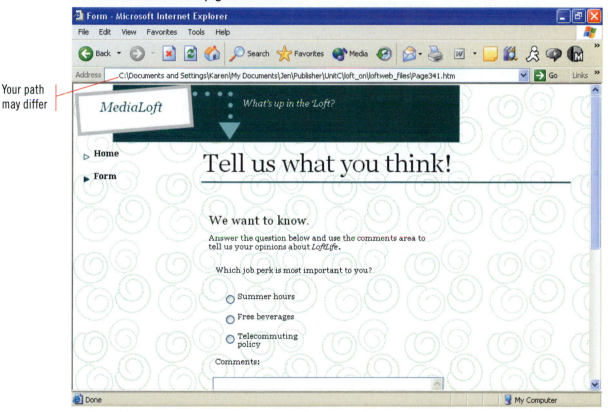

Your path may differ

Clues to Use

Formatting Web publications for different audiences

When you create a Web page, you want to make it available to the largest possible audience. Publisher allows you to create Web pages for Internet Explorer 4.0 or later, or Netscape Navigator 4.0 or later. Some features, such as tables and cascading style sheets, may not be viewed properly if viewed in early browser versions. If your site is going to be viewed only on an intranet where all users have Internet Explorer 5.5, you might want to optimize your site and include features that can only be viewed with this version of the browser. However, if your site is being viewed on the Internet by a wide range of users, you will want to make sure that you optimize the site for an earlier browser version. It is important to test your site using a variety of browser versions before making it available to a wide audience to ensure that it can be read by all.

Sending a Publication as an E-mail

Using Publisher, you can send a page of a document as an e-mail message or an entire document as an attachment if you have Microsoft Outlook or Microsoft Outlook Express (version 5.0 or later) as your default e-mail program. Many e-mail programs (although not all) can read e-mails that have formatting, graphics, and links to Web sites. This can be an effective way to distribute an electronic newsletter. When converting a publication for e-mail, you should always use the preview feature, and also send a test copy to yourself to check for any formatting issues before sending it to your audience. You may need to adjust the width of your publication. Publisher also provides e-mail templates that are formatted specifically for e-mail. You want to explore making the *LoftLife* newsletter available as an e-mail to MediaLoft employees. You start by converting page 1 of a recent issue to an e-mail.

STEPS

1. **Click File on the menu bar, click Open, then open the file PB C-3.pub from the drive and folder where your Data Files are stored**
   The first page of *LoftLife* appears in the workspace.

2. **Click File on the menu bar, point to Send E-mail, then click E-Mail Preview**
   The first page of the newsletter appears in your browser, as shown in Figure C-15. Although the margins look good, you know that you will have to create links to other articles and do more work on the newsletter before you can send it as an e-mail. You decide to send it to yourself as an e-mail to see what it would look like.

3. **Return to the Publisher file, click File on the menu bar, point to Send E-mail, then click Send This Page as Message**
   A toolbar appears with text boxes for e-mail addresses and a subject, as shown in Figure C-16.

   TROUBLE
   If you do not have Microsoft Outlook 2003 or Microsoft Outlook Express 5.0 or later, you will not be able to complete this lesson.

4. **Type your e-mail address in the To text box, then click the Send button** 📧 Send
   An Outlook status dialog box opens while the e-mail is sent. After a few minutes, check your e-mail to see if it appears in your inbox. Open the e-mail, then delete it.

5. **Close the PB C-3 file without saving changes, then exit Publisher**

FIGURE C-15: First page of *LoftLife* issue viewed as an e-mail preview

Your path will differ

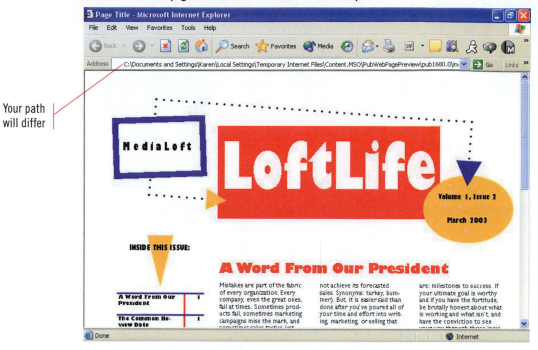

FIGURE C-16: Sending a publication as an e-mail

Send button

Enter your e-mail address here

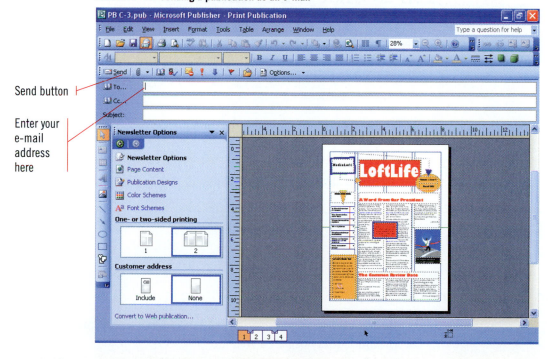

Clues to Use

Converting a print publication to a Web site

When you create a Web site from scratch, you format the text, preview it using the Web Page Preview button, make adjustments as necessary, and then save it as a Web page. You can use this same process to convert print publications such as flyers and newsletters into Web pages. Each page in your publication becomes a separate page in the Web site, and you can add a navigation bar and other links easily. To convert a print publication to a Web site, click Convert to Web publication at the bottom of the *Document Type* Options task page (where Document Type is newsletter, or whatever type of document you are working with). A Wizard opens, asking if you want to save your print publication first and save your Web publication as a new document. Click Next, choose the appropriate navigation bar option, then click Finish in the Wizard. You will need to reposition some objects, and create links to the navigation bar, but creating a Web site from an existing publication is easy.

Practice

▼ CONCEPTS REVIEW

Label each item marked in Figure C-17.

FIGURE C-17

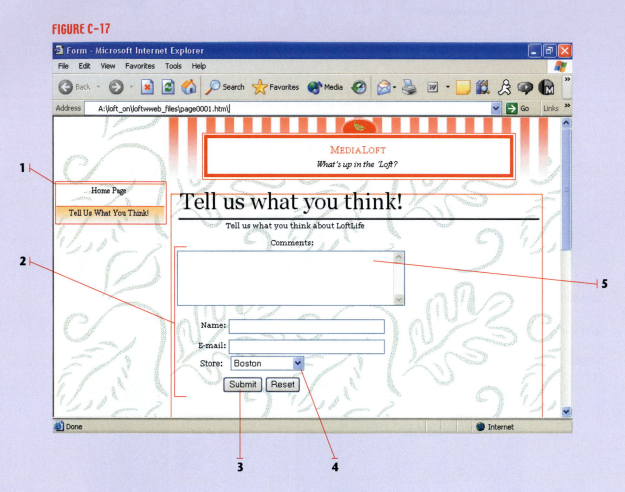

Match each item with its definition.

6. **HTML**

7. **Web form**

8. **Web site**

9. **home page**

10. **navigation bar**

11. **browser**

a. A means for users of a Web page to enter and submit information

b. The introductory page of a Web site

c. Special software for viewing Web pages and Web sites

d. The programming language in which all Web pages are created

e. Area on a Web page that provides links to the most important pages in a Web site, in the same location on each page

f. A group of associated Web pages

Select the best answer from the list of choices.

12. Which Web page control would most commonly be found in a form?
- **a.** Image box
- **b.** Check box
- **c.** Navigation bar
- **d.** Link

13. Which is *not* true about Web pages and Web sites?
- **a.** They can be created and added to the network by anyone with Internet access.
- **b.** They are written in a common programming language called Hypertext Markup Language (HTML).
- **c.** They can be viewed with special software called Web browsers.
- **d.** They can be created only by using software designed exclusively for that purpose.

14. If you want a user to open a Web page by clicking on text or graphics, you insert a(n):
- **a.** Form control
- **b.** User input field
- **c.** Hyperlink
- **d.** HTML code fragment

15. You can create a Web publication from a print publication by:
- **a.** Using the Publish to the Web command
- **b.** Selecting the Page Setup command
- **c.** Using the Web Publishing Wizard
- **d.** Using the Convert to Web layout command

▼ SKILLS REVIEW

1. Create a new Web publication.
- **a.** Start Publisher, then, if necessary, open the New Publication task pane.
- **b.** In the New from a design list in the task pane, click Web Sites and E-mail, click the Spotlight Easy Web Site design in the Publication Gallery, then click OK in the Easy Web Site Builder dialog box.
- **c.** In the Web Site Options task pane, verify that Vertical and Bottom is selected in the Navigation bar area.
- **d.** Insert a new page with a sign-up form.
- **e.** Choose the Shamrock color scheme.
- **f.** Choose the Impact font scheme, then close the task pane.

2. Format a Web publication.
- **a.** Zoom in on the top of page 1, click the image of the pagoda at the top of the page twice, make sure the pagoda is selected, right-click, point to Change Picture, click From File, select the file PB C-4.jpg from the drive and folder where your Data Files are stored, then click Insert. (*Hint:* If the Format Object dialog box opens, close it and try selecting the pagoda again.)
- **b.** Replace the graphic of a dragon with a clip art image of your choice relating to sports, and size it appropriately and delete the caption placeholder.
- **c.** Select the text Home, then type **MediaLoft Recreation**.
- **d.** Select the text Your business tag line here above MediaLoft Recreation, then type **And you thought your job was fun!**
- **e.** Delete the Business Name text box at the top of the page and the pyramid placeholder logo and graphic.
- **f.** Right-click the paragraph placeholder text, point to Change Text, click Text File, then insert the file PB C-5.doc from the drive and folder where your Data Files are stored. Click No in the Autoflow alert window. Move the bottom green line, contact information boxes, and navigation bar down, drag the bottom of the text frame down until all text is visible and the Text in Overflow icon disappears, then press Tab where necessary to align the location entries. (*Hint:* Seattle is the last entry.)
- **g.** Select the text sign-up form in the last line of the paragraph before Boston, then click the Insert Hyperlink button on the Standard toolbar.
- **h.** Click the Place in This Document option, click Page 2. Form, then click OK.

Publisher 2003

i. Scroll to the bottom of the page, then type the following information in the two text boxes below To contact us:, then position them side-by-side and delete the black line. (*Hint*: Change the font to Verdana 8 point.)

<table>
<tr><td>**MediaLoft, Inc.**
Your Name
821 Post Street
San Francisco, CA 94108</td><td>**Phone: (415) 555-2398**
Fax: (415) 555-2399
E-mail: Recreation@media-loft.com</td></tr>
</table>

j. Resize the text boxes as necessary to make the text fit, reposition the navigation bar if necessary, then save your publication as **recsite** to the drive and folder where your Data Files are stored. Do not save the logo if asked.

3. **Modify a Web form.**

a. Open page 2 of the publication and zoom in on the top of the page.

b. Delete the Business name text box and replace the picture on the right with the MediaLoft logo. Delete the placeholder logo.

c. Select the text Sign Up Form, type **Event Registration**, delete the text box below Event Registration, then replace Sign-up form title with **Sign up today for your store's event!**

d. Drag a selection rectangle to select all the controls and text labels from the Sign up for: label through the Total: control, then press [Delete].

e. Select and delete the text labels and controls from Method of Payment through Exp. Date. (*Hint*: Make sure you delete the text box containing security information.)

f. Replace the text in the label Address with **Event**, then add a label and textbox form for **Number of Guests** below the E-mail text box and label.

g. Drag the Submit and Reset buttons up so they are positioned just below the Number of Guests control.

4. **Add form controls.**

a. Click the Event: text area, then press [Delete]. (*Hint*: Do not delete the Event label.)

b. Click the Form Control button, click List Box, drag to create a one-line list box in the space formerly occupied by the Event text box, then double-click the list box you inserted.

c. Make sure Item One is selected in the Appearance section, click Modify, replace the text in the Item text box with **Boston**, click the Not Selected option button, then click OK.

d. Replace the Item text with **Chicago** for Item Two, and with **Houston** for Item Three.

e. Click Add, type **Park City** in the Item text box, click OK, create four new items with the text **New York**, **San Diego**, **San Francisco**, and **Seattle**, then click OK to close the List Box Properties dialog box.

f. Double-click the Submit button, click Form Properties, click the Save the data in a file on my Web server option button, click OK, click OK, then save your changes.

5. **Preview a Web publication.**

a. Click the Web Page Preview button.

b. Scroll down your home page to view the entire contents, click Home on the navigation bar to open the first page, then scroll to view all the page's contents.

c. Click the Publisher program button on the taskbar.

d. Drag a selection rectangle to select all objects from the Name label to the Reset button, then drag them up to just below Sign up today for your store's event!

e. Click the Page 1 navigation button, drag to select the three text boxes containing MediaLoft contact information at the bottom of the page, click the Copy button on the Standard toolbar, click the Page 2 navigation button, click the Paste Button on the Standard toolbar, then position the contact information below the Submit and Reset buttons.

f. Select the navigation bar, then drag it up to just below the contact information.

g. Save your changes, click the Web Page Preview button, then review your changes.

h. Close the browser window.

▼ SKILLS REVIEW (CONTINUED)

6. Convert a Web publication to a Web site.

  a. Click the Publisher program button on the taskbar if it is not open to view the recsite publication.

  b. Click File on the menu bar, then click Publish to the Web.

  c. Locate the drive and folder where your Data Files are stored, click the Create New Folder button, type **mediarec** as the new folder name, click OK, name the .html file **recsite**, click Save, then click OK in the dialog box.

  d. Open your default Web browser. Click File on the menu bar, click Open, open the mediarec folder, double-click the file recsite.htm, then click OK.

  e. Click the Form button on the navigation bar.

  f. Type **your name** in the Name field, then click the Print button on the browser toolbar. Click the home Page link, then print that page.

  g. Close the browser window.

  h. Close the recsite.htm file, but keep Publisher open.

7. Send a publication as an e-mail.

  a. Click File on the menu bar, click Open, then open the file PB C-6.pub from the drive and folder where your Data Files are stored. (*Hint*: If you do not have Microsoft Outlook 2003 or Microsoft Outlook Express 5.0 or later, you will not be able to complete this lesson.)

  b. Click File on the menu bar, point to Send E-mail, then click E-mail Preview.

  c. Close the e-mail preview (if necessary), click File on the menu bar, point to Send E-mail, then click Send This Page as Message.

  d. Type your e-mail address in the To text box, then click the Send button.

  e. Check your e-mail to see if it appears in your inbox. Open the e-mail, then delete it.

▼ INDEPENDENT CHALLENGE 1

You have been hired by a local café to advertise their Saturday Karaoke Night series. You have decided to create a Web page describing the series that the café can publish on their ISP's (Internet service provider's) Web server. You start by creating a Web publication.

  a. Start Publisher, then create a new Web publication using the Accent Bar Easy Web Site design.

  b. Choose Vertical and Bottom navigation bars, then insert a sign-up form on the second page.

  c. Choose a color scheme and font scheme that appeal to you.

  d. Replace the text Home with **Sing at Java Jerry's Café!**, delete the business tag line and business name placeholders, replace the main paragraph text with the contents of the file PB C-7.doc. Expand the text box so you can see all the text, if necessary.

  e. Delete the placeholder logo at the top of the page and replace the graphic with an appropriate piece of clip art.

  f. Scroll to the bottom of the page, and insert the following text in the text box below To contact us:, then delete the phone number text box.

    Your Name, Karaoke Coordinator
    Phone: 415-555-5232
    E-mail: javajerryscafe@isp-services.com
    98 Danvers Street
    San Francisco, CA 94114

  g. Save the publication with the name **karaoke**.

  h. Open page 2 of the publication, delete the business tag line and business name placeholders, replace the text Sign Up Form with **Karaoke Night Registration**, replace the Sign-up form title text with **Sing at Java Jerry's!**, delete all the labels and controls from Sign up for through Total, then delete all the labels and controls from Method of Payment through Exp. date: and the placeholder logo. (*Hint*: Make sure you delete the text box containing security information.)

  i. Just below the E-mail label, insert a text box for a label, type **Song style** in it to create a song style label, then format it to match the other labels.

j. Insert a list box to the right of the Song style label that contains the following items: **Country**, **R&B**, **Pop**, **Showtunes**, **Hip Hop**, and **Other**, and resize the list box so that only the first item is showing.

k. Drag the remaining controls and labels up to fill in the empty space on the page, double-click the Submit button, click Form Properties, click the Save the data in a file on my Web server option button, click OK twice, then save your publication.

l. Preview your pages in a Web browser, then make any necessary formatting adjustments in Publisher, and save your publication as a Web page named **karaoke.htm** in a folder called **karaoke** in the drive and folder where your Data Files are stored.

m. Print the pages, close your browser, close the publication, then exit Publisher.

▼ INDEPENDENT CHALLENGE 2

You are the human resources director for Jasmine Herbal Harvest, a producer of herbal products. You are conducting a contest for your sales force, offering prizes for the best success story relating to your line of herbal products. You will post the information about the contest on your company intranet.

a. Start Publisher. Create a Web site named **jasmine** using one of the Web site designs in the New Publication task pane.

b. Add a horizontal navigation bar and a response form.

c. Choose a color and font scheme that you like, and replace any graphics with appropriate ones.

d. Insert the following text on your home page, replacing the placeholder text as appropriate:
Jasmine Herbal Harvest, Inc., 2230 Red Rock Way, Sedona, Arizona 86336, (520) 555-9010

e. Type your name somewhere on the home page, and delete the placeholder logos on both pages.

f. On the home page, replace the paragraph text with the file PB C-8.doc. Don't use Autoflow and be sure you can view all the text in the text box, and format the text as necessary. (*Hint*: You may have to insert a text box depending on what template you choose.)

g. Create a link from Contest Form at the end of the paragraph to the contest form on page 2.

Form heading placeholder	Replace with:
Response Form	Success Story Contest
Response Form Title	Win a Caribbean Cruise for two!
Briefly describe your desired feedback	Describe the best success story you've heard from a customer about Jasmine Herbal Harvest products.

h. On page 2, replace the placeholder Form headings with the following:

i. Delete all the placeholder questions, and the comments label, then drag the Comment text box control up to close up the empty space.

j. Modify the remaining placeholder controls and labels so that the form contains only an E-mail label and text box and Submit and Reset buttons. Create a list box below the E-mail text box with four items as follows: **North, South, East,** and **West**, then add a label with the text **Sales Territory**.

k. Drag all the remaining elements up to close the space.

l. Double-click the Submit button, click Form Properties, click the save data in a file on my Web server option button, then click OK twice.

Advanced Challenge Exercise

- ■ Right-click the navigation bar, then click Delete Object.
- ■ Click Insert on the menu bar, point to Navigation Bar, then click New.
- ■ Choose a navigation bar from the Design Gallery, click Insert Object, then position it as necessary.
- ■ Copy and paste this new navigation bar onto every page of your Web page as necessary.

▼ INDEPENDENT CHALLENGE 2

m. Preview your Publication in a browser using the Web Page Preview button, then make necessary changes. Save the publication as a Web page called **jasmine.htm**, in a new folder called **jasmine** in the drive and folder where your Data Files are stored.

n. View the pages in your browser, print both pages, close the browser, then exit Publisher.

▼ INDEPENDENT CHALLENGE 3

Create a Web site called **myweb** about yourself using your Publisher Web site creation skills.

a. Start by planning the information you want to include in your site. Remember that you can include several pages in your site, so you should plan on breaking the information up logically into separate Web pages. Make a list of information you want your site to contain, and create an outline of the site showing what information will appear on each page.

b. Start Publisher, choose a Web Site design from the New Publication task pane, then select the options you want to use for your Web site. In addition to your home page, include at least one form page and one other page. You may include other pages if you want.

c. Replace the placeholder text and graphics on your Web site with graphics that are appropriate for you. If you need to add additional pages, click Insert a page on the Web Site Options task pane.

d. Save your publication with the name **myweb.pub**.

e. Preview your publication in a browser using the Web Page Preview button, make necessary changes, then use the Publish to the Web command to save the file as myweb.htm to a new folder called **mywebpg**.

f. View the pages in a browser, print the pages, close the browser, close the file, then exit Publisher. Do not save the modified logo.

▼ INDEPENDENT CHALLENGE 4

There are many organizations that help people worldwide. Pick a cause that is important to you that affects the global community. It could be a health issue, a political cause, or a charitable organization. Create a Web site about this topic.

a. Log on to the Internet, go to a search engine site such as Google (www.google.com), and research your chosen topic. Be sure to find out how organizations work around the world to help and support this cause.

b. To create the Web site, choose a Web site design, color scheme, and font scheme that appeal to you, and appropriate graphics. Your site should have at least three pages, including a home page, a response form page, and a related links page. On the home page, include a paragraph written by you that provides an overview of the topic. Insert links from the paragraph to the related links page and the response form page. Save the Publisher file as **myweb**.

c. On the related links page, insert at least five links to other Web sites that relate to your topic.

d. On the response form page, include at least one survey question for your viewers to answer relating to your cause.

e. Type your name somewhere on the Web page, use the Web page preview button to preview your work, then make any necessary adjustments in Publisher. Save your publication as **mycause.pub**, then save it as a Web page named **mycause.htm** in a folder called **my_cause**.

Advanced Challenge Exercise

■ Click Format on the menu bar, click Background, then click the More backgrounds link on the task pane.

■ In the Effects dialog box, choose a textured or patterned background, then click OK.

■ Apply the same background or choose a different background for every page in your Web site.

f. View the page in Publisher, and then view the page in your default browser. Print your pages.

g. Exit Publisher.

Publisher 2003

▼ VISUAL WORKSHOP

Use Publisher to create the Web page shown in Figure C-18. Use the Orbits Easy Web design, the Berry color scheme, and the Wizard font scheme. Insert or replace any existing graphics with the coffee cup graphic, resize and move it to the position shown in the figure, then import the paragraph text from the file PB C-9.doc. Format the paragraph text in 10-point Arial. Resize the text box so that the paragraph fits as shown. Create the controls shown using the Form Control button. Add the E-mail label. Save the publication as **inn_site.pub**, then save it as a Web page called **inn_site.htm** in a new folder titled **inn**. Make any other changes based on Figure C-18. View the publication in your default browser, type your name in the E-mail text box on the page, then print it. Close the browser, then exit Publisher.

FIGURE C-18

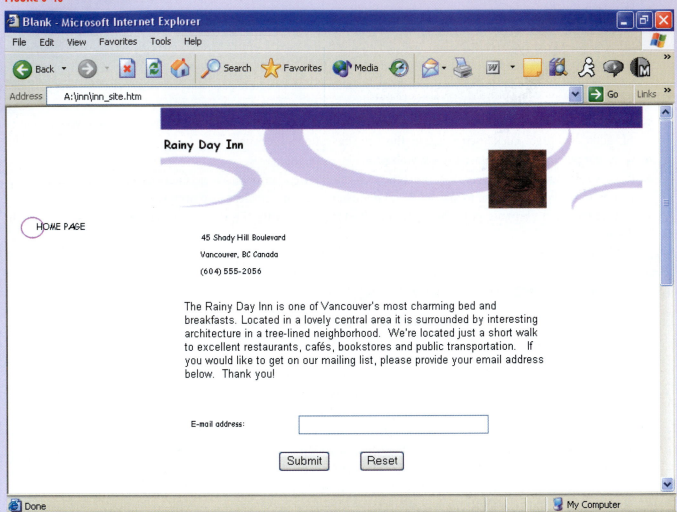

Glossary

3-D reference A reference that uses values on other sheets or workbooks, effectively creating another dimension to a workbook.

Absolute cell reference A cell reference that contains a dollar sign before the column letter and/or row number to indicate the absolute, or fixed, contents of specific cells. For example, the formula $A$1+$B$1 calculates only the sum of these specific cells no matter where the formula is copied in the workbook.

Access database file All of the objects (tables, queries, forms, reports, macros, modules) created in an Access database are stored in one file with an .mdb extension.

Action button An on-screen control button that you click in Slide Show view to perform an activity, such as advancing to the next slide.

Active cell A selected cell in a Graph datasheet or an Excel worksheet. The current location of the cell pointer.

ActiveX control A control that follows ActiveX standards.

ActiveX standards Programming standards developed by Microsoft to allow developers to more easily share software components and functionality across multiple applications.

Adjustment handle The yellow diamond that appears when certain AutoShapes are selected; used to change the shape, but not the size, of an AutoShape. Also, a small yellow diamond that changes the appearance of an object's most prominent feature.

Aggregate function A function such as Sum, Avg, and Count used in a summary query to calculate information about a group of records.

Align To place two or more objects' edges or centers on the same plane.

Align Left Button you click to align selected text or controls along a left margin.

Alignment (Access) Commands used in Form or Report Design View to either left-, center-, or right-align a value within its control, or to align the top, bottom, right, or left edge of the control with respect to other controls.

Alignment (Excel) The placement of cell contents; for example, left, center, or right.

Alignment (Word) The position of text in a document relative to the margins.

Anchored The state of a floating graphic that moves with a paragraph or other item if the item is moved; an anchor symbol appears with the floating graphic when formatting marks are displayed.

AND criteria Criteria placed in the same row of the query design grid. All criteria on the same row must be true for a record to appear on the resulting datasheet.

AND query A query that contains AND criteria—two or more criteria present on the same row of the query design grid. All criteria must be true for the record to appear on the resulting datasheet.

Animated GIF File format used to display animations in Web pages.

Animation The illusion of making a static object appear to move. Some graphics, such as an animated .gif (Graphics Interchange Format) file, have motion when you run a slide show.

Animation scheme A set of predefined visual effects for a slide transition, title text, and bullet text of the slides in a PowerPoint presentation.

Animation tag Identifies the order in which objects are animated on a slide during a slide show.

Annotate A freehand drawing on the screen made by using the Annotation tool. You can annotate only in Slide Show view.

Application *See* Program.

Area chart A line chart in which each area is given a solid color or pattern to emphasize the relationship between the pieces of charted information.

Argument Information that a function needs to calculate an answer. In an expression, multiple arguments are separated by commas. All of the arguments are enclosed in parentheses; for example, =SUM(A1:B1).

Argument ScreenTip The yellow box that appears as you build a function. As you build the function using different elements, the box displays these elements. You can click each element to display its online help.

Arithmetic operator Plus (+), minus (–), multiply (*), divide (/), or exponentiation (^) character used in a mathematical calculation.

Ascending order Lists data alphabetically or sequentially (from A to Z, 0 to 9, or earliest to latest).

Ask a Question box Text box at the top right side of the menu bar in which you can type a question to access the program's Help system.

Asterisk Wildcard character that represents any group of characters.

Attributes The styling features such as bold, italics, and underlining that can be applied to cell contents.

AutoCalculate value Value displayed in the status bar that represents the sum of values in the selected range.

AutoComplete A feature that automatically completes entries based on other entries in the same column, or suggests text to insert.

AutoContent Wizard A wizard that helps you get a presentation started by supplying a sample outline and a design template.

AutoCorrect A feature that automatically detects and corrects typing errors, minor spelling errors, and capitalization, or inserts certain typographical symbols as you type.

AutoCorrect Options button Smart Tag that helps you correct typos or, when it appears as Property Update Options, helps you apply property changes to other areas of the database where a field is used.

AutoFill A feature that creates a series of text entries or numbers when a range is selected using the fill handle.

AutoFill Options button Allows you to specify what you want to fill and whether or not you want to include formatting.

AutoFilter An Excel list feature that lets you click a list arrow and select criteria by which to display certain types of records.

AutoFilter list arrows Small triangles that appear next to field names in an Excel list; used to display portions of your data.

AutoFit A feature that automatically adjusts the width of a column to accommodate its widest entry when the boundary to the right of the column selector is double-clicked.

AutoFit (Publisher) A formatting feature that automatically sizes text to fit in a frame.

Autoflow A feature that automatically flows text from one existing empty text frame to the next, asking for confirmation before it flows to the next frame.

AutoForm Tool to quickly create a form that displays all of the fields of the selected record source.

AutoFormat (Access) Predefined format that you can apply to a form or report to set the background picture, font, color, and alignment formatting choices.

AutoFormat (Excel) Preset schemes that can be applied to format a range instantly. Excel comes with 16 AutoFormats that include colors, fonts, and numeric formatting.

Automatic page break A page break that is inserted automatically at the bottom of a page.

AutoNumber A field data type in which Access enters a sequential integer for each record added to the datasheet. Numbers cannot be reused even if the record is deleted.

AutoShape A drawing object, such as a rectangle, oval, triangle, line, block arrow, or other shape that you create using the tools on the Drawing toolbar.

AutoSum A feature that automatically creates totals using the SUM function when you click the AutoSum button.

AutoText A feature that stores frequently used text and graphics so they can be easily inserted into a document.

Avg function Built-in Access function used to calculate the average of the values in a given field.

Background (Publisher) Layer that appears behind every page in a publication where you put objects such as headers that you want repeated on each page.

Background (PowerPoint) The area behind the text and graphics on a slide.

Background color The color applied to the background of a cell.

Backup An up-to-date copy of an Access database.

Bar chart A chart that shows information as a series of horizontal bars.

Bitmap graphic A graphic that is composed of a series of small dots called "pixels."

.bmp The abbreviation for the bitmap graphics file format.

Body text Subpoints or bullet points on a slide under the slide title.

Body text placeholder A reserved box on a slide for the main text points.

Boilerplate text Text that appears in every version of a merged document.

Bold Formatting applied to text to make it thicker and darker.

Border (Word) A line that can be added above, below, or to the sides of a paragraph, text, or a table cell; a line that divides the columns and rows of a table.

Border (Excel) The edge of a cell, an area of a worksheet, or a selected object; you can change its color or line style.

Bound control A control used in either a form or report to display data from the underlying record source; also used to edit and enter new data in a form.

Bound object frame A bound control used to show OLE data such as a picture on a form or report.

Browser A software program used to access and display Web pages.

Bullet A small graphic symbol, usually a round or square dot, often used to identify items in a list.

Calculated control A control that uses information from existing controls to calculate new data such as subtotals, dates, or page numbers; used in either a form or report.

Calculated field A field created in Query Design View that results from an expression of existing fields, Access functions, and arithmetic operators. For example, the entry Profit: [RetailPrice]-[WholesalePrice] in the field cell of the query design grid creates a calculated field called Profit that is the difference between the values in the RetailPrice and WholesalePrice fields.

Calculation A new value that is created by entering an expression in a text box on a form or report.

Calendar control An ActiveX control that shows the current date selected on a small calendar. You can use this control to find or display a date in the past or future.

Caption A field property used to override the technical field name with an easy-to-read caption entry when the field name appears on datasheets, forms, and reports.

Catalog Merge A feature that lets you insert text and pictures from a data source such as a spreadsheet or database in order to create catalogs, address books, or other publications that include multiple records.

Category axis The horizontal axis in a chart, also known as the x-axis in a 2-dimensional chart. On a PivotChart, the horizontal axis. Also called the x-axis.

Category field On a PivotChart, the field that supplies the values for the horizontal axis. Analogous to the Row Field on a PivotTable and the Row Heading field for a crosstab query.

Cell The intersection of a column and row in a worksheet, datasheet, or table.

Cell address The location of a cell expressed by the column and row coordinates; the cell address of the cell in column A, row 1, is A1.

Cell pointer A highlighted rectangle around a cell that indicates the active cell.

Cell reference A code that identifies a cell's position in a table or a worksheet. Each cell reference contains a letter (A, B, C, and so on) to identify its column and a number (1, 2, 3, and so on) to identify its row. Cell references in worksheets can be used in formulas and are relative or absolute.

Center Alignment in which an item is centered between the margins or within a cell.

Character spacing Formatting that changes the width or scale of characters, expands or condenses the amount of space between characters, raises or lowers characters relative to the line of text, and adjusts kerning (the space between standard combinations of letters).

Character style A named set of character format settings that can be applied to text to format it all at once.

Chart A graphic representation of worksheet information. Types include 2-D and 3-D column, bar, pie, area, and line charts usually used to illustrate trends, patterns, or relationships.

Chart boxes In Organization Chart, the placeholders for text. The placeholders can contain names and positions in an organization's structure.

Chart Field List A list of the fields in the underlying record source for a PivotChart.

Chart sheet A separate sheet that contains only a chart linked to worksheet data.

Chart Wizard (Excel) A series of dialog boxes that helps you create or modify a chart.

Chart Wizard (Access) A series of dialog boxes that steps you through the process of creating charts within forms and reports.

Check box Bound control used to display "yes" or "no" answers for a field. If the box is "checked" it indicates "yes" information in a form or report.

Child record In a pair of tables that have a one-to-many relationship, the "many" table contains the child records.

Click and Type A feature that allows you to automatically apply the necessary paragraph formatting to a table, graphic, or text when you insert the item in a blank area of a document in Print Layout or Web Layout view.

Click and Type pointer A pointer used to move the insertion point and automatically apply the paragraph formatting necessary to insert text at that location in the document.

Clip A media file, such as a graphic, photograph, sound, movie, or animation, that can be inserted into a document.

Clip art A collection of graphic images that can be inserted into documents, presentations, Web pages, spreadsheets, and other Office files.

Clip Organizer A library of art, pictures, sounds, video clips, and animations that all Office applications share.

Clipboard A temporary storage area for items that are cut or copied from any Office file and are available for pasting. *See also* Office Clipboard and System Clipboard.

Clipboard task pane A task pane that shows the contents of the Office Clipboard; contains options for copying and pasting items.

Code *See* Program Code.

Color scheme (Publisher) A named set of five colors that can be applied consistently throughout a publication. There are 66 professionally selected color schemes provided in Publisher.

Color scheme (Powerpoint) The series of eight coordinated colors that make up a presentation; a color scheme assigns colors for text, lines, objects, and background. You can change the color scheme in any presentation at any time.

Column break A break that forces text following the break to begin at the top of the next column.

Column chart The default chart type in Excel, which displays information as a series of vertical columns.

Column Field On a PivotTable, the field that supplies values for each column. Analogous to the Series field in a PivotChart and the Column Heading field of a crosstab query.

Column heading (Access) Gray boxes along the top of a datasheet.

Column heading (Excel) The gray box containing the letter above the column in a worksheet.

Combination chart Combines a column and line chart to compare data requiring different scales of measure.

Combo box A bound control used to display a list of possible entries for a field in which you can also type an entry from the keyboard. It is a "combination" of the list box and text box controls.

Combo box wizard A series of dialog boxes that steps you through the process of creating a combo box.

Command button An unbound control used to provide an easy way to initiate an action or run a macro.

Command Button wizard A wizard that steps you through the process of creating a command button.

Comment An embedded note or annotation that an author or reviewer adds to a document.

Comments In a Visual Basic procedure, notes that explain the purpose of the macro or procedure; they are preceded by a single apostrophe and appear in green on a color monitor.

Compact and Repair Database Option on the Database Utilities menu that allows you to compact and repair an open database.

Compact on Close Feature found on the General tab of the Options dialog box, which compacts and repairs your database each time you close it.

Compacting Rearranging the data and objects on the storage medium so space formerly occupied by deleted objects is eliminated. Compacting a database doesn't change the data, but reduces the overall size of the database.

Comparison operators Characters such as > (greater than) and < (lesser than) that allow you to find or filter data based on specific criteria.

Complex formula An equation that uses more than one type of arithmetic operator.

Conditional formatting Formatting that is based on specified criteria. For example, a text box may be conditionally formatted to display its value in red if the value is a negative number. A cell format that is based on the cell's value or the outcome of a formula.

Conditional formula A formula that makes calculations based on stated conditions, such as calculating a rebate based on a particular purchase amount.

Connected text box A text box whose text flows either from or to another text box.

Consolidate To combine data on multiple worksheets and display the result on another worksheet.

Continued notice A phrase that identifies where the overflow text continues from or continues to.

Control Any element such as a label, text box, line, or combo box, on a form or report. Controls can be bound, unbound, or calculated.

Control menu box A box in the upper-left corner of a window used to resize or close a window.

Copy To place a copy of an item on the Clipboard without removing it from a document.

Count Aggregate function that calculates the number of values in a field (not counting null values).

Criteria Entries (rules and limiting conditions) that determine which records are displayed when finding or filtering records in a datasheet or form, or when building a query.

Criteria syntax Rules by which criteria need to be entered in Query Design View.

Crop To hide part of a picture or object using the Cropping tool; to trim away part of a graphic.

Crosstab query A query that presents data in a cross-tabular layout (fields are used for both column and row headings), similar to PivotTables in other database and spreadsheet products.

Crosstab Query Wizard A wizard used to create crosstab queries that helps identify fields that will be used for row and column headings, and fields that will be summarized within the datasheet.

Crosstab row A row in the query design grid used to specify the column and row headings and values for the crosstab query.

Currency A field data type used for monetary values.

Current record box *See* Record selector box.

Current record symbol A black triangle symbol that appears in the record selector box to the left of the record that has the focus in either a datasheet or a form.

Cut To remove an item from a document and place it on the Clipboard.

Cut and paste To move text or graphics using the Cut and Paste commands.

D

DAP *See* page.

Data The unique information you enter into the fields of records.

Data access page (DAP) *See* page.

Data entry area The unlocked portion of a worksheet where users are able to enter and change data.

Data field A category of information, such as last name, first name, street address, city, or postal code. On a PivotChart, the field that supplies the values that are summarized as bars or lines within the PivotChart. Analogous to the Totals or Details field on a PivotTable and a Value field in a crosstab query.

Data form In an Excel list (or database), a dialog box that displays one record at a time.

Data label Information that identifies the data in a column or row in a datasheet.

Data marker A graphical representation of a data point, such as a bar or column.

Data point Individual piece of data plotted in a chart.

Data record A complete set of related information for a person or an item, such as a person's name and address.

Data series The selected range in a datasheet or worksheet that is converted into a graphic and shown as a chart.

Data series marker A graphical representation of a data series, such as a bar or column.

Data source In a mail merge, the file with the unique data for individual people or items.

Data type A required property for each field that defines the type of data that can be entered in each field. Valid data types include AutoNumber, Text, Number, Currency, Date/Time, OLE Object, and Memo.

Database A collection of tables associated with a general topic (for example, sales of products to customers). Also, an organized collection of related information. In Excel, a database is called a list.

Database toolbar Toolbar that contains buttons for common tasks that affect the entire database or are common to all database objects.

Database window The window that includes common elements such as the Access title bar, menu bar, and toolbar.

Database window toolbar Toolbar that contains buttons used to open, modify, create, delete, and view objects.

Database Wizard An Access wizard that creates a sample database file for a general purpose such as inventory control, event tracking, or expenses. The objects created by the Database Wizard can be used and modified.

Datasheet A spreadsheet-like grid that displays fields as columns, and records as rows.

Datasheet View A view that lists the records of the object in a datasheet. Table, query, and most form objects have a Datasheet View.

Date function Built-in Access function used to display the current date on a form or report.

Date/Time A field data type used for date and time data.

Decimal Places A field property that determines the number of digits that should be displayed to the right of the decimal point (for Number or Currency fields).

Default Value A field property that provides a default value, automatically entered for a given field when a new record is created.

Default View A form property that determines whether a subform automatically opens in Datasheet or Continuous Forms View.

Delete To permanently remove an item from a document.

Descending order Lists data in reverse alphabetical or sequential order (Z to A, 9 to 0, or latest to earliest).

Design Gallery A collection of Publisher-designed objects such as logos, calendars, sidebars, Web page components, and other design elements that you can use to enhance your publications.

Design grid *See* Query design grid.

Design Set A group of sample designs provided by Publisher applied to a broad range of publication types including business cards, letterhead, and fax cover sheets to ensure a consistent and professional look.

Design template Predesigned slide design with formatting and color schemes that you can apply to an open presentation.

Design View A view in which the structure of the object can be manipulated. Every Access object has a Design View.

Desktop publishing program A program for creating publications containing text and graphics.

Desktop workspace The area around the publication page you can use to store text and graphics prior to placing them in a publication.

Destination file The file that receives the copied information. For example, a query table created in Access, the source file, can be copied to and edited in a Word document, an Excel worksheet, or a PowerPoint presentation, the destination file.

Destination program The program a file or object is embedded into.

Detail section The section of a form or report that contains the controls that are printed for each record in the underlying query or table.

Dialog box A window that opens when a program needs more information to carry out a command.

Display When A control property that determines whether the control will appear only on the screen, only when printed, or at all times.

Document The electronic file you create using Word.

Document properties Details about a file, such as author name or the date the file was created, that are used to organize and search for files.

Document window The workspace in the program window that displays the current document.

Drag and drop To move text or a graphic by dragging it to a new location using the mouse.

Drag-and-drop technique Method in which you drag the contents of selected cells to a new location.

Drawing canvas A workspace for creating graphics.

Drawing toolbar A toolbar that contains buttons that let you create lines, shapes, and special effects.

Drop area A position on a PivotChart or PivotTable where you can drag and place a field. Drop areas on a PivotTable include the Filter field, Row field, Column field, and Totals or Detail field. Drop areas on a PivotChart include the Filter field, Category field, Series field, and Data field.

Drop cap A large dropped initial capital letter that is often used to set off the first paragraph of an article.

Dummy column/row Blank column or row included at the end of a range that enables a formula to adjust when columns or rows are added or deleted.

Dynamic Data Exchange (DDE) link The connection between the source file and the destination file when an object is pasted as a link into the destination file.

Dynamic page breaks In a larger workbook, horizontal or vertical dashed lines that represent the place where pages print separately. They also adjust automatically when you insert or delete rows or columns, or change column widths or row heights.

Dynamic Web page A Web page automatically updated with the latest changes to the database each time it is opened. Web pages created by the page object are dynamic.

Edit mode The mode in which Access assumes you are trying to edit a particular field, so keystrokes such as [Ctrl][End], [Ctrl][Home], [↑] and [↓] move the insertion point within the field.

Edit record symbol A pencil symbol that appears in the record selector box to the left of the record that is currently being edited in either a datasheet or a form.

Electronic spreadsheet A computer program that performs calculations on data and organizes information into worksheets. A worksheet is divided into columns and rows, which form individual cells.

Embedded chart A chart displayed as an object in a worksheet.

Embedded object An object that is created in one application and copied to another. Embedded objects remain connected to the original program file in which they were created for easy editing.

Embedded object An object that maintains a link to the source program, but not to the source file. When you double-click an embedded object, the source program opens and you can edit the object. The source file that the object originally represented does not change.

Enabled Control property that determines whether the control can have the focus in Form View.

Error Indicator button Smart Tag that helps identify potential design errors in Report or Form Design View.

Exception A Formatting change that differs from the slide master.

Exploding pie slice A slice of a pie chart that has been pulled away from the whole pie to add emphasis.

Exporting A process to quickly convert data from Access to another file format such as an Excel workbook, a Word document, or a static Web page.

Expression A combination of values, functions, and operators that calculates to a single value. Access expressions start with an equal sign and are placed in a text box in either Form Design View or Report Design View.

External reference indicator The exclamation point (!) used in a formula to indicate that a referenced cell is outside the active sheet.

Field (Word) A code that serves as a placeholder for data that changes in a document, such as a page number.

Field (Excel) In a list (an Excel database), a column that describes a characteristic about records, such as first name or city.

Field (Access) The smallest piece of information in a database, for example, the customer's name, city, or phone number.

Field list A list of the available fields in the table or query that the list represents.

Field name (Access) The name of a data field.

Field names The names given to each field in Table Design or Table Datasheet View.

Field Properties pane The lower half of Table Design View that shows you the properties for the currently selected field.

Field property *See* Properties.

Field selector button The button to the left of a field in Table Design View that indicates which field is currently selected. Also the thin gray bar above each field in the query grid.

Field Size A field property that determines the largest number that can be entered in a field (for Number or Currency fields) or the number of characters that can be entered in a field (for Text fields).

File An electronic collection of information that has a unique name, distinguishing it from other files.

File format A file type, such as .bmp, .jpg, or .gif.

Filename The name given to a document when it is saved.

Fill color The cell background color.

Fill handle A small square in the lower-right corner of the active cell used to copy cell contents.

Fill/Back Color Button on the Formatting toolbar that you click to change the background color of a selected object or area.

Filter (Access) A temporary view of a subset of records. A filter can be saved as a query object if you wish to apply the same filter later without re-creating it.

Filter (Word) In a mail merge, to pull out records that meet specific criteria and include only those records in the merge.

Filter (Excel) To display data in an Excel list that meet specified criteria.

Filter field On a PivotTable or PivotChart, the field in the upper-left corner, but neither a row nor column heading.

Filter window A window that appears when you click the Filter By Form button when viewing data in a datasheet or in a form window. The Filter window allows you to define the filter criteria.

Find A command used to locate specific data within a field.

Find Duplicates Query Wizard A wizard used to create a query that determines whether a table contains duplicate values in one or more fields.

Find Unmatched Query Wizard A wizard used to create a query that finds records in one table that don't have related records in another table.

First Aggregate function that returns the field value from the first record in a table or query.

First line indent A type of indent in which the first line of a paragraph is indented more than the subsequent lines.

Fit (print option) An option that automatically adjusts a preview to display all pages in a report.

Floating graphic A graphic to which a text wrapping style has been applied, making the graphic independent of text and able to be moved anywhere on a page.

Focus The property that indicates which field would be edited if you were to start typing.

Folder A subdivision of a disk that works like a filing system to help you organize files.

Font The typeface or design of a set of characters (letters, numbers, symbols, and punctuation marks).

Font effect Font formatting that applies a special effect to text, such as a shadow, an outline, small caps, or superscript.

Font scheme A named set of two fonts, a major font and a minor font, that are applied consistently throughout a publication.

Font size The size of characters, measured in units called points (pts).

Font/Fore Color Button on the Formatting toolbar that you click to change the foreground color of a selected object or text.

Footer Information that prints at the bottom of each printed page; on screen, a footer is visible only in Print Preview.

Foreground The layer that sits on top of the background layer and consists of the objects that appear on a specific page of a publication.

Foreign key field In a one-to-many relationship between two tables, the foreign key field is the field in the "many" table that links the table to the primary key field in the "one" table.

Form An Access object that provides an easy-to-use data entry screen that generally shows only one record at a time.

Form control An item in a form that's used for gathering information from a user, such as a text box, list box, command button, or check box.

Form Design toolbar When working in Form Design View, the toolbar that appears with buttons that help you modify a form's controls.

Form Design View The view of a form in which you add, delete, and modify the form's properties, sections, and controls.

Form Footer A section that appears at the bottom of the screen in Form View for each record, but prints only once at the end of all records when the form is printed.

Form Header A section that appears at the top of the screen in Form View for each record, but prints only once at the top of all records when the form is printed.

Form View View of a form object that displays data from the underlying recordset and allows you to enter and update data.

Form Wizard An Access wizard that helps you create a form.

Format (Access) Field property that controls how information will be displayed and printed.

Format The appearance of text and numbers, including color, font, attributes, borders, and shading. *See also* Number format.

Format Painter A feature used to copy the format settings applied to the selected text or cell to other text or another range of cells you want to format the same way.

Format Painter (Access) A tool that you can use within Form Design View and Report Design View to copy formatting characteristics from one control, and paint them on another.

Formatting Enhancing the appearance of the information through font, size, and color changes.

Formatting marks Nonprinting characters that appear on screen to indicate the ends of paragraphs, tabs, and other formatting elements.

Formatting toolbar A toolbar that contains buttons for frequently used formatting commands.

Formula A set of instructions used to perform numeric calculations (adding, subtracting, averaging, etc.).

Formula bar The area below the menu bar and above the Excel workspace where you enter and edit data in a worksheet cell. The formula bar becomes active when you start typing or editing cell data. It includes the Enter button and the Cancel button.

Formula prefix An arithmetic symbol, such as the equal sign (=), used to start a formula.

Frame A section of a Web page window in which a separate Web page is displayed. Also, an object that contains text or graphics and that can be moved or resized.

Freeze To hold in place selected columns or rows when scrolling in a worksheet that is divided in panes. *See also* panes.

Full screen view A view that shows only the document window on screen.

Function A special, predefined formula that provides a shortcut for a commonly used calculation, for example, SUM or COUNT.

Getting Started task pane A task pane that contains shortcuts for opening documents, for creating new documents, and for accessing information on the Microsoft Web site.

Getting Started task pane Lets you quickly open new or existing workbooks.

.gif The abbreviation for the graphic interchange format; the standard format for displaying images on Web pages.

Glossary terms Words in the Help system that are shown as blue hyperlinks and display the word's definition when clicked.

Graphic image *See* Image.

Grid Evenly spaced horizontal and vertical lines that appear on a slide when it is being created to help place objects. Lines do not appear when the slide is shown or printed.

Gridlines Horizontal and/or vertical lines within a chart that make the chart easier to read. Also, nonprinting lines that show the boundaries of table cells.

Group (n) A collection of objects.

Group (v) To combine multiple objects into a single object so you can easily move and resize them as a unit.

Group Footer A section of the report that contains controls that print once at the end of each group of records.

Group Header A section of the report that contains controls that print once at the beginning of each group of records.

Group selection handles Selection handles that surround grouped controls.

Grouping To sort records in a particular order, plus provide a section before and after each group of records.

Grouping controls Allow you to identify several controls as a group to quickly and easily apply the same formatting properties to them.

Grouping records In a report, to sort records based on the contents of a field, plus provide a group header section that precedes the group of records and provide a group footer section that follows the group of records.

Groups bar Located just below the Objects bar in the database window, the Groups bar displays the Favorites and any user-created groups, which in turn contain shortcuts to objects. Groups are used to organize the database objects into logical sets.

Groups button Button on the Groups bar that expands or collapses that section of the database window.

Gutter Extra space left for a binding at the top, left, or inside margin of a document.

Handles Small circles that appear around a selected object that you can drag to resize or rotate the selected object.

Handles *See* Sizing handles.

Handout master The master view for printing handouts.

Hanging indent A type of indent in which the second and subsequent lines of a paragraph are indented more than the first.

Hanging indent The first line of a paragraph begins to the left of all subsequent lines of text.

Hard page break *See* Manual page break.

Header Information, such as text, a page number, or a graphic, that appears at the top of every page in a document or a section.

Header row The first row of a table that contains the column headings.

Help system A utility that gives you immediate access to definitions, steps, explanations, and useful tips.

Hide To make rows, columns, formulas, or sheets invisible to workbook users.

Hide Duplicates Control property that when set to "Yes," hides duplicate values for the same field from record to record in the Detail section.

Highlighting Transparent color that can be applied to text to call attention to it.

Home page The main page of a Web site and the first Web page viewers see when they visit a site.

Horizontal ruler A ruler that appears at the top of the document window in Print Layout, Normal, and Web Layout view.

Host A location where you can store the files for a Web site.

Hotspot An object that, when clicked, will run a macro or open a file.

HTML HyperText Markup Language, a set of codes inserted into a text file that browser software such as Internet Explorer can use to determine the way text, hyperlinks, images, and other elements appear on a Web page.

Hyperlink (Access) A field data type that stores World Wide Web addresses. A hyperlink can also be a control on a form that when clicked, opens another database object, external file, or external Web page.

Hyperlink An object or link (a filename, word, phrase, or graphic) that, when clicked, "jumps to" another location in the current file or opens another PowerPoint presentation, a Word, Excel, or Access file, or an address on the World Wide Web. Also called a link.

HyperText Markup Language *See* HTML.

I-beam pointer The pointer used to move the insertion point and select text.

Image A nontextual piece of information such as a picture, piece of clip art, drawn object, or graph. Because images are graphical (and not numbers or letters), they are sometimes referred to as graphical images.

Image control A control used to store a single piece of clip art, a photo, or a logo on a form or report.

Importing A process to quickly convert data from an external source, such as Excel or another database application, into an Access database.

Indent The space between the edge of a line of text or a paragraph and the margin.

Indent levels Text levels in the master text placeholder. Each level is indented a certain amount from the left margin, and you control their placement by dragging indent markers on the ruler.

Indent marker A marker on the horizontal ruler that shows the indent settings for the active paragraph.

Inline graphic A graphic that is part of a line of text in which it was inserted.

Input Information that produces desired results, or output, in a worksheet.

Input Mask Field property that provides a visual guide for users as they enter data.

Insert row The last row in an Excel list, where a record can be entered.

Insertion point (PowerPoint) A blinking vertical line that indicates where text appears in a text placeholder.

Insertion point (Excel) The blinking vertical line that appears in the formula bar or in a cell during editing.

Insertion point (Word) The blinking vertical line that shows where text will appear when you type in a document.

Integration The ability to use information across multiple programs. For example, you can include a chart created in Excel in a document created in Word.

Internet A system of connected computers and computer networks located around the world by telephone lines, cables, satellites, and other telecommunications media.

Intranet An internal network site used by a particular group of people who work together.

Is Not Null Criterion that finds all records in which any entry has been made in the field.

Is Null Criterion that finds all records in which no entry has been made in the field.

Italic Formatting applied to text to make the characters slant to the right.

Jpg The abbreviation for the JPEG (Joint Photographic Experts Group) File Interchange Format.

Junction table A table created for the purpose of establishing separate one-to-many relationships to two tables that have a many-to-many relationship.

Justify Alignment in which an item is flush with both the left and right margins.

Key field *See* Primary key field.

Key field combination Two or more fields that as a group contain unique information for each record.

Key field symbol *See* Key symbol.

Key symbol In Table Design View, the symbol that appears as a miniature key in the field indicator box to the left of the field name. It identifies the field that contains unique information for each record.

Keyboard shortcut A combination of keys or a function key that can be pressed to perform a command.

Keyword A representative word on which the Help system can search to find information on your area of interest.

Kiosk A freestanding computer used to display information, usually in a public area.

Label (Access) An unbound control that displays static text on forms and reports.

Label (Excel) Descriptive text or other information that identifies the rows and columns of a worksheet. Labels are not included in calculations.

Label prefix A character, such as the apostrophe, that identifies an entry as a label and controls the way it appears in the cell.

Landscape orientation A print setting that positions the worksheet on the page so the page is wider than it is tall.

Last Aggregate function that returns the field value from the last record in a table or query.

Layout The general arrangement in which a form will display the fields in the underlying recordset. Layout types include Columnar, Tabular, Datasheet, Chart, and PivotTable. Columnar is most popular for a form, and Datasheet is most popular for a subform.

Layout guides Nonprinting lines that appear in every page of your publication to help you to align text, pictures, and other objects into columns and rows so that your publication will have a consistent look across all pages.

Leading The spacing between lines of text in a text object.

Left function Access function that returns a specified number of characters starting with the left side of a value in a Text field.

Left indent A type of indent in which the left edge of a paragraph is moved in from the left margin.

Left-align Alignment in which the item is flush with the left margin.

Legend A key explaining how information is represented by colors or patterns in a chart.

Like operator An Access comparison operator that allows queries to find records that match criteria that include a wildcard character.

Limit to List Combo box control property that allows you to limit the entries made by that control to those provided by the combo box list.

Line chart A graph of data that is mapped by a series of lines. Line charts show changes in data or categories of data over time and can be used to document trends.

Line control An unbound control used to draw lines on a form or report that divide it into logical groupings.

Line spacing The amount of space between lines of text.

Link A connection to the original file. For example, when you link an object to a PowerPoint slide, a representation, or picture, of the object is placed on the slide instead of the actual object. This representation of the object is connected, or linked, to the original file. Changes made to the source file are reflected in the linked object. Can also refer to a hyperlink (*see also* Hyperlink).

Link Child Fields A subform property that determines which field will serve as the "many" link between the subform and main form.

Link Master Fields A subform property that determines which field will serve as the "one" link between the main form and the subform.

Linked object An object that maintains a connection to the source file so that the object is updated when the data in the source file changes.

Linking The dynamic referencing of data in other workbooks, so that when data in the other workbooks is changed, the references in the current workbook are automatically updated.

List The Excel term for a database, an organized collection of related information.

List box A bound control that displays a list of possible choices for the user. Used mainly on forms.

List style A named set of format settings, such as indents and outline numbering, that can be applied to a list to format it all at once.

Lock To secure a row, column, or sheet so that data in that location cannot be changed.

Locked property A control property specifies whether you can edit data in a control in Form View.

Logical test The first part of an IF function; if the logical test is true, then the second part of the function is applied, and if it is false, then the third part of the function is applied.

Logical view The datasheet of a query is sometimes called a logical view of the data because it is not a copy of the data, but rather, a selected view of data from the underlying tables.

Lookup A reference table or list of values used to populate the values of a field.

Lookup field A field that has lookup properties. Lookup properties are used to create a drop-down list of values to populate the field.

Lookup properties Field properties that allow you to supply a drop-down list of values for a field.

Lookup Wizard A wizard used in Table Design View that allows one field to "look up" values from another table or entered list. For example, you might use the Lookup Wizard to specify that the CustomerNumber field in the Sales table display the CustomerName field entry from the Customers table.

Macro A set of instructions recorded or written in the Visual Basic programming language used to automate worksheet tasks.

Macro (Access) An Access object that stores a collection of keystrokes or commands such as those for printing several reports in a row or providing a toolbar when a form opens.

Main document In a mail merge, the document with the standard text which is the text, that remains the same for each recipient in a merge.

Main form A form that contains a subform control.

Manual page break A page break inserted to force the text following the break to begin at the top of the next page.

Many-to-many relationship The relationship between two tables in an Access database in which one record of one table relates to many records in the other table and vice versa. You cannot directly create a many-to-many relationship between two tables in Access. To relate two tables with such a relationship, you must establish a third table called a junction table that creates separate one-to-many relationships with the two original tables.

Margin Perimeter of the page outside of which nothing will print. The blank area between the edge of the text and the edge of a page.

Master page The page where you place any object that you want to repeat on every page of a publication.

Master text placeholder The placeholder on the Slide Master that controls the formatting and placement of the Main text placeholder on each slide. If you modify the Master text placeholder, each Main text placeholder is affected in the entire presentation.

Master title placeholder The placeholder on the Slide Master that controls the formatting and placement of the Title placeholder on each slide. If you modify the Master title placeholder, each Title placeholder is affected in the entire presentation.

Master view A specific view in a presentation that stores information about font styles, text placeholders, and color scheme. There are three master views: Slide Master view, Handout Master view, and Notes Master view.

Max Aggregate function that returns the maximum value in the field.

Memo A field data type used for lengthy text such as comments or notes. It can hold up to 64,000 characters of information.

Menu bar The bar beneath the title bar that contains the names of menus, that when clicked, open menus from which you choose program commands.

Merge The process of combining data from a data source such as an Access database with a document created in Word. The data could consist of the names, addresses, and other information about a company's customers, contacts, and suppliers. The document in Word could be a form letter. You can merge data from the database with a form letter to create a series of individually addressed form letters.

Merge cells To combine adjacent cells into a single larger cell.

Merge field A placeholder that you insert in the main document to indicate where the data from each record should be inserted when you perform a mail merge.

Microsoft Graph The program that creates a datasheet and chart to graphically depict numerical information in Powerpoint.

Min Aggregate function that returns the minimum value in the field.

Minor gridlines Gridlines that show the values between the tick marks.

Mirror margins Margins used in documents with facing pages, where the inside and outside margins are mirror images of each other.

Mixed reference A formula containing both a relative and absolute reference.

Mode indicator A box located in the lower-left corner of the status bar that informs you of a program's status. For example, when Excel is performing a task, the word "Wait" appears.

Module (Access) An object that stores Visual Basic programming code that extends the functions of automated Access processes.

Module (Excel) In Visual Basic, a module is stored in a workbook and contains macro procedures.

Movie Live action captured in digital format.

Moving border The dashed line that appears around a cell or range that is copied to the Clipboard.

Name box The left-most area in the formula bar that shows the cell reference or name of the active cell. For example, A1 refers to cell A1 of the active worksheet. You can also display a list of names in a workbook using the Name list arrow.

Name property Property of a text box that gives the text box a meaningful name.

Named range A range of cells given a meaningful name; it retains its name when moved and can be referenced in a formula.

Navigation bar (Access) A bar containing buttons that let you move from one record to another. On a data access page, the navigation bars also contain buttons to edit, sort, and filter data.

Navigation bar The bar that provides a set of links to pages in a Web site.

Navigation buttons Buttons in the lower-left corner of a datasheet or form that allow you to quickly navigate between the records in the underlying object as well as add a new record.

Navigation mode A mode in which Access assumes that you are trying to move between the fields and records of the datasheet (rather than edit a specific field's contents), so keystrokes such as [Ctrl][Home] and [Ctrl][End] move you to the first and last field of the datasheet.

Navigation toolbar Toolbar at the lower-left corner of Datasheet View, Form View, or a Web page that helps you navigate between records.

Negative indent A type of indent in which the left edge of a paragraph is moved to the left of the left margin.

Nested table A table inserted in a cell of another table.

New Record button Button you click to add records to a database.

Normal view (PowerPoint) A presentation view that divides the presentation window into three sections: Slides or Outline tab, Slide pane, and Notes pane.

Normal view (Word) A view that shows a document without margins, headers and footers, or graphics.

Notes master The master view for Notes Page view.

Notes Page view A presentation view that displays a reduced image of the current slide above a large text box where you can type notes.

Notes pane The area in Normal view that shows speaker notes for the current slide; also in Notes Page view, the area below the slide image that contains speaker notes.

Nudge To move a graphic a small amount in one direction using the arrow keys.

Number A field data type used for numeric information used in calculations, such as quantities.

Number format A format applied to values to express numeric concepts, such as currency, date, and percentage.

Object A chart or graphic image that can be moved and resized and that contains handles when selected.

Object (Access) A table, query, form, report, page, macro, or module in an Access database.

Object (PowerPoint) An item you place or draw on a slide that can be manipulated. Objects are drawn lines and shapes, text, clip art, imported pictures, and embedded objects.

Object (Publisher) Any element in a publication that contains text or graphics and that can be moved or resized.

Object buttons Buttons on the Objects bar that provide access to the different types of objects (tables, queries, forms, reports, macros, modules) in the current database.

Object Position indicator An indicator on the status bar used to precisely position an object.

Object Size indicator An indicator on the status bar used to accurately gauge the size of an object.

Objects button Button on the Objects bar that expands or collapses that section of the database window.

Office Assistant An animated character that offers tips and provides access to the program's Help system.

Office Clipboard A temporary storage area shared by all Office programs that can be used to cut, copy and paste multiple items within and between Office programs. The Office Clipboard can hold up to 24 items collected from any Office program. *See also* Clipboard, System Clipboard, and System Clipboard task pane.

OLE Object *See* One-to-many line.

One-to-many join line *See* One-to-many line.

One-to-many line The line that appears in the Relationships window and shows which field is duplicated between two tables to serve as the linking field. The one-to-many line displays a "1" next to the field that serves as the "one" side of the relationship and displays an infinity symbol next to the field that serves as the "many" side of the relationship when referential integrity is specified for the relationship. Also called the one-to-many join line.

One-to-many relationship The relationship between two tables in an Access database in which a common field links the tables together. The linking field is usually the primary key field in the "one" table of the relationship and the foreign key field in the "many" table of the relationship.

Open To use one of the methods for opening a document to retrieve it and display it in the document window.

Option button A bound control used to display a limited list of mutually exclusive choices for a field such as "female" or "male" for a gender field in a form or report.

Option group A bound control placed on a form that is used to group together several option buttons that provide a limited number of values for a field.

Option Group wizard An Access wizard that guides you through the process of developing an option group with option buttons.

Option Value property Property of an option button that identifies the numeric value that will be placed in the field to which the associated option group is bound.

OR criteria Criteria placed on different rows of the query design grid. A record will appear in the resulting datasheet if it is true for any single row.

OR query A query that contains OR criteria—two or more criteria present on different rows in the query design grid. A record will appear on the resulting datasheet if it is true for any of the criteria.

Order of precedence The order in which Excel calculates parts of a formula: (1) exponents, (2) multiplication and division, and (3) addition and subtraction.

Organization chart A diagram of connected boxes that shows reporting structure in a company or organization.

Orphan record A record in a "many" table that doesn't have a linking field entry in the "one" table. Orphan records can be avoided by using referential integrity.

Outdent *See* Negative indent.

Outline tab The section in Normal view that displays your presentation text in the form of an outline, without graphics.

Outline view A view that shows the headings of a document organized as an outline.

Output The end result of a worksheet.

Overflow text Text that won't fit in a text frame.

Overtype mode A feature that allows you to overwrite existing text as you type.

Pack and Go Wizard A wizard that lets you package your publication to take to another computer or to a commercial printing service.

Page An Access object that creates Web pages from Access objects as well as provides Web page connectivity features to an Access database. Also called data access page (DAP).

Page Design View A view that allows you to modify the structure of a data access page.

Page Footer A section of a form or report that contains controls that print once at the bottom of each page.

Page function Built-in Access function used to display the current page number on a report.

Page Header A section of a form or report that contains controls that print once at the top of each page. On the first page of the report, the Page Header section prints below the Report Header section.

Page Navigation buttons The buttons at the bottom of the publication window that are used to jump to a specific page in your publication.

Page View A view that allows you to see how your dynamic Web page will appear when opened in Internet Explorer.

Pane A section of the PowerPoint window, such as the Slide or Notes pane.

Panes Sections into which you can divide a worksheet when you want to work on separate parts of the worksheet at the same time; one pane freezes, or remains in place, while you scroll in another pane until you see the desired information.

Paragraph spacing The amount of space between paragraphs.

Paragraph style A named set of paragraph and character format settings that can be applied to a paragraph to format it all at once.

Parent/Child relationship The relationship between the main form and subform. The main form acts as the parent, displaying the information about the "one" side of a one-to-many relationship between the forms. The subform acts as the "child," displaying as many records as exist in the "many" side of the one-to-many relationship.

Paste To insert items stored on the Clipboard into a document.

Paste Function A series of dialog boxes that helps you build functions; it lists and describes all Excel functions.

Personal macro workbook A workbook that can contain macros that are available to any open workbook. By default, the personal macro workbook is hidden.

Personal stationery sets Design sets used to create coordinating labels, envelopes, and letterheads in Publisher.

Personalized menus/toolbars The menus and toolbars that modify themselves to reflect those features that you use most often.

Photo album A type of presentation that displays photographs.

Picture caption Text that appears next to, above, or below a picture to describe or elaborate on the picture.

Pie chart A circular chart that represents data as slices of a pie. A pie chart is useful for showing the relationship of parts to a whole; pie slices can be extracted for emphasis. *See also* Exploding pie slice.

PivotChart A graphical presentation of the data in a PivotTable.

PivotChart View The view in which you build a PivotChart.

PivotTable An arrangement of data that uses one field as a column heading, another as a row heading, and summarizes a third field, typically a Number field, in the body.

PivotTable List A control on a Web page that summarizes data by columns and rows to make it easy to analyze.

PivotTable View The view in which you build a PivotTable.

PivotTable Wizard Form creation tool that provides a series of steps to create a summarized arrangement of data in a PivotTable arrangement.

Pixels Small dots that define color and intensity on the screen or in a graphic.

Placeholder A dashed line box where you place text or objects.

Plot area The area inside the horizontal and vertical chart axes.

Point A unit of measure used for fonts and row height. One inch equals 72 points, or a point is equal to ½ of an inch.

Pointing method Specifying formula cell references by selecting the desired cell with the mouse instead of typing its cell reference; it eliminates typing errors. Also known as Pointing.

Portrait orientation A print setting that positions the worksheet on the page so the page is taller than it is wide.

Portrait orientation Page orientation in which the page is taller than it is wide.

Pound sign Wildcard that stands for a single-number digit.

PowerPoint Viewer A special application designed to run a PowerPoint slide show on any compatible computer that does not have PowerPoint installed.

PowerPoint window A window that contains the running PowerPoint application. The PowerPoint window includes the PowerPoint menus, toolbars, and Presentation window.

Presentation software A software program used to organize and present information.

Preview A view of the document exactly as it will appear on paper.

Primary key field A field that contains unique information for each record. A primary key field cannot contain a null entry.

Primary sort field In a query grid, the leftmost field that includes sort criteria. It determines the order in which the records will appear and can be specified "ascending" or "descending."

Print area A portion of a worksheet that you can define using the Print Area command on the File menu; after you define a print area, clicking the Print icon on the Standard toolbar prints only that worksheet area.

Print Layout view A view that shows a document as it will look on a printed page.

Print Preview A view of a file as it will appear when printed.

Print title In a list that spans more than one page, the field names that print at the top of every printed page.

Program Task-oriented software (such as Excel or Word) that enables you to perform a certain type of task such as data calculation or word processing.

Program code Macro instructions, written in the Visual Basic for Applications programming language.

Properties Characteristics that further define the field (if field properties), control (if control properties), section (if section properties), or object (if object properties).

Property sheet A window that displays an exhaustive list of properties for the chosen control, section, or object within the Form Design View or Report Design View.

Publication A file created in Publisher.

Publication Gallery A pane that displays thumbnails of Publisher ready-made designs for the selected category in the New Publication task pane.

Publication page A visual representation of your publication that appears in the publication window.

Publication window The area that includes the workspace for the publication page or pages and a desktop workspace for storing text and graphics prior to placing them in your publication.

Publish (Excel) To place an Excel workbook or worksheet on a Web site or an intranet in HTML format so that others can access it using their Web browsers.

Publish (PowerPoint) To save a version of a presentation in HTML format. You can save the HTML files to a disk or save them directly to an intranet or Web server.

Publishing a Web site Process of making a Web site available to World Wide Web users by storing all files on a web server.

Pull quote A quotation from a story that is pulled out and treated like a graphic.

Query An Access object that provides a spreadsheet-like view of the data, similar to that in tables. It may provide the user with a subset of fields and/or records from one or more tables. Queries are created when the user has a "question" about the data in the database.

Query Datasheet View The view of a query that shows the selected fields and records as a datasheet.

Query design grid The bottom pane of the Query Design View window in which you specify the fields, sort order, and limiting criteria for the query.

Query Design View The window in which you develop queries by specifying the fields, sort order, and limiting criteria that determine which fields and records are displayed in the resulting datasheet.

Query grid *See* Query design grid.

Question mark Wildcard character that stands for any single character.

Range A group of adjacent cells.

Range finder A feature that outlines an equation's arguments in blue and green.

Raw data *See* Data.

Reading Layout view A view that shows a document so that it is easy to read and annotate.

Record A group of related fields, such as all demographic information for one customer. In a list (an Excel database), data about an object or a person.

Record number box *See* Specific record box.

Record selector box The small square to the left of a record in a datasheet that marks the current record or the edit record symbol when the record has the focus or is being edited.

Record Source In a form or report, the property that determines which table or query object contains the fields and records that the form or report will display. It is the most important property of the form or report object. A bound control on a form or report also has a Record Source property. In this case, the Record Source property identifies the field to which the control is bound.

Recordset The value of the Record Source property.

Rectangle control An unbound control used to draw rectangles on the form that divide the other form controls into logical groupings.

Referential integrity Ensures that no orphan records are entered or created in the database by making sure that the "one" side of a linking relationship (CustomerNumber in a Customer table) is entered before that same value can be entered in the "many" side of the relationship (CustomerNumber in a Sales table).

Relational database A database in which more than one table, such as the customer, sales, and inventory tables, can share information. The term "relational database" means the tables are linked or "related" with a common field of information. An Access database is relational.

Relational database software Software such as Access that is used to manage data organized in a relational database.

Relative cell reference A type of cell reference used to indicate a relative position in the worksheet. It allows you to copy and move formulas from one area to another of the same dimensions. Excel automatically changes the column and row numbers to reflect the new position. Also known as Relative reference.

Report An Access object that creates a professional printout of data that may contain such enhancements as headers, footers, and calculations on groups of records.

Report Design View View of a report in which you add, delete, and edit the report's properties, sections, and controls.

Report Footer On a report, a section that contains controls that print once at the end of the last page of the report.

Report Header On a report, a section that contains controls that print once at the top of the first page of the report.

Report section properties Properties that determine what information appears in different report sections and how it is formatted.

Report Wizard An Access wizard that helps you create a report.

Required A field property that determines if an entry is required for a field.

Research services Reference information available through the Research task pane that can be inserted into your document.

Right indent A type of indent in which the right edge of a paragraph is moved in from the right margin.

Right-align Alignment in which an item is flush with the right margin.

Rotate handle A green circular handle at the top of a selected object that you can drag to rotate the selected object upside-down, sideways, or to any angle in between.

Rotation handle A green circular handle at the top of a selected object that you can drag to rotate the selected object to any angle between 0 to 360 degrees.

Row field On a PivotTable, the field that supplies values for the row headings. Analogous to the Category field on a PivotChart and a Row Heading field on a crosstab query.

Row heading The gray box containing the row number to the left of the row.

Row height The vertical dimension of a cell.

Row selector The small square to the left of a field in Table Design View or the Tab Order dialog box.

Row Source The Lookup property that defines the list of values for the Lookup field.

Ruler guides Nonprinting lines that appear on a single page of your publication that help you align text, pictures, and other objects into columns and rows.

Rulers (Publisher) Vertical and horizontal bars in the publication window marked in inches, centimeters, picas, or points that help you position text and graphics in your publications.

Rulers (Access) Vertical and horizontal guides that appear in Form and Report Design View to help you position controls. Also, to play, as a macro.

Run To play, as a macro. Also, to open a query and view the fields and records that you have selected for the query presented as a datasheet.

Sans serif font A font, such as Arial, whose characters do not include serifs, which are small strokes at the ends of letters.

Save To store a file permanently on a disk or to overwrite the copy of a file that is stored on a disk with the changes made to the file.

Save As Command used to save a file for the first time or to create a new file with a different filename, leaving the original file intact.

Scale To change the size of a graphic to a specific percentage of its original size.

ScreenTip A descriptive message that appears when you point to a toolbar button.

Scroll To use the scroll bars or the arrow keys to display different parts of a document in the document window.

Scroll arrows The arrows at the ends of the scroll bars that are clicked to scroll a document one line at a time.

Scroll bars The bars on the right edge (vertical scroll bar) and bottom edge (horizontal scroll bar) of the document window that are used to display different parts of the document in the document window.

Scroll box The box in a scroll bar that can be dragged to scroll a document.

Secondary sort field In a query grid, the second field from the left that includes sort criteria. It determines the order in which the records will appear if there is a "tie" on the primary sort field. (For example, the primary sort field might be the State field. If two records both contained the data "IA" in that field, the secondary sort field, which might be the City field, would determine the order of the IA records in the resulting datasheet.)

Section (Access) A location of a form or report that contains controls. The section in which a control is placed determines where and how often the control prints.

Section (Word) A portion of a document that is separated from the rest of the document by section breaks.

Section break A formatting mark inserted to divide a document into sections.

Select To click or highlight an item in order to perform some action on it.

Select query The most common type of query that retrieves data from one or more linked tables and displays the results in a datasheet.

Selection box A slanted line border that appears around a text object or placeholder, indicating that it is ready to accept text.

Selection handles Small boxes or circles that appear around a selected object that are used for moving and resizing the object.

Series On a PivotChart, the area that is also called the legend.

Series field On a PivotChart, the field that supplies the values for the legend. Analogous to the Column field in a PivotTable and the Column Heading field of a crosstab query.

Series in Columns The information in the columns of a datasheet that are on the Value axis; the row labels are on the Category axis.

Series in Rows The information in the datasheet rows that are on the Value axis; the column labels are the Category axis.

Series of labels Preprogrammed series, such as days of the week and months of the year. They are formed by typing the first word of the series, then dragging the fill handle to select and fill the desired range of cells.

Serif font A font, such as Times New Roman, whose characters include serifs, which are small strokes at the ends of letters.

Shading A background color or pattern that can be applied to text, tables, or graphics.

Sheet A term used for a worksheet.

Sheet tab A description at the bottom of each worksheet that identifies it in a workbook. In an open workbook, move to a worksheet by clicking its sheet tab. Also known as Worksheet tab.

Sheet tab scrolling buttons Buttons that enable you to move among sheets within a workbook.

Shortcut key See Keyboard shortcut.

Sidebar Text that is set apart from the major text but in some way relates to that text.

Simple Query Wizard A wizard used to create a select query.

Single-file Web page A Web page that integrates all of the worksheets and graphical elements from a workbook into a single file in the MHTML file format, making it easier to publish to the Web. Users who have IE 4.0 or higher can open a Web page saved in MHTML format.

Sizing handles Small boxes appearing along the corners and sides of charts and graphic images that are used for moving and resizing.

Sizing handles (Access) Small squares at each corner of a selected control in Access. Dragging a handle resizes the control. Also known as handles.

Slide layout Determines how all of the elements on a slide are arranged, including text and content placeholders.

Slide Master A template for all slides in a presentation except the title slides. Text and design elements you place on the slide master appear on every slide of the presentation. See also Title Master, Notes Master, and Handout Master.

Slide pane The section of Normal view that contains the current slide.

Slide Show view A view that shows a presentation as an electronic slide show; each slide fills the screen.

Slide Sorter view A view that displays a thumbnail of all slides in the order in which they appear in a presentation; used to rearrange slides and add special effects.

Slide timing The amount of time a slide is visible on the screen during a slide show. You can assign specific slide timings to each slide, or use the PowerPoint Rehearse Timings feature to simulate the amount of time you will need to display each slide in a slide show.

Slide transition The special effect that moves one slide off the screen and the next slide on the screen during a slide show. Each slide can have its own transition effect.

Slide-title master pair The title master and the slide master slides in Slide Master view.

Slides tab The section in Normal View that displays the slides of a presentation as small thumbnails.

Smart tag A purple dotted line that appears under text that Word identifies as a date, name, address, or place.

Smart Tag Actions button The button that appears when you point to a smart tag.

Smart Tags (Access) Buttons that provide a small menu of options and automatically appear when certain conditions are present to help you work with the task at hand, such as correcting errors. For example, the AutoCorrect Options button, which helps you correct typos and update properties, as well as the Error Indicator button, which helps identify potential design errors in Form and Report Design View, are Smart Tags.

Soft page break See Automatic page break.

Sort (Access) Reorder records in either ascending or descending order based on the values of a particular field.

Sort (Excel) To change the order of records in a list according to one or more fields, such as Last Name.

Sort To organize data, such as table rows, items in a list, or records in a mail merge, in ascending or descending order.

Sort keys Criteria on which a sort, or a reordering of data, is based.

Source document Original paper document, such as an employment application or medical history form, upon which data is recorded.

Source file The file from which information is copied.

Source program The program in which a file was created.

Specific record box Part of a box in the lower-left corner in Datasheet view and Form view of the Navigation buttons and which indicates the current record number. You can click in the specific record box, then type a record number to quickly move to that record. Also called the current record box or record number box.

Split To divide a cell into two or more cells.

SQL See Structured Query Language (SQL).

Standard toolbar The toolbar containing the buttons that perform some of the most commonly used commands such as Cut, Copy, Paste, Save, Open, and Print.

Static Web page Web pages created by exporting a query or report to HTML from an Access database are static because they never change after they are created.

Status bar (Access) The bar at the bottom of the window that provides informational messages and other status information (such as whether the Num Lock is active).

Status bar (Excel) The bar at the bottom of the window that provides information about various keys, commands, and processes.

Status bar (PowerPoint) The bar at the bottom of the window that contains messages about what you are doing and seeing in PowerPoint, such as the current slide number or a description of a command or button.

Status bar (Publisher) The bar at the bottom of the publication window that indicates the current page, the position and size of the selected object in a publication.

Status bar (Word) The bar at the bottom of the program window that shows the vertical position, section, and page number of the insertion point, the total number of pages in a document, and the on/off status of several Word features.

StDev Aggregate function that returns the standard deviation of values in a field.

Story A single article that is contained in either one text box or a series of connected text boxes.

Storyboard A detailed outline of a Web site, including position of elements, necessary links, and graphics placement.

Structured Query Language (SQL) A standard programming language for selecting and manipulating data stored in a relational database.

Style A named collection of character and/or paragraph formats that are stored together and can be applied to text to format it quickly.

Style A named combination of formatting characteristics, such as bold, italic, and zero decimal places.

Subform A form placed within a form that shows related records from another table or query. A subform generally displays many records at a time in a datasheet arrangement.

Subscript A font effect in which text is formatted in a smaller font size and placed below the line of text.

Subtitle text placeholder A box on the title slide reserved for subpoint text.

Sum Aggregate function that returns the total of values in a field.

SUM The most frequently used function, this adds columns or rows of cells.

Summary query A query used to calculate and display information about records grouped together.

Superscript A font effect in which text is formatted in a smaller font size and placed above the line of text.

Symbols Special characters that can be inserted into a document using the Symbol command.

System Clipboard A clipboard that stores only the last item cut or copied from a document. *See* Clipboard, Clipboard task pane, and Office Clipboard.

Tab *See* Tab stop.

Tab control An unbound control used to create a three-dimensional aspect to a form so that other controls can be organized and shown in Form View by clicking the "tabs."

Tab indicator Cycles through the tab alignment options.

Tab leaders Lines that appear in front of tabbed text.

Tab order The sequence in which the controls on the form receive the focus when the user presses [Tab] or [Enter] in Form view.

Tab stop A location on the horizontal ruler that indicates where to align text.

Table (Access) A collection of records for a single subject, such as all of the customer records.

Table (Word) A grid made up of rows and columns of cells that you can fill with text and graphics.

Table (Publisher) Information that appears in columns and rows for quick reference and analysis.

Table Datasheet toolbar The toolbar that appears when you are viewing a table's datasheet.

Table Design View The view in which you can add, delete, or modify fields and their associated properties.

Table style A named set of table format settings that can be applied to a table to format it all at once.

Table Wizard An interactive tool used to create a new table from a list of sample tables and sample fields.

Tags HTML codes placed around the elements of a Web page to describe how each element should appear when viewed with a browser.

Target The location that a hyperlink displays after you click it.

Task pane (PowerPoint) A separate pane available in all the PowerPoint views except Slide Show view that contains sets of menus, lists, options, and hyperlinks for commonly used commands.

Task pane (Excel) A window area to the right of the worksheet that provides worksheet options, such as creating a new workbook, conducting a search, inserting Clip Art, and using the Office Clipboard.

Task pane (Publisher) A window that provides quick access to the common tasks organized by categories such as Publication Designs, Web Site Options, Insert Clip Art, Color Schemes, and Font Schemes to help you perform tasks in Publisher.

Task pane (Word) An area of the Word program window that contains shortcuts to Word formatting, editing, research, Help, clip art, mail merge, and other features.

Task pane list arrow Lets you switch between different task panes.

Template (Word) A formatted document that contains placeholder text you can replace with your own text.

Template (Publisher) A model for a publication that contains formatting specifications for text, fonts, and colors that can be used as a basis for a new publication.

Template (Excel) An Excel file saved with a special format that lets you open a new file based on an existing workbook's design and/or content.

Text A field data type that allows text information or combinations of text and numbers such as a street address. By default, it is 50 characters but can be changed. The maximum length of a text field is 255 characters.

Text anchor The location in a text object that determines the location of the text within the placeholder.

Text annotations Labels added to a chart to draw attention to a particular area.

Text box A container that you can fill with text and graphics, which can be moved or resized.

Text box (Word) Any text object you create using the Text Box button. A word processing box and a text label are both examples of a text box. Text box text does not appear in the Outline tab.

Text color The color applied to text in a cell or on a chart.

Text flow icon An icon that appears in a text box to indicate whether the text in the text box flows to another text box, or whether it fits in the text box.

Text label A text box you create using the Text Box button, where the text does not automatically wrap inside the box. Text box text does not appear in the Outline tab.

Text placeholder A box with a dashed-line border and text that you replace with your own text.

Text style A set of formatting characteristics that you can quickly apply to text on a paragraph-by-paragraph basis.

Theme A set of complementary design elements that you can apply to Web pages, e-mail messages, and other documents that are viewed on screen.

Thumbnail A small image of a slide. Thumbnails are visible on the Slides tab and in Slide Sorter view.

Tick marks Notations of a scale of measure on a chart axis.

Timing *See* slide timing.

Title The first line or heading on a slide.

Title bar The bar at the top of the program window that indicates the program name and the name of the current file.

Title Master A template for all title slides in a presentation. Text and design elements you place on the Title Master appear on all slides in the presentation that use the title slide layout.

Title placeholder A box on a slide reserved for the title of a presentation or slide.

Title slide The first slide in a presentation.

Toggle button (Access) A bound control used to indicate "yes" or "no" answers for a field. If the button is "pressed" it displays "yes" information.

Toggle button A button that turns a feature on and off.

Toggle key A key that switches between two options – press once to turn the option on, press again to turn it off.

Toolbar A bar that contains buttons that you can click to perform commands.

Toolbar Options button A button you click on a toolbar to view toolbar buttons not currently visible.

Toolbox toolbar The toolbar that has common controls that you can add to a report or form when working in Report Design View or Form Design View.

Total row Row in the query design grid used to specify how records should be grouped and summarized with aggregate functions.

Totals or Detail Field On a PivotTable, the field that supplies the data that is summarized in the body of the report. Analogous to the Data field in a PivotChart and the Value field in a crosstab query.

Tracked change A mark that shows where an insertion, deletion, or formatting change has been made in a document.

Truncate To shorten the display of cell information because a cell is too wide.

Two-page spread Pages that will face each other when the publication is printed.

Type a question for help box The box at the right end of the menu bar that is used to query the Help system.

Unbound control A control that does not change from record to record and exists only to clarify or enhance the appearance of the form, using element such as labels, lines, and clip art.

Unbound object frame An unbound control that is used to display clip art, a sound clip, or other multimedia content and that doesn't change as you navigate from record to record on a form or report.

Undo To reverse a change by using the Undo button or command.

Undo button Button that allows you to undo your last action.

URL (Uniform Resource Locator) A Web address.

Validation rule A field property that helps eliminate unreasonable entries by establishing criteria for an entry before it is accepted into the database.

Validation text A field property that determines what message will appear if a user attempts to make a field entry that does not pass the validation rule for that field.

Value A number, formula, or function used in calculations.

Value axis Also known as the y-axis in a 2-dimensional chart, this area often contains numerical values that help you interpret the size of chart elements. On a PivotChart, the vertical axis, or y-axis.

Var Aggregate function that returns the variance of values in a field.

Vertex The point where two straight lines meet or the highest point in a curve.

Vertical alignment The position of text in a document relative to the top and bottom margins.

Vertical ruler A ruler that appears on the left side of the document window in Print Layout view.

View (Excel) A set of display or print settings that you can name and save for access at another time. You can save multiple views of a worksheet.

View (Word) A way of displaying a document in the document window; each view provides features useful for editing and formatting different types of documents.

View (PowerPoint) A way of displaying a presentation, such as Normal view, Notes Page view, Slide Sorter view, and Slide Show view.

View buttons (Word) Buttons to the left of the horizontal scroll bar that are used to change views.

View buttons (PowerPoint) The buttons at the bottom of the Outline tab and the Slides tab that you click to switch among views.

Virus Destructive software that can damage your computer files.

Visual Basic Editor A program that lets you display and edit macro code.

Visual Basic for Applications (VBA) A programming language used to create macros in Excel.

Web browser Software used to view Web pages and Web sites.

Web discussion Comments attached to an Excel worksheet that you will save as an HTML document, allowing people viewing your worksheet on the Web to review and reply to your comments.

Web forms Forms that provide an easy way for a user to submit information via the Web.

Web Layout view A view that shows a document as it will look when viewed with a Web browser.

Web page A document that can be stored on a computer called a Web server and viewed on the World Wide Web or on an intranet using a browser.

Web Page Preview Viewing a Web page created by a data access page in Internet Explorer.

Web publication A publication that you can convert to either a Web page or a Web site.

Web server A computer with a permanent connection to the Internet; it runs Web server software and it makes Web pages available to anyone with Web access.

Web site A group of associated Web pages that are linked together with hyperlinks.

What-if analysis A decision-making feature in which data is changed and formulas based on it are automatically recalculated.

Wildcards Special characters used in criteria to find, filter, and query data. The asterisk (*) stands for any group of characters. For example, the criteria I* in a State field criterion cell would find all records where the state entry was IA, ID, IL, IN, or Iowa. The question mark (?) wildcard stands for only one character.

Window A rectangular area of a screen where you view and work on the open file.

Wizard An interactive set of dialog boxes that guides you through a task.

.wmf The abbreviation for the Windows metafile file format, which is the format of some clip art.

Word processing box A text box you create using the Text Box button, where the text automatically wraps inside the box.

Word processing program A software program that includes tools for entering, editing, and formatting text and graphics.

Word program window The window that contains the Word program elements, including the document window, toolbars, menu bar, and status bar.

Word-wrap A feature that automatically moves the insertion point to the next line as you type.

WordArt A drawing object, treated as a graphic, that contains text formatted with special shapes, patterns, and orientations.

Workbook A collection of related worksheets contained within a single file.

Worksheet An electronic spreadsheet containing 256 columns by 65,536 rows.

Worksheet tab *See* Sheet tab.

Worksheet window Includes the tools that enable you to create and work with worksheets.

Workspace An Excel file with an .xlw extension containing information about the identity, view, and placement of a set of open workbooks. Instead of opening each workbook individually, you can open the workspace file instead.

World Wide Web (WWW) A collection of electronic documents available to people around the world via the Internet, commonly referred to as the Web.

Wrapping The flow of text around an object rather than over it or behind it.

X-axis The horizontal axis in a chart; because it often shows data categories, such as months, it is also called the category axis.

X-axis label A label describing a chart's x-axis.

XY (scatter) chart Compares trends over uneven time or measurement intervals; used in scientific and engineering disciplines for trend spotting and extrapolation.

Y-axis The vertical axis in a chart; because it often shows numerical values in a 2-dimensional chart, it is also called the value axis.

Y-axis label A label describing the y-axis of a chart.

Yes/No A field data type that stores only one of two values, "Yes" or "No."

Zoom A feature that enables you to focus on a larger or smaller part of the document in Print Preview.

Zoom pointers Mouse pointers displayed in Print Preview that allow you to change the zoom magnification of a printout.

Index